Mitsubishi Galant Automotive Repair Manual

**by John A Wegmann
and John H Haynes**

Member of the Guild of Motoring Writers

Models covered:
Mitsubishi Galant - 1994 through 2012

(68035 - 2S6)

ABCDE
F

Haynes Publishing Group
Sparkford Nr Yeovil
Somerset BA22 7JJ England

Haynes North America, Inc
861 Lawrence Drive
Newbury Park
California 91320 USA

Acknowledgements

Wiring diagrams originated exclusively for Haynes North America, Inc. by Valley Forge Technical Information Services. Technical writers who contributed to this project include Mike Stubblefield, Robert Maddox and Larry Warren. Technical consultants include Jamie Sarté, Jr. and Brad Conn.

© **Haynes North America, Inc. 2003, 2011, 2014**

With permission from J.H. Haynes & Co. Ltd.

A book in the Haynes Automotive Repair Manual Series

Printed in the U.S.A.

ISBN-13: 978-1-62092-092-3
ISBN-10: 1-62092-092-1

Library of Congress Control Number: 2014932479

Contents

Haynes mechanic, author and photographer with a 2000 Mitsubishi Galant

About this manual

Its purpose

The purpose of this manual is to help you get the best value from your vehicle. It can do so in several ways. It can help you decide what work must be done, even if you choose to have it done by a dealer service department or a repair shop; it provides information and procedures for routine maintenance and servicing; and it offers diagnostic and repair procedures to follow when trouble occurs.

We hope you use the manual to tackle the work yourself. For many simpler jobs, doing it yourself may be quicker than arranging an appointment to get the vehicle into a shop and making the trips to leave it and pick it up. More importantly, a lot of money can be saved by avoiding the expense the shop must pass on to you to cover its labor and overhead costs. An added benefit is the sense of satisfaction and accomplishment that you feel after doing the job yourself.

Using the manual

The manual is divided into Chapters. Each Chapter is divided into numbered Sections, which are headed in bold type between horizontal lines. Each Section consists of consecutively numbered paragraphs.

At the beginning of each numbered Section you will be referred to any illustrations which apply to the procedures in that Section. The reference numbers used in illustration captions pinpoint the pertinent Section and the Step within that Section. That is, illustration 3.2 means the illustration refers to Section 3 and Step (or paragraph) 2 within that Section.

Procedures, once described in the text, are not normally repeated. When it's necessary to refer to another Chapter, the reference will be given as Chapter and Section number. Cross references given without use of the word "Chapter" apply to Sections and/or paragraphs in the same Chapter. For example, "see Section 8" means in the same Chapter.

References to the left or right side of the vehicle assume you are sitting in the driver's seat, facing forward.

Even though we have prepared this manual with extreme care, neither the publisher nor the author can accept responsibility for any errors in, or omissions from, the information given.

NOTE

A **Note** provides information necessary to properly complete a procedure or information which will make the procedure easier to understand.

CAUTION

A **Caution** provides a special procedure or special steps which must be taken while completing the procedure where the Caution is found. Not heeding a Caution can result in damage to the assembly being worked on.

WARNING

A **Warning** provides a special procedure or special steps which must be taken while completing the procedure where the Warning is found. Not heeding a Warning can result in personal injury.

Introduction to the Mitsubishi Galant

The Mitsubishi Galant is available in a four-door sedan body style only. It features transversely mounted four-cylinder and V6 engines.

All models are equipped with an electronically controlled multi-port electronic fuel injection system.

The engine transmits power to the front wheels through either a five-speed manual transaxle or a four-speed automatic transaxle via independent driveaxles.

All models feature an all steel unibody design and independent front and rear suspension. The front suspension on 1998 and earlier models incorporates a shock absorber/coil spring assembly with upper and lower control arms. The front suspension on 1999 and later models use a MacPherson strut design. The rear suspension on all models utilizes a shock absorber/coil spring assembly and upper control arm in combination with a trailing arm and lateral links.

The standard power rack-and-pinion steering unit is mounted behind the engine on the front suspension crossmember.

All models are equipped with power assisted front disc and rear disc or drum brakes with an Anti-lock Brake System (ABS) available as an option.

Vehicle identification numbers

Modifications are a continuing and unpublicized process in vehicle manufacturing. Since spare parts manuals and lists are compiled on a numerical basis, the individual vehicle numbers are essential to correctly identify the component required.

Vehicle Identification Number (VIN)

This very important identification number is located on a plate attached to the dashboard inside the windshield on the driver's side of the vehicle (see illustration). The VIN also appears on the Vehicle Certificate of Title and Registration. It contains information such as where and when the vehicle was manufactured, the model year and the body style.

VIN engine and model year codes

Two particularly important pieces of information found in the VIN are the engine code and the model year code. Counting from the left, the engine code letter designation is the 8th digit and the model year code designation is the 10th digit.

On the models covered by this manual the engine codes are:

1994
- G .... 2.4L 4-cyl SOHC
- L .... 2.4L 4-cyl DOHC

1995
- G .... 2.4L 4-cyl SOHC
- L .... 2.4L 4-cyl DOHC

1996
- G .... 2.4L 4-cyl SOHC

1997
- G .... 2.4L 4-cyl SOHC

1998
- G .... 2.4L 4-cyl SOHC

1999
- G .... 2.4L 4-cyl SOHC
- L .... 3.0L V6 SOHC

2000
- G .... 2.4L 4-cyl SOHC
- L .... 3.0L V6 SOHC

2001
- G .... 2.4L 4-cyl SOHC
- H .... 3.0L V6 SOHC

2002
- G .... 2.4L 4-cyl SOHC
- H .... 3.0L V6 SOHC

2003
- G .... 2.4L 4-cyl SOHC
- H .... 3.0L V6 SOHC

2004
- F .... 2.4L 4-cyl MIVEC
- S 3.8L V6

2005
- F .... 2.4L 4-cyl MIVEC
- S 3.8L V6

2006
- F .... 2.4L 4-cyl MIVEC
- S 3.8L V6

2007
- F .... 2.4L 4-cyl MIVEC
- S 3.8L V6
- T .... 3.8L V6 MIVEC

2008
- F .... 2.4L 4-cyl MIVEC
- S 3.8L V6
- T .... 3.8L V6 MIVEC

2009
- F .... 2.4L 4-cyl MIVEC
- S 3.8L V6
- T .... 3.8L V6 MIVEC

2010
- F .... 2.4L 4-cyl MIVEC
- S 3.8L V6
- T .... 3.8L V6 MIVEC

2011
- F .... 2.4L 4-cyl MIVEC

2012
- F .... 2.4L 4-cyl MIVEC

On the models covered by this manual the model year codes are:

- R 1994
- S 1995
- T 1996
- V 1997
- W 1998
- X 1999
- Y 2000
- 1 2001
- 2 2002
- 3 2003

The Vehicle Identification Number (VIN) is stamped into a metal plate fastened to the dashboard on the driver's side - it's visible through the windshield

- 4 2004
- 5 2005
- 6 2006
- 7 2007
- 8 2008
- 9 2009
- A 2010
- B 2011
- C 2012

Body Code Plate

The Body Code Plate is a stamped metal plate attached in the engine compartment (see illustration). It contains more specific information about the manufacturing of the vehicle such as the paint code, trim code and vehicle order number, as well as the VIN.

Vehicle Safety Certification label

The Vehicle Safety Certification label is attached to the driver's side door pillar (see illustration). The label contains the name of the manufacturer, the month and year of production, the Gross Vehicle Weight Rating (GVWR), the Gross Axle Weight Rating (GAWR) and the certification statement.

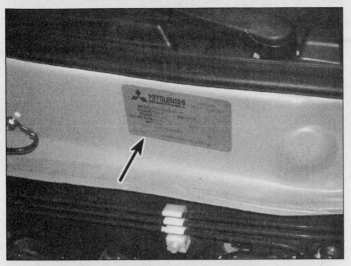

The body code plate is located on the firewall in the engine compartment

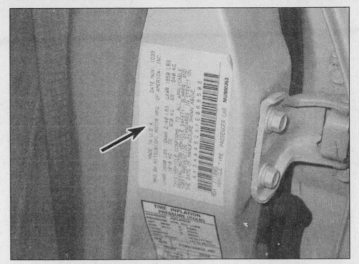

The Vehicle Safety Certification label is affixed to the driver's door pillar

On four-cylinder engines, the engine identification number is stamped on the side of the engine block

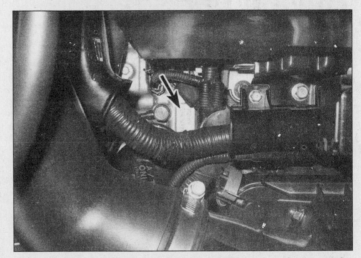

The transaxle identification number can be found on the top of the case (as shown) or the side of the bellhousing

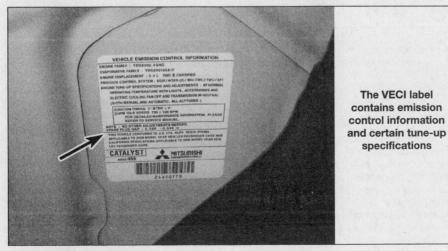

The VECI label contains emission control information and certain tune-up specifications

it'll be on the back side of the engine, but on 1999 and later models it'll be on the front side of the engine. V6 engine identification is located on the front side of the engine block, just below the cylinder head, near the left end of the engine.

Transaxle identification numbers

The transaxle identification information can be found stamped on a pad on the top or side of the case or bellhousing (see illustration).

Vehicle Emissions Control Information (VECI) label

The emissions control information label is found on the underside of the hood (see illustration). This label contains information on the emissions control equipment installed on the vehicle, as well as tune-up specifications (see Chapter 6 for more information).

Engine identification numbers

The four-cylinder engine identification numbers can be found stamped on a machined pad below the cylinder head on the side of the engine block at the drivebelt end (see illustration); on 1998 and earlier models

Buying parts

Replacement parts are available from many sources, which generally fall into one of two categories - authorized dealer parts departments and independent retail auto parts stores. Our advice concerning these parts is as follows:

Retail auto parts stores: Good auto parts stores will stock frequently needed components which wear out relatively fast, such as clutch components, exhaust systems, brake parts, tune-up parts, etc. These stores often supply new or reconditioned parts on an exchange basis, which can save a considerable amount of money. Discount auto parts stores are often very good places to buy materials and parts needed for general vehicle maintenance such as oil, grease, filters, spark plugs, belts, touch-up paint, bulbs, etc. They also usually sell tools and general accessories, have convenient hours, charge lower prices and can often be found not far from home.

Authorized dealer parts department: This is the best source for parts which are unique to the vehicle and not generally available elsewhere (such as major engine parts, transmission parts, trim pieces, etc.).

Warranty information: If the vehicle is still covered under warranty, be sure that any replacement parts purchased - regardless of the source - do not invalidate the warranty!

To be sure of obtaining the correct parts, have engine and chassis numbers available and, if possible, take the old parts along for positive identification.

Maintenance techniques, tools and working facilities

Maintenance techniques

There are a number of techniques involved in maintenance and repair that will be referred to throughout this manual. Application of these techniques will enable the home mechanic to be more efficient, better organized and capable of performing the various tasks properly, which will ensure that the repair job is thorough and complete.

Fasteners

Fasteners are nuts, bolts, studs and screws used to hold two or more parts together. There are a few things to keep in mind when working with fasteners. Almost all of them use a locking device of some type, either a lockwasher, locknut, locking tab or thread adhesive. All threaded fasteners should be clean and straight, with undamaged threads and undamaged corners on the hex head where the wrench fits. Develop the habit of replacing all damaged nuts and bolts with new ones. Special locknuts with nylon or fiber inserts can only be used once. If they are removed, they lose their locking ability and must be replaced with new ones.

Rusted nuts and bolts should be treated with a penetrating fluid to ease removal and prevent breakage. Some mechanics use turpentine in a spout-type oil can, which works quite well. After applying the rust penetrant, let it work for a few minutes before trying to loosen the nut or bolt. Badly rusted fasteners may have to be chiseled or sawed off or removed with a special nut breaker, available at tool stores.

If a bolt or stud breaks off in an assembly, it can be drilled and removed with a special tool commonly available for this purpose. Most automotive machine shops can perform this task, as well as other repair procedures, such as the repair of threaded holes that have been stripped out.

Flat washers and lockwashers, when removed from an assembly, should always be replaced exactly as removed. Replace any damaged washers with new ones. Never use a lockwasher on any soft metal surface (such as aluminum), thin sheet metal or plastic.

Fastener sizes

For a number of reasons, automobile manufacturers are making wider and wider use of metric fasteners. Therefore, it is important to be able to tell the difference between standard (sometimes called U.S. or SAE) and metric hardware, since they cannot be interchanged.

All bolts, whether standard or metric, are sized according to diameter, thread pitch and length. For example, a standard 1/2 - 13 x 1 bolt is 1/2 inch in diameter, has 13 threads per inch and is 1 inch long. An M12 - 1.75 x 25 metric bolt is 12 mm in diameter, has a thread pitch of 1.75 mm (the distance between threads) and is 25 mm long. The two bolts are nearly identical, and easily confused, but they are not interchangeable.

In addition to the differences in diameter, thread pitch and length, metric and standard bolts can also be distinguished by examining the bolt heads. To begin with, the distance across the flats on a standard bolt head is measured in inches, while the same dimension on a metric bolt is sized in millimeters (the same is true for nuts). As a result, a standard wrench should not be used on a metric bolt and a metric wrench should not be used on a standard bolt. Also, most standard bolts have slashes radiating out from the center of the head to denote the grade or strength of the bolt, which is an indication of the amount of torque that can be applied to it. The greater the number of slashes, the greater the strength of the bolt. Grades 0 through 5 are commonly used on automobiles. Metric bolts have a property class (grade) number, rather than a slash, molded into their heads to indicate bolt strength. In this case, the higher the number, the stronger the bolt. Property class numbers 8.8, 9.8 and 10.9 are commonly used on automobiles.

Strength markings can also be used to distinguish standard hex nuts from metric hex nuts. Many standard nuts have dots stamped into one side, while metric nuts are marked with a number. The greater the number of dots, or the higher the number, the greater the strength of the nut.

Metric studs are also marked on their ends according to property class (grade). Larger studs are numbered (the same as metric bolts), while smaller studs carry a geometric code to denote grade.

It should be noted that many fasteners, especially Grades 0 through 2, have no distinguishing marks on them. When such is the case, the only way to determine whether it is standard or metric is to measure the thread pitch or compare it to a known fastener of the same size.

Standard fasteners are often referred to as SAE, as opposed to metric. However, it should be noted that SAE technically refers to a non-metric fine thread fastener only. Coarse thread non-metric fasteners are referred to as USS sizes.

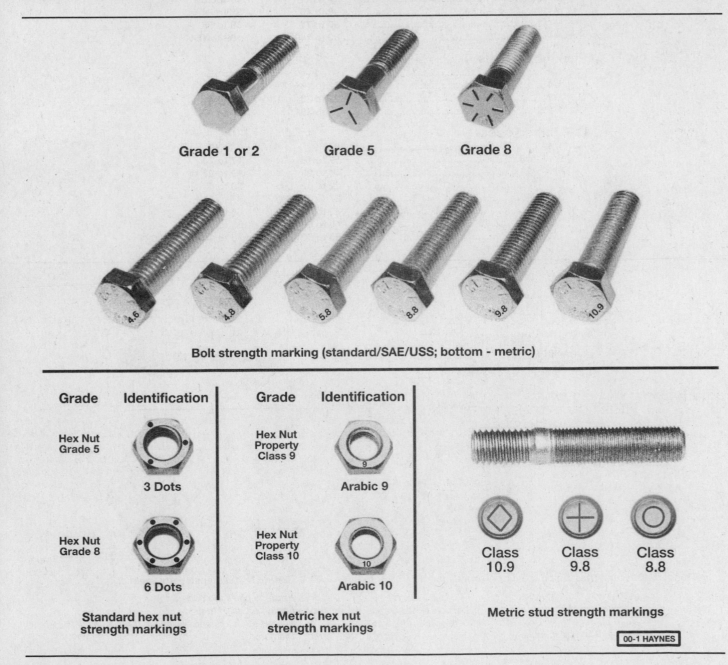

Since fasteners of the same size (both standard and metric) may have different strength ratings, be sure to reinstall any bolts, studs or nuts removed from your vehicle in their original locations. Also, when replacing a fastener with a new one, make sure that the new one has a strength rating equal to or greater than the original.

Tightening sequences and procedures

Most threaded fasteners should be tightened to a specific torque value (torque is the twisting force applied to a threaded component such as a nut or bolt). Overtightening the fastener can weaken it and cause it to break, while undertightening can cause it to eventually come loose. Bolts, screws and studs, depending on the material they are made of and their thread diameters, have specific torque values, many of which are noted in the Specifications at the beginning of each Chapter. Be sure to follow the torque recommendations closely. For fasteners not assigned a specific torque, a general torque value chart is presented here as a guide. These torque values are for dry (unlubricated) fasteners threaded into steel or cast iron (not aluminum). As was previously mentioned, the size and grade of a fastener determine the amount of torque that can safely be applied to it. The figures listed here are approximate for Grade 2 and Grade 3 fasteners. Higher grades can tolerate higher torque values.

Fasteners laid out in a pattern, such as cylinder head bolts, oil pan bolts, differential cover bolts, etc., must be loosened or tightened in sequence to avoid warping the component. This sequence will normally be shown in the appropriate Chapter. If a specific pattern is not given, the following procedures can be used to prevent warping.

Metric thread sizes	Ft-lbs	Nm
M-6	6 to 9	9 to 12
M-8	14 to 21	19 to 28
M-10	28 to 40	38 to 54
M-12	50 to 71	68 to 96
M-14	80 to 140	109 to 154
Pipe thread sizes		
1/8	5 to 8	7 to 10
1/4	12 to 18	17 to 24
3/8	22 to 33	30 to 44
1/2	25 to 35	34 to 47
U.S. thread sizes		
1/4 - 20	6 to 9	9 to 12
5/16 - 18	12 to 18	17 to 24
5/16 - 24	14 to 20	19 to 27
3/8 - 16	22 to 32	30 to 43
3/8 - 24	27 to 38	37 to 51
7/16 - 14	40 to 55	55 to 74
7/16 - 20	40 to 60	55 to 81
1/2 - 13	55 to 80	75 to 108

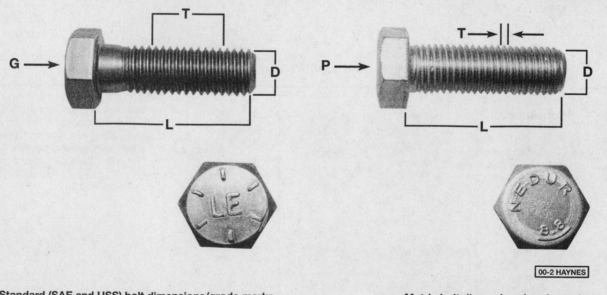

00-2 HAYNES

Standard (SAE and USS) bolt dimensions/grade marks

G   Grade marks (bolt strength)
L   Length (in inches)
T   Thread pitch (number of threads per inch)
D   Nominal diameter (in inches)

Metric bolt dimensions/grade marks

P   Property class (bolt strength)
L   Length (in millimeters)
T   Thread pitch (distance between threads in millimeters)
D   Diameter

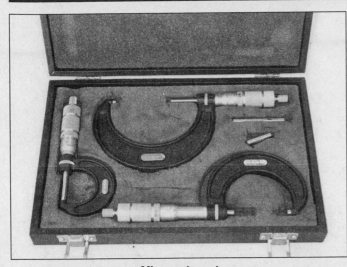

Micrometer set

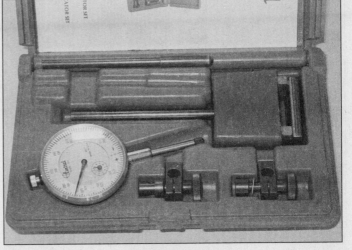

Dial indicator set

Initially, the bolts or nuts should be assembled finger-tight only. Next, they should be tightened one full turn each, in a criss-cross or diagonal pattern. After each one has been tightened one full turn, return to the first one and tighten them all one-half turn, following the same pattern. Finally, tighten each of them one-quarter turn at a time until each fastener has been tightened to the proper torque. To loosen and remove the fasteners, the procedure would be reversed.

Component disassembly

Component disassembly should be done with care and purpose to help ensure that the parts go back together properly. Always keep track of the sequence in which parts are removed. Make note of special characteristics or marks on parts that can be installed more than one way, such as a grooved thrust washer on a shaft. It is a good idea to lay the disassembled parts out on a clean surface in the order that they were removed. It may also be helpful to make sketches or take instant photos of components before removal.

When removing fasteners from a component, keep track of their locations. Sometimes threading a bolt back in a part, or putting the washers and nut back on a stud, can prevent mix-ups later. If nuts and bolts cannot be returned to their original locations, they should be kept in a compartmented box or a series of small boxes. A cupcake or muffin tin is ideal for this purpose, since each cavity can hold the bolts and nuts from a particular area (i.e. oil pan bolts, valve cover bolts, engine mount bolts, etc.). A pan of this type is especially helpful when working on assemblies with very small parts, such as the carburetor, alternator, valve train or interior dash and trim pieces. The cavities can be marked with paint or tape to identify the contents.

Whenever wiring looms, harnesses or connectors are separated, it is a good idea to identify the two halves with numbered pieces of masking tape so they can be easily reconnected.

Gasket sealing surfaces

Throughout any vehicle, gaskets are used to seal the mating surfaces between two parts and keep lubricants, fluids, vacuum or pressure contained in an assembly.

Many times these gaskets are coated with a liquid or paste-type gasket sealing compound before assembly. Age, heat and pressure can sometimes cause the two parts to stick together so tightly that they are very difficult to separate. Often, the assembly can be loosened by striking it with a soft-face hammer near the mating surfaces. A regular hammer can be used if a block of wood is placed between the hammer and the part. Do not hammer on cast parts or parts that could be easily damaged. With any particularly stubborn part, always recheck to make sure that every fastener has been removed.

Avoid using a screwdriver or bar to pry apart an assembly, as they can easily mar the gasket sealing surfaces of the parts, which must remain smooth. If prying is absolutely necessary, use an old broom handle, but keep in mind that extra clean up will be necessary if the wood splinters.

After the parts are separated, the old gasket must be carefully scraped off and the gasket surfaces cleaned. Stubborn gasket material can be soaked with rust penetrant or treated with a special chemical to soften it so it can be easily scraped off. **Caution:** *Never use gasket removal solutions or caustic chemicals on plastic or other composite components.* A scraper can be fashioned from a piece of copper tubing by flattening and sharpening one end. Copper is recommended because it is usually softer than the surfaces to be scraped, which reduces the chance of gouging the part. Some gaskets can be removed with a wire brush, but regardless of the method used, the mating surfaces must be left clean and smooth. If for some reason the gasket surface is gouged, then a gasket sealer thick enough to fill scratches will have to be used during reassembly of the components. For most applications, a non-drying (or semi-drying) gasket sealer should be used.

Hose removal tips

Warning: *If the vehicle is equipped with air conditioning, do not disconnect any of the A/C hoses without first having the system depressurized by a dealer service department or a service station.*

Hose removal precautions closely parallel gasket removal precautions. Avoid scratching or gouging the surface that the hose mates against or the connection may leak. This is especially true for radiator hoses. Because of various chemical reactions, the rubber in hoses can bond itself to the metal spigot that the hose fits over. To remove a hose, first loosen the hose clamps that secure it to the spigot. Then, with slip-joint pliers, grab the hose at the clamp and rotate it around the spigot. Work it back and forth until it is completely free, then pull it off. Silicone or other lubricants will ease removal if they can be applied between the hose and the outside of the spigot. Apply the same lubricant to the inside of the hose and the outside of the spigot to simplify installation.

As a last resort (and if the hose is to be replaced with a new one anyway), the rubber can be slit with a knife and the hose peeled from the spigot. If this must be done, be careful that the metal connection is not damaged.

If a hose clamp is broken or damaged, do not reuse it. Wire-type clamps usually weaken with age, so it is a good idea to replace them with screw-type clamps whenever a hose is removed.

Tools

A selection of good tools is a basic requirement for anyone who plans to maintain and repair his or her own vehicle. For the owner who has few tools, the initial investment might seem high, but when compared to the spiraling costs of professional auto maintenance and repair, it is a wise one.

To help the owner decide which tools are needed to perform the tasks detailed in this manual, the following tool lists are offered: *Maintenance and minor repair,*

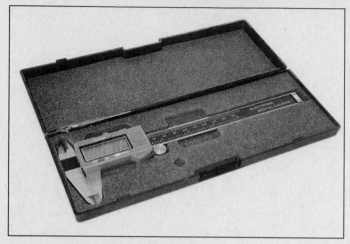

Dial caliper

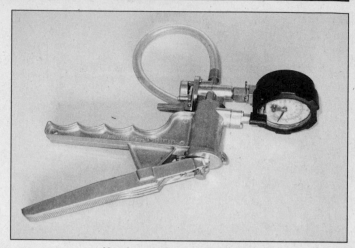

Hand-operated vacuum pump

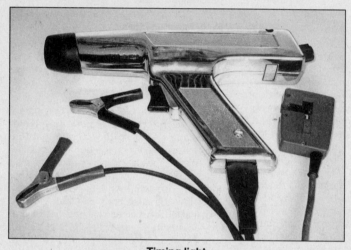

Timing light

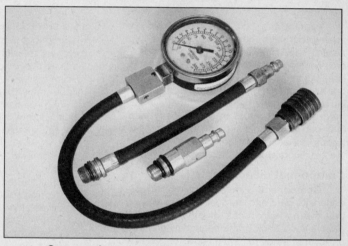

Compression gauge with spark plug hole adapter

Damper/steering wheel puller

General purpose puller

Hydraulic lifter removal tool

Repair/overhaul and *Special*.

The newcomer to practical mechanics should start off with the *maintenance and minor repair* tool kit, which is adequate for the simpler jobs performed on a vehicle. Then, as confidence and experience grow, the owner can tackle more difficult tasks, buying additional tools as they are needed.

Eventually the basic kit will be expanded into the *repair and overhaul* tool set. Over a period of time, the experienced do-it-yourselfer will assemble a tool set complete enough for most repair and overhaul procedures and will add tools from the special category when it is felt that the expense is justified by the frequency of use.

Maintenance and minor repair tool kit

The tools in this list should be considered the minimum required for performance of routine maintenance, servicing and minor repair work. We recommend the purchase of combination wrenches (box-end and open-end com-

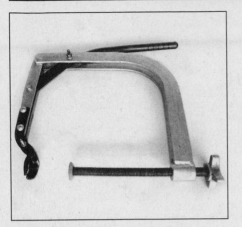

Valve spring compressor

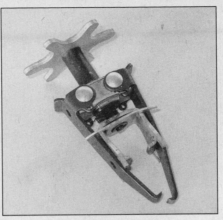

Valve spring compressor

Ridge reamer

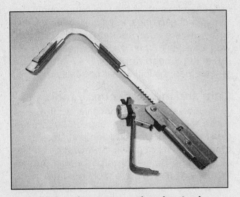

Piston ring groove cleaning tool

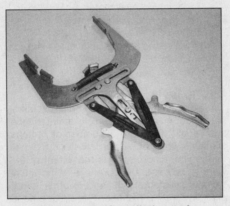

Ring removal/installation tool

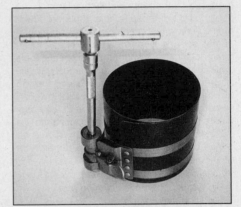

Ring compressor

bined in one wrench). While more expensive than open end wrenches, they offer the advantages of both types of wrench.

> Combination wrench set (1/4-inch to
>   1 inch or 6 mm to 19 mm)
> Adjustable wrench, 8 inch
> Spark plug wrench with rubber insert
> Spark plug gap adjusting tool
> Feeler gauge set
> Brake bleeder wrench
> Standard screwdriver (5/16-inch x
>   6 inch)
> Phillips screwdriver (No. 2 x 6 inch)
> Combination pliers - 6 inch
> Hacksaw and assortment of blades
> Tire pressure gauge
> Grease gun
> Oil can
> Fine emery cloth
> Wire brush
> Battery post and cable cleaning tool
> Oil filter wrench
> Funnel (medium size)
> Safety goggles
> Jackstands (2)
> Drain pan

Note: *If basic tune-ups are going to be part of routine maintenance, it will be necessary to purchase a good quality stroboscopic timing light and combination tachometer/dwell meter. Although they are included in the list of special tools, it is mentioned here because* they are absolutely necessary for tuning most vehicles properly.

Repair and overhaul tool set

These tools are essential for anyone who plans to perform major repairs and are in addition to those in the maintenance and minor repair tool kit. Included is a comprehensive set of sockets which, though expensive, are invaluable because of their versatility, especially when various extensions and drives are available. We recommend the 1/2-inch drive over the 3/8-inch drive. Although the larger drive is bulky and more expensive, it has the capacity of accepting a very wide range of large sockets. Ideally, however, the mechanic should have a 3/8-inch drive set and a 1/2-inch drive set.

> Socket set(s)
> Reversible ratchet
> Extension - 10 inch
> Universal joint
> Torque wrench (same size drive as
>   sockets)
> Ball peen hammer - 8 ounce
> Soft-face hammer (plastic/rubber)
> Standard screwdriver (1/4-inch x 6 inch)
> Standard screwdriver (stubby -
>   5/16-inch)
> Phillips screwdriver (No. 3 x 8 inch)
> Phillips screwdriver (stubby - No. 2)
> Pliers - vise grip

> Pliers - lineman's
> Pliers - needle nose
> Pliers - snap-ring (internal and external)
> Cold chisel - 1/2-inch
> Scribe
> Scraper (made from flattened copper
>   tubing)
> Centerpunch
> Pin punches (1/16, 1/8, 3/16-inch)
> Steel rule/straightedge - 12 inch
> Allen wrench set (1/8 to 3/8-inch or
>   4 mm to 10 mm)
> A selection of files
> Wire brush (large)
> Jackstands (second set)
> Jack (scissor or hydraulic type)

Note: *Another tool which is often useful is an electric drill with a chuck capacity of 3/8-inch and a set of good quality drill bits.*

Special tools

The tools in this list include those which are not used regularly, are expensive to buy, or which need to be used in accordance with their manufacturer's instructions. Unless these tools will be used frequently, it is not very economical to purchase many of them. A consideration would be to split the cost and use between yourself and a friend or friends. In addition, most of these tools can be obtained from a tool rental shop on a temporary basis.

This list primarily contains only those

Cylinder hone

Brake hold-down spring tool

Torque angle gauge

tools and instruments widely available to the public, and not those special tools produced by the vehicle manufacturer for distribution to dealer service departments. Occasionally, references to the manufacturer's special tools are included in the text of this manual. Generally, an alternative method of doing the job without the special tool is offered. However, sometimes there is no alternative to their use. Where this is the case, and the tool cannot be purchased or borrowed, the work should be turned over to the dealer service department or an automotive repair shop.

Valve spring compressor
Piston ring groove cleaning tool
Piston ring compressor
Piston ring installation tool
Cylinder compression gauge
Cylinder ridge reamer
Cylinder surfacing hone
Cylinder bore gauge
Micrometers and/or dial calipers
Hydraulic lifter removal tool
Balljoint separator
Universal-type puller
Impact screwdriver
Dial indicator set
Stroboscopic timing light (inductive pick-up)
Hand operated vacuum/pressure pump

Tachometer/dwell meter
Universal electrical multimeter
Cable hoist
Brake spring removal and installation tools
Floor jack

Buying tools

For the do-it-yourselfer who is just starting to get involved in vehicle maintenance and repair, there are a number of options available when purchasing tools. If maintenance and minor repair is the extent of the work to be done, the purchase of individual tools is satisfactory. If, on the other hand, extensive work is planned, it would be a good idea to purchase a modest tool set from one of the large retail chain stores. A set can usually be bought at a substantial savings over the individual tool prices, and they often come with a tool box. As additional tools are needed, add-on sets, individual tools and a larger tool box can be purchased to expand the tool selection. Building a tool set gradually allows the cost of the tools to be spread over a longer period of time and gives the mechanic the freedom to choose only those tools that will actually be used.

Tool stores will often be the only source of some of the special tools that are needed,

but regardless of where tools are bought, try to avoid cheap ones, especially when buying screwdrivers and sockets, because they won't last very long. The expense involved in replacing cheap tools will eventually be greater than the initial cost of quality tools.

Care and maintenance of tools

Good tools are expensive, so it makes sense to treat them with respect. Keep them clean and in usable condition and store them properly when not in use. Always wipe off any dirt, grease or metal chips before putting them away. Never leave tools lying around in the work area. Upon completion of a job, always check closely under the hood for tools that may have been left there so they won't get lost during a test drive.

Some tools, such as screwdrivers, pliers, wrenches and sockets, can be hung on a panel mounted on the garage or workshop wall, while others should be kept in a tool box or tray. Measuring instruments, gauges, meters, etc. must be carefully stored where they cannot be damaged by weather or impact from other tools.

When tools are used with care and stored properly, they will last a very long time. Even with the best of care, though, tools will wear out if used frequently. When a tool is

Clutch plate alignment tool

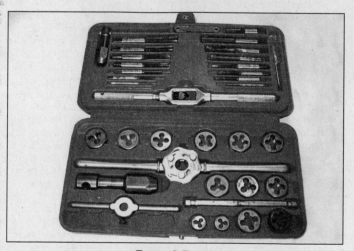

Tap and die set

damaged or worn out, replace it. Subsequent jobs will be safer and more enjoyable if you do.

How to repair damaged threads

Sometimes, the internal threads of a nut or bolt hole can become stripped, usually from overtightening. Stripping threads is an all-too-common occurrence, especially when working with aluminum parts, because aluminum is so soft that it easily strips out.

Usually, external or internal threads are only partially stripped. After they've been cleaned up with a tap or die, they'll still work. Sometimes, however, threads are badly damaged. When this happens, you've got three choices:

1) *Drill and tap the hole to the next suitable oversize and install a larger diameter bolt, screw or stud.*
2) *Drill and tap the hole to accept a threaded plug, then drill and tap the plug to the original screw size. You can also buy a plug already threaded to the original size. Then you simply drill a hole to the specified size, then run the threaded plug into the hole with a bolt and jam nut. Once the plug is fully seated, remove the jam nut and bolt.*

3) *The third method uses a patented thread repair kit like Heli-Coil or Slimsert. These easy-to-use kits are designed to repair damaged threads in straight-through holes and blind holes. Both are available as kits which can handle a variety of sizes and thread patterns. Drill the hole, then tap it with the special included tap. Install the Heli-Coil and the hole is back to its original diameter and thread pitch.*

Regardless of which method you use, be sure to proceed calmly and carefully. A little impatience or carelessness during one of these relatively simple procedures can ruin your whole day's work and cost you a bundle if you wreck an expensive part.

Working facilities

Not to be overlooked when discussing tools is the workshop. If anything more than routine maintenance is to be carried out, some sort of suitable work area is essential.

It is understood, and appreciated, that many home mechanics do not have a good workshop or garage available, and end up removing an engine or doing major repairs outside. It is recommended, however, that the overhaul or repair be completed under the cover of a roof.

A clean, flat workbench or table of comfortable working height is an absolute necessity. The workbench should be equipped with a vise that has a jaw opening of at least four inches.

As mentioned previously, some clean, dry storage space is also required for tools, as well as the lubricants, fluids, cleaning solvents, etc. which soon become necessary.

Sometimes waste oil and fluids, drained from the engine or cooling system during normal maintenance or repairs, present a disposal problem. To avoid pouring them on the ground or into a sewage system, pour the used fluids into large containers, seal them with caps and take them to an authorized disposal site or recycling center. Plastic jugs, such as old antifreeze containers, are ideal for this purpose.

Always keep a supply of old newspapers and clean rags available. Old towels are excellent for mopping up spills. Many mechanics use rolls of paper towels for most work because they are readily available and disposable. To help keep the area under the vehicle clean, a large cardboard box can be cut open and flattened to protect the garage or shop floor.

Whenever working over a painted surface, such as when leaning over a fender to service something under the hood, always cover it with an old blanket or bedspread to protect the finish. Vinyl covered pads, made especially for this purpose, are available at auto parts stores.

Booster battery (jump) starting

Observe these precautions when using a booster battery to start a vehicle:

a) *Before connecting the booster battery, make sure the ignition switch is in the OFF position.*
b) *Turn off the lights, heater and other electrical loads.*
c) *Your eyes should be shielded. Safety goggles are a good idea.*
d) *Make sure the booster battery is the same voltage as the dead one in the vehicle.*
e) *The two vehicles MUST NOT TOUCH each other!*
f) *Make sure the transaxle is in Neutral (manual) or Park (automatic).*
g) *If the booster battery is not a maintenance-free type, remove the vent caps and lay a cloth over the vent holes.*

Connect the red colored jumper cable to the positive (+) terminal of booster battery and the other end to the positive (+) terminal of the dead battery. Then connect one end of the black colored jumper cable to the negative (-) terminal of the booster battery and other end of the cable to a good ground on the vehicle to be started, such as a bolt or bracket on the engine.

Start the engine using the booster battery and then with the engine running at idle speed, disconnect the jumper cables in the reverse order of connection.

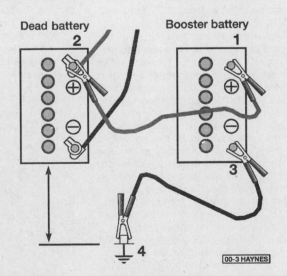

Make the booster cable connections in the numerical order shown (note that the negative cable of the booster battery is NOT attached to the negative terminal of the dead battery)

Jacking and towing

Jacking

Warning: *The jack supplied with the vehicle should only be used for changing a tire or placing jackstands under the frame. Never work under the vehicle or start the engine while this jack is being used as the only means of support.*

The vehicle should be on level ground. Place the shift lever in Park, if you have an automatic, or Reverse if you have a manual transaxle. Block the wheel diagonally opposite the wheel being changed. Set the parking brake.

Remove the spare tire and jack from stowage. Remove the wheel cover and trim ring (if so equipped) with the tapered end of the lug nut wrench by inserting and twisting the handle and then prying against the back of the wheel cover. Loosen the wheel lug nuts about 1/4-to-1/2 turn each.

Place the scissors-type jack under the side of the vehicle and adjust the jack height until it fits in the notch in the vertical rocker panel flange nearest the wheel to be changed. There is a front and rear jacking point on each side of the vehicle **(see illustration)**.

Turn the jack handle clockwise until the tire clears the ground. Remove the lug nuts and pull the wheel off. Install the spare.

Install the lug nuts with the beveled edges facing in. Tighten them snugly. Don't attempt to tighten them completely until the vehicle is lowered or it could slip off the jack. Turn the jack handle counterclockwise to lower the vehicle. Remove the jack and tighten the lug nuts in a diagonal pattern.

Install the cover (and trim ring, if used) and be sure it's snapped into place all the way around.

Stow the tire, jack and wrench. Unblock the wheels.

Towing

As a general rule, the vehicle should be towed with the front (drive) wheels off the ground. If they can't be raised, place them on a dolly. The ignition key must be in the ACC position, since the steering lock mechanism isn't strong enough to hold the front wheels straight while towing.

Vehicles equipped with an automatic transaxle can be towed from the rear, with the front wheels on the ground, provided that speeds don't exceed 25 mph and the distance is not over 15 miles. Before towing, check the transmission fluid level (see Chapter 1). If the level is below the HOT line on the dipstick, add fluid or use a towing dolly.

When towing a vehicle equipped with a manual transaxle with all four wheels on the ground, be sure to place the shift lever in Neutral and release the parking brake.

Equipment specifically designed for towing should be used. It should be attached to the main structural members of the vehicle, not the bumpers, brackets or suspension. Safety is a major consideration when towing and all applicable state and local laws must be obeyed. A safety chain system must be used at all times.

The jack fits over the rocker panel flange (there are two jacking points on each side of the vehicle, indicated by a pair of notches, front and rear, in the rocker panel flange)

Automotive chemicals and lubricants

A number of automotive chemicals and lubricants are available for use during vehicle maintenance and repair. They include a wide variety of products ranging from cleaning solvents and degreasers to lubricants and protective sprays for rubber, plastic and vinyl.

Cleaners

Carburetor cleaner and choke cleaner is a strong solvent for gum, varnish and carbon. Most carburetor cleaners leave a dry-type lubricant film which will not harden or gum up. Because of this film it is not recommended for use on electrical components.

Brake system cleaner is used to remove brake dust, grease and brake fluid from the brake system, where clean surfaces are absolutely necessary. It leaves no residue and often eliminates brake squeal caused by contaminants.

Electrical cleaner removes oxidation, corrosion and carbon deposits from electrical contacts, restoring full current flow. It can also be used to clean spark plugs, carburetor jets, voltage regulators and other parts where an oil-free surface is desired.

Demoisturants remove water and moisture from electrical components such as alternators, voltage regulators, electrical connectors and fuse blocks. They are non-conductive and non-corrosive.

Degreasers are heavy-duty solvents used to remove grease from the outside of the engine and from chassis components. They can be sprayed or brushed on and, depending on the type, are rinsed off either with water or solvent.

Lubricants

Motor oil is the lubricant formulated for use in engines. It normally contains a wide variety of additives to prevent corrosion and reduce foaming and wear. Motor oil comes in various weights (viscosity ratings) from 0 to 50. The recommended weight of the oil depends on the season, temperature and the demands on the engine. Light oil is used in cold climates and under light load conditions. Heavy oil is used in hot climates and where high loads are encountered. Multi-viscosity oils are designed to have characteristics of both light and heavy oils and are available in a number of weights from 0W-20 to 20W-50.

Gear oil is designed to be used in differentials, manual transmissions and other areas where high-temperature lubrication is required.

Chassis and wheel bearing grease is a heavy grease used where increased loads and friction are encountered, such as for wheel bearings, balljoints, tie-rod ends and universal joints.

High-temperature wheel bearing grease is designed to withstand the extreme temperatures encountered by wheel bearings in disc brake equipped vehicles. It usually contains molybdenum disulfide (moly), which is a dry-type lubricant.

White grease is a heavy grease for metal-to-metal applications where water is a problem. White grease stays soft under both low and high temperatures (usually from -100 to +190-degrees F), and will not wash off or dilute in the presence of water.

Assembly lube is a special extreme pressure lubricant, usually containing moly, used to lubricate high-load parts (such as main and rod bearings and cam lobes) for initial start-up of a new engine. The assembly lube lubricates the parts without being squeezed out or washed away until the engine oiling system begins to function.

Silicone lubricants are used to protect rubber, plastic, vinyl and nylon parts.

Graphite lubricants are used where oils cannot be used due to contamination problems, such as in locks. The dry graphite will lubricate metal parts while remaining uncontaminated by dirt, water, oil or acids. It is electrically conductive and will not foul electrical contacts in locks such as the ignition switch.

Moly penetrants loosen and lubricate frozen, rusted and corroded fasteners and prevent future rusting or freezing.

Heat-sink grease is a special electrically non-conductive grease that is used for mounting electronic ignition modules where it is essential that heat is transferred away from the module.

Sealants

RTV sealant is one of the most widely used gasket compounds. Made from silicone, RTV is air curing, it seals, bonds, waterproofs, fills surface irregularities, remains flexible, doesn't shrink, is relatively easy to remove, and is used as a supplementary sealer with almost all low and medium temperature gaskets.

Anaerobic sealant is much like RTV in that it can be used either to seal gaskets or to form gaskets by itself. It remains flexible, is solvent resistant and fills surface imperfections. The difference between an anaerobic sealant and an RTV-type sealant is in the curing. RTV cures when exposed to air, while an anaerobic sealant cures only in the absence of air. This means that an anaerobic sealant cures only after the assembly of parts, sealing them together.

Thread and pipe sealant is used for sealing hydraulic and pneumatic fittings and vacuum lines. It is usually made from a Teflon compound, and comes in a spray, a paint-on liquid and as a wrap-around tape.

Chemicals

Anti-seize compound prevents seizing, galling, cold welding, rust and corrosion in fasteners. High-temperature ant-seize, usually made with copper and graphite lubricants, is used for exhaust system and exhaust manifold bolts.

Anaerobic locking compounds are used to keep fasteners from vibrating or working loose and cure only after installation, in the absence of air. Medium strength locking compound is used for small nuts, bolts and screws that may be removed later. High-strength locking compound is for large nuts, bolts and studs which aren't removed on a regular basis.

Oil additives range from viscosity index improvers to chemical treatments that claim to reduce internal engine friction. It should be noted that most oil manufacturers caution against using additives with their oils.

Gas additives perform several functions, depending on their chemical makeup. They usually contain solvents that help dissolve gum and varnish that build up on carburetor, fuel injection and intake parts. They also serve to break down carbon deposits that form on the inside surfaces of the combustion chambers. Some additives contain upper cylinder lubricants for valves and piston rings, and others contain chemicals to remove condensation from the gas tank.

Miscellaneous

Brake fluid is specially formulated hydraulic fluid that can withstand the heat and pressure encountered in brake systems. Care must be taken so this fluid does not come in contact with painted surfaces or plastics. An opened container should always be resealed to prevent contamination by water or dirt.

Weatherstrip adhesive is used to bond weatherstripping around doors, windows and trunk lids. It is sometimes used to attach trim pieces.

Undercoating is a petroleum-based, tar-like substance that is designed to protect metal surfaces on the underside of the vehicle from corrosion. It also acts as a sound-deadening agent by insulating the bottom of the vehicle.

Waxes and polishes are used to help protect painted and plated surfaces from the weather. Different types of paint may require the use of different types of wax and polish. Some polishes utilize a chemical or abrasive cleaner to help remove the top layer of oxidized (dull) paint on older vehicles. In recent years many non-wax polishes that contain a wide variety of chemicals such as polymers and silicones have been introduced. These non-wax polishes are usually easier to apply and last longer than conventional waxes and polishes.

Conversion factors

Length (distance)

Inches (in)	X 25.4	= Millimeters (mm)	X 0.0394	= Inches (in)
Feet (ft)	X 0.305	= Meters (m)	X 3.281	= Feet (ft)
Miles	X 1.609	= Kilometers (km)	X 0.621	= Miles

Volume (capacity)

Cubic inches (cu in; in³)	X 16.387	= Cubic centimeters (cc; cm³)	X 0.061	= Cubic inches (cu in; in³)
Imperial pints (Imp pt)	X 0.568	= Liters (l)	X 1.76	= Imperial pints (Imp pt)
Imperial quarts (Imp qt)	X 1.137	= Liters (l)	X 0.88	= Imperial quarts (Imp qt)
Imperial quarts (Imp qt)	X 1.201	= US quarts (US qt)	X 0.833	= Imperial quarts (Imp qt)
US quarts (US qt)	X 0.946	= Liters (l)	X 1.057	= US quarts (US qt)
Imperial gallons (Imp gal)	X 4.546	= Liters (l)	X 0.22	= Imperial gallons (Imp gal)
Imperial gallons (Imp gal)	X 1.201	= US gallons (US gal)	X 0.833	= Imperial gallons (Imp gal)
US gallons (US gal)	X 3.785	= Liters (l)	X 0.264	= US gallons (US gal)

Mass (weight)

Ounces (oz)	X 28.35	= Grams (g)	X 0.035	= Ounces (oz)
Pounds (lb)	X 0.454	= Kilograms (kg)	X 2.205	= Pounds (lb)

Force

Ounces-force (ozf; oz)	X 0.278	= Newtons (N)	X 3.6	= Ounces-force (ozf; oz)
Pounds-force (lbf; lb)	X 4.448	= Newtons (N)	X 0.225	= Pounds-force (lbf; lb)
Newtons (N)	X 0.1	= Kilograms-force (kgf; kg)	X 9.81	= Newtons (N)

Pressure

Pounds-force per square inch (psi; lbf/in²; lb/in²)	X 0.070	= Kilograms-force per square centimeter (kgf/cm²; kg/cm²)	X 14.223	= Pounds-force per square inch (psi; lbf/in²; lb/in²)
Pounds-force per square inch (psi; lbf/in²; lb/in²)	X 0.068	= Atmospheres (atm)	X 14.696	= Pounds-force per square inch (psi; lbf/in²; lb/in²)
Pounds-force per square inch (psi; lbf/in²; lb/in²)	X 0.069	= Bars	X 14.5	= Pounds-force per square inch (psi; lbf/in²; lb/in²)
Pounds-force per square inch (psi; lbf/in²; lb/in²)	X 6.895	= Kilopascals (kPa)	X 0.145	= Pounds-force per square inch (psi; lbf/in²; lb/in²)
Kilopascals (kPa)	X 0.01	= Kilograms-force per square centimeter (kgf/cm²; kg/cm²)	X 98.1	= Kilopascals (kPa)

Torque (moment of force)

Pounds-force inches (lbf in; lb in)	X 1.152	= Kilograms-force centimeter (kgf cm; kg cm)	X 0.868	= Pounds-force inches (lbf in; lb in)
Pounds-force inches (lbf in; lb in)	X 0.113	= Newton meters (Nm)	X 8.85	= Pounds-force inches (lbf in; lb in)
Pounds-force inches (lbf in; lb in)	X 0.083	= Pounds-force feet (lbf ft; lb ft)	X 12	= Pounds-force inches (lbf in; lb in)
Pounds-force feet (lbf ft; lb ft)	X 0.138	= Kilograms-force meters (kgf m; kg m)	X 7.233	= Pounds-force feet (lbf ft; lb ft)
Pounds-force feet (lbf ft; lb ft)	X 1.356	= Newton meters (Nm)	X 0.738	= Pounds-force feet (lbf ft; lb ft)
Newton meters (Nm)	X 0.102	= Kilograms-force meters (kgf m; kg m)	X 9.804	= Newton meters (Nm)

Vacuum

Inches mercury (in. Hg)	X 3.377	= Kilopascals (kPa)	X 0.2961	= Inches mercury
Inches mercury (in. Hg)	X 25.4	= Millimeters mercury (mm Hg)	X 0.0394	= Inches mercury

Power

Horsepower (hp)	X 745.7	= Watts (W)	X 0.0013	= Horsepower (hp)

Velocity (speed)

Miles per hour (miles/hr; mph)	X 1.609	= Kilometers per hour (km/hr; kph)	X 0.621	= Miles per hour (miles/hr; mph)

Fuel consumption*

Miles per gallon, Imperial (mpg)	X 0.354	= Kilometers per liter (km/l)	X 2.825	= Miles per gallon, Imperial (mpg)
Miles per gallon, US (mpg)	X 0.425	= Kilometers per liter (km/l)	X 2.352	= Miles per gallon, US (mpg)

Temperature

Degrees Fahrenheit = (°C x 1.8) + 32

Degrees Celsius (Degrees Centigrade; °C) = (°F - 32) x 0.56

*It is common practice to convert from miles per gallon (mpg) to liters/100 kilometers (l/100km), where mpg (Imperial) x l/100 km = 282 and mpg (US) x l/100 km = 235

DECIMALS to MILLIMETERS

Decimal	mm	Decimal	mm
0.001	0.0254	0.500	12.7000
0.002	0.0508	0.510	12.9540
0.003	0.0762	0.520	13.2080
0.004	0.1016	0.530	13.4620
0.005	0.1270	0.540	13.7160
0.006	0.1524	0.550	13.9700
0.007	0.1778	0.560	14.2240
0.008	0.2032	0.570	14.4780
0.009	0.2286	0.580	14.7320
		0.590	14.9860
0.010	0.2540		
0.020	0.5080		
0.030	0.7620		
0.040	1.0160	0.600	15.2400
0.050	1.2700	0.610	15.4940
0.060	1.5240	0.620	15.7480
0.070	1.7780	0.630	16.0020
0.080	2.0320	0.640	16.2560
0.090	2.2860	0.650	16.5100
		0.660	16.7640
0.100	2.5400	0.670	17.0180
0.110	2.7940	0.680	17.2720
0.120	3.0480	0.690	17.5260
0.130	3.3020		
0.140	3.5560		
0.150	3.8100		
0.160	4.0640	0.700	17.7800
0.170	4.3180	0.710	18.0340
0.180	4.5720	0.720	18.2880
0.190	4.8260	0.730	18.5420
		0.740	18.7960
0.200	5.0800	0.750	19.0500
0.210	5.3340	0.760	19.3040
0.220	5.5880	0.770	19.5580
0.230	5.8420	0.780	19.8120
0.240	6.0960	0.790	20.0660
0.250	6.3500		
0.260	6.6040		
0.270	6.8580	0.800	20.3200
0.280	7.1120	0.810	20.5740
0.290	7.3660	0.820	21.8280
		0.830	21.0820
0.300	7.6200	0.840	21.3360
0.310	7.8740	0.850	21.5900
0.320	8.1280	0.860	21.8440
0.330	8.3820	0.870	22.0980
0.340	8.6360	0.880	22.3520
0.350	8.8900	0.890	22.6060
0.360	9.1440		
0.370	9.3980		
0.380	9.6520		
0.390	9.9060	0.900	22.8600
0.400	10.1600	0.910	23.1140
0.410	10.4140	0.920	23.3680
0.420	10.6680	0.930	23.6220
0.430	10.9220	0.940	23.8760
0.440	11.1760	0.950	24.1300
0.450	11.4300	0.960	24.3840
0.460	11.6840	0.970	24.6380
0.470	11.9380	0.980	24.8920
0.480	12.1920	0.990	25.1460
0.490	12.4460	1.000	25.4000

FRACTIONS to DECIMALS to MILLIMETERS

Fraction	Decimal	mm	Fraction	Decimal	mm
1/64	0.0156	0.3969	33/64	0.5156	13.0969
1/32	0.0312	0.7938	17/32	0.5312	13.4938
3/64	0.0469	1.1906	35/64	0.5469	13.8906
1/16	0.0625	1.5875	9/16	0.5625	14.2875
5/64	0.0781	1.9844	37/64	0.5781	14.6844
3/32	0.0938	2.3812	19/32	0.5938	15.0812
7/64	0.1094	2.7781	39/64	0.6094	15.4781
1/8	0.1250	3.1750	5/8	0.6250	15.8750
9/64	0.1406	3.5719	41/64	0.6406	16.2719
5/32	0.1562	3.9688	21/32	0.6562	16.6688
11/64	0.1719	4.3656	43/64	0.6719	17.0656
3/16	0.1875	4.7625	11/16	0.6875	17.4625
13/64	0.2031	5.1594	45/64	0.7031	17.8594
7/32	0.2188	5.5562	23/32	0.7188	18.2562
15/64	0.2344	5.9531	47/64	0.7344	18.6531
1/4	0.2500	6.3500	3/4	0.7500	19.0500
17/64	0.2656	6.7469	49/64	0.7656	19.4469
9/32	0.2812	7.1438	25/32	0.7812	19.8438
19/64	0.2969	7.5406	51/64	0.7969	20.2406
5/16	0.3125	7.9375	13/16	0.8125	20.6375
21/64	0.3281	8.3344	53/64	0.8281	21.0344
11/32	0.3438	8.7312	27/32	0.8438	21.4312
23/64	0.3594	9.1281	55/64	0.8594	21.8281
3/8	0.3750	9.5250	7/8	0.8750	22.2250
25/64	0.3906	9.9219	57/64	0.8906	22.6219
13/32	0.4062	10.3188	29/32	0.9062	23.0188
27/64	0.4219	10.7156	59/64	0.9219	23.4156
7/16	0.4375	11.1125	15/16	0.9375	23.8125
29/64	0.4531	11.5094	61/64	0.9531	24.2094
15/32	0.4688	11.9062	31/32	0.9688	24.6062
31/64	0.4844	12.3031	63/64	0.9844	25.0031
1/2	0.5000	12.7000	1	1.0000	25.4000

Safety first!

Regardless of how enthusiastic you may be about getting on with the job at hand, take the time to ensure that your safety is not jeopardized. A moment's lack of attention can result in an accident, as can failure to observe certain simple safety precautions. The possibility of an accident will always exist, and the following points should not be considered a comprehensive list of all dangers. Rather, they are intended to make you aware of the risks and to encourage a safety conscious approach to all work you carry out on your vehicle.

Essential DOs and DON'Ts

DON'T rely on a jack when working under the vehicle. Always use approved jackstands to support the weight of the vehicle and place them under the recommended lift or support points.

DON'T attempt to loosen extremely tight fasteners (i.e. wheel lug nuts) while the vehicle is on a jack - it may fall.

DON'T start the engine without first making sure that the transmission is in Neutral (or Park where applicable) and the parking brake is set.

DON'T remove the radiator cap from a hot cooling system - let it cool or cover it with a cloth and release the pressure gradually.

DON'T attempt to drain the engine oil until you are sure it has cooled to the point that it will not burn you.

DON'T touch any part of the engine or exhaust system until it has cooled sufficiently to avoid burns.

DON'T siphon toxic liquids such as gasoline, antifreeze and brake fluid by mouth, or allow them to remain on your skin.

DON'T inhale brake lining dust - it is potentially hazardous (see *Asbestos* below).

DON'T allow spilled oil or grease to remain on the floor - wipe it up before someone slips on it.

DON'T use loose fitting wrenches or other tools which may slip and cause injury.

DON'T push on wrenches when loosening or tightening nuts or bolts. Always try to pull the wrench toward you. If the situation calls for pushing the wrench away, push with an open hand to avoid scraped knuckles if the wrench should slip.

DON'T attempt to lift a heavy component alone - get someone to help you.

DON'T *rush or take unsafe shortcuts to finish a job.*

DON'T allow children or animals in or around the vehicle while you are working on it.

DO wear eye protection when using power tools such as a drill, sander, bench grinder, etc. and when working under a vehicle.

DO keep loose clothing and long hair well out of the way of moving parts.

DO make sure that any hoist used has a safe working load rating adequate for the job.

DO get someone to check on you periodically when working alone on a vehicle.

DO carry out work in a logical sequence and make sure that everything is correctly assembled and tightened.

DO keep chemicals and fluids tightly capped and out of the reach of children and pets.

DO remember that your vehicle's safety affects that of yourself and others. If in doubt on any point, get professional advice.

Steering, suspension and brakes

These systems are essential to driving safety, so make sure you have a qualified shop or individual check your work. Also, compressed suspension springs can cause injury if released suddenly - be sure to use a spring compressor.

Airbags

Airbags are explosive devices that can **CAUSE** injury if they deploy while you're working on the vehicle. Follow the manufacturer's instructions to disable the airbag whenever you're working in the vicinity of airbag components.

Asbestos

Certain friction, insulating, sealing, and other products - such as brake linings, brake bands, clutch linings, torque converters, gaskets, etc. - may contain asbestos or other hazardous friction material. Extreme care must be taken to avoid inhalation of dust from such products, since it is hazardous to health. If in doubt, assume that they do contain asbestos.

Fire

Remember at all times that gasoline is highly flammable. Never smoke or have any kind of open flame around when working on a vehicle. But the risk does not end there. A spark caused by an electrical short circuit, by two metal surfaces contacting each other, or even by static electricity built up in your body under certain conditions, can ignite gasoline vapors, which in a confined space are highly explosive. Do not, under any circumstances, use gasoline for cleaning parts. Use an approved safety solvent.

Always disconnect the battery ground (-) cable at the battery before working on any part of the fuel system or electrical system. Never risk spilling fuel on a hot engine or exhaust component. It is strongly recommended that a fire extinguisher suitable for use on fuel and electrical fires be kept handy in the garage or workshop at all times. Never try to extinguish a fuel or electrical fire with water.

Fumes

Certain fumes are highly toxic and can quickly cause unconsciousness and even death if inhaled to any extent. Gasoline vapor falls into this category, as do the vapors from some cleaning solvents. Any draining or pouring of such volatile fluids should be done in a well ventilated area.

When using cleaning fluids and solvents, read the instructions on the container carefully. Never use materials from unmarked containers.

Never run the engine in an enclosed space, such as a garage. Exhaust fumes contain carbon monoxide, which is extremely poisonous. If you need to run the engine, always do so in the open air, or at least have the rear of the vehicle outside the work area.

The battery

Never create a spark or allow a bare light bulb near a battery. They normally give off a certain amount of hydrogen gas, which is highly explosive.

Always disconnect the battery ground (-) cable at the battery before working on the fuel or electrical systems.

If possible, loosen the filler caps or cover when charging the battery from an external source (this does not apply to sealed or maintenance-free batteries). Do not charge at an excessive rate or the battery may burst.

Take care when adding water to a non maintenance-free battery and when carrying a battery. The electrolyte, even when diluted, is very corrosive and should not be allowed to contact clothing or skin.

Always wear eye protection when cleaning the battery to prevent the caustic deposits from entering your eyes.

Household current

When using an electric power tool, inspection light, etc., which operates on household current, always make sure that the tool is correctly connected to its plug and that, where necessary, it is properly grounded. Do not use such items in damp conditions and, again, do not create a spark or apply excessive heat in the vicinity of fuel or fuel vapor.

Secondary ignition system voltage

A severe electric shock can result from touching certain parts of the ignition system (such as the spark plug wires) when the engine is running or being cranked, particularly if components are damp or the insulation is defective. In the case of an electronic ignition system, the secondary system voltage is much higher and could prove fatal.

Hydrofluoric acid

This extremely corrosive acid is formed when certain types of synthetic rubber, found in some O-rings, oil seals, fuel hoses, etc. are exposed to temperatures above 750-degrees F (400-degrees C). The rubber changes into a charred or sticky substance containing the acid. *Once formed, the acid remains dangerous for years. If it gets onto the skin, it may be necessary to amputate the limb concerned.*

When dealing with a vehicle which has suffered a fire, or with components salvaged from such a vehicle, wear protective gloves and discard them after use.

Troubleshooting

Contents

This section provides an easy reference guide to the more common problems which may occur during the operation of your vehicle. These problems and their possible causes are grouped under headings denoting various components or systems, such as Engine, Cooling system, etc. They also refer you to the chapter and/or section that deals with the problem.

Remember that successful troubleshooting is not a mysterious art practiced only by professional mechanics. It is simply the result of the right knowledge combined with an intelligent, systematic approach to the problem. Always work by a process of elimination, starting with the simplest solution and working through to the most complex - and never overlook the obvious. Anyone can run the gas tank dry or leave the lights on overnight, so don't assume that you are exempt from such oversights.

Finally, always establish a clear idea of why a problem has occurred and take steps to ensure that it doesn't happen again. If the electrical system fails because of a poor connection, check the other connections in the system to make sure that they don't fail as well. If a particular fuse continues to blow, find out why - don't just replace one fuse after another. Remember, failure of a small component can often be indicative of potential failure or incorrect functioning of a more important component or system.

Engine

1 Engine will not rotate when attempting to start

1   Battery terminal connections loose or corroded (Chapters 1 and 5).
2   Battery discharged or faulty (Chapter 1).
3   Automatic transaxle not completely engaged in Park (Chapter 7B) or clutch pedal not completely depressed (Chapter 8).
4   Broken, loose or disconnected wiring in the starting circuit (Chapters 5 and 12).
5   Starter motor pinion jammed in flywheel ring gear (Chapter 5).
6   Starter solenoid faulty (Chapter 5).
7   Starter motor faulty (Chapter 5).
8   Ignition switch faulty (Chapter 12).
9   Starter pinion or flywheel teeth worn or broken (Chapter 5).
10   Defective fusible link (see Chapter 12).

2 Engine rotates but will not start

1   Fuel tank empty.
2   Battery discharged (engine rotates slowly) (Chapter 5).
3   Battery terminal connections loose or corroded (Chapters 1 and 5).
4   Leaking fuel injector(s), faulty fuel pump,

pressure regulator, etc. (Chapter 4).
5   Broken or stripped timing belt (Chapter 2).
6   Ignition components damp or damaged (Chapter 5).
7   Worn, faulty or incorrectly gapped spark plugs (Chapter 1).
8   Broken, loose or disconnected wiring in the starting circuit (Chapter 5).
9   Broken, loose or disconnected wires at the ignition coil(s) or faulty coil(s) (Chapter 5).
10   Defective crankshaft sensor, camshaft sensor or PCM (see Chapter 6).

3 Engine hard to start when cold

1   Battery discharged or low (Chapter 1).
2   Malfunctioning fuel system (Chapter 4).
3   Faulty coolant temperature sensor or intake air temperature sensor (Chapter 6).
4   Fuel injector(s) leaking (Chapter 4).
5   Faulty ignition system (Chapter 5).
6   Defective MAP sensor (see Chapter 6).

4 Engine hard to start when hot

1   Air filter clogged (Chapter 1).
2   Fuel not reaching the fuel injection system (Chapter 4).
3   Corroded battery connections, especially ground (Chapters 1 and 5).
4   Faulty coolant temperature sensor or intake air temperature sensor (Chapter 6).

5 Starter motor noisy or excessively rough in engagement

1   Pinion or flywheel gear teeth worn or broken (Chapter 5).
2   Starter motor mounting bolts loose or missing (Chapter 5).

6 Engine starts but stops immediately

1   Loose or faulty electrical connections at ignition coil (Chapter 5).
2   Insufficient fuel reaching the fuel injector(s) (Chapters 4).
3   Vacuum leak at the gasket between the intake manifold/plenum and throttle body (Chapter 4).
4   Fault in the engine control system (Chapter 6).
5   Intake air leaks, broken vacuum lines (see Chapter 4).

7 Oil puddle under engine

1   Oil pan gasket and/or oil pan drain bolt washer leaking (Chapter 2).

2   Oil pressure sending unit leaking (Chapter 2).
3   Oil filter or adapter block leaking (Chapter 1).
4   Valve cover(s) leaking (Chapter 2).
5   Engine oil seals leaking (Chapter 2).

8 Engine lopes while idling or idles erratically

1   Vacuum leakage (Chapters 2 and 4).
2   Leaking EGR valve or EGR vacuum lines (Chapter 6).
3   Air filter clogged (Chapter 1).
4   Fuel pump not delivering sufficient fuel to the fuel injection system (Chapter 4).
5   Leaking head gasket (Chapter 2).
6   Timing belt and/or sprocket(s) worn (Chapter 2).
7   Camshaft lobes worn (Chapter 2).

9 Engine misses at idle speed

1   Spark plugs worn or not gapped properly (Chapter 1).
2   Faulty spark plug wires (Chapter 1).
3   Vacuum leaks (Chapters 2 and 4).
4   Faulty ignition coil(s) (Chapter 5).
5   Uneven or low compression (Chapter 2).
6   Faulty fuel injector(s) (Chapter 4).

10 Engine misses throughout driving speed range

1   Fuel filter clogged and/or impurities in the fuel system (Chapter 4).
2   Low fuel output at the fuel injector(s) (Chapter 4).
3   Faulty or incorrectly gapped spark plugs (Chapter 1).
4   Defective spark plug wires (Chapters 1 or 5).
5   Faulty emission system components (Chapter 6).
6   Low or uneven cylinder compression pressures (Chapter 2).
7   Burned valves (Chapter 2).
8   Weak or faulty ignition system (Chapter 5).
9   Vacuum leak in fuel injection system, throttle body, intake manifold or vacuum hoses (Chapter 4).

11 Engine stumbles on acceleration

1   Spark plugs fouled (Chapter 1).
2   Problem with fuel injection system (Chapter 4).
3   Fuel filter clogged (Chapter 4).
4   Fault in the engine control system (Chapter 6).
5   Intake air leak (Chapters 2 and 4).
6   EGR system malfunction (Chapter 6).

12 Engine surges while holding accelerator steady

1 Intake air leak (Chapter 4).
2 Fuel pump or fuel pressure regulator faulty (Chapter 4).
3 Problem with the fuel injection system (Chapter 4).
4 Problem with the emissions control system (Chapter 6).

13 Engine stalls

1 Idle speed incorrect (Chapter 1).
2 Fuel filter clogged and/or water and impurities in the fuel system (Chapter 4).
3 Ignition components damp or damaged (Chapter 5).
4 Faulty emissions system components (Chapter 6).
5 Faulty or incorrectly gapped spark plugs (Chapter 1).
6 Faulty spark plug wires (Chapter 1).
7 Vacuum leak in the fuel injection system, intake manifold or vacuum hoses (Chapters 2 and 4).

14 Engine lacks power

1 Worn camshaft lobes (Chapter 2).
2 Burned valves or incorrect valve timing (Chapter 2).
3 Faulty spark plug wires or faulty coil(s) (Chapters 1 and 5).
4 Faulty or incorrectly gapped spark plugs (Chapter 1).
5 Problem with the fuel injection system (Chapter 4).
6 Plugged air filter (Chapter 1).
7 Brakes binding (Chapter 9).
8 Automatic transaxle fluid level incorrect (Chapter 1).
9 Clutch slipping (Chapter 8).
10 Fuel filter clogged and/or impurities in the fuel system (Chapter 4).
11 Emission control system not functioning properly (Chapter 6).
12 Low or uneven cylinder compression pressures (Chapter 2).
13 Restricted exhaust system or catalytic converter (Chapter 4).

15 Engine backfires

1 Emission control system not functioning properly (Chapter 6).
2 Faulty spark plug wires or coil(s) (Chapter 5).
3 Problem with the fuel injection system (Chapter 4).
4 Vacuum leak at fuel injector(s), intake manifold or vacuum hoses (Chapters 2 and 4).
5 Burned valves or incorrect valve timing (Chapter 2).

16 Pinging or knocking engine sounds during acceleration or uphill

1 Incorrect grade of fuel.
2 Problem with the engine control system (Chapter 6).
3 Fuel injection system faulty (Chapter 4).
4 Improper or damaged spark plugs or wires (Chapter 1).
5 EGR valve not functioning (Chapter 6).
6 Vacuum leak (Chapters 2 and 4).

17 Engine runs with oil pressure light on

1 Low oil level (Chapter 1).
2 Idle rpm below specification (Chapter 1).
3 Short in wiring circuit (Chapter 12).
4 Faulty oil pressure sender (Chapter 2).
5 Worn engine bearings and/or oil pump (Chapter 2).

18 Engine diesels (continues to run) after switching off

1 Idle speed too high (Chapter 1).
2 Excessive engine operating temperature (Chapter 3).
3 Excessive carbon deposits on valves and pistons (see Chapter 2)

Engine electrical system

19 Alternator light fails to come on when key is turned on

1 Warning light bulb defective (Chapter 12).
2 Fault in the printed circuit, dash wiring or bulb holder (Chapter 12).

20 Alternator light fails to go out

1 Faulty alternator or charging circuit (Chapter 5).
2 Alternator drivebelt defective or out of adjustment (Chapter 1).
3 Alternator voltage regulator fault (Chapter 5).

21 Battery will not hold a charge

1 The alternator drivebelt defective or not adjusted properly (slipping) (Chapter 1).
2 Battery electrolyte level low (not applicable on maintenance-free batteries) (Chapter 1).
3 Battery terminals loose or corroded (Chapters 1 and 5).
4 Alternator not charging properly (Chapter 5).

5 The wiring in the charging circuit is loose, broken or faulty (Chapter 5).
6 Short in vehicle wiring (Chapter 12).
7 The battery is internally defective (Chapters 1 and 5).

Fuel and emissions systems

22 CHECK ENGINE or SERVICE ENGINE SOON light remains on or is flashing

1 Light remains on:
a) *Fuel filler cap (gas cap) is not seated or tightened properly.*
b) *On-Board Diagnostic (OBD-II) computer has detected an emissions or fuel injection component fault (Chapter 6).*
2 Light is flashing:
a) *If the CHECK ENGINE or SERVICE ENGINE SOON light is flashing, severe catalytic converter damage has occurred and engine power loss will soon result. Take the vehicle to your nearest dealer service department or other qualified shop for immediate repair.*

23 Excessive fuel consumption

1 Dirty or clogged air filter element (Chapter 1).
2 Emissions system not functioning properly (Chapter 6).
3 The fuel injection system not functioning properly (Chapter 4).
4 Low tire pressure or incorrect tire size (Chapter 1).
5 Dragging brakes (Chapter 9).

24 Fuel leakage and/or fuel odor

1 Leaking fuel feed or return line (Chapters 1 and 4).
2 Fuel tank overfilled.
3 Clogged evaporative canister filter (Chapters 1 and 6).
4 Problem with the fuel injection system (Chapter 4).

Cooling system

25 Overheating

1 There is insufficient coolant in the system (Chapter 1).
2 Water pump defective (Chapter 3).
3 Radiator core blocked or grille restricted (Chapter 3).
4 The thermostat is faulty (Chapter 3).
5 Electric cooling fan inoperative or the blades are broken (Chapter 3).
6 Radiator cap not maintaining proper pressure (Chapter 3).

26 Overcooling

1   The thermostat is faulty (Chapter 3).
2   The temperature gauge sending unit is inaccurate (Chapter 3)

27 External coolant leakage

1   Deteriorated/damaged hoses; loose clamps (Chapters 1 and 3).
2   Water pump defective (Chapter 3).
3   Leakage from radiator core or coolant reservoir (Chapter 3).
4   Engine drain or water jacket core plugs leaking (Chapter 2).

28 Internal coolant leakage

1   Leaking cylinder head gasket (Chapter 2).
2   Cracked cylinder bore or cylinder head (Chapter 2).

29 Coolant loss

1   Too much coolant in system (Chapter 1).
2   Coolant boiling away because of overheating (Chapter 3).
3   Internal or external leakage (Chapter 3).
4   Faulty radiator cap (Chapter 3).

30 Poor coolant circulation

1   Inoperative water pump (Chapter 3).
2   Restriction in cooling system (Chapters 1 and 3).
3   Thermostat sticking (Chapter 3).

Clutch

31 Pedal travels to floor - no pressure or very little resistance

1   Broken release bearing or fork (Chapter 8).
2   Faulty clutch master cylinder or release cylinder (Chapter 8).

32 Unable to select gears

1   Faulty transaxle (Chapter 7A).
2   Faulty clutch disc or pressure plate (Chapter 8).
3   Faulty clutch master cylinder or release cylinder (Chapter 8).
4   Faulty release lever or release bearing (Chapter 8).
5   Faulty shift lever assembly or cables (Chapter 8).

33 Clutch slips (engine speed increases with no increase in vehicle speed)

1   Clutch plate worn (Chapter 8).
2   Clutch plate is oil soaked by leaking rear main seal (Chapters 2 and 8).
3   Clutch plate not seated (Chapter 8).
4   Warped pressure plate or flywheel (Chapter 8).
5   Weak clutch diaphragm springs (Chapter 8).
6   Clutch plate overheated. Allow to cool.

34 Grabbing (chattering) as clutch is engaged

1   Oil on clutch plate lining, burned or glazed facings (Chapter 8).
2   Worn or loose engine or transaxle mounts (Chapters 2 and 7).
3   Worn splines on clutch plate hub (Chapter 8).
4   Warped pressure plate or flywheel (Chapter 8).
5   Burned or smeared resin on flywheel or pressure plate (Chapter 8).

35 Transaxle rattling (clicking)

Release fork loose (Chapter 8).

36 Noise in clutch area

Faulty throw-out bearing (Chapter 8).

37 Clutch pedal stays on floor

1   Broken release bearing or fork (Chapter 8).
2   Faulty clutch master cylinder or release cylinder (Chapter 8).
3   Faulty pressure plate (Chapter 8).

38 High pedal effort

Pressure plate faulty (Chapter 8).

Manual transaxle

39 Knocking noise at low speeds

1   Worn driveaxle constant velocity (CV) joints (Chapter 8).
2   Worn side gear shaft counterbore in differential case (Chapter 7A).*

40 Noise most pronounced when turning

Differential gear noise (Chapter 7A).*

41 Clunk on acceleration or deceleration

1   Loose engine or transaxle mounts (Chapters 2 and 7A).
2   Worn differential pinion shaft in case.*
3   Worn side gear shaft counterbore in differential case (Chapter 7A).*
4   Worn or damaged driveaxle inboard CV joints (Chapter 8).

42 Clicking noise in turns

Worn or damaged outboard CV joint (Chapter 8).

43 Vibration

1   Rough wheel bearing (Chapters 1 and 10).
2   Damaged driveaxle (Chapter 8).
3   Out of round tires (Chapter 1).
4   Tire out of balance (Chapters 1 and 10).
5   Worn CV joint (Chapter 8).

44 Noisy in Neutral with engine running

1   Damaged input gear bearing (Chapter 7A).*
2   Damaged clutch release bearing (Chapter 8).

45 Noisy in one particular gear

1   Damaged or worn constant mesh gears (Chapter 7A).*
2   Damaged or worn synchronizers (Chapter 7A).*
3   Bent reverse fork (Chapter 7A).*
4   Damaged fourth speed gear or output gear (Chapter 7A).*
5   Worn or damaged reverse idler gear or idler bushing (Chapter 7A).*

46 Noisy in all gears

1   Insufficient lubricant (Chapters 1 and 7A).
2   Damaged or worn bearings (Chapter 7A).*
3   Worn or damaged input gear shaft and/or output gear shaft (Chapter 7A).*

47 Slips out of gear

1 Worn or improperly adjusted linkage (Chapter 7A).
2 Transaxle loose on engine (Chapter 7A).
3 Shift linkage does not work freely, binds (Chapter 7A).
4 Input gear bearing retainer broken or loose (Chapter 7A).*
5 Worn shift fork (Chapter 7A).*

48 Leaks lubricant

1 Driveaxle seals worn (Chapter 7A).
2 Excessive amount of lubricant in transaxle (Chapters 1 and 7A).
3 Loose or broken input gear shaft bearing retainer (Chapter 7A).*
4 Input gear bearing retainer O-ring and/or lip seal damaged (Chapter 7A).*
5 Vehicle speed sensor O-ring leaking (Chapter 7A).

49 Hard to shift

Shift linkage loose or worn (Chapter 7A).
Although the corrective action necessary to remedy the symptoms described is beyond the scope of this manual, the above information should be helpful in isolating the cause of the condition so that the owner can communicate clearly with a professional mechanic.

Automatic transaxle

Note: *Due to the complexity of the automatic transaxle, it is difficult for the home mechanic to properly diagnose and service this component. For problems other than the following, the vehicle should be taken to a dealer service department or other qualified transmission shop.*

50 Fluid leakage

1 Automatic transaxle fluid is a deep red color. Fluid leaks should not be confused with engine oil, which can easily be blown onto the transaxle by air flow.
2 To pinpoint a leak, first remove all built-up dirt and grime from the transaxle housing with degreasing agents and/or steam cleaning. Then drive the vehicle at low speeds so air flow will not blow the leak far from its source. Raise the vehicle and determine where the leak is coming from. Common areas of leakage are:
   a) *Pan (Chapters 1 and 7)*
   b) *Dipstick tube (Chapters 1 and 7)*
   c) *Transaxle oil cooler lines (Chapter 7)*
   d) *Speed sensor (Chapter 7)*
   e) *Driveaxle oil seals (Chapter 7).*

51 Transaxle fluid brown or has a burned smell

Transaxle fluid overheated - change fluid and filter (Chapter 1).

52 General shift mechanism problems

1 Chapter 7, Part B, deals with checking and adjusting the shift linkage on automatic transaxles. Common problems that may be attributed to poorly adjusted linkage are:
   a) *Engine starting in gears other than Park or Neutral.*
   b) *Indicator on shifter pointing to a gear other than the one actually being used.*
   c) *Vehicle moves when in Park.*
2 Refer to Chapter 7B for the shift linkage adjustment procedure.

53 Transaxle will not downshift with accelerator pedal pressed to the floor

The transaxle is electronically controlled. This type of problem - which is caused by a malfunction in the Transmission Control Module (TCM), a sensor or solenoid, or the circuit itself - is beyond the scope of this manual. Have the problem diagnosed by a dealer service department or other qualified automatic transmission shop.

54 Engine will start in gears other than Park or Neutral

Neutral start switch out of adjustment or malfunctioning (Chapter 7B).

55 Transaxle slips, shifts roughly, is noisy or has no drive in forward or reverse gears

There are many probable causes for the above problems, but the home mechanic should be concerned with only one possibility - fluid level. Before taking the vehicle to a repair shop, check the level and condition of the fluid and/or filter as described in Chapter 1. Correct the fluid level as necessary or change the fluid and filter if needed. If the problem persists, have a professional diagnose the cause.

Driveaxles

56 Clicking noise in turns

Worn or damaged outboard CV joint (Chapter 8).

57 Shudder or vibration during acceleration

1 Excessive toe-in (Chapter 10).
2 Incorrect spring heights (Chapter 10).
3 Worn or damaged inboard or outboard CV joints (Chapter 8).
4 Sticking inboard CV joint assembly (Chapter 8).

58 Vibration at highway speeds

1 Out-of-balance front wheels and/or tires (Chapters 1 and 10).
2 Out-of-round front tires (Chapters 1 and 10).
3 Worn CV joint(s) (Chapter 8).

Brakes

Note: *Before assuming that a brake problem exists, make sure that:*
   a) *The tires are in good condition and properly inflated (Chapter 1).*
   b) *The front end alignment is correct (Chapter 10).*
   c) *The vehicle weight is not loaded in an unequal manner.*

59 Vehicle pulls to one side during braking

1 Incorrect tire pressures (Chapter 1).
2 Front end out-of-alignment (have the front end aligned).
3 Front tire sizes or tread types not matched to one another.
4 Restricted brake lines or hoses (Chapter 9).
5 Malfunctioning/leaking brake wheel cylinder or caliper assembly (Chapter 9).
6 Loose suspension parts (Chapter 10).
7 Loose calipers (Chapter 9).
8 Excessive wear of brake shoe or pad material or disc/drum on one side.

60 Noise (high-pitched squeal when the brakes are applied)

Front disc brake pads worn out. Replace pads with new ones immediately (Chapter 9).

61 Brake roughness or chatter (pedal pulsates)

1 Excessive lateral runout (Chapter 9).
2 Uneven pad wear (Chapter 9).

3   Defective disc (Chapter 9).
4   If the vehicle is equipped with an anti-lock brake system (ABS), brake pedal pulsation and associated noises are normal when severe braking is required.

62   Excessive brake pedal effort required to stop vehicle

1   Malfunctioning power brake booster (Chapter 9).
2   Partial system failure (Chapter 9).
3   Excessively worn pads or shoes (Chapter 9).
4   Piston in caliper or wheel cylinder stuck or sluggish (Chapter 9).
5   Brake pads or shoes contaminated with oil or grease (Chapter 9).
6   Brake disc grooved and/or glazed (Chapter 1).
7   New pads or shoes installed and not yet seated. It will take a while for the new material to seat against the disc or drum.

63   Excessive brake pedal travel

1   Partial brake system failure (Chapter 9).
2   Insufficient fluid in master cylinder (Chapters 1 and 9).
3   Air trapped in system (Chapters 1 and 9).

64   Dragging brakes

1   Incorrect adjustment of brake light switch (Chapter 9).
2   Master cylinder pistons not returning correctly (Chapter 9).
3   Restricted brakes lines or hoses (Chapters 1 and 9).
4   Incorrect parking brake adjustment (Chapter 9).

65   Grabbing or uneven braking action

1   Malfunction of proportioning valve (Chapter 9).
2   Malfunction of power brake booster unit (Chapter 9).
3   Binding brake pedal mechanism (Chapter 9).

66   Brake pedal feels spongy when depressed

1   Air in hydraulic lines (Chapter 9).
2   Master cylinder mounting bolts loose (Chapter 9).
3   Master cylinder defective (Chapter 9).

67   Brake pedal travels to the floor with little resistance

1   Little or no fluid in the master cylinder reservoir caused by leaking caliper piston(s) (Chapter 9).
2   Loose, damaged or disconnected brake lines (Chapter 9).

68   Parking brake does not hold

Parking brake cables improperly adjusted (Chapter 9).

Suspension and steering systems

Note: *Before attempting to diagnose suspension and steering system problems, perform the following preliminary checks:*
a) Tires for wrong pressure and uneven wear.
b) Steering universal joints from the column to the rack and pinion for loose connectors or wear.
c) Front and rear suspension and the rack and pinion assembly for loose or damaged parts.
d) Out-of-round or out-of-balance tires, bent rims and loose and/or rough wheel bearings.

69   Vehicle pulls to one side

1   Mismatched or uneven tires (Chapter 10).
2   Broken or sagging coil springs (Chapter 10).
3   Wheel alignment out of specification (Chapter 10).
4   Front brake dragging (Chapter 9).
5   Tire pressure(s) incorrect (Chapter 1).

70   Abnormal or excessive tire wear

1   Wheel alignment out of specification (Chapter 10).
2   Sagging or broken coil springs (Chapter 10).
3   Tire out-of-balance (Chapter 10).
4   Worn shock absorber (Chapter 10).
5   Overloaded vehicle.
6   Tires not rotated regularly (Chapter 1).
7   Tire pressure(s) incorrect (Chapter 1).

71   Wheel makes a thumping noise

1   Blister or bump on tire (Chapter 10).
2   Faulty shock absorber(s) (Chapter 10).

72   Shimmy, shake or vibration

1   Tire or wheel out-of-balance or out-of-round (Chapter 10).
2   Loose or worn wheel bearings (Chapters 1, 8 and 10).
3   Worn tie-rod ends (Chapter 10).
4   Worn lower balljoints (Chapters 1 and 10).
5   Excessive wheel runout (Chapter 10).
6   Blister or bump on tire (Chapter 10).

73   Hard steering

1   Lack of lubrication at balljoints, tie-rod ends and rack and pinion assembly (Chapter 10).
2   Low power steering fluid level (Chapter 1).
3   Faulty power steering pump (Chapter 10).
4   Front wheel alignment out of specifications (Chapter 10).
5   Low tire pressure(s) (Chapter 1).

74   Poor returnability of steering to center

1   Lack of lubrication at balljoints and tie-rod ends (Chapter 10).
2   Binding in balljoints (Chapter 10).
3   Binding in steering column (Chapter 10).
4   Lack of lubricant in steering gear assembly (Chapter 10).
5   Front wheel alignment out of specifications (Chapter 10).

75   Abnormal noise at the front end

1   Lack of lubrication at balljoints and tie-rod ends (Chapters 1 and 10).
2   Damaged strut mounting (Chapter 10).
3   Worn control arm bushings or tie-rod ends (Chapter 10).
4   Loose stabilizer bar (Chapter 10).
5   Loose wheel nuts (Chapters 1).
6   Loose suspension bolts (Chapter 10)

76   Wander or poor steering stability

1   Mismatched or unevenly worn tires (Chapter 10).
2   Lack of lubrication at balljoints and tie-rod ends (Chapters 1 and 10).
3   Bad strut(s) or shock absorber(s) (Chapter 10).
4   Loose stabilizer bar (Chapter 10).
5   Broken or sagging coil springs (Chapter 10).
6   Wheels out of alignment (Chapter 10).
7   Tire pressure(s) incorrect (Chapter 1).

77 Erratic steering when braking

1   Wheel bearings worn (Chapter 10).
2   Broken or sagging coil springs (Chapter 10).
3   Leaking wheel cylinder or caliper (Chapter 9).
4   Warped discs or drums (Chapter 9).

78 Excessive pitching and/or rolling around corners or during braking

1   Loose stabilizer bar (Chapter 10).
2   Worn shock absorbers or mountings (Chapter 10).
3   Broken or sagging coil springs (Chapter 10).
4   Overloaded vehicle.

79 Suspension bottoms

1   Overloaded vehicle.
2   Worn shock absorbers (Chapter 10).
3   Incorrect, broken or sagging coil springs (Chapter 10).

80 Cupped tires

1   Front wheel or rear wheel alignment out of specifications (Chapter 10).
2   Worn shock absorbers (Chapter 10).
3   Wheel bearings worn (Chapter 10).
4   Excessive tire or wheel runout (Chapter 10).
5   Worn balljoints (Chapter 10).

81 Excessive tire wear on outside edge

1   Inflation pressures incorrect (Chapter 1).
2   Excessive speed during turns.
3   Front end alignment incorrect (excessive toe-in). Have professionally aligned.
4   Suspension arm bent or twisted (Chapter 10).

82 Excessive tire wear on inside edge

1   Inflation pressures incorrect (Chapter 1).
2   Front end alignment incorrect (toe-out). Have professionally aligned.

3   Loose or damaged steering components (Chapter 10).

83 Tire tread worn in one place

1   Tires out-of-balance.
2   Damaged or buckled wheel. Inspect and replace if necessary.
3   Defective tire (Chapter 1).

84 Excessive play or looseness in steering system

1   Wheel bearing(s) worn (Chapter 10).
2   Tie-rod end loose (Chapter 10).
3   Steering gear loose or worn (Chapter 10).
4   Worn or loose steering intermediate shaft (Chapter 10).

85 Rattling or clicking noise in steering gear

Steering gear loose or worn (Chapter 10).

Notes

Chapter 1 Tune-up and routine maintenance

Contents

Specifications

Recommended lubricants and fluids

Engine oil	
Type	"API Certified for gasoline engines"
Viscosity	See accompanying chart
Manual transaxle lubricant	SAE 75W-90 or 75W-85 API GL-4 gear lubricant
Automatic transaxle fluid	
1996 and earlier models	DIAMOND ATF SP or equivalent
1997 through 1999 models	DIAMOND ATF SP II or equivalent
2000 models	DIAMOND ATF SP II or DIAMOND ATF SP II M, or equivalent
2001 models	DIAMOND ATF SP III or DIAMOND ATF SP II M, or equivalent
2002 and later models	DIAMOND ATF SP III or equivalent
Power steering fluid	
2001 and earlier models	DEXRON III automatic transmission fluid, or equivalent
2002 models	DIAMOND ATF or equivalent
2003 and later models	Genuine Mitsubishi power steering fluid
Brake and clutch fluid	DOT 3 OR DOT 4 brake fluid
Engine coolant	50/50 mixture of ethylene glycol-based antifreeze and water
Parking brake mechanism grease	White lithium-based grease NLGI no. 2
Hood, door and trunk hinge lubricant	Engine oil
Hood latch, door hinge and check spring grease	NLGI no. 2 multi-purpose grease
Key lock cylinder lubricant	Graphite spray

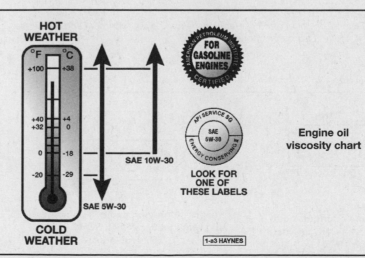

Engine oil viscosity chart

Capacities*

Engine oil (including filter)..	4.5 quarts (4.3L)
Fuel tank	
2003 and earlier models...	16.3 gallons (6.0L)
2004 and later models	17.7 gallons (6.7L)
Automatic transaxle (dry fill)	
1994 and 1995	
SOHC engine..	6.3 quarts (6.0L)
DOHC engine...	8.0 quarts (7.5L)
1996 through 1998..	6.3 quarts (6.0L)
1999 and later	
Four-cylinder engine..	8.2 quarts (7.7L)
V6 engine..	9.0 quarts (8.5L)

Note 1: *Since this is a dry-fill specification, the amount required during a routine fluid change will be substantially less. The best way to determine the amount of fluid to add during a routine fluid change is to measure the amount drained. Begin the refill procedure by initially adding 1/3rd of the amount drained. Then, with the engine running, add 1/2-pint at a time (cycling the shifter through each gear position between additions) until the level is correct on the dipstick. It is important to not overfill the transaxle.*

Note 2: *On 1999 and later models, additional fluid will be required because the fluid changing procedure involves flushing the system.*

Manual transaxle	
Four-cylinder engine...	2.2 quarts (2.1L)
V6 engine	3.0 quarts (2.8L)
Cooling System	
2003 and earlier models	
Four-cylinder engine..	7.4 quarts (7.0L)
V6 engine..	8.5 quarts (8.0L)
2004 and later models	
Four-cylinder engine..	8.1 quarts (7.7L)
V6 engine..	9.2 quarts (8.7L)

*All capacities approximate. Add as necessary to bring to appropriate level.

Brakes

Disc brake pad wear limit...	1/8 inch (3.2 mm)
Drum brake shoe wear limit...	1/16 inch (1.5 mm)
Parking brake lever travel	
Rear drum brake	5 to 7 clicks
Rear disc brake	3 to 5 clicks

Ignition system

Spark plug type and gap*	
Type	
Four-cylinder engines	
2003 and earlier models...	NGK BK5RE-11 or equivalent
2004 and later models...	NGK LZFR6AI or equivalent
V6 engines	
1999 through 2001 models	NGK PFR6G-11 or equivalent
2002 and 2003 models	NGK PFR5G-11 or equivalent
2004 through 2008 models without MIVEC	NGK FR6EI or equivalent
2008 and later models with MIVEC...................................	NGK IFR6B-K or equivalent
Gap	
2003 and earlier models	0.039 to 0.043 inch (1.0 to 1.1 mm)
2004 and later models..	0.028 to 0.031 inch (0.7 to 0.8 mm)

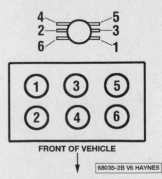

FRONT ↓

Cylinder numbering and coil terminal locations (2.4L DOHC engine, 1994 and 1995)

*Refer to the Vehicle Emission Control Information label in the engine compartment and follow the information on the label if it differs from that shown here.

Firing order	
Four-cylinder engines	1-3-4-2
V6 engines	1-2-3-4-5-6

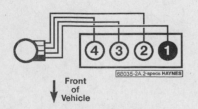

Front of Vehicle ↓

Cylinder numbering and distributor cap terminal locations (2.4L SOHC engine, 1994 through 1998)

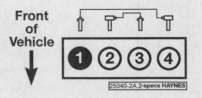

Front of Vehicle ↓

Cylinder numbering and coil pack/spark plug wire locations (2.4L SOHC engine, 1999 and later)

FRONT OF VEHICLE ↓

V6 engine cylinder numbering; the distributor cap terminal locations shown apply to 2003 and earlier models

Valve adjustment

Four-cylinder engines, adjust at operating temperature
    2003 and earlier models.. Not applicable, hydraulic actuators
    2004 models
        Intake... 0.008 inch (0.20 mm)
        Exhaust
            Special California emission models*..................................... 0.013 inch (0.33 mm)
            All except above... 0.012 inch (0.30 mm)
    2005 and later models
        Intake... 0.008 inch (0.20 mm)
        Exhaust.. 0.012 inch (0.30 mm)
V6 engines, adjust cold
    2009 and earlier models without MIVEC.. Not applicable, hydraulic actuators
    2004 and later models with MIVEC
        Intake... 0.004 inch (0.10 mm)
        Exhaust.. Not applicable, hydraulic actuators
*These are California-only models and are further identified by an absence of a white paint stripe at the rear of the camshaft and a "G" stamping

Torque specifications

Note: One foot-pound (ft-lb) of torque is equivalent to 12 inch-pounds (in-lbs) of torque. Torque values below approximately 15 foot-pounds are expressed in inch-pounds, because most foot-pound torque wrenches are not accurate at these smaller values.

	Ft-lbs (unless otherwise indicated)	Nm
Automatic transaxle		
Fluid pan bolts	96 in-lbs	11
Fluid filter bolts (1998 and earlier models)	61 in-lbs	7
Drain plug(s)	24	33
Engine oil pan drain plug	29	39
Fuel filter banjo bolt	21	29
Manual transaxle fill and drain plugs	24	34
Rocker arm adjustment lock nuts	71 to 89 in-lbs	8 to 10
Spark plugs	18	25
Wheel lug nuts	66 to 81	88 to 108

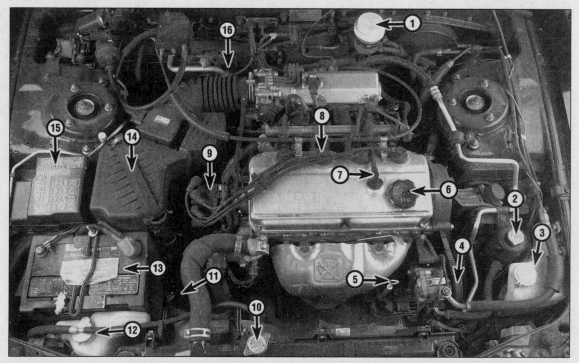

Engine compartment layout (1998 and earlier 2.4L SOHC four-cylinder engine shown)

1	Brake fluid reservoir	5	Engine oil dipstick	10	Radiator cap	14	Air filter housing
2	Power steering fluid reservoir	6	Engine oil filler cap	11	Automatic transaxle	15	Power Distribution Center
3	Windshield washer reservoir	7	PCV valve		fluid dipstick		(PDC) - fuses and relays
4	Power steering pump	8	Spark plug and plug wire	12	Engine coolant reservoir	16	Fuel filter (under air
	drivebelt	9	Distributor cap and rotor	13	Battery		intake duct)

Engine compartment layout (1999 through 2003 2.4L SOHC four-cylinder engine shown)

1	Windshield washer fluid reservoir	7	Battery	12	Automatic transaxle filter
2	Power steering fluid reservoir	8	Brake fluid reservoir	13	Upper radiator hose
3	Engine coolant reservoir	9	Power Distribution Center (PDC) -	14	Ignition coil pack
4	Engine oil dipstick		fuses and relays	15	Engine oil filler cap
5	PCV valve	10	Air filter housing	16	Radiator cap
6	Spark plug boot	11	Automatic transaxle fluid dipstick	17	Drivebelt

Typical engine compartment underside components (1999 and later model shown)

1	Disc brake caliper	6	Brake hose	11	Exhaust pipe
2	Drivebelt	7	Strut/coil spring assembly	12	Engine oil drain plug
3	Air conditioning compressor	8	Brake disc	13	Driveaxle outer CV joint
4	Catalytic converter	9	Control arm	14	Engine oil filter
5	Automatic transaxle	10	Driveaxle inner CV joint		

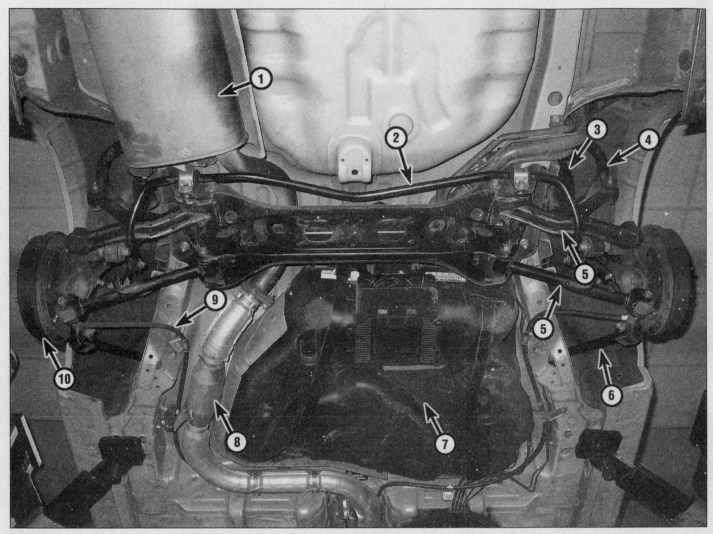

Typical rear underside components (1999 and later model shown)

1	Muffler	5	Lateral control arms	8	Exhaust pipe
2	Rear stabilizer bar	6	Trailing arm	9	Parking brake cable
3	Coil spring/shock absorber assembly	7	Fuel tank	10	Rear drum brake
4	Upper control arm				

1   Mitsubishi Galant maintenance schedule

The following maintenance intervals are based on the assumption that the vehicle owner will be doing the maintenance or service work, as opposed to having a dealer service department do the work. Although the time/mileage intervals are loosely based on factory recommendations, most have been shortened to ensure, for example, that such items as lubricants and fluids are checked/changed at intervals that promote maximum engine/driveline service life. Also, subject to the preference of the individual owner interested in keeping his or her vehicle in peak condition at all times, and with the vehicle's ultimate resale in mind, many of the maintenance procedures may be performed more often than recommended in the following schedule. We encourage such owner initiative.

When the vehicle is new it should be serviced initially by a factory authorized dealer service department to protect the factory warranty. In many cases the initial maintenance check is done at no cost to the owner (check with your dealer service department for more information).

Every 250 miles (400 km) or weekly, whichever comes first

Check the engine oil level (see Section 4)
Check the engine coolant level (see Section 4)
Check the windshield washer fluid level (see Section 4)
Check the brake fluid level (see Section 4)
Check the tires and tire pressures (see Section 5)
Check the automatic transaxle fluid level (see Section 6)
Check the power steering fluid level (see Section 7)
Check the operation of all lights
Check the horn operation

Every 7500 miles (12,000 km) or 6 months, whichever comes first

Change the engine oil and filter (see Section 8)*
Check and clean the battery and terminals (see Section 9)
Check the cooling system hoses and connections for leaks and damage (see Section 10)
Check the condition of all vacuum hoses and connections (see Section 11)
Check the wiper blade condition (see Section 12)
Rotate the tires (see Section 13)
Check for freeplay in the steering linkage and balljoints (see Section 14)
Check the suspension components and driveaxle boots (see Section 14)
Check the exhaust pipes and hangers (see Section 15)
Check the manual transaxle fluid level (see Section 16)

Every 15,000 miles (24,000 km) or 12 months, whichever comes first

All items listed above, plus:
Replace the interior ventilation filter (1999 and later models) (see Section 17)
Check the brake system (see Section 18)
Check the fuel system hoses and connections for leaks and damage (see Section 19)
Check the drivebelts and adjust if necessary (see Section 20)

Every 30,000 miles (48,000 km) or 24 months, whichever comes first

All items listed above, plus:
Lubricate the parking brake cable and hood, door and trunk lid hinges (see Section 21)*
Replace the air filter element (see Section 22)*
Change the automatic transaxle fluid and (if equipped) filter (see Section 23)*
Change the manual transaxle lubricant (see Section 24)*
Drain and replace the engine coolant (see Section 25)
Check the fuel evaporative emission system and hoses (see Section 26)
Replace the spark plugs (non-platinum type) (see Section 27)
Check the spark plug wires (see Section 29)
Adjust the valves on MIVEC-equipped models (see Section 31)

Every 60,000 miles (96,000 km) or 48 months, whichever comes first

All items listed above, plus:
Replace the drivebelts (see Section 20)
Check and replace, if necessary, the PCV valve (see Section 28)*
Replace spark plug wires (see Section 29)

Every 100,000 miles (160,000 km) or 84 months, whichever comes first

Replace the spark plugs (platinum-tipped spark plugs) (see Section 27)*
Replace the spark plug wires, distributor cap and rotor (see Section 29)*
Replace the timing belt (see Chapter 2)

This item is affected by "severe" operating conditions as described below. If the vehicle in question is operated under "severe" conditions, perform all maintenance procedures marked with an asterisk (*) at the intervals specified by the mileage headings below.

Consider the conditions "severe" if most driving is done . . .
In dusty areas
Towing a trailer
Idling for extended periods and/or low-speed operation
When outside temperatures remain below freezing and most trips are less than four miles
In heavy city traffic where outside temperatures regularly reach 90-degrees F or higher

Every 3000 miles (4,800 km)

Change the engine oil and filter (see Section 8)

Every 15,000 miles (24,000 km)

Check and replace, if necessary, the air filter element (see Section 22)
Change the automatic transaxle fluid and filter (see Section 23)
Change the manual transaxle lubricant (see Section 24)

Every 30,000 miles (48,000 km)

Check and replace, if necessary, the PCV valve (see Section 28)

Every 75,000 miles (120,000 km)

Replace the spark plugs (see Section 27)
Replace the spark plug wires (distributor-equipped engine) (see Section 29)

2   Introduction

This Chapter is designed to help the home mechanic maintain the Mitsubishi Galant with the goals of maximum performance, economy, safety and reliability in mind.

Included is a master maintenance schedule, followed by procedures dealing specifically with each item on the schedule. Visual checks, adjustments, component replacement and other helpful items are included. Refer to the accompanying illustrations of the engine compartment and the underside of the vehicle for the locations of various components.

Adhering to the mileage/time maintenance schedule and following the step-by-step procedures, which is simply a preventive maintenance program, will result in maximum reliability and vehicle service life. Keep in mind that it's not possible for this comprehensive program to produce the same results if you maintain some items at the specified intervals but not others.

As you service the vehicle, you'll discover that many of the procedures can - and should - be grouped together because of the nature of the particular procedure you're performing or because of the close proximity of two otherwise unrelated components to one another.

For example, if the vehicle is raised, you should inspect the exhaust, suspension, steering and fuel systems while you're under the vehicle. When you're rotating the tires, it makes good sense to check the brakes, since the wheels are already removed. Finally, let's suppose you have to borrow or rent a torque wrench. Even if you only need it to tighten the spark plugs, you might as well check the torque of as many critical fasteners as time allows.

The first step in this maintenance program is to prepare before the actual work begins. Read through all the procedures you're planning, then gather together all the parts and tools needed. If it looks like you might run into problems during a particular job, seek advice from a mechanic or an experienced do-it-yourselfer.

Owner's Manual and VECI label information

Your vehicle owner's manual was written for your year and model and contains very specific information on component locations, specifications, fuse ratings, part numbers, etc. The Owner's Manual is an important resource for the do-it-yourselfer to have; if one was not supplied with your vehicle, it can generally be ordered from a dealer parts department.

Among other important information, the Vehicle Emissions Control Information (VECI) label contains specifications and procedures for applicable tune-up adjustments and, in some instances, spark plugs (see Chapter 6 for more information on the VECI label). The information on this label is the exact maintenance data recommended by the manufacturer. This data often varies by intended operating altitude, local emissions regulations, month of manufacture, etc.

This Chapter contains procedural details, safety information and more ambitious maintenance intervals than you might find in manufacturer's literature. However, you may also find procedures or specifications in your Owner's Manual or VECI label that differ with what's printed here. In these cases, the Owner's Manual or VECI label can be considered correct, since it is specific to your particular vehicle.

3   Tune-up general information

The term "tune-up" is used in this manual to represent a combination of individual operations rather than one specific procedure.

The engine will be kept in relatively good running condition and the need for additional work will be minimized if the routine maintenance schedule is followed closely and frequent checks are made of fluid levels and high wear items, as suggested throughout this manual, from the time the vehicle is new.

More likely than not, however, there will be times when the engine is running poorly due to lack of regular maintenance. This is even more likely if a used vehicle, which hasn't received regular and frequent maintenance checks, is purchased. In such cases, an engine tune-up will be needed outside of the regular routine maintenance intervals.

The first step in any tune-up or diagnostic procedure to help correct a poor running engine is a cylinder compression check. A compression check (see Chapter 2, Part C) will help determine the condition of internal engine components and should be used as a guide for tune-up and repair procedures. For instance, if a compression check indicates serious internal engine wear, a conventional tune-up will not improve the performance of the engine and would be a waste of time and money. Because of its importance, someone with the right equipment and the knowledge to use it properly should do the compression check.

The following procedures are those most often needed to bring a generally poor running engine back into a proper state of tune:

Minor tune-up

Check all engine related fluids (see Section 4)
Clean, inspect and test the battery (see Section 9)
Check all underhood hoses (see Section 11)
Check and adjust the drivebelts (see Section 20)
Check the air filter (see Section 22)
Service the cooling system (see Section 25)
Check the PCV valve (see Section 28)
Inspect the spark plug wires (see Section 29)

Major tune-up

All items listed under Minor tune-up plus . . .
Check the fuel system (see Section 19)
Replace the air filter (see Section 22)
Replace the spark plugs (see Section 27)
Check the charging system (see Chapter 5)

4   Fluid level checks (every 250 miles [400 km] or weekly)

Note: *The following are fluid level checks to be done on a 250 mile or weekly basis. Additional fluid level checks can be found in specific maintenance procedures that follow. Regardless of the intervals, develop the habit of checking under the vehicle periodically for evidence of fluid leaks.*

1   Fluids are an essential part of the lubrication, cooling, brake and window washer systems. Because the fluids gradually become depleted and/or contaminated during normal operation of the vehicle, they must be replenished periodically. See *Recommended lubricants and fluids* at the beginning of this Chapter before adding fluid to any of the following components. **Note:** *The vehicle must be on level ground when fluid levels are checked.*

Engine oil

Refer to illustrations 4.2, 4.4 and 4.5

2   Engine oil level is checked with a dipstick that is located on the side of the engine facing the front of the vehicle (V6 engines and 1998 and earlier four-cylinder engines) or at the right rear of the engine compartment **(see accompanying illustration and the underhood views at the beginning of this Chap-**

4.2 The engine oil dipstick is located at the right rear (passenger's) side of the engine on 1999 and later four-cylinder engines (shown) or the front side on V6 engines and 1998 and earlier four cylinder engines, and is clearly marked

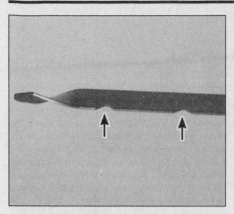

4.4 The oil level should be between the two marks on the dipstick - if it isn't, add enough oil to bring the level up to or near the upper mark (do not overfill)

4.5 Turn the oil filler cap counterclockwise to remove it

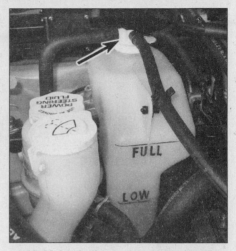

4.10 Maintain the coolant level near the upper line on the reservoir

ter). The dipstick extends through a tube and into the oil pan at the bottom of the engine.

3   The oil level should be checked before the vehicle has been driven, or about 5 minutes after the engine has been shut off. If the oil is checked immediately after driving the vehicle, some of the oil will remain in the upper engine components, resulting in an inaccurate reading on the dipstick.

4   Pull the dipstick out of the tube and wipe all the oil off the end with a clean rag or paper towel. Insert the clean dipstick all the way back into the tube, then pull it out again. Note the oil level at the end of the dipstick. Add oil as necessary to bring the oil level to the upper notch or mark in the dipstick **(see illustration)**.

5   Oil is added to the engine after removing a cap located on the valve cover **(see illustration)**. The cap will be marked "OIL". Use a funnel to prevent spills as the oil is added.

6   Don't allow the level to drop below the lower notch or mark on the dipstick or engine damage may occur. On the other hand, don't overfill the engine by adding too much oil - it may result in oil aeration and loss of oil pressure and also could result in oil fouled spark plugs, oil leaks or seal failures.

7   Checking the oil level is an important preventive maintenance step. A consistently low oil level indicates oil leakage through damaged seals, defective gaskets or past worn rings or valve guides. If the oil looks milky in color or has water droplets in it, the block or head may be cracked and leaking coolant is entering the crankcase. The engine should be checked immediately. The condition of the oil should also be checked. Each time you check the oil level, slide your thumb and index finger up the dipstick before wiping off the oil. If you see small dirt or metal particles clinging to the dipstick, the oil should be changed (see Section 8).

Engine coolant

Refer to illustration 4.10
Warning: *Do not allow coolant (antifreeze) to come in contact with your skin or painted surfaces of the vehicle. Flush contaminated areas*

immediately with plenty of water. Don't store new coolant or leave old coolant lying around where it's accessible to children or pets - they're attracted by its sweet smell. Ingestion of even a small amount of coolant can be fatal! Wipe up garage floor and drip pan spills immediately. Keep antifreeze containers covered and repair cooling system leaks as soon as they are noticed. Check with local authorities about the disposal of used antifreeze. Many communities have collection centers, which will see that antifreeze is disposed of properly.

8   All vehicles covered by this manual are equipped with a coolant recovery system. A coolant reservoir is attached to the right side of the engine compartment and is connected by a hose to the radiator filler neck. As the engine warms up, the system pressure increases causing some coolant to escape through a valve in the radiator cap and travel through the hose and into the coolant reservoir. As the engine cools, the coolant in the reservoir is automatically drawn back into the cooling system via the vacuum created by the contracting coolant. This recovery type system maintains the maximum amount of coolant available at all times.

9   **Warning:** *Never remove the radiator cap to add coolant while the engine is warm! If the cap feels even slightly warm, wrap a towel or rag around the cap and open it very slowly.* With the engine cold, remove the radiator cap. The coolant level should be up to the cap seat inside the filler neck. If it is low, add a mixture of high-quality antifreeze/coolant and water in the ratio specified on the antifreeze container or in this Chapter's Specification Section to bring it up to the correct level.

10   The coolant level in the reservoir should be checked while the engine is at normal operating temperature. Simply note the fluid level in the reservoir - it should be at or close to the FULL HOT or MAX mark when the engine is at normal operating temperature **(see illustration)**.

11   If only a small amount of coolant is required to bring the system up to the proper level, ordinary tap water may be used. However, to maintain the proper antifreeze/water mixture in the system, a blend of high-quality antifreeze/coolant and water in the ratio specified on the antifreeze container or in this Chapter's Specification Section should be added.

12   As the coolant level is checked, note the condition of the coolant as well. It should be relatively clean and the color of new antifreeze. If it's brown or rust colored, the system should be drained, flushed and re-filled (see Section 25).

13   If the coolant level drops consistently, there is a leak in the system. Check the radiator, hoses, filler cap, drain plugs and water pump (see Section 10). If no leaks are noted, have the radiator cap and coolant system pressure tested by your dealer service department or other qualified service station.

Windshield washer fluid

Refer to illustration 4.14
14   The fluid for the windshield washer sys-

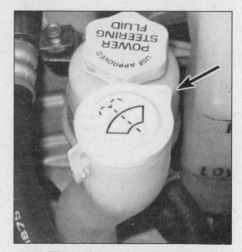

4.14 Flip up the cap to add washer fluid

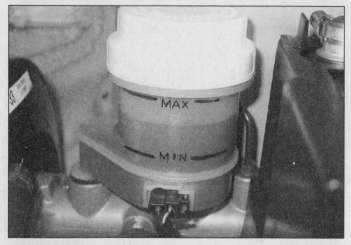

4.17 Brake fluid level, indicated on the translucent white plastic brake fluid reservoir, should be kept at the upper (MAX) mark

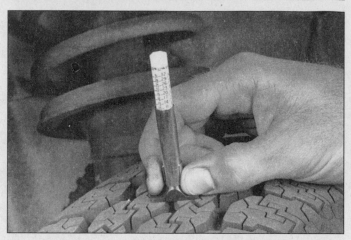

5.2 Use a tire tread depth indicator to monitor tire wear - they are available at auto parts stores or service stations and are relatively inexpensive

tem is stored in a plastic reservoir. The reservoir level should be maintained about one inch below the filler cap. The reservoir is located on either the right or left side of the engine compartment, depending on model year **(see illustration)**.

15   In milder climates, plain water can be used in the reservoir, but it should be kept no more than two-thirds full to allow for expansion if the water freezes. In colder climates, use windshield washer system antifreeze, available at any auto parts store, to lower the freezing point of the fluid. Mix the antifreeze with water in accordance with the manufacturer's directions on the container. **Caution:** *DO NOT use cooling system antifreeze - it will damage the vehicle's paint. To help prevent icing in cold weather, warm the windshield with the defroster before using the washer.*

Brake and clutch fluid

Refer to illustration 4.17

16   On early models the brake fluid reservoir is mounted on the firewall, next to the power brake booster. On later models it's located on top of the brake master cylinder. The clutch fluid reservoir is located on the clutch master cylinder, next to the power brake booster.

17   The fluid level should be maintained at the upper (FULL or MAX) mark on the reservoir **(see illustration)**.

18   If additional fluid is necessary to bring the level up, use a rag to clean all dirt off the top of the reservoir to prevent contamination of the system. Also, make sure all painted surfaces around the reservoir are covered, since brake fluid will ruin paint. Carefully pour new, clean brake fluid obtained from a sealed container into the reservoir. Be sure the specified fluid is used; mixing different types of brake fluid can cause damage to the system. See *Recommended lubricants and fluids* at the beginning of this Chapter or your owner's manual.

19   At this time the fluid and the master cylinder should be inspected for contamination. Normally the brake hydraulic system won't

need periodic draining and refilling, but if rust deposits, dirt particles or water droplets are observed in the fluid, the system should be disassembled, cleaned and refilled with fresh fluid. Over time brake fluid will absorb moisture from the air. Moisture in the fluid lowers the fluid boiling point; if the fluid boils, the brakes will become ineffective. Normal brake fluid is clear in color. If the brake fluid is dark brown in color or is over three years old, it's a good idea to flush the system and refill it with new fluid.

20   Reinstall the fluid reservoir cap.

21   The brake fluid in the reservoir will drop slightly as the brake shoes and pads at each wheel wear down during normal operation. If the master cylinder requires repeated replenishing to maintain the correct level, there is a leak in the brake system that should be corrected immediately. Check all brake lines and connections, along with the calipers, wheel cylinders and vacuum booster (see Section 18 and Chapter 9 for more information).

22   If you discover that the reservoir is empty or nearly empty, the system should be thoroughly inspected, refilled and then bled (see Chapter 8 for clutch system bleeding and Chapter 9 for brake system bleeding).

5   Tire and tire pressure checks (every 250 miles [400 km] or weekly)

Refer to illustrations 5.2, 5.3, 5.4a, 5.4b and 5.8

1   Periodic inspection of the tires may spare you the inconvenience of being stranded with a flat tire. It can also provide you with vital information regarding possible problems in the steering and suspension systems before major damage occurs.

2   Original tires on this vehicle are equipped with 1/2-inch wide bands that will appear when tread depth reaches 1/16-inch, at which point the tires can be considered worn out. Tread wear can be monitored with a simple,

inexpensive device known as a tread depth indicator **(see illustration)**.

3   Note any abnormal tread wear **(see illustration)**. Tread pattern irregularities such as cupping, flat spots and more wear on one side than the other are indications of front end alignment and/or balance problems. If any of these conditions are noted, take the vehicle to a tire shop or service station to correct the problem.

4   Look closely for cuts, punctures and embedded nails or tacks. Sometimes a tire will hold air pressure for a short time or leak down very slowly after a nail has embedded itself in the tread. If a slow leak persists, check the valve stem core to make sure it's tight **(see illustration)**. Examine the tread for an object that may have embedded itself in the tire or for a "plug" that may have begun to leak (radial tire punctures are repaired with a plug that's installed in the puncture). If a puncture is suspected, it can be easily verified by spraying a solution of soapy water onto the puncture area **(see illustration)**. The soapy solution will bubble if there's a leak. Unless the puncture is unusually large, a tire shop or service station can usually repair the tire.

5   Carefully inspect the inner sidewall of each tire for evidence of brake fluid leakage. If you see any, inspect the brakes immediately.

6   Correct air pressure adds miles to the life span of the tires, improves mileage and enhances overall ride quality. Tire pressure cannot be accurately estimated by looking at a tire, especially if it's a radial. A tire pressure gauge is essential. Keep an accurate gauge in the vehicle. The pressure gauges attached to the nozzles of air hoses at gas stations are often inaccurate.

7   Always check tire pressure when the tires are cold. Cold, in this case, means the vehicle has not been driven over a mile in the three hours preceding a tire pressure check. A pressure rise of four to eight pounds is not uncommon once the tires are warm.

8   Unscrew the valve cap protruding from the wheel or hubcap and push the gauge

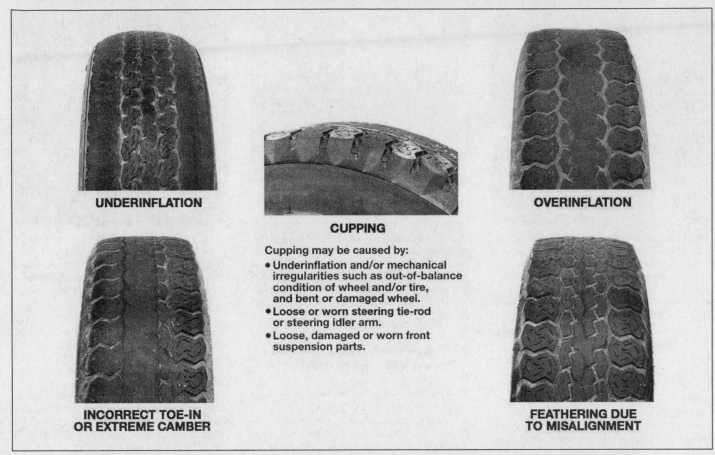

UNDERINFLATION

OVERINFLATION

CUPPING

Cupping may be caused by:
- Underinflation and/or mechanical irregularities such as out-of-balance condition of wheel and/or tire, and bent or damaged wheel.
- Loose or worn steering tie-rod or steering idler arm.
- Loose, damaged or worn front suspension parts.

INCORRECT TOE-IN OR EXTREME CAMBER

FEATHERING DUE TO MISALIGNMENT

5.3 This chart will help you determine the condition of the tires, the probable cause(s) of abnormal wear and the corrective action necessary

firmly onto the valve stem **(see illustration)**. Compare the reading on the gauge to the recommended tire pressure shown on the placard on the driver's side door pillar. Be sure to reinstall the valve cap to keep dirt and moisture out of the valve stem mechanism. Check all four tires and, if necessary, add enough air to bring them up to the recommended pressure.

9   Don't forget to keep the spare tire inflated to the specified pressure (refer to your owner's manual or the tire sidewall). Note that the pressure recommended for the compact spare is higher than for the other tires on the vehicle.

5.4a If a tire loses air on a steady basis, check the valve stem core first to make sure it's snug (special inexpensive wrenches are commonly available at auto parts stores)

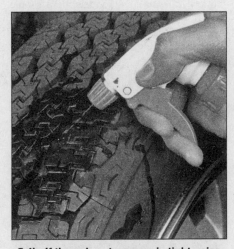

5.4b If the valve stem core is tight, raise the corner of the vehicle with the low tire and spray a soapy water solution onto the tread as the tire is turned slowly - leaks will cause small bubbles to appear

5.8 To extend the life of the tires, check the air pressure at least once a week with an accurate gauge (don't forget the spare!)

6.3 The automatic transaxle dipstick on later models is located on the left side of the engine compartment next to the spin-on type fluid filter

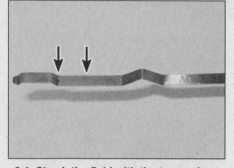

6.4 Check the fluid with the transaxle at normal operating temperature - the level should be kept in the HOT range

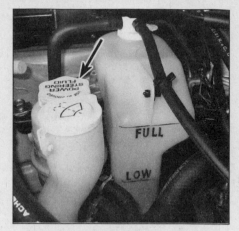

7.2 The power steering reservoir is located in the right front corner of the engine compartment on later models and the fluid reservoir is translucent plastic - keep the level between the MIN and MAX marks

6   Automatic transaxle fluid level check (every 250 miles [400 km] or weekly)

Refer to illustrations 6.3 and 6.4

1   Fluid inside the transaxle should be at normal operating temperature to get an accurate reading on the dipstick. This is done by driving the vehicle for several miles, making frequent starts and stops to allow the transaxle to shift through all gears.

2   Park the vehicle on a level surface and apply the parking brake. With the engine running, apply the brakes and place the gear selector lever momentarily in Reverse, then Drive and repeat the sequence again ending with the gear selector in the Park position.

3   With the engine still running locate the transaxle fluid dipstick; **(see accompanying illustration and the underhood photos at the front of this Chapter)**. Remove the dipstick and wipe the fluid from the end with a clean rag.

4   Insert the dipstick back into the transaxle until the cap seats completely. Remove the dipstick again and note the fluid level on the end. The level should be in the area marked HOT **(see illustration)**.

5   If the fluid level is below the HOT mark on the dipstick, add just enough of the specified fluid (see *Recommended lubricants and fluids* at the beginning of this Chapter) to raise the level to between the marks in the HOT range. Fluid should be slowly added into the dipstick tube, using a funnel to prevent spills.

6   DO NOT overfill the transaxle. Never allow the fluid level to go above the upper mark on the dipstick - it could cause internal transaxle damage. The best way to prevent overfilling is to add fluid a little at a time, cycle the shifter through each gear range and checking the level between additions.

7   Use only transaxle fluid specified by the manufacturer. This information can be found in the *Recommended lubricants and fluids* Section at the beginning of this Chapter or in your owner's manual.

8   The condition of the fluid should also be checked along with the level. If it's a dark reddish-brown color, or if it smells burned, it should be changed. If you're in doubt about the condition of the fluid, purchase some new fluid and compare the two for color and odor.

7   Power steering fluid level check (every 250 miles [400 km] or weekly)

Refer to illustrations 7.2, 7.6a and 7.6b

1   Unlike manual steering, the power steering system relies on hydraulic fluid that may, over a period of time, require replenishing.

2   The fluid reservoir for the power steering pump is located at the left front corner of the engine compartment on 1998 and earlier models, and in the right front corner of the engine compartment on 1999 and later models **(see illustration)**.

3   The power steering fluid level can be checked with the engine either hot or cold.

4   On later models the power steering fluid reservoir is translucent and the level can be checked without removing the cap **(see illustration 7.2)**. On these models it's a simple matter to make sure the fluid level is within the proper range.

5   On earlier models the fluid level is

checked with a dipstick. With the engine off, use a rag to clean the reservoir cap and the area around the cap. This will help prevent foreign material from falling into the reservoir when the cap is removed.

6   Turn and pull out the reservoir cap, which has a dipstick attached to it **(see illustration)**. Wipe the fluid at the bottom of the dipstick with a clean rag. Reinstall the cap to get a fluid level reading. Remove the cap again and note the fluid level. It should be at the appropriate mark on the dipstick in relation to the engine temperature; near the MIN mark if the fluid is cold, and near the MAX mark if the fluid is hot **(see illustration)**.

7   If additional fluid is required, pour the specified type fluid (see *Recommended lubricants and fluids* at the beginning of this Chapter or your owner's manual) directly into the reservoir using a funnel to prevent spills.

8   If the reservoir requires frequent topping up, all power steering hoses, hose connections, the power steering pump and the steering gear should be carefully examined for leaks.

7.6a On earlier models, remove the cap/ dipstick to check the fluid level

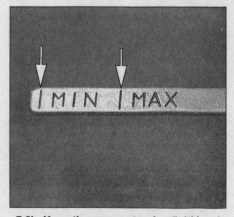

7.6b Keep the power steering fluid level between the MIN and MAX marks on the dipstick

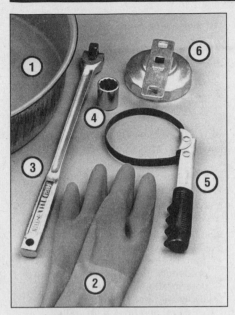

8.8 **To avoid rounding off the corners, use the correct size box-end wrench or a socket to remove the engine oil drain plug**

8.13 **Since the oil filter is probably very tight, you'll need a special wrench for removal**

8.3 **These tools are required when changing the engine oil and filter**

1   *Drain pan - It should be fairly shallow in depth, but wide to prevent spills and capable of holding at least 5 quarts*
2   *Rubber gloves - When removing the drain plug and filter, you will get oil on your hands (the gloves will prevent burns)*
3   *Breaker bar - Sometimes the oil drain plug is tight, and a long breaker bar is needed to loosen it*
4   *Socket - To be used with the breaker bar or a ratchet*
5   *Filter wrench - This is a metal band-type wrench, which requires clearance around the filter to be effective*
6   *Filter wrench - This type fits on the bottom of the filter and can be turned with a ratchet or breaker bar (different size wrenches are available for different types of filters)*

8 Engine oil and filter change (every 7500 miles [12,000 km] or 6 months)

Refer to illustrations 8.3, 8.8, 8.13 and 8.18

1   Frequent oil changes are the most important preventive maintenance procedures that can be performed by the home mechanic. When engine oil ages, it gets diluted and contaminated, which ultimately leads to premature engine wear.
2   Although some sources recommend oil filter changes every other oil change, a new filter should be installed every time the oil is changed.
3   Gather together all necessary tools and materials before beginning this procedure **(see illustration)**. **Note:** *To avoid rounding off the corners of the drain plug, use a box-end type wrench or socket.* In addition, you should have plenty of clean rags and newspapers handy to mop up any spills.

4   Raise the front of the vehicle and support it securely on jackstands. **Warning:** *Never work under a vehicle that is supported only by a jack!*
5   If this is your first oil change on the vehicle, familiarize yourself with the locations of the oil drain plug and the oil filter. Since the engine and exhaust components will be warm during the actual work, it's a good idea to figure out any potential problems beforehand.
6   Allow the engine to warm up to normal operating temperature. If oil or tools are needed, use the warm-up time to gather everything necessary for the job. The correct type of oil to buy for your application can be found in the *Recommended lubricants and fluids* Section at the beginning of this Chapter or your owner's manual.
7   Move all necessary tools, rags and newspapers under the vehicle. Place a drain pan capable of holding at least 5 quarts under the drain plug. Keep in mind that the oil will initially flow from the engine with some force, so position the pan accordingly.
8   Being careful not to touch any of the hot exhaust components, use the breaker bar and socket or box-end wrench to remove the drain plug **(see illustration)**. It's a good idea to wear oil-resistant gloves while unscrewing the plug to prevent contact with the hot, contaminated oil.
9   Allow the oil to drain into the pan. It may be necessary to move the pan further under the engine when the oil flow slows to a trickle.
10   After all the oil has completely drained, clean the plug thoroughly with a rag. Small metal particles may cling to it and would immediately contaminate the new oil.
11   Clean the area around the drain plug opening and reinstall the plug. Tighten it to the torque listed in this Chapter's Specifications.
12   Next, carefully move the drain pan into position under the oil filter.
13   Now use the filter wrench to loosen the oil filter in a counterclockwise direction **(see illustration)**.

14   Sometimes the oil filter is on so tight it cannot be loosened, or it's positioned in an area inaccessible with a conventional filter wrench. Other types of tools which fit over the end of the filter and turned with a ratchet or breaker bar, are available and may be better for removing the filter.
15   Completely unscrew the old filter. Be careful, it's full of oil. Empty the old oil inside the filter into the drain pan.
16   Compare the old filter with the new one to make sure they're identical.
17   Use a clean rag to remove all oil, dirt and sludge from the area where the oil filter seals on the engine. Check the old filter to make sure the rubber gasket isn't stuck to the engine mounting surface.
18   Apply a light coat of clean engine oil to the rubber gasket on the new oil filter **(see illustration)**.
19   Attach the new filter to the engine, following the tightening directions printed on the filter canister or packing box. Most filter manufacturers recommend against using a filter wrench due to the possibility of over-tightening and damage to the seal.
20   Remove all tools and materials from

8.18 **Lubricate the oil filter gasket with clean engine oil before installing the filter on the engine**

9.1 Tools and materials required for battery maintenance

1   *Face shield/safety goggles - When removing corrosion with a brush, the acidic particles can easily fly up into your eyes*
2   *Baking soda - A solution of baking soda and water can be used to neutralize corrosion*
3   *Petroleum jelly - A layer of this on the battery posts will help prevent corrosion*
4   *Battery post/cable cleaner - This wire brush cleaning tool will remove all traces of corrosion from the battery posts and cable clamps*
5   *Treated felt washers - Placing one of these on each post, directly under the cable clamps, will help prevent corrosion*
6   *Puller - Sometimes the cable clamps are very difficult to pull off the posts, even after the nut/bolt has been completely loosened. This tool pulls the clamp straight up and off the post without damage*
7   *Battery post/cable cleaner - Here is another cleaning tool, which is a slightly different version of Number 4 above, but it does the same thing*
8   *Rubber gloves - Another safety item to consider when servicing the battery; remember that's acid inside the battery!*

under the vehicle, being careful not to spill the oil in the drain pan. Lower the vehicle.
21   Working inside the engine compartment, locate and remove the oil filler cap from the valve cover **(see illustration 4.5)**.
22   Using a funnel to prevent spills, pour the specified type and amount of new oil required into the engine. Wait a few minutes to allow the oil to drain down to the pan, then check the level on the dipstick (see Section 4 if necessary). If the oil level is at or above the first notch or lower mark on the dipstick, start the engine and allow the new oil to circulate.
23   Run the engine for only about a minute then shut it off. Immediately look under the

vehicle and check for leaks at the oil pan drain plug and around the oil filter. If either one is leaking, tighten it with a bit more force.
24   With the new oil circulated and the filter now completely full, wait a few minutes for the oil to drain back down into the pan then recheck the oil level on the dipstick. If necessary, add enough oil to bring the level to the second notch or upper mark on the dipstick. DO NOT overfill!
25   During the first few trips after an oil change make it a point to check for leaks and keep a close watch on the oil level.
26   The old oil drained from the engine cannot be reused in its present state and should be disposed of. Check with your local auto parts store, disposal facility or environmental agency to see if they will accept the oil for recycling. After the oil has cooled it can be drained into a container (capped plastic jugs, topped bottles, milk cartons, etc.) for transport to one of these disposal sites. Don't dispose of the oil by pouring it on the ground or down a drain!

---

9   Battery check, maintenance and charging (every 7,500 miles [12,000 km] or 6 months)

Warning: *Certain precautions must be followed when checking and servicing the battery. The battery produces hydrogen gas, which is highly explosive. Keep lighted tobacco, open flames, bare light bulbs or other possible sources of ignition away from the battery. Furthermore, the electrolyte inside the battery is sulfuric acid, which is highly corrosive, and can burn your skin and cause severe injury to your eyes. Always wear eye protection! It will also destroy clothing and ruin painted surfaces.*

Servicing
Refer to illustrations 9.1, 9.5a, 9.5b, 9.6a and 9.6b

1   A routine preventive maintenance program for the battery in your vehicle is the only way to ensure quick and reliable starts. But

9.5a Battery terminal corrosion usually appears as light, fluffy powder

9.5b Removing the cable from a battery post with a wrench - sometimes special battery pliers are required for this procedure if corrosion has caused deterioration of the nut or bolt hex (always remove the ground [-] cable first and hook it up last!)

before performing any battery maintenance, make sure that you have the proper equipment necessary to work safely around the battery **(see illustration)**.
2   Prior to servicing the battery always turn the engine and all accessories off and disconnect the cable from the negative terminal of the battery.
3   The battery is located on the right side of the engine compartment on 1998 and earlier models and on the left side of the engine compartment on 1998 and later models.
4   Inspect the external condition of the battery. Check the battery case for cracks or other damage.
5   If corrosion, which looks like white, fluffy deposits **(see illustration)** is evident, particularly around the terminals, the battery should be removed for cleaning. Loosen the cable clamp bolts or nuts with a wrench, being careful to remove the ground (negative) cable first, and slide them off the terminals **(see illustration)**. Then disconnect the hold-down clamp bolt and nut, remove the clamp and lift the battery from the engine compartment.
6   Clean the cable clamps thoroughly with a battery brush or a terminal cleaner and a solution of warm water and baking soda **(see illustration)**. Wash the terminals and the top of the battery case with the same solution but make sure that the solution doesn't get into the battery. When cleaning the cables, terminals and battery top, wear safety goggles and rubber gloves to prevent any solution from coming in contact with your eyes or hands. Wear old clothes too - even diluted, sulfuric acid splashed onto clothes will burn holes in them. If the terminals have been extensively corroded, clean them up with a terminal cleaner **(see illustration)**. Thoroughly wash all cleaned areas with plain water.
7   Inspect the battery carrier. If it's dirty or covered with corrosion, clean it with the same solution of warm water and baking soda and rinse it with clean water.

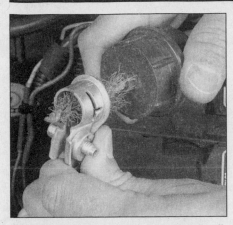

9.6a When cleaning the cable clamps, all corrosion must be removed

9.6b Regardless of the type of tool used on the battery post, a clean, shiny surface should be the result (the inside of the clamp is tapered to match the taper on the post, so don't remove too much material)

8   If the battery is a maintenance-type, it has removable cell caps which allow you to add water (use distilled water only) to the battery when the electrolyte level gets low.

9   If you are not sure what type of battery you have (some maintenance-types have recessed cell caps that resemble maintenance-free batteries), one simple way to confirm your type of battery is to look for a built-in hydrometer. Most maintenance-free batteries have built-in hydrometers that indicate the state of charge by the color displayed in the hydrometer window since measuring the specific gravity of the electrolyte is not possible. Also check for cut-outs near the cell caps - if the caps can be removed, cut-outs are usually provided to assist with prying off the caps.

10   If your battery is a maintenance-type, remove the cell caps and check the level of the electrolyte. It should be up to the split-ring inside the battery. If the level is low, add distilled water (distilled water is mineral-free, tap water contains minerals that will shorten the life of your battery) to bring the electrolyte up to the proper level.

11   Next, check the entire length of each battery cable for cracks worn insulation and frayed conductors. Replace the cable(s) if necessary.

12   Reinstall the battery by reversing the removal procedure. Be sure to connect the positive cable first and the negative cable last.

Charging

Warning: *When batteries are being charged, hydrogen gas, which is very explosive and flammable, is produced. Do not smoke or allow open flames near a charging or a recently charged battery. Wear eye protection when near the battery during charging. Also, make sure the charger is unplugged before connecting or disconnecting the battery from the charger.*

13   Slow-rate charging is the best way to restore a battery that's discharged to the point where it will not start the engine. It's also a good way to maintain the battery charge in a vehicle that's only driven a few miles between starts. Maintaining the battery charge is particularly important in the winter

when the battery must work harder to start the engine and electrical accessories that drain the battery are in greater use.

14   It's best to use a one or two-amp battery charger (sometimes called a "trickle" charger). They are the safest and put the least strain on the battery. They are also the least expensive. For a faster charge, you can use a higher amperage charger, but don't use one rated more than 1/10th the amp/hour rating of the battery. Rapid boost charges that claim to restore the power of the battery in one to two hours are hardest on the battery and can damage batteries not in good condition. This type of charging should only be used in emergency situations.

15   The average time necessary to charge a battery should be listed in the instructions that come with the charger. As a general rule, a trickle charger will charge a battery in 12 to 16 hours.

16   On maintenance-type batteries remove the cell caps. Make sure the electrolyte level is OK before beginning to charge the battery. Cover the holes with a clean cloth to prevent spattering electrolyte.

17   Connect the battery charger leads to the battery posts (positive to positive, negative to negative), then plug in the charger. Make sure it is set at 12 volts if it has a selector switch. If the battery charger does not have a built-in timer, it's a good idea to use one in case you forget - so you won't over charge the battery.

18   If you're using a charger with a rate higher than two amps, check the battery regularly during charging to make sure it doesn't overheat. If you're using a trickle charger, you can safely let the battery charge overnight after you've checked it regularly for the first couple of hours.

19   If the battery has removable cell caps, measure the specific gravity with a hydrometer every hour during the last few hours of the charging cycle. Hydrometers are available inexpensively from auto parts stores - follow the instructions that come with the hydrometer. Consider the battery charged when

there's no change in the specific gravity reading for two hours and the electrolyte in the cells is outgassing (bubbling) freely. The specific gravity reading from each cell should be very close to the others. If not, the battery probably has a bad cell(s).

20   Most batteries with sealed tops have built-in hydrometers on the top that indicate the state of charge by the color displayed in the hydrometer window. Normally, a bright-colored hydrometer indicates a full charge and a dark hydrometer indicates the battery still needs charging. Check the battery manufacturer's instructions to be sure you know what the colors mean. **Note:** *It may be necessary to jiggle the battery to bring the test indicator fluid into view.*

21   If the battery has a sealed top and does not have a built-in hydrometer, you can hook up a voltmeter across the battery terminals to check the charge. A fully charged battery should read approximately 12.6 volts or higher.

22   Further information on the battery and jump starting can be found in Chapter 5 and at the front of this manual, respectively.

10   Cooling system check (every 7,500 miles [12,000 km] or 6 months)

Refer to illustrations 10.3 and 10.4
Warning 1: *The engine must be completely cool before beginning this procedure.*
Warning 2: *The electric cooling fan(s) on these models can activate at any time the ignition switch is in the ON position. Make sure the ignition is OFF when working in the vicinity of the fan(s).*

1   Many major engine failures can be attributed to a faulty cooling system. If the vehicle is equipped with an automatic transaxle, a transmission fluid cooler is incorporated inside the radiator bottom tank.

2   The cooling system must be checked with the engine cold. Do this before the vehicle is driven for the day or after it has been shut off for three or four hours and the upper radiator hose feels cool to the touch.

3   Remove the radiator cap (see illustra-

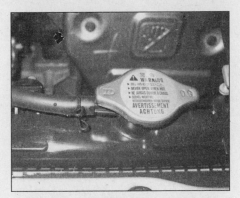

10.3 With the engine cold, remove the radiator cap, wash it and inspect it for damage

tion) and thoroughly clean the cap with water. Also clean the filler neck. All traces of corrosion and gum should be removed.

4   Carefully check the upper and lower radiator hoses along with the smaller diameter heater hoses. Inspect the entire length of each hose, replacing any that are cracked, swollen or deteriorated. Some cracks may become more apparent when a hose is squeezed **(see illustration)**.

5   Also check that all hose connections are tight. If the vehicle came equipped with spring-type hose clamps, which lose their tension over time, replace them with the more reliable screw-type clamps when new hoses are installed. A leak in the cooling system will usually show up as white or rust-colored deposits on the areas adjoining the leak.

6   Use compressed air, water or a soft brush to remove bugs, leaves, and other debris from the front of the radiator or air conditioning condenser. Be careful not to damage the delicate cooling fins, or cut yourself on them.

7   Finally, have the cap and system pressure tested. If you do not have a pressure tester available, most gas stations and repair shops will do this for a minimal charge.

11   Underhood hose check and replacement (every 7,500 miles [12,000 km] or 6 months)

Warning: *Replacement of air conditioning hoses must be left to a dealer service department or air conditioning shop equipped to depressurize the system safely. Never remove air conditioning components or hoses until the system has been depressurized.*

General

1   High temperatures under the hood can cause the deterioration of the rubber and plastic hoses used for engine, accessory and emission systems operation. Periodic inspection should be made for cracks, loose clamps, material hardening and leaks.

2   Information specific to the cooling system hoses can be found in Section 10.

3   Some hoses use clamps to secure the hoses to fittings. Where clamps are used, check to be sure that they haven't lost their tension, allowing the hose to leak. Where clamps are not used, make sure the hose hasn't expanded and/or hardened where it slips over the fitting, allowing it to leak.

Vacuum hoses

4   It's quite common for vacuum hoses, especially those in the emissions system, to be color coded or identified by colored stripes molded into the hose. Various systems require hoses with different wall thickness, collapse resistance and temperature resistance. When replacing hoses, make sure the new ones are made of the same material as the original.

5   Often the only effective way to check a hose is to remove it completely from the vehi-

Check for a chafed area that could fail prematurely.

Check for a soft area indicating the hose has deteriorated inside.

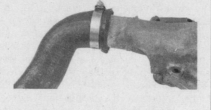

Overtightening the clamp on a hardened hose will damage the hose and cause a leak.

Check each hose for swelling and oil-soaked ends. Cracks and breaks can be located by squeezing the hose.

10.4 Hoses, like drivebelts, have a habit of failing at the worst possible time - to prevent the inconvenience of a blown radiator or heater hose, inspect them carefully as shown here

cle. Where more than one hose is removed, be sure to label the hoses and their attaching points to insure proper reattachment.

6   Include plastic T-fittings in the check of vacuum hoses. Check the fittings for cracks and the hose where it fits over the fitting for enlargement, which could cause leakage.

7   A small piece of vacuum hose (1/4-inch inside diameter) can be used as a stethoscope to detect vacuum leaks. Hold one end of the hose to your ear and probe around vacuum hoses and fittings, listening for the "hissing" sound characteristic of a vacuum leak. **Warning:** *When probing with the vacuum hose stethoscope, be careful not to allow your body or the hose to come into contact with moving engine components such as the drivebelt, cooling fan, etc.*

Fuel hose

Warning: *Gasoline is extremely flammable, so take extra precautions when you work on any part of the fuel system. Don't smoke or allow open flames or bare light bulbs near the work area, and don't work in a garage where a gas-type appliance (such as a water heater or clothes dryer) is present. If you spill any fuel on your skin, rinse it off immediately with soap and water. When you perform any kind of work on the fuel system, wear safety glasses and have a Class B type fire extinguisher on hand. Before working on any part of the fuel system, relieve the fuel system pressure (see Chapter 4).*

8   Check all rubber fuel hoses for damage and deterioration. Check especially for cracks in areas where the hose bends and just before clamping points, such as where a hose attaches to the fuel injection system.

9   High quality fuel line, specifically designed for fuel injection systems, should be used for fuel line replacement. **Warning:** *Never use vacuum line, clear plastic tubing or water hose for fuel lines.*

Brake hoses

10   The hoses used to connect the brake calipers or wheel cylinders to the metal lines are subject to extreme working conditions. They must endure high hydraulic pressures, heat and still maintain flexibility. The brake hoses typically can be inspected without removing the wheels. Carefully examine each hose for leakage, cracks, bulging, delaminating and damage. If any damage is found, the hose must be replaced immediately (see Chapter 9).

Fuel and brake system metal lines

11   Sections of metal line are often used for fuel line between the fuel tank and fuel injection system. Carefully check to be sure the line has not been bent and crimped and that no cracks have started in the line.

12   If a section of metal fuel line must be replaced, only seamless steel tubing should be used, since copper and aluminum tubing do not have the strength necessary to withstand normal engine operating vibration.

13   Check the metal brake lines where they enter the master cylinder and brake proportioning or ABS unit (if equipped) for cracks in the lines or loose fittings. Any sign of brake fluid leakage calls for an immediate thorough inspection of the brake system.

12   Windshield wiper blade inspection and replacement (every 7,500 miles [12,000 km] or 6 months)

Refer to illustrations 12.3, 12.5a and 12.5b

1   The windshield wiper blade elements should be checked periodically for cracks and deterioration.

12.3 Pry off the plastic cover for access to the wiper nut

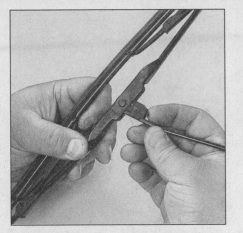

12.5a Depress the release lever and . . .

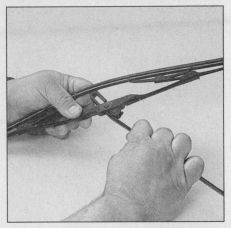

12.5b . . . slide the wiper element down out of the hook in the end of the arm

2   Road film can build up on the wiper blades and affect their efficiency, so they should be washed regularly with a mild detergent solution.

3   The action of the wiping mechanism can loosen the wiper arm retaining nuts, so they should be checked and tightened at the same time the wiper blades are checked **(see illustration)**.

4   Lift the wiper blade assembly away from the windshield.

5   Press the release lever and slide the blade assembly out of the hook in the end of the wiper arm **(see illustrations)**. Carefully rest the wiper arm on the windshield.

6   The rubber wiper element is secured to the blade assembly at one end of the blade element channel. Compress the locking feature on the element so it clears the tangs on the blade assembly channel claw and then slide the element out of the frame.

7   Installation is the reverse of removal. Make sure the rubber element and blade assembly is securely attached.

---

13 Tire rotation (every 7,500 miles [12,000 km] or 6 months)

Refer to illustrations 13.2a and 13.2b

1   The tires should be rotated at the specified intervals and whenever uneven wear is noticed. Since the vehicle will be raised and the tires removed, this is a good time to check the brakes also (see Section 18).

2   Radial tires must be rotated in a specific pattern **(see illustrations)**. **Note:** *Most vehicles are sold with non-directional radial tires, but some performance tires are directional, and have an arrow on the sidewall indicating the direction they must turn when mounted on the vehicle.*

3   See the information in *Jacking and towing* at the front of this manual for the proper procedures to follow when raising the vehicle and changing a tire; however, if the brakes are to be checked, don't apply the parking brake as stated. Make sure the tires are blocked to prevent the vehicle from rolling.

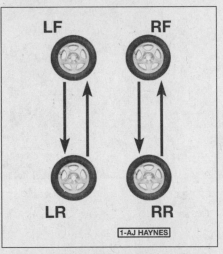

13.2a The recommended four-tire rotational pattern for *directional* **radial tires**

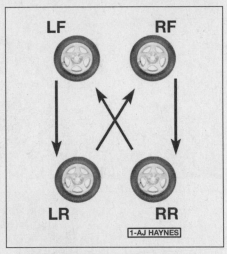

13.2b The recommended four-tire rotational pattern for *non-directional* **radial tires**

Note: *Prior to raising the vehicle, loosen all lug nuts a quarter turn.*

4   Preferably, the entire vehicle should be raised at the same time. This can be done on a hoist or by jacking up each corner of the vehicle and lowering it onto jackstands. Always use jackstands and make sure the vehicle is safely supported. **Warning:** *Never work under a vehicle that is supported only by a jack!*

5   After the tire rotation check and adjust the tire pressures as necessary and tighten the wheel lug nuts to the torque listed in this Chapter's Specifications.

---

14 Steering, suspension and driveaxle boot check (every 7,500 miles [12,000 km] or 6 months)

Note 1: *The steering linkage and suspension components should be checked periodically. Worn or damaged suspension and steering components can result in excessive and*

abnormal tire wear, poor ride quality and vehicle handling and reduced fuel economy. For detailed illustrations of the steering and suspension components, refer to Chapter 10. **Note 2:** *The front suspension on 1999 and later models is a MacPherson strut design. The front suspension on all other models, as well as the rear suspension on all models, uses coil-over shock absorber assemblies.*

Shock absorber/strut check

1   Park the vehicle on level ground, turn the engine off and set the parking brake. Check the tire pressures.

2   Push down at one corner of the vehicle, then release it while noting the movement of the body. It should stop moving and come to rest in a level position within one or two bounces.

3   If the vehicle continues to move up-and-down or if it fails to return to its original position, a worn or weak shock absorber or strut assembly is probably the reason.

4   Repeat the above check at each of the three remaining corners of the vehicle.

14.9a Front suspension components (1998 and earlier models)

1   Upper control arm
2   Coil spring
3   Steering knuckle
4   Shock absorber
5   Shock absorber damper fork
6   Tie-rod end
7   Lower control arm
8   Steering gear boot

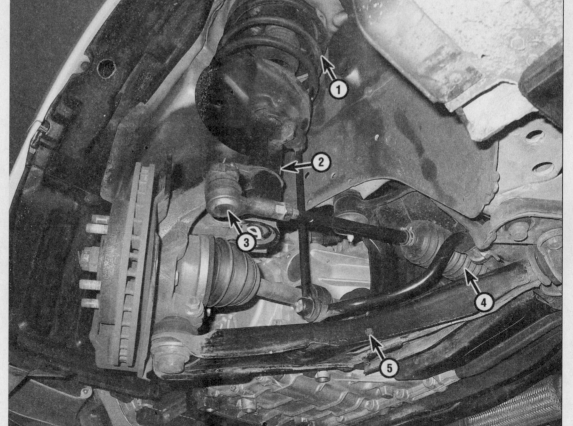

14.9b Front suspension components (1999 and later models)

1   Coil spring
2   Strut body
3   Tie-rod end
4   Steering gear boot
5   Lower control arm

14.10 Check for tie-rod endplay by moving the wheel/tire front and rear, then move the top and bottom of the tire to check for play in the balljoint

14.13 Check the steering gear boots for damage

14.16 Check the inner and outer boot on each driveaxle for cracks and/or leaking grease

5   Raise the vehicle and support it securely on jackstands.

6   Check the shock absorbers/struts for evidence of fluid leakage. A light film of fluid is no cause for concern. Make sure that any fluid noted is from the shocks/struts and not from some other source. If leakage is noted, replace the shocks/struts as a set.

7   Check the shocks/struts to be sure that they are securely mounted and undamaged. Check the upper mounts for damage and wear. If damage or wear is noted, replace the shocks or struts as a set (front or rear).

8   If the shocks or struts must be replaced, refer to Chapter 10 for the procedure.

Suspension and steering check

Refer to illustrations 14.9a, 14.9b, 14.10 and 14.13

9   Raise the vehicle and support it securely on jackstands. **Warning:** *Never work under a vehicle that is supported only by a jack!* Visually inspect the steering and suspension components (front and rear) for damage and distortion. Look for damaged seals, boots and bushings and leaks of any kind. Examine the bushings where the lower control arm meets the chassis and on the stabilizer bar connections **(see illustration)**.

10   Clean the lower end of the steering knuckle. Have an assistant grasp the lower edge of the tire and move the wheel in-and-out while you look for movement at the steering knuckle-to-control arm balljoint **(see illustration)**. If there is any movement, the suspension balljoint(s) must be replaced.

11   Grasp each front tire at the front and rear edges, push in at the front, pull out at the rear and feel for play in the steering system components. If any freeplay is noted, check the tie-rod ends for looseness.

12   Additional steering and suspension system information and illustrations can be found in Chapter 10.

13   Inspect the steering gear boots for cracks as well as loose clamps **(see illustra-**

tion). If there is any evidence of cracks, they must be replaced as described in Chapter 8. If you find leaking lubricant, the rack seal(s) have failed and the steering gear will have to be replaced with a new or rebuilt unit (see Chapter 10).

Driveaxle boot check

Refer to illustration 14.16

14   If the driveaxle boots are damaged, letting grease out and dirt and water in, serious (not to mention costly) damage can occur to the CV joints. The boots should be inspected very carefully at the recommended intervals or anytime the vehicle is raised.

15   Raise the front of the vehicle and support it securely on jackstands. **Warning:** *Never work under a vehicle that is supported only by a jack!*

16   Place the transaxle in Neutral. While rotating the wheels, inspect the four driveaxle boots (two on each driveaxle) very carefully for cracks, tears, holes, deteriorated rubber and loose or missing clamps **(see illustration)**. If the boots are dirty, wipe them clean before beginning the inspection.

17   If damage or deterioration is evident, replace the boots and check the CV joints for damage (see Chapter 8).

18   Place the transaxle in Park or in-gear as applicable, then lower the vehicle.

15   Exhaust system check (every 7,500 miles [12,000 km] or 6 months)

Refer to illustration 15.3
Warning: *Perform the following procedure with the engine cold.*

1   Raise the vehicle and support it securely on jackstands. **Warning:** *Never work under a vehicle that is supported only by a jack!*

2   With the engine cold (at least three hours after the vehicle has been driven) check the complete exhaust system from its starting point at the engine to the end of the tailpipe.

3   Check the pipes and connections for

signs of leakage and/or corrosion indicating a potential failure. Make sure that all brackets and hangers are in good condition and tight **(see illustration)**.

4   At the same time, inspect the underside of the body for holes, corrosion and open seams which may allow exhaust gases to enter the passenger compartment. Seal all body openings with silicone sealant or body putty.

5   Rattles and other noises can often be traced to the exhaust system, especially the mounts and hangers. Try to move the pipes, muffler and catalytic converter. If the components can come into contact with the body, secure the exhaust system with new mounts.

6   This is also an ideal time to check the running condition of the engine by inspecting the very end of the tailpipe. The exhaust deposits here are an indication of the engine's state-of-tune. If the pipe is black and sooty or coated with white deposits, the engine may be in need of a tune-up (including a thorough fuel injection system inspection).

15.3 Check the exhaust system connections, the clamps, the mounting bolts and brackets and particularly the rubber hangers for damage

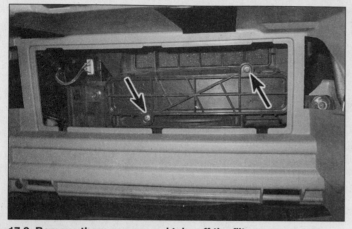

17.2 Remove these screws and take off the filter access cover . . .

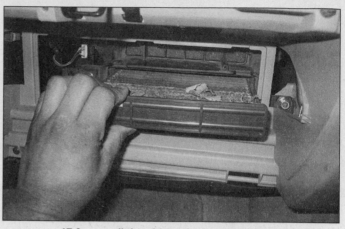

17.3 . . . pull the old ventilation filter out . . .

16 Manual transaxle lubricant level check (every 7500 miles [12,000 km] or 6 months)

1   Manual transaxles do not have a fluid dipstick. The lubricant level is checked by removing the plug from the side of the transaxle case. The lubricant level should be checked with the engine cold and the vehicle level.

2   Raise the vehicle and support it securely on jackstands in a level position. **Warning:** *Never work under a vehicle that is supported only by a jack!*

3   Locate the fill plug on the front of the transaxle. Use a rag to clean it and the surrounding area. It may be necessary to remove the under-vehicle splash shield for access to the plug. Place a drain pan under the transaxle.

4   Use a socket or wrench to unscrew the plug. If oil begins to run out, let it find its own level (presuming the vehicle is relatively level). If oil does not run out, insert your finger to feel the lubricant level. It should be within 3/16-inch of the bottom of the plug hole.

5   If the transaxle requires additional lubricant, use a funnel with a rubber tube or a syringe to pour or squeeze the recommended lubricant into the plug hole to restore the level.

17.4 . . . and install the new filter. This one has an integral access cover

If you overfill it, let the fluid run out until it is level with the plug hole. **Caution:** *Use only the specified transaxle lubricant - see* Recommended lubricants and fluids *at the beginning of this Chapter or your owner's manual.* **Note:** *Most auto parts stores sell pumps that screw into the oil containers which make this job much easier and less messy.*

6   Install the plug and tighten to the torque listed in this Chapter's Specifications, then lower the vehicle. Test drive the vehicle and check for leaks.

17 Interior ventilation filter replacement (every 15,000 miles [24,000 km] or 12 months)

Refer to illustrations 17.2 and 17.3
Note: *This procedure applies to 1999 through early 2001 models only. On mid-year 2001 and later models, no filter is installed, but one can be retrofitted. It will be necessary to cut the block-off plate from the HVAC housing using a sharp cutting tool. The filter can then be installed in the housing, and the block-off plate can be secured with self-tapping screws.*

1   Open the glove box door, push in on the sides, swing the door down and remove it (see Chapter 11 if necessary).

2   Remove the two screws and take off the access cover **(see illustration)**.

3   Pull the filter element straight out of the housing **(see illustration)**.

4   Installation is the reverse of removal. **Note:** *Some replacement filters are equipped with an integral access cover* **(see illustration)**. *It would be a good idea to save the old cover, however, just in case you obtain another filter in the future that doesn't have the cover attached to it.*

18 Brake system check (eve4ry 15,000 miles [24,000 km] or 12 months)

Warning: *Dust created by the brake system is harmful to your health. Never blow it out with*

compressed air and don't inhale any of it. An approved filtering mask should be worn when working on brakes. Do not, under any circumstances, use petroleum-based solvents to clean brake parts. Use brake system cleaner only!

1   The brakes should be inspected every time the wheels are removed or whenever a defect is suspected. Indications of a potential brake system problem include the vehicle pulling to one side when the brake pedal is depressed, noises coming from the brakes when they are applied, excessive brake pedal travel, a pulsating pedal and leakage of fluid, usually seen on the inside of the tire or wheel. **Note:** *It is normal for a vehicle equipped with an Anti-lock Brake System (ABS) to exhibit brake pedal pulsation's during severe braking conditions.*

Disc brakes

Refer to illustrations 18.5a, 18.5b and 18.8

2   Disc brakes can be visually checked without removing any parts except the wheels. Remove the hub caps (if applicable) and loosen the wheel lug nuts a quarter turn each.

3   Raise the vehicle and place it securely on jackstands. **Warning:** *Never work under a vehicle that is supported only by a jack!*

4   Remove the wheels. Now visible is the disc brake caliper that contains the pads. There is an outer brake pad and an inner pad. Both must be checked for wear.

5   Measure the thickness of the outer pad at each end of the caliper and the inner pad through the inspection hole in the caliper body **(see illustrations)**. Compare the measurement with the limit given in this Chapter's Specifications; if any brake pad thickness is less than specified, then all brake pads on the front or rear must be replaced (see Chapter 9).

6   If you're in doubt as to the exact pad thickness or quality, remove them for measurement and further inspection (see Chapter 9).

7   Check the disc for score marks, wear and burned spots. If any of these conditions

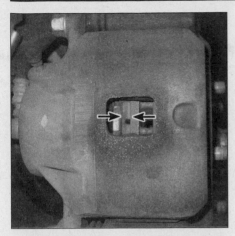

18.5a With the wheel off, measure the thickness of the inner pad lining material through the inspection hole

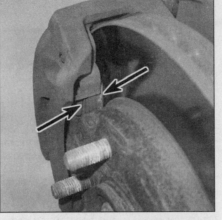

18.5b Measure the thickness of the outer brake pad from the metal backing

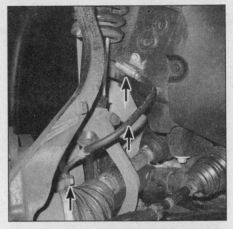

18.8 Check the brake line connection at the caliper, look along the brake hose for signs of cracking or fluid leakage, and check where the flexible brake hose meets the steel line on the chassis

exist, the disc should be removed for servicing or replacement (see Chapter 9).

8   Before installing the wheels, check all the brake lines and hoses for damage, wear, deformation, cracks, corrosion, leakage, bends and twists, particularly in the vicinity of the rubber hoses and calipers (see illustration).

9   Install the wheels, lower the vehicle and tighten the wheel lug nuts to the torque given in this Chapter's Specifications.

Drum brakes

Refer to illustrations 18.14 and 18.17

10   Remove the hub caps (if applicable) and loosen the wheel lug nuts a quarter turn each.

11   Raise the rear of the vehicle and support it securely on jackstands. Warning: Never work under a vehicle that is supported only by a jack! Block the front wheels to prevent the vehicle from rolling, however, do not apply the parking brake or it will lock the drums in

place. Remove the rear wheels.

12   Remove the brake drum as described in Chapter 9.

13   With the drum removed, carefully clean off any accumulations of dirt and dust using brake system cleaner. Warning: DO NOT blow the dust out with compressed air and don't inhale any of it.

14   Measure the thickness of the lining material on both leading and trailing brake shoes (see illustration). Compare the measurement with the limit given in this Chapter's Specifications; if any brake shoe thickness is less than specified, then all brake shoes must be replaced (see Chapter 9).

15   Inspect the brake shoes for uneven wear patterns cracks, glazing and delaminating and replace if necessary. If the shoes have been saturated with brake fluid, oil or grease, this also necessitates replacement (see Chapter 9).

16   Make sure all the brake assembly springs are connected and in good condition.

17   Check the brake wheel cylinder for signs of fluid leakage. Carefully pull back the rubber dust boots on the wheel cylinder (see illustration). Any leakage here is an indication that the wheel cylinders must be replaced immediately (see Chapter 9). Also, check all hoses and connections for signs of leakage.

18   Clean the inside of the drum with brake system cleaner. Again, be careful not to breathe the dust.

19   Inspect the inside of the drum for cracks, score marks, deep scratches and "hard spots" which will appear as small-discolored areas. If imperfections cannot be removed with emery cloth or sandpaper, the drum must be taken to an automotive machine shop for resurfacing.

20   Repeat the procedure for the remaining wheel.

21   Install the wheels, lower the vehicle and tighten the wheel lug nuts to the torque given in this Chapter's Specifications.

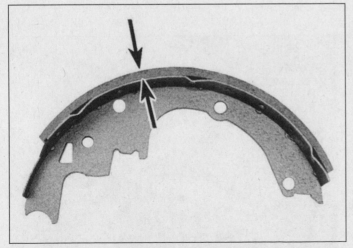

18.14 If the lining is bonded to the brake shoe, measure the lining thickness from the outer surface to the metal shoe; if the lining is riveted to the shoe, measure from the lining outer surface to the rivet head

18.17 Pull the boot away from the cylinder and check for fluid leakage

Parking brake

22   Slowly pull up on the parking brake and count the number of clicks you hear until the handle is up as far as it will go. The adjustment is correct if you hear the specified number of clicks (see this Chapter's Specifications). If you hear more or fewer clicks, it's time to adjust the parking brake (see Chapter 9).

23   An alternative method of checking the parking brake is to park the vehicle on a steep hill with the engine running (so you can apply the brakes if necessary) with the parking brake set and the transaxle in Neutral. If the parking brake cannot prevent the vehicle from rolling, it needs adjustment (see Chapter 9).

19   Fuel system hoses and connections check (every 15,000 miles [24,000 km] or 12 months)

Refer to illustration 19.5

Warning: *Gasoline is extremely flammable, so take extra precautions when you work on any part of the fuel system. Don't smoke or allow open flames or bare light bulbs near the work area, and don't work in a garage where a gas-type appliance (such as a water heater or clothes dryer) is present. If you spill any fuel on your skin, rinse it off immediately with soap and water. When you perform any kind of work on the fuel system, wear safety glasses and have a Class B type fire extinguisher on hand.*

1   If the smell of gasoline is noticed while driving, or after the vehicle has been parked in the sun, the fuel system and evaporative emissions control system (see Section 26) should be thoroughly inspected immediately.

2   The fuel system is under pressure even when the engine is off. Consequently, the fuel system must be depressurized before servicing the system (see Chapter 4). Even after depressurization, if any fuel lines are disconnected for servicing, be prepared to catch some fuel as it spills out. Plug all disconnected fuel lines immediately to prevent the

tank from emptying itself.

3   Remove the gas tank filler cap and check for damage, corrosion and a proper sealing imprint on the gasket. Replace the cap with a new one if necessary.

4   Raise the vehicle and support it securely on jackstands. **Warning:** *Never work under a vehicle that is supported only by a jack!*

5   Inspect the gas tank and filler neck for punctures, cracks and other damage. The hose connection between the filler neck and the tank is especially critical **(see illustration)**. Sometimes the filler neck hose will leak due to loose clamps or deteriorated rubber; problems a home mechanic can usually rectify.

6   Carefully inspect all rubber hoses and metal lines leading to-and-from the fuel tank. Check for loose connections, deteriorated hoses, crimped lines and damage of any kind. Follow the lines up to the front of the vehicle, carefully inspecting them all the way. Repair or replace damaged sections as necessary (see Chapter 4).

20   Drivebelt check, adjustment and replacement (every 15,000 miles [24,000 km] or 12 months)

Warning: *The electric cooling fan(s) on these models can activate at any time the ignition switch is in the ON position. Make sure the ignition is OFF when working in the vicinity of the fan(s).*

1   The drivebelts are located at the front of the engine and play an important role in the operation of the vehicle and its components. Due to their function and material makeup, the belts are prone to failure after a period of time and should be inspected and adjusted periodically to prevent major damage.

2   A number of belt arrangements can be used, depending on the engine and accessories. 1998 and earlier models with air conditioning have three belts: one for the power steering pump, one for the water pump and alternator, and one for the air conditioning

19.5 Check the fuel filler neck-to-tank hose and clamp

compressor. 1999 and later models with a four cylinder engine have two belts: one for the water pump and alternator, and one for the air conditioning compressor and power steering pump. 1999 and later models with a V6 engine also have two belts: one for the water pump and power steering pump, and one for the alternator and air conditioning compressor.

Check

Refer to illustrations 20.3 and 20.4

3   With the engine off, open the hood and use your fingers (and a flashlight, if necessary), to move along the belt checking for cracks and separation of the belt plies. Also check for fraying and glazing, which gives the belt a shiny appearance. Also check the ribs on the underside of the belt. They should all be the same depth, with none of the surface uneven **(see illustration)**.

4   The tension of each belt is checked by pushing on it at a distance halfway between the pulleys. Apply about 20 pounds of force with your thumb and see how much the belt moves down (deflects). Measure the deflection with a ruler **(see illustration)**. The belt should deflect about 1/4-inch if the distance between pulleys is between 7 and 11 inches and around 1/2-inch if the distance is between 12 and 16 inches.

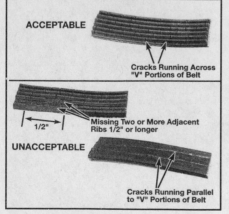

20.3 Here are some of the more common problems associated with drivebelts (check the belts very carefully to prevent an untimely breakdown)

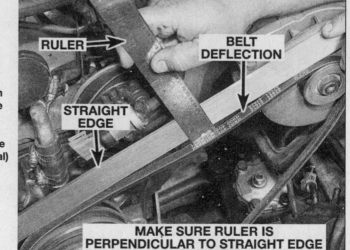

20.4 Measure drivebelt deflection with a straightedge and ruler - make sure the ruler is perpendicular to the straight edge (typical)

20.6a To adjust the alternator/water pump belt on a 1999 or later four-cylinder model, loosen this pivot bolt nut (seen from below) . . .

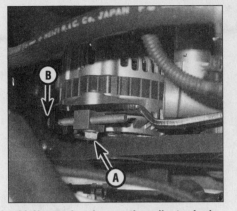

20.6b . . . then loosen the adjuster lock bolt (A) and turn the adjusting bolt (B) to adjust the drivebelt tension

20.7 Rotate the tensioner to align the holes, then slip a drill into the holes to lock it in position while you route a new belt onto the pulleys

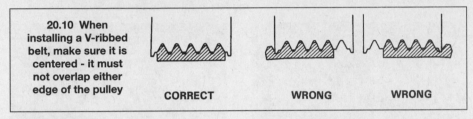

20.10 When installing a V-ribbed belt, make sure it is centered - it must not overlap either edge of the pulley

CORRECT   WRONG   WRONG

they are routed correctly and properly centered in each pulley **(see illustration)**.

11 Adjust the drivebelts as described earlier in this Section. After the drivebelts have been in service for approximately fifteen minutes, check the drivebelt tension again and adjust if necessary, as new drivebelts tend to stretch after initial installation.

Adjustment

Refer to illustrations 20.6a, 20.6b and 20.7

5   Depending on the belt being adjusted, you may have to raise the vehicle and support it securely on jackstands.

6   On some drivebelts the tension adjustment is made by moving the component position with an adjuster after loosening the pivot bolt **(see illustration)**. Loosen the adjuster lock bolt and turn the adjuster bolt as necessary to move the component away from the engine (to tighten the belt) or toward the engine (to loosen the belt) to achieve the correct drivebelt tension **(see illustration)**. Tighten the pivot bolt/nut and lock bolt securely. Some drivebelts are adjusted in a similar manner, but instead of moving the driven component, an idler wheel is moved within its bracket.

7   Other belts have a spring-loaded automatic tensioner. On these belts, put a wrench or a ratchet and socket on the tensioner hex and rotate it to release tension for belt removal. A pin can be inserted into the tensioner holes to hold it in the released position while the new belt is installed **(see illustration)**. There is an arrow on the tensioner that should point between two lines when the belt is operating properly. If the arrow is outside the lines, then the belt has stretched and should be replaced.

Replacement

Refer to illustration 20.10

8   To replace a drivebelt, follow the procedures for drivebelt adjustment, except loosen the adjustment enough to allow you to slip the drivebelt off the pulleys to remove it. Because drivebelts tend to wear out equally, it's a good idea to replace all belts at the same time. As they are removed, identify each belt as to its appropriate drive function (PS or ALT-A/C) so the replacement belts can be installed in their proper positions.

9   Take the old drivebelts with you when you go to the auto parts store in order to make a direct comparison for length, width and design.

10   Install the new drivebelts. Make sure

21   Chassis lubrication (every 30,000 miles [48,000 km] or 24 months)

Refer to illustration 21.1

1   Although the tie-rod ends and front suspension lower balljoints on these models are not serviceable, a grease gun or container of grease, an oil can filled with engine oil and graphite spray will be necessary to lubricate the components which do require periodic lubrication **(see illustration)**.

2   Raise the vehicle and support it securely on jackstands. **Warning:** *Never work under a vehicle that is supported only by a jack!*

3   Lubricate the sliding contact and pivot points of the parking brake cable along with the cable guides and levers. Smearing some of the chassis grease onto the cable and related parts with your fingers can do this. Be careful of frayed wires!

4   Lower the vehicle to the ground.

5   Open the hood and smear a little chassis grease on the hood latch mechanism and striker. Have an assistant pull the hood release lever from inside the vehicle as you lubricate the cable at the latch.

6   Lubricate all the hinges (door, hood, trunk, etc.) with the recommended lubricant (see *Recommended lubricants and fluids* at the beginning of this Chapter) to keep them in proper working order.

7   The key lock cylinders can be lubricated with spray-type graphite or silicone lubricant which is available at auto parts stores.

8   Lubricate the door weatherstripping with silicone spray. This will reduce chafing and retard wear.

21.1 Materials required for chassis and body lubrication

1   **Engine oil** - *Light engine oil in a can like this can be used for door and hood hinges*

2   **Graphite spray** - *Used to lubricate lock cylinders*

3   **Grease** - *Grease, in a variety of types and weights, is available for use in a grease gun. Check the Specifications for your requirements*

4   **Grease gun** - *A common grease gun, shown here with a detachable hose and nozzle, is a handy source of grease. After use, clean it thoroughly*

22.2a Release the latches to remove the air cleaner cover . . .

22.2b . . . then detach the cover and lift out the filter element (1999 and later models shown; the housing on earlier models is split side-to-side)

22 Air filter replacement (every 30,000 miles [48,000 km] or 24 months)

Refer to illustrations 22.2a and 22.2b

1   The air filter element is located in a housing on either the right (1998 and earlier models) or the left (1999 and later models) side of the engine compartment.

2   Detach the latch clips securing the cover of the air cleaner housing, then separate the housing halves and lift the filter element out **(see illustrations)**.

3   Inspect the inside of the air cleaner housing for dirt, debris or damage. If necessary, clean the inside of the housing with a rag or shop vacuum. If the air cleaner housing is damaged and requires replacement, refer to Chapter 4.

23 Automatic transaxle fluid and filter change (every 30,000 miles [48,000 km] or 24 months)

1   The automatic transaxle fluid and filter (if equipped) should be changed and the magnet (if equipped) cleaned at the recommended intervals.

2   Raise the front of the vehicle and support it securely on jackstands. **Warning:** *Never work under a vehicle that is supported only by a jack!* Remove the transaxle splash shield.

3   Position a large drain pan under the transaxle.

1997 and earlier models
Refer to illustrations 23.4a, 23.4b, 23.6a, 23.6b, 23.7a, 23.7b, 23.8a, 23.8b and 23.8c

4   Remove the drain plugs in the fluid pan and the transaxle housing and allow the fluid to drain into the container **(see illustrations)**. Measure the amount of fluid drained and write down this figure for reference when refilling.

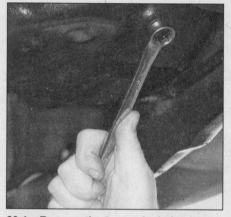

23.4a Remove the transaxle drain plug . . .

23.4b . . . and the differential drain plug

5   After the fluid has completely drained, install the drain plugs and tighten them to the torque given in this Chapter's Specifications.

6   Remove the pan bolts and lower the pan from the transaxle **(see illustrations)**. Tap the corners of the pan using a soft-faced mallet to break the seal and detach the pan.

7   Remove the filter (if equipped) **(see illustrations)**.

8   Carefully remove all traces of the old gasket sealant from the pan and transaxle body (be careful not to nick or gouge the sealing surfaces) **(see illustrations)**.

9   Clean the pan and the magnet located inside the pan with a clean, lint-free cloth moistened with solvent. Don't forget to place the magnet back in its proper location at the bottom of the pan.

10   Install the new filter in place on the transaxle valve body. Tighten the filter mount-

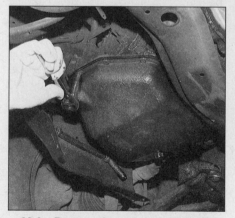

23.6a Remove the pan retaining bolts

23.6b Detach the pan and lower it from the transaxle

23.7a Remove the filter retaining bolts . . .

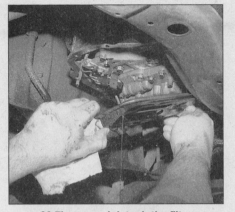

23.7b . . . and detach the filter
from the transaxle

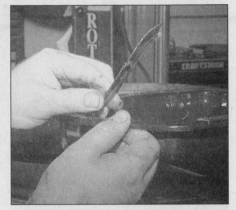

23.8a Remove the old gasket
from the pan . . .

ing bolts to the torque listed in this Chapter's Specifications.

11   Using a new gasket, install the pan and tighten the bolts to the torque given in this Chapter's Specifications.

12   Fill the transaxle with the recommended lubricant (see Section 6). Begin the refill procedure by initially adding 1/3 of the amount drained. Then, with the engine running, add 1/2-pint at a time (cycling the shifter through each gear position between additions) until the level is correct on the dipstick. It is important to not overfill the transaxle.

1998 models

13   Locate the oil cooler hose connected to the transaxle that is closest to the rear of the vehicle. Disconnect the hose from the tube and point it into the drain pan. Cap off the metal tube on the transaxle to keep out dirt. Be sure to drain any fluid from the hose.

14   Apply the parking brake and block the front wheels. Have an assistant start the engine and let it idle in neutral while you watch the hose. Let the engine run until the fluid (about 2-1/2 quarts) stops coming out, then shut the engine off immediately (but in any case, don't let the engine run longer than one minute).

15   Remove the drain plugs from the

transaxle and drain the fluid (see illustrations 23.4a and 23.4b). After the fluid has completely drained, install the drain plugs and tighten them to the torque given in this Chapter's Specifications. Measure the total amount of fluid drained and write down this figure for reference when refilling.

16   Refer to Steps 6 through 11 to replace the filter.

17   Begin the refill procedure by initially adding 1/3 of the amount drained. Then, with the engine running, add 1/2-pint at a time (cycling the shifter through each gear position between additions) until the level is correct on the dipstick. It is important to not overfill the transaxle.

18   Repeat Step 14 to pump more fluid into the drain pan, then drain a small amount from the drain plug and check it for contamination. If it's contaminated, add more fluid, then repeat Step 14 and this Step again.

19   Reconnect the fluid hose to the metal tube at the transaxle.

20   Start the engine and let it idle for one to two minutes. Shift the selector into all positions from P through L, then shift into P and apply the parking brake.

21   With the engine idling, check the fluid level. It should be up to the Cold mark on the dipstick. Add fluid slowly to bring the level up

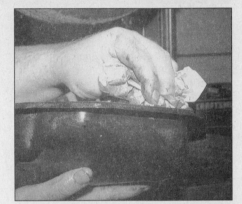

23.8b . . . then carefully clean the contact
surfaces of the pan . . .

if necessary.

22   Operate the vehicle to bring transaxle temperature up to normal, then recheck the level on the dipstick. It should be within the Hot range. Add fluid as necessary.

1999 and later models

Refer to illustrations 23.23 and 23.25

23   Locate the oil cooler hose that connects to the metal tube at the radiator (see illustration). Disconnect the hose from the tube and

23.8c . . . and the transaxle case

23.23 On 1999 and later models, disconnect the fluid cooler line
at the radiator and direct it into the drain pan, then start the
engine to pump the fluid out

23.25 Remove the automatic transaxle drain plug (1999 and later models)

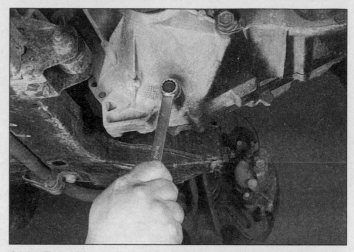

24.2a To avoid rounding off the corners, use the correct size box-end wrench or a socket to remove the drain plug . . .

point it into the drain pan. Cap off the metal tube to keep out dirt.

24   Apply the parking brake and block the front wheels. Have an assistant start the engine and let it idle in neutral while you watch the hose. Let the engine run until the fluid stops coming out (about 3-1/2 quarts), then shut the engine off immediately (but in any case, don't let the engine run longer than one minute).

25   Remove the drain plug from the transaxle case and drain the fluid **(see illustration)**. Install the drain plug and tighten it to the torque listed in this Chapter's Specifications. Measure the total amount of fluid drained and write down this figure for reference when refilling.

26   Using an oil filter wrench, unscrew the spin-on type filter located next to the dipstick tube **(see illustration 6.3)**. Clean the fulter mounting surface. Lubricate the O-ring of the new filter with clean transmission fluid, then thread the filter onto the transaxle and tighten it according to the instructions on the filter canister or box (usually 3/4 of a turn after the gasket contacts the transaxle. **DO NOT** use an engine oil filter, and don't use the wrench to tighten the filter.

27   Begin the refill procedure by initially adding 1/3 of the amount drained. Then, with the engine running, add 1/2-pint at a time (cycling the shifter through each gear position between additions) until the level is correct on the dipstick. It is important to not overfill the transaxle.

28   Repeat Step 24 to pump more fluid into the drain pan, then drain a small amount from the drain plug and check it for contamination. If it's contaminated, add more fluid, then repeat Step 24 and this Step again.

29   Reconnect the fluid hose to the metal tube at the radiator.

30   Start the engine and let it idle for one to two minutes. Shift the selector into all positions from P through L, then shift into P and apply the parking brake.

31   With the engine idling, check the fluid level. It should be up to the Cold mark on the dipstick. Add fluid slowly to bring the level up if necessary.

32   Operate the vehicle to bring transmission temperature up to normal, then recheck level on the dipstick. It should be within the Hot range. Add fluid as necessary.

All models

33   Old fluid drained from the transaxle cannot be reused in its present state and should be disposed of. Check with your local auto parts store, disposal facility or environmental agency to see if they will accept the fluid for recycling. After the fluid has cooled it can be drained into a container (capped plastic jugs, topped bottles, milk cartons, etc.) for transport to one of these disposal sites. Don't dispose of the fluid by pouring it on the ground or down a drain!

---

24   Manual transaxle lubricant change (every 30,000 miles [48,000 km] or 24 months)

Refer to illustrations 24.2a and 24.2b

1   Raise the vehicle and support it securely on jackstands in a level position. **Warning:** *Never work under a vehicle that is supported only by a jack!*

2   Position a drain pan under the transaxle. Using a box-end wrench or socket to prevent rounding off the flats of the drain plug and fill plug, remove the fill plug, then the drain plug **(see illustrations)**.

3   After the fluid has completely drained, install the drain plug and tighten it to the torque given in this Chapter's Specifications.

4   Fill the transaxle with the recommended lubricant up to the bottom of the check/fill plug hole (see *Recommended lubricants and fluids* at the front of this Chapter). Reinstall the check/fill plug and tighten it to the torque listed in this Chapter's Specifications.

5   Old lubricant drained from the transaxle cannot be reused in its present state and should be disposed of. Check with your local

24.2b . . . and allow the lubricant to drain

auto parts store, disposal facility or environmental agency to see if they will accept the lubricant for recycling. After the lubricant has cooled it can be drained into a container (capped plastic jugs, topped bottles, milk cartons, etc.) for transport to one of these disposal sites. Don't dispose of the lubricant by pouring it on the ground or down a drain!

---

25   Cooling system servicing (draining, flushing and refilling) (every 30,000 miles [48,000 km] or 24 months)

Warning 1: *Wait until the engine is completely cool before beginning this procedure.*
Warning 2: *Do not allow engine coolant (antifreeze) to come in contact with your skin or painted surfaces of the vehicle. Rinse off spills immediately with plenty of water. Antifreeze is highly toxic if ingested. Never leave antifreeze lying around in an open container or in puddles on the floor; children and pets are attracted by its sweet smell and may drink it. Check with local authorities about disposing of used antifreeze. Many communities have*

25.4 The drain fitting is located at the lower corner of the radiator

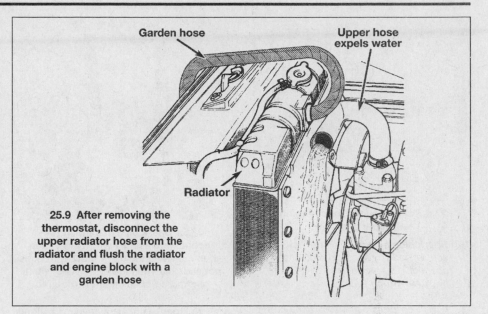

25.9 After removing the thermostat, disconnect the upper radiator hose from the radiator and flush the radiator and engine block with a garden hose

collection centers that will see that antifreeze is disposed of safely.

Warning 3: *The electric cooling fan(s) can come on at any time the ignition switch is in the ON position. Make sure the ignition is OFF when working in the vicinity of the fan(s).*

Note: *Non-toxic antifreeze is available at most auto parts stores. Although the antifreeze is non-toxic when fresh, proper disposal is still required.*

1   Periodically, the cooling system should be drained, flushed and refilled to replenish the antifreeze mixture and prevent formation of rust and corrosion, which can impair the performance of the cooling system and cause engine damage. When the cooling system is serviced, all hoses and the cooling system pressure cap should be checked and replaced if necessary.

Draining

Refer to illustration 25.4

Warning: *Wait until the engine is completely cool before beginning this procedure.*

2   Apply the parking brake and block the wheels. If the vehicle has just been driven, wait several hours to allow the engine to cool down before beginning this procedure.

3   Once the engine is completely cool, remove the radiator cap.

4   Move a large container under the radiator drain to catch the coolant, then open the drain fitting at the bottom of the radiator (a pair of pliers may be required to turn it) **(see illustration)**.

5   While the coolant is draining, check the condition of the radiator hoses, heater hoses and clamps (refer to Section 13 if necessary). Replace any damaged clamps or hoses.

6   Remove the coolant reservoir and drain it, too.

Flushing

Refer to illustration 25.9

7   Once the system is completely drained, remove the thermostat from the engine (see Chapter 3). Then reinstall the thermostat housing without the thermostat. This will

allow the system to be flushed.

8   Tighten the radiator drain fitting. Turn your heating system controls to Hot, so that the heater core will be flushed at the same time as the rest of the cooling system. Install the radiator cap.

9   Disconnect the upper radiator hose from the radiator. Place a garden hose in the upper radiator inlet, turn the water on and flush the system until the water runs clear out of the upper radiator hose **(see illustration)**.

10   In severe cases of contamination or clogging of the radiator, remove the radiator (see Chapter 3) and have a radiator repair facility clean and repair it if necessary. Many deposits can be removed by the chemical action of a cleaner available at auto parts stores. Follow the procedure outlined in the manufacturer's instructions. **Note:** *When the coolant is regularly drained and the system refilled with the correct antifreeze/water mixture, there should be no need to use chemical cleaners or descalers.*

11   After flushing, drain the radiator once again to drain the water from the system.

Refilling

12   Tighten the radiator drain fitting. Reinstall the thermostat and the coolant reservoir.

13   Make sure the heater temperature control is in the maximum heat position.

14   On 1998 and earlier models, open the air bleed bolt (it's located on the water outlet fitting or thermostat housing).

15   Remove the radiator cap and slowly add new coolant (a 50/50 mixture of water and antifreeze) until it's full. On 1998 and earlier models, tighten the bleed bolt securely after coolant begins flowing from the bleed bolt hole. Add coolant to the reservoir up to the FULL mark.

16   Install the radiator cap and run the engine in a well-ventilated area until the thermostat opens (coolant will begin flowing through the radiator and the upper radiator hose will become hot).

17   Increase the engine speed to 3000 rpm three times.

18   Turn the engine off and let it cool. Remove the radiator cap and add more coolant mixture to bring the level back up to the lip on the radiator filler neck.

19   Squeeze the upper radiator hose to expel air, then add more coolant mixture if necessary. Reinstall the radiator cap.

20   Start the engine, allow it to reach normal operating temperature and check for leaks.

26   Evaporative emissions control system check (every 30,000 miles [48,000 km] or 24 months)

1   The function of the evaporative emissions control system is to prevent fuel vapors from escaping the fuel system and being released into the atmosphere. Vapors from the fuel tank are temporarily stored in a charcoal canister. The Powertrain Control Module (PCM) monitors the system and allows the vapors to be drawn into the intake manifold when the engine reaches normal operating temperature.

2   The charcoal canister on 1998 and earlier models is mounted to a bracket below the battery. On 1999 and later models, it's located on top of the fuel tank. The canister is maintenance-free and should last the life of the vehicle.

3   The most common symptom of a fault in the evaporative emissions system is a strong fuel odor coming from the area where the charcoal canister is mounted or raw fuel leaking from the canister. These indications are usually more prevalent in hot temperatures.

4   1997 and later California models and all 1998 and later models are equipped with an EVAP ventilation solenoid. This solenoid is normally open, but when the PCM conducts an OBD-II system leak check it turns the solenoid ON, which closes the charcoal canister

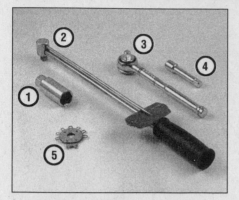

27.2 Tools required for changing spark plugs

1   **Spark plug socket** - *This will have special padding inside to protect the spark plug's porcelain insulator*
2   **Torque wrench** - *Although not mandatory, using this tool is the best way to ensure the plugs are tightened properly*
3   **Ratchet** - *Standard hand tool to fit the spark plug socket*
4   **Extension** - *Depending on model and accessories, you may need special extensions and universal joints to reach one or more of the plugs*
5   **Spark plug gap gauge** - *This gauge for checking the gap comes in a variety of styles. Make sure the gap for your engine is included*

27.5a Spark plug manufacturers recommend using a wire-type gauge when checking the gap - if the wire does not slide between the electrodes with a slight drag, adjustment is required

27.5b To change the gap, bend the side electrode only, as indicated by the arrows, and be very careful not to crack or chip the porcelain insulator surrounding the center electrode

vent to atmospheric pressure, which effectively seals the system. The pressure of the trapped fuel vapors is monitored by the fuel tank differential pressure sensor; if the sensor detects a leak, the PCM will store the appropriate fault code and illuminate the CHECK ENGINE light on the instrument panel. The most common cause of system pressure loss is a loose or poor-sealing gas cap.
5   For more information and replacement procedures see Chapter 6.

27   Spark plug check and replacement (see *Maintenance schedule* for intervals)

All models
Refer to illustrations 27.2, 27.5a and 27.5b
1   The spark plugs are located in the cylinder heads and are accessed through long tubes in the top of the valve cover(s).
2   In most cases the tools necessary for spark plug replacement include a spark plug socket which fits onto a ratchet (this special socket is padded inside to protect the porcelain insulators on the new plugs and hold them in place), various extensions and a feeler gauge to check and adjust the spark plug gap **(see illustration)**. A special plug wire removal tool is available for separating the wire boot from the spark plug, but it isn't absolutely necessary. Since these engines

are equipped with an aluminum cylinder head(s), a torque wrench should be used when tightening the spark plugs.
3   The best approach when replacing the spark plugs is to purchase the new spark plugs beforehand, adjust them to the proper gap and then replace each plug one at a time. When buying the new spark plugs, be sure to obtain the correct plug for your specific engine. This information can be found in the Specification Section at the front of this Chapter or in your owner's manual.
4   Allow the engine to cool completely before attempting to remove any of the plugs. During this cooling off time, each of the new spark plugs can be inspected for defects and the gaps can be checked.
5   The gap is checked by inserting the proper thickness gauge between the electrodes at the tip of the plug **(see illustration)**. The gap between the electrodes should be as specified on the VECI label in the engine compartment or as listed in this Chapter's Specifications. The wire should touch each of the electrodes. If the gap is incorrect, use the adjuster on the thickness gauge body to bend the curved side electrode slightly until the proper gap is obtained **(see illustration)**. **Caution:** *The manufacturer recommends against checking the gap on platinum- or iridium-tipped spark plugs; the coating could be*

scraped off. Also, at this time check for cracks in the spark plug body (if any are found, the plug must not be used). If the side electrode is not exactly over the center one, use the adjuster to align the two.
6   Cover the fender to prevent damage to the paint, fender covers are available from auto parts stores but an old blanket will work just fine.

Four-cylinder engines
1994 through 1998 SOHC engines and 1994 and 1995 DOHC engines
7   Remove the center cover from the valve cover, if applicable. Grasp the spark plug boot securely, twist it back and forth and detach it from the spark plug. Proceed to Step 13. **Note:** *It's a good idea to remove one spark plug wire and replace one spark plug at a time to prevent mixing up the wires.*

1999 through 2003 engines
Refer to illustrations 27.8a, 27.8b, 27.9a and 27.9b
8   These models use a combination of coil-over-plug ignition coil and spark plug wires connections. On cylinders 1 and 3, the spark plug wires are connected to the coil-over spark plug units on cylinders 2 and 4 **(see illustration)**. Detach the spark plug wires first

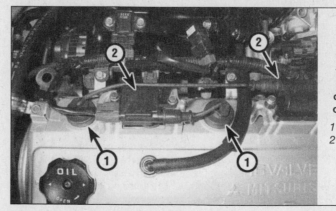

27.8a 1999 and later four-cylinder engines use a combination of conventional and coil-over-plug connections

1   *Spark plug wire/boot*
2   *Coil-over-plug type ignition coil*

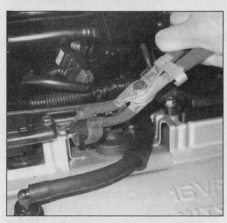

27.8b Disconnect the spark plug wire from the ignition coil, then twist and pull the boot off the spark plug

27.9a Disconnect the electrical connector and remove the bolts . . .

27.9b . . . then pull the coil pack out of the valve cover

from the coil pack/coil over units, then detach them from the spark plugs **(see illustration)**.
9   On cylinders 2 and 4, disconnect the electrical connectors, remove the retaining bolts and detach the coil unit from the spark plug **(see illustrations)**.

2004 and later SOHC engines
10   These vehicles have an individual ignition coil mounted on top of each spark plug.
11   Refer to Chapter 5 and remove the ignition coils.

V6 engines
2003 and earlier models
Refer to illustration 27.14
12   Remove the upper intake manifold for access to the rear spark plugs (see Chapter 2B).
13   To prevent dirt or other foreign debris from entering the engine, place clean rags into the openings in the lower intake manifold.
14   Detach any clips securing the spark plug wires. Using a twisting motion, loosen the boot/wire at the valve cover then pull the boot from the cover **(see illustration)**. **Note:** *It's a good idea to remove one spark plug wire and replace one spark plug at a time to prevent mixing up the wires.*

2004 and later models
15   These vehicles have an individual ignition coil mounted on top of each spark plug.
16   Refer to Chapter 5 and remove the ignition coils.

All models
Refer to illustrations 27.18, 27.20 and 27.21
17   If compressed air is available, use it to blow any dirt or foreign material away from the spark plug area. **Warning:** *Use proper eye protection!* A pressurized can of air of the type used for dusting computer or camera equipment will also work. The idea here is to eliminate the possibility of material falling into the cylinder through the spark plug hole as the spark plug is removed.
18   Place the spark plug socket over the plug and remove it from the engine by turning it in a counterclockwise direction **(see illustration)**.
19   Compare the spark plug with the chart on the inside back cover of this manual to get an indication of the overall running condition of the engine.
20   It's a good idea to lightly coat the threads of the spark plugs with an anti-seize compound **(see illustration)** to insure that the spark plugs do not seize in the aluminum cylinder head. Be careful not to get any of the

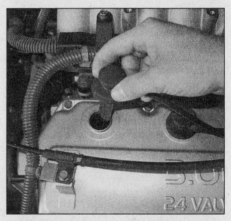

27.14 Twist the spark plug boot back-and-forth to detach it from the spark plug

anti-seize compound on the plug electrodes!
21   It's often difficult to insert spark plugs into their holes without cross-threading them. To avoid this possibility, fit a piece of rubber hose over the end of the spark plug **(see illustration)**. The flexible hose acts as a universal joint to help align the plug with the plug hole. Should the plug begin to cross-thread, the hose will slip on the spark plug, preventing thread damage. Install the spark plug and

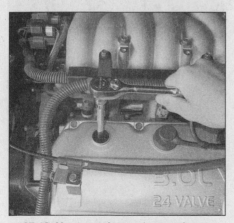

27.18 Use a ratchet and extension to remove the spark plugs

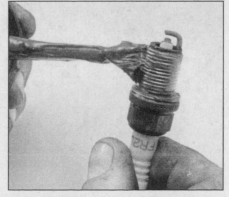

27.20 Apply a thin coat of anti-seize compound to the spark plug threads - DO NOT get any on the electrodes!

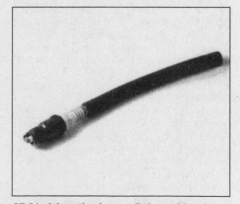

27.21 A length of snug-fitting rubber hose will save time and prevent damaged threads when installing the spark plugs

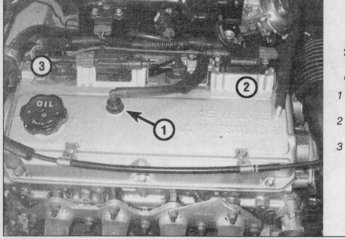

28.2a PCV valve location - four cylinder engines

1   1999 and later SOHC engine
2   1998 and earlier SOHC engine
3   1994 and 1995 DOHC engine (threaded into valve cover)

tighten it to the torque listed in this Chapter's Specifications.

22   Attach the plug wire or coil to the new spark plug, again using a twisting motion on the boot until it is firmly seated on the end of the spark plug.

23   Follow the above procedure for the remaining spark plugs, replacing them one at a time to prevent mixing up the spark plug wires.

24   On V6 models remove the rags from the lower intake manifold and install the upper intake manifold (see Chapter 2B).

---

28   Positive Crankcase Ventilation (PCV) valve check and replacement (every 60,000 miles [96,000 km] or 48 months)

Refer to illustrations 28.2a, 28.2b and 28.4

1   The PCV valve controls the amount of crankcase vapors allowed to enter the intake manifold. Inside the PCV valve is a spring-loaded valve that opens in relation to intake manifold vacuum, which allows crankcase vapors to be drawn from the valve cover back into the engine combustion chamber.

2   The PCV valve is on top of the valve cover on SOHC four-cylinder engines, and threaded into the right rear of the valve cover on DOHC four-cylinder engines **(see illustration)**. On V6 models, it's located in the end of the valve cover **(see illustration)**.

3   Check the operation of the PCV valve by removing the valve from the valve cover, with the hose attached. On DOHC four-cylinder engines you'll have to detach the hose, unscrew the valve, then reattach the hose.

4   Start the engine and listen for a hissing sound coming from the PCV valve. Place your finger over the valve opening - you should feel vacuum **(see illustration)**. If there's no vacuum at the valve, check for a plugged hose, plenum port or valve. Replace any plugged or deteriorated hoses.

5   Check the spring-loaded valve located inside the valve for freedom of movement by using a small screwdriver or equivalent to

push the valve off its seat and see if it returns to the fully seated position. If the valve is sluggish or the inside of the valve is contaminated with gum and carbon deposits, the valve must be replaced.

6   When purchasing a replacement PCV valve, make sure it's for your particular vehicle and engine size. Compare the old valve with the new one to make sure they're the same.

7   Installation is the reverse of removal.

---

29   Spark plug wires, distributor cap and rotor check and replacement (see Maintenance schedule for intervals)

Note: *Distributor cap and rotor replacement applies to 1998 and earlier SOHC four-cylinder engines and 2008 and earlier non-MIVEC V6 engines. Other engines have distributorless ignitions.*

All models

1   The spark plug wires should be checked at the recommended intervals or whenever a misfire-type driveability problem is present.

28.2b The PCV valve on V6 engines is located in the end of the front valve cover

2   Begin this procedure by making a visual check of the spark plug wires while the engine is running. In a darkened garage (make sure there is adequate ventilation) or at night, start the engine and observe each plug wire. Be careful not to come into contact with any moving engine parts. If possible, use an insulated or non-conductive object to wiggle each wire. If there is a break in the wire, you will see arcing or a small blue spark coming from the damaged area. Secondary ignition voltage increases with engine speed and sometimes a damaged wire will not produce an arc at idle speed. Have an assistant press the accelerator pedal to raise the engine speed to approximately 2000 rpm. Check the spark plug wires for arcing as stated previously. If arcing is noticed, replace all spark plug wires.

DOHC four-cylinder and 1999 and later four-cylinder engines

3   Perform the following checks with the engine OFF. The wires should be inspected one at a time to prevent mixing up the order that is essential for proper engine operation. **Note:** *Due to the short length of the spark plug wire, always disconnect the spark plug wire from the ignition coil pack first.*

4   With the engine cool, disconnect the spark plug wire from the ignition coil pack or coil-over-plug ignition coil. Pull only on the boot at the end of the wire; don't pull on the wire itself. Use a twisting motion to free the boot/wire from the coil. Disconnect the same spark plug wire from the spark plug, using the same twisting method while pulling on the boot. Disconnect the spark plug wire from any retaining clips as necessary and remove it from the engine.

5   Check inside the boot for corrosion, which will look like a white, crusty powder (don't mistake the white dielectric grease used on some plug wire boots for corrosion protection).

6   Now push the wire and boot back onto the end of the spark plug. It should be a tight fit on the plug end. If not, remove the wire and use a pair of pliers to carefully crimp the

28.4 You should be able to feel the vacuum at the PCV valve with the engine idling

29.15a Loosen the distributor cap
retaining screws . . .

29.15b . . . and detach the cap
from the distributor

29.15c Grasp the rotor securely and pull it
straight off the distributor shaft

metal connector inside the wire boot until the fit is snug.

7   Now push the wire and boot back into the end of the ignition coil terminal. It should be a tight fit in the terminal. If not, remove the wire and use a pair of pliers to carefully crimp the metal connector inside the wire boot until the fit is snug.

8   Now, using a cloth, clean each wire along its entire length. Remove all built-up dirt and grease. As this is done, inspect for burned areas, cracks and any other form of damage. Repeat the procedure for the remaining wires.

9   If new spark plug wires are required, purchase a complete set for your particular engine. The terminals and rubber boots should already be installed on the wires. Replace the wires one at a time to avoid mixing up the firing order and make sure the terminals are securely seated on the coil pack and the spark plugs.

10   Attach the plug wire to the new spark plug and to the ignition coil using a twisting motion on the boot until it is firmly seated. Attach the spark plug wire to any retaining clips to keep the wires in their proper location on the valve cover.

Distributor-equipped four-cylinder and V6 engines

Refer to illustrations 29.15a, 29.15b, 29.15c, 29.15d, 29.15e and 29.15f

11   Remove the air intake duct and air filter housing connected to it, as a unit.

12   On V6 engines, remove the upper intake manifold (see Chapter 2B).

13   To prevent dirt or other foreign debris from entering the engine, place duct tape or rags over the openings of the lower intake manifold.

14   Disconnect one spark plug wire from the distributor cap. Pull only on the boot at the end of the wire; don't pull on the wire itself. Use a twisting motion to free the boot/wire from the distributor. Install the removed wire into the new distributor cap in the exact same location. Repeat this procedure until all spark plug wires are installed in the new cap.

15   Loosen the screws and remove the old distributor cap and rotor **(see illustrations)**. Inspect them for wear, cracks and other damage **(see illustrations)**.

16   Unless they are in as-new condition, it's a good idea to install a new rotor and distributor cap.

17   Replace the spark plugs as described in Section 27, but don't yet reattach the spark plug wires to the retaining clips.

18   Replace the spark plug wires one at a time to avoid mixing up the firing order. Install the plug wires using a twisting motion on the boot until it is firmly seated. Make sure the terminals are securely seated on the distributor cap and the spark plugs. Attach the spark plug wire to any retaining clips as required.

19   Install the air intake duct and air filter housing.

20   If you're working on a V6 engine, remove the duct tape or rags from the lower intake manifold, then install the upper intake manifold (see Chapter 2B).

---

30   Fuel filter replacement (1998 and earlier models) (every 60,000 miles [96,000 km] or 48 months)

Warning: *Gasoline is extremely flammable, so take extra precautions when you work on any part of the fuel system (see the* **Warning** *in Section 19).*

Note: *The manufacturer does not suggest*

29.15d Note that the distributor rotor flat
must align with the flat of the shaft

29.15e Inspect the distributor cap and
contacts for damage, wear and corrosion
(if in doubt about its condition,
install a new one)

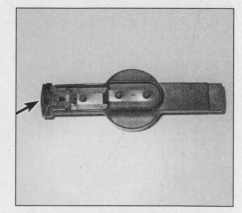

29.15f Check the end of the distributor
rotor for damage, wear and corrosion (if in
doubt about its condition,
install a new one)

30.3a Use an open-end wrench to hold the filter while unscrewing the fuel line fitting with a flare nut wrench

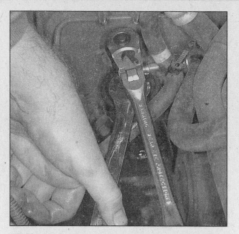

30.3b Use an open-end wrench to prevent the filter from turning while loosening the banjo bolt at the top of the filter

30.3c Remove the banjo bolt and detach the fuel line

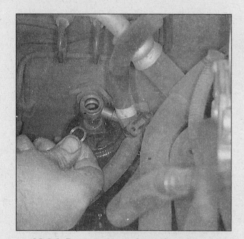

30.3d Be sure to replace the copper washers on either side of the banjo fitting with new ones when installing the new filter

30.4a Remove the filter mounting bolts . . .

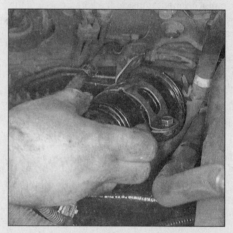

30.4b . . . and lift the filter from the engine

periodic fuel filter replacement on 1999 and later models because the fuel filter is integrated with the fuel pump assembly. See Chapter 4 if the fuel filter requires replacement due to a fuel restriction or fuel contamination problem.

Removal

Refer to illustrations 30.3a, 30.3b, 30.3c, 30.3d, 30.4a and 30.4b

1   The fuel filter mounts to the firewall below the air intake duct. Remove the air intake duct for access (see Chapter 4).

2   Relieve the fuel system pressure, then disconnect the cable from the negative terminal of the battery (see Chapter 4).

3   Prevent the filter from turning with an open-end wrench, then unscrew the fuel line fitting at the bottom of the filter with a flare nut wrench, if available, to prevent rounding-off the corners of the fitting nut **(see illustration)**. Now hold the filter with an open-end wrench and unscrew the banjo bolt at the top of the filter **(see illustrations)**. Note: *Have*

some rags or a container to catch or wipe up the fuel that will spill from the filter.

4   Remove the filter mounting bolts and detach the filter from the firewall.

5   Installation is the reverse of removal. Tighten the mounting bolts and fuel line fitting securely. Use new sealing washers on either

side of the banjo fitting, and tighten the banjo bolt to the torque listed in this Chapter's Specifications.

6   Connect the cable to the negative terminal of the battery, then pressurize the system by turning the ignition key to the RUN position a few times and check for leaks.

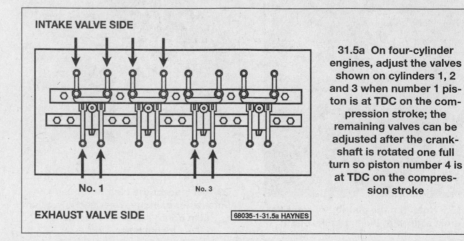

31.5a On four-cylinder engines, adjust the valves shown on cylinders 1, 2 and 3 when number 1 piston is at TDC on the compression stroke; the remaining valves can be adjusted after the crankshaft is rotated one full turn so piston number 4 is at TDC on the compression stroke

INTAKE VALVE SIDE

No. 1   No. 3

EXHAUST VALVE SIDE

68035-1-31.5a HAYNES

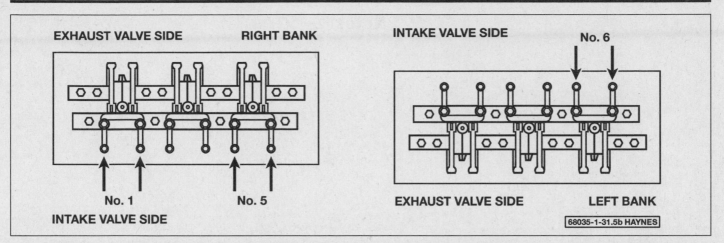

EXHAUST VALVE SIDE   RIGHT BANK   INTAKE VALVE SIDE   No. 6

No. 1   No. 5

INTAKE VALVE SIDE   EXHAUST VALVE SIDE   LEFT BANK

68035-1-31.5b HAYNES

31.5b On V6 engines, adjust the intake valves on cylinders 1, 5 and 6 when the number 1 piston is at TDC on the compression stroke; the remaining valves can be adjusted after the crankshaft is rotated one full turn so piston number 4 is at TDC on the compression stroke

31 Valve clearance check and adjustment - MIVEC engines only (every 30,000 miles [48,000 km] or 36 months)

Refer to illustrations 31.5a, 31.5b and 31.5c
Note: *This procedure should also be performed whenever there is noticeable valve-train noise.*
Note: *This procedure applies only to MIVEC-equipped engines. All other engines have hydraulic lash adjusters that don't need adjustment.*
1   If you're working on a four-cylinder engine, start the engine and let it reach normal operating temperature. **Warning:** *You will be working on a hot engine. Be very careful to avoid touching components that could burn you.* If you're working on a V6 engine, make sure that it's cool before proceeding.
2   Disconnect the cable from the negative battery terminal (see Chapter 5).
3   Refer to Chapter 2 and remove the valve cover(s). Remove any other components that will interfere with valve adjustment.
4   Refer to Chapter 2 and position the number 1 piston near TDC on the compression stroke. The notch on the crankshaft pulley must be aligned with the "T" on the timing indicator. **Note:** *On four-cylinder engines, all rocker arms of the number 1 cylinder will be*

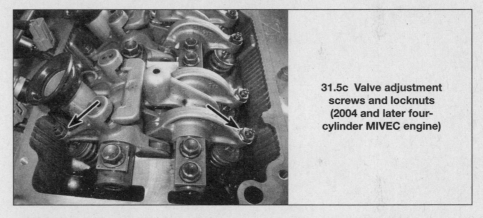

31.5c Valve adjustment screws and locknuts (2004 and later four-cylinder MIVEC engine)

loose when it is near TDC on the compression stroke. On V6 engines, the intake rocker arms for the number 6 cylinder will be loose when number 1 cylinder is at TDC on the compression stroke.
5   Measure the clearance of the indicated valves with a feeler gauge of the specified thickness **(see illustrations)**. You should feel a slight drag as the feeler gauge is pulled through the gap between the adjuster screw and the valve tip. See this Chapter's Specifications for the correct clearances.
6   If a valve needs adjustment, loosen the rocker arm lock nut and adjust the clearance with the adjusting screw. **Note:** *Exhaust valves on V6 engines are not adjustable. They*

have hydraulic lash adjusters.
7   When the feeler gauge slides with a modest amount of drag, hold the adjustment screw and tighten the lock nut to the torque listed in this Chapter's Specifications.
8   On all engines, rotate the crankshaft one full turn so that the number 1 cylinder is near TDC on the exhaust stroke and the notch on the crankshaft pulley is aligned with the "T" on the timing indicator. Check the remaining valves and adjust them if necessary.
9   When you're confident of the valve adjustments, refer to Chapter 2 and assemble the engine in the reverse order of disassembly.

Notes

Chapter 2 Part A
Four-cylinder engines

Contents

Specifications

2.4L DOHC engine

General
Displacement	143 cubic inches (2.4 liters)
Bore	3.41 inches (86.5 mm)
Stroke	3.94 inches (100 mm)
Compression ratio	10:1
Compression pressure	See Chapter 2C
Oil pressure	See Chapter 2C
Firing order	1-3-4-2

Camshaft
Lobe height	
Intake	
Identification marks A and D	1.378 to 1.397 inches (34.99 to 35.49 mm)
Identification marks B and E	1.366 to 1.386 inches (34.70 to 35.20 mm)
Identification mark K	1.373 to 1.393 inches (34.88 to 35.38 mm)
Exhaust	
Identification mark A	1.366 to 1.386 inches (34.70 to 35.20 mm)
Identification mark C	1.378 to 1.397 inches (34.99 to 35.49 mm)
Identification marks H	1.355 to 1.374 inches (34.41 to 34.49 mm)
Bearing journal diameter	1.022 (25.96 mm)
Endplay	0.004 to 0.008 inch (0.10 to 0.20 mm)

Cylinder head
Head gasket surface warpage limit	0.002 inch maximum (0.05 mm)

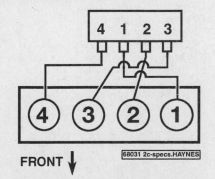

Cylinder numbering and coil terminal locations (2.4L DOHC engines)

68031 2c-specs.HAYNES

2.4L DOHC engine (continued)

Intake and exhaust manifolds
Warpage limit .... 0.008 inch maximum (0.20 mm)

Oil pump side clearance
Drive gear .... 0.0031 to 0.0055 inch (0.080 to 0.140 mm)
Driven gear .... 0.0024 to 0.0047 inch (0.060 to 0.120 mm)

Timing belt
Automatic tensioner pushrod movement (@ 22 to 44 lbs force) .... 0.03 inch (0.08 mm)
Automatic tensioner protrusion... 0.15 to 0.18 inch (3.8 to 4.5 mm)
Balance shaft belt deflection.. 0.25 inch (6.0 mm)

Torque specifications (DOHC engine)

Note: *One foot-pound (ft-lb) of torque is equivalent to 12 inch-pounds (in-lbs) of torque. Torque values below approximately 15 foot-pounds are expressed in inch-pounds, because most foot-pound torque wrenches are not accurate at these smaller values.*

	Ft-lbs (unless otherwise indicated)	Nm
Air conditioner idler pulley bolt	17 to 19	23 to 26
Balance shaft sprocket bolt	33	46
Camshaft bearing cap bolt	14 to 16	19 to 21
Camshaft sprocket bolt	56 to 72	79 to 96
Crankshaft pulley center bolt	80 to 94	108 to 127
Flywheel-to-crankshaft bolts	94 to 101	127 to 137
Driveplate-to-crankshaft bolts	94 to 101	127 to 137
Crankshaft pulley-to-damper bolts	18	25
Cylinder head bolts **(in sequence - see illustration 13.14a)**		
Step 1	58	78
Step 2	Fully loosen each cylinder head bolt (in the reverse of the tightening sequence)	
Step 3	15	20
Step 4	Tighten 1/4 turn (90-degrees)	
Step 5	Tighten an additional 1/4 turn (90-degrees)	
Exhaust manifold-to-cylinder head bolts	20	28
Exhaust manifold-to-exhaust pipe bolts	25	34
Intake manifold bolts	15	20
Intake manifold brace bolts	19 to 24	26 to 33
Oil pan bolts	60 to 72 in-lbs	7 to 8
Oil filter bracket bolts	168 in-lbs	19
Oil pump front cover (front case) bolts	168 in-lbs	19
Oil pump cover (back of case)		
Bolts	144 in-lbs	17
Screws	87 in-lbs	10
Oil pump pick-up tube bolt	168 in-lbs	19
Oil pump drive gear bolt	27	36
Oil pump drive gear plug	17	24
Timing belt components		
Cover bolts	84 in-lbs	10
Guide pulley bolt	26	36
Oil pump sprocket nut	40	55
Tensioner assembly		
Tensioner pulley bolt	35	48
Tensioner mounting bolts	17	24
Timing belt B		
Pulley bolt	168 in-lbs	19
Balance shaft sprocket bolt	33	46
Valve cover bolts	36 in-lbs	3.5
Center cover bolts	24 in-lbs	2.5

Refer to Part C for additional torque specifications

2.4L SOHC engine

General
Displacement	143 cubic inches (2.4 liters)	
Bore	3.41 inches (86.5 mm)	
Stroke	3.94 inches (100 mm)	
Compression ratio		
1994 through 1999	9.5:1	
2000 and later	9.0:1	
Compression pressure	See Chapter 2C	
Oil pressure	See Chapter 2C	
Firing order	1-3-4-2	

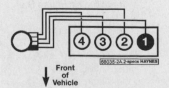

Cylinder numbering and distributor terminal locations (1994 through 1998 2.4L SOHC engine)

Camshaft

Lobe height

1994 through 1998 models

Intake

Identification mark D .... 1.650 to 1.669 inches (41.90 to 42.40 mm)

Identification marks 1 and 2 .... 1.452 to 1.472 inches (36.89 to 37.39 mm)

Exhaust

Identification mark D .... 1.650 to 1.669 inches (41.90 to 42.40 mm)

Identification marks 1 and 2 .... 1.456 to 1.475 inches (36.97 to 37.47 mm)

1999 through 2003 models

Intake .... 1.452 to 1.472 inches (36.89 to 37.39 mm)

Exhaust

1999 and 2000 models .... 1.443 to 1.462 inches (36.64 to 37.14 mm)

2001 through 2003 models .... 1.430 to 1.450 inches (36.33 to 36 83 mm)

2004 and later models

Intake

Low speed cam A .... 1.355 inches (34.41 mm)

Low speed cam B .... 1.475 inches (37.47 mm)

High speed cam .... 1.465 inches (37.21 mm)

Exhaust .... 1.491 inches (37.86 mm)

Bearing journal diameter

1994 through 1998 models .... 1.768 (44.93 mm)

1999 and later models .... 1.80 (45.0 mm)

Cylinder head

Cylinder head gasket surface warpage limit

2003 and earlier models .... 0.002 inch (0.05 mm)

2004 and later models .... 0.007 inch (0.2 mm)

Intake and exhaust manifolds

Warpage limit .... 0.008 inch maximum (0.20 mm)

Timing belt

Automatic tensioner pushrod movement (@ 22 to 44 lbs force) .... 0.03 inch (0.8 mm)

Automatic tensioner protrusion .... 0.15 to 0.18 inch (3.8 to 4.5 mm)

Balance-shaft belt deflection .... 0.25 inch (6.4 mm)

Oil pump side clearance

Drive gear .... 0.004 to 0.006 inch (0.10 to 0.15 mm)

Driven gear .... 0.003 to 0.004 inch (0.08 to 0.10 mm)

Cylinder numbering and coil pack/spark plug wire terminal locations (1999 and later 2.4L SOHC engine)

Torque specifications (SOHC engines)	Ft-lbs (unless otherwise noted)	Nm

Note: *One foot-pound (ft-lb) of torque is equivalent to 12 inch-pounds (in-lbs) of torque. Torque values below approximately 15 foot-pounds are expressed in inch-pounds, because most foot-pound torque wrenches are not accurate at these smaller values.*

Item	Ft-lbs	Nm
Air conditioner idler pulley bolt	18	25
Camshaft sprocket bolt	65	90
Crankshaft pulley center bolt		
2003 and earlier models	87	120
2004 and later models	123	167
Flywheel-to-crankshaft bolts	98	135
Driveplate-to-crankshaft bolts	98	135
Crankshaft pulley-to-damper bolts	18	25
Cylinder head bolts **(in sequence - see illustration 13.14b)**		
Step 1	58	78
Step 2	Fully loosen each cylinder head bolt (in the reverse of the tightening sequence)	
Step 3	15	20
Step 4	Tighten 1/4 turn (90-degrees)	
Step 5	Tighten an additional 1/4 turn (90-degrees)	
Exhaust manifold-to-cylinder head nuts		
M8 nuts	21	29
M10 nuts		
1994 through 1998	22	31
1999 and later	36	49
Exhaust manifold heat shield mounting bolts	122 inch-lbs	14
Exhaust manifold-to-exhaust pipe bolts	32	44
Intake manifold fasteners		
2003 and earlier models	15	20
2004 and later models		
Nuts	15	20
Bolts	18	24

2.4L SOHC engine Torque specifications (continued)

Ft-lbs (unless otherwise noted)   **Nm**

Note: One foot-pound (ft-lb) of torque is equivalent to 12 inch-pounds (in-lbs) of torque. Torque values below approximately 15 foot-pounds are expressed in inch-pounds, because most foot-pound torque wrenches are not accurate at these smaller values.

	Ft-lbs	Nm
Intake manifold brace bolts	22	30
Rocker arm shaft bolts		
2003 and earlier models	23	31
2004 and later models		
Intake side	23	31
Exhaust side	115 in-lbs	13
Oil pan bolts	62 in-lbs	7
Oil filter bracket bolts	168 in-lbs	19
Oil pump front cover (front case) bolts	144 in-lbs	17
Oil pump cover (back of case)		
Bolts	144 in-lbs	17
Screws	87 in-lbs	10
Oil pump pick-up tube bolt	168 in-lbs	19
Oil pump drive gear bolt	27	36
Oil pump drive gear plug	17	24
Timing belt components		
Guide pulley bolt	26	36
Oil pump sprocket nut	40	55
Tensioner assembly		
Tensioner pulley bolt	35	48
Tensioner mounting bolts	17	24
Timing belt B		
Pulley bolt	168 in-lbs	19
Balance shaft sprocket bolt	33	46
Valve cover bolts		
2003 and earlier models		
Outer bolts	36 in-lbs	3.5
Center cover bolts	24 in-lbs	2.5
2004 and later models	27 to 35 in-lbs	2.5 to 3.5

Refer to Part C for additional torque specifications

1   General information

This Part of Chapter 2 is devoted to in-vehicle engine repair procedures. Information concerning engine removal and installation can be found in Part C of this Chapter.

The following repair procedures are based on the assumption that the engine is installed in the vehicle. If the engine has been removed from the vehicle and mounted on a stand, many of the steps outlined in this Part of Chapter 2 will not apply.

The Specifications included in this Part of Chapter 2 apply only to the procedures contained in this Part.

There are two types of four-cylinder engines installed in the models covered in this book: 2.4L DOHC and 2.4L SOHC engine. The 2.4L DOHC is used in 1994 and 1995 models only.

2   Repair operations possible with the engine in the vehicle

Many major repair operations can be accomplished without removing the engine from the vehicle.

Clean the engine compartment and the exterior of the engine with some type of degreaser before any work is done. It will make the job easier and help keep dirt out of the internal areas of the engine.

Depending on the components involved, it may be helpful to remove the hood to improve access to the engine as repairs are performed (refer to Chapter 11 if necessary). Cover the fenders to prevent damage to the paint. Special pads are available, but an old bedspread or blanket will also work.

If vacuum, exhaust, oil or coolant leaks develop, indicating a need for gasket or seal replacement, the repairs can generally be made with the engine in the vehicle. The intake and exhaust manifold gaskets, oil pan gasket, camshaft and crankshaft oil seals and cylinder head gasket are all accessible with the engine in place.

Exterior engine components, such as the intake and exhaust manifolds, the oil pan, the oil pump, the water pump, the starter motor, the alternator, the distributor and the fuel system components can be removed for repair with the engine in place.

Since the camshaft(s) and cylinder head can be removed without pulling the engine, valve component servicing can also be accomplished with the engine in the vehicle. Replacement of the timing belt and sprockets is also possible with the engine in the vehicle.

In extreme cases caused by a lack of necessary equipment, repair or replacement of piston rings, pistons, connecting rods and rod bearings is possible with the engine in the vehicle. However, this practice is not recommended because of the cleaning and preparation work that must be done to the components involved.

3.7 With the number one piston beginning its compression stroke, continue to turn the crankshaft and align the timing notch on the edge of the crankshaft pulley with the "T" mark on the timing indicator scale

3   Top Dead Center (TDC) for number one piston - locating

Refer to illustration 3.7

1   Top Dead Center (TDC) is the highest point in the cylinder that each piston reaches as it travels up-and-down when the crankshaft turns. Each piston reaches TDC on the compression stroke and again on the exhaust stroke, but TDC generally refers to piston

4.5a Gradually and evenly loosen the valve cover bolts (2.4L SOHC engine shown)

4.5b Remove the valve cover mounting bolts and lift the valve cover off the cylinder head

position on the compression stroke. The timing mark on the crankshaft pulley and front cover are referenced to the number one piston at TDC.

2   Positioning a specific piston at TDC is an essential part of many procedures such as camshaft(s) removal, rocker arm removal, and timing belt and sprocket replacement.

3   In order to bring any piston to TDC, the crankshaft must be turned using one of the methods outlined below. When looking at the front of the engine, normal crankshaft rotation is clockwise. **Warning:** *Before beginning this procedure, be sure to set the emergency brake, place the transmission in Park or Neutral and disable the ignition system by disconnecting the primary electrical connector from the ignition coil pack.*

a) *The preferred method is to turn the crankshaft with a large socket and breaker bar attached to the crankshaft balancer hub bolt that is threaded into the front of the crankshaft.*

b) *A remote starter switch, which may save some time, can also be used. Attach the switch leads to the S (switch) and B (battery) terminals on the starter solenoid. Once the piston is close to TDC, discontinue with the remote switch and use a socket and breaker bar as described in the previous paragraph.*

c) *If an assistant is available to turn the ignition switch to the Start position in short bursts, you can get the piston close to TDC without a remote starter switch. Use a socket and breaker bar as described in Paragraph a) to complete the procedure.*

4   Remove all spark plugs as this will make it easier to rotate the engine by hand.

5   Insert a compression gauge (screw-in type with a hose) in the number 1 spark plug hole. Place the gauge dial where you can see it while turning the crankshaft balancer hub bolt. **Note:** *The number one cylinder is located at the front (timing belt end) of the engine.*

6   Turn the crankshaft clockwise until you see compression building up on the gauge - you are on the compression stroke for that cylinder. If you did not see compression build up, continue with one more complete revolution to achieve TDC for the number one cylinder.

7   Continue to turn the crankshaft in the normal direction of rotation (clockwise) until the notch on the edge of the crankshaft pulley is aligned with the TDC mark on the lower timing belt cover **(see illustration)**. **Note:** *On some models it may be necessary to remove the inner fender splash shield to view the timing mark.* At this point the number one piston is at the TDC position.

8   After the number one piston has been positioned at TDC on the compression stroke, TDC for any of the remaining cylinders can be located by turning the crankshaft 180-degrees (1/2-turn) at a time and following the firing order (refer to the Specifications).

---

4   Valve cover - removal and installation

Removal

Refer to illustrations 4.5a, 4.5b and 4.6

1   Disconnect the cable from the negative battery terminal (see Chapter 5).

2   Remove the ignition coil pack(s) from the valve cover, on models so equipped (see Chapter 5). **Note:** *1994 through 1998 2.4L SOHC engines are equipped with a distributor. All other four cylinder models are equipped with distributorless ignition systems (DIS).*

3   Clearly label and detach any electrical wiring harnesses which connect to or cross over the valve cover.

4   Disconnect the PCV valve hose and breather hose from the valve cover (see Chapter 6).

5   Remove the valve cover bolts **(see illus-**

tration) and lift off the cover **(see illustration)**. If the cover sticks to the cylinder head, tap on it with a soft-face hammer or place a wood block against the cover and tap on the wood with a hammer. **Caution:** *If you have to pry between the valve cover and the cylinder head, be extremely careful not to gouge or nick the gasket surfaces of either part. A leak could develop after reassembly.*

6   Remove the valve cover perimeter rubber gasket **(see illustration)**. Thoroughly clean the valve cover and remove all traces of old gasket material. Gasket removal solvents are available from auto parts stores and may prove helpful. After cleaning the surfaces, degrease them with a rag soaked in lacquer thinner or acetone.

Spark plug tube replacement (2.4L SOHC engine only)

Refer to illustration 4.9

7   Grasp the spark plug tube with locking pliers, carefully twist back and forth and remove the tube from the cylinder head.

8   Clean any locking agent from the tube receptacle in the cylinder head with solvent and allow it to dry.

9   Apply a small amount of red Loctite No. 271, or equivalent, around the lower end

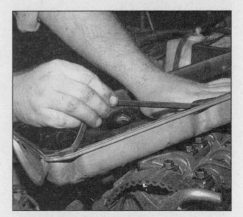

4.6 Remove the old valve cover gasket

4.9 After applying a small amount of red Loctite No. 271, or equivalent, to the lower end of the tube, install it and carefully tap the tube into place until it is seated (2.4L SOHC engine only)

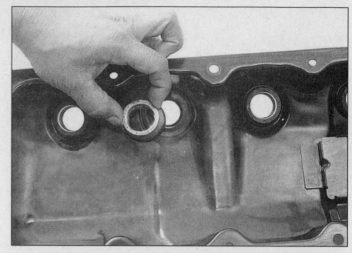

4.10 Remove and inspect each spark plug tube seal for deterioration and hardness; install new seals as a set and make sure that they're correctly seated in the cover

of the tube and install the tube into the cylinder head. Carefully tap the tube into the receptacle with a wood block and mallet. Tap the tube in until it seats against the cylinder head **(see illustration)**.

Installation

Refer to illustration 4.10

10 Inspect the spark plug tube seals **(see illustration)** for deterioration and hardness. Replace them if necessary.

11 Install a new gasket on the cover, using RTV sealant to hold it in place. On 2.4L DOHC models, apply RTV sealant to the camshaft cap corners and the top edges of the half-round seal.

12 Place the cover on the engine and install the cover bolts.

13 Starting from the center and working to the outer bolts, tighten the bolts to the torque listed in this Chapter's Specifications. The remaining steps are the reverse of removal. When finished, run the engine and check for oil leaks.

5   Intake manifold - removal and installation

Warning: *Wait until the engine is completely cool before beginning this procedure.*

Removal

1   Relieve the fuel system pressure (see Chapter 4)

2   Disconnect the cable from the negative battery terminal (see Chapter 5).

3   Drain the engine cooling system (see Chapter 1).

4   Remove the air intake hose (see Chapter 4).

5   On 2003 and earlier models, disconnect the cable(s) from the throttle lever (see Chapter 4). On 2004 and later models, disconnect

the wiring from the throttle body.

2.4L DOHC engine

6   Unplug the electrical connectors from the Idle Air Control (IAC) motor, the Throttle Position Sensor (TPS), the Engine Coolant Temperature (ECT) sensor, the Knock sensor, the Camshaft and Crankshaft Position sensors, the EGR temperature sensor and the Intake Air Temperature (IAT) sensor (see Chapter 6).

7   Remove the fuel rail, fuel pressure regulator and fuel injectors as a single assembly (see Chapter 4).

8   Remove the breather hose and the PCV valve from the intake system (see Chapter 6).

9   Disconnect the ignition coil harness connector (see Chapter 5).

10   Disconnect the vacuum lines from the fuel pressure regulator, the brake booster, the vacuum pipes, etc. and label them for correct reassembly.

11   Disconnect the heater hoses (see Chapter 3).

12   Disconnect the ignition power transistor and coils (see Chapter 5).

13   Remove the EGR pipe bolts at the EGR valve and at the intake manifold (see Chapter 6), then remove the EGR pipe.

14   If you're planning to *replace* or *service* the intake manifold, remove the throttle body (see Chapter 4). **Note:** *If you're simply removing the intake manifold to remove or service the cylinder head, it's not necessary to remove the throttle body from the intake manifold.*

15   Remove the intake manifold support bracket.

16   Remove the intake manifold fasteners and washers, then remove the intake manifold and the manifold gasket.

2.4L SOHC engine

Refer to illustrations 5.30a, 5.30b and 5.31

17   Unplug the electrical connectors from

the Throttle Position Sensor (TPS), the Engine Coolant Temperature (ECT) sensor, the Heated Oxygen sensor, the EGR temperature sensor and the Intake Air Temperature (IAT) sensor (see Chapter 6).

18   Disconnect the vacuum lines from the brake booster, the vacuum pipes, etc. and label them for correct reassembly.

19   Remove the throttle body (see Chapter 4). **Note:** *If you're simply removing the intake manifold to remove or service the cylinder head, it's not necessary to remove the throttle body from the intake manifold.*

2003 and earlier models

20   Remove the fuel rail, fuel pressure regulator and fuel injectors as a single assembly (see Chapter 4). Remove the fuel rail mounting bolt insulators and store them in a plastic bag.

21   Disconnect the wiring harness bracket at the radiator.

22   Disconnect the electrical connector from the air conditioning refrigerant temperature switch connector, if equipped.

23   Remove the thermostat housing assembly (see Chapter 3).

24   On early models, unplug the electrical connector from the Purge Solenoid Valve connector and the Exhaust Gas Recirculation (EGR) valve (see Chapter 6). **Note:** *California models are equipped with certain emission control systems not equipped on Federal models. Check the VECI label for status.*

25   Remove the engine oil dipstick and then remove the dipstick tube retaining bolt and remove the tube.

26   Disconnect and remove the PCV hose (see Chapter 6).

27   Remove the EGR valve (see Chapter 6).

2004 and later models

28   Remove the EGR valve and the MAP sensor (see Chapter 6).

29   Refer to Chapter 3 and remove the thermostat housing assembly.

5.30a Remove the intake manifold bracket bolts (1998 and earlier 2.4L SOHC engine shown)

5.30b Remove the intake manifold bracket bolts (1999 and later 2.4L SOHC engine shown)

All models

30 Remove the intake manifold support bracket bolts and then remove the support bracket from underneath the intake manifold **(see illustrations)**.

31 Remove the intake manifold fasteners **(see illustration)**, then remove the intake manifold and discard the old manifold gasket.

Inspection

32 Using a straightedge and feeler gauge, check the intake manifold mating surface for warpage. Check the intake manifold surface on the cylinder head also. If the warpage on either surface exceeds the limit listed in this Chapter's Specifications, the intake manifold and/or the cylinder head must be resurfaced at an automotive machine shop or, if the warpage is too excessive for resurfacing, replaced.

Installation

33 Using a new intake manifold gasket, place the intake manifold in position, install and hand-tighten the fasteners. Then, working from the center outward, gradually and evenly tighten them to the torque listed in this Chapter's Specifications.

34 The remainder of installation is the reverse of removal.

35 Refill the cooling system (see Chapter 1), run the engine and verify proper operation.

---

6   Exhaust manifold - removal and installation

Refer to illustrations 6.3 and 6.6
Warning: *Allow the engine to cool completely before beginning this procedure.*

Removal

1 Raise the vehicle and place it securely on jackstands.

2 Remove the exhaust manifold-to-exhaust pipe flange nuts and then detach the exhaust pipe from the exhaust manifold (see Chapter 4). Remove and discard the old flange gasket.

3 Unplug the electrical connector for the oxygen sensor(s) and remove the oxygen sensor(s) from the exhaust manifold (see Chapter 6).

4 Lower the vehicle and remove the exhaust manifold heat shield **(see illustration)**.

5 Remove the exhaust manifold bracket, if equipped.

6 Remove the exhaust manifold mounting fasteners, then remove the exhaust manifold and the old manifold gasket **(see illustration)**.

Inspection

7 Inspect the exhaust manifold for cracks and any other obvious damage. If the manifold is cracked or damaged in any way, replace it.

8 Using a wire brush, clean up the threads of the exhaust manifold bolts and/or studs and inspect the threads for damage. Replace any bolts or studs that have thread damage.

9 Using a scraper, remove all traces of gasket material from the mating surfaces and inspect them for wear and cracks. **Caution:** *When removing gasket material from any surface, especially aluminum, be very careful not to scratch or gouge the gasket surface. Any damage to the surface may leak after reassembly. Gasket removal solvents are available from auto parts stores and may prove helpful.*

10 Using a straightedge and feeler gauge, inspect the exhaust manifold mating surface for warpage. Check the exhaust manifold surface on the cylinder head also. If the warpage on any surface exceeds the limits listed in this Chapter's Specifications, the exhaust manifold and/or cylinder head must be replaced or resurfaced at an automotive machine shop.

Installation

11 Coat the threads of the exhaust manifold bolts and studs with an anti-seize compound. Install a new gasket, install the manifold and install the fasteners. Tighten the bolts and nuts in several stages, working from the center out, to the torque listed in this Chapter's Specifications.

12 The remainder of installation is the reverse of removal. When you're done, be sure to run the engine and check for exhaust leaks.

5.31 Location of the intake manifold mounting bolts (2000 2.4L SOHC engine shown) - lower bolts not visible

6.3 To detach the heat shield from the exhaust manifold, remove these bolts

6.6 Location of the exhaust manifold mounting nuts on a 2000 2.4L SOHC engine (others similar)

7 Timing belt and balance shaft belt - removal, inspection and installation

Refer to illustrations 7.6 and 7.7

Caution 1: *If the timing belt failed with the engine operating, damage to the valves (and possibly to the pistons) most likely has occurred. One way this can be verified is by performing a compression check or a leak-down check on all cylinders, but in order to do so you'll have to first install a new timing belt (and chances are you'll be wasting your time doing this, because most likely you'll just have to remove the belt and cylinder head). Bent valves can sometimes be confirmed visually by removing the valve cover, camshaft(s) and rocker arms and comparing the height of the valve stems. If one or more valve stems sit lower than the others, bent valves are indicated.*

Caution 2: *Do not try to turn the crankshaft with a camshaft sprocket bolt and do not rotate the crankshaft counterclockwise.*

Caution 3: *Do not turn the crankshaft or camshaft(s) after the timing belt has been removed. Doing so will damage the valves from contact with the pistons. Do not try to turn the crankshaft with the camshaft sprocket bolt(s) and do not rotate the crankshaft counterclockwise.*

Note: *In order to perform this procedure, you'll need a special tool (MD 998767 for 2003 and earlier models, 998738 for 2004 and later models) to tension the timing belt. This tool is available from automotive specialty tool companies such as Miller tools.*

1   Position the number one piston at Top Dead Center (see Section 3).

2   Disconnect the cable from the negative battery terminal (see Chapter 5).

3   Remove the accessory drivebelts (see Chapter 1).

4   Set the parking brake and block the rear wheels. Raise the front of the vehicle and support it securely on jackstands.

5   Remove the inner fender splash shield, if equipped.

6   Loosen the large bolt in the center of the crankshaft damper pulley. It might be very tight; to break it loose insert a large screwdriver or bar through the opening in the pulley to keep the pulley stationary and loosen the bolt with a socket and breaker bar **(see illustration)**.

7   Install a 3-jaw puller onto the damper pulley and remove the pulley from the crankshaft **(see illustration)**. Use the proper insert to keep the puller from damaging the crankshaft bolt threads. If the pulley is difficult to remove, tap the center bolt of the puller with a brass mallet to break it loose. Reinstall the bolt with a spacer so you can rotate the crankshaft later.

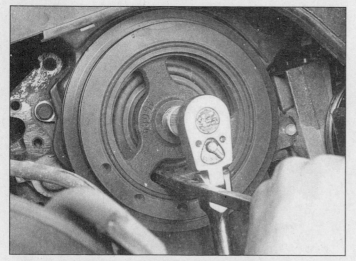

7.6 Insert a large screwdriver or bar through the opening in the pulley and wedge it against the engine block, then loosen the bolt with a socket and breaker bar

7.7 Install a 3-jaw puller onto the damper pulley, position the center post of the puller on the crankshaft end (use the proper insert to keep from damaging the crankshaft threads), tighten the puller and remove the pulley from the crankshaft

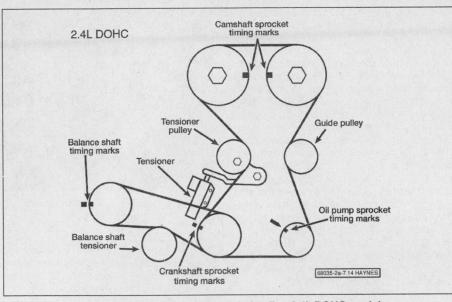

7.14 Timing belt alignment mark details - 2.4L DOHC models

7.15a Make sure that the oil pump sprocket timing mark is aligned with the stationary mark on the engine

7.15b To verify that the oil pump-driven balance shaft is in the correct position, and to lock the shaft in this position until the timing belt is reinstalled, remove the plug on the side of the engine block and insert a screwdriver through the hole in the block and into the hole in the balance shaft (it's not necessary to remove the oil pan; it's removed here so that you can clearly see how the screwdriver holds the balance shaft)

2.4L DOHC engine

Removal

Note: *There are two timing belts on the 2.4L DOHC engine; the longer one drives the camshafts and the oil pump (which, in turn, drives one of the balance shafts), and the shorter one drives the other balance shaft. When you replace one belt, always replace the other belt at the same time.*

Timing belt

Refer to illustrations 7.14, 7.15a and 7.15b

Caution: *The timing system is complex. Severe engine damage will occur if you make any mistakes. Do not attempt this procedure unless you are highly experienced with this type of repair. If you are at all unsure of your abilities, consult an expert. Double-check all your work and be sure everything is correct before you attempt to start the engine.*

8   Remove the air conditioning idler pulley bolts, if equipped, then remove the pulley assembly.

9   Remove the water pump pulley (see Chapter 3) and the power steering pump pulley (see Chapter 10).

10   Support the engine with a floor jack under the oil pan. Place a wood block on the jack head to prevent the floor jack from denting or damaging the oil pan.

11   Working on the timing belt side of the engine block, remove the engine mount (see Section 18), then remove the engine mount support bracket.

12   Remove the upper timing belt cover bolts and the upper timing belt cover. Note the position of the wiring harness clips that are secured by the upper bolts.

13   Remove the lower and center timing belt cover bolts and the timing belt covers.

14   Rotate the crankshaft in a clockwise direction until the timing marks on the camshaft sprockets are aligned, pointing at each other and even with the top surface of the cylinder head **(see illustration)**.

15   Verify that the oil pump sprocket timing mark is aligned with the stationary mark **(see illustration)**. The oil pump, of course, is not timed, but the balance shafts are, and the oil pump drives one of the balance shafts. There are timing marks on the oil pump drive and driven gears, but you can't see them unless the pump is removed. To verify that the balance shaft is in the correct position - and to lock the shaft in this position until the timing belt is reinstalled - remove the plug on the side of the engine block and insert an 8 mm (no. 3) Phillips head screwdriver through the hole in the block **(see illustration)**. When the shaft is in the correct position, the screwdriver will go about 2-1/2 inches into the hole in the block (the screwdriver goes over the top of the balance shaft, preventing it from turning). **Caution:** *Do NOT remove the screwdriver until the timing belt and balance shaft belt have been reinstalled.*

16   If you're going to reuse the timing belt, put an arrow on the belt indicating the (clockwise) direction of rotation to ensure that it will be reinstalled in the same direction.

17   Loosen the timing belt tensioner pulley bolt and remove the timing belt tensioner bolts. Remove the tensioner from the engine. Push the tensioner pulley toward the water pump to create slack in the belt. Make sure that the timing marks are still aligned, then remove the timing belt.

Balance shaft belt

Refer to illustrations 7.19 and 7.20

18   If you're going to reuse the balance shaft belt, put an arrow on the belt indicating the (clockwise) direction of rotation to ensure that it will be reinstalled in the same direction.

19   If you're planning to replace the balance shaft seal, you'll need to remove the balance shaft sprocket to do so. Try to loosen the bolt

7.19 Use this tool to lock the balance shaft sprocket to the engine block and remove the retaining bolt

now, before removing the balance shaft belt. The tensioned belt helps to hold the sprocket while you're breaking the bolt loose. If you're unable to loosen the bolt this way, wait until after you have removed the balance shaft belt and then, using a sprocket holding tool **(see illustration)** or a strap wrench, try again.

20   Make sure that the timing marks on the crankshaft sprocket and the balance shaft sprocket are aligned with their respective stationary marks on the engine **(see illustration 7.14)**. Then loosen the tensioner pulley bolt **(see illustration)**, swing the tensioner in a counterclockwise direction and remove the balance shaft belt.

21   If you were unable to remove the balance shaft sprocket, hold the balance shaft sprocket with a suitable sprocket holding tool or strap wrench and then loosen and remove the sprocket bolt and the sprocket.

22   If you're planning to replace the crankshaft front oil seal, remove the Crankshaft Position (CKP) sensor (see Chapter 6), the outer crankshaft sprocket, the CKP sensing blade and the rear crank sprocket. **Caution:** *Note that the concave side of the CKP sensing blade faces toward the engine. When installing the CKP sensing blade, make sure that it is oriented correctly.*

Inspection

Refer to illustration 7.24

23   Rotate the tensioner pulley and guide pulley by hand and move them side-to-side to detect roughness and excess play. Visually inspect the sprockets for any signs of damage and wear. Replace parts as necessary.

24   Inspect the timing belt for cracks, separation, wear, missing teeth and oil contamination. Replace the belt if it's in questionable condition **(see illustration)**. If the timing belt is excessively worn or damaged on one side, it might be due to incorrect tracking (misalignment). If the belt looks like it was misaligned, be sure to replace the belt tensioner assembly.

25   Check the automatic tensioner for leaks or any obvious damage to the body.

Installation

Caution: *Before starting the engine, carefully rotate the crankshaft by hand through at least two full revolutions (use a socket and breaker bar on the crankshaft pulley center bolt). If you feel any resistance, STOP! There is something wrong - most likely, valves are contacting the pistons. You must find the problem before proceeding. Check your work and see if any updated repair information is available.*

Balance shaft belt

26   If the crankshaft sprockets were removed, degrease both sides of the crankshaft sensing blade and the crank sprockets and clean out the bolt hole in the nose of the crank with degreaser as well. Degreasing these areas will help prevent the crankshaft sprocket bolt from loosening, which might allow the sensing blade to waver slightly, which would affect the output signal from the CKP sensor. Be sure to install the CKP sensing blade between the inner and outer crankshaft sprockets, with its concave side facing *toward* the engine.

27   If you removed the balance shaft sprocket to replace the seal, install the

sprocket and tighten the sprocket retaining bolt to the torque listed in this Chapter's Specifications.

28   Make sure that the timing marks on the crankshaft sprocket and the balance shaft sprocket are still correctly aligned **(see illustration 7.14)**, then install the balance shaft belt. After installing the balance shaft belt, make sure that the tension side (the upper run) of the belt has no slack.

29   Install the balance shaft belt tensioner pulley and bolt, but don't tighten the bolt completely at this time. First, make sure that the center of the tensioner pulley for the balance shaft belt is located to the left of the pulley. Holding up the tensioner in this position with one hand to tension the belt, tighten the tensioner pulley bolt to the torque listed in this Chapter's Specifications. **Note:** *After tightening the bolt, use your index finger and press firmly on the balance shaft belt. The belt should deflect about 1/4-inch.*

Timing belt

Refer to illustrations 7.31a, 7.31b, 7.31c, 7.36 and 7.38

30   Make sure that the timing marks on the camshaft sprockets are still in alignment and that the timing marks on the crankshaft and oil pump sprockets are also still aligned **(see illustration 7.14)**. When aligning the oil pump sprocket marks, it is critical that the weighted part of the balance shaft is facing *down*. If you used a screwdriver to verify that the balance shaft was in the correct position before removing the timing belt, the shaft is still in the correct position. If you didn't, or if you removed it and then accidentally turned the oil pump sprocket, then you can no longer be sure which direction the weighted part of the shaft is facing. It's possible that the balance shaft weight could be facing up, *even with the timing marks aligned*. If this happens, severe engine vibration will result. If you find yourself in this predicament, try the following check: Before installing the timing belt, slightly rock the oil pump sprocket by hand and, watching closely,

7.20 Loosen the balance shaft tensioner bolt

note whether the sprocket has a tendency to remain stationary (return to the timing-marks-aligned position) when the sprocket is rotated. If it does, this means that the balance shaft is CORRECTLY timed. If the sprocket has a tendency to rotate clockwise when spun lightly, the shaft is INCORRECTLY timed. If there is any doubt about whether or not the balance shaft is in the correct position, insert a Phillips screwdriver through the hole in the side of the cylinder block **(see illustration 7.15b)**. Make sure the screwdriver extends about 2-1/2 inches into the hole and verify that the sprocket cannot be rotated with the screwdriver in place. Now you can be sure the timing is correct. If the screwdriver can only be inserted about one inch into the hole, the timing is not correct. Rotate the sprocket until the marks are aligned again and insert the screwdriver again. It should now go in the full 2-1/2 inches. The balance shaft is now in the correct position.

31   The automatic tensioner should have a fair amount of resistance. Here's an easy way to test the tensioner before preparing it for installation: Grasp the tensioner firmly and press the plunger against a hard surface (like the engine block). You shouldn't be able to compress the plunger more than 3/64-inch (1 mm) **(see illustration)**. If the plunger com-

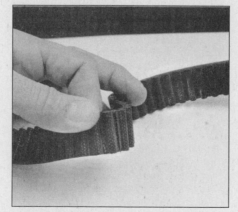

7.24 Carefully inspect the timing belt; bending it backwards will often make wear or damage more apparent

7.31a The tensioner pin must be compressed into the tensioner housing prior to installation

7.31b Place the tensioner in the vise so the hole faces up

7.31c Compress the pin with the vise and place a small Allen wrench, or something similar, through the hole to keep the pin retracted for reassembly on the engine

presses much more than that, or is easily compressed, replace it with a new unit. To prepare the tensioner for installation, place it in a vise **(see illustration)** and compress the plunger until the hole in the tensioner body and the hole in the plunger are aligned. **Caution:** *Make sure that the tensioner is in a level position when it is in the vise. Also, put a washer over the plug on the bottom of the tensioner to prevent the vise from contacting the plug.* When the holes are lined up, insert a small Allen wrench or pin through the holes to keep the plunger retracted during installation **(see illustration)**.

32   Install the automatic tensioner on the engine, install the tensioner mounting bolts and tighten them to the torque listed in this Chapter's Specifications. Make sure that the plunger remains in the compressed position, i.e. leave the Allen wrench or pin in place for now.

33   Install the tensioner pulley on the tensioner arm, install the pulley bolt and tighten the pulley bolt finger tight. Don't remove the pin from the automatic tensioner yet.

34   Make sure the timing marks on the camshaft, oil pump sprocket and crankshaft sprocket are still correctly aligned **(see illustration 7.14)**

35   Install the timing belt in the following sequence:

a) *Start at the crankshaft sprocket.*
b) *Then go around the oil pump sprocket.*
c) *Then go to the inside of the guide pulley and around the camshaft sprockets*
d) *Then go to the inside of the tensioner pulley.*
e) *Set the tensioner pulley so that the two holes in the pulley hub are below the pulley bolt and horizontal, lightly push the tensioner pulley against the timing belt, then temporarily tighten the pulley bolt just enough to hold the tensioner pulley in this position.*
f) *Remove the screwdriver from the engine block hole and install the plug.*

36   Adjust the timing belt tension in the fol-

lowing sequence:

a) *Turn the crankshaft 90-degrees (1/4-turn) in a counterclockwise direction, then turn it clockwise until the timing marks are realigned.*
b) *Loosen the tensioner pulley bolt and attach the special tool **(see illustration)** (No. MD998767, or a suitable equivalent; see your special tool dealer about this tool) to an inch-pound torque wrench.* **Note:** *This special tool attaches to the front of the tensioner pulley and allows the pulley to rotate against the timing belt, while the inch pound torque wrench applies the belt tension. Your torque wrench must be capable of measuring increments between 0 and 40 inch-lbs. Apply 30 inch-lbs. to the tensioner.*
c) *While holding tension on the timing belt tensioner, tighten the tensioner pulley bolt to the torque listed in this Chapter's Specifications.*
d) *Remove the special tool.*
e) *Pull the Allen wrench or pin out of the automatic tensioner.*
f) *Rotate the crankshaft two complete (clockwise) turns and wait about 15 minutes to allow the plunger in the automatic tensioner to fully extend.* **Caution:** *If you feel resistance while turning the crankshaft, the valves may be hitting the*

pistons from incorrect valve timing. Stop and re-check the valve timing.
g) *After 15 minutes measure how far the tensioner plunger protrudes from the tensioner body (the distance between the automatic tensioner body and the tensioner arm). It should be between 5/32 and 3/16-inch (3.9 to 4.7 mm).*
h) *Verify that all timing marks are still aligned.*

37   If the protrusion of the tensioner plunger is incorrect, repeat the belt adjustment procedure.

38   Install the timing belt covers and tighten the fasteners to the torque listed in this Chapter's Specifications. Note that the timing belt cover bolts come in different lengths; make sure they're reinstalled in the correct holes **(see illustration)**.

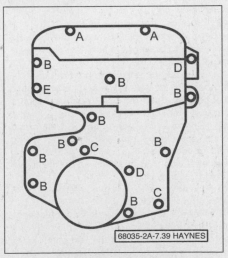

7.38 Timing belt cover bolt locations and lengths on the 2.4L DOHC engine

A	16 mm
B	18 mm
C	25 mm (bolt with washer)
D	25 mm
E	45 mm

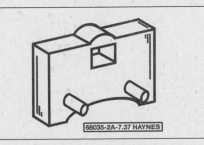

7.36 Insert the dowels of the timing belt tensioner tool into the tensioner pulley holes and insert the torque wrench into the 3/8 inch square drive

7.44 Remove the bolts that attach the timing belt
cover to the engine

7.46 Rotate the crankshaft in a clockwise direction until the
timing mark on the camshaft sprocket is aligned with
the stationary index mark on the engine

39   The remainder of installation is the reverse of removal.
40   Start the engine and road test the vehicle.

2.4L SOHC engine

Removal

Note: *There are two timing belts on the 2.4L SOHC engine; the longer one drives the camshafts and the oil pump (which, in turn, drives one of the balance shafts), and the shorter one drives the other balance shaft. When you replace one belt, always replace the other belt at the same time.*

Timing belt

Refer to illustrations 7.44, 7.46 and 7.48

41   Remove the air conditioning idler pulley assembly bolts, if equipped, then remove the pulley assembly.
42   Support the engine with a floor jack under the oil pan. Place a wood block on the jack head to prevent the floor jack from denting or damaging the oil pan.
43   Remove the engine mount from the timing belt side of the engine compartment (see Section 18), then remove the engine mount support bracket.
44   Remove the upper timing belt cover bolts **(see illustration)** and the upper timing belt cover. Note the position of the wiring harness clips that are secured by the upper timing cover bolts.
45   Remove the lower timing belt cover bolts and remove the cover.
46   Rotate the crankshaft in a clockwise direction until the timing mark on the camshaft sprocket is aligned with the stationary index mark on the engine **(see illustration)**.
47   Verify that the oil pump sprocket timing mark is aligned with the stationary mark **(see illustration 7.15a)**. The oil pump, of course, is not timed, but the balance shafts are, and the oil pump drives one of the balance shafts. There are timing marks on the oil pump drive and driven gears, but you can't see them

unless the pump is removed. To verify that the balance shaft is in the correct position - and to lock the shaft in this position until the timing belt is reinstalled - remove the plug on the side of the engine block and insert an 8 mm (no. 3) Phillips head screwdriver through the hole in the block **(see illustration 7.15b)**. When the shaft is in the correct position, the screwdriver will go about 2-1/2 inches into the hole in the block (the screwdriver goes over the top of the balance shaft, preventing it from turning). **Caution:** *Do NOT remove the screwdriver until the timing belt and balance shaft belt have been reinstalled.*
48   If you're going to reuse the timing belt, put an arrow on the belt indicating the (clockwise) direction of rotation to ensure that it will

be reinstalled in the same direction.
49   Loosen the timing belt tensioner pulley bolt and push the tensioner pulley toward the water pump to create slack in the belt. **Note:** *The special tool MD 998738 can be used to move the tensioner. Screw it in slowly by hand to gradually release belt tension.* Make sure that the timing marks are still aligned, and then remove the timing belt.

Balance shaft belt

50   If you're going to reuse the balance shaft belt, put an arrow on the belt indicating the (clockwise) direction of rotation to ensure that it will be reinstalled in the same direction.
51   If you're planning to replace the balance shaft seal, you'll need to remove the balance

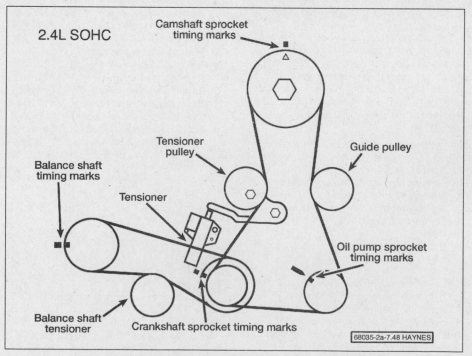

7.48 Timing belt alignment mark details - 2.4L SOHC models

shaft sprocket to do so. Try to loosen the bolt now, before removing the balance shaft belt. The tensioned belt helps to hold the sprocket while you're breaking the bolt loose. If you're unable to loosen the bolt this way, wait until after you have removed the balance shaft belt and then, using a sprocket holding tool **(see illustration 7.19)** or a strap wrench, try again.

52   Make sure that the timing marks on the crankshaft sprocket and the balance shaft sprocket are aligned with their respective stationary marks on the engine **(see illustration 7.47)**. Then loosen the tensioner pulley bolt, swing the tensioner in a counterclockwise direction and remove the balance shaft belt **(see illustration 7.20)**.

53   If you were unable to remove the balance shaft sprocket in Step 51, hold the balance shaft sprocket with a suitable sprocket holding tool or strap wrench, then loosen and remove the sprocket bolt and the sprocket.

54   If you're planning to replace the crankshaft front oil seal, remove the outer crankshaft sprocket, then pull off the rear sprocket (the balance shaft drive sprocket).

Inspection
55   Refer to Steps 23 through 25.

Installation
Balance shaft belt
56   If the crankshaft sprockets were removed, degrease both sides of the crank sprockets and clean out the bolt hole in the nose of the crank with degreaser as well. Degreasing these areas will help prevent the crankshaft sprocket bolt from loosening.

57   If you removed the balance shaft sprocket to replace the seal, install the sprocket and tighten the sprocket retaining bolt to the torque listed in this Chapter's Specifications.

58   Make sure that the timing marks on the crankshaft sprocket and the balance shaft sprocket are still correctly aligned **(see illustration 7.47)**, then install the balance shaft belt. After installing the balance shaft belt, make sure that the tension side (the upper run) of the belt has no slack.

59   Install the balance shaft belt tensioner pulley and bolt, but don't tighten the bolt completely at this time. First, make sure that the center of the tensioner pulley for the balance shaft belt is located to the left of the pulley. Holding up the tensioner in this position with one hand to tension the belt, tighten the tensioner pulley bolt to the torque listed in this Chapter's Specifications. **Note:** *After tightening the bolt, use your index finger and press firmly on the balance shaft belt. The belt should deflect about 1/4-inch.*

Timing belt
Refer to illustrations 7.68a and 7.68b

60   Make sure that the timing mark on the camshaft sprocket is still aligned with the mark on the valve cover and that the timing marks on the crankshaft and oil pump sprockets are also still aligned **(see illustration 7.47)**. When aligning the oil pump sprocket marks, it is critical that the weighted part of the balance shaft is facing *down*. If you used a screwdriver to verify that the balance shaft was in the correct position before removing the timing belt, the shaft is still in the correct position. But, if you didn't insert the screwdriver into the balance shaft, or if you removed it and then accidentally turned the oil pump sprocket, then you can no longer be sure which direction the weighted part of the shaft is facing. It's possible that the balance shaft weight could be facing up, *even with the timing marks aligned*. If this happens, severe engine vibration will result. If you find yourself in this predicament, try the following check: Before installing the timing belt, slightly rock the oil pump sprocket by hand and, watching closely, note whether the sprocket has a tendency to remain stationary (return to the timing-marks-aligned position) when the sprocket is rotated. If it does, this means that the balance shaft is CORRECTLY timed. If the sprocket has a tendency to rotate clockwise when spun lightly, the shaft is INCORRECTLY timed. If there is any doubt about whether or not the balance shaft is in the correct position, insert a Phillips screwdriver through the hole in the side of the cylinder block **(see illustration 7.15b)**. Make sure the screwdriver extends about 2-1/2 inches into the hole and verify that the sprocket cannot be rotated with the screwdriver in place. Now you can be sure the timing is correct. If the screwdriver can only be inserted about one inch into the hole, the timing is not correct. Rotate the sprocket until the marks are aligned again and insert the screwdriver again. It should now go in the full 2-1/2 inches. The balance shaft is now in the correct position.

61   The automatic tensioner should have a fair amount of resistance. Here's an easy way to test the tensioner before preparing it for installation: Grasp the tensioner firmly and press the plunger against a hard surface (like the engine block). You shouldn't be able to compress the plunger more than 3/64-inch (1 mm). If the plunger compresses much more than that, or is easily compressed, replace it with a new unit. To prepare the tensioner for installation, place it in a vise and compress the plunger until the hole in the tensioner body and the hole in the plunger are aligned. **Caution:** *Make sure that the tensioner is in a level position when it is in the vise. Also, put a washer over the plug on the bottom of the tensioner to prevent the vise from contacting the plug.* When the holes are lined up, insert a small Allen wrench or pin through the holes to keep the plunger retracted during installation **(see illustrations 7.31b and 7.31c)**.

62   Install the automatic tensioner on the engine, install the tensioner mounting bolts and tighten them to the torque listed in this Chapter's Specifications. Make sure that the plunger remains in the compressed position, i.e. leave the Allen wrench or pin in place for now.

63   Install the tensioner pulley on the tensioner arm, install the pulley bolt and tighten the pulley bolt finger tight. Don't remove the pin from the automatic tensioner yet.

64   Make sure the timing marks on the camshaft, oil pump sprocket and crankshaft sprocket are still correctly aligned **(see illustration 7.47)**

65   Install the timing belt in the following sequence:
a) *Start at the crankshaft sprocket.*
b) *Then go around the oil pump sprocket.*
c) *Then go inside the guide pulley and around the camshaft sprocket*
d) *Then go inside the tensioner pulley.*
e) *Set the tensioner pulley so that the two holes in the pulley hub are below the pulley bolt and horizontal, lightly push the tensioner pulley against the timing belt, then temporarily tighten the pulley bolt just enough to hold the tensioner pulley in this position.*
f) *Remove the screwdriver from the engine block hole and install the plug.*

66   Adjust the timing belt tension in the following sequence:
a) *Turn the crankshaft 90-degrees (1/4-turn) in a counterclockwise direction, then turn it clockwise until the timing marks are realigned.*
b) *Loosen the tensioner pulley bolt and attach the special tool* **(see illustration 7.36)** *(No. MD998738 / MD998767 or a suitable equivalent; see your special tool dealer about this tool) to an inch-pound torque wrench.* **Note:** *This special tool attaches to the front of the tensioner pulley and allows the pulley to rotate against the timing belt, while the inch pound torque wrench applies the belt tension. Your torque wrench must be capable of measuring increments between 0 and 40 inch-lbs. Apply 30 inch-lbs. to the tensioner.*
c) *While holding tension on the timing belt tensioner, tighten the tensioner pulley bolt to the torque listed in this Chapter's Specifications.*
d) *Remove the special tool.*
e) *Pull the Allen wrench or pin out of the automatic tensioner.*
f) *Rotate the crankshaft two complete (clockwise) turns and wait about 15 minutes to allow the plunger in the automatic tensioner to fully extend.* **Caution:** *If you feel resistance while turning the crankshaft, the valves may be hitting the pistons from incorrect valve timing. Stop and re-check the valve timing.*
g) *After 15 minutes measure how far the tensioner plunger protrudes from the tensioner body (the distance between the automatic tensioner body and the tensioner arm). It should be between 5/32 and 3/16-inch (3.9 to 4.7 mm).*
h) *Verify that all timing marks are still aligned.*

67   If the protrusion of the tensioner plunger is incorrect, repeat the belt adjustment procedure.

68   Install the timing covers and then tighten the timing belt cover fasteners securely. Note that the timing belt cover bolts come in differ-

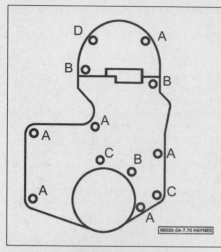

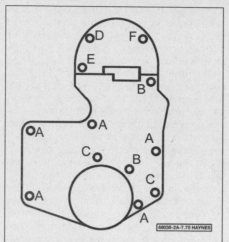

7.68a Timing belt cover bolt locations and lengths on 1994 and 1995 2.4L SOHC engine

A   18 mm
B   25 mm
C   25 mm (bolt with washer)
D   50 mm

7.68b Timing belt cover bolt locations and lengths on 1996 and later 2.4L SOHC engines

A   18 mm
B   25 mm
C   25 mm (bolt with washer)
D   50 mm
E   35 mm
F   28 mm

8.2 Attach a bolt-type gear puller to the crankshaft sprocket and remove the sprocket from the crankshaft

8.3 Working from below the right inner fender, use the screwdriver to pry the seal out of its bore

8.5 Lubricate the new seal with engine oil and drive the seal into place with a hammer and socket

ent lengths; make sure they're reinstalled in the correct holes (see illustration).

69   The remainder of installation is the reverse of removal.

70   Start the engine, check the ignition timing (models with distributors; see Chapter 5), then road test the vehicle.

8   Crankshaft front oil seal - replacement

Refer to illustrations 8.2, 8.3 and 8.5
Caution: *Do not rotate the camshaft(s) or crankshaft when the timing belt is removed or damage to the engine may occur.*

1   Remove the timing belts and crankshaft sprockets (see Section 7).

2   Pull the crankshaft sprocket from the crankshaft with a bolt-type gear puller (see illustration). Remove the Woodruff key.

3   Wrap the tip of a small screwdriver with tape. Use the screwdriver to pry the seal out of its bore (see illustration). Take care to prevent damaging the front case, the crankshaft and the seal bore.

4   Thoroughly clean and inspect the seal bore and sealing surface on the crankshaft. Minor imperfections can be removed with emery cloth. If there is a groove worn in the crankshaft sealing surface (from contact with the seal), installing a new seal will probably not stop the leak.

5   Lubricate the new seal with engine oil and drive the seal into place with a hammer and seal driver or an appropriate size socket (see illustration).

6   The remaining steps are the reverse of removal. **Caution:** *Be careful when installing the crank sprockets and the CKP sensing blade, which is installed between the two sprockets. Make sure that you follow the procedure in Section 7 for degreasing the sensing blade and the sprockets.*

7   Run the engine and check for oil leaks.

9   Camshaft oil seal - replacement

Refer to illustrations 9.5, 9.7 and 9.9
Caution: *Do not rotate the camshaft(s) or crankshaft when the timing belt is removed or damage to the engine may occur.*

1   Position the engine at TDC for cylinder no.1 (see Section 3). Remove the timing belt cover and timing belt (see Section 7).

2   Rotate the crankshaft counterclockwise until the crankshaft sprocket is three notches BTDC (see illustrations 7.14 and 7.47). This will prevent engine damage if the camshaft sprocket is inadvertently rotated during removal.

3   Immobilize the camshaft sprocket with a pin spanner or by inserting a large screwdriver through one of the openings in the sprocket, then remove the camshaft sprocket bolt. Using two large screwdrivers, lever the sprocket(s) off the camshaft.

4   If the engine is equipped with a rear tim-

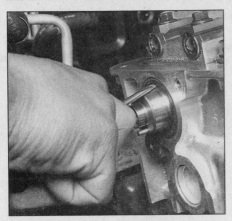

9.5 Carefully pry the camshaft seal out of the bore - DO NOT nick or scratch the camshaft or seal bore

9.7 Gently tap the new seal into place with the spring side toward the engine

9.9 When installing a camshaft sprocket on a DOHC engine, make sure the pin in the camshaft is aligned with the hole in the sprocket

ing belt cover, remove the upper part.

5   Note how far the seal is seated in the bore, then carefully pry it out with a small screwdriver **(see illustration)**. Don't scratch the bore or damage the camshaft in the process (if the camshaft is damaged, the new seal will end up leaking).

6   Clean the bore and coat the outer edge of the new seal with engine oil or multi-purpose grease. Also lubricate the seal lip.

7   Using a seal driver or a socket with an outside diameter slightly smaller than the outside diameter of the seal **(see illustration)**, carefully drive the new seal into place with a hammer. Make sure it's installed squarely and driven in to the same depth as the original.

8   If the engine is equipped with a rear timing belt cover, install the upper part.

9   Install the camshaft sprocket, aligning the Woodruff key on the camshaft with the slot in the sprocket (SOHC models) or the dowel pin on the camshaft with the hole in the sprocket **(see illustration)**. Use an appropriate tool to hold the camshaft sprocket while tightening the bolt to the torque listed in this Chapter's Specifications.

10   Reinstall the timing belt (see Section 7).

11   Run the engine and check for oil leaks at the camshaft seal.

10 Camshaft(s) - removal, inspection and installation

2.4L DOHC engine

Removal

1   Remove the valve cover (see Section 4).

2   Remove the timing belt (see Section 7).

3   Remove the camshaft sprockets (see Section 9) and the rear timing belt cover.

4   The camshaft bearing caps are identified with their numbered location in the cylinder head. Note the location of each camshaft bearing cap on paper.

5   Remove the bearing caps at each end of the camshafts, then remove the remaining camshaft bearing caps. Loosen the bolts a

little at a time to prevent distorting the camshafts. When the bearing caps have all been loosened enough for removal, they may still be difficult to remove. Use the bearing cap bolts for leverage and move the cap back and forth to loosen the cap from the cylinder head. If they are still difficult to remove you can tap them gently with a soft face mallet until they can be lifted off. **Caution:** *Store them in order so they can be returned to their original locations, with the same side facing forward.*

6   Carefully lift the camshafts out of the cylinder head. Mark the camshafts INTAKE and EXHAUST. They are not interchangeable.

7   Remove the front seal from each camshaft. **Note:** *Inspect the rocker arms and lash adjusters at this time* (see Section 11).

Inspection

Refer to illustration 10.9

8   Clean the camshaft(s) and the bearing surfaces. Inspect the camshaft for wear and/or damage to the lobe surfaces, bearing journals, and seal contact surfaces. Inspect the camshaft bearing surfaces in the cylinder head and bearing caps for scoring and other damage.

9   Measure the camshaft bearing journal

diameters and lobe heights **(see illustration)**. Compare your readings with the values listed this Chapter's Specifications.

10   Replace the camshaft if it fails any of the inspections. **Note:** *If the lobes are worn, replace the rocker arms and lash adjusters along with the camshaft.* The cylinder head may need to be replaced, if the camshaft bearing surfaces in the head are damaged or excessively worn.

11   Clean and inspect the cylinder head.

Camshaft endplay measurement

Refer to illustration 10.14

12   Lubricate the camshaft(s) and cylinder head bearing journals with clean engine oil.

13   Place the camshaft in its original location in the cylinder head. **Note:** *Do not install the rocker arms for this check.* Install the thrust bearing cap and tighten the bolts to the torque listed in this Chapter's Specifications.

14   Install a dial indicator on the cylinder head and place the indicator tip on the camshaft at the sprocket end **(see illustration)**.

15   Use a screwdriver to carefully pry the camshaft fully to the rear until it stops. Zero the dial indicator and pry the camshaft fully to

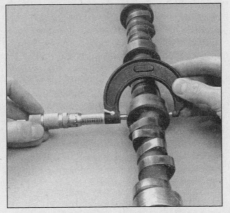

10.9 Measure the camshaft bearing journal diameters with a micrometer

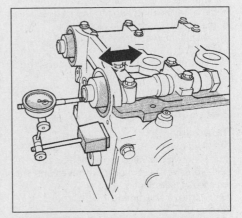

10.14 Measure the camshaft endplay with a dial indicator positioned on the sprocket end of the camshaft as shown

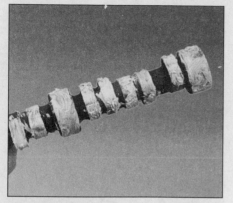

10.17 Prior to installing each camshaft, lubricate the bearing journals, thrust surfaces and lobes with assembly lube or clean engine oil

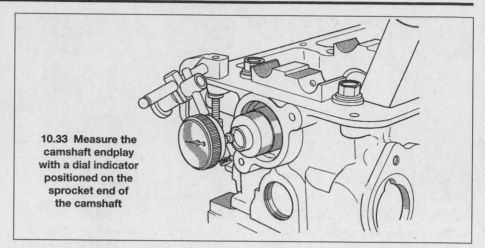

10.33 Measure the camshaft endplay with a dial indicator positioned on the sprocket end of the camshaft

the front (toward the dial indicator end). The amount of indicator travel is the camshaft endplay. Compare the endplay with the tolerance given in this Chapter's Specifications. If the endplay is excessive, check the camshaft and cylinder head bearing journals for wear. Replace as necessary.

Installation

Refer to illustration 10.17

16   Install the valve lash adjusters and rocker arms (see Section 11).

17   Clean the camshaft and bearing journals and caps. Liberally coat the journals, lobes, and thrust portions of the camshaft with assembly lube or engine oil **(see illustration)**.

18   Carefully install the camshafts in the cylinder head in their original location. Temporarily install the camshaft sprockets and rotate the camshafts so that their timing marks align **(see illustrations 7.14)**. Make sure the crankshaft is positioned with the crankshaft sprocket timing mark at three notches BTDC. **Caution:** *If the pistons are at TDC when tightening the camshaft bearing caps, damage to the engine may occur.*

19   Install the bearing caps.

20   Tighten the bolts in several steps, starting with the inner bearing caps and working to the outer bearing caps to the torque listed in this Chapter's Specifications.

21   Install new camshaft oil seals (see Section 9).

22   Install the timing belt, covers, and related components (see Section 7).

23   Install the valve cover (see Section 4).

2.4L SOHC engine

Removal

24   Remove the PCV valve (see Chapter 6).

25   Remove the valve cover (see Section 4).

26   Remove the timing belt cover and the timing belt (see Section 7).

27   Remove the timing belt sprocket (see Section 9).

28   Remove the rocker arm assemblies (see Section 11).

29   Remove the distributor (1994 through

1998 models) (see Chapter 5) or the Camshaft Position Sensor (CMP) and housing (1999 and later models) (see Chapter 6).

30   Carefully remove the camshaft through the opening in the rear of the cylinder head. Be careful not to damage the camshaft lobes or bearing journals during removal. **Note:** *On 2004 and later models, it will be necessary to disconnect the transaxle mounts and use a jack under the transaxle to slightly raise the left side of the engine for clearance.*

Inspection

Refer to illustration 10.33

31   Remove the old seal from the cylinder head and thoroughly clean the camshaft. Inspect the camshaft lobes, bearing journals and seal contact surfaces for wear and damage. Also inspect the camshaft bearing surfaces in the cylinder head for scoring and other damage.

32   Measure the camshaft bearing journal diameters and lobe heights **(see illustration 10.9)**. Measure the inside diameter of the camshaft bearing surfaces in the cylinder head, using a telescoping gauge. Subtract the journal measurement from the bearing measurement to obtain the camshaft bearing oil clearance. Compare your readings with the values listed in this Chapter's Specifications.

Camshaft endplay measurement

33   Lubricate the camshaft journals with clean engine oil, install the camshaft in the cylinder head and then install the distributor (1994 through 1998 models) or the camshaft oil seal (1999 and later models). Set up a dial indicator and measure the camshaft endplay **(see illustration)**. Compare your measurement with the value listed in this Chapter's Specifications.

34   Replace the camshaft if it fails any of the above inspections. **Note:** *If the lobes are worn, replace the rocker arms along with the camshaft.* Cylinder head replacement may be necessary if the camshaft bearing surfaces in the head are damaged or excessively worn or if the endplay is excessive.

Installation

35   Very carefully clean the camshaft and bearing journals. Liberally coat the journals,

lobes and thrust portions of the camshaft with assembly lube or engine oil.

36   Carefully install the camshaft in the cylinder head.

37   Install a new camshaft oil seal (see Section 9).

38   Install the CMP sensor housing and the CMP sensor (see Chapter 6).

39   Install the rocker arm shaft assemblies (see Section 11).

40   Install the timing belt and covers (see Section 7).

41   Install the valve cover (see Section 4).

---

11 Rocker arm assembly - removal, inspection and installation

---

2.4L DOHC engine

Removal

1   Remove the valve cover (see Section 4).

2   Remove both camshafts (see Section 10).

3   Once the camshafts have been removed, the rocker arms can be lifted off. **Caution:** *Each rocker arm must be placed back in the same location it was removed from, so mark each rocker arm or place them in a container (such as an egg carton) so they won't get mixed up.* The lash adjusters can remain in the head at this time, unless they are being replaced (see Section 12).

Inspection

4   Inspect the rocker arm tip, roller and lash adjuster pocket for wear. Replace them if evidence of wear or damage is found.

5   Carefully inspect each lash adjuster for signs of wear and damage, particularly on the ball tip that contacts the rocker arm. The lash adjusters can become clogged as they age, so it's a good idea to replace them if you're concerned about their condition or if the engine is making valve "tapping" noises.

Installation

6   Installation is the reverse of removal. When reinstalling the rocker arms, make sure that you install them in the same locations from which they were removed.

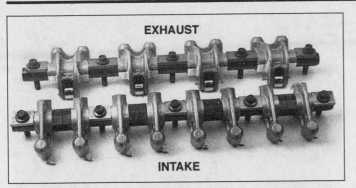

EXHAUST

INTAKE

11.10 Intake and exhaust rocker arms and shaft assemblies are unique - don't intermix any of the parts (2003 and earlier models)

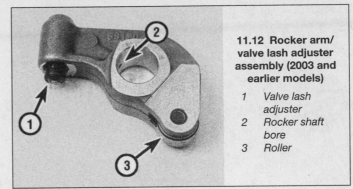

11.12 Rocker arm/ valve lash adjuster assembly (2003 and earlier models)

1 Valve lash adjuster
2 Rocker shaft bore
3 Roller

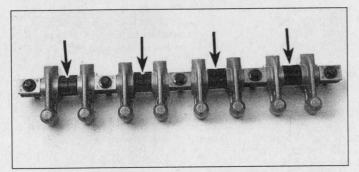

11.16 The intake rocker arm shafts and the plastic spacers must be installed in the correct locations (2003 and earlier models)

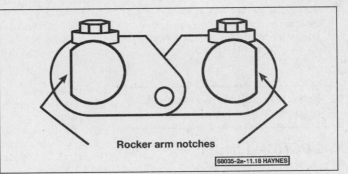

Rocker arm notches

68035-2a-11.18 HAYNES

11.17 Both rocker arm shafts must be positioned with their notches facing out, away from each other (2003 and earlier models)

2.4L SOHC engine

Removal

Refer to illustration 11.10

7   Remove the valve cover (see Section 4).

8   Prior to removing the rocker arm shafts, mark the shafts INTAKE and EXHAUST. **Caution:** *Do not interchange the rocker arms onto a different shaft as this could lead to premature wear.*

9   Loosen each rocker arm shaft bolt 1/4-turn at a time until the spring pressure is relieved, in the *reverse* order of the TIGHTENING sequence **(see illustration 11.19)**. Completely loosen the bolts, but do not remove them, since leaving them in place will prevent the assembly from falling apart when it is lifted off the cylinder head.

10   Lift off the rocker arm assemblies from

the cylinder head and then set them on the workbench **(see illustration)**.

Inspection

Refer to illustration 11.12

11   Disassemble the rocker arm shaft components. **Caution:** *Prior to disassembly, mark every component to ensure that all the parts are reassembled in the same locations from which they were removed. To keep the rocker arms and related parts in order, it's a good idea to remove them and put them onto two pieces of wire (like coat hangers) in the order in which they're removed. Mark each wire (which serves as the rocker shaft) with respect to the front of the engine.*

12   Inspect the rocker arms for wear **(see illustration)**. Replace them if evidence of wear or damage is found.

13   Inspect the rocker shafts and all parts

on the shafts. Look for wear and scoring on the shafts. Replace all damaged parts.

Installation

Refer to illustrations 11.16, 11.17 and 11.18

14   Prior to installation, make sure that each lash adjuster is at least partially full of oil.

15   When reassembling the parts, make sure that they all go back on in the same locations they were removed from.

16   On 2003 and earlier models without the MIVEC system, make sure that the plastic spacers are installed on the intake rocker arm shaft in the correct locations **(see illustration)**. On 2004 and later models with the MIVEC system, take care to ensure that all rocker shaft components have been installed in the positions from which they were removed.

17   On 2003 and earlier models, install the rocker arm assemblies with the notch in each rocker arm shaft (located at the timing belt end of the engine) facing out, away from each other **(see illustration)**. The oiling hole in the 2004 and later rocker shafts must face down.

18   Tighten the rocker arm shaft bolts in the recommended sequence if you're working on a 2003 or earlier model **(see illustration)**. On 2004 and later models, tighten the bolts a little at a time, working from the center to the shaft ends. In both engines, use the torque listed in this Chapter's Specifications.

19   On 2004 and later models, refer to Chapter 1 and adjust the valve clearances.

20   The rest of the procedure is the reverse of disassembly. Run the engine and listen for valve noise (indicating an improper adjustment on 2004 and later models), then check for leaks.

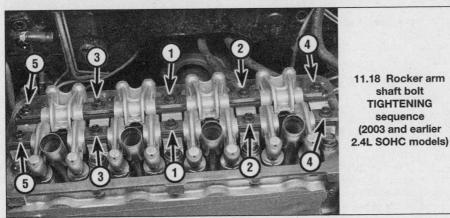

11.18 Rocker arm shaft bolt TIGHTENING sequence (2003 and earlier 2.4L SOHC models)

12.3 After removing the rocker arm(s), the lash adjuster(s) can be pulled out of the head

13.4 Cover the intake ports with duct tape to keep out debris before removing the cylinder head

13.10a Carefully lift the cylinder head straight up and place the head on wood blocks to prevent damage to the sealing surfaces

12 Valve lash adjusters - removal, inspection and installation

2.4L DOHC engine

Refer to illustration 12.3

1   Remove the camshafts (see Section 10).

2   Remove the rocker arms (see Section 11).

3   If the lash adjusters aren't already removed from the head, lift them out now **(see illustration)**. **Caution:** *Be sure to keep the adjusters in order so they can be placed back in the same location in the cylinder head they were removed from.*

4   Inspect each adjuster carefully for signs of wear and damage, particularly on the ball tip that contacts the rocker arm. Since the lash adjusters can become clogged (especially on high-mileage engines), we recommend replacing them if you're concerned about their condition or if the engine is exhibiting valve "tapping" noises.

5   The lash adjusters must be partially full of engine oil - indicated by little or no plunger action when the adjuster is depressed. If there's excessive plunger travel, place the lash adjuster into clean engine oil and pump the plunger until the plunger travel is eliminated. **Note:** *If the plunger still travels within the lash adjuster when full of oil it's defective and the lash adjuster must be replaced.*

6   When re-starting the engine after replacing the adjusters, the adjusters will normally make "tapping" noises. After warm-up, raise the speed of the engine from idle to 3,000 rpm for one minute. If the adjuster(s) do not become silent, replace the defective ones.

2.4L SOHC engine

Note: *This procedure applies only to 2003 and earlier engines without the MIVEC system. Later MIVEC-equipped engines use screw-type lash adjustment.*

Note: *The hydraulic valve adjuster is an integral part of each rocker arm and can't be replaced separately.*

7   Remove the rocker arm shafts (see Section 11). Don't remove the rocker arms from the shafts.

8   Turn the rocker arm assembly upside down on the workbench. Inspect each lash adjuster carefully for signs of wear and damage, particularly on the surface that contacts the valve tip. Since the lash adjusters can become clogged (especially on high-mileage engines), we recommend replacing any rocker arm/lash adjuster assembly if you're concerned about its condition or if the engine is exhibiting valve "tapping" noises.

9   If any are removed, assemble the rocker arms onto their shaft(s) (see Section 11).

10   The lash adjusters must be partially full of engine oil - indicated by little or no plunger action when the adjuster is depressed. If there's excessive plunger travel, place the rocker arm assembly into clean engine oil and pump the plunger until the plunger travel is eliminated. **Note:** *If the plunger still travels within the rocker arm when full of oil it's defective and the rocker arm assembly must be replaced.*

11   When re-starting the engine after replacing the rocker arm/lash adjusters, the adjusters will normally make "tapping" noises. After warm-up, raise the speed of the engine from idle to 3,000 rpm for one minute. If the adjuster(s) do not become silent, replace the defective rocker arm/lash adjuster(s).

13 Cylinder head - removal and installation

Warning: *Allow the engine to cool completely before beginning this procedure.*

Removal

Refer to illustrations 13.4, 13.10a and 13.10b

1   Position the number one piston at Top Dead Center (see Section 3).

2   Disconnect the cable from the negative battery terminal (see Chapter 5).

3   Drain the cooling system and remove the spark plugs (see Chapter 1).

4   Remove the intake manifold (see Sec-

tion 5). Cover the intake ports with duct tape to keep out debris **(see illustration)**.

5   If necessary, remove the exhaust manifold (see Section 6). **Note:** *On some models, the exhaust manifold is easier to remove after the cylinder head is removed.*

6   Remove the ignition system components (see Chapter 5).

7   Remove the timing belt (see Section 7).

8   Remove the valve cover (see Section 4).

9   Loosen the cylinder head bolts 1/4-turn at a time in the reverse of the tightening sequence **(see illustration 13.14a or 13.14b)** until they can be removed by hand. Write down the locations of the different length bolts so they can be installed in the same locations if you're working on a 2003 or earlier engine. **Note:** *Mitsubishi tool MB991654 or its equivalent must be used to remove the bolts on 2004 and later engines. On 2004 and later engines, discard the bolts and replace them with new ones on reassembly. On earlier engines, check the bolts for damage or wear and replace them as necessary.*

10   Carefully lift the cylinder head **(see illus-**

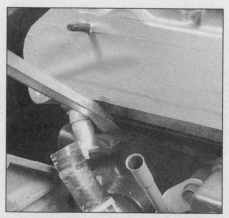

13.10b If the head sticks to the engine block, dislodge it by placing a wood block against the head casting and tapping the wood with a hammer or by prying the head with a prybar placed carefully on a casting protrusion

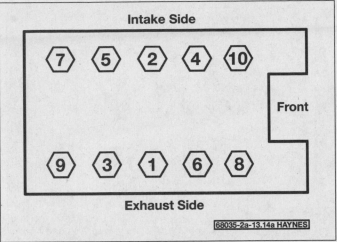

13.14a Cylinder head bolt TIGHTENING sequence
(2.4L DOHC engine)

13.14b Cylinder head bolt TIGHTENING sequence
(2.4L SOHC engine)

tration) straight up and place the head on wood blocks to prevent damage to the sealing surfaces. If the head sticks to the engine block, dislodge it by placing a wood block against the head casting and tapping the wood with a hammer or by prying the head with a prybar placed carefully on a casting protrusion (see illustration). Caution: *The cylinder head is aluminum, so you must be very careful not to gouge the sealing surfaces.* Note: *It's a good idea to have the head checked for warpage, even if you're just replacing the gasket.*

11 Special gasket removal solvents that soften gaskets and make removal much easier are available at auto parts stores. Remove all traces of old gasket material from the block and head. Do not allow anything to fall into the engine. Clean and inspect all threaded fasteners and be sure the threaded holes in the block are clean and dry.

Installation

Refer to illustrations 13.14a and 13.14b

12 Place a new gasket and the cylinder head in position on the engine block.

13 Apply clean engine oil to the bolt threads, under the heads and to the washers prior to installation. On 2004 and later models, be sure to install new bolts.

14 Tighten the cylinder head bolts in several stages in the recommended sequence (see illustrations) to the torque listed in this Chapter's Specifications. Note: *The final two steps in the tightening procedure requires you to tighten the bolts a specific number of degrees. An angle-torque gauge that fits on your torque wrench is available at most auto parts stores and is highly recommended for this procedure. If the tool is not available, paint marks on the bolt heads and tighten them in sequence until the mark is the specified number of degrees from the starting point.*

15 Reinstall the timing belt (see Section 7).

16 Reinstall the remaining parts in the reverse order of removal.

17 Change the engine oil and filter and refill the cooling system (see Chapter 1). Rotate the crankshaft clockwise slowly by hand through six complete revolutions. Recheck the camshaft timing marks (see Section 7).

18 Start the engine and run it until normal operating temperature is reached. Check for leaks and proper operation.

14 Oil pan - removal and installation

Removal

Refer to illustrations 14.6a, 14.6b, 14.6c, 14.7a, 14.7b and 14.8

1 Disconnect the cable from the negative battery terminal (see Chapter 5).

2 Raise the vehicle and support it securely on jackstands.

3 Drain the engine oil (see Chapter 1).

4 Remove the front exhaust pipe (see Chapter 4).

5 Remove the flywheel/driveplate inspection cover.

6 Remove the mounting bolts and lower the oil pan from the vehicle (see illustrations). If the pan is stuck, tap it with a soft-

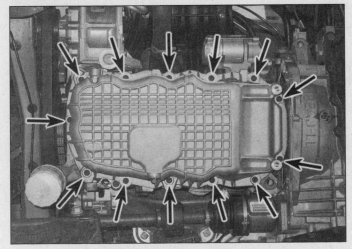

14.6a Using a criss-cross pattern, loosen and remove the oil pan bolts . . .

14.6b . . . then lower the pan carefully (there might still be some residual oil in the pan)

14.6c If the pan is stuck, tap it with a soft-face hammer or place a wood block against the pan and tap the wood block with a hammer

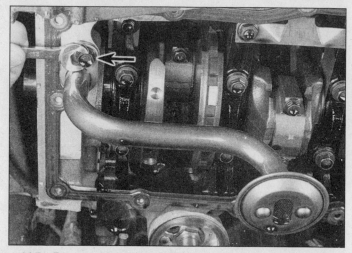

14.7a Remove the bolt and remove the oil pump pick-up tube and screen assembly - clean both the tube and screen thoroughly before reassembly

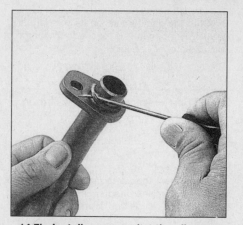

14.7b Install a new seal at the oil pump pick-up tube mounting flange

14.8 Thoroughly clean the oil pan and sealing surfaces on the engine block and oil pan with a scraper to remove all traces of old gasket material

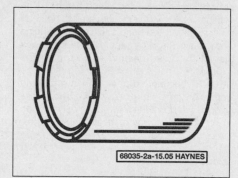

15.5 Use a special tool to remove the plug cap from the oil pump driven gear bolt

face hammer **(see illustration)** or place a wood block against the pan and tap the wood block with a hammer. **Caution:** *If you're wedging something between the oil pan and the engine block to separate the two, be extremely careful not to gouge or nick the gasket surface of either part; an oil leak could result.*

7   Remove the oil pump pick-up tube and screen assembly **(see illustration)** and clean both the tube and screen thoroughly. Install the pick-up tube and screen with a new seal **(see illustration)**.

8   Thoroughly clean the oil pan and sealing surfaces on the block and pan **(see illustration)**. Use a scraper to remove all traces of old gasket material. Gasket removal solvents are available at auto parts stores and may prove helpful. Check the oil pan sealing surface for distortion. Straighten or replace as necessary. After cleaning and straightening (if necessary), wipe the gasket surfaces of the pan and block clean with a rag soaked in lacquer thinner or acetone.

Installation

9   Apply a 1/8-inch bead of RTV sealant at the cylinder block-to-oil pump assembly joint at

the oil pan flange. Install a new oil pan gasket.

10   Place the oil pan into position and install the bolts finger tight. Working side-to-side from the center out, tighten the bolts to the torque listed in this Chapter's Specifications.

11   The remainder of installation is the reverse of removal.

12   Refill the crankcase with the correct quantity and grade of oil (see Chapter 1), run the engine and check for leaks.

13   Road test the vehicle and check for leaks again.

---

15   Oil pump - removal, inspection and installation

Removal

Refer to illustration 15.5

1   Disconnect the battery cable from the negative battery terminal (see Chapter 5).

2   Raise the vehicle and place it securely on jackstands.

3   Remove the oil pan and pick-up tube/strainer assembly (see Section 14).

4   Remove the timing belt, the crankshaft sprockets and tensioner assembly (see Section 7).

5   Remove the plug cap with a special tool **(see illustration)**. If the special tool is not available, strike the face of the plug squarely with a hammer two or three times to break it loose and then the plug can be removed using a pair of pliers.

6   Remove the bolt from the side of the block and insert a Phillips screwdriver or a small punch to keep the balance shaft from turning **(see illustration 7.15b)**.

7   Remove the bolt that secures the oil pump driven gear to the balance shaft.

8   Remove the bolts from the oil pump/front case. Separate the oil pump/front case from the engine. **Caution:** *If the pump doesn't come off by hand, tap it gently with a soft-faced hammer or pry on a casting boss.* **Caution:** *Because each bolt varies in length, be sure to label each bolt and its corresponding location to insure correct installation.*

9   Remove the mounting screws on the backside of the oil pump/front cover and remove the cover. **Caution:** *Be very careful with these parts. Close tolerances are critical*

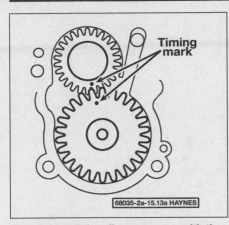

15.13 Install the oil pump gears with the marks lined up - if they do not line up, the balance shaft will be out of phase and severe engine vibration will result

16.4 Mark the relative position of the flywheel or driveplate to the crankshaft and, using an appropriate tool to hold the flywheel, remove the bolts

16.5 Remove the flywheel/driveplate from the crankshaft

in creating the correct oil pressure. Any nicks or other damage will require replacement of the complete pump assembly.

Inspection

Refer to illustration 15.13

10   Clean all components including the block surfaces with solvent, then inspect all surfaces for chips, score marks or possible overheating (a bluish discoloration of the gears). Replace the gears if necessary.

11   Inspect the front case housing where the gears ride and look for wear indications such as scoring, galling or evidence of an overheating situation. If any of these are found in the pump housing, the oil pump/ front cover will have to be replaced.

12   Disassemble the relief valve, unscrew the cap bolt and remove the bolt, washer, spring and relief valve. Check the oil pressure relief valve piston sliding surface and valve spring. If either the spring or the valve is damaged, they must be replaced as a set. If no damage is found reassemble the relief valve parts. Make sure to install the relief valve into the pump body with the grooved end going in first. Coating the parts with oil, and reinstall them in the oil pump body. Tighten the cap bolt securely.

13   Install the oil pump outer and inner gears and align the oil pump marks **(see illustration)**. Measure the side clearance of each rotor. Compare the clearances to the values listed in this Chapter's Specifications. Replace parts as necessary. Pack the pump cavity with petroleum jelly and install the cover. Tighten the bolts to the torque listed in this Chapter's Specifications. **Caution:** *You must line up the oil pump gear marks on reassembly. If you don't, the balance shaft will be out of phase and severe engine vibration will result.*

Installation

14   Install the pressure regulator valve components and tighten the plug securely.

15   Install the pump cover. Tighten the fasteners to the torque listed in this Chapter's Specifications.

16   Install the front case (making sure to install the bolts in their proper locations, according to length), using a new gasket coated with a light film of RTV sealant. Tighten the bolts to the torque listed in this Chapter's Specifications.

17   Reinstall the remaining parts in the reverse order of removal.

18   Add oil and change the oil filter (see Chapter 1), start the engine and check for oil pressure and leaks.

16   Flywheel/driveplate - removal and installation

Removal

Refer to illustrations 16.4 and 16.5

1   Raise the vehicle and support it securely on jackstands, then refer to Chapter 7 and remove the transaxle assembly.

2   If the vehicle has a manual transaxle, remove the pressure plate and clutch disc (see Chapter 8). Now is a good time to check/ replace the clutch components.

3   To ensure correct alignment during reinstallation, mark the position of the flywheel/ driveplate to the crankshaft before removal.

4   Remove the bolts that secure the flywheel/driveplate to the crankshaft **(see illustration)**. A tool is available at most auto parts stores to hold the flywheel/driveplate while loosening the bolts. If the tool is not available, wedge a screwdriver in the ring gear teeth to jam the flywheel.

5   Remove the flywheel/driveplate from the crankshaft **(see illustration)**. Since the flywheel is fairly heavy, be sure to support it while removing the last bolt.

6   Clean the flywheel to remove grease and oil. To inspect the flywheel, see Chapter 8.

7   Clean and inspect the mating surfaces of the flywheel/driveplate and the crankshaft. If the crankshaft rear main seal is leaking, replace it before reinstalling the flywheel/ driveplate (see Section 17).

Installation

8   Position the flywheel/driveplate against the crankshaft. Align the previously applied match marks. Before installing the bolts, apply thread locking compound to the threads.

9   Hold the flywheel/driveplate with the holding tool, or wedge a screwdriver in the ring gear teeth to keep the flywheel/driveplate from turning as you tighten the bolts to the torque listed in this Chapter's Specifications.

10   The remainder of installation is the reverse of the removal procedure.

17   Rear main oil seal - replacement

Refer to illustrations 17.2 and 17.4

1   The one-piece rear main oil seal is pressed into a bore machined into the rear main bearing cap and engine block. Remove the transaxle (see Chapter 7), the clutch components, if equipped (see Chapter 8) and the flywheel or driveplate (see Section 16).

2   **Note:** *Observe that the oil seal is installed flush with the outer surface of the block.* Pry out the old seal with a 3/16-inch flat blade screwdriver **(see illustration)**. **Caution:** *To*

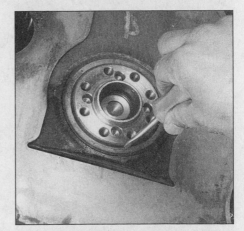

17.2 Carefully pry the crankshaft seal out of the bore - DO NOT nick or scratch the crankshaft or seal bore

17.4 Position the new seal with the words THIS SIDE OUT facing out, toward the rear of the engine. Gently drive the seal into the cylinder block until it is flush with the outer surface of the block. Do not drive it past flush or there will be an oil leak - the seal must be flush

prevent an oil leak after the new seal is installed, be very careful not to scratch or otherwise damage the crankshaft sealing surface or the bore in the engine block.

3   Clean the crankshaft and seal bore in the block thoroughly and de-grease these areas by wiping them with a rag soaked in lacquer thinner or acetone. Do not lubricate the lip or outer diameter of the new seal - it must be installed as it comes from the manufacturer.

4   Position the new seal onto the crankshaft. **Note:** *When installing the new seal, if so marked, the words THIS SIDE OUT on the seal must face out, toward the rear of the engine*. Using an appropriate size driver and pilot tool, drive the seal into the cylinder block until it is flush with the outer surface of the block. If the seal is driven in past flush, there will be a oil leak. Check that the seal is flush **(see illustration)**.

5   The remainder of installation is the reverse of removal.

18   Engine mounts - check and replacement

1   Engine mounts seldom require attention, but broken or deteriorated mounts should be replaced immediately or the added strain placed on the driveline components may cause damage or wear.

Check

2   During the check, the engine must be raised slightly to remove the weight from the mounts.

3   Raise the vehicle and support it securely on jackstands, then position a jack under the engine oil pan. Place a large wood block between the jack head and the oil pan to prevent oil pan damage, then carefully raise the engine just enough to take the weight off the mounts. **Warning:** *DO NOT place any part of your body under the engine when it's supported only by a jack!*

18.9a Remove the left engine mount upper (vertical) bolts (1998 and earlier 2.4L SOHC engines)

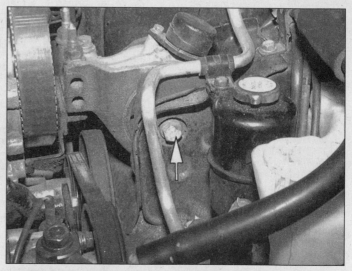

18.9b Next, remove the through (horizontal) bolt from the left engine mount (1998 2.4L SOHC and earlier engines)

18.9c Lift the mount from the engine compartment (1998 and earlier 2.4L SOHC engines)

18.9d Remove the right engine mount bolts (1999 and later 2.4L SOHC engines)

4   Check the mounts to see if the rubber is cracked, hardened or separated from the metal backing. Sometimes the rubber will split right down the center.

5   Check for relative movement between the mount plates and the engine or frame. Use a large screwdriver or pry bar to attempt to move the mounts. If movement is noted, lower the engine and tighten the mount fasteners.

6   Rubber preservative may be applied to the mounts to slow deterioration.

Replacement

Refer to illustrations 18.9a, 18.9b, 18.9c and 18.9d

Note: *Refer to Chapter 7 for information on the roll stoppers (transaxle mounts) located on the center support member.*

7   Disconnect the cable from the negative battery terminal, then raise the vehicle and support it securely on jackstands (if not already done).

8   Place a floor jack under the engine with a wood block between the jack head and oil pan and raise the engine slightly to relieve the weight from the mounts.

9   Remove the fasteners and detach the mount from the frame and engine **(see illustrations)**. **Caution:** *Do not disconnect more than one mount at a time, except during engine removal.*

10   Installation is the reverse of removal.

19.2 MIVEC system components consist of conventional exhaust rocker arms (A), low-lift rocker arms (B) and MIVEC high-lift T-bar unit (C)

Use thread locking compound on the mount bolts and be sure to tighten them securely.

19   MIVEC system - description

Refer to illustration 19.2

1   MIVEC stands for Mitsubishi Innovative Valve Electronic Control and is used on later model four-cylinder and V6 engines. This system is activated by the PCM and varies the lift and timing of the intake valves for additional power.

2   A mild intake cam profile is used at engine speeds below about 3500 rpm for smooth idling and low emissions. At higher engine speeds, the PCM opens an engine oil control valve that is mounted near the oil pressure sensor on the end of the cylinder head. This valve allows oil to flow through the intake camshaft, moving T bars located in each intake rocker arm **(see illustration)**. These T bars engage the high speed cam lobes which give more valve lift, opening duration and overlap.

Notes

Chapter 2 Part B
V6 engines

Contents

Specifications

General

Displacement
    2003 and earlier models .... 181 cubic inches (3.0 liters)
    2004 and later models .... 234 cubic inches (3.8 liters)
Bore
    3.0L models .... 3.59 inches (91.1 mm)
    3.8L models .... 3.74 inches (95.0 mm)
Stroke
    3.0L models .... 2.99 inches (76.0 mm)
    3.8L models .... 3.54 inches (90.0 mm)
Firing order 1-2-3-4-5-6
Compression ratio
    2003 and earlier models 9.0:1
    2004 and later non-MIVEC models 10.0:1
    MIVEC models 10.5:1
Compression pressure .... See Chapter 2C
Oil pressure .... See Chapter 2C
Cylinder numbers (drivebelt end-to-transaxle end)
    Rear (firewall side) 1-3-5
    Front (radiator side) 2-4-6

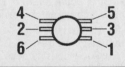

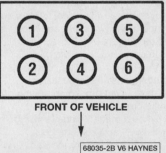

FRONT OF VEHICLE

68035-2B V6 HAYNES

V6 cylinder numbering - spark plug terminal locations are for 2003 and earlier models

Camshaft

Cam lobe height
    1999 and 2000 models
        Intake
            Standard .... 1.480 inches (37.58 mm)
            Minimum .... 1.460 inches (37.08 mm
        Exhaust
            Standard .... 1.455 inches (36.95 mm)
            Minimum .... 1.435 inches (36.45 mm)
    2001 and later non-MIVEC models
        Intake
            Standard .... 1.485 inches (37.71 mm)
            Minimum .... 1.465 inches (37.21 mm
        Exhaust
            Standard .... 1.462 inches (37.14 mm)
            Minimum .... 1.443 inches (36.64 mm)

Camshaft (continued)

Cam lobe height (continued)
    2007 and later MIVEC models
        Intake low speed cam A
            Standard... 1.321 inches (33.55 mm)
            Minimum.. 1.301 inches (33.05 mm)
        Intake low speed cam B
            Standard... 1.4705 inches (37.35 mm)
            Minimum.. 1.451 inches (36.85 mm)
        Intake high speed cam
            Standard... 1.465 inches (37.21 mm)
            Minimum.. 1.471 inches (37.37 mm)
        Exhaust cam
            Standard... 1.491 inches (37.87 mm)
            Minimum.. 1.471 inches (37.37 mm)
Cam journal diameter .... 1.8 inches (45 mm)

Intake and exhaust manifolds

Intake manifold warpage limit .... 0.008 inch (0.02 mm)
Exhaust manifold warpage limit .... 0.008 inch (0.02 mm)

Oil pump

Body clearance
    Standard .... 0.004 to 0.007 inch (0.10 to 0.18 mm)
    Service limit.. 0.013 inch (0.35 mm)
Side clearance.. 0.002 to 0.003 inch (0.05 to 0.07 mm)
Tip clearance.. 0.003 to 0.007 inch (0.07 to 0.18 mm)

Timing belt

Automatic tensioner pushrod movement (@ 22 to 44 lbs pressure) .... 0.03 inch (1.0 mm)
Automatic tensioner protrusion.. 0.15 to 0.20 inch (3.8 to 5.0 mm)

Torque specifications

Note: *One foot-pound (ft-lb) of torque is equivalent to 12 inch-pounds (in-lbs) of torque. Torque values below approximately 15 foot-pounds are expressed in inch-pounds, because most foot-pound torque wrenches are not accurate at these smaller values.*

	Ft-lbs (unless otherwise indicated)	Nm
Camshaft sprocket bolt	65	88
Camshaft thrust case bolts	109 in-lbs	12
Coolant crossover housing bolts	168 in-lbs	19
Crankshaft pulley/vibration damper bolt	134	182
Crankshaft rear main seal retainer bolts	95 in-lbs	11
Cylinder head bolts **(in sequence - see illustration 12.24)**		
Step 1	80	108
Step 2	Back off bolts to 0	
Step 3	80	108
Drivebelt tensioner mounting nut	36	49
Engine support bracket mounting bolts **(see illustration 7.30)**	33	44
Exhaust manifold		
Exhaust manifold heat shield bolts		
1999 and 2000 models	117 in-lbs	13
2001 and later models	122 in-lbs	14
Exhaust manifold-to-cylinder head nuts		
Federal models		
1999 through 2000 models	33	44
2001 and later models	36	49
California models	36	49
Exhaust pipe-to-exhaust manifold nuts	26	35
Flywheel/driveplate mounting bolts*	55	74
Intake manifold		
Upper intake manifold bolts/nuts	156 in-lbs	17
Lower intake manifold nuts		
2003 and earlier models **(see illustration 5.31)**		
Step 1 (Bolts A [rear])	56 in-lbs	6
Step 2 (Bolts D [front])	16	22
Step 3 (Bolts A [rear])	16	22
Step 4 (Bolts D [front])	16	22
Step 5 (Bolts A [rear])	16	22
2004 and later models	18 to 24	24 to 32
Oil pan bolts		
Lower oil pan-to-upper pan bolts	96 in-lbs	11
Upper oil pan bolts	52 in-lbs	5.9

Torque specifications

	Ft-lbs (unless otherwise indicated)	Nm
Oil pump		
Mounting bolts		
M8 bolts		
2003 and earlier models	122 in-lbs	14
2004 and later models	17	23
M10 bolts	30	41
Cover retaining bolts	87 in-lbs	10
Pick-up tube bolts	168 in-lbs	19
Relief valve plug	33	44
Rocker arm shaft bolts	23	31
Timing belt **(see illustration 7.12a)**		
Timing belt cover bolts		
Upper timing cover		
M6 bolt	95 in-lbs	11
M8 bolt	122 in-lbs	14
Lower timing cover	95 in-lbs	11
Auto-tensioner retaining bolts	17	24
Tensioner arm retaining bolt	33	44
Guide pulley retaining bolt	33	44
Tensioner pulley bolt	35	48
Valve cover bolts		
2003 and earlier models	26 in-lbs	3
2004 and later models	27 to 35 in-lbs	3 to 4

* Apply a thread locking compound to the threads prior to installation

1   General information

This Part of Chapter 2 is devoted to in-vehicle engine repair procedures. Information concerning engine removal and installation can be found in Part C of this Chapter.

The following repair procedures are based on the assumption that the engine is installed in the vehicle. If the engine has been removed from the vehicle and mounted on a stand, many of the steps outlined in this Part of Chapter 2 will not apply.

The Specifications included in this Part of Chapter 2 apply only to the procedures contained in this Part.

2   Repair operations possible with the engine in the vehicle

Many major repair operations can be accomplished without removing the engine from the vehicle.

Clean the engine compartment and the exterior of the engine with some type of degreaser before any work is performed. It will make the job easier and help keep dirt out of the internal areas of the engine.

Depending on the components involved, it may be helpful to remove the hood to improve access to the engine as repairs are performed (refer to Chapter 11 if necessary). Cover the fenders to prevent damage to the paint. Special pads are available, but an old bedspread or blanket will also work.

If vacuum, exhaust, oil or coolant leaks develop, indicating a need for gasket or seal replacement, the repairs can generally be made with the engine in the vehicle. The intake and exhaust manifold gaskets, oil pan gasket, camshaft and crankshaft oil seals and cylinder head gasket are all accessible with the engine in place.

Exterior engine components, such as the intake and exhaust manifolds, the oil pan, the oil pump, the water pump, the starter motor, the alternator, the distributor and the fuel system components can be removed for repair with the engine in place.

Since the camshafts and cylinder heads can be removed without pulling the engine, valve component servicing can also be accomplished with the engine in the vehicle. Replacement of the timing belt and sprockets is also possible with the engine in the vehicle.

In extreme cases caused by a lack of necessary equipment, repair or replacement of piston rings, pistons, connecting rods and rod bearings is possible with the engine in the vehicle. However, this practice is not recommended because of the cleaning and preparation work that must be done to the components involved.

3   Top Dead Center (TDC) for number one piston - locating

Note: *The crankshaft timing marks on both engines aren't visible until after the timing belt cover has been removed. The number one cylinder can be positioned at TDC by using this procedure without removing the timing belt cover.*

1   Top Dead Center (TDC) is the highest point in the cylinder that each piston reaches as it travels up-and-down when the crankshaft turns. Each piston reaches TDC on the compression stroke and again on the exhaust stroke, but TDC generally refers to piston position on the compression stroke.

2   Positioning a specific piston at TDC is an essential part of many procedures such as camshaft(s) removal, rocker arm removal, timing belt and sprocket replacement.

3   In order to bring any piston to TDC, the crankshaft must be turned using one of the methods outlined below. When looking at the front of the engine, normal crankshaft rotation is clockwise. **Warning:** *Before beginning this procedure, be sure to set the emergency brake, place the transmission in Park or Neutral and disable the ignition system by disconnecting the primary electrical connector from the ignition coil pack.*

a) *The preferred method is to turn the crankshaft with a large socket and breaker bar attached to the crankshaft balancer hub bolt that is threaded into the front of the crankshaft.*

b) *A remote starter switch, which may save some time, can also be used. Attach the switch leads to the S (switch) and B (battery) terminals on the starter solenoid. Once the piston is close to TDC, discontinue with the remote switch and use a socket and breaker bar as described in the previous paragraph.*

c) *If an assistant is available to turn the ignition switch to the Start position in short bursts, you can get the piston close to TDC without a remote starter switch. Use a socket and breaker bar as described in Paragraph a) to complete the procedure.*

4   Remove all spark plugs as this will make it easier to rotate the engine by hand.

5   Insert a compression gauge (screw-in type with a hose) in the number 1 spark plug hole. Place the gauge dial where you can see it while turning the crankshaft balancer hub bolt. **Note:** *The number one cylinder is located at the front (timing belt end) of the engine, on the rear cylinder bank.*

6   Turn the crankshaft clockwise until you

4.4 To detach the breather hose between the valve covers, loosen these hose clamps and pull the hose off both valve cover pipes

4.5 If you're removing the rear valve cover, remove these nuts and detach these emissions vacuum lines

4.6a Front valve cover mounting bolts

4.6b Rear valve cover mounting bolts

see compression building up on the gauge - you are on the compression stroke for that cylinder. If you did not see compression build up, continue with one more complete revolution to achieve TDC for the number one cylinder.

7   If your engine is equipped with a notch in the crankshaft pulley, align the notch in the pulley with the 0 or T mark on the timing belt cover. At this point the number one piston is at TDC on the compression stroke.

8   If your engine is not equipped with a timing scale or a notch in the crankshaft pulley, remove the compression gauge. Through the number one cylinder spark plug hole insert a length of wooden dowel or plastic rod and

slowly push it down until it reaches the top surface of the piston crown. **Caution:** *Don't insert a metal or sharp object into the spark plug hole as the piston crown may be damaged*. With the dowel or rod in place on top of the piston crown, slowly rotate the crankshaft clockwise until the dowel or rod is pushed upward, stops, and then starts to move back down. Now, rotate the crankshaft slightly counterclockwise until the dowel or rod has reached it upper most travel. At this point the number one piston is at the TDC position.

9   After the number one piston has been positioned at TDC on the compression stroke,

TDC for any of the remaining cylinders can be located by turning the crankshaft 120-degrees (1/3-turn) at a time and following the firing order (refer to the Specifications).

4   Valve cover - removal and installation

Removal

Refer to illustrations 4.4, 4.5, 4.6a, 4.6b, 4.7 and 4.8

1   Disconnect the cable from the negative battery terminal (see Chapter 5).

2   If you're going to remove the rear valve cover, remove the upper intake manifold (see Section 5).

3   Clearly label and disconnect any spark plug wires (see Chapter 1). Also label and disconnect any electrical harnesses that connect to or cross over the valve cover.

4   Disconnect the breather hose **(see illustration)** and the PCV hose from the valve cover (see Chapter 6).

5   Detach the emission vacuum lines from the rear cover, if equipped **(see illustration)**.

6   Remove the valve cover bolts **(see illustrations)** and lift off the cover. If the cover sticks to the cylinder head, tap on it with a soft-face hammer or place a wood block against the cover and tap on the wood with a hammer. **Caution:** *If you have to pry between the valve cover and the cylinder head, be*

4.7 Remove the spark plug tube seals and, even if they look okay, replace them

4.8 Remove the old valve cover gasket and clean off all traces of old gasket material

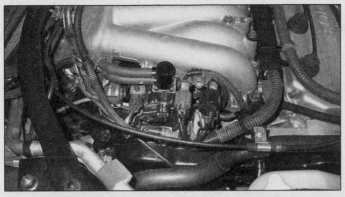

5.6a Disconnect the hoses and the electrical connectors at the timing belt end of the engine . . .

5.6b . . . and the distributor end of the engine

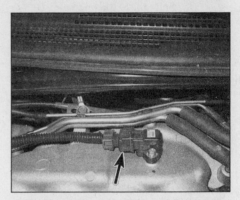

5.6c Disconnect the hoses and electrical connectors at the rear of the engine

5.7a Unbolt the EGR tube and remove it from the manifold

5.7b Disconnect the differential pressure sensor at the rear of the intake manifold

extremely careful not to gouge or nick the gasket surfaces of either part. A leak could develop after reassembly.

7   Remove the spark plug tube seals. Even if they look OK, they should be replaced **(see illustration)**.

8   Remove the old gasket **(see illustration)**. Thoroughly clean the valve cover and remove all traces of old gasket material. Gasket removal solvents are available from auto parts stores and may prove helpful. After cleaning the surfaces, degrease them with a rag soaked in lacquer thinner or acetone.

Installation

9   Install the new spark plug seals onto the tubes.

10   Install a new gasket on the cover, using anaerobic RTV sealant to hold it in place.

11   Tighten the valve cover bolts in 3 steps to the torque listed in this Chapter's Specifications using a criss-cross pattern starting in the middle of the cover and working outwards.

12   The remaining installation steps are the reverse of removal. When complete, run the engine and check for oil leaks.

Spark plug tube replacement

13   Remove the applicable valve cover.

14   Grasp the spark plug tube firmly with locking pliers, carefully twist it back and forth and simultaneously pull up, then remove the tube from the cylinder head.

15   Clean the locking agent from the tube

and the recess in the cylinder head with solvent, then dry it thoroughly.

16   Apply a small amount of Loctite No. 271, or equivalent, around the lower end of the tube and install the tube into the cylinder head. Carefully tap the tube into the recess with a wood block and mallet until it is fully seated in the cylinder head.

5   Intake manifold - removal and installation

Warning: *Wait until the engine is completely cool before beginning this procedure.*

Upper intake manifold
Removal

Refer to illustrations 5.6a, 5.6b, 5.6c, 5.7a, 5.7b, 5.14 and 5.15

2003 and earlier models

1   Relieve the fuel pressure (see Chapter 4). Disconnect the cable from the negative battery terminal (see Chapter 5).

2   Drain the engine coolant (see Chapter 1).

3   Remove the air intake duct from the throttle body (see Chapter 4).

4   Disconnect the accelerator cable and cruise control cable (if applicable) from the throttle body (see Chapter 4).

5   If you're going to replace the upper intake manifold, remove the throttle body (see Chapter 4). If you're just removing the upper

intake manifold to get to the lower intake manifold or to perform some other service procedure, it's not necessary to remove the throttle body.

6   Clearly label and disconnect all vacuum hoses, pipes and lines that would interfere with removal **(see illustrations)**.

7   Clearly label and disconnect the following fuel, electrical and emission control electrical connectors and components (see Chapter 4, 5 or 6):

a) *Volume airflow sensor connector*
b) *Control wiring harness and power steering wiring harness combination connector*
c) *Exhaust Gas Recirculation (EGR) solenoid valve connector*
d) *Evaporative emission (EVAP) purge solenoid valve connector*
e) *Knock sensor connector*
f) *Crankshaft Position (CKP) sensor connector*
g) *Right heated oxygen sensor connector*
h) *Fuel injector connector*
i) *Distributor connector*
j) *Control wiring harness and injector wiring harness combination connector*
k) *EGR solenoid valve, evaporative emission purge solenoid valve and vacuum valve*
l) *EGR valve and EGR pipe* **(see illustration)**
m) *Manifold differential pressure sensor* **(see illustration)**

8   Remove the power steering pump drivebelt (see Chapter 1), then remove the power steering pump bracket stay.

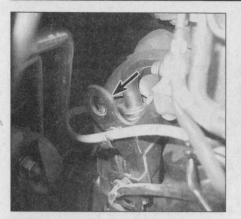

5.14 Unbolt the support stays at the front and rear of the engine

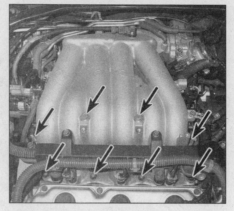

5.15 Remove the upper intake manifold bolts and nuts

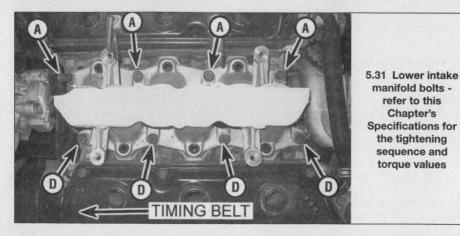

5.18 Check the intake manifold gasket surfaces for warpage

2004 and later models

9   Remove the intake duct and any other interfering components.

10   Disconnect the vacuum line and wiring from the throttle body. The throttle body can be left attached to the upper intake manifold.

11   Disconnect the wiring from the purge control solenoid valve, then remove the valve and its bracket.

12   Remove the EGR tube and the EGR valve.

13   Disconnect any remaining interfering wiring or hoses.

All models

14   Remove the bolts securing the upper intake manifold to the right and left side support stays **(see illustration)**.

15   Remove the upper intake manifold bolts/ nuts **(see illustration)**, remove the upper intake manifold, then remove the manifold gasket. If it sticks, tap the manifold with a soft-face hammer or carefully pry it from the lower intake manifold. **Caution:** *Do not pry between gasket sealing surfaces.*

16   To minimize the chance of gasket debris or other contamination from getting into the engine, place clean rags into the lower intake manifold passages.

17   Remove all traces of gasket material from both the upper and lower intake manifold by carefully scraping them using a suitable gasket scraper. **Caution:** *The intake manifold components are made of aluminum*

and are easily nicked or gouged. Do not damage the gasket surfaces or a leak may result after the work is complete. Gasket removal solvents are available from auto parts stores and may prove helpful.

Inspection

Refer to illustration 5.18

18   Using a precision straightedge and feeler gauge, check the upper and lower intake manifold mating surfaces for warpage **(see illustration)**. If the warpage on any surface exceeds the limits listed in this Chapter's Specifications, the discrepant intake manifold must be replaced or resurfaced by an automotive machine shop.

Installation

19   Remove the rags from the lower intake manifold. Use a shop vacuum to remove any contamination that may be present.

20   Install the upper intake manifold, using a new gasket. Tighten the bolts in 3 stages, working from the center out, to the torque listed in this Chapter's Specifications.

21   The remainder of installation is the reverse of removal. Refill the cooling system (see Chapter 1).

Lower intake manifold

Removal

22   Relieve the fuel pressure (see Chapter 4).

23   Remove the upper intake manifold (see Steps 1 through 17).

24   Remove the fuel rail and injector assembly (see Chapter 4).

25   Loosen the lower intake manifold nuts in the reverse order of the tightening sequence **(see illustration 5.31)**, 1/4 turn at a time until they can be removed by hand. Remove the washers.

26   Remove the lower intake manifold from the engine. If it sticks, tap the manifold with a soft-face hammer or carefully pry it from the heads. **Caution:** *Do not pry between gasket sealing surfaces.*

27   To minimize the chance of gasket debris or other contamination from getting into the engine, place clean rags into the cylinder head intake passages.

28   Remove all traces of gasket material from the upper and lower intake manifold and cylinder heads by carefully scraping them using a suitable gasket scraper. **Caution:** *The intake manifold components and cylinder heads are made of aluminum and are easily nicked or gouged. Do not damage the gasket surfaces or a leak may result after the work is complete. Gasket removal solvents are available from auto parts stores and may prove helpful.*

Inspection

29   Using a precision straightedge and feeler gauge, check the upper and lower intake manifold gasket surfaces for warpage **(see illustration 5.18)**. Check the gasket surface on the cylinder head also. If the warpage on any surface exceeds the limits listed in this Chapter's Specifications, the discrepant component must be replaced or resurfaced by an automotive machine shop.

Installation

Refer to illustration 5.31

30   Remove the rags from the cylinder head intake passages. Use a shop vacuum to remove any contamination that may be present.

31   Install the lower intake manifold, using a new gasket. Tighten the nuts **(see illustration)** in five stages, following the sequence listed in this Chapter's Specifications, to the final torque.

5.31 Lower intake manifold bolts - refer to this Chapter's Specifications for the tightening sequence and torque values

6.2 To detach the heat shield from the front exhaust manifold, remove these bolts

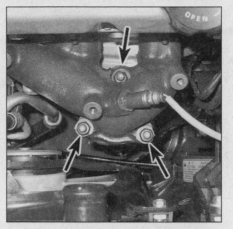

6.3 To detach the upstream catalytic converter or exhaust pipe from the exhaust manifold, remove these three nuts (front exhaust manifold-to-catalyst flange shown, rear manifold-to-catalyst flange similar)

6.5 Location of the engine oil dipstick tube bracket bolt (left) and the engine hanger bolt (right)

32   Install the fuel rail and fuel injector assembly (see Chapter 4).

33   Install the upper intake manifold, using a new gasket (see Steps 19 through 21).

34   The remainder of installation is the reverse of removal.

35   Refill the cooling system (see Chapter 1).

6   Exhaust manifolds - removal and installation

Warning: *Allow the engine to cool completely before beginning this procedure.*

Note: *This procedure can be used to remove one or both of the exhaust manifolds as required.*

Removal

Refer to illustrations 6.2, 6.3 and 6.5

1   Disconnect the cable from the negative battery terminal (see Chapter 5).

2   Remove the upper and lower exhaust manifold heat shields **(see illustration)**. On the front exhaust manifold of some models, there are two heat shields: the upper shield and the lower shield, which must be removed from below. On the rear exhaust manifold of some models, there are three heat shields: the upper shield, the side shield and the lower shield, which must be removed from below.

3   Remove the front exhaust pipe/catalytic converter assembly **(see illustration)**.

4   Remove the air filter housing (see Chapter 4).

5   Remove the engine oil dipstick tube and the front engine lifting bracket **(see illustration)**. If the vehicle is equipped with an automatic transaxle, remove the automatic transmission fluid level dipstick tube.

6   Disconnect the electrical connector for the upstream oxygen sensor (see Chapter 6).

7   If you're removing the rear exhaust manifold, disconnect the EGR pipe from the intake manifold, back off the threaded fitting at the lower end of the pipe and then unscrew the

pipe from the exhaust manifold. If the EGR pipe-to-exhaust manifold fitting is difficult to loosen, apply some penetrating oil to the fitting, wait awhile and then try again.

8   To make removal easier, apply penetrating oil to the exhaust manifold and to the manifold-to-upstream catalytic converter fasteners.

9   Detach the upstream catalytic converter from the manifold.

10   Unscrew the exhaust manifold mounting nuts, remove the exhaust manifold, then remove and discard the old manifold gasket.

11   Using a wire brush, clean the exhaust manifold studs, replacing any that show thread damage.

12   Using a scraper, remove all traces of gasket material from the exhaust manifold, cylinder head, and exhaust pipe mating surfaces and inspect them for wear and cracks. **Caution:** *When removing gasket material from any surface, especially aluminum, be very careful not to scratch or gouge the gasket surface. Any damage to the surface may cause a leak after reassembly. Gasket removal solvents are available from auto parts stores and may prove helpful.*

Inspection

13   Using a precision straightedge and feeler gauge, check the exhaust manifold gasket surfaces for warpage. Check the surface on the cylinder head also. If the warpage on any surface exceeds the limits listed in this Chapter's Specifications, the exhaust manifold and/or cylinder head must be replaced or resurfaced by an automotive machine shop.

Installation

14   Install a new exhaust gasket on the cylinder head.

15   Apply Loctite No. 271 to the exhaust manifold mounting stud threads.

16   Install the manifold, washers and nuts. Tighten the nuts in three stages, working from the center out, to the torque listed in this Chapter's Specifications.

17   The remaining installation steps are the

reverse of removal. Install a new gasket(s) between the exhaust manifold and exhaust pipe(s). Tighten the nuts to the torque listed in this Chapter's Specifications.

18   Run the engine and check for exhaust leaks.

7   Timing belt - removal, inspection and installation

Note: *If the timing belt failed with the engine operating, damage to the valves (and possibly to the pistons) most likely has occurred. One way this can be verified is by performing a compression check or a leak-down check on all cylinders, but in order to do so you'll have to first install a new timing belt (and chances are you'll be wasting your time doing this, because most likely you'll just have to remove the belt and cylinder heads). Bent valves can sometimes be confirmed visually by removing the valve covers, camshafts and rocker arms and comparing the height of the valve stems. If one or more valve stems sit lower than the others, bent valves are indicated.*

Removal

Refer to illustrations 7.4a, 7.4b, 7.8, 7.12a, 7.12b, 7.13 and 7.14

Caution: *The timing system is complex. Severe engine damage will occur if you make any mistakes. Do not attempt this procedure unless you are highly experienced with this type of repair. If you are at all unsure of your abilities, consult an expert. Double-check all your work and be sure everything is correct before you attempt to start the engine.*

Caution: *Do not turn the crankshaft or camshafts after the timing belt has been removed, as this will damage the valves from contact with the pistons. Do not try to turn the crankshaft with the camshaft sprocket bolt(s) and do not rotate the crankshaft counterclockwise as viewed from the timing belt end of the engine.*

7.4a To keep the crankshaft from turning, insert a large screwdriver or bar through the opening in the damper/pulley and wedge it against the engine block, then loosen the bolt with a socket and breaker bar

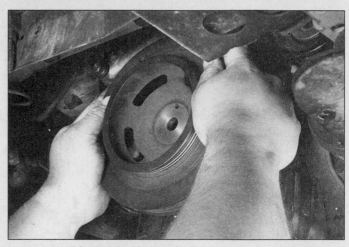

7.4b Remove the damper/pulley from the crankshaft

Note: *In order to perform this procedure, you'll need a special tool (MD 998767 or equivalent) to tension the timing belt. This tool number is available from automotive specialty tool companies such as Miller Special Tools.*

1   Position the number one piston at Top Dead Center (see Section 3), then disconnect the cable from the negative battery terminal (see Chapter 5).
2   Raise the vehicle, place it securely on jackstands, remove the right front wheel

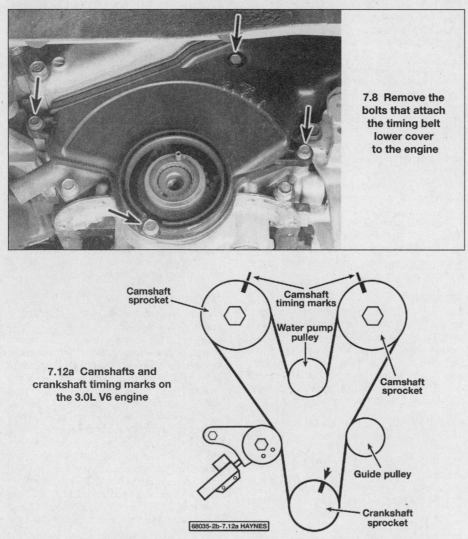

7.8 Remove the bolts that attach the timing belt lower cover to the engine

7.12a Camshafts and crankshaft timing marks on the 3.0L V6 engine

Camshaft sprocket

Camshaft timing marks

Water pump pulley

Camshaft sprocket

Guide pulley

Crankshaft sprocket

68035-2b-7.12a HAYNES

and the drivebelt splash shield (see Chapter 11).
3   Remove the drivebelts (see Chapter 1).
4   Loosen the large bolt in the center of the crankshaft pulley. To break it loose, insert a large screwdriver or bar through the opening in the pulley to keep the crankshaft stationary, then loosen the bolt with a socket and breaker bar. Remove the bolt, washer and pulley from the crankshaft **(see illustrations)**.
5   After removing the crankshaft pulley, reinstall the crankshaft bolt using an appropriate spacer. This will enable you to turn the crankshaft later.
6   Remove the alternator (see Chapter 5).
7   Remove the upper left timing belt cover.
8   Remove the lower timing belt cover **(see illustration)**.
9   Remove the engine support bracket from the right cylinder bank.
10   Remove the upper right timing belt cover.
11   Remove the right (passenger side) engine mount (see Section 17) and the engine support bracket from the engine. **Caution:** *Make sure the engine is supported with a floor jack placed under the oil pan. Place a wood block on the jack head to prevent the floor jack from denting or damaging the oil pan.*
12   Make sure the timing marks on the crankshaft sprocket and camshaft sprockets align with their respective marks before removing the timing belt **(see illustrations)**.
13   If you plan to reuse the timing belt, paint an arrow on it to indicate the direction of rotation (clockwise) **(see illustration)**.
14   Unscrew the timing belt tensioner mounting bolts and remove the tensioner **(see illustration)**. **Note:** *The tensioner piston will extend when the assembly is removed.*
15   Carefully slip the timing belt off the sprockets and set it aside. If you plan to reuse the timing belt, place it in a plastic bag - do not allow the belt to come in contact with any type of oil or water as this will greatly shorten belt life.

7.12b Crankshaft timing belt sprocket and oil pump housing timing marks

7.13 Paint an arrow on the timing belt in the direction of rotation (clockwise) so it may be reinstalled in the same direction

7.14 Timing belt tensioner mounting bolts

Inspection

Refer to illustration 7.19

16   With the timing belt covers removed, now is a good time to inspect the front crankshaft and camshaft seals for leakage. If leakage is evident, replace them (see Sections 8 and 9).

17   Inspect the water pump for evidence of leakage, usually indicated by a trail of wet or dried coolant. Check the pulley for excessive radial play and bearing roughness. Replace if necessary (see Chapter 3).

18   Rotate the tensioner pulley and guide pulley by hand and move them side-to-side to detect bearing roughness and/or excessive play. Visually inspect all timing belt sprockets for any signs of damage or wear. Replace as necessary.

19   Inspect the timing belt for cracks, separation, wear, missing teeth and oil contamination **(see illustration)**. Replace the belt if it's in questionable condition or the engine mileage is close to that referenced in the *Maintenance Schedule* (see Chapter 1).

20   Check the timing belt tensioner unit for leaks or any other obvious damage; replace if necessary.

Installation

Refer to illustrations 7.23, 7.24, 7.26 and 7.30

Caution: *Before starting the engine, carefully rotate the crankshaft by hand through at least two full revolutions (use a socket and breaker bar on the crankshaft pulley center bolt). If you feel any resistance, STOP! There is something wrong - most likely, valves are contacting the pistons. You must find the problem before proceeding. Check your work and see if any updated repair information is available.*

21   Confirm that the timing marks on both camshaft sprockets are aligned with their respective marks on the rear timing belt covers **(see illustration 7.12a)**. Reposition the camshafts if required. **Caution:** *If it is necessary to rotate the camshafts to align the timing marks, first rotate the crankshaft slightly counterclockwise (three notches on the sprocket) to ensure the valves do not contact the pistons.*

22   Position the crankshaft sprocket with

the timing marks aligned **(see illustration 7.12b)**.

23   Before installation, the timing belt tensioner piston must be compressed into the tensioner housing. Place the tensioner in a vise so the surface with the pin hole is facing up. Slowly compress the tensioner using the vise, then install an appropriate size Allen wrench or drill bit through the body and into the piston to retain the piston in this position **(see illustration)**. Remove the tensioner from

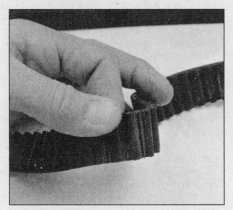

7.19 Carefully inspect the timing belt for damage or wear - bending it backwards will often make defects more apparent

the vise and install it, tightening the mounting bolts to the torque listed in this Chapter's Specifications. Using special tool MD 998767 (or equivalent), turn the tensioner pulley into the timing belt, then tighten the tensioner pulley bolt temporarily.

24   Install the timing belt as follows: First onto the crankshaft sprocket and up around the guide pulley, then over the front camshaft sprocket; clamp the belt to the sprocket with a binder clip **(see illustration)**. Now route the

7.23 Using a vise (lined with soft-jaws), compress the timing belt tensioner piston until the holes in the housing and piston align. Then place a small Allen wrench or drill bit, through the holes to keep the piston in position for installation

7.24 Binder clips can be used to retain the timing belt in position on the camshaft sprockets during installation

68035-2A-7.37 HAYNES

7.26 Using special tool MD 998767 (or equivalent) attached to a torque wrench, apply 39 in-lbs of torque (in a counterclockwise direction) to the tensioner pulley, then move the tensioner unit up against the tensioner pulley bracket and tighten the tensioner mounting bolts to the torque listed in this Chapter's Specifications

belt under the water pump pulley and over the rear camshaft sprocket, clamping it to the sprocket with a binder clip. Finally, pass the belt around the tensioner pulley. Once the belt is in place, remove the binder clips.

25   Using the crankshaft pulley bolt, turn the crankshaft 1/4-turn counterclockwise, then clockwise 1/4 turn until the timing marks are all in alignment. Make sure the timing belt is tight between the front camshaft sprocket and the crankshaft sprocket, all the slack is at the tensioner pulley and all the timing marks are aligned.

26   Loosen the tensioner pulley bolt and, using special tool MD 998767 (or equivalent) **(see illustration)**, apply 39 inch-lbs of force (in a counterclockwise direction) to properly tension the belt, then tighten the tensioner pulley bolt to the torque listed in this Chapter's Specifications. Remove the torque wrench and special tool from the tensioner.

27   Remove the Allen wrench or drill bit retaining the piston from the tensioner, then wait for five minutes. The timing belt tension

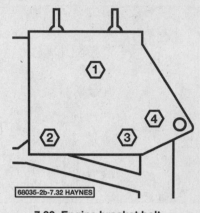

68035-2b-7.32 HAYNES

7.30 Engine bracket bolt tightening sequence

is correct when the tensioner plunger extends from the tensioner body the amount listed in this Chapter's Specifications. If it doesn't, repeat Steps 25 through 28. Verify that the timing marks on the camshaft sprockets and crankshaft sprocket are still aligned with their respective timing marks **(see illustrations 7.12a and 7.12b)**.

28   Using the bolt in the center of the crankshaft sprocket, slowly turn the crankshaft clockwise two complete revolutions. **Caution:** *If you feel strong resistance while turning the crankshaft - STOP, the valves may be hitting the pistons from incorrect valve timing. Stop and re-check the valve timing.* **Note:** *The camshafts and crankshaft sprocket marks will align every two revolutions of the crankshaft.* Recheck the alignment of the timing marks **(see illustrations 7.12a and 7.12b)**. If the marks do not align properly, remove the timing belt tensioner, slip the belt off the camshaft sprockets, realign the marks, reinstall the belt and tensioner, then check the alignment again.

29   The remaining installation steps are the reverse of removal.

30   Tighten the engine support bracket in

the correct sequence **(see illustration)**. Tighten the bolts to the torque listed in this Chapter's Specifications.

31   Tighten the crankshaft pulley bolt to the torque listed in this Chapter's Specifications.

8   Crankshaft front oil seal - replacement

Refer to illustrations 8.2, 8.3 and 8.5
Caution: *Do not rotate the camshafts or crankshaft when the timing belt is removed or damage to the engine may occur.*

1   Remove the timing belt (see Section 7).

2   Remove the crankshaft timing belt sprocket using a gear puller. Remove the Woodruff key from the crankshaft keyway **(see illustration)**.

3   Wrap the tip of a small screwdriver with vinyl tape. Carefully use the screwdriver to pry the seal out of its bore **(see illustration)**. Take care to prevent damaging the oil pump assembly, the crankshaft and the seal bore.

4   Thoroughly clean and inspect the seal bore and sealing surface on the crankshaft. Minor imperfections can be removed with fine emery cloth. If there is a groove worn in the crankshaft sealing surface (from contact with the seal), installing a new seal will probably not stop the leak.

5   Lubricate the new seal with engine oil and using a hammer and the appropriate size socket, drive the seal into the bore until it's flush with the oil pump housing **(see illustration)**.

6   Install the Woodruff key into the slot in the crankshaft. Place the crankshaft timing belt sprocket onto the crankshaft with the timing belt retaining lip facing inward (toward the engine).

7   The remaining installation steps are the reverse of removal. Tighten the crankshaft pulley bolt to the torque listed in this Chapter's Specifications.

8   Start the engine and check for oil leaks.

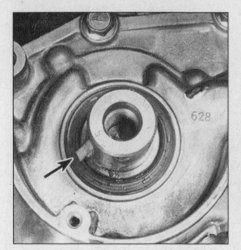

8.2 After removing the timing belt sprocket, remove the Woodruff key from the crankshaft

8.3 Using a hooked tool or screwdriver, carefully pry the crankshaft front seal out of its bore - DO NOT nick or scratch the crankshaft or seal bore

8.5 Lubricate the new seal with clean engine oil and drive it into place using a hammer and socket

9.3 To hold the camshaft while removing the sprocket bolt, use an old piece of timing belt wrapped around the sprocket and a chain wrench as shown

9.4 Using a hooked tool or screwdriver, carefully pry the camshaft seal out of the bore - DO NOT nick or scratch the camshaft or seal bore

9 Camshaft oil seal - replacement

Refer to illustrations 9.3, 9.4, 9.6a and 9.6b
Caution: *Do not rotate the camshafts or crankshaft when the timing belt is removed or damage to the engine may occur.*

1 Remove the timing belt (see Section 7).
2 Rotate the crankshaft counterclockwise until the crankshaft sprocket is three notches BTDC. This will prevent engine damage if the camshaft sprocket is inadvertently rotated during removal.
3 While keeping the camshaft from rotating, remove the camshaft sprocket bolt. Then using two large screwdrivers, lever the sprocket off the camshaft. **Note:** *A strap-type damper/pulley holder tool is available at most auto parts stores and is recommended for this procedure, however, if you are not going to reuse the old timing belt, you can wrap a piece of it around the sprocket and use a chain wrench to hold the sprocket in place as shown* **(see illustration)**.

4 Carefully pry out the camshaft oil seal using a small hooked tool or screwdriver **(see illustration)**. Don't scratch the bore or damage the camshaft in the process (if the camshaft is damaged, the new seal will end up leaking).
5 Clean the bore and coat the outer edge of the new seal with engine oil or multi-purpose grease. Also lubricate the seal lip.
6 Using a socket with an outside diameter slightly smaller than the outside diameter of the seal and a hammer **(see illustration)**, carefully drive the new seal into the cylinder head until it's flush with the face of the cylinder head. If a socket isn't available, a short section of pipe will also work. **Note:** *If engine location makes it difficult to use a hammer to install the camshaft seal, fabricate a seal installation tool from a piece of pipe cut to the appropriate length, a bolt and a large washer* **(see illustration)**. *Place the section of pipe over the seal and thread the bolt into the camshaft. The seal can now be pressed into the bore by tightening the bolt.*
7 Install the camshaft sprocket, aligning the pin in the camshaft with the hole in the sprocket. Using an appropriate tool to hold the camshaft sprocket, tighten the camshaft sprocket bolt to the torque listed in this Chapter's Specifications.
8 Install the timing belt (see Section 7).
9 Run the engine and check for oil leaks.

10 Rocker arm and hydraulic valve lash adjuster assembly - removal, inspection and installation

Removal

1 Disconnect the cable from the negative battery terminal (see Chapter 5).
2 Position the number one piston at Top Dead Center (see Section 3).
3 Remove the valve cover(s) (see Section 4).
4 Prior to removing the rocker arm shafts, identify each rocker arm and shaft as to its proper location (cylinder number and intake or exhaust). **Caution:** *Do not interchange the rocker arms onto a different shaft or shaft assemblies onto a different location as this could lead to premature wear.*
5 Loosen the rocker arm shaft bolts 1/4-turn at a time, until they can be loosened by hand, in the reverse order of the tightening sequence **(see illustration 10.17)**. Completely loosen the bolts, but do not remove them; leaving them in place will prevent the assembly from falling apart when it is lifted off the cylinder head. **Note:** *Install special hydraulic actuator holders (tool # MD998443 or equivalent) onto each lash adjuster to prevent the adjuster from falling into the engine. Use vinyl tape if the special tool holders are not available.*

9.6a Using a hammer and the appropriate size socket, drive the camshaft seal into the bore until it is flush with the cylinder head

9.6b If the space is too confined to use a hammer to drive the seal in place, fabricate a tool using a bolt, washer and section of pipe. Place the section of pipe over the seal and thread the bolt into the camshaft to press the seal into the bore

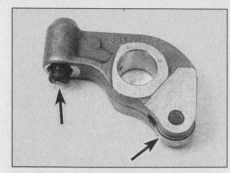

10.8 Visually inspect the hydraulic lash adjuster and roller for damage and excessive play - check the rocker arm shaft bore for score marks or excessive wear

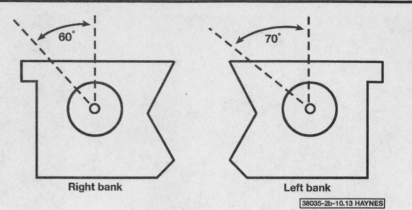

10.13 Rotate the engine until the dowel pin on the front of each camshaft is in the correct off-set location

Right bank   Left bank

38035-2b-10.13 HAYNES

10.14 The intake rocker arm shaft springs must be installed as shown - 3.0L engine

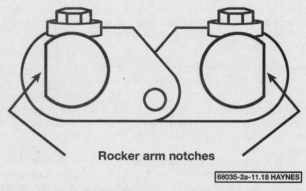

Rocker arm notches

68035-2a-11.18 HAYNES

10.16 The rocker arm notches must be positioned opposite and facing out (2003 and earlier models)

6   Lift the rocker arms and shaft assemblies from the cylinder head and set them on the workbench.

7   It's okay to disassemble the rocker arm shaft components, but pay close attention to the relationship of the parts to each other. **Note:** *To keep the rocker arms and related parts in order, it's a good idea to remove them and put them onto two lengths of wire in the same order as they're removed, marking each wire (which simulates the rocker shaft) as to which end would be the front of the engine.*

Inspection
Refer to illustration 10.8
Note: *The valve lash adjuster is an integral part of each rocker arm and cannot be replaced separately. If defective, both must be replaced.*

8   Visually check the rocker arms for excessive wear or damage **(see illustration)**. Replace them if evidence of wear or damage is found.

9   Inspect each lash adjuster carefully for signs of wear and damage, particularly on the surface that contacts the valve tip. Use a small diameter wire to check the oil holes for restrictions.

10   Since the hydraulic lash adjusters can become clogged, we recommend replacing the rocker arm/lash adjuster assembly if you're concerned about their condition or if the engine is exhibiting valve "tapping" noises.

11   Inspect all rocker arm shaft components. Look for cracks, worn or scored surfaces or other damage. Replace any parts found to be damaged or worn excessively.

Installation
Refer to illustrations 10.13, 10.14, 10.16 and 10.17
12   Prior to installation, the hydraulic lash adjusters must be partially full of engine oil - indicated by little or no plunger action when the adjuster is depressed. If there's excessive plunger travel, place the rocker arm assembly into clean engine oil and pump the plunger until the plunger travel is eliminated. **Note:** *If the plunger still travels within the rocker arm when full of oil, it's defective and the rocker*

arm assembly must be replaced.

13   Rotate the engine until the dowel pin on the front of each camshaft is in the correct off-set location **(see illustration)**. This will allow the camshaft lobes to be positioned down and away to ease the rocker arm and shaft installation.

14   Install all of the rocker shaft components onto the shafts in their original order **(see illustration)**. **Note:** *On 2004 and later 3.8L engines, the intake rocker shaft has 4 bolt holes and the exhaust shaft has 6.*

15   On 2003 and earlier models, install the rocker shaft clips onto the rocker shafts with the open sides of the clips sliding over the shaft facing the valves.

16   On 2003 and earlier 3.0L engines, install

10.17 Rocker arm shaft bolt TIGHTENING sequence

11.5 On the left (front) cylinder head, remove the thrust case and carefully withdraw the camshaft

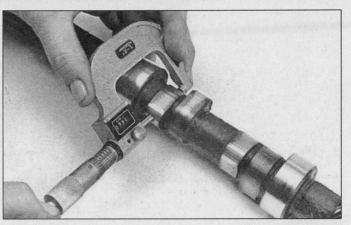

11.15 Check the camshaft lobes for wear with a micrometer

the rocker arm assemblies with the rocker shaft notches positioned properly **(see illustration)**. The slotted shaft oil holes on the 3.8L intake rocker shafts must face downward. There are notches at the ends of the exhaust rocker shafts on 2004 and later 3.8L engines. These notches must be positioned toward the outer edge of the engine.

17 Tighten the rocker arm shaft bolts in the sequence shown **(see illustration)** in three steps to the torque listed in this Chapter's Specifications. On 2007 and later MIVEC engines, refer to Chapter 1 and adjust the intake valves.

18 The remaining installation steps are the reverse of removal. Run the engine and check for oil leaks and proper operation.

19 When re-starting the engine after replacing the rocker arm/lash adjusters, the adjusters will normally make "tapping" noises due to air in the lubrication system. To bleed air from the lash adjusters, start the engine and allow it to reach operating temperature, slowly raise the speed of the engine from idle to 3,000 rpm and back to idle over a one minute period. If, after several attempts, the adjuster(s) do not become silent, replace the defective rocker arm/lash adjuster assembly.

---

11 Camshafts - removal, inspection and installation

Removal

Refer to illustration 11.5

1 Refer to Section 12 and remove the cylinder head(s). **Note:** *Camshaft removal clearance may exist on some models. Check your vehicle before removing the cylinder heads.*

2 If you're working on the rear cylinder head on a 2003 or earlier model, remove the distributor.

3 Remove the rocker arm shaft assemblies (see Section 10) and all other interfering components.

2003 and earlier models

4 Carefully withdraw the camshaft from the distributor opening in the rear of the cylinder head. **Caution:** *Do not damage the cam-*

shaft lobes or bearing journals during removal. **Note:** *If you are removing both camshafts, identify each one as it is removed from the cylinder head so that it may be installed back in its original location.*

5 On the front cylinder head, remove the thrust case from the rear of the cylinder head and withdraw the camshaft **(see illustration)**. **Caution:** *Do not damage the camshaft lobes or bearing journals during removal.*

2004 and later models
Left cylinder head

6 Remove the camshaft position sensor, its O-ring, support and the CMP sensor cylinder (see Chapter 6).

7 Remove the camshaft sprocket.

Right cylinder head

8 Remove the camshaft sprocket.

9 Disconnect the wiring from the oil control valve assembly on MIVEC engines. Also remove the MIVEC oil tube and the oil control valve assembly. On non-MIVEC engines, remove the thrust case from the rear of the cylinder head.

Both cylinder heads

10 Carefully slide the camshaft out of the opening in the rear of the cylinder head. **Caution:** *Do not damage the camshaft lobes or bearing journals.* **Note:** *If you're removing both camshafts, identify them so they can be installed in their original positions.*

All models

11 Remove the camshaft seal(s) from the cylinder head(s) (see Section 9).

Inspection

Refer to illustration 11.15

12 Using a suitable scraper, remove all traces of gasket material from all gasket surfaces. **Caution:** *When removing gasket material from any surface, especially aluminum, be very careful not to scratch or gouge the gasket surface. Any damage to the surface may a leak after reassembly. Gasket removal solvents are available from auto parts stores and may prove helpful.*

13 Thoroughly clean the camshaft(s) with a

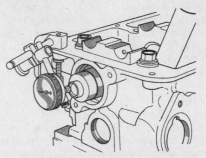

11.18 Measure the camshaft endplay with a dial indicator positioned on the sprocket end of the camshaft as shown

rag soaked in lacquer thinner or acetone. Visually inspect the camshaft(s) for wear and/or damage to the lobe surfaces, bearing journals and seal contact surfaces. Visually inspect the camshaft bearing surfaces in the cylinder head(s) for scoring and other damage. Cylinder head replacement may be necessary if the camshaft bearing surfaces in the head are damaged or excessively worn.

14 Replace any component that fails the above inspections.

15 Using a micrometer, check the camshaft lobes for excessive wear by measuring the center of the lobe (the area the rocker arm roller rides on) and comparing it with the edges of the lobes (the area the rocker arm roller does not ride on) **(see illustration)**. If any wear is indicated, check the corresponding rocker arm. Replace the camshaft and rocker arms if necessary.

Camshaft endplay measurement

Refer to illustration 11.18

16 Lubricate the camshaft(s) and cylinder head bearing journals with clean engine oil.

17 Carefully insert the camshaft into the cylinder head and install the thrust case or distributor as applicable. Tighten the bolts to the torque listed in this Chapter's Specifications.

18 Install a dial indicator set up on the cylinder head and place the indicator tip on the camshaft at the sprocket end **(see illustration)**.

11.20 Prior to installing the camshaft, lubricate the bearing journals, thrust surfaces and lobes with engine assembly lube or clean engine oil

19   Using a screwdriver, carefully pry the camshaft to the rear of the cylinder head until it stops. Zero the dial indicator and pry the camshaft forward. The amount of indicator travel is the camshaft endplay. Compare the endplay measurement with the tolerance listed in this Chapter's Specifications. If the endplay is excessive, check the camshaft and cylinder head thrust bearing surfaces for wear and replace components as necessary.

Installation

Refer to illustration 11.20

20   Very carefully clean the camshaft and bearing journals. Liberally coat the bearing journals, lobes and thrust bearing surfaces of the camshaft with engine assembly lube or engine oil **(see illustration)**.

21   Carefully insert the camshaft into the cylinder head. On the left side cylinder head,

install the thrust case, using a new O-ring, and tighten the bolts to the torque listed in this Chapter's Specifications.

22   Install a new camshaft oil seal in the cylinder head (see Section 9).

23   Inspect the cylinder head bolts and install the cylinder head(s) (see Section 12).

24   If removed from 2003 and earlier models, install the distributor using a new O-ring (see Chapter 5).

25   The remaining installation steps are the reverse of removal. Check and adjust the ignition timing (see Chapter 5). Check for leaks and proper operation.

12   Cylinder head - removal and installation

Warning: *Allow the engine to cool completely before beginning this procedure.*

Removal

Refer to illustrations 12.19a and 12.19b

1   Position the number one piston at Top Dead Center (see Section 3).

2   Disconnect the cable from the negative battery terminal (see Chapter 5).

3   Drain the cooling system, remove the spark plugs and spark plug wires (see Chapter 1). **Note:** *Leave the plug wires attached to the distributor cap.*

4   Remove the upper and lower intake manifolds (see Section 5).

5   If you are removing the rear cylinder

head, remove the distributor (see Chapter 5).

6   Remove the coolant crossover housing bolts and separate the assembly from the rear of the cylinder heads.

7   Remove the rocker arm shaft assemblies (see Section 10).

8   If you are removing the rear cylinder head, remove the bolts securing the power steering reservoir and hoses to the cylinder head and position them out of the way.

9   Remove the engine bracket from the front of the rear cylinder head.

10   Remove the exhaust manifold(s) (see Section 6).

11   Remove the EGR solenoid/transducer assembly and EGR valve from the rear cylinder head (see Chapter 6).

12   Remove the timing belt (see Section 7).

13   Remove the camshaft sprocket(s) (see Section 9).

14   Clearly label and disconnect any hoses, lines, brackets or electrical connections that may interfere with cylinder head removal.

15   Loosen the cylinder head bolts, 1/4-turn at a time, in the reverse order of the tightening sequence **(see illustration 12.24)** until they can be removed by hand. **Note:** *Mitsubishi tool MD998051 or its equivalent is recommended.*

16   Carefully lift the cylinder head straight up and place it on wood blocks to prevent damage to the sealing surfaces. If the head sticks to the engine block, dislodge it by placing a wood block against the head casting and tapping the wood with a hammer or by prying the head with a prybar placed carefully on a casting protrusion.

17   Remove all traces of old gasket material from the block and head. Special gasket removal solvents that soften gaskets and make removal much easier are available at auto parts stores. **Caution:** *The cylinder head is aluminum, be very careful not to gouge the sealing surfaces.* When working on the block, place clean shop rags into the cylinders to help keep out debris. Use a vacuum to remove any contamination from the engine. Use a tap of the correct size to chase the threads in the engine block. Clean and inspect all threaded fasteners for damage.

18   Inspect the cylinder head bolt threads for "necking," where the diameter of threads

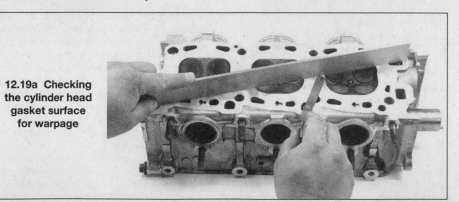

12.19a Checking the cylinder head gasket surface for warpage

12.19b Checking the engine block head gasket surface for warpage

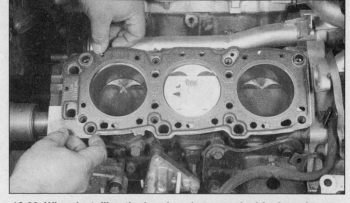

12.22 When installing the head gasket onto the block, make sure all passages in the block align with the holes in the gasket

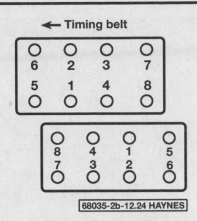

12.24 Cylinder head bolt
TIGHTENING sequence

13.5 Engine oil dipstick tube
mounting bolt

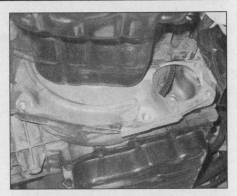

13.8 After removing the starter motor and
the engine-to-transmission support
brackets, remove the flywheel/
driveplate inspection cover

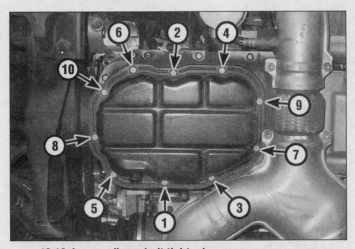

13.10 Lower oil pan bolt tightening sequence - reverse
sequence for removal

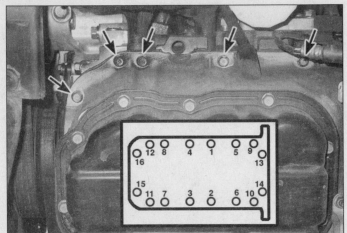

13.11 Upper oil pan bolt tightening sequence - reverse
sequence for removal

narrow due to bolt stretching. If any cylinder head bolt exhibits damage or necking, it must be replaced. **Note:** *Be sure to check each cylinder head bolt for any signs of stretching or thread damage. Consult with a dealer parts department or machine shop/auto parts department. Replace any damaged cylinder head bolts with new head bolts.*

19   Using a precision straightedge and feeler gauge, check all gasket surfaces for warpage **(see illustrations)**.

20   If the warpage on any surface exceeds the limits listed in this Chapter's Specifications, the discrepant component must be replaced or resurfaced by an automotive machine shop.

Installation

Refer to illustrations 12.22 and 12.24

21   Install the camshaft(s) if removed (see Section 11).

22   Place a new gasket on the engine block **(see illustration)**. Use no sealer unless indicated by the gasket manufacturer. Note any directions printed on the gasket such as "Front" or "This side up." Place the cylinder head(s) in position on the engine block.

23   Install the washers onto the cylinder head bolts with the rounded shoulders facing

up. Apply clean engine oil to the cylinder head bolt threads, under their heads and to any washers. Install the washers (if used) with the chamfers facing up.

24   Tighten the cylinder head bolts in the sequence shown **(see illustration)** progressing in three stages to the torque listed in this Chapter's Specifications.

25   Install the coolant crossover housing onto the rear of the cylinder heads. Be sure to install a new O-ring onto the coolant inlet pipe. Torque the coolant crossover housing to the Specifications listed in this Chapter.

26   The remaining installation steps are the reverse of removal.

27   Change the engine oil and filter, then refill the cooling system (see Chapter 1).

28   Start the engine and let it run until normal operating temperature is reached. Check for leaks and proper operation.

13   Oil pan - removal and installation

Removal

Refer to illustrations 13.5, 13.8, 13.10, 13.11, 13.12a, 13.12b, 13.14a and 13.14b

1   Disconnect the cable from the negative

battery terminal (see Chapter 5).

2   Raise the vehicle and support it securely on jackstands.

3   Remove the accessory drivebelt splash shield (see Chapter 1).

4   Drain the engine oil (see Chapter 1).

5   Remove the dipstick tube **(see illustration)**.

6   Remove the starter motor (see Chapter 5).

7   Remove the engine-to-transaxle support brackets.

8   Remove the flywheel/driveplate inspection cover **(see illustration)**.

9   Remove the front exhaust pipe/catalytic converter assembly (see Chapter 4).

10   Remove the lower oil pan mounting bolts **(see illustration)**. If the pan is stuck, tap it with a soft-face hammer or place a wood block against the pan and tap the wood block with a hammer.

11   Remove the upper oil pan mounting bolts **(see illustration)** and separate the oil pan from the engine block enough to facilitate oil pump pick-up tube removal. **Caution:** *If you're wedging something between the oil pan and the engine block to separate them, be extremely careful not to gouge or nick the gasket surface of either part; an oil leak could result.*

13.12a Lower the front of the oil pan to access the oil pump pick-up tube and remove the mounting bolts . . .

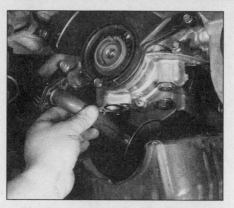

13.12b . . . then remove the oil pump pick-up tube from the pump body

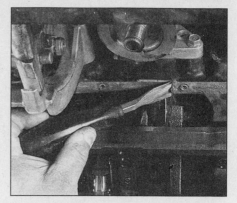

13.14a Thoroughly clean the oil pan and engine block gasket surfaces with a scraper to remove all traces of old gasket material

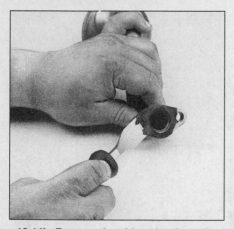

13.14b Remove the old gasket from the oil pump pick-up tube

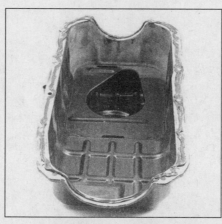

13.15 Apply a 1/8-inch bead of RTV sealant to the oil pan sealing surface as shown - stay on the inside of the bolt holes

12   Remove the oil pump pick-up tube and screen assembly **(see illustrations)**.
13   Remove the oil pan from the vehicle.
14   Thoroughly clean all gasket sealing surfaces. Use a scraper to remove all traces of old gasket material **(see illustrations)**. Gasket removal solvents are available at auto parts stores and may prove helpful. Check the oil pan sealing surface for distortion. Straighten or replace as necessary. After cleaning and straightening (if necessary), wipe the gasket surfaces of the pan and block clean with a rag soaked in lacquer thinner or acetone.

Installation

Refer to illustration 13.15
15   Apply a 1/8-inch bead of RTV sealant to the oil pan as shown **(see illustration)**. Also apply a light coating of RTV sealant to the underside of the oil pan bolt heads.
16   Install the oil pump pick-up tube. Tighten the bolts to the torque listed in this Chapter's Specifications.
17   Place the upper oil pan against the engine block and install the bolts. Tighten the bolts to the torque listed in this Chapter's Specifications following the torque sequence

shown in **illustration 13.11**.
18   Place the lower oil pan against the upper oil pan. Tighten the bolts to the torque listed in this Chapter's Specifications following the sequence shown in **illustration 13.10**.
19   The remaining installation steps are the reverse of removal.
20   Lower the vehicle and fill the crankcase with the proper quantity and grade of engine oil (see *Recommended lubricants and fluids* at the beginning of Chapter 1) and run the engine, checking for leaks. Road test the vehicle and check for leaks again.

14 Oil pump - removal, inspection and installation

Removal

Refer to illustrations 14.7, 14.8, 14.9 and 14.10
1   Disconnect the cable from the negative battery terminal (see Chapter 5).
2   Raise the vehicle and support it securely on jackstands.
3   Remove the drivebelts (see Chapter 1).
4   Remove the timing belt (see Section 7)

and crankshaft sprocket and Woodruff key (see Section 8).
5   Remove the oil pan (see Section 13).
6   If equipped, remove the air conditioning compressor bracket from the engine. **Warning:** *The air conditioning system is under high pressure. Don't disconnect any of the refrigerant lines. After unbolting the air conditioning compressor from its bracket, position it out of the way and secure it with wire or rope.*
7   On 2004 and later models, remove the oil filter, the filter shield, the oil filter housing and its gasket from the front of the engine. Remove the bolts and detach the oil pump assembly from the engine **(see illustration)**. **Caution:** *If the pump doesn't come off by hand, tap it gently with a soft-faced hammer or pry on a casting boss*.
8   Remove the oil filter passage O-ring seals and discard them. They may stick to the engine block **(see illustration)** or remain in the oil pump housing.
9   Remove the oil pump rotor cover **(see illustration)**.
10   New rotors are manufactured with arrows on them which are aligned at installation. If both arrows are not clearly visible **(see illustration)**, use a permanent marker to match-mark the rotors so they can be installed back in their original position. Remove the inner and outer rotor from the body. **Caution:** *Be very careful with these components. Close tolerances are critical in creating the correct oil pressure. Any nicks or other damage will require replacement of the complete pump assembly.*
11   Using a hammer and drift, carefully and evenly drive the crankshaft front seal from the oil pump housing and discard it.
12   Disassemble the oil pressure relief valve assembly, taking note of the way the relief valve piston is installed. Unscrew the cap bolt **(see illustration 14.10)** and remove the bolt, washer, spring and relief valve.
13   Thoroughly clean all gasket sealing surfaces. Use a scraper to remove all traces of old gasket material. Gasket removal solvents are available at auto parts stores and may prove helpful. Check the oil pan sealing sur-

14.7 Remove the oil pump assembly mounting bolts and detach it from the engine - bolt (A) also secures an additional bracket (if equipped)

14.8 The oil filter passage O-ring seals might remain attached to the engine block - be sure to install new ones

face for distortion. Straighten or replace as necessary. After removing the residual gasket material, wipe the gasket surfaces of the oil pan and block clean with a rag soaked in lacquer thinner or acetone.

Inspection

Refer to illustrations 14.16a, 14.16b and 14.16c

14   Clean all oil pump components with sol-vent and inspect them for excessive wear and/or damage. Replace as required. **Note:** *If either rotor is damaged, they must be replaced as a set.*

15   Inspect the oil pressure relief valve piston sliding surface and valve spring for damage. **Note:** *If either the spring or the valve is damaged, they must be replaced as a set.*

16   Install the rotors into the pump housing with the match-marks aligned. Check the oil pump rotor clearances using a precision straightedge and feeler gauges **(see illustrations)**. Compare the results to the tolerances listed in this Chapter's Specifications. Replace both rotors if any clearance is out of tolerance.

14.9 Remove the rotor cover mounting screws

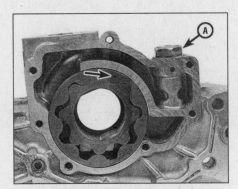

14.10 The alignment mark has worn off the inner rotor on this oil pump; in this case, use a permanent marker to match-mark the rotors for reinstallation; to remove the oil pressure relief spring and valve, remove this bolt (A)

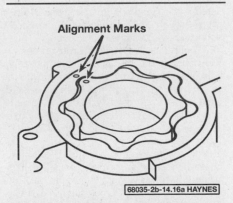

14.16a Install the rotors into the oil pump body with the match-marks aligned

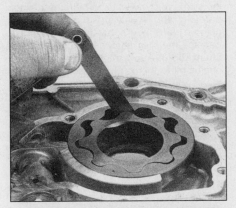

14.16b Use a feeler gauge to measure the inner rotor-to-outer rotor lobe clearance

14.16c Measuring the outer rotor-to-pump body clearance

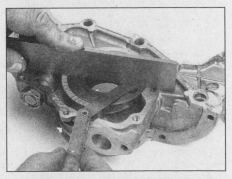

14.16d Place a precision straightedge over the rotors and measure the clearance between the rotors and the straightedge to determine the rotor-to-cover clearance

14.19 Install new O-ring seals on the oil filter passages

15.4 Remove the driveplate from the crankshaft

Installation

Refer to illustration 14.19

17   Lubricate the relief valve piston, piston bore and spring with clean engine oil. Install the relief valve piston into the bore maintaining original orientation followed by the spring and cap bolt. Tighten the cap bolt to the torque listed in this Chapter's Specifications. **Note:** *If the relief valve piston is installed incorrectly, serious engine damage could occur.*

18   Lubricate the oil pump rotor recess in the housing and the inner and outer rotors with clean engine oil. Install the rotors into the pump housing with the match-marks aligned. Next, fill the rotor cavity with clean engine oil and install the cover. Tighten the cover screws to the torque listed in this Chapter's Specifications.

19   Install new O-ring seals in the oil pump passages located on the pump body **(see illustration)**. If necessary, apply a light coating of grease on the O-rings to hold them in place.

20   Install the new crankshaft front seal into the oil pump housing (see Section 8).

21   Apply a 1/8-inch bead of RTV sealant to the oil pump body sealing surface (along the grooves in the case and passing around the inside edge of the bolt holes), and position the pump assembly on the block, aligning the inner rotor and crankshaft drive flats. Install the mounting bolts.

22   If equipped, install the air conditioning bracket onto the engine (one bolt secures both the air conditioning bracket and the oil pump housing).

23   Tighten the oil pump attaching bolts **(see illustration 14.7)** to the torque listed in this Chapter's Specifications.

24   Install the Woodruff key, crankshaft timing belt sprocket (see Section 8) and timing belt (see Section 7).

25   Install the oil pan (see Section 13).

26   The remaining installation steps are the reverse of removal.

27   Allow the sealant to cure the amount of time indicated by the manufacturer before adding oil to the engine.

28   Change the oil filter then lower the vehicle and fill the crankcase with the proper quantity and grade of oil (see Chapter 1).

29   Connect the negative battery cable to the battery.

30   Start the engine and check for leaks.

15   Driveplate - removal and installation

Removal

Refer to illustration 15.4

1   Remove the transaxle (see Chapter 7).

2   To ensure correct alignment during reinstallation, match-mark the backing plate and driveplate to the crankshaft before removal.

3   Remove the bolts securing the driveplate to the crankshaft. A tool is available a most auto parts stores to hold the driveplate while loosening the bolts, if the tool is not available, wedge a screwdriver in the ring gear teeth to jam the driveplate.

4   Remove the driveplate from the crankshaft **(see illustration)**.

5   Clean the driveplate to remove any grease and oil. Inspect it for cracks, distortion and missing or excessively worn ring gear teeth. Replace if necessary.

6   Clean and inspect the mating surfaces of the driveplate and the crankshaft. Check the crankshaft rear main seal for leakage; if leakage is evident replace it before reinstalling the driveplate (see Section 16).

Installation

8   Position the driveplate and backing plate against the crankshaft. Align the previously applied match-marks. Before installing the bolts, apply thread locking compound to the threads.

9   Hold the driveplate with the special holding tool, or wedge a screwdriver in the ring gear teeth to keep the driveplate from turning as you tighten the bolts in a crisscross pattern to the torque listed in this Chapter's Specifications.

10   The remaining installation steps are the reverse of removal.

16   Rear main oil seal - replacement

Refer to illustrations 16.3, 16.6 and 16.12

1   The crankshaft rear main oil seal is pressed into a retainer and bolted to the rear of the engine block.

2   Remove the driveplate (see Section 15).

3   The crankshaft rear main oil seal can be replaced without removing the oil pan or seal retainer. However, this method is NOT recommended because the lip of the seal is quite stiff and it's possible to cock the seal in the retainer bore or damage it during installation. If you want to take the chance, carefully and evenly pry out the old seal using a flat blade screwdriver - do not to damage the crankshaft sealing surface **(see illustration)**. Apply a light coating of clean engine oil to the crankshaft seal journal and the lip of the new seal then carefully tap the new seal into place using a hammer and socket. The seal lip is stiff, so carefully work it onto the seal journal of the crankshaft with a smooth object like the rounded end of a socket extension as you tap the seal into place **(see illustration 16.12)**. Don't force it or you may damage the seal.

4   The following method is recommended and requires removal of the oil pan (see Section 13).

5   Remove the mounting bolts from the

crankshaft rear seal retainer and separate the retainer from the engine block.

6   Using a hammer and drift, carefully drive the old seal out of the retainer and discard it **(see illustration)**.

7   Thoroughly clean all gasket sealing surfaces. Use a scraper to remove all traces of old gasket material. Gasket removal solvents are available at auto parts stores and may prove helpful. Check the oil pan sealing surface for distortion. Straighten or replace as necessary. After removing the residual gasket material, wipe the gasket surfaces clean using a rag soaked in lacquer thinner or acetone.

8   Thoroughly clean and inspect the seal bore and sealing surface on the crankshaft. Minor imperfections can be removed with fine emery cloth. If there is a groove worn in the crankshaft sealing surface (from contact with the seal), installing a new seal will probably not stop the leak.

9   Install the new seal into the retainer using a socket or block of wood and a hammer. Drive it in until it's flush with the retainer.

10   Apply a 1/8-inch bead of RTV sealant to the retainer gasket sealing surface.

11   Lubricate the lip of the new seal and the crankshaft sealing surface with a light coat of clean engine oil.

12   Place the seal retainer in position on the engine block and install the mounting bolts. The seal lip is stiff, so carefully work it onto the seal journal of the crankshaft with a smooth object like the rounded end of a socket extension as you tap the seal into place **(see illustration)**. Don't force it or you may damage the seal. Tighten the bolts to the torque listed in this Chapter's Specifications.

13   Install the oil pan (see Section 13).

14   The remaining installation steps are the reverse of removal.

16.3 Carefully pry the crankshaft seal out of the bore - DO NOT nick or scratch the crankshaft or seal bore

17   Engine mounts - check and replacement

1   Engine mounts seldom require attention, but broken or deteriorated mounts should be replaced immediately or the added strain placed on the driveline components may cause damage or wear.

Check

2   During the check, the engine must be raised slightly to relieve the weight from the mounts.

3   Raise the vehicle and support it securely on jackstands, then position a jack under the engine oil pan. Place a large wood block between the jack head and the oil pan to prevent oil pan damage, then carefully raise the engine just enough to take the weight off the mounts. **Warning:** *DO NOT place any part of your body under the engine when it's supported only by a jack!*

4   Inspect the mounts to see if the rubber is cracked, hardened or separated from the metal backing. Sometimes the rubber will split right down the center.

5   Check for relative movement between the mount plates and the engine or frame. Use a large screwdriver or pry bar to attempt to move the mounts. If movement is noted, lower the engine and tighten the mount fasteners.

6   Rubber preservative may be applied to the mounts to slow deterioration.

Replacement
Refer to illustrations 17.10a, 17.10b, 17.10c, 17.10d, 17.11a and 17.11b

7   Disconnect the negative battery cable (see Chapter 5).

8   Raise the vehicle and support it securely on jackstands.

9   Place a floor jack under the engine with a wood block between the jack head and oil pan and raise the engine slightly to relieve the weight from the mount to be replaced.

16.6 With the seal retainer supported on wood blocks, use a hammer and drift to drive the seal out of the retainer

16.12 Using a rounded object like a socket extension, carefully work the seal onto the crankshaft

10   Remove the fasteners and detach the mount from the frame and engine **(see illustrations)**. **Caution:** *Do not disconnect more than one mount at a time, except during engine/transaxle removal.*

11   Installation is the reverse of removal. Install the engine mount and transaxle mount with the arrow marks pointing in the proper direction **(see illustrations)**. Install the front roll stopper with the small hole in its bracket

toward the front of the vehicle. Use thread locking compound on the mount bolts and be sure to tighten them securely.

17.10a Passenger's side engine mount through-bolt

17.10b Transaxle mount details

17.10c Front roll stopper through-bolt

17.10d Rear roll stopper through-bolt

17.11a Position the engine mount with the arrows in the direction shown for proper alignment

17.11b Position the transaxle mount with the arrows in the direction shown for proper alignment

Chapter 2 Part C
General engine overhaul procedures

Contents

Specifications

General

Displacement
- 2.4L DOHC and 2.4L SOHC models ... 143 cubic inches
- 3.0L V6 models ... 181 cubic inches
- 3.8L V6 models ... 234 cubic inches

Bore and Stroke
- 2.4L DOHC and 2.4L SOHC models ... 3.41 x 3.94 inches (86.5 x 100 mm)
- 3.0L V6 models ... 3.59 x 2.99 inches (91.1 x 76.0 mm)
- 3.8L V6 models ... 3.74 x 3.54 inches (95.0 x 90.0 mm)

Cylinder compression
- 2.4L DOHC models
  - Standard ... 206 psi (1,450 kPa)
  - Minimum ... 157 psi (1,105 kPa)
- 2.4L SOHC models
  - Standard ... 192 psi (1,350 kPa)
  - Minimum ... 145 psi (1,020 kPa)
- 3.0L V6 models
  - Standard ... 119 psi (824 kPa)
  - Minimum ... 83 psi (575 kPa)
- 3.8L V6 models
  - Standard ... 225 psi (1,550 kPa)
  - Minimum ... 161 psi (1,110 kPa)

Oil pressure
- 2.4L DOHC models
  - At curb idle ... 4 psi (25 kPa)
  - At 3,000 rpm ... 25 to 80 psi (170 to 550 kPa)
- 2.4L SOHC models
  - At curb idle ... 4.2 psi (29 kPa)
  - At 3,000 rpm ... 43 to 100 psi (294 to 686 kPa)
- V6 models
  - At curb idle ... 11 psi (80 kPa)
  - At 3,000 rpm ... 43 to 100 psi (294 to 686 kPa)

Torque specifications

	Ft-lbs	Nm

Note: *One foot-pound (ft-lb) of torque is equivalent to 12 inch-pounds (in-lbs) of torque. Torque values below approximately 15 foot-pounds are expressed in inch-pounds, because most foot-pound torque wrenches are not accurate at these smaller values.*

Connecting rod bearing cap bolts
- 2.4L DOHC and 2.4L SOHC models
  - Step 1 ... 168 in-lbs — 19
  - Step 2 ... Tighten an additional 1/4-turn (90-degrees)
- 3.0L V6 models ... 37 — 51
- 3.8L V6 models
  - Step 1 ... 19 to 21 — 25 to 29
  - Step 2 ... Tighten an additional 90-degrees

Main bearing assembly
- 2.4L DOHC and 2.4L SOHC models
  - Step 1 ... 18 — 25
  - Step 2 ... Tighten an additional 1/4-turn (90-degrees)
- 3.0L V6 models ... 69 — 93
- 3.8L V6 models
  - Step 1 ... 51 to 57 — 70 to 78
  - Step 2 ... Tighten an additional 90-degrees

1.3 A crankshaft having a main bearing journal ground

1.1 An engine block being bored. An engine rebuilder will use special machinery to recondition the cylinder bores

1.2 If the cylinders are bored, the machine shop will normally hone the engine on a machine like this

1   General information - engine overhaul

Refer to illustrations 1.1, 1.2, 1.3, 1.4, 1.5 and 1.6

Included in this portion of Chapter 2 are general information and diagnostic testing procedures for determining the overall mechanical condition of your engine.

The information ranges from advice concerning preparation for an overhaul and the purchase of replacement parts and/or components to detailed, step-by-step procedures covering removal and installation.

The following Sections have been written to help you determine whether your engine needs to be overhauled and how to remove and install it once you've determined it needs to be rebuilt. For information concerning in-vehicle engine repair, see Chapter 2A or 2B.

The Specifications included in this Part are general in nature and include only those necessary for testing the oil pressure and checking the engine compression. Refer to Chapter 2A or 2B for additional engine Specifications.

It's not always easy to determine when, or if, an engine should be completely overhauled, because a number of factors must be considered.

High mileage is not necessarily an indication that an overhaul is needed, while low mileage doesn't preclude the need for an overhaul. Frequency of servicing is probably the most important consideration. An engine that's had regular and frequent oil and filter changes, as well as other required maintenance, will most likely give many thousands of miles of reliable service. Conversely, a neglected engine may require an overhaul very early in its service life.

Excessive oil consumption is an indication that piston rings, valve seals and/or valve guides are in need of attention. Make sure that oil leaks aren't responsible before deciding that the rings and/or guides are bad. Perform a cylinder compression check to determine the extent of the work required (see Section 3). Also check the vacuum readings under various conditions (see Section 4).

Check the oil pressure with a gauge installed in place of the oil pressure sending unit and compare it to this Chapter's Specifications (see Section 2). If it's extremely low, the bearings and/or oil pump are probably worn out.

Loss of power, rough running, knocking or metallic engine noises, excessive valve train noise and high fuel consumption rates may also point to the need for an overhaul, especially if they're all present at the same time. If a complete tune-up doesn't remedy the situation, major mechanical work is the only solution.

An engine overhaul involves restoring the internal parts to the specifications of a new engine. During an overhaul, the piston rings are replaced and the cylinder walls are reconditioned (rebored and/or honed) **(see illustrations 1.1 and 1.2)**. If a rebore is done by an automotive machine shop, new oversize pistons will also be installed. The main bearings, connecting rod bearings and camshaft bearings are generally replaced with new ones and, if necessary, the crankshaft may be reground to restore the journals **(see illustration 1.3)**. Generally, the valves are serviced as well, since they're usually in less-than-perfect condition at this point. While the engine is being overhauled, other components, such as the distributor, starter and alternator, can be rebuilt as well. The end result should be similar to a new engine

1.4 A machinist checks for a bent connecting rod, using specialized equipment

that will give many trouble free miles. **Note:** *Critical cooling system components such as the hoses, drivebelts, thermostat and water pump should be replaced with new parts when an engine is overhauled. The radiator should be checked carefully to ensure that it isn't clogged or leaking (see Chapter 3). If you purchase a rebuilt engine or short block, some rebuilders will not warranty their engines unless the radiator has been professionally flushed. Also, we don't recommend overhauling the oil pump - always install a new one when an engine is rebuilt.*

Overhauling the internal components on today's engines is a difficult and time-consuming task which requires a significant amount of specialty tools and is best left to a professional engine rebuilder **(see illustrations 1.4, 1.5 and 1.6)**. A competent engine rebuilder will handle the inspection of your old parts and offer advice concerning the reconditioning or replacement of the original engine, never purchase parts or have machine work done on other components until the block has been thoroughly inspected by a professional machine shop. As a gen-

1.5 A bore gauge being used to check the main bearing bore

1.6 Uneven piston wear like this indicates a bent connecting rod

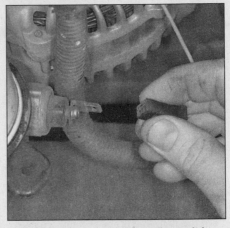

2.2a The oil pressure sending unit is located on the front of the engine block near the oil filter housing (2.4L DOHC and 1994 through 1998 2.4L SOHC engines)

2.2b The oil pressure sending unit is located on the front of the engine block near the timing belt (1999 and later 2.4L SOHC engines)

2.2c The oil pressure sending unit is located on the front of the engine block near the oil filter housing (3.0L V6 engines)

2.3 The oil pressure can be checked by removing the sending unit and installing a pressure gauge in its place

eral rule, time is the primary cost of an overhaul, especially since the vehicle may be tied up for a minimum of two weeks or more. Be aware that some engine builders only have the capability to rebuild the engine you bring them while other rebuilders have a large inventory of rebuilt exchange engines in stock. Also be aware that many machine shops could take as much as two weeks time to completely rebuild your engine depending on shop workload. Sometimes it makes more sense to simply exchange your engine for another engine that's already rebuilt to save time.

2 Oil pressure check

Refer to illustration 2.2a, 2.2b, 2.2c and 2.3

1   Low engine oil pressure can be a sign of an engine in need of rebuilding. A "low oil pressure" indicator (often called an "idiot light") is not a test of the oiling system. Such indicators only come on when the oil pres-

sure is dangerously low. Even a factory oil pressure gauge in the instrument panel is only a relative indication, although much better for driver information than a warning light. A better test is with a mechanical (not electrical) oil pressure gauge.

2   Locate the oil pressure sending unit:

a)   *On 2.4L DOHC and 1994 through 1998 2.4L SOHC engines, the oil pressure sending unit is located on the front side of the block on the oil filter housing* **(see illustration)**.

b)   *On 1999 and later 2.4L SOHC engines, the sending unit is located at the front side of the block* **(see illustration)**.

c)   *On V6 engines, the sending unit is located on the oil filter housing, on the front side of the block* **(see illustration)**.

3   Unscrew the oil pressure sending unit and screw in the hose for your oil pressure gauge **(see illustration)**. If necessary, install an adapter fitting. Use Teflon tape or thread sealant on the threads of the adapter and/or the fitting on the end of your gauge's hose.

4   Connect an accurate tachometer to the

engine, according to the tachometer manufacturer's instructions.

5   Check the oil pressure with the engine running (normal operating temperature) at the specified engine speed, and compare it to this Chapter's Specifications. If it's extremely low, the bearings and/or oil pump are probably worn out.

3 Cylinder compression check

Refer to illustration 3.6

1   A compression check will tell you what mechanical condition the upper end of your engine (pistons, rings, valves, head gaskets) is in. Specifically, it can tell you if the compression is down due to leakage caused by worn piston rings, defective valves and seats or a blown head gasket. **Note:** *The engine must be at normal operating temperature and the battery must be fully charged for this check.*

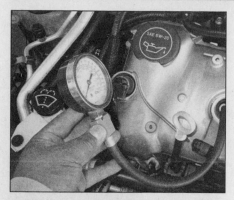

3.6 Use a compression gauge with a threaded fitting for the spark plug hole, not the type that requires hand pressure to maintain the seal

4.4 A simple vacuum gauge can be handy in diagnosing engine condition and performance

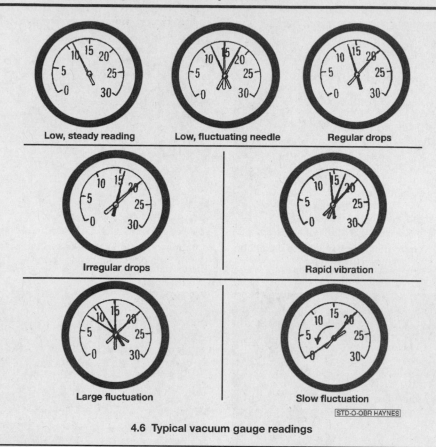

4.6 Typical vacuum gauge readings

2   Begin by cleaning the area around the spark plugs before you remove them (compressed air should be used, if available). The idea is to prevent dirt from getting into the cylinders as the compression check is being done.

3   Remove all of the spark plugs from the engine (see Chapter 1).

4   Block the throttle wide open.

5   Disconnect the primary (low voltage) wires from the distributor (1994 through 1998 2.4L SOHC or 3.0L V6 engines) or the ignition coils (2.4L DOHC and 1999 and later 2.4L SOHC engines) (see Chapter 5). Remove the fuel pump relay (see Chapter 4). The relays are located in the power distribution center in the engine compartment (see Chapter 12).

6   Install a compression gauge in the spark plug hole **(see illustration)**.

7   Crank the engine over at least seven compression strokes and watch the gauge. The compression should build up quickly in a healthy engine. Low compression on the first stroke, followed by gradually increasing pressure on successive strokes, indicates worn piston rings. A low compression reading on the first stroke, which doesn't build up during successive strokes, indicates leaking valves or a blown head gasket (a cracked head could also be the cause). Deposits on the

undersides of the valve heads can also cause low compression. Record the highest gauge reading obtained.

8   Repeat the procedure for the remaining cylinders and compare the results to this Chapter's Specifications.

9   Add some engine oil (about three squirts from a plunger-type oil can) to each cylinder, through the spark plug hole, and repeat the test.

10   If the compression increases after the oil is added, the piston rings are definitely worn. If the compression doesn't increase significantly, the leakage is occurring at the valves or head gasket. Leakage past the valves may be caused by burned valve seats and/or faces or warped, cracked or bent valves.

11   If two adjacent cylinders have equally low compression, there's a strong possibility that the head gasket between them is blown. The appearance of coolant in the combustion chambers or the crankcase would verify this condition.

12   If one cylinder is slightly lower than the others, and the engine has a slightly rough idle, a worn lobe on the camshaft could be the cause.

13   If the compression is unusually high, the combustion chambers are probably coated with carbon deposits. If that's the case, the cylinder head(s) should be removed and decarbonized.

14   If compression is way down or varies greatly between cylinders, it would be a good idea to have a leak-down test performed by

an automotive repair shop. This test will pinpoint exactly where the leakage is occurring and how severe it is.

4   Vacuum gauge diagnostic checks

Refer to illustrations 4.4 and 4.6

1   A vacuum gauge provides inexpensive but valuable information about what is going on in the engine. You can check for worn rings or cylinder walls, leaking head or intake manifold gaskets, incorrect carburetor adjustments, restricted exhaust, stuck or burned valves, weak valve springs, improper ignition or valve timing and ignition problems.

2   Unfortunately, vacuum gauge readings are easy to misinterpret, so they should be used in conjunction with other tests to confirm the diagnosis.

3   Both the absolute readings and the rate of needle movement are important for accurate interpretation. Most gauges measure vacuum in inches of mercury (in-Hg). The following references to vacuum assume the diagnosis is being performed at sea level. As elevation increases (or atmospheric pressure decreases), the reading will decrease. For every 1,000 foot increase in elevation above approximately 2000 feet, the gauge readings will decrease about one inch of mercury.

4   Connect the vacuum gauge directly to the intake manifold vacuum, not to ported (throttle body) vacuum **(see illustration)**. Be sure no hoses are left disconnected during

the test or false readings will result.

5   Before you begin the test, allow the engine to warm up completely. Block the wheels and set the parking brake. With the transaxle in Park, start the engine and allow it to run at normal idle speed. **Warning:** *Keep your hands and the vacuum gauge clear of the fans.*

6   Read the vacuum gauge; an average, healthy engine should normally produce about 17 to 22 in-Hg with a fairly steady needle **(see illustration)**. Refer to the following vacuum gauge readings and what they indicate about the engine's condition:

7   A low steady reading usually indicates a leaking gasket between the intake manifold and cylinder head(s) or throttle body, a leaky vacuum hose, late ignition timing or incorrect camshaft timing. Check ignition timing with a timing light and eliminate all other possible causes, utilizing the tests provided in this Chapter before you remove the timing chain cover to check the timing marks.

8   If the reading is three to eight inches below normal and it fluctuates at that low reading, suspect an intake manifold gasket leak at an intake port or a faulty fuel injector.

9   If the needle has regular drops of about two-to-four inches at a steady rate, the valves are probably leaking. Perform a compression check or leak-down test to confirm this.

10   An irregular drop or down-flick of the needle can be caused by a sticking valve or an ignition misfire. Perform a compression check or leak-down test and read the spark plugs.

11   A rapid vibration of about four in-Hg vibration at idle combined with exhaust smoke indicates worn valve guides. Perform a leak-down test to confirm this. If the rapid vibration occurs with an increase in engine speed, check for a leaking intake manifold gasket or head gasket, weak valve springs, burned valves or ignition misfire.

12   A slight fluctuation, say one inch up and down, may mean ignition problems. Check all the usual tune-up items and, if necessary, run the engine on an ignition analyzer.

13   If there is a large fluctuation, perform a compression or leak-down test to look for a weak or dead cylinder or a blown head gasket.

14   If the needle moves slowly through a wide range, check for a clogged PCV system, incorrect idle fuel mixture, throttle body or intake manifold gasket leaks.

15   Check for a slow return after revving the engine by quickly snapping the throttle open until the engine reaches about 2,500 rpm and let it shut. Normally the reading should drop to near zero, rise above normal idle reading (about 5 in-Hg over) and then return to the previous idle reading. If the vacuum returns slowly and doesn't peak when the throttle is snapped shut, the rings may be worn. If there is a long delay, look for a restricted exhaust system (often the muffler or catalytic converter). An easy way to check this is to temporarily disconnect the exhaust ahead of the suspected part and redo the test.

5   Engine rebuilding alternatives

The do-it-yourselfer is faced with a number of options when purchasing a rebuilt engine. The major considerations are cost, warranty, parts availability and the time required for the rebuilder to complete the project. The decision to replace the engine block, piston/connecting rod assemblies and crankshaft depends on the final inspection results of your engine. Only then can you make a cost effective decision whether to have your engine overhauled or simply purchase an exchange engine for your vehicle.

Some of the rebuilding alternatives include:

Individual parts - If the inspection procedures reveal that the engine block and most engine components are in reusable condition, purchasing individual parts and having a rebuilder rebuild your engine may be the most economical alternative. The block, crankshaft and piston/connecting rod assemblies should all be inspected carefully by a machine shop first.

Short block - A short block consists of an engine block with a crankshaft and piston/connecting rod assemblies already installed. All new bearings are incorporated and all clearances will be correct. The existing camshafts, valve train components, cylinder head and external parts can be bolted to the short block with little or no machine shop work necessary.

Long block - A long block consists of a short block plus an oil pump, oil pan, cylinder head, valve cover, camshaft and valve train components, timing sprockets and chain or gears and timing cover. All components are installed with new bearings, seals and gaskets incorporated throughout. The installation of manifolds and external parts is all that's necessary.

Low-mileage used engines - Some companies now offer low-mileage used engines which is a very cost effective way to get your vehicle up and running again. These engines often come from vehicles which have been in totaled in accidents or come from other countries which have a higher vehicle turn over rate. A low-mileage used engine also usually has a similar warranty like the newly remanufactured engines.

Give careful thought to which alternative is best for you and discuss the situation with local automotive machine shops, auto parts dealers and experienced rebuilders before ordering or purchasing replacement parts.

6   Engine removal - methods and precautions

Refer to illustrations 6.1, 6.2, 6.3 and 6.4

If you've decided that an engine must be removed for overhaul or major repair work, several preliminary steps should be taken. Read all removal and installation procedures carefully prior to committing to this job.

Locating a suitable place to work is extremely important. Adequate work space,

6.1 After tightly wrapping water-vulnerable components, use a spray cleaner on everything, with particular concentration on the greasiest areas, usually around the valve cover and lower edges of the block. If one section dries out, apply more cleaner

6.2 Depending on how dirty the engine is, let the cleaner soak in according to the directions and then hose off the grime and cleaner. Get the rinse water down into every area you can get at; then dry important components with a hair dryer or paper towels

6.3 Get an engine stand sturdy enough to firmly support the engine while you're working on it. Stay away from three-wheeled models: they have a tendency to tip over more easily, so get a four-wheeled unit.

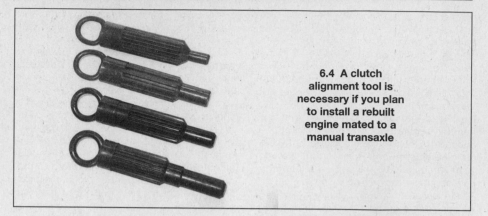

6.4 A clutch alignment tool is necessary if you plan to install a rebuilt engine mated to a manual transaxle

along with storage space for the vehicle, will be needed. If a shop or garage isn't available, at the very least a flat, level, clean work surface made of concrete or asphalt is required.

Cleaning the engine compartment and engine before beginning the removal procedure will help keep tools clean and organized **(see illustrations 6.1 and 6.2)**.

An engine hoist will also be necessary. Make sure the hoist is rated in excess of the combined weight of the engine and transaxle. Safety is of primary importance, considering the potential hazards involved in removing the engine from the vehicle.

If you're a novice at engine removal, get at least one helper. One person cannot easily do all the things you need to do to remove a big heavy engine and transaxle assembly from the engine compartment. Also helpful is to seek advice and assistance from someone who's experienced in engine removal.

Plan the operation ahead of time. Arrange for or obtain all of the tools and equipment you'll need prior to beginning the job **(see illustrations 6.3 and 6.4)**. Some of the equipment necessary to perform engine removal and installation safely and with relative ease are (in addition to a vehicle hoist and an engine hoist) a heavy duty floor jack (preferably fitted with a transmission jack head adapter), complete sets of wrenches and sockets as described in the front of this manual, wooden blocks, plenty of rags and cleaning solvent for mopping up spilled oil, coolant and gasoline.

Plan for the vehicle to be out of use for quite a while. A machine shop can do the work that is beyond the scope of the home mechanic. Machine shops often have a busy schedule, so before removing the engine, consult the shop for an estimate of how long it will take to rebuild or repair the components that may need work.

7 Engine - removal and installation

Refer to illustrations 7.8, 7.33 and 7.36

Warning 1: *Gasoline is extremely flammable, so take extra precautions when you work on any part of the fuel system. Don't smoke or allow open flames or bare light bulbs near the work area, and don't work in a garage where a gas-type appliance (such as a water heater or clothes dryer) is present. Since gasoline is carcinogenic, wear fuel-resistant gloves when there's a possibility of being exposed to fuel, and, if you spill any fuel on your skin, rinse it off immediately with soap and water. Mop up any spills immediately and do not store fuel-soaked rags where they could ignite. The fuel system is under constant pressure, so, if any fuel lines are to be disconnected, the fuel pressure in the system must be relieved first (see Chapter 4 for more information). When you perform any kind of work on the fuel system, wear safety glasses and have a Class B type fire extinguisher on hand.*

Warning 2: *The engine must be completely cool before beginning this procedure.*

Removal

1   Have the air conditioning system discharged by an automotive air conditioning technician.

2   Relieve the fuel system pressure (see Chapter 4).

3   Disconnect the cable from the negative battery terminal (see Chapter 5).

4   Place protective covers on the fenders and cowl and remove the hood (see Chapter 11).

5   Remove the air filter housing (see Chapter 4).

6   Disconnect the accelerator cable (and cruise control cable, if equipped) and bracket from the engine and position them aside.

7   Remove the battery and the battery tray (see Chapter 5).

8   Clearly label and disconnect all vacuum lines, emissions hoses, wiring harness connectors, ground straps and fuel lines. Masking tape and/or a touch up paint applicator work well for marking items **(see illustration)**. Take instant photos or sketch the locations of components and brackets.

9   Disconnect the electrical connectors

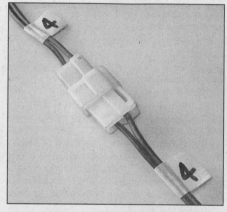

7.8 Label both ends of each wire and hose before disconnecting it

from the PCM (see Chapter 6). Also detach any other electrical connectors between the engine and the vehicle.

10   Detach the positive cable from the engine compartment fuse/relay box and the ground cable from the vehicle. Unbolt the fuse/relay box and position it out of the way.

11   Detach the electrical connectors from the battery tray support.

12   Loosen the front wheel lug nuts, then raise the vehicle and support it securely on jackstands.

13   Drain the cooling system (see Chapter 1).

14   Drain the engine oil and remove the drivebelts (see Chapter 1).

15   Remove the alternator and its brackets (see Chapter 5).

16   Remove the power steering pump and bracket (see Chapter 10).

17   Detach the lower radiator hose from the engine.

18   Lower the vehicle and detach the heater hoses at the firewall.

19   Detach the upper radiator hose from the thermostat housing.

20   Remove the radiator support brackets (see Chapter 3).

21   Remove the cooling fan(s), shroud(s) and radiator (see Chapter 3).

22   Disconnect the shift cable(s) from the transaxle (see Chapter 7A or 7B). Also disconnect any wiring harness connectors from the transaxle.

7.33 Paint an alignment mark on the driveplate and the torque converter to insure correct installation

7.36 Attach the chain to the lifting hangers - be sure the chain or sling, and the hardware used to attach it, are of adequate strength

23   Disconnect the upper air conditioning line from the condenser.

24   Disconnect the air conditioning lines at the compressor. Remove the air conditioning compressor (see Chapter 3).

25   Remove the power steering pump (see Chapter 10).

26   Raise the vehicle and support it securely on jackstands. Remove the front wheels.

27   Remove the driveaxles (see Chapter 8).

28   If equipped with a manual transaxle, disconnect the hydraulic line at the clutch release cylinder (see Chapter 8).

29   Unplug the oxygen sensor electrical connector(s).

30   Detach the exhaust pipe from the exhaust manifold(s) (see Chapter 4).

31   Detach the pressure hose from the power steering gear (see Chapter 10).

32   Remove the inspection cover from the bellhousing on the transaxle.

33   If equipped with an automatic transaxle, remove the torque converter bolts **(see illustration)**.

34   Remove the starter motor (see Chapter 5).

35   Locate the lifting brackets on the engine.

36   Roll the engine hoist into position and attach it to the lifting brackets with a length of heavy-duty chain or an engine lifting sling **(see illustration)**. Take up the slack in the sling or chain, but don't lift the engine. **Warning:** *DO NOT place any part of your body under the engine when it's supported only by a hoist or other lifting device.*

37   Remove the transaxle (see Chapter 7).

38   Remove the engine mount fasteners (see Chapter 2A or 2B).

39   Recheck to be sure nothing is still connecting the engine to the transaxle or vehicle. Disconnect anything still remaining.

40   Raise the engine slightly and inspect it thoroughly once more to make sure that *nothing* is still attached, then slowly raise the engine out of the engine compartment. Check

carefully to make sure nothing is hanging up.

41   Remove the flywheel/driveplate (see Chapter 2A or 2B) and mount the engine on an engine stand **(see illustration 6.3)**.

42   Inspect the engine and transaxle mounts (see Chapter 2A or 2B). If they're worn or damaged, replace them.

Installation

43   Install the flywheel/driveplate (see Chapter 2A or 2B).

44   If you're working on a vehicle with manual transaxle, install the clutch and pressure plate (see Chapter 8). Now is a good time to install a new clutch.

45   Carefully lower the engine into the engine compartment and then reattach it to the engine mounts (see Chapter 2A or 2B).

46   Install the transaxle (see Chapter 7) If you're working on a vehicle with an automatic transaxle, guide the torque converter into the crankshaft following the procedure outlined in Chapter 7B. Install the transaxle-to-engine bolts and tighten them securely. **Caution:** *DO NOT use the bolts to force the transaxle and engine together!*

47   Reinstall the remaining components in the reverse order of removal.

48   Add coolant, oil and transaxle fluid as needed.

49   Run the engine and check for leaks and proper operation of all accessories, then install the hood and test drive the vehicle.

50   Have the air conditioning system recharged and leak tested, if it was discharged.

---

8   Engine overhaul - disassembly sequence

---

1   It's much easier to remove the external components if it's mounted on a portable engine stand. A stand can often be rented quite cheaply from an equipment rental yard.

Before the engine is mounted on a stand, the flywheel/driveplate should be removed from the engine.

2   If a stand isn't available, it's possible to remove the external engine components with it blocked up on the floor. Be extra careful not to tip or drop the engine when working without a stand.

3   If you're going to obtain a rebuilt engine, all external components must come off first, to be transferred to the replacement engine. These components include:

> *Clutch and flywheel (models with manual transaxle)*
> *Driveplate (models with automatic transaxle)*
> *Ignition system components*
> *Emissions-related components*
> *Engine mounts and mount brackets*
> *Engine rear cover (spacer plate between flywheel/driveplate and engine block)*
> *Intake/exhaust manifolds*
> *Fuel injection components*
> *Oil filter*
> *Spark plug wires and spark plugs*
> *Thermostat and housing assembly*
> *Water pump*

Note: *When removing the external components from the engine, pay close attention to details that may be helpful or important during installation. Note the installed position of gaskets, seals, spacers, pins, brackets, washers, bolts and other small items.*

4   If you're going to obtain a short block (assembled engine block, crankshaft, pistons and connecting rods), then remove the timing belt, cylinder head, oil pan, oil pump pick-up tube, oil pump and water pump from your engine so that you can turn in your old short block to the rebuilder as a core. See *Engine rebuilding alternatives* for additional information regarding the different possibilities to be considered.

9.1 Before you try to remove the pistons, use a ridge reamer to remove the raised material (ridge) from the top of the cylinders

9.3 Checking the connecting rod endplay (side clearance)

9.4 If the connecting rods and caps are not marked, use permanent ink or paint to mark the caps to the rods by cylinder number (for example, this would be the No. 4 connecting rod)

9   Pistons and connecting rods - removal and installation

Removal

Refer to illustrations 9.1, 9.3, 9.4 and 9.6

Note: *Prior to removing the piston/connecting rod assemblies, remove the cylinder head and oil pan (see Chapter 2A).*

1   Use your fingernail to feel if a ridge has formed at the upper limit of ring travel (about 1/4-inch down from the top of each cylinder). If carbon deposits or cylinder wear have produced ridges, they must be completely removed with a special tool **(see illustration)**. Follow the manufacturer's instructions provided with the tool. Failure to remove the ridges before attempting to remove the piston/connecting rod assemblies may result in piston breakage.

2   After the cylinder ridges have been removed, turn the engine so the crankshaft is facing up.

3   Before the main bearing cap assembly and connecting rods are removed, check the connecting rod endplay with feeler gauges. Slide them between the first connecting rod and the crankshaft throw until the play is removed **(see illustration)**. Repeat this procedure for each connecting rod. The endplay is equal to the thickness of the feeler gauge(s). Check with an automotive machine shop for the endplay service limit (a typical end play limit should measure between 0.005 to 0.015 inch [0.127 to 0.369 mm]). If the play exceeds the service limit, new connecting rods will be required. If new rods (or a new crankshaft) are installed, the endplay may fall under the minimum allowable. If it does, the rods will have to be machined to restore it. If necessary, consult an automotive machine shop for advice.

4   Check the connecting rods and caps for identification marks. If they aren't plainly marked, use paint or marker to clearly identify each rod and cap (1, 2, 3, etc., depending

on the cylinder they're associated with) **(see illustration)**.

5   Loosen each of the connecting rod cap nuts 1/2-turn at a time until they can be removed by hand.

6   Remove the number one connecting rod cap and bearing insert. Don't drop the bearing insert out of the cap. Slip a short length of plastic or rubber hose over each connecting rod bolt to protect the crankshaft journal and cylinder wall as the rod is removed **(see illustration)**.

7   Remove the bearing insert and push the connecting rod/piston assembly out through the top of the engine. Use a wooden or plastic hammer handle to push on the upper bearing surface in the connecting rod. If resistance is felt, double-check to make sure that all of the ridge was removed from the cylinder.

8   Repeat the procedure for the remaining cylinders.

9   After removal, reassemble the connecting rod caps and bearing inserts in their respective connecting rods and install the cap bolts finger tight. Leaving the old bearing inserts in place until reassembly will help prevent the connecting rod bearing surfaces from being accidentally nicked or gouged.

10   The pistons and connecting rods are now ready for inspection and overhaul at an automotive machine shop. Be sure to include the connecting rod bolts in this check, if they are damaged in any way, or are "necked down," meaning slightly smaller in diameter in the threaded area, replace them (and the cap nuts) with new ones.

Piston ring installation

Refer to illustrations 9.13, 9.14, 9.15, 9.19a, 9.19b and 9.22

11   Before installing the new piston rings, the ring end gaps must be checked. It's assumed that the piston ring side clearance has been checked and verified correct.

12   Lay out the piston/connecting rod assemblies and the new ring sets so the ring sets will be matched with the same piston

9.6 Push a short section of plastic or rubber hose over the connecting rod bolts to prevent damage to the crankshaft journals during piston/rod removal

9.13 Install the piston ring into the cylinder then push it down into position using a piston so the ring will be square in the cylinder

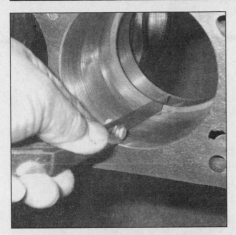

9.14 With the ring square in the cylinder, measure the ring end gap with a feeler gauge

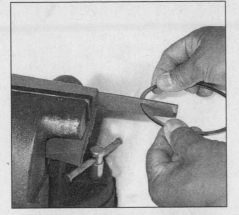

9.15 If the ring end gap is too small, clamp a file in a vise as shown and file the piston ring ends - be sure to remove all raised material

9.19a Installing the spacer/expander in the oil ring groove

and cylinder during the end gap measurement and engine assembly.

13   Insert the top (number one) ring into the first cylinder and square it up with the cylinder walls by pushing it in with the top of the piston **(see illustration)**. The ring should be near the bottom of the cylinder, at the lower limit of ring travel.

14   To measure the end gap, slip feeler gauges between the ends of the ring until a gauge equal to the gap width is found **(see illustration)**. The feeler gauge should slide between the ring ends with a slight amount of drag. A typical ring gap should fall between 0.010 and 0.020 inch [0.25 to 0.50 mm] for compression rings and up to 0.030 inch [0.76 mm] for the oil ring steel rails. If the gap is larger or smaller than specified, double-check to make sure you have the correct rings before proceeding.

15   If the gap is too small, it must be enlarged or the ring ends may come in contact with each other during engine operation, which can cause serious damage to the engine. If necessary, increase the end gaps by filing the ring ends very carefully with a fine file. Mount the file in a vise equipped with soft jaws, slip the ring over the file with the ends contacting the file face and slowly move the ring to remove material from the ends. When performing this operation, file only by pushing the ring from the outside end of the file towards the vise **(see illustration)**.

16   Excess end gap isn't critical unless it's greater than 0.040 inch (1.01 mm). Again, double-check to make sure you have the correct ring type.

17   Repeat the procedure for each ring that will be installed in the first cylinder and for each ring in the remaining cylinders. Remember to keep rings, pistons and cylinders matched up.

18   Once the ring end gaps have been checked/corrected, the rings can be installed on the pistons.

19   The oil control ring (lowest one on the piston) is usually installed first. It's composed of three separate components. Slip the

9.19b DO NOT use a piston ring installation tool when installing the oil control side rails

spacer/expander into the groove **(see illustration)**. If an anti-rotation tang is used, make sure it's inserted into the drilled hole in the ring groove. Next, install the upper side rail in the same manner **(see illustration)**. Don't use a piston ring installation tool on the oil ring side rails, as they may be damaged. Instead, place one end of the side rail into the groove between the spacer/expander and the ring land, hold it firmly in place and slide a finger around the piston while pushing the rail into the groove. Finally, install the lower side rail.

20   After the three oil ring components have been installed, check to make sure that both the upper and lower side rails can be rotated smoothly inside the ring grooves.

21   The number two (middle) ring is installed next. It's usually stamped with a mark which must face up, toward the top of the piston. Do not mix up the top and middle rings, as they have different cross-sections. **Note:** *Always follow the instructions printed on the ring package or box - different manufacturers may require different approaches.* Typically on the engines covered by this manual, the top ring

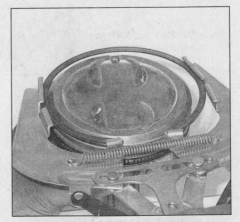

9.22 Use a piston ring installation tool to install the number 2 and the number 1 (top) rings - be sure the directional mark on the piston ring(s) is facing toward the top of the piston

will be marked with *1R* (four-cylinder) or *T* (V6), while the middle ring will be marked *2R* (four-cylinder) or *2T* (V6).

22   Use a piston ring installation tool and make sure the identification mark is facing the top of the piston, then slip the ring into the middle groove on the piston **(see illustration)**. Don't expand the ring any more than necessary to slide it over the piston.

23   Install the number one (top) ring in the same manner. Make sure the mark is facing up. Be careful not to confuse the number one and number two rings.

24   Repeat the procedure for the remaining pistons and rings.

Installation

25   Before installing the piston/connecting rod assemblies, the cylinder walls must be perfectly clean, the top edge of each cylinder bore must be chamfered, and the crankshaft must be in place.

26   Remove the cap from the end of the number one connecting rod (refer to the

ENGINE BEARING ANALYSIS

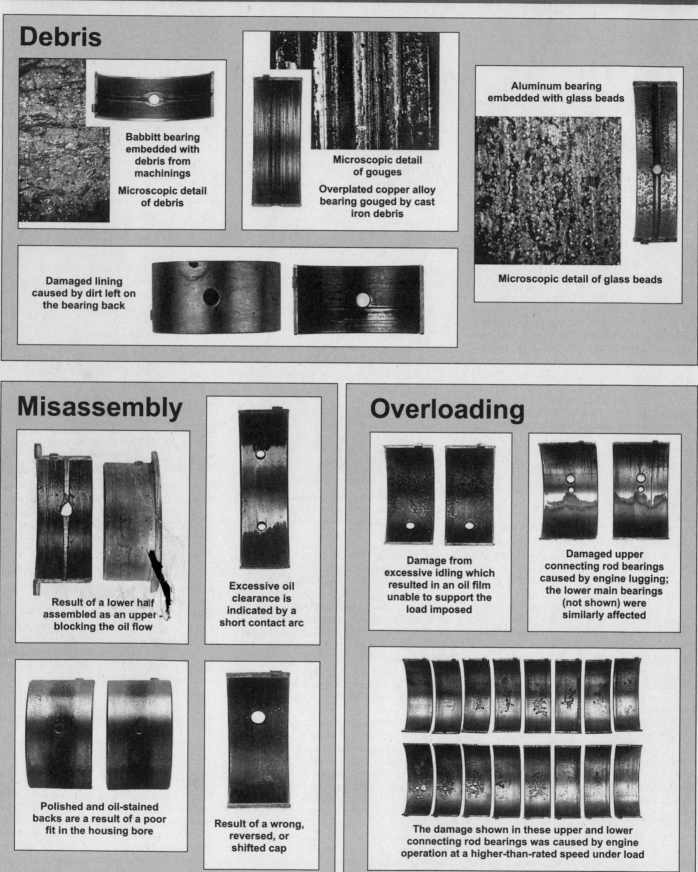

Debris

Babbitt bearing embedded with debris from machinings

Microscopic detail of debris

Microscopic detail of gouges

Overplated copper alloy bearing gouged by cast iron debris

Aluminum bearing embedded with glass beads

Microscopic detail of glass beads

Damaged lining caused by dirt left on the bearing back

Misassembly

Result of a lower half assembled as an upper blocking the oil flow

Excessive oil clearance is indicated by a short contact arc

Polished and oil-stained backs are a result of a poor fit in the housing bore

Result of a wrong, reversed, or shifted cap

Overloading

Damage from excessive idling which resulted in an oil film unable to support the load imposed

Damaged upper connecting rod bearings caused by engine lugging; the lower main bearings (not shown) were similarly affected

The damage shown in these upper and lower connecting rod bearings was caused by engine operation at a higher-than-rated speed under load

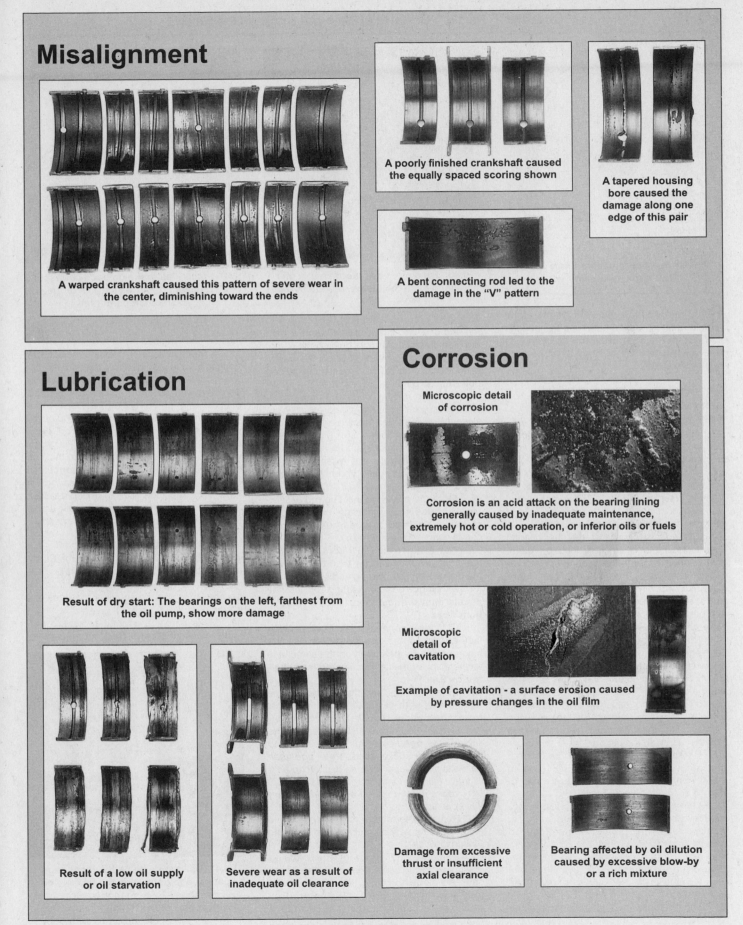

Misalignment

A warped crankshaft caused this pattern of severe wear in the center, diminishing toward the ends

A poorly finished crankshaft caused the equally spaced scoring shown

A bent connecting rod led to the damage in the "V" pattern

A tapered housing bore caused the damage along one edge of this pair

Lubrication

Result of dry start: The bearings on the left, farthest from the oil pump, show more damage

Result of a low oil supply or oil starvation

Severe wear as a result of inadequate oil clearance

Corrosion

Microscopic detail of corrosion

Corrosion is an acid attack on the bearing lining generally caused by inadequate maintenance, extremely hot or cold operation, or inferior oils or fuels

Microscopic detail of cavitation

Example of cavitation - a surface erosion caused by pressure changes in the oil film

Damage from excessive thrust or insufficient axial clearance

Bearing affected by oil dilution caused by excessive blow-by or a rich mixture

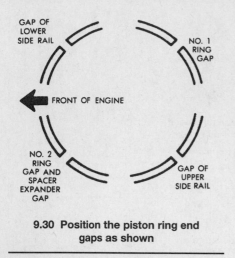

9.30 Position the piston ring end gaps as shown

9.35 Use a plastic or wooden hammer handle to push the piston into the cylinder

9.37 Place Plastigage on each connecting rod bearing journal parallel to the crankshaft centerline

marks made during removal). Remove the original bearing inserts and wipe the bearing surfaces of the connecting rod and cap with a clean, lint-free cloth. They must be kept spotlessly clean.

Connecting rod bearing oil clearance check

Refer to illustrations 9.30, 9.35, 9.37 and 9.41

27   Clean the back side of the new upper bearing insert, then lay it in place in the connecting rod.

28   Make sure the tab on the bearing fits into the recess in the rod. Don't hammer the bearing insert into place and be very careful not to nick or gouge the bearing face. Don't lubricate the bearing at this time.

29   Clean the back side of the other bearing insert and install it in the rod cap. Again, make sure the tab on the bearing fits into the recess in the cap, and don't apply any lubricant. It's critically important that the mating surfaces of the bearing and connecting rod are perfectly clean and oil free when they're assembled.

30   Position the piston ring gaps at 90-degree intervals around the piston as shown **(see illustration)**.

31   Lubricate the piston and rings with clean engine oil and attach a piston ring compressor to the piston. Leave the skirt protruding about 1/4-inch to guide the piston into the cylinder. The rings must be compressed until they're flush with the piston.

32   Rotate the crankshaft until the number one connecting rod journal is at BDC (bottom dead center) and apply a liberal coat of engine oil to the cylinder walls.

33   With the mark on top of the piston facing the front (timing belt end) of the engine, gently insert the piston/connecting rod assembly into the number one cylinder bore and rest the bottom edge of the ring compressor on the engine block. Install the pistons with the cavity mark(s) facing toward the timing belt.

34   Tap the top edge of the ring compressor to make sure it's contacting the block around its entire circumference.

35   Gently tap on the top of the piston with the end of a wooden or plastic hammer handle **(see illustration)** while guiding the end of the connecting rod into place on the crankshaft journal. The piston rings may try to pop out of the ring compressor just before entering the cylinder bore, so keep some downward pressure on the ring compressor. Work slowly, and if any resistance is felt as the piston enters the cylinder, stop immediately. Find out what's hanging up and fix it before proceeding. Do not, for any reason, force the piston into the cylinder - you might break a ring and/or the piston.

36   Once the piston/connecting rod assembly is installed, the connecting rod bearing oil clearance must be checked before the rod cap is permanently installed.

37   Cut a piece of the appropriate size Plastigage slightly shorter than the width of the connecting rod bearing and lay it in place on the number one connecting rod journal, parallel with the journal axis **(see illustration)**.

38   Clean the connecting rod cap bearing face and install the rod cap. Make sure the mating mark on the cap is on the same side as the mark on the connecting rod **(see illustration 9.4)**.

39   Install the nuts, and tighten them to the torque listed in this Chapter's Specifications. **Note:** *Use a thin-wall socket to avoid erroneous torque readings that can result if the socket is wedged between the rod cap and the nut. If the socket tends to wedge itself between the fastener and the cap, lift up on it slightly until it no longer contacts the cap. DO NOT rotate the crankshaft at any time during this operation.*

40   Remove the fasteners and detach the rod cap, being very careful not to disturb the Plastigage.

41   Compare the width of the crushed Plastigage to the scale printed on the Plastigage envelope to obtain the oil clearance **(see illustration)**. The connecting rod oil clearance is usually about 0.001 to 0.002 inch. Consult an automotive machine shop for the clearance specified for the rod bear-

ings on your engine.

42   If the clearance is not as specified, the bearing inserts may be the wrong size (which means different ones will be required). Before deciding that different inserts are needed, make sure that no dirt or oil was between the bearing inserts and the connecting rod or cap when the clearance was measured. Also, recheck the journal diameter. If the Plastigage was wider at one end than the other, the journal may be tapered. If the clearance still exceeds the limit specified, the bearing will have to be replaced with an undersize bearing. **Caution:** *When installing a new crankshaft always use a standard size bearing.*

Final installation

43   Carefully scrape all traces of the Plastigage material off the rod journal and/or bearing face. Be very careful not to scratch the bearing - use your fingernail or the edge of a plastic card.

44   Make sure the bearing faces are perfectly clean, then apply a uniform layer of

9.41 Use the scale on the Plastigage package to determine the bearing oil clearance - be sure to measure the widest part of the Plastigage and use the correct scale; it comes with both standard and metric scales

10.1 Checking crankshaft endplay with a dial indicator

10.3 Checking the crankshaft endplay with feeler gauges at the thrust bearing journal

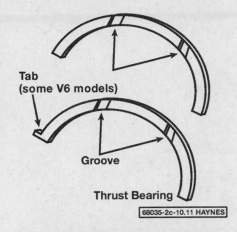

10.11 The thrust bearing grooves must face toward the crankshaft webs (away from the main bearing saddle/cap)

clean moly-base grease or engine assembly lube to both of them. You'll have to push the piston into the cylinder to expose the face of the bearing insert in the connecting rod.

45   Slide the connecting rod back into place on the journal, install the rod cap, install the nuts and tighten them to the torque listed in this Chapter's Specifications. Again, work up to the torque in three steps.

46   Repeat the entire procedure for the remaining pistons/connecting rods.

47   The important points to remember are:

a) *Keep the back sides of the bearing inserts and the insides of the connecting rods and caps perfectly clean when assembling them.*

b) *Make sure you have the correct piston/rod assembly for each cylinder.*

c) *The mark on the piston must face the front (timing belt end) of the engine.*

d) *Lubricate the cylinder walls liberally with clean oil.*

e) *Lubricate the bearing faces when installing the rod caps after the oil clearance has been checked.*

48   After all the piston/connecting rod assemblies have been correctly installed, rotate the crankshaft a number of times by hand to check for any obvious binding.

49   As a final step, check the connecting rod endplay, as described in Step 3. If it was correct before disassembly and the original crankshaft and rods were reinstalled, it should still be correct. If new rods or a new crankshaft were installed, the endplay may be inadequate. If so, the rods will have to be removed and taken to an automotive machine shop for resizing.

10   Crankshaft - removal and installation

Removal

Refer to illustrations 10.1 and 10.3
Note: *The crankshaft can be removed only after the engine has been removed from the vehicle. It's assumed that the flywheel or*

driveplate, crankshaft pulley, timing belt, oil pan, oil pump body, oil filter and piston/connecting rod assemblies have already been removed. The rear main oil seal retainer must be unbolted and separated from the block before proceeding with crankshaft removal.

1   Before the crankshaft is removed, measure the endplay. Mount a dial indicator with the indicator in line with the crankshaft and just touching the end of the crankshaft as shown **(see illustration)**.

2   Pry the crankshaft all the way to the rear and zero the dial indicator. Next, pry the crankshaft to the front as far as possible and check the reading on the dial indicator. The distance traveled is the endplay. A typical crankshaft endplay will fall between 0.003 to 0.010 inch (0.076 to 0.254 mm). If it is greater than that, check the crankshaft thrust surfaces for wear after it's removed. If no wear is evident, new main bearings should correct the endplay.

3   If a dial indicator isn't available, feeler gauges can be used. Gently pry the crankshaft all the way to the front of the engine. Slip feeler gauges between the crankshaft and the front face of the thrust bearing or washer to determine the clearance **(see illustration)**.

4   Loosen the main bearing cap assembly (bedplate) bolts 1/4-turn at a time each, until they can be removed by hand.

5   Gently tap the main bearing cap assembly with a soft-face hammer around the perimeter of the assembly. Pull the main bearing cap assembly straight up and off the cylinder block. Try not to drop the bearing inserts if they come out with the assembly.

6   Carefully lift the crankshaft out of the engine. It may be a good idea to have an assistant available, since the crankshaft is quite heavy and awkward to handle. With the bearing inserts in place inside the engine block and main bearing caps, reinstall the main bearing cap assembly onto the engine block and tighten the bolts finger tight. Make sure you install the main bearing cap assembly with the arrow facing the front end of the engine.

Installation

7   Crankshaft installation is the first step in

engine reassembly. It's assumed at this point that the engine block and crankshaft have been cleaned, inspected and repaired or reconditioned.

8   Position the engine block with the bottom facing up.

9   Remove the mounting bolts and lift off the main bearing cap assembly.

10   If they're still in place, remove the original bearing inserts from the block and from the main bearing cap assembly. Wipe the bearing surfaces of the block and main bearing cap assembly with a clean, lint-free cloth. They must be kept spotlessly clean. This is critical for determining the correct bearing oil clearance.

Main bearing oil clearance check

Refer to illustrations 10.11, 10.17, 10.19a, 10.19b, 10.19c and 10.21

11   Without mixing them up, clean the back sides of the new upper main bearing inserts (with grooves and oil holes) and lay one in each main bearing saddle in the engine block. Each upper bearing (engine block) has an oil groove and oil hole in it. **Caution:** *The oil holes in the block must line up with the oil holes in the upper bearing inserts.* The thrust washer or thrust bearing insert must be installed in the number 3 **(see illustrations 10.19a, 10.19b and 10.19c)**. **Note:** *The four thrust bearings on the 3.0L V6 have an upper thrust bearing and a lower thrust bearing located in pairs on the number 3 main bearing saddle and cap. Be sure the tab on the thrust bearing is correctly positioned* **(see illustration)**; *on the block side, one of the thrust washers with a tab fits into the rear side of the number three main bearing saddle (the tab fits into a notch). On the main bearing assembly side one of the tabbed thrust washers fits into the front side of the number three main bearing cap (the tab fits into a notch here, too). The two thrust bearings on the 2.4L SOHC models are located next to the upper*

10.17 Place the Plastigage onto the crankshaft bearing journal as shown

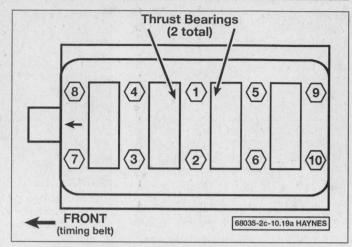

10.19a Main bearing cap assembly tightening sequence on four-cylinder models

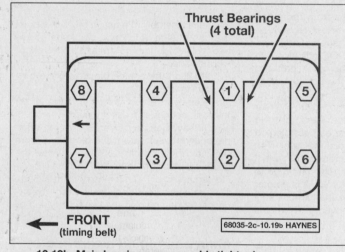

10.19b Main bearing cap assembly tightening sequence on 3.0L V6 models

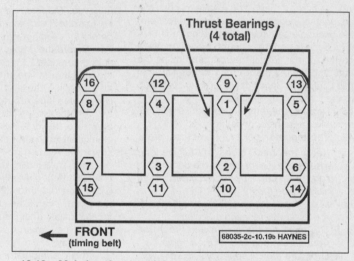

10.19c Main bearing cap tightening sequence - 3.8L V6 models

main bearing inserts in the engine block. On all models the grooves must face the crankshaft webs. Clean the back sides of the lower main bearing inserts and lay them in the corresponding location in the main bearing cap assembly. Make sure the tab on the bearing insert fits into the recess in the block or main bearing cap assembly. The upper bearings with the oil holes are installed into the engine block while the lower bearings without the oil holes are installed in the crankshaft bedplate (main bearing assembly). **Caution:** *Do not hammer the bearing insert into place and don't nick or gouge the bearing faces. DO NOT apply any lubrication at this time.*

12   Clean the faces of the bearing inserts in the block and the crankshaft main bearing journals with a clean, lint-free cloth.

13   Check or clean the oil holes in the crankshaft, as any dirt here can go only one way - straight through the new bearings.

14   Once you're certain the crankshaft is clean, carefully lay it in position in the cylinder block.

15   Before the crankshaft can be permanently installed, the main bearing oil clearance must be checked.

16   Cut several strips of the appropriate size of Plastigage. They must be slightly shorter than the width of the main bearing journal.

17   Place one piece on each crankshaft main bearing journal, parallel with the journal axis as shown **(see illustration)**.

18   Clean the faces of the bearing inserts in

10.21 Use the scale on the Plastigage package to determine the bearing oil clearance - be sure to measure the widest part of the Plastigage and use the correct scale; it comes with both standard and metric scales

the main bearing cap assembly. Hold the bearing inserts in place and install the assembly onto the crankshaft and cylinder block. DO NOT disturb the Plastigage. Make sure you install the main bearing cap assembly with the arrow facing the front (timing belt end) of the engine.

19   Apply clean engine oil to all bolt threads prior to installation, then install all bolts finger-tight. Tighten main bearing cap assembly bolts in the sequence shown **(see illustrations)** progressing in steps, to the torque listed in this Chapter's Specifications. DO NOT rotate the crankshaft at any time during this operation.

20   Remove the bolts in the *reverse* order of the tightening sequence and carefully lift the main bearing cap assembly straight up and off the block. Do not disturb the Plastigage or rotate the crankshaft. If the main bearing cap assembly is difficult to remove, tap it gently from side-to-side with a soft-face hammer to loosen it.

21   Compare the width of the crushed Plastigage on each journal to the scale printed on the Plastigage envelope to determine the main bearing oil clearance **(see illustration)**. Check with an automotive machine shop for the oil clearance for your engine.

22   If the clearance is not as specified, the bearing inserts may be the wrong size (which means different ones will be required). Before deciding if different inserts are needed, make sure that no dirt or oil was between the bearing inserts and the cap assembly or block when the clearance was measured. If the Plastigage was wider at one end than the other, the crankshaft journal may be tapered. If the clearance still exceeds the limit specified, the bearing insert(s) will have to be replaced with an undersize bearing insert(s). **Caution:** *When installing a new crankshaft always install a standard bearing insert set.*

23   Carefully scrape all traces of the Plastigage material off the main bearing journals and/or the bearing insert faces. Be sure to remove all residue from the oil holes. Use your fingernail or the edge of a plastic card - don't nick or scratch the bearing faces.

Final installation

24   Carefully lift the crankshaft out of the cylinder block.

25   Clean the bearing insert faces in the cylinder block, then apply a thin, uniform layer of moly-base grease or engine assembly lube to each of the bearing surfaces. Be sure to coat the thrust faces as well as the journal face of the thrust bearing.

26   Make sure the crankshaft journals are clean, then lay the crankshaft back in place in the cylinder block.

27   Clean the bearing insert faces and apply the same lubricant to them. Clean the engine block and the bedplate thoroughly. The surfaces must be free of oil residue.

28   Hold the bedplate (main bearing assembly) and bearings in place and install the main bearing assembly onto the crankshaft and cylinder block. Make sure the arrow on the front of the main bearing assembly faces the front of the engine.

29   Prior to installation, apply clean engine oil to all bolt threads, wiping off any excess, then install all bolts finger-tight.

30   Tighten the main bearing cap assembly following the correct torque sequence **(see illustrations 10.19a, 10.19b and 10.19c)**, to the torque listed in this Chapter's Specifications.

31   Recheck the crankshaft endplay with a feeler gauge or a dial indicator. The endplay should be correct if the crankshaft thrust faces aren't worn or damaged and if new bearings have been installed.

32   Rotate the crankshaft a number of times by hand to check for any obvious binding. It should rotate with a running torque of 50 in-lbs or less (without the pistons/connecting rods installed). If the running torque is too high, correct the problem at this time.

33   Install a new rear main oil seal (see Chapter 2A or 2B).

11   Engine overhaul - reassembly sequence

1   Before beginning engine reassembly, make sure you have all the necessary new parts, gaskets and seals as well as the following items on hand:

Common hand tools
A 1/2-inch drive torque wrench
New engine oil
Gasket sealant
Thread locking compound

2   If you obtained a short block it will be necessary to install the cylinder head(s), the oil pump and pick-up tube, the oil pan, the water pump, the timing belt and timing covers, and the valve cover(s) (see Chapter 2A or 2B). In order to save time and avoid problems, the external components must be installed in the following general order:

Thermostat and housing
Water pump
Intake and exhaust manifolds
Fuel injection components
Emission control components
Spark plug wires and spark plugs
Distributor (if equipped)
Ignition coil(s)
Oil filter
Engine mounts and mount brackets
Flywheel and clutch (manual transaxle)
Driveplate (automatic transaxle)

12   Initial start-up and break-in after overhaul

Warning: *Have a fire extinguisher handy when starting the engine for the first time.*

1   Once the engine has been installed in the vehicle, double-check the engine oil and coolant levels.

2   With the spark plugs out of the engine and the ignition system and fuel pump disabled, crank the engine until oil pressure registers on the gauge or the light goes out.

3   Install the spark plugs, hook up the plug wires and restore the ignition system and fuel pump functions.

4   Start the engine. It may take a few moments for the fuel system to build up pressure, but the engine should start without a great deal of effort.

5   After the engine starts, it should be allowed to warm up to normal operating temperature. While the engine is warming up, make a thorough check for fuel, oil and coolant leaks.

6   Shut the engine off and recheck the engine oil and coolant levels.

7   Drive the vehicle to an area with minimum traffic, accelerate from 30 to 50 mph, then allow the vehicle to slow to 30 mph with the throttle closed. Repeat the procedure 10 or 12 times. This will load the piston rings and cause them to seat properly against the cylinder walls. Check again for oil and coolant leaks.

8   Drive the vehicle gently for the first 500 miles (no sustained high speeds) and keep a constant check on the oil level. It is not unusual for an engine to use oil during the break-in period.

9   At approximately 500 to 600 miles, change the oil and filter.

10   For the next few hundred miles, drive the vehicle normally. Do not pamper it or abuse it.

11   After 2000 miles, change the oil and filter again and consider the engine broken in.

COMMON ENGINE OVERHAUL TERMS

B

Backlash - The amount of play between two parts. Usually refers to how much one gear can be moved back and forth without moving the gear with which it's meshed.

Bearing Caps - The caps held in place by nuts or bolts which, in turn, hold the bearing surface. This space is for lubricating oil to enter.

Bearing clearance - The amount of space left between shaft and bearing surface. This space is for lubricating oil to enter.

Bearing crush - The additional height which is purposely manufactured into each bearing half to ensure complete contact of the bearing back with the housing bore when the engine is assembled.

Bearing knock - The noise created by movement of a part in a loose or worn bearing.

Blueprinting - Dismantling an engine and reassembling it to EXACT specifications.

Bore - An engine cylinder, or any cylindrical hole; also used to describe the process of enlarging or accurately refinishing a hole with a cutting tool, as to bore an engine cylinder. The bore size is the diameter of the hole.

Boring - Renewing the cylinders by cutting them out to a specified size. A boring bar is used to make the cut.

Bottom end - A term which refers collectively to the engine block, crankshaft, main bearings and the big ends of the connecting rods.

Break-in - The period of operation between installation of new or rebuilt parts and time in which parts are worn to the correct fit. Driving at reduced and varying speed for a specified mileage to permit parts to wear to the correct fit.

Bushing - A one-piece sleeve placed in a bore to serve as a bearing surface for shaft, piston pin, etc. Usually replaceable.

C

Camshaft - The shaft in the engine, on which a series of lobes are located for operating the valve mechanisms. The camshaft is driven by gears or sprockets and a timing chain. Usually referred to simply as the cam.

Carbon - Hard, or soft, black deposits found in combustion chamber, on plugs, under rings, on and under valve heads.

Cast iron - An alloy of iron and more than two percent carbon, used for engine blocks and heads because it's relatively inexpensive and easy to mold into complex shapes.

Chamfer - To bevel across (or a bevel on) the sharp edge of an object.

Chase - To repair damaged threads with a tap or die.

Combustion chamber - The space between the piston and the cylinder head, with the piston at top dead center, in which air-fuel mixture is burned.

Compression ratio - The relationship between cylinder volume (clearance volume) when the piston is at top dead center and cylinder volume when the piston is at bottom dead center.

Connecting rod - The rod that connects the crank on the crankshaft with the piston. Sometimes called a con rod.

Connecting rod cap - The part of the connecting rod assembly that attaches the rod to the crankpin.

Core plug - Soft metal plug used to plug the casting holes for the coolant passages in the block.

Crankcase - The lower part of the engine in which the crankshaft rotates; includes the lower section of the cylinder block and the oil pan.

Crank kit - A reground or reconditioned crankshaft and new main and connecting rod bearings.

Crankpin - The part of a crankshaft to which a connecting rod is attached.

Crankshaft - The main rotating member, or shaft, running the length of the crankcase, with offset throws to which the connecting rods are attached; changes the reciprocating motion of the pistons into rotating motion.

Cylinder sleeve - A replaceable sleeve, or liner, pressed into the cylinder block to form the cylinder bore.

D

Deburring - Removing the burrs (rough edges or areas) from a bearing.

Deglazer - A tool, rotated by an electric motor, used to remove glaze from cylinder walls so a new set of rings will seat.

E

Endplay - The amount of lengthwise movement between two parts. As applied to a crankshaft, the distance that the crankshaft can move forward and back in the cylinder block.

F

Face - A machinist's term that refers to removing metal from the end of a shaft or the face of a larger part, such as a flywheel.

Fatigue - A breakdown of material through a large number of loading and unloading cycles. The first signs are cracks followed shortly by breaks.

Feeler gauge - A thin strip of hardened steel, ground to an exact thickness, used to check clearances between parts.

Free height - The unloaded length or height of a spring.

Freeplay - The looseness in a linkage, or an assembly of parts, between the initial application of force and actual movement. Usually perceived as slop or slight delay.

Freeze plug - See Core plug.

G

Gallery - A large passage in the block that forms a reservoir for engine oil pressure.

Glaze - The very smooth, glassy finish that develops on cylinder walls while an engine is in service.

H

Heli-Coil - A rethreading device used when threads are worn or damaged. The device is installed in a retapped hole to reduce the thread size to the original size.

I

Installed height - The spring's measured length or height, as installed on the cylinder head. Installed height is measured from the spring seat to the underside of the spring retainer.

J

Journal - The surface of a rotating shaft which turns in a bearing.

K

Keeper - The split lock that holds the valve spring retainer in position on the valve stem.

Key - A small piece of metal inserted into matching grooves machined into two parts fitted together - such as a gear pressed onto a shaft - which prevents slippage between the two parts.

Knock - The heavy metallic engine sound, produced in the combustion chamber as a result of abnormal combustion - usually detonation. Knock is usually caused by a loose or worn bearing. Also referred to as detonation, pinging and spark knock. Connecting rod or main bearing knocks are created by too much oil clearance or insufficient lubrication.

L

Lands - The portions of metal between the piston ring grooves.

Lapping the valves - Grinding a valve face and its seat together with lapping compound.

Lash - The amount of free motion in a gear train, between gears, or in a mechanical assembly, that occurs before movement can begin. Usually refers to the lash in a valve train.

Lifter - The part that rides against the cam to transfer motion to the rest of the valve train.

M

Machining - The process of using a machine to remove metal from a metal part.

Main bearings - The plain, or babbit, bearings that support the crankshaft.

Main bearing caps - The cast iron caps, bolted to the bottom of the block, that support the main bearings.

O

O.D. - Outside diameter.

Oil gallery - A pipe or drilled passageway in the engine used to carry engine oil from one area to another.

Oil ring - The lower ring, or rings, of a piston; designed to prevent excessive amounts of oil from working up the cylinder walls and into the combustion chamber. Also called an oil-control ring.

Oil seal - A seal which keeps oil from leaking out of a compartment. Usually refers to a dynamic seal around a rotating shaft or other moving part.

O-ring - A type of sealing ring made of a special rubberlike material; in use, the O-ring is compressed into a groove to provide the sealing action.

Overhaul - To completely disassemble a unit, clean and inspect all parts, reassemble it with the original or new parts and make all adjustments necessary for proper operation.

P

Pilot bearing - A small bearing installed in the center of the flywheel (or the rear end of the crankshaft) to support the front end of the input shaft of the transmission.

Pip mark - A little dot or indentation which indicates the top side of a compression ring.

Piston - The cylindrical part, attached to the connecting rod, that moves up and down in the cylinder as the crankshaft rotates. When the fuel charge is fired, the piston transfers the force of the explosion to the connecting rod, then to the crankshaft.

Piston pin (or wrist pin) - The cylindrical and usually hollow steel pin that passes through the piston. The piston pin fastens the piston to the upper end of the connecting rod.

Piston ring - The split ring fitted to the groove in a piston. The ring contacts the sides of the ring groove and also rubs against the cylinder wall, thus sealing space between piston and wall. There are two types of rings: Compression rings seal the compression pressure in the combustion chamber; oil rings scrape excessive oil off the cylinder wall.

Piston ring groove - The slots or grooves cut in piston heads to hold piston rings in position.

Piston skirt - The portion of the piston below the rings and the piston pin hole.

Plastigage - A thin strip of plastic thread, available in different sizes, used for measuring clearances. For example, a strip of plastigage is laid across a bearing journal and mashed as parts are assembled. Then parts are disassembled and the width of the strip is measured to determine clearance between journal and bearing. Commonly used to measure crankshaft main-bearing and connecting rod bearing clearances.

Press-fit - A tight fit between two parts that requires pressure to force the parts together. Also referred to as drive, or force, fit.

Prussian blue - A blue pigment; in solution, useful in determining the area of contact between two surfaces. Prussian blue is commonly used to determine the width and location of the contact area between the valve face and the valve seat.

R

Race (bearing) - The inner or outer ring that provides a contact surface for balls or rollers in bearing.

Ream - To size, enlarge or smooth a hole by using a round cutting tool with fluted edges.

Ring job - The process of reconditioning the cylinders and installing new rings.

Runout - Wobble. The amount a shaft rotates out-of-true.

S

Saddle - The upper main bearing seat.

Scored - Scratched or grooved, as a cylinder wall may be scored by abrasive particles moved up and down by the piston rings.

Scuffing - A type of wear in which there's a transfer of material between parts moving against each other; shows up as pits or grooves in the mating surfaces.

Seat - The surface upon which another part rests or seats. For example, the valve seat is the matched surface upon which the valve face rests. Also used to refer to wearing into a good fit; for example, piston rings seat after a few miles of driving.

Short block - An engine block complete with crankshaft and piston and, usually, camshaft assemblies.

Static balance - The balance of an object while it's stationary.

Step - The wear on the lower portion of a ring land caused by excessive side and back-clearance. The height of the step indicates the ring's extra side clearance and the length of the step projecting from the back wall of the groove represents the ring's back clearance.

Stroke - The distance the piston moves when traveling from top dead center to bottom dead center, or from bottom dead center to top dead center.

Stud - A metal rod with threads on both ends.

T

Tang - A lip on the end of a plain bearing used to align the bearing during assembly.

Tap - To cut threads in a hole. Also refers to the fluted tool used to cut threads.

Taper - A gradual reduction in the width of a shaft or hole; in an engine cylinder, taper usually takes the form of uneven wear, more pronounced at the top than at the bottom.

Throws - The offset portions of the crankshaft to which the connecting rods are affixed.

Thrust bearing - The main bearing that has thrust faces to prevent excessive endplay, or forward and backward movement of the crankshaft.

Thrust washer - A bronze or hardened steel washer placed between two moving parts. The washer prevents longitudinal movement and provides a bearing surface for thrust surfaces of parts.

Tolerance - The amount of variation permitted from an exact size of measurement. Actual amount from smallest acceptable dimension to largest acceptable dimension.

U

Umbrella - An oil deflector placed near the valve tip to throw oil from the valve stem area.

Undercut - A machined groove below the normal surface.

Undersize bearings - Smaller diameter bearings used with re-ground crankshaft journals.

V

Valve grinding - Refacing a valve in a valve-refacing machine.

Valve train - The valve-operating mechanism of an engine; includes all components from the camshaft to the valve.

Vibration damper - A cylindrical weight attached to the front of the crankshaft to minimize torsional vibration (the twist-untwist actions of the crankshaft caused by the cylinder firing impulses). Also called a harmonic balancer.

W

Water jacket - The spaces around the cylinders, between the inner and outer shells of the cylinder block or head, through which coolant circulates.

Web - A supporting structure across a cavity.

Woodruff key - A key with a radiused backside (viewed from the side).

Notes

Chapter 3
Cooling, heating and air conditioning systems

Contents

Specifications

General

Radiator cap pressure rating
- 2.4L DOHC models .... 11 to 15 psi (75 to 105 kPa)
- 2.4L SOHC models
  - 1994 through 2002 models .... 11 to 15 psi (75 to 105 kPa)
  - 2003 and later models .... 14 to 18 psi (93 to 123 kPa)
- 3.0L V6 models
  - 1999 through 2002 models .... 11 to 15 psi (75 to 105 kPa)
  - 2003 and later models .... 14 to 18 psi (93 to 123 kPa)

Thermostat rating (opening to fully open temperature range)
- 2.4L DOHC models .... 180 to 203 degrees F (82 to 95 degrees C)
- 2.4L SOHC models
  - 1994 through 1998 .... 180 to 203 degrees F (82 to 95 degrees C)
  - 1999 and later .... 190 to 212 degrees F (88 to 100 degrees C)
- V6 models .... 190 to 212 degrees F (88 to 100 degrees C)

Cooling system capacity .... See Chapter 1
Refrigerant capacity .... Refer to HVAC specification tag (usually located on the firewall)

Torque specifications

Ft-lbs (unless otherwise indicated) **Nm**

Note: *One foot-pound (ft-lb) of torque is equivalent to 12 inch-pounds (in-lbs) of torque. Torque values below approximately 15 foot-pounds are expressed in inch-pounds, because most foot-pound torque wrenches are not accurate at these smaller values.*

	Ft-lbs	Nm
Thermostat housing bolts		
Four-cylinder engines		
1994 through 1998 models	120 in-lbs	13
1999 and later models	106 in-lbs	12
V6 engines	168 in-lbs	19
Water pump mounting bolts		
Four-cylinder engines	115 in-lbs	13
V6 engines	30	40

1   General information

Engine cooling system

All vehicles covered by this manual employ a pressurized engine cooling system with thermostatically controlled coolant circulation. An impeller-type water pump mounted on the front of the engine pumps coolant through the engine. The pump mounts directly on the engine block and is driven by a drivebelt (four-cylinder models) or the timing belt (V6 models). The coolant flows around the combustion chambers and toward the rear of the engine. Cast-in coolant passages direct coolant near the intake ports, exhaust ports, and spark plug areas.

A wax pellet-type thermostat is located in a housing near the front of the engine. During warm-up, the closed thermostat prevents coolant from circulating through the radiator. As the engine nears normal operating temperature, the thermostat opens and allows hot coolant to travel through the radiator, where it's cooled before returning to the engine.

The cooling system is sealed by a pressure-type cap, which raises the boiling point of the coolant and increases the cooling efficiency of the system. If the system pressure exceeds the cap pressure relief value, the excess pressure in the system forces the spring-loaded valve inside the cap off its seat and allows the coolant to escape through the overflow tube into a coolant reservoir. When the system cools the excess coolant is automatically drawn from the reservoir back into the radiator.

The coolant reservoir serves as both the point at which fresh coolant is added to the cooling system to maintain the proper fluid level and as a holding tank for overheated coolant. This type of cooling system is known as a closed design because coolant that escapes past the pressure cap is saved and reused.

Heating system

The heating system consists of a blower fan and heater core located in the heater housing, with hoses connecting the heater core to the engine cooling system. Hot engine coolant is circulated through the heater core. When the heater mode on the heater/air conditioning control panel on the instrument panel is activated, a flap door opens to expose the heater core to the passenger compartment. A fan switch on the control panel activates the blower motor, which forces air through the core, heating the air.

Air conditioning system

The air conditioning system consists of a condenser mounted in front of the radiator, an evaporator mounted adjacent to the heater core, a compressor mounted on the engine, receiver/drier which contains a high pressure relief valve and the plumbing connecting all of the above components.

A blower fan forces the warmer air of the

2.4 Use a hydrometer to test the coolant

passenger compartment through the evaporator core, transferring the heat from the air to the refrigerant (sort of a "radiator in reverse"). The liquid refrigerant boils off into low pressure vapor, taking the heat with it when it leaves the evaporator.

2   Antifreeze - general information

Refer to illustration 2.4

Warning: *Do not allow antifreeze to come in contact with your skin or painted surfaces of the vehicle. Rinse off spills immediately with plenty of water. Antifreeze is highly toxic if ingested. Never leave antifreeze lying around in an open container or in puddles on the floor; children and pets are attracted by it's sweet smell and may drink it. Antifreeze is also flammable, so don't store or use it near open flames. Check with local authorities about disposing of used antifreeze. Many communities have collection centers which will see that antifreeze is disposed of safely. Never dump used anti-freeze on the ground or into drains.*

Note: *Non-toxic coolant is available at local auto parts stores. Although the coolant is non-toxic when fresh, proper disposal is still required.*

The cooling system should be filled with a water/ethylene glycol based antifreeze solution, which will prevent freezing down to at least 20 degrees F, or lower if local climate requires it. It also provides protection against corrosion and increases the coolant boiling point.

The cooling system should be drained, flushed and refilled at the specified intervals (see Chapter 1). Old or contaminated antifreeze solutions are likely to cause damage and encourage the formation of rust and scale in the system. Use distilled water with the antifreeze.

Before adding antifreeze, check all hose connections, because antifreeze tends to leak through very minute openings. Engines don't normally consume coolant, so if the level goes down, find the cause and correct it.

The exact mixture of antifreeze-to-water

which you should use depends on the relative weather conditions. The mixture should contain at least 50 percent antifreeze, but should never contain more than 70 percent antifreeze. Consult the mixture ratio chart on the antifreeze container before adding coolant. Use a hydrometer, available at auto parts stores, to test the coolant **(see illustration)**. Use antifreeze that meets the vehicle manufacturer's specifications.

3   Thermostat - check and replacement

Warning: *Do not remove the radiator cap, drain the coolant or replace the thermostat until the engine has cooled completely.*

Check

1   Before assuming the thermostat is to blame for a cooling system problem, check the coolant level, drivebelt tension (see Chapter 1) and temperature gauge operation.
2   If the engine seems to be taking a long time to warm up, based on heater output or temperature gauge operation, the thermostat is probably stuck open. Replace the thermostat with a new one.
3   If the engine runs hot, use your hand to check the temperature of the lower radiator hose. If the hose isn't hot, but the engine is, the thermostat is probably stuck closed, preventing the coolant inside the engine from escaping to the radiator. Replace the thermostat. **Caution:** *Don't drive the vehicle without a thermostat. The computer may stay in open loop and emissions and fuel economy will suffer.*
4   If the lower radiator hose is hot, it means that the coolant is flowing and the thermostat is open. Consult the *Troubleshooting* section at the front of this manual for cooling system diagnosis.

Replacement

Refer to illustration 3.8

5   Disconnect the cable from the negative battery terminal (see Chapter 5).
6   Drain the cooling system (see Chapter 1). If the coolant is relatively new and still in good condition, save it and reuse it.
7   Follow the lower radiator hose to the engine to locate the thermostat housing. On 1998 and earlier models it will be necessary to remove the air filter housing for access to the thermostat (see Chapter 4). On 1999 and later models it'll be necessary to remove the battery for access (see Chapter 5).
8   Loosen the hose clamp, then detach the hose from the fitting **(see illustration)**. If it's stuck, grasp it near the end with a pair of adjustable pliers and twist it to break the seal, then pull it off. If the hose is old or if it has deteriorated, cut it off and install a new one.
9   If the outer surface of the thermostat housing cover, which mates with the hose, is already corroded, pitted, or otherwise deteriorated, it might be damaged even more by

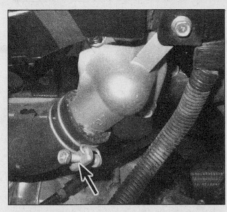

3.8 Loosen the hose clamp and twist the hose to break it loose from the thermostat housing (2000 2.4L SOHC engine shown)

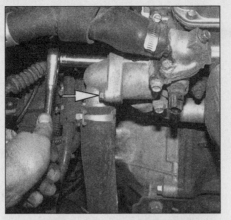

3.10a Remove the thermostat housing bolts (1998 2.4L SOHC engine shown)

3.10b Remove the thermostat housing cover from the engine block (1998 2.4L SOHC engine shown)

3.10c Remove the thermostat housing bolts (2000 2.4L SOHC engine shown)

3.10d Remove the thermostat housing cover from the engine block (2000 2.4L SOHC engine shown)

3.11 Before removing the thermostat, note how it's installed, with the spring facing in, toward the engine

hose removal. If it is, replace the thermostat housing cover.

Four-cylinder models

Refer to illustrations 3.10a, 3.10b, 3.10c, 3.10d and 3.11

10   Remove the fasteners and detach the thermostat housing cover (**see illustrations**). If the cover is stuck, tap it with a soft-face hammer to jar it loose. Be prepared for some coolant to spill as the gasket seal is broken.
11   Note how it's installed (which end is facing up or out), then remove the thermostat (**see illustration**).

V6 models

Refer to illustrations 3.12 and 3.13

12   Remove the fasteners and detach the thermostat housing cover (**see illustration**). If the cover is stuck, tap it with a soft-face hammer to jar it loose. Be prepared for some coolant to spill as the gasket seal is broken.
13   Note how it's installed (which end is facing up or out), then remove the thermostat (**see illustration**).

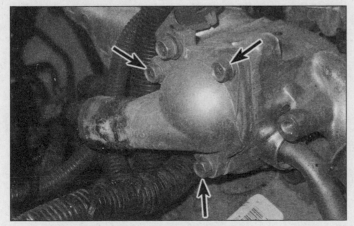

3.12 Location of the thermostat housing cover bolts on a V6 engine

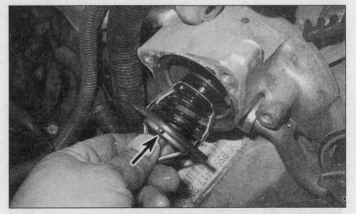

3.13 Before removing the thermostat, note how it is installed, with the spring facing in toward the engine, and also note the orientation of the "jiggle valve" (arrow) in relation to the housing

3.15a Be sure to install a new rubber O-ring type gasket on the thermostat

All models

Refer to illustrations 3.15a and 3.15b

14   Remove all traces of old gasket material and sealant from the housing and cover with

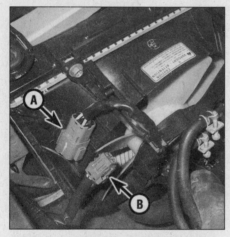

4.1a Typical early model (1994 through 1998) radiator fan motor and condenser fan motor electrical connector halves unplugged; make sure that you connect the jumper wires to the fan motor side of the connector (A), not the harness side (B)

3.15b When installing the thermostat, make sure that the jiggle valve is at 12 o'clock

a gasket scraper.

15   Install a new rubber gasket on the thermostat **(see illustration)**, then install the thermostat, spring-end first (facing the engine). On housings that face out instead of up, make sure that you install the thermostat with the "jiggle valve" at 12 o'clock **(see illustration)**. If the thermostat housing cover uses a paper gasket, dip the new gasket in water and position it on the thermostat housing with the holes in the gasket aligned with the bolt holes in the housing.

16   Install the thermostat housing cover and bolts, then tighten the bolts to the torque listed in this Chapter's Specifications.

17   Reattach the hose to the thermostat housing cover. Make sure that the hose clamp is still tight. If it isn't, replace it.

18   Refill the cooling system (see Chapter 1). Reinstall the air filter housing or battery, as applicable.

19   Start the engine and allow it to reach normal operating temperature, then check for leaks and proper thermostat operation (as described in Steps 2 through 4). See Chapter 1 for the cooling system air-bleeding procedure.

4   Engine cooling fans - check and replacement

Warning: *To avoid possible injury or damage, DO NOT operate the engine with a damaged fan. Do not attempt to repair fan blades - replace a damaged fan with a new one.*
Note 1: *Always be sure to check for blown fuses before attempting to diagnose an electrical circuit problem.*
Note 2: *1994 through 1998 models are equipped with high and low speed cooling fan relays. 1999 and later models are equipped with a single cooling fan relay that is controlled by the PCM. 1994 through 1998 models and 3.0L V6 models with A/C are equipped with a condenser fan mounted adjacent to the engine cooling fan. 1999 and later 2.4L SOHC models with A/C are equipped with a single cooling fan and cooling fan module.*

Check

Refer to illustrations 4.1a, 4.1b and 4.3

1   If the engine is overheating and the cooling fan is not coming on when the engine temperature rises to an excessive level, unplug the fan motor electrical connector **(see illustrations)** and connect the motor directly to the battery with fused jumper wires. If the fan motor doesn't come on, replace the motor. On some air-conditioned models, there is a separate fan for the condenser. If the radiator fan motor checks out okay, be sure to test the condenser fan motor.

2   If the radiator fan motor is okay, but it isn't coming on when the engine gets hot, the fan relay might be defective. A relay is used to control a circuit by turning it on and off in response to a control decision by the Powertrain Control Module (PCM). These control circuits are fairly complex, and checking them should be left to a dealer service department or other qualified repair shop. Sometimes, the control system can be fixed by simply identifying and replacing a bad relay.

3   Locate the fan relays in the engine com-

4.1b Typical late model (1999 and later) radiator fan control module and harness connector

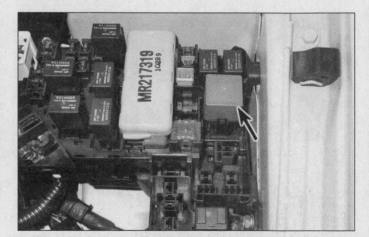

4.3 The fan motor relay is located inside the engine compartment fuse/relay box (2000 2.4L SOHC model shown)

partment fuse/relay box **(see illustration)**.

4   Test the relay (see Chapter 12).

5   If the relay is okay, check all wiring and connections to the fan motor. Refer to the wiring diagrams at the end of Chapter 12. If no obvious problems are found, the problem could be the engine coolant temperature (ECT) sensor or the Powertrain Control Module (PCM). Have the cooling fan system and circuit diagnosed by a dealer service department or repair shop with the proper diagnostic equipment.

Replacement

Refer to illustrations 4.10, 4.12a, 4.12b, 4.12c, 4.12d, 4.14 and 4.15

Warning: *Wait until the engine is completely cool before beginning this procedure.*

6   Disconnect the cable from the negative battery terminal (see Chapter 5). On 1999 and later models, remove the fresh air intake duct.

7   Disconnect the fan motor electrical connector **(see illustration 4.1a or 4.1b)**.

8   Raise the vehicle and secure it on jackstands.

9   Drain the cooling system (see Chapter 1). If the coolant is relatively new and still in good condition, save it and reuse it. On 2004 and later models, refer to Section 5 and remove the coolant reservoir.

10   Detach the upper radiator hose from the radiator. Loosen the hose clamp by squeezing the ends together. Hose clamp pliers work best **(see illustration)**, but regular pliers will work also. If the radiator hose is stuck, grasp it near the end with a pair of adjustable pliers and twist it to break the seal, then pull it off. If the hose is old or if it has deteriorated, cut it off and install a new one.

11   Disconnect any oil cooler lines or brackets from the bottom of the radiator that would interfere with removal of the fan shroud.

12   Detach the wire harness from the fan shroud, remove the upper and lower fan shroud mounting bolts **(see illustrations)**, then carefully lift the fan motor and shroud out of the engine compartment as a single assembly.

13   Remove the fan mounting screws.

14   To detach the fan blade from the motor, remove the nut or retaining clip from the

4.10 To disconnect the upper radiator hose from the radiator, loosen the hose clamp and carefully pull off the hose (the special pliers used here are designed for this type of hose clamp, which is known as a constant-tension-spring type)

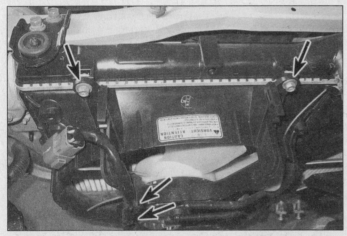

4.12a Detach the fan motor wiring harness from the clips (lower arrows) that attach it to the fan shroud; to detach the upper end of the engine cooling fan shroud from the radiator, remove these bolts from the left side (upper arrows) . . .

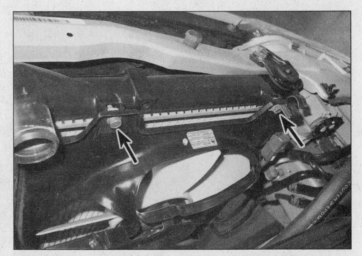

4.12b . . . and these bolts from the right side - 2003 and earlier models

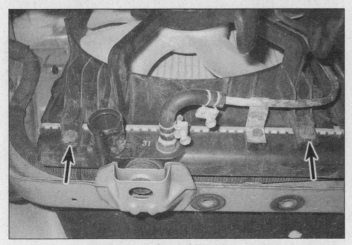

4.12c To detach the lower end of the engine cooling fan shroud from the radiator, remove these bolts

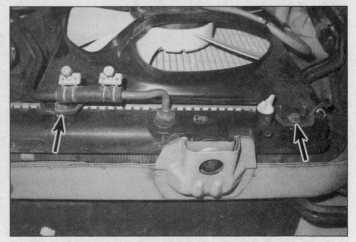

4.12d To detach the lower end of the condenser cooling fan shroud from the radiator, remove these bolts

4.14 The fan blade is retained to the motor with either a nut or a clip

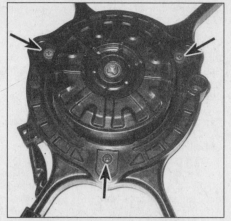

4.15 To remove the fan motor from the shroud, remove the three screws

6.4 Disconnect the automatic transaxle oil cooler lines from the lower section of the radiator

motor shaft **(see illustration)**. Remove the fan blade from the motor.

15 To detach the motor from the shroud, remove the retaining nuts or screws **(see illustrations)**. Remove the motor from the shroud.

16 Installation is the reverse of removal. **Note:** *When reinstalling the fan assembly, make sure the rubber air shields around the shroud are still in place - without them, the cooling system may not work efficiently.*

17 Refill the cooling system (see Chapter 1).

5   Coolant reservoir - removal and installation

Warning: *Wait until the engine is completely cool before beginning this procedure.*

2003 and earlier models

1 Disconnect the hose from the coolant reservoir.

2 Remove the coolant reservoir by lifting up and sliding the reservoir off its bracket.

3 Clean out the reservoir with soapy water

and a brush to remove any deposits inside. Inspect the reservoir carefully for cracks. If you find a crack, replace the reservoir.

4 Installation is the reverse of removal.

2004 and later models

5 Raise the vehicle and support it securely on jackstands. Remove the engine lower splash shield.

6 Refer to Chapter 4 and remove the air intake duct.

7 Remove the reservoir hose, then disconnect the fan motors. On California models, also disconnect the radiator sensor connector.

8 Remove the reservoir. Installation is the reverse of removal.

6   Radiator - removal and installation

Warning: *Wait until the engine is completely cool before beginning this procedure.*

Removal

Refer to illustration 6.4, 6.5a, 6.5b, 6.6a, 6.6b, 6.13 and 6.14

1 Disconnect the cable from the negative battery terminal (see Chapter 5).

6.5a Loosen the hose clamp and separate the upper radiator hose from the radiator (2000 2.4L SOHC engine shown)

6.5b Remove the lower radiator hose clamp - constant tension spring clamp shown

6.6a Remove the radiator support bracket bolts from the left side . . .

6.6b . . . and the right side of the radiator support beam (2003 and earlier models)

6.11 The front bumper cover must be removed to access the cross bar bolts

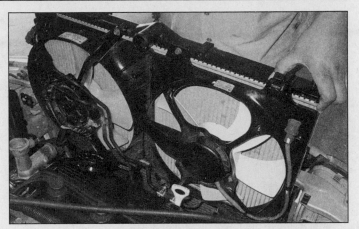

6.13 Remove the radiator, the cooling fans and shroud as a single assembly

6.14 Make sure that the rubber insulators don't come out with the radiator; if they do, inspect them to make sure that they're in good condition, then install them in their holes in the lower crossmember

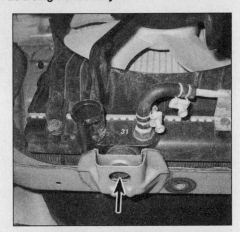

6.16a When installing the radiator, make sure the left positioning pin is correctly seated in the left insulator . . .

2   Raise the vehicle and place it securely on jackstands.

3   Drain the cooling system (see Chapter 1). If the coolant is relatively new and in good condition, save it and reuse it.

2003 and earlier models

4   On automatic transaxle models, disconnect the transaxle oil cooler lines **(see illustration)** from the radiator. Also disconnect the wiring from the fans.

5   Disconnect the upper and lower radiator hoses from the radiator **(see illustrations)**. If the radiator hose is stuck, grasp it near the end with a pair of adjustable pliers and twist it to break the seal, then pull it off. If the hose is old or if it has deteriorated, cut it off and install a new one.

6   Remove the radiator mounting brackets from the radiator support and the radiator **(see illustrations)**.

2004 and later models

Refer to illustration 6.11

7   Refer to Chapter 4 and remove the air intake ducting.

8   Disconnect the upper and lower radiator hoses (see Step 5).

9   Disconnect the wiring from the fans. Also disconnect the wiring from the radiator sensor on California cars.

10   Refer to Chapter 11 and remove the hood latch.

11   Remove the radiator cover plate and vertical cross bar unit **(see illustration)**.

12   Remove the radiator mounting bolts at the front of the condenser.

All models

13   Carefully lift out the radiator as a single assembly **(see illustration)**.

14   Don't spill coolant on the vehicle or scratch the paint. Make sure the rubber radiator seals or insulators that fit on the bottom of the radiator and into the sockets in the body remain in place in the body for proper reinstallation of the radiator **(see illustration)**.

15   Remove bugs and dirt from the radiator with compressed air and a soft brush. Don't bend the cooling fins. Inspect the radiator for leaks and damage. If it needs repair, have a radiator shop or a dealer service department do the work.

Installation

Refer to illustrations 6.16a and 6.16b

16   Inspect the rubber insulators in the lower crossmember **(see illustrations)** for cracks and deterioration. Make sure that they're free of dirt and gravel. When installing the radiator, make sure that it's correctly seated on the insulators before fastening the top brackets.

17   Installation is otherwise the reverse of the removal procedure. After installation, fill the cooling system with the correct mixture

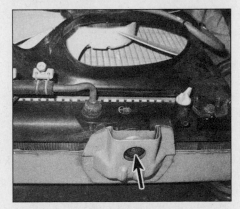

6.16b . . . and the right pin is seated in the right insulator

of antifreeze and water (see Chapter 1).

18   Start the engine, allow it to reach normal operating temperature then check for leaks.

19   Allow the engine to cool completely, then recheck the coolant level, adding as necessary to bring it to the appropriate level (see Chapter 1).

20   If you're working on an automatic transaxle equipped vehicle, check and add fluid as needed (see Chapter 1).

8.8a Remove the lower mounting bolts securing the water pump . . .

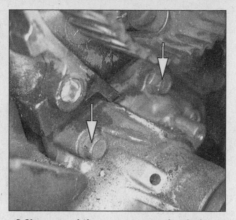

8.8b . . . and the upper mounting bolts - 1998 2.4L SOHC engine shown

8.8c Separate the water pump from the engine block

8.14 Location of the water pump mounting bolts on V6 engines

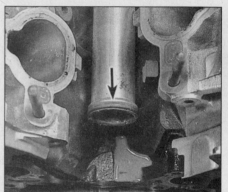

8.17 Install a new O-ring on the water inlet pipe

7   Water pump - check

1   A failure in the water pump can cause serious engine damage due to overheating.
2   If a failure occurs in the pump seal, coolant will leak from the front of the engine.

Four-cylinder engines

3   Water pumps are equipped with weep or vent holes. On four-cylinder engines it is possible to check the water pump weep hole using a flashlight. If a failure occurs in the pump seal, coolant will leak from the hole. **Note:** *Some small black staining around the weep hole is normal. If the stain is heavy brown or actual coolant is evident, replace the pump.*
4   If the water pump shaft bearings fail there may be a howling sound at the front of the engine while it's running. With the engine off and the drivebelt removed, shaft wear can be felt if the water pump pulley is rocked up-and-down. Don't mistake drivebelt slippage, which causes a squealing sound, for water pump bearing failure.

V6 engines

5   The water pump on V6 engines is driven by the timing belt and is concealed by the timing belt cover. If the water pump seal fails, coolant will leak from the bottom of the timing belt cover. This can be verified by removing the timing belt cover and inspecting the pump with a flashlight and a mirror.

8   Water pump - replacement

Warning: *Wait until the engine is completely cool before beginning this procedure.*
Caution: *If the water pump has failed and soaked the timing belt with coolant, install a new timing belt also (see Chapter 2A or 2B).*
1   Disconnect the cable from the negative battery terminal (see Chapter 5).
2   Drain the cooling system (see Chapter 1).
3   Remove the accessory drivebelts (see Chapter 1).

Four-cylinder engines

Refer to illustration 8.8a, 8.8b and 8.8c
4   Remove the water pump pulley.
5   Remove the alternator bracket (see Chapter 5).
6   Remove the timing belt (see Chapter 2A).
7   Remove the timing belt tensioner pulley (see Chapter 2A).
8   Remove the bolts attaching the water pump to the engine block and remove the pump from the engine **(see illustrations)**. If the water pump is stuck, gently tap it with a soft-faced hammer to break the seal.
9   Clean the bolt threads and the threaded holes in the engine to remove the corrosion and sealant. Remove all traces of old gasket material from the sealing surfaces.
10   Clean the O-ring surfaces on the pump and the water inlet pipe.
11   Install a new O-ring on the water inlet

pipe. Wet the O-ring with clean coolant to facilitate assembly.

V6 engines

Refer to illustrations 8.14 and 8.17
12   Remove the alternator bracket (see Chapter 5).
13   Remove the timing belt (see Chapter 2B). On 2004 and later models, remove the crankshaft position sensor (see Chapter 6).
14   Remove the water pump mounting bolts **(see illustration)**.
15   Separate the pump from the water inlet pipe and remove the pump.
16   Clean all the gasket and O-ring surfaces on the pump and the water inlet pipe.
17   Install a new O-ring on the water inlet pipe. Wet the O-ring with clean coolant to facilitate assembly **(see illustration)**.

All models

18   Compare the new pump to the old one to make sure that they're identical.
19   Apply a thin film of RTV sealant to hold the new gasket in place during installation. **Caution:** *Make sure that the gasket is correctly positioned on the water pump and the engine block surface is clean and free of old gasket material.* Carefully mate the pump to the engine.
20   Install the water pump bolts and tighten them to the torque listed in this Chapter's Specifications.

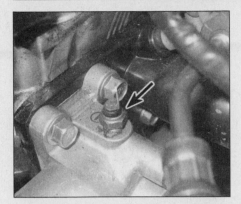

9.4a The coolant temperature sending unit is located on the thermostat housing (1999 and later four-cylinder model shown)

21 The remainder of installation is the reverse of removal. Refill the cooling system (see Chapter 1) when you're done.
22 Operate the engine to check for leaks.

9 Coolant temperature sending unit - check and replacement

Check

Refer to illustrations 9.4a and 9.4b
Note: *This procedure applies only to 2003 and earlier models. The coolant temperature gauge on later models is controlled by the Engine Coolant Temperature (ECT) sensor and the PCM. See Chapter 6 for additional information.*

1 The coolant temperature indicator system consists of a temperature gauge on the instrument cluster and a coolant temperature sending unit mounted on the thermostat housing.
2 If an overheating indication occurs, check the coolant level (see Chapter 1) and make sure all connectors in the wiring harness between the sending unit and the instrument cluster are in good condition and tight.
3 If you're working on a 1999 or later model, remove the air intake duct for access to the sending unit (see Chapter 4).
4 Unplug the electrical connector from the sending unit **(see illustration)**. Using a 12-volt test light connected to a good ground, probe the electrical connector (on the harness side)

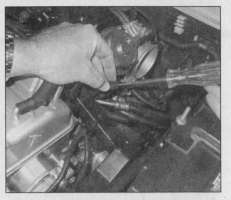

9.4b The coolant temperature gauge and circuit can be checked with a test light; if the gauge and circuit are okay, the light will come on and the gauge needle will deflect when the key is turned to the On position

and have an assistant turn the ignition key On (but don't crank the engine) **(see illustration)**:

a) *If the gauge itself is functioning properly, the test light will light and the gauge needle will deflect; this would indicate that the sending unit is faulty.*
b) *If the test light comes on but the gauge needle doesn't move at all, the gauge is faulty.*
c) *If the test light doesn't come on and the needle doesn't move, the problem lies in the wiring harness.*

5 The sending unit can be checked with an ohmmeter. Unplug the electrical connector from the sending unit and attach the positive probe of an ohmmeter to the terminal of the sending unit; connect the negative probe to a good ground. If the engine is warm (not hot - approximately 150-degrees F [65-degrees C]), the resistance should be approximately 104 ohms, plus or minus 14 ohms. As the engine temperature INCREASES the resistance of the sending unit should DECREASE. Conversely, as the engine temperature DECREASES the resistance of the sending unit should INCREASE. If the sensor fails either of these tests, replace it.

Replacement

Warning: *Wait until the engine is completely*

cool before beginning this procedure.
6 Prepare the new sending unit by coating the threads with thread sealant. Remove the radiator cap to release any residual pressure in the cooling system, then reinstall the cap.
7 If you're working on a 1999 through 2003 model, remove the air intake duct for access to the sending unit (see Chapter 4).
8 Unscrew the sending unit from the thermostat housing and install the new one as quickly as possible to minimize coolant loss. Tighten the sending unit securely.
9 Reinstall the air intake duct, if removed.
10 Check the engine coolant, adding as necessary to bring it to the appropriate level (see Chapter 1).

10 Blower motor resistor and blower motor - replacement

Warning: *These models are equipped with airbags. Always disable the airbag system before working in the vicinity of airbag system components to avoid the possibility of accidental deployment of the airbag, which could cause personal injury (see Chapter 12).*

Blower motor resistor

Refer to illustrations 10.2 and 10.3
1 Remove the glove box and lower trim panel from the passenger compartment (see Chapter 11).
2 Disconnect the electrical connector from the blower motor resistor **(see illustration)**.
3 Remove the blower motor resistor mounting screws **(see illustration)**, then remove the resistor from the joint duct (1994 through 1998 models without air conditioning and all 1999 and later models) or from the evaporator housing (1994 through 1998 models with air conditioning).
4 Installation is the reverse of removal.

Blower motor

Refer to illustrations 10.5, 10.7 and 10.8
5 Remove the glove box and the lower trim panel **(see illustration)** from the passenger compartment (see Chapter 11).
6 On 1994 through 1998 air-conditioned

10.2 Unplug the electrical connector from the blower motor resistor

10.3 Remove the screws from the blower motor resistor

10.5 Remove this cover for access to the blower motor on 2004 and later models

10.7 Unplug the electrical connector from the blower motor

10.8 Location of the blower motor mounting screws

models, remove the changeover damper module from the blower motor housing.

7   Disconnect the blower motor electrical connector **(see illustration)**.

8   Remove the blower motor mounting screws **(see illustration)** and remove the blower motor.

9   Installation is the reverse of removal.

11   Heater/air conditioner control assembly - removal and installation

Refer to illustrations 11.4a, 11.4b, 11.5 and 11.6
Warning: *These models are equipped with airbags. Always disable the airbag system before working in the vicinity of airbag system*

components to avoid the possibility of acci-dental deployment of the airbag, which could cause personal injury (see Chapter 12).

1   Disconnect the cable from the negative battery terminal (see Chapter 5).

2   Refer to Chapter 11 and remove the center instrument panel trim bezel.

3   On 1998 and earlier models, remove the radio (see Chapter 12).

4   Remove the heater control mounting screws or, on 2004 and later models, pry it out with a trim tool **(see illustrations)**.

5   On 2003 and earlier models, disconnect the control cables from the levers **(see illustration)**.

6   Disconnect the wiring from the control unit **(see illustration)**.

7   On 2003 and earlier models, disconnect the cables from the control unit.

8   Remove the control assembly.

12   Heater core - replacement

Refer to illustrations 12.2, 12.4a, 12.4b, 12.4c, 12.5a, 12.5b, 12.6, 12.7, 12.8, 12.9, 12.10a, 12.10b, 12.10c, 12.11a, 12.11b, 12.11c, 12.12, 12.13a, 12.13b, 12.22, 12.23 and 12.24
Warning 1: *These models are equipped with airbags. Always disable the airbag system before working in the vicinity of airbag system components to avoid the possibility of acci-dental deployment of the airbag, which could cause personal injury (see Chapter 12).*
Warning 2: *The heating/ventilation/air condi-tioning (HVAC) housing must be removed before the heater core or the air conditioning evaporator can be removed. So if you are going to remove the heater core, have the air conditioning system discharged by an auto-motive air conditioning shop BEFORE begin-ning this procedure. Do NOT loosen any refrig-erant line fittings until the system has been discharged. The system is under high pressure and could cause a serious injury if opened while still pressurized. You will not be able to drive the vehicle to an automotive air condi-*

11.4a To detach the air conditioning and heater control assembly from the instrument panel, remove these screws

11.4b Use a plastic trim tool or a screw-driver wrapped with tape to carefully release the hooks on the heater/radio control assembly (2004 and later models)

11.5 Disconnect the control cables from the air mix damper lever and the air outlet changeover lever

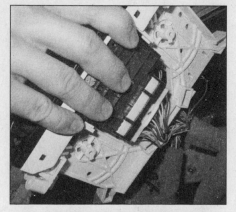

11.6 To remove the air conditioning and heater control assembly, unplug the electrical connector

12.2 Trace the heater hoses to the firewall, loosen the hose clamps, then disconnect the hoses from the heater core pipes

12.4a First, remove the bolts from the right side of the center bracket (2003 and earlier models)

12.4b Next, remove the bolts from the upper section of the center bracket

12.4c Finally, remove the bolts from the left side of the center bracket assembly

12.5a Remove the harness fasteners from the center bracket (2003 and earlier models)

12.5b Remove the harness fasteners from the center bracket on the upper, left side of the dash area

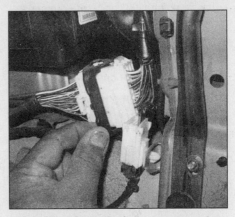

12.6 Disconnect the harness connector

tioning shop to have the system discharged once you have begun this procedure because the instrument panel must be removed and the vehicle will not be driveable.

1 Have the air conditioning system discharged by a dealer service department or an automotive air conditioning shop before proceeding (see **Warning 2**).

2 Drain the cooling system (see Chapter 1) and disconnect the heater hoses from the heater core inlet and outlet pipes at the fire-wall **(see illustration)**.

3 Remove the instrument panel (see Chapter 11).

2003 and earlier models

4 Remove the center bracket bolts **(see illustrations)**.

5 Remove the harness push-on fasteners from the center bracket **(see illustrations)** and remove the center bracket from the passenger compartment.

6 Disconnect the harness connector **(see illustration)**.

7 Remove the right side vent and the joint duct **(see illustration)**.

8 Remove the automatic compressor controller **(see illustration)**. **Note:** *V6 models are equipped with an automatic belt lock controller.*

12.7 Remove the right side vent and the joint duct from the heater control unit and the blower housing

12.8 Disconnect the harness connector and remove the automatic compressor controller

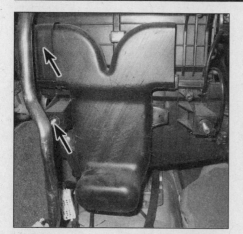

12.9 Remove the mounting nut and separate the center vent from the heater control unit (2003 and earlier models)

12.10a Remove the upper mounting nuts from the heater control unit

12.10b Remove the mounting nuts from the front of the heater control unit . . .

9   Remove the center vent (see illustration).
10   Remove the heater control unit mounting nuts (see illustrations).

1999 through 2003 models
11   Remove the center reinforcement mounting bolts and nuts (see illustrations).
12   Remove the blower unit (see illustration).
13   Without removing the center reinforcement, install guide bolts (see illustrations) and pull the reinforcement bar four inches forward for clearance.

2004 and later models
14   Move the steering column out of the way (see Chapter 10). Also remove the suspension strut support bar from the engine compartment.
15   Refer to Chapter 11 and remove the center console and the front seats.
16   Refer to Chapter 5 and remove the battery.
17   Refer to Chapter 4 and remove the air filter housing assembly.
18   Disconnect the air conditioning system

refrigerant lines. Cover the ends to prevent contamination.
19   Remove the heater ducts that supply the rear of the vehicle.
20   Remove the fuse block and set it out of the way. Also make sure the ECU is set aside.
21   Unbolt and remove the crossmember support bar. **Note:** *There are several wiring connectors that must be disconnected. Be sure to make notes and label any that could be confusing during assembly.* **Note:** *It may be possible on some models to keep the crossmember in position using guide bolts instead of removing it completely* (see illustration 12.13a). Remove the data link connector bracket.

All models
22   Carefully remove the heater unit (see illustration).
23   Remove the heater core retaining screws (see illustration).
24   Pull the heater core out of the housing (see illustration).
25   Remove the clips from the heater housing, separate the two halves of the housing,

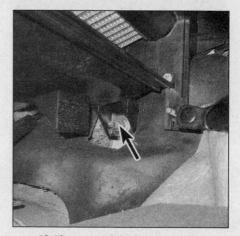

12.10c . . . and the lower section

then clean the coolant from the housing.
26   Installation is the reverse of removal. Don't forget to reconnect the heater core inlet and outlet hoses at the firewall.
27   Refill the cooling system (see Chapter 1), then have the air conditioning system evacuated, recharged and leak tested by the shop that discharged it.

12.11a Remove the center reinforcement bolts from the right side of the passenger compartment . . .

12.11b . . . the center section of the dash area . . .

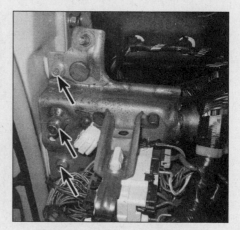

12.11c . . . and the left side of the center reinforcement

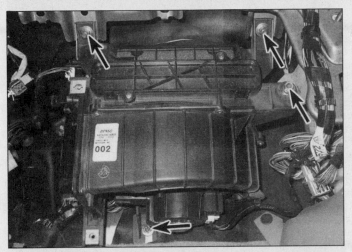

12.12 Remove the blower housing mounting nuts and bolts, then remove the assembly from the passenger compartment

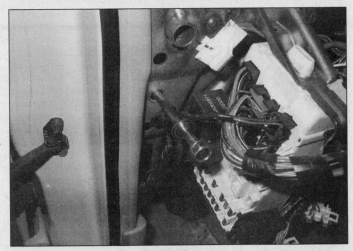

12.13a Install a guide bolt into the left side of the center reinforcement . . .

13 Air conditioning and heating system - check and maintenance

Refer to illustration 13.1

Warning: *The air conditioning system is under high pressure. Do not loosen any hose fittings or remove any components until after the system has been discharged by a dealer service department or service station. Always wear eye protection when disconnecting air conditioning system fittings.*

1   The following maintenance checks should be performed on a regular basis to ensure the air conditioner continues to operate at peak efficiency.

a) *Check the compressor drivebelt. If it's worn or deteriorated, replace it (see Chapter 1).*

b) *Check the drivebelt tension and, if necessary, adjust it (see Chapter 1).*

c) *Check the system hoses. Look for cracks, bubbles, hard spots and deterioration. Inspect the hoses and all fittings for oil bubbles and seepage. If there's any evidence of wear, damage or leaks, replace the hose(s).*

12.13b . . . and the right side to keep the center reinforcement in position

d) *Inspect the condenser fins for leaves, bugs and other debris. Use a "fin comb" or compressed air to clean the condenser.*

e) *Make sure the system has the correct refrigerant charge.*

12.22 Remove the heater unit from the dash area

f) *Check the evaporator housing drain tube* **(see illustration)** *for blockage.*

2   It's a good idea to operate the system for about 10 minutes at least once a month, particularly during the winter. Long term non-

12.23 To remove the heater core, remove the mounting screw from the bracket (2003 and earlier models)

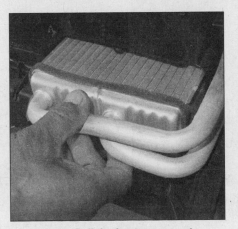

12.24 Pull the heater core out of the housing

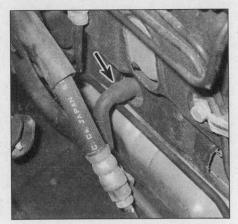

13.1 Look for the evaporator drain hose on the firewall; to remove it for cleaning or for removing the evaporator, simply pull it off

13.7 If the air conditioning system is properly charged, the low-pressure line (suction line) should feel cold and the high-pressure line (discharge line) should feel warm

A   Low-pressure line (should feel cold)
B   High-pressure line (should feel warm)

use can cause hardening, and subsequent failure, of the seals.

3   Because of the complexity of the air conditioning system and the special equipment necessary to service it, in-depth troubleshooting and repairs are not included in this manual (refer to the *Haynes Automotive Heating and Air Conditioning Repair Manual*). However, simple checks and component replacement procedures are provided in this Chapter.

4   The most common cause of poor cooling is simply a low system refrigerant charge. If a noticeable drop in cool air output occurs, the following quick check will help you determine if the refrigerant level is low.

Checking the refrigerant charge

Refer to illustration 13.7
5   Warm the engine up to normal operating temperature.

6   Place the air conditioning temperature selector at the coldest setting and the blower at the highest setting. Open the doors (to make sure the air conditioning system doesn't cycle off as soon as it cools the passenger compartment.

7   With the compressor engaged - the clutch will make an audible click and the center of the clutch will rotate - feel the lines going to and from the evaporator **(see illustration)**. The high-pressure (small diameter) line should feel warm and the low-pressure (large diameter) line should feel cold. If so, the system is properly charged.

8   Place a thermometer in the dashboard vent nearest the evaporator and operate the system until the indicated temperature is around 40 to 45-degrees F. If the ambient (outside) air temperature is very high, say 110-degrees F, the duct air temperature may be as high as 60-degrees F, but generally the air conditioning is 30 to 50-degrees F cooler than the ambient air. **Note:** *Humidity of the ambient air also affects the cooling capacity of the system. Higher ambient humidity lowers the effectiveness of the air conditioning system.*

Adding refrigerant

Refer to illustrations 13.12 and 13.15
9   Buy an automotive charging kit at an auto parts store. A charging kit includes a 14-ounce can of refrigerant, a tap valve and a short section of hose that can be attached between the tap valve and the system low side service valve. Because one can of refrigerant may not be sufficient to bring the system charge up to the proper level, it's a good idea to buy an additional can. Make sure that one of the cans contains red refrigerant dye. If the system is leaking, the red dye will leak out with the refrigerant and help you pinpoint the location of the leak. **Caution:** *There are two types of refrigerant used in automotive systems; R-12 - which has been widely used on earlier models and the more environmentally-friendly R-134a used in all models cov-*

ered by this manual. These two refrigerants (and their appropriate refrigerant oils) are not compatible and must never be mixed or components will be damaged. Use only R-134a refrigerant in the models covered by this manual.

10   Hook up the charging kit by following the manufacturer's instructions. **Warning:** *DO NOT hook the charging kit hose to the system high side! The fittings on the charging kit are designed to fit **only** on the low side of the system.*

11   Back off the valve handle on the charging kit and screw the kit onto the refrigerant can, making sure first that the O-ring or rubber seal inside the threaded portion of the kit is in place. **Warning:** *Wear protective eyewear when dealing with pressurized refrigerant cans.*

12   Remove the dust cap from the low-side charging connection and attach the quick-connect fitting on the kit hose **(see illustration)**.

13   Warm up the engine and turn on the air conditioner. Keep the charging kit hose away from the fan and other moving parts. **Note:** *The charging process requires the compressor to be running. Your compressor may cycle off if the pressure is low due to a low charge. If the clutch cycles off, you can pull the low-pressure cycling switch plug and attach a jumper wire. This will keep the compressor ON.*

14   Turn the valve handle on the kit until the stem pierces the can, then back the handle out to release the refrigerant. You should be able to hear the rush of gas. Add refrigerant to the low side of the system until both the receiver-drier surface and the evaporator inlet pipe feel about the same temperature . Allow stabilization time between each addition.

15   If you have an accurate thermometer, place it in the center air conditioning vent **(see illustration)** and note the temperature of the air coming out of the vent. A fully-charged system which is working correctly should cool down to about 40-degrees F. Generally, an air conditioning system will put out air that

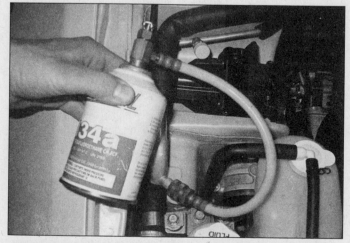

13.12 Cans of R-134A refrigerant (available at auto parts stores) can be added to the low side of the air conditioning system with a simple recharging kit (2000 2.4L SOHC engine shown)

13.15 Insert a thermometer in the center vent, turn on the air conditioning system and wait for it to cool down; depending on the humidity, the output air should be 30 to 40-degrees cooler than the ambient air temperature

is 30 to 40 degrees F cooler than the ambient air. For example, if the ambient (outside) air temperature is very high (over 100-degrees F), the temperature of air coming out of the registers should be 60 to 70-degrees F.

16 When the can is empty, turn the valve handle to the closed position and release the connection from the low-side port. Replace the dust cap. **Warning:** *Never add more than two cans of refrigerant to the system.*

17 Remove the charging kit from the can and store the kit for future use with the piercing valve in the UP position, to prevent inadvertently piercing the can on the next use.

Heating systems

18 If the carpet under the heater core is damp, or if antifreeze vapor or steam is coming through the vents, the heater core is leaking. Remove it (see Section 12) and install a new unit (most radiator shops will not repair a leaking heater core).

19 If the air coming out of the heater vents isn't hot, the problem could stem from any of the following causes:

a) *The thermostat is stuck open, preventing the engine coolant from warming up enough to carry heat to the heater core. Replace the thermostat (see Section 3).*

b) *There is a blockage in the system, preventing the flow of coolant through the heater core. Feel both heater hoses at the firewall. They should be hot. If one of them is cold, there is an obstruction in one of the hoses or in the heater core, or the heater control valve is shut. Detach the hoses and back flush the heater core with a water hose. If the heater core is clear but circulation is impeded, remove the two hoses and flush them out with a water hose.*

c) *If flushing fails to remove the blockage from the heater core, the core must be replaced (see Section 12).*

Eliminating air conditioning odors

20 Unpleasant odors that often develop in air conditioning systems are caused by the growth of a fungus, usually on the surface of the evaporator core. The warm, humid environment there is a perfect breeding ground for mildew to develop..

21 The evaporator core on most vehicles is difficult to access, and factory dealerships have a lengthy, expensive process for eliminating the fungus by opening up the evaporator case and using a powerful disinfectant and rinse on the core until the fungus is gone. You can service your own system at home, but it takes something much stronger than basic household germ-killers or deodorizers.

22 Aerosol disinfectants for automotive air conditioning systems are available in most auto parts stores, but remember when shopping for them that the most effective treatments are also the most expensive. The basic procedure for using these sprays is to start by running the system in the RECIRC mode for ten minutes with the blower on its highest speed. Use the highest heat mode to dry out the system and keep the compressor from engaging by disconnecting the wiring connector at the compressor (see Section 14).

23 Make sure that the disinfectant can comes with a long spray hose. Point the nozzle through the air recirculation door so that it protrudes inside the evaporator housing **(see illustration)**, and then spray according to the manufacturer's recommendations. Try to cover the whole surface of the evaporator core, by aiming the spray up, down and sideways. Follow the manufacturer's recommendations for the length of spray and waiting time between applications.

24 Once the evaporator has been cleaned, the best way to prevent the mildew from coming back again is to make sure your evaporator housing drain tube is clear **(see illustration 13.1)**.

14 Air conditioning compressor - removal and installation

Warning: *The air conditioning system is under high pressure. DO NOT disassemble any part of the system (hoses, compressor, line fittings, etc.) until after the system has been discharged by a dealer service department or by an automotive air conditioning shop.*
Note: *If you're replacing the compressor, also replace the receiver-drier (see Section 15).*

Removal

Refer to illustrations 14.6 and 14.10

1 Have the system discharged (see the **Warning** above).

2 Disconnect the cable from the negative battery terminal (see Chapter 5).

3 Remove the engine compartment protection cover from below the vehicle.

4 Remove the fender splash shield.

5 Remove the air conditioning compressor drivebelt (see Chapter 1).

6 Unplug the electrical connector **(see illustration)** from the compressor clutch.

7 Disconnect the refrigerant lines from the compressor. Plug the open fittings to prevent entry of dirt and moisture. Be sure to remove and discard the old refrigerant line fitting O-rings.

8 On 1994 through 1998 models, remove the tensioner pulley retaining nut and the tensioner pulley. Remove the tensioner pulley bracket bolts and separate the tensioner bracket from the compressor bracket. Inspect the threads on the pulley bolt and nut, particularly on the adjusting bolt. Make sure that both nut/bolt are in good condition before re-using them. **Note:** *On 1999 and later models, it is not necessary to remove the tensioner pulley or the tensioner pulley bracket. The compressor bolts are accessible.*

9 On 3.0L V6 models, remove the condenser cooling fan from the radiator (see Section 4).

13.23 Remove the glove box (see Chapter 11) and insert the nozzle of the disinfectant can into the evaporator housing by shoving it through the air recirculation door

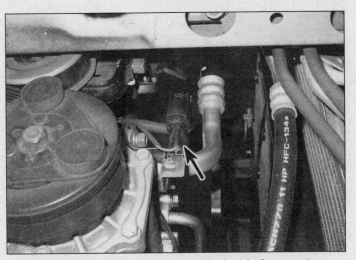

14.6 Unplug the compressor clutch electrical connector

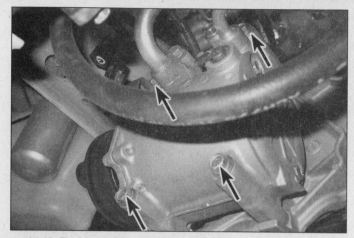

14.10 To detach the compressor from its mounting bracket, remove these bolts

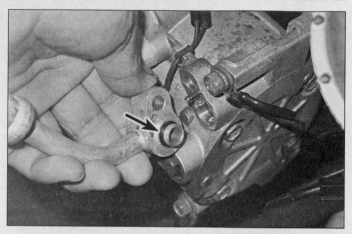

14.14 Be sure to discard the old O-ring on each refrigerant line fitting

10   Remove the compressor mounting bolts **(see illustration)** and remove it from the vehicle.

Installation

Refer to illustration 14.14

11   If a new compressor is being installed, pour out the oil from the old compressor into a graduated container and add that amount of new refrigerant oil to the new compressor. Also follow any directions included with the new compressor.

12   The clutch might have to be transferred from the original compressor to the new unit.

13   Installation is the reverse of removal. Replace all O-rings with new ones **(see illustration)** specifically made for use with R-134a refrigerant and lubricate them with R-134a-compatible refrigerant oil.

14   Have the system evacuated, recharged and leak tested by the shop that discharged it.

15   Air conditioning receiver-drier - removal and installation

Warning: *The air conditioning system is under high pressure. DO NOT disassemble any part*

of the system (hose, compressor, line fittings, etc.) until after the system has been evacuated and the refrigerant recovered by a dealer service department or service station.
Caution: *Replacement receiver-drier units are so effective at absorbing moisture that they can quickly saturate upon exposure to the atmosphere. When installing a new unit, have all tools and supplies ready for quick reassembly to avoid having the system open any longer than necessary.*

Removal

Refer to illustration 15.3

1   The receiver-drier acts as a reservoir for the system refrigerant. It's located on the right side of the engine compartment, next to the radiator and condenser.

2   Have the system discharged (see the **Warning** at the beginning of this Section).

2003 and earlier models

3   Disconnect the dual pressure switch electrical connector **(see illustration)** from the receiver-drier.

4   Disconnect the refrigerant lines from the

receiver-drier. Be sure to discard and replace the old O-rings in the fittings and then plug the open fittings to prevent entry of dirt and moisture.

5   Remove the bracket bolts at the receiver/drier.

2004 and later models

Refer to illustration 15.7

6   Refer to Section 16 and remove the condenser. **Note:** *On some models, it may be possible to remove the receiver/drier without first removing the condenser. On these models, remove the front bumper cover only.*

7   Disconnect the lower rear mounting bracket. Disconnect the refrigerant fittings **(see illustration)**. Unclamp the receiver/drier from the side of the condenser and lift it off. Remove the O-rings and discard them so they can be replaced with new ones.

Installation

8   Installation is the reverse of removal. If a new receiver-drier is being installed add one ounce of refrigerant oil to it before installation.

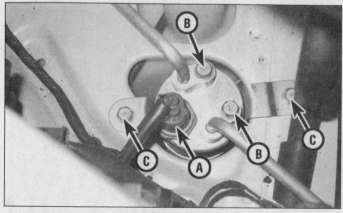

15.3 To remove the receiver-drier, unplug the dual-pressure switch electrical connector (A), remove the refrigerant line inlet and outlet fitting bolts (B) and then remove the receiver-drier mounting bolts (C) (2003 and earlier models)

15.7 Refrigerant line fittings, 2004 and later models - the receiver/drier is also secured by a bracket at the rear

16.11a Disconnect the refrigerant lines at the condenser; remove the nuts then pull off the fittings (2003 and earlier models)

16.11b Be sure to discard and replace the O-rings with new ones

9   Take the vehicle back to the shop that discharged it. Have the system evacuated, recharged and leak tested.

16   Air conditioning condenser - removal and installation

Refer to illustrations 16.11a, 16.11b, 16.12b and 16.12b

Warning: *The air conditioning system is under high pressure. Do not loosen any hose fittings or remove any components until after the system has been discharged by a dealer service department or service station. Always wear eye protection when disconnecting air conditioning system components.*

Note: *The receiver-drier should be replaced if the condenser was damaged, causing the system to be open for some time (see Section 15).*

1   Have the system discharged (see the **Warning** at the beginning of this Section).
2   Disconnect the cable from the negative battery terminal (see Chapter 5).

2003 and earlier models

3   Remove the engine cooling fans (see Section 4).
4   Remove the radiator mounting brackets (see Section 6).
5   Remove the radiator (see Section 6).

2004 and later models

6   Refer to Chapter 4 and remove the interfering air intake duct.
7   Refer to Chapter 11 and remove the radiator grille.
8   Remove the hood latch and radiator top support structure.
9   Remove the condenser fan, if so equipped.
10   Raise the vehicle and support it securely

on jackstands. Remove the engine lower splash shield.

All models

11   Disconnect the refrigerant liquid lines **(see illustration)**. Be sure to remove and discard the old O-rings **(see illustration)**.
12   Remove the condenser mounting bolts **(see illustrations)** and remove the condenser from the vehicle.
13   Be sure to inspect the rubber mounting bolt insulators for cracks and deterioration. Replace them if they're worn or damaged.
14   Installation is the reverse of removal. Be sure to use new O-rings when reconnecting the refrigerant line fittings. If a new condenser is being installed add one ounce of refrigerant oil to it before installation.
15   Take the vehicle back to the shop that discharged it. Have the system evacuated, recharged and leak tested.

16.12a Remove the condenser mounting bolts (2003 and earlier models)

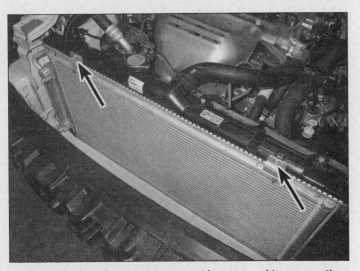

16.12b The front bumper cover must be removed to access the condenser mounting bolts (arrows) and the receiver/drier fittings

**17.3 Disconnect the dual-pressure switch electrical connector
(2000 2.4L SOHC model shown, others similar)**

**17.4 Remove the dual-pressure switch using a deep socket
(2003 and earlier models)**

17 Air conditioning dual-pressure switch - replacement

Refer to illustrations 17.3 and 17.4

Warning: *The air conditioning system is under high pressure. Do not loosen any hose fittings or remove any components until after the system has been discharged by a dealer service department or service station. Always wear eye protection when disconnecting air conditioning system components.*

Note: *The dual-pressure switch detects high* refrigerant pressure at 426 psi, turns off the compressor clutch and activates the clutch again at 341 psi. If the system pressure drops too low, it shuts off at 28 psi and then back on again at 32 psi. 1994 models are equipped with a four-terminal switch called the triple-pressure switch. 2004 and later models use an A/C pressure sensor located near the receiver/drier.

1   Have the system discharged (see the **Warning** at the beginning of this Section).

2   Disconnect the cable from the negative battery terminal (see Chapter 5).

3   Disconnect the electrical connector from the dual-pressure switch **(see illustration)**.

4   Unscrew the dual-pressure switch **(see illustration)**.

5   Lubricate the switch O-ring with clean refrigerant oil of the correct type.

6   Screw the new switch onto the threads until hand tight, and then tighten it securely.

7   Reconnect the electrical connector.

8   Have the system evacuated, charged and leak tested by the shop that discharged it.

Chapter 4
Fuel and exhaust systems

Contents

Specifications

General

Accelerator cable freeplay	
2003 and earlier models	0.04 to 0.08 inch (1 to 2 mm)
2004 and later models	Not applicable, electronically operated
Fuel pressure	
2003 and earlier models	
Vacuum hose connected	38 psi (270 kPa)
Vacuum hose disconnected	47 to 50 psi (330 to 350 kPa)
2004 and later models, at idle	47 psi (330 kPa)
Fuel system hold pressure (fuel pressure after engine is shut off)	Should not drop within two minutes after shut-off
Fuel injector resistance at 68-degrees F (20-degrees C)	
2003 and earlier models	13 to 16 ohms
2004 and later models	10.5 to 13.5 ohms

Torque specifications

Note: *One foot-pound (ft-lb) of torque is equivalent to 12 inch-pounds (in-lbs) of torque. Torque values below approximately 15 foot-pounds are expressed in inch-pounds, because most foot-pound torque wrenches are not accurate at these smaller values.*

	Ft-lbs (unless otherwise indicated)	Nm
Fuel rail mounting bolts	106 in-lbs	12
Fuel pressure regulator bolts	78 in-lbs	9
Fuel tank retaining nuts	19	26
Throttle body mounting bolts		
2003 and earlier models	168 in-lbs	19
2004 and later models	21	28

1 General information

Multiport Fuel Injection (MFI) system

Refer to illustration 1.1

The vehicles covered by this manual are equipped with a sequential Multiport Fuel Injection (MFI) system **(see illustration)**. This system uses timed impulses to sequentially inject the fuel directly into the intake ports of each cylinder. The injectors are controlled by the Powertrain Control Module (PCM). The PCM monitors various engine parameters and delivers the exact amount of fuel, in the correct sequence, to the intake ports. This Chapter's information pertains to the air and fuel delivery components of the fuel injection system only. Refer to Chapter 6 for additional general information concerning the emissions and engine control systems.

Fuel pump and lines

All models are equipped with an in-tank electric fuel pump. The fuel pump can be removed and installed through an access cover under the rear seat. The in-tank fuel level sending unit is an integral part of the fuel pump module.

On 2003 and earlier models, there is a fuel pressure regulator that is mounted on the fuel rail. It is a spring-loaded valve that maintains proper fuel pressure. When the fuel pressure rises, the regulator opens and allows unneeded fuel to return to the fuel tank via a steel line. On 2004 and later models, the fuel pressure regulator is a part of the fuel pump module, which is mounted in the fuel tank.

The fuel filter is located in the engine compartment, on the firewall, on 1994 through 1998 models. Refer to Chapter 1 for the replacement procedure. The fuel filter is located inside the fuel tank along with the fuel pump on 1999 and later models. Fuel filter replacement on 1999 and later models is covered in the fuel pump replacement procedure in this Chapter.

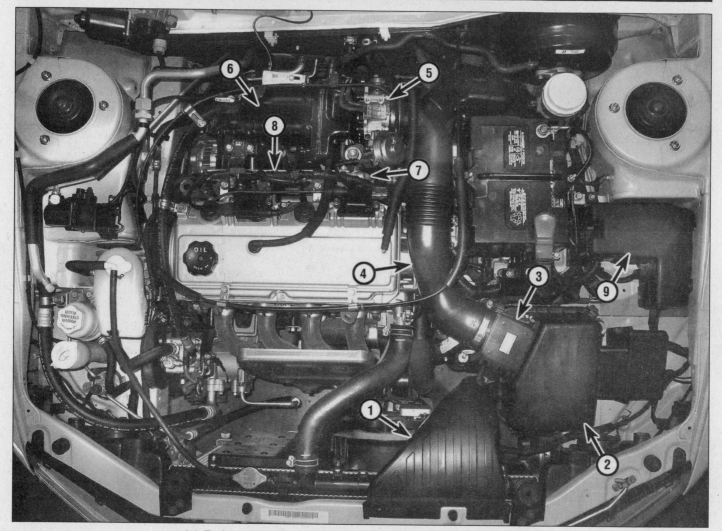

1.1 Typical fuel system components (1999 through 2003 2.4L models)

1   Fresh air intake
2   Air filter housing
3   Volume Air Flow sensor
4   Air intake duct

5   Throttle body
6   Intake manifold
7   Fuel supply line (test fuel pressure here)

8   Fuel rail and fuel injectors (fuel injectors not visible in this photo)
9   Underhood fuse/relay panel

Exhaust system

The exhaust system consists of the exhaust manifold(s), the catalytic converter(s), the exhaust pipes and a muffler. Each of these components is replaceable. For further information regarding the catalytic converter, refer to Chapter 6.

2   Fuel pressure relief procedure

Refer to illustration 2.3
Warning: *Gasoline is extremely flammable, so take extra precautions when you work on any part of the fuel system. Don't smoke or allow open flames or bare light bulbs near the work area, and don't work in a garage where a gas-type appliance (such as a water heater or a clothes dryer) is present. Since gasoline is carcinogenic, wear latex gloves when there's a possibility of being exposed to fuel,*

and if you spill any on your skin, rinse it off immediately with soap and water. Mop up any spills immediately and do not store fuel-soaked rags where they could ignite. The fuel system is under constant pressure, so, if any fuel lines are to be disconnected, the pressure must be relieved first. When you perform any kind of work on the fuel system, wear safety glasses and have a Class B type fire extinguisher on hand.

1   Remove the fuel filler cap to relieve the fuel tank pressure.
2   On 1994 through 1998 models, remove the rear seat cushion (see Chapter 11), remove the fuel pump access cover and disconnect the electrical connector from the fuel pump (see Section 5).
3   On 1999 and later models locate the fuel pump relay and remove it from the fuse and relay panel. On 1999 through 2001 models, the fuel pump relay is located in the engine compartment fuse and relay panel **(see illus-**

tration). On 2002 and later models, the fuel pump relay is located in the passenger compartment fuse and relay panel, which is located at the left end of the dash.
4   Start the engine and allow it to run until it stops. After the engine dies, crank it again to verify that the fuel pressure is completely relieved.
5   Before working on any part of the fuel system, be sure to disconnect the cable from the negative battery terminal (see Chapter 5).
6   Even after the fuel pressure has been relieved, always lay a shop towel over any fuel connection that is to be separated to absorb the residual fuel that will leak out.
7   When you are finished working on the fuel system, reconnect the fuel pump electrical connector (1994 through 1998 models) or plug the fuel pump relay into the fuse and relay panel (1999 and later models).
8   Reconnect the cable to the negative battery terminal (see Chapter 5).

2.3 The fuel pump relay is located in the engine compartment fuse/relay panel on 1999 through 2001 models

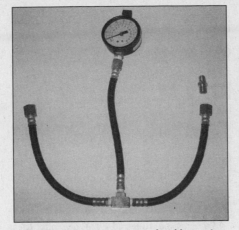

3.7a Typical fuel pressure checking setup

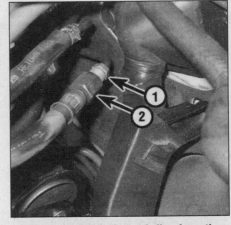

3.7b Trace the fuel supply line from the fuel rail back to the firewall and unscrew this fitting (after you have relieved the system fuel pressure)

1 *Fuel supply line fitting (firewall side of connection)*
2 *Fuel supply line fitting (fuel rail side of connection)*

9   Turn the ignition key to the ON position a few times to pressurize the system, then check the fittings of the fuel system component that you serviced for leaks.
10   Install the fuel filler cap and tighten it securely.

---

3   Fuel pump/fuel pressure - check

Warning: *Gasoline is extremely flammable, so take extra precautions when you work on any part of the fuel system (see the Warning in Section 2).*
Note: *To check the fuel pressure, you will need a fuel pressure gauge capable of reading fuel pressures up to 70 psi. The fuel rail is not equipped with a Schrader valve type fuel pressure test port, so you will also need to obtain an adapter suitable for tee-ing into the fuel supply line at the fuel rail.*

General checks

1   If you suspect poor fuel delivery, check the following items first:
   a) *Check the battery and make sure it's fully charged (see Chapter 5).*
   b) *Check the fuel pump fuse (if equipped, it's in the fuse box in the engine compartment).*
   c) *Check the fuel filter for restriction (on the firewall on 1994 through 1998 models; part of the in-tank fuel pump module on 1999 and later models).*
   d) *Inspect all fuel lines to verify that the problem is not caused by a leaking fuel line or connection.*

2   Verify that the fuel pump actually runs as follows: Place the transaxle in Park (automatic) or Neutral (manual) and apply the parking brake. Remove the fuel filler cap, then have an assistant turn the ignition key to the ON (*not* the START) position while you stand next to the open fuel filler neck and listen. When the key is turned to ON, you should hear a brief (about two seconds) whirring noise as the pump comes on and pressurizes the system. If the fuel pump makes no sound, check the

fuel pump relay, fuse and electrical circuit. If the fuel pump runs, but you still suspect that the fuel system is not functioning correctly, continue with the fuel pump pressure check.
3   If the pump does not come on with the ignition key in the ON position, check the fuel pump relay (see Chapter 12). On 1994 through 1998 models, the fuel pump relay is located in the dash, where it's sandwiched between the Powertrain Control Module (PCM) and the Transaxle Control Module (TCM), both of which are located in the space directly ahead of the radio. To access the fuel pump relay on these models, you'll have to remove the center console trim panel (see Chapter 11), the radio (see Chapter 12), the storage receptacle, the cup holder and the PCM (see Chapter 6). On 1999 through 2001 models, the fuel pump relay is located in the engine compartment fuse and relay panel **(see illustration 2.3)**. On 2002 and later models, the fuel pump relay is located in the passenger compartment fuse and relay panel, which is located on the left end of the dash.
4   If the relay is good but the fuel pump does not operate, check for voltage to the fuel pump with the engine cranking.
5   If the fuel pump circuit wiring and connectors are good, replace the fuel pump (see Section 6).

Fuel pump pressure check

2003 and earlier models
Refer to illustrations 3.7a, 3.7b, 3.7c and 3.7d
Warning: *Make sure the fuel pressure gauge hose is positioned away from the engine drivebelt before starting the engine.*
6   Relieve the system fuel pressure (see Section 2).
7   In order to measure the fuel pressure, you'll need a fuel pressure gauge **(see illustration)** capable of reading up to 70 psi and a T-type adapter suitable for tee-ing into the fuel system. The fuel supply line is not equipped with a fuel pressure test port (Schrader valve fitting). At dealerships a special fuel pressure adapter is installed between the fuel supply line and the flange at the end of the fuel rail. However, this adapter is expensive, and it's not critical that the fuel pressure be measured at this location. Instead, trace the fuel supply line back to the threaded fitting at the firewall **(see illustration)**. Unscrew this fitting and

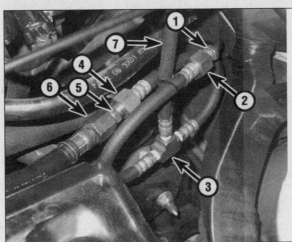

3.7c The easiest way to "tee" the fuel pressure gauge into the fuel supply line:

1 *Fuel supply line fitting (firewall side)*
2 *Fuel pressure test hose fitting*
3 *T-type adapter*
4 *Fuel pressure test hose fitting*
5 *Threaded male fitting between female test hose fitting and female fuel supply line fitting*
6 *Hose to fuel rail*

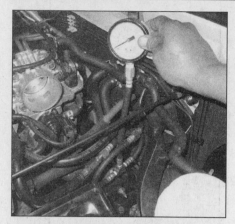

3.7d Your setup should look like this when it's installed (the air intake duct has been removed for access here - be sure to reinstall it before starting the engine so a trouble code is not set)

4.2a A typical fuel and EVAP line clip; to remove it, simply remove this bolt

then, using the T-type adapter, tee the fuel pressure gauge into the fuel supply line between the metal line (firewall side) and the high pressure hose from the fitting to the fuel rail **(see illustrations)**.

8   Turn off all accessories, then turn the ignition key to ON (engine not running). The fuel pump should run for about two seconds to pressurize the system. Check your fuel pressure test gauge setup and make sure that none of the fittings are leaking.

9   Start the engine and allow it to warm it up until it's idling at its normal operating temperature. Note the reading on the gauge and compare your measurement to the fuel pressure listed in this Chapter's Specifications.

10   If the fuel pressure is lower than the specified range, turn the ignition key to OFF, pinch off the fuel return line, then turn the key to ON again. **Caution:** *Use special pliers designed specifically for pinching a rubber fuel hose (available at most auto parts stores). Using any other type of pliers might damage the fuel line.* **Caution:** *Do not allow the fuel pressure to rise above the specified range any longer than necessary to get a reading. Block-*

ing the fuel return hose for too long could damage the fuel pump or cause a leak. If the fuel pressure is now above the specified pressure, replace the fuel pressure regulator (see Section 14). If the fuel pressure is still lower than specified, inspect the fuel injectors, the fuel filter (if equipped with an external filter) and the fuel supply and return lines for leaks. If no leak is found, remove the fuel pump assembly (see Section 5) and inspect the fuel pump inlet "sock" (strainer) for restrictions. Also check the fuel pump wiring for high resistance. If no problems are found, replace the fuel pump.

11   If the fuel pressure recorded in Step 9 is higher than specified, check the fuel return line for restrictions. If no restrictions are found, replace the fuel pressure regulator (see Section 14).

12   Start the engine, let it idle at normal operating temperature and disconnect the vacuum hose to the fuel pressure regulator. The fuel pressure should be within the range listed in this Chapter's Specifications. If it isn't, verify there is 12 to 14 in-Hg of vacuum present at the hose. If vacuum is not present at the hose, check the hose for a restriction or a break. If vacuum is present, reconnect

the hose to the fuel pressure regulator. If the fuel pressure regulator does not decrease the fuel pressure with engine vacuum applied, replace the fuel pressure regulator.

13   Turn off the engine and note the indicated pressure on the fuel pressure gauge. It should not drop below the minimum listed in this Chapter's Specifications for about two minutes. If it does drop in less than two minutes, the fuel pump or fuel pressure regulator could be defective, or a fuel injector could be leaking.

14   When you're done, relieve the fuel pressure (see Section 2), remove the fuel pressure gauge and reconnect the fuel supply line fittings.

2004 and later models

15   To measure the fuel pressure, you'll need a fuel pressure gauge capable of reading up to 70 psi (414 kPa), some fuel hose and an adapter suitable for connecting the gauge to the fuel rail. Fuel pressure gauges and adapters are available at most auto parts stores.

16   Relieve the system fuel pressure (see Section 2), then disconnect the cable from the negative battery terminal (see Chapter 5, Section 1).

17   Connect the fuel pressure gauge to the fuel rail.

18   Reconnect the cable to the negative battery terminal (see Chapter 5, Section 1).

19   Turn the ignition switch to ON (don't start the engine yet). The fuel pump should run for about two seconds - pressure should register on the gauge and should hold steady. Make sure there are no leaks.

20   Start the engine and let it warm up until it's idling at its normal operating temperature, then measure the fuel pressure and compare your reading to the fuel pressure listed in this Chapter's Specifications.

a) *If the indicated fuel pressure is low, inspect the fuel supply hose and line for an obstruction. If the hose and line are clear, replace the fuel filter, then recheck the fuel pressure. If the indicated fuel pressure is still low, replace the fuel pressure regulator, then recheck the fuel*

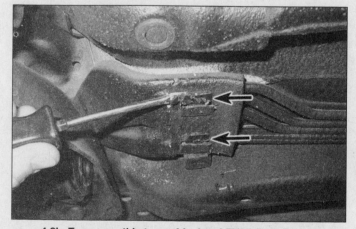

4.2b To remove this type of fuel and EVAP line clip, pry these locking tabs open slightly . . .

4.2c . . . then pry the clip sideways to release it from the tabs

4.5 Typical two-tab type quick-connect fitting (this one's located just ahead of the fuel tank, and connects the fuel supply line from the in-tank fuel pump to the metal fuel supply line running underneath the vehicle to the engine compartment)

pressure. If the fuel pressure is still low, replace the fuel pump.

b) *If the indicated fuel pressure is high, replace the fuel pump module (see Section 5), then recheck the fuel pressure. If the fuel pressure is still high, have the fuel system diagnosed by a dealer service department or other qualified repair shop.*

21   After the test is complete, relieve the system fuel pressure (see Section 2), then disconnect the cable from the negative battery terminal (see Chapter 5, Section 1).

22   Remove the fuel pressure gauge.

23   Reconnect the cable to the negative battery terminal (see Chapter 5, Section 1).

24   Start the engine and check for fuel leaks.

---

4   Fuel lines and fittings - general information

Warning: *Gasoline is extremely flammable, so take extra precautions when you work on any part of the fuel system (see the* **Warning** *in Section 2).*

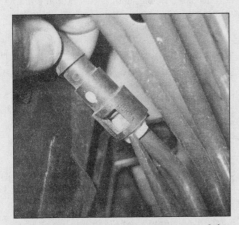

4.9a To disconnect a two-tab type quick-connect fitting, squeeze the two plastic retainer tabs together . . .

General information

Refer to illustrations 4.2a, 4.2b and 4.2c

1   Always relieve the system fuel pressure (see Section 2) before servicing the fuel lines or their fittings.

2   The fuel supply, return and Evaporative Emission Control (EVAP) lines extend from the fuel tank to the engine compartment. The fuel supply lines are constructed of steel or rubber, the fuel return hoses are rubber and the EVAP lines are plastic. The lines are secured to the underbody with clips and brackets **(see illustrations)**. These lines should be inspected for leaks, kinks and dents anytime the vehicle is raised for service.

3   If evidence of dirt is found in the fuel system or fuel filter during service, the affected line should be disconnected and blown out. Check the fuel inlet strainer on the fuel pump for blockage or contamination (see Section 6).

Quick-connect fittings

4   These models use various types of quick-connect fittings to join various fuel lines and components. The first type uses a single-tab retainer, the second type uses a two-tab retainer and the third type incorporates a plastic retainer ring (usually black in color) which connects/disconnects much like a common compressed air hose fitting. Some are equipped with safety latch clips. The fittings are equipped with non-serviceable O-ring seals located in the female part of the fitting. In the event the fitting or tubing becomes damaged or develops a leak, replace the entire fuel line/quick-connect fitting as an assembly. Always use original equipment parts, or parts that meet or exceed the original equipment standards.

Single and two-tab retainer fittings

Disassembly

Refer to illustrations 4.5, 4.9a and 4.9b

5   These quick-connect fittings have one or two windows (depending on type) located in the side(s) of the female fitting. When the male fitting is inserted into the female, the tab(s) on

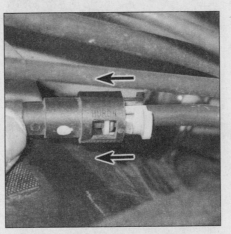

4.9b . . . and pull the metal line out of the quick-connect fitting

the male engage in the window(s) and lock the fitting together **(see illustra-tion)**.

6   Relieve the system fuel pressure (see Section 2).

7   Remove all fasteners, brackets or clips securing the lines as applicable.

8   Clean the area around the fitting to remove dirt and foreign debris.

9   Depress the retaining tab(s) on the quick-connect fitting and pull it apart **(see illustrations)**. Note: *The retaining tabs and shoulder should remain on the metal fuel line after separation.*

Assembly

10   Clean the male part of the fitting and lightly lubricate it with clean engine oil.

11   Position the retaining tab ears on the tube so they align with the windows in the female fitting and push them together. You should hear the fitting snap into place as the retaining tab ears lock into the windows.

12   Verify that the fitting is correctly fastened by trying to pull the lines apart.

13   Secure the fuel line using any clips or brackets as applicable.

14   Pressurize the system and check for leaks.

Plastic retainer ring fittings

Disassembly

15   Relieve the system fuel pressure (see Section 2).

16   Remove all fasteners, brackets or clips securing the lines as applicable.

17   Clean the area around the fitting to remove dirt and foreign debris.

18   Grasp the male line and push it in (towards the fitting). While applying pressure on the male line, press the plastic retainer ring into the female fitting and then pull the male line from the female fitting. **Note:** *The plastic retainer ring must be pushed into the female fitting squarely! If it gets cocked, the fitting will be difficult to separate. If necessary, use an open-end wrench applied to the plastic retainer to assist in evenly pressing it into the female fitting. The plastic retainer ring should remain attached to the female fitting after separation.*

Assembly

19   Clean the male part of the fitting and lightly lubricate it with clean engine oil.

20   Insert the male end into the female and push them together. You should hear the retainer ring snap into place as it locks the fitting together. Make sure the retainer ring is fully extended after assembly.

21   Verify that the fitting is correctly fastened by trying to pull the lines apart.

22   Secure the fuel line using any clips or brackets as applicable.

23   Pressurize the system and check for leaks.

Fuel lines - replacement

Steel tubing

24   If replacement of a metal line is required, disassemble the applicable quick-connect fittings

as described above and remove the line from the vehicle. If the quick-connect fitting is damaged or leaks, replace the affected section of fuel line/ quick-connect fittings as an assembly.

25 If the quick-connect fittings are acceptable, a new piece of steel tubing may be spliced-in to replace a damaged section by flaring the tubing ends and joining them with a union. Use tubing that meets or exceeds original equipment standards. Do not use copper or aluminum tubing to replace steel tubing. These materials cannot withstand normal vehicle vibration. Do not use a rubber hose to replace a damaged section of steel tubing!

26 When installing the replacement section into the line, assemble the quick-connect fittings first, then tighten the unions. **Warning:** *Make sure that no metal lines are rubbing against other components or against each other. Maintain a minimum of 1/4-inch clearance around the lines to prevent them from contacting other parts or each other.*

27 After replacing the line or section, pressurize the system and check for leaks.

Plastic lines

28 If replacement of a plastic line is required, disassemble the applicable quick-connect fittings as described above and

remove the line from the vehicle. The plastic lines used on these vehicles are not serviceable. If replacement is required, the affected section of fuel line/quick-connect fittings must be replaced as an assembly.

29 Install the new line onto the vehicle and assemble the quick-connect fittings as applicable (see above). Secure the line to the vehicle as required. **Warning:** *Do not route plastic fuel lines within four inches of any part of the exhaust system or within ten inches of the catalytic converter. Make sure that no plastic lines are rubbing against other components or against each other. Maintain a minimum of 1/4-inch clearance around the lines to prevent them from contacting other parts or each other.*

30 After replacing the line pressurize the system and check for leaks.

Rubber hoses

Warning: *Use only original equipment hoses or hoses that meet or exceed original equipment standards. Any other hoses might have a lower fatigue threshold.*

31 Relieve the system fuel pressure (see Section 2).

32 Loosen the clamps securing the hose and remove it from the vehicle.

33 Installation is the reverse of removal.

Warning: *Do not route rubber fuel hoses within four inches of any part of the exhaust system or within ten inches of the catalytic converter. And do not allow rubber fuel hoses to rub against other components or against each other. Maintain a minimum of 1/4-inch clearance around the hoses to prevent them from contacting other components or each other.*

34 After replacing the hose, pressurize the system and check for leaks.

---

5 Fuel pump/fuel level sending unit - removal and installation

Removal

Warning: *Gasoline is extremely flammable, so take extra precautions when you work on any part of the fuel system (see the* **Warning** *in Section 2).*

Note: *2004 and later models have a secondary fuel level sender mounted in the right side of the fuel tank. Refer to Section 6 for more information.*

1 Relieve the system fuel pressure (see Section 2).

2 Disconnect the cable from the negative battery terminal (see Chapter 5).

3 Remove the rear seat cushion (see Chapter 11).

1994 through 1998 models (except California)

Refer to illustrations 5.4, 5.5, 5.6 and 5.8

4 Remove the fuel pump service hole cover **(see illustration)**.

5 Disconnect the electrical connector from the fuel pump **(see illustration)**.

6 Disconnect the fuel supply line **(see illustration)** and the fuel return hose from the fuel pump.

7 Remove the fuel pump retaining bolts.

8 Carefully withdraw the fuel pump assembly from the fuel tank **(see illustra-tion)**. Then remove and discard the old gasket. If you're *replacing* the pump, refer to Section 6.

9 Installation is the reverse of removal. Be sure to use a new gasket and tighten the fuel pump retaining bolts to the torque listed in this Chapter's Specifications.

1994 through 1998 models (California only)

10 On these models, the fuel pump and the fuel level sending unit are an integral assembly. The location of the fuel pump/fuel level sending unit assembly is the same location as the fuel pump on non-California models and the removal and installation procedure is identical to the procedure described in Steps 4 through 9.

1999 and later models

Refer to illustrations 5.11, 5.12, 5.13a, 5.13b, 5.14a, 5.14b, 5.15a and 5.15b

11 Remove the fuel pump service hole cover **(see illustration)**.

5.4 To remove the fuel pump service hole cover (A) on 1994 through 1998 models, remove these four screws (this is also the location for the fuel level sending unit, which is an integral part of the pump on 1994 through 1998 California models); to remove the fuel level sending unit service hole cover (B) on 1994 through 1998 non-California models, remove these four screws

5.5 Disconnect the electrical connector from the fuel pump (1994 through 1998 non-California models) or from the fuel pump/fuel level sending unit (1994 through 1998 California models)

5.6 To disconnect the fuel supply line from the fuel pump on 1994 through 1998 models, use a back-up wrench to hold one nut while you loosen the other one; to disconnect the fuel return hose, simply open the spring clamp by squeezing the ends together and pull off the hose

12   Disconnect the fuel pump/fuel level sending unit electrical connectors **(see illustration)**.
13   Disconnect the fuel line(s) from the fuel pump **(see illustrations)**.
14   Unscrew the fuel pump/fuel level sending unit lock ring **(see illustrations)**.
15   Carefully withdraw the fuel pump/fuel level sending unit assembly from the fuel tank **(see illustration)**. The fuel pump uses a rubber seal around its circumference. This seal might come out with the pump or it might remain in the opening when the pump is removed. Remove the rubber seal from the pump **(see illustration)** or from the opening and inspect it for cracks, tears, deterioration and deformation. If it's damaged or deformed, replace it.

5.8 Carefully lift the fuel pump assembly from the fuel tank (1994 through 1998 models)

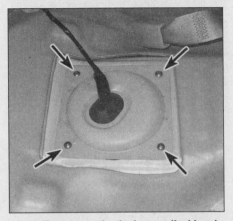

5.11 To remove the fuel pump/fuel level sending unit service hole cover on 1999 and later models, remove these four screws

5.12 Disconnect the fuel pump/fuel level sending unit electrical connector (1999 and later models)

5.13a To disconnect the fuel supply line connector from the fuel pump, squeeze these two locking tangs together and separate the fitting from the pump (1999 and later models)

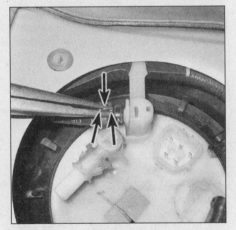

5.13b To disconnect the fuel return hose from the fuel pump, squeeze the ends of this spring clamp together to expand the clamp, then pull off the hose (1999 and later models)

5.14a Use a hammer and punch to loosen the fuel pump/fuel level sending unit lock ring . . .

5.14b . . . then unscrew and remove the lock ring (1999 and later models)

5.15a Carefully remove the fuel pump/fuel level sending unit from the fuel tank . . .

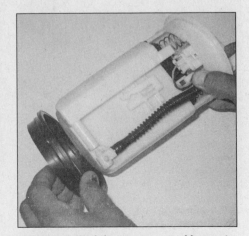

5.15b . . . and then remove and inspect the rubber seal (1999 and later models)

5.17a When installing the rubber seal on 1999 and later models, install the seal in the fuel pump opening, not on the pump itself

5.17b On 1999 and later models, be sure to coat the inside of the rubber seal with clean engine oil so that the pump module will slide into place without deforming the seal

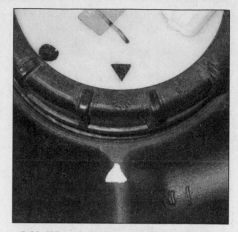

5.20 When installing the fuel pump/fuel level sending unit on 1999 and later models, be sure to align the arrow on top of the fuel pump with the arrow on the top of the fuel tank

Installation (all models)

Refer to illustrations 5.17a, 5.17b and 5.20

16   Clean the area on top of the fuel tank around the opening for the fuel pump (or fuel pump/fuel level sending unit on California models), then install a new fuel pump gasket on 1994 through 1998 models.

17   On 1999 and later models, install the rubber seal *in the fuel tank opening* **(see illustration)**. **Caution:** *If you install the rubber seal on the fuel pump/fuel level sending unit on these models, it might be deformed when the pump assembly is installed and the lock ring is tightened, which will result in a leak.* Lightly lubricate the inside walls of the rubber seal on these models with clean engine oil **(see illustration)** to ensure that the pump module slides freely into place without catching and deforming the rubber seal.

18   Carefully insert the fuel pump/fuel level sending unit into the fuel tank.

19   On 1994 through 1998 models install the fuel pump/fuel level sending unit mounting bolts and tighten them to the torque listed in this Chapter's Specifications.

20   On 1999 and later models, align the arrow on the fuel pump/fuel level sending unit with the arrow on the fuel tank **(see illustration)**. Then, holding the fuel pump in place, install the ring nut and tighten it securely. **Caution:** *Over-tightening the ring nut will deform the rubber seal and might cause a leak.*

21   The remaining installation steps are the reverse of removal.

6   Fuel pump/fuel level sending unit - component replacement

Warning: *Gasoline is extremely flammable, so take extra precautions when you work on any part of the fuel system (see the Warning in Section 2).*

1   Relieve the fuel system pressure (see Section 2).

2   Disconnect the cable from the negative battery terminal (see Chapter 5).

3   Remove the fuel pump (1994 through 1998 non-California models) or the fuel pump/ fuel level sending unit (1994 through 1998 California models and all 1999 through 2003 models) from the fuel tank (see Section 5). On 1994 through 1998 *non-California* models, the fuel pump and the fuel level sending unit are separate components, so it's not necessary to separate the two when replacing either of them. However, some disassembly is required after removing the fuel pump; the procedure for doing so begins with Step 4. To replace the fuel level sending unit on 1994 through 1998 non-California models (see Steps 9 through 15) or the secondary fuel level sender on 2004 and later models (see Steps 26 through 28), simply remove it and install a new unit. On 1994 through 1998 *California* models and on all 1999 and later models, the fuel pump and the fuel level sending unit are an integral assembly, but in order to replace either component you'll have to separate them once they're out of the tank.

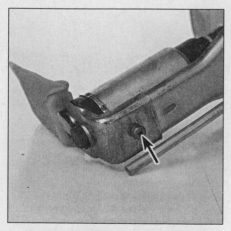

6.4a Remove the mounting screw and separate the bracket from the frame (1994 through 1998 non-California models)

6.4b Remove the clip . . .

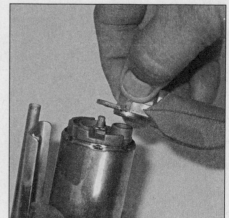

6.4c . . . and detach the inlet strainer from the fuel pump (1994 through 1998 non-California models)

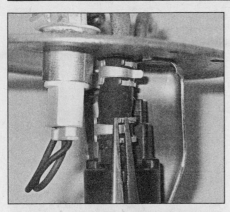

6.5 Remove the hose clamp (1994 through 1998 non-California models)

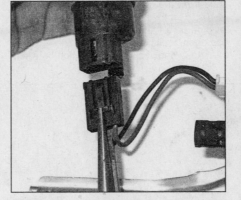

6.6 Unplug the electrical connector (1994 through 1998 non-California models)

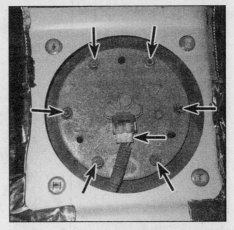

6.11 To remove the fuel level sending unit from the fuel tank on 1994 through 1998 models (except California), disconnect the electrical connector and remove the retaining nuts

1994 through 1998 models (except California)

Fuel pump

Refer to illustrations 6.4a, 6.4b, 6.4c, 6.5 and 6.6

4   Remove the fuel pump from its "frame" (support bracket). Remove the screw from the bracket at the lower section of the frame **(see illustration)**. Remove the clip securing the inlet strainer to the pump **(see illustration)**. Remove the inlet strainer **(see illustration)**.
5   Remove the hose clamp and pull the lower end of the fuel pump loose from the bracket **(see illustration)**. Withdraw the pump from the hose.
6   Disconnect the electrical connector from the fuel pump **(see illustration)**. Separate the fuel pump from the frame.
7   Inspect the fuel strainer for contamination. If it is dirty, replace it.
8   Installation is the reverse of removal.

Fuel level sending unit

Refer to illustration 6.11

9   Remove the rear seat (see Chapter 11).

10   Pull back the carpet and access the fuel level sending unit service hole cover. **Note:** *There are two separate covers under the rear seat. The service hole cover on the passenger side of the vehicle is for the fuel pump while the service hole cover toward the center of the vehicle is for the fuel level sending unit.*
11   Disconnect the electrical connector for the fuel level sending unit **(see illustration)**.
12   Remove the fuel level sending unit retaining nuts from the fuel tank **(see illustration 6.11)**.
13   Carefully remove the fuel level sending unit assembly from the fuel tank.
14   Remove the fuel level sending unit retaining screws and separate it from the assembly.
15   Install the fuel level sending unit onto the frame. Installation is the reverse of removal.

1994 through 1998 California models

16   On these models, the fuel pump and the fuel level sending unit are an integral assembly, but the components are virtually identical

to the separate components used on 1994 through 1998 non-California models. Refer to the previous procedures (Steps 4 through 8 and 9 through 15) when separating the pump and the fuel level sending unit.

1999 through 2003 models

Refer to illustrations 6.17a, 6.17b, 6.17c, 6.18, 6.19a, 6.19b, 6.19c, 6.19d, 6.19e, 6.19f, 6.20a, 6.20b, 6.20c, 6.20d, 6.20e, 6.21a, 6.21b, 6.22, 6.23a, 6.23b, 6.24a and 6.24b

17   Remove the fuel level sending unit **(see illustrations)**.
18   Remove the rubber seal **(see illustration)**. Inspect the seal for cracks, tears, deterioration and deformation. If it's damaged or deformed, discard it and replace it with a new seal.
19   Separate the pump support assembly

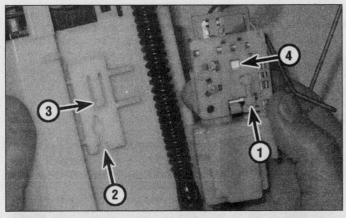

6.17a The fuel level sending unit on 1999 and later models is attached to the outside of the fuel pump reservoir by a small raised guide (1) on the sender that fits into a slot (2) on the reservoir, and it's locked into place by a tab (3) on the reservoir that fits into a hole (4) on the sending unit; to install the sender, line up the guide with the slot, then slide the sender into position until the locking tab on the reservoir snaps into the hole on the sender

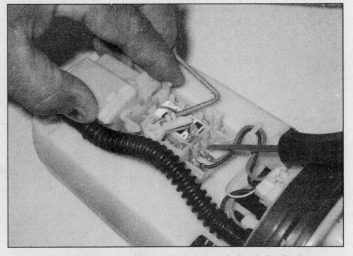

6.17b To detach the fuel level sending unit from the fuel pump reservoir cup, insert the tip of a small slotted screwdriver between the sending unit and the reservoir and *carefully* pry it loose (1999 through 2003 models)

from the fuel reservoir cup **(see illustrations)**.
20　Separate the fuel pump from the fuel filter **(see illustrations)**.
21　If you're replacing the fuel pump or the pump inlet fuel sock (strainer), remove the

sock from the fuel pump **(see illustration)**. Also inspect the spacer on the fuel pump outlet pipe **(see illustration)** for damage. If it's damaged, replace it.
22　An O-ring seals the connection between

the fuel filter and the fuel supply hose. Remove this O-ring from the fuel filter **(see illustration)** and inspect it for cracks, tears and deterioration. If it's damaged or worn, replace it.

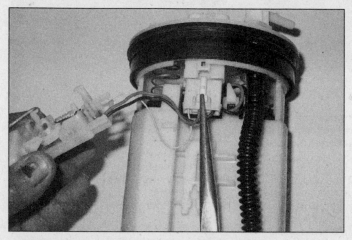

6.17c Release the locking tab and disconnect the fuel level sending unit electrical connector (1999 through 2003 models)

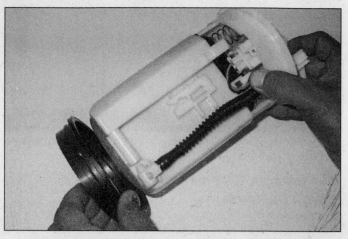

6.18 Remove the rubber seal from the fuel pump/fuel level sending unit and inspect it for cracks, tears and deterioration; replace the seal if it's damaged (1999 through 2003 models)

6.19a To separate the pump support assembly from the fuel filter, release this locking tab . . .

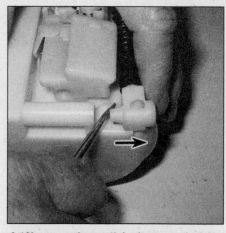

6.19b . . . and pry off the lower end of the fuel return hose from the reservoir with a small screwdriver . . .

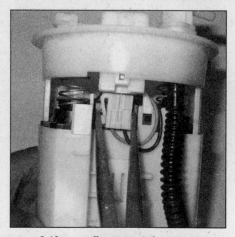

6.19c . . . disconnect the pump electrical connector . . .

6.19d . . . release these two locking tangs . . .

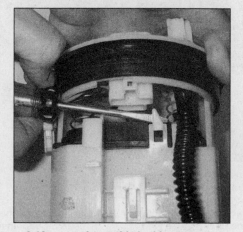

6.19e . . . release this locking tang . . .

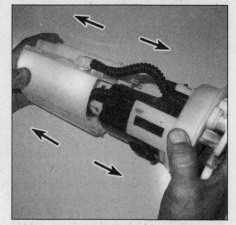

6.19f . . . then separate the pump support assembly from the fuel reservoir cup

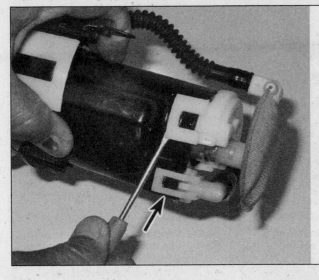

6.20a To separate the fuel pump from the fuel filter, release this locking tab, and the two locking tabs (not visible in this photo) on the other side; if you're going to *replace the fuel filter*, release the locking tab indicated by the arrow, and the other locking tab (not visible in this photo) on the other side and disconnect the fuel supply hose from the filter (if you're not replacing the filter, releasing these two tabs is unnecessary)

6.20b Once you have released the three locking tabs, remove the lock bracket (the white part)

6.20c To disconnect the ground wire, push *down* on the (bent-back) end of the spade connector (A) with a small screwdriver and carefully pull out the connector with a pair of needle nose pliers

6.20d If you're going to *replace the fuel filter*, disconnect the fuel pump electrical connector from the upper end of the fuel filter (if you're just replacing the pump, it's not necessary to disconnect this connector)

6.20e To separate the fuel pump from the fuel filter, grasp the filter firmly and carefully but firmly pull out the pump, being careful not to damage the fuel inlet sock (strainer)

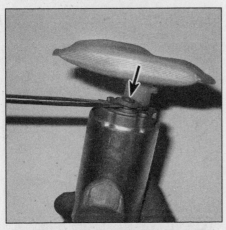

6.21a To separate the fuel inlet sock (strainer) from the fuel pump, pry it off with a small screwdriver; be sure to replace the small clip on top when installing the sock

6.21b Also inspect the spacer on the end of the fuel pump outlet pipe; if it's damaged, replace it

6.22 Remove this O-ring from the fuel filter and inspect it for cracks, tears and damage; if it's damaged, replace it

6.23a This grommet seals the connection between the fuel filter and the fuel pump outlet pipe (which inserts into the grommet when the fuel pump and fuel filter are assembled)

6.23b To replace the grommet, simply pry it out and then push another grommet into place

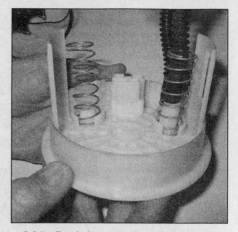

6.24a Don't forget to install these two springs on the pump support assembly before reattaching the fuel pump to the pump support

23   A grommet inside the upper end of the fuel filter **(see illustration)** seals the connection between the fuel pump and the fuel filter. Remove the grommet **(see illustration)** and inspect it for cracks, tears and deterioration. If it's damaged, replace it.

24   When reattaching the fuel pump/filter assembly to the pump support assembly, don't forget to install the two springs and make sure that the locking tabs on the pump support are aligned between the guide rails on the pump/filter **(see illustrations)**.

25   Reassembly is otherwise the reverse of disassembly.

2004 and later models

Note: *There are two fuel level sending units on these vehicles due to the shape of the tank. The primary unit is attached to the fuel pump module in the left side of the fuel tank; the secondary sender is mounted in the right side of the fuel tank.*

Secondary fuel level sender

Refer to illustration 6.26

26   On early models with an access cover under the rear seat, remove the right floor hole access cover, then disconnect the electrical connector **(see illustration)**. On later models with no access cover, refer to Section 7 and remove the fuel tank.

27   Remove the secondary fuel level sender mounting bolts. Carefully pull the sender out of the fuel tank. Be sure not to bend any of the components.

28   Inspect the gasket and replace it if necessary. Installation is the reverse of removal.

Fuel pump and primary fuel level sender

Refer to illustration 6.29

29   Refer to Section 5 and remove the fuel pump module from the fuel tank **(see illustration)**.

30   Unplug the level sender wiring. Remove the attaching screw, then lift the sender off.

31   Installation is the reverse of removal. Be careful when installing the module to avoid bending the arm of the float.

---

7   Fuel tank - removal and installation

Refer to illustrations 7.9a, 7.9b, 7.9c and 7.12
Warning: *Gasoline is extremely flammable, so take extra precautions when you work on any part of the fuel system (see the Warning in Section 2).*
Refer to illustrations

1   Relieve the fuel system pressure (see Section 2).

2   Disconnect the cable from the negative battery terminal (see Chapter 5).

3   Remove the rear seat (see Chapter 11).

4   Remove the service hole cover(s) for the fuel pump and fuel level sending unit (see Section 5). **Note:** *1994 through 1998 non-California models have a separate fuel pump and fuel level sending unit, so there are two*

6.24b When reattaching the fuel pump/filter assembly to the pump support assembly, make sure that the locking tabs on the pump support assembly are aligned between the guide rails of the fuel pump/filter assembly

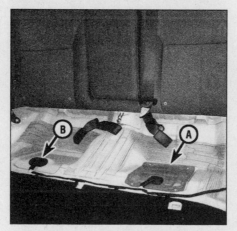

6.26 Fuel pump module access cover (A) and secondary fuel level sender connector (B) - many models also have an access cover at B

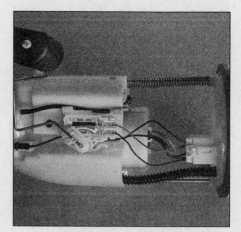

6.29 Fuel pump module (2004 and later models)

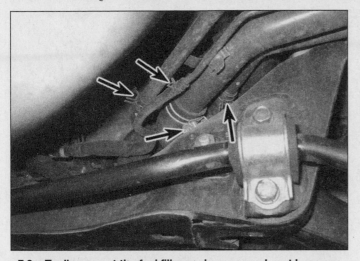

7.9a To disconnect the fuel filler neck, vapor and vent hoses up top, loosen these clamps and pull off the hoses; there are a lot of vent and vapor hoses on these vehicles so it's a good idea to label the hoses before disconnecting them

7.9b To disconnect the fuel filler neck, vapor and vent hoses at the tank, loosen these clamps and pull off the hoses

service covers **(see illustration 5.4)**. *1994 through 1998 California models and all 1999 through 2003 models have an integral fuel pump/fuel level sending unit with one single access cover* **(see illustration 5.11)**. *Most 2004 and later models have two access covers. The right one is for the secondary fuel level sending unit and the left side is for the fuel pump module. Some 2004 and later models only have an access cover on the left side; on these vehicles, the fuel tank must be removed in order to service the secondary fuel level sensor.*

5 Disconnect the electrical connector(s) from the fuel pump and the fuel level sending unit and position them out of the way (see Section 5).
6 Disconnect the fuel line fittings from the fuel pump (see Section 5).
7 Raise the vehicle and support it securely on jackstands.

8 Using a siphon pump, drain the fuel tank into a large container. **Warning:** *Never start the siphoning action by mouth!*
9 Loosen the clamps and disconnect the filler neck hose, and the vent and vapor hoses, from the fuel tank **(see illustrations)**. **Warning:** *There might be some residual fuel inside the filler neck and hose, so be prepared to catch any spilled fuel and protect your eye and skin accordingly.* Also, detach the EVAP system (ventilation solenoid/vent valve/air filter) support bracket **(see illustration)**. (It's much easier to lower the EVAP system components with the tank than it is to try to remove them separately. And, unless you're planning to *replace* the fuel tank, it's not necessary to detach any of these components from the fuel tank just to lower it.)
10 Support the fuel tank with a floor jack. Place a piece of wood between the jack head and the fuel tank to protect the tank.

11 On 1999 and later models, remove the center exhaust pipe (see Section 16). On 2004 and later models, disconnect the parking brake cable clamps.
12 Remove the fuel tank mounting nuts (1994 through 1998 models) or the fuel tank retaining strap nuts **(see illustration)**.
13 Lower the fuel tank slightly and make sure that every electrical harness and fuel, vapor or vent hose connecting the tank to the vehicle is disconnected. If you discover any wiring, hoses or lines that still need to be disconnected, clearly label them to ensure that they will be correctly reconnected.
14 Lower the fuel tank and maneuver it out from under the vehicle.
15 Installation is the reverse of removal. Be sure to tighten the fuel tank mounting nuts or strap nuts to the torque listed in this Chapter's Specifications.

7.9c To detach the EVAP system (ventilation solenoid/vent valve/ air filter) support bracket, remove these three bolts

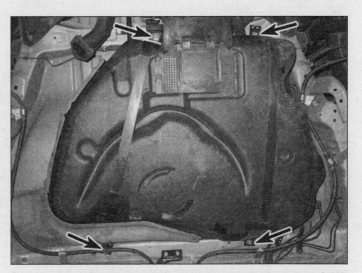

7.12 To detach the tank from the vehicle, remove these nuts (1999 and later model shown; earlier models also have four nuts, but no straps)

9.1a To disconnect the air intake duct from the air filter housing, loosen this clamp screw

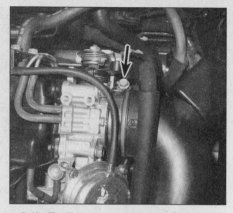

9.1b To disconnect the air intake duct from the throttle body, loosen this clamp screw

9.1c Look for any wiring harness brackets and/or clips and either detach them from the air filter housing, or detach the wire harness from the clip (1999 and later model shown)

8 Fuel tank cleaning and repair - general information

Warning: *Gasoline is extremely flammable, so take extra precautions when you work on any part of the fuel system (see the* **Warning** *in Section 2).*

1   The fuel tank on some models is made of plastic and is not repairable.

2   A professional who has experience in this critical and potentially dangerous work should do all repair work on metal fuel tanks. Even after cleaning and flushing of the fuel system, explosive fumes can remain and ignite during repair of the tank.

3   If the fuel tank is removed from the vehicle, do not place it in an area where sparks or open flames could ignite the fuel vapors escaping from the tank. Be especially careful inside a garage where a gas-type appliance is located, because it could cause an explosion.

9 Air filter housing - removal and installation

Refer to illustrations 9.1a, 9.1b, 9.1c, 9.3, 9.4a, 9.4b, 9.5a and 9.5b

1   Loosen the air intake duct clamps **(see**

illustrations**)** and remove the air intake duct. Detach any wiring harness clips that are attached to the air filter housing **(see illustration)**. On 2004 and later models, refer to Chapter 6 and remove the powertrain control module (PCM).

2   Disconnect the electrical connector from the Volume Air Flow sensor (see Chapter 6), then remove the Volume Air Flow sensor and air filter housing cover and remove the air filter element (see Chapter 1).

3   Remove the air filter housing retaining bolts **(see illustration)**.

4   Remove the air filter housing and fresh air inlet as a single assembly **(see illustration)**. You'll probably feel a little resistance when pulling out the air filter housing because it's connected to a large resonator underneath on most models, which is bolted to the left inner wheel well. However, the air filter housing and the resonator are not bolted or fastened together. If the housing "sticks," pull firmly and it will come loose. While the housing is removed, inspect the condition of the fresh air inlet and the air filter housing. If either part is damaged, replace it. The fresh air inlet and the air filter housing are two parts. To separate them, simply squeeze the locking tangs that secure the fresh air inlet to the air filter housing **(see illustration)** and pull out

the fresh air inlet.

5   The connection between the upper end of the resonator and the oblong hole in the floor of the air filter housing is sealed by a large foam seal **(see illustration)**. This seal deteriorates over time from engine vibration. So be sure to inspect the seal for deterioration. If it's damaged, detach the front part of the inner fenderwell cover (see Chapter 11) and remove the resonator **(see illustration)**.

6   Installation is the reverse of removal.

10 Accelerator cable - removal and installation

Replacement
Refer to illustrations 10.1, 10.2, 10.3, 10.4a, 10.4b, 10.5a, 10.5b and 10.6

Note: *This procedure applies only to 2003 and earlier models. The throttles on later vehicles are controlled by the accelerator pedal position sensor and the PCM.*

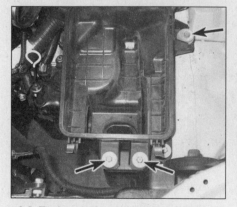

9.3 To detach the air filter housing from the vehicle, remove these bolts (1999 and later models)

9.4a Remove the air filter housing and fresh air inlet as a single assembly (1999 through 2003 model shown)

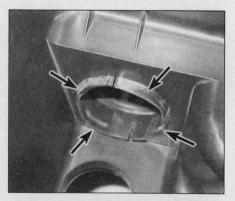

9.4b To separate the fresh air inlet from the air filter housing, depress these locking tangs and pull out the fresh air inlet; when installing the air inlet, insert it into the air filter housing until it snaps into place, indicating that it's fully seated (1999 through 2003 models)

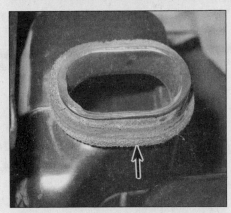

9.5a On 1999 through 2003 models, be sure to inspect the condition of this foam seal around the mouth of the big resonator that's located underneath the air filter housing; if the seal is damaged, replace the resonator

9.5b To detach the resonator from a 1999 through 2003 model, detach the front part of the inner fenderwell cover (see Chapter 11), then remove these three bolts (this photo was taken front directly underneath the resonator, looking straight up)

10.1 To disengage the accelerator cable from the cable bracket, loosen the locknut with a wrench while holding the adjustment nut with a back-up wrench, then slide the cable out of its slot in the bracket (1999 through 2003 model shown)

1   Remove the accelerator cable from the cable bracket (see illustration).
2   Disconnect the accelerator cable from the slot in the throttle valve cam (see illustration).

3   Detach the accelerator cable from any clips securing it to the engine (see illustration).
4   Disconnect the accelerator cable from the firewall (see illustrations).

5   Working inside the vehicle, disconnect the lower end of the accelerator cable from the accelerator pedal (see illustrations).
6   Push the cable through the firewall into

10.2 To disengage the accelerator cable from the throttle valve cam, slide the end plug out of its slot in the cam (1999 through 2003 model shown)

10.3 To detach the accelerator cable from these clips, simply pull it out of each clip (it's not necessary to actually detach the clips themselves) (1999 through 2003 model shown)

10.4a To detach the accelerator cable from the firewall, remove these two bolts . . .

10.4b . . . and pull the cable-to-firewall mounting flange away from the firewall (1999 through 2003 model shown, earlier models similar)

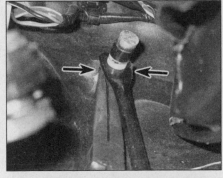

10.5a To disengage the lower end of the accelerator cable from the accelerator pedal, squeeze the tangs on the front side (facing toward the firewall) of the retainer, then slide the retainer out of the way . . .

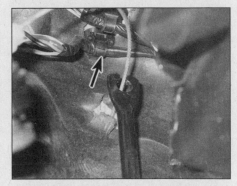

10.5b . . . and pull the accelerator cable out of its slot in the top of the pedal (2003 and earlier models)

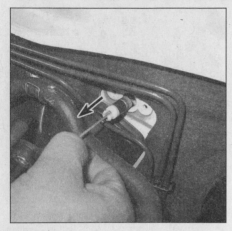

10.6 To remove the accelerator cable, pull it out, from the engine compartment side, through the hole in the firewall

10.8 To adjust accelerator cable freeplay, loosen the cable bracket bolts and slide the bracket left or right as necessary

the engine compartment and remove it from the vehicle **(see illustration)**.

7　Installation is the reverse of removal.

Adjustment

Refer to illustration 10.8

8　To adjust the cable:

a) *Turn off the air conditioning system, the headlights and interior lights.*

b) *Start the engine and allow it to reach operating temperature.*

c) *Check the idle speed. Refer to the VECI label in the engine compartment.*

d) *Turn the engine off.*

e) *Check the cable deflection between the throttle lever and the cable sheathing (the outside covering that protects the cable from dirt, moisture, etc.). Deflection should be 0.04 to 0.08-inch (1 to 2 mm). If deflection is not within specifications, loosen the cable bracket adjusting bolts* **(see illustration)** *and slide the bracket as necessary until the deflection is as specified.*

f) *After you have adjusted the accelerator cable, have an assistant help you verify that the throttle valve opens all the way when you depress the accelerator pedal to the floor and that it returns to the idle position when you release the accelerator. Also verify that the cable operates smoothly. It must not bind or stick.*

11　Multiport Fuel Injection (MFI) system - general information

The Multiport Fuel Injection (MFI) system consists of a computerized electronic engine control system, the air intake system and the fuel delivery system. The MFI system uses a Powertrain Control Module (PCM) and an array of information sensors to determine the correct air/fuel ratio under all operating conditions. The MFI system and the emission control systems are interrelated. For more information about the PCM and its sensors, and the emission control systems used on the vehicles covered in this manual, refer to Chapter 6.

Air intake system

The air intake system consists of the air filter housing, the air intake duct, the throttle body and the intake manifold (see Chapter 2 for more information about the intake manifolds used on the vehicles covered by this manual).

2003 and earlier models

The PCM controls engine idle speed with an output actuator known as the Idle Air Control (IAC) motor, which is mounted on the throttle body. When the engine is idling, the IAC motor meters the amount of air bypassing the closed throttle valve (inside the bore of the throttle body) in accordance with the "load" imposed on the engine. (Typical loads at idle include warm-up, running the air conditioning system, turning the wheels at low-speed or putting an automatic transaxle into gear.) The PCM uses data from an array of information sensors to determine the correct amount of air needed to maintain idle speed during these and all other conditions. For information on the PCM and the engine management system, see Chapter 6.

2004 and later models

The throttle on theses vehicles is controlled electronically by the PCM. The PCM controls idle speed, cruise control operation and overall throttle position by monitoring sensors such as the accelerator pedal position sensor. There is no idle air control system on these models.

Fuel delivery system

The fuel delivery system consists of an electric fuel pump, a fuel filter, a fuel pressure regulator, a fuel rail, the fuel injectors and metal or plastic lines and rubber hoses connecting these components.

All models are equipped with an electric fuel pump. The fuel pump is mounted inside the fuel tank. The fuel pump is accessible through a service hole cover under the rear seat. The fuel level sending unit is also accessible through a separate service hole cover under the rear seat on 1994 through 1998 non-California models. On 1994 through 1998 California models, and on all 1999 through 2003 models, the fuel level sending unit is an integral part of the fuel pump assembly and is accessed through the same service hole cover as the pump. All 2004 and later models have a fuel pump module in the left part of the fuel tank that includes a level sensor, regulator, filter and pump. There is a secondary fuel level sensor in the right section of the fuel tank on these vehicles. All pumps are equipped with a small fuel inlet "sock" (strainer) that protects the pump from debris in the fuel.

The fuel pump circuit is controlled by the fuel pump relay. When the ignition key is turned to ON, the fuel pump relay closes the circuit for the fuel pump for a second or two in order to "prime" (pressurize) the system, then it shuts off unless the ignition key is turned to START. The fuel pump relay keeps the fuel pump circuit energized when the engine is running; when the ignition key is turned to OFF, the fuel pump relay opens the fuel pump circuit, turning off the pump. The fuel pump relay on 1994 through 1998 models is located in the center of the dash, below the PCM and above the Transaxle Control Module (TCM) and in the fuse/relay center in the engine compartment on 1999 and later models.

The actual fuel filter for the rest of the system is located on the outlet, or pressurized, side of the fuel pump. The fuel filter removes debris in the fuel that might clog the fuel system, especially the valves inside the fuel injectors. The fuel filter is located on the firewall on 1994 through 1998 models, and is an integral part of the fuel pump/fuel level sending unit on 1999 and later models. The fuel filter replacement procedure for 1994 through 1998 models is in Chapter 1. The fuel filter replacement procedure for 1999 and later models is in Section 6 of this Chapter.

The pressurized and filtered fuel is pumped into the fuel rail, which serves as a fuel reservoir for the fuel injectors. Each of the PCM-controlled injectors consists of a solenoid, plunger, needle valve and housing. When the PCM sends a voltage signal to an fuel injector, the solenoid winding produces an electromagnetic field that raises the needle valve off its seat, allowing pressurized fuel to be sprayed into the intake port for that injector. The amount of fuel injected is determined by the length of time during which current is supplied to the injector solenoid winding. 2003 and earlier models have a fuel pressure regulator mounted on the fuel rail. This regulator maintains proper pressure and returns unneeded fuel to the

12.7 Use a stethoscope to determine if the injectors are working properly - they should make a steady clicking sound that rises and falls with engine speed changes

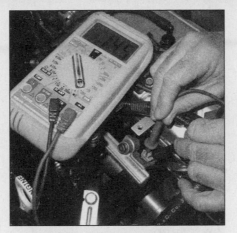

12.8 To check the resistance of a fuel injector, disconnect the injector electrical connector and measure the resistance across the terminals of the injector

tank through a steel line. 2004 and later models have a fuel pressure regulator that is a part of the fuel pump module in the fuel tank. These vehicles don't have a fuel return system.

12 Fuel injection system - general check

Refer to illustrations 12.7 and 12.8
Warning: *Gasoline is extremely flammable, so take extra precautions when you work on any part of the fuel system (see the* **Warning** *in Section 2).*

1   Check all electrical connectors that are related to the system. Check the ground wire connections for tightness. Loose connectors and poor grounds can cause many

problems that resemble more serious malfunctions.

2   Check to see that the battery is fully charged, as the control unit and sensors depend on an accurate supply voltage in order to properly meter the fuel.

3   Check the air filter element. A dirty or partially blocked filter will severely impede performance and economy (see Chapter 1).

4   Check the related fuses. If a blown fuse is found, replace it and see if it blows again. If it does, search for a wire shorted to ground in the harness.

5   Check the air intake duct to the intake manifold for leaks, which will result in an excessively lean mixture. Also check the condition of all vacuum hoses connected to the intake manifold and/or throttle body.

6   Remove the air intake duct from the throttle body and check for dirt, carbon, varnish, or other residue in the throttle body,

particularly around the throttle plate. If it's dirty, clean it with carburetor cleaner spray, a toothbrush and shop towel.

7   With the engine running, place an automotive stethoscope against each injector, one at a time, and listen for a clicking sound that indicates operation **(see illustration)**. If you don't have a stethoscope, you can place the tip of a long screwdriver against the injector and listen through the handle. If you hear the injectors operating but there is a misfire condition present, the electrical circuits are functioning, but the injectors may be dirty or fouled from carbon deposits - commercial cleaning products may help, or the injectors may require replacement.

8   If you can't hear the injector operating, disconnect the injector electrical connectors and measure the resistance across the terminals of each injector connector with an ohmmeter **(see illustration)**. Compare your measurement with the resistance value listed in this Chapter's Specifications. Replace any injector whose resistance value does not fall within the specifications.

9   If the injector is not operating, but the resistance reading is within specifications, the PCM or the circuit between the PCM and the injector might be faulty.

13 Throttle body - check, removal and installation

Check
Refer to illustrations 13.2a and 13.2b
Note: *This procedure applies to 2003 and earlier models only.*

1   Verify that the throttle linkage operates smoothly.

2   Remove the air intake duct from the throttle body and inspect the bore for carbon and residue build-up. If it's dirty, clean it with aerosol carburetor cleaner **(see illustration)**. Make sure the can specifically states that it is safe with oxygen sensor systems and catalytic converters. **Caution:** *Do not clean the Throttle Position (TP) sensor or the Idle Air Control (IAC) motor with the solvent. Also, do NOT allow solvent to enter the air bypass passages located in front of the throttle valve* **(see illustration)**. *The IAC motor plunger and pintle valve must not become contaminated by solvent or debris. If the area in front of the throttle valve is so dirty that it will require extensive cleaning, remove the IAC motor (see Chapter 6) so that it won't be damaged if any solvent gets into the air bypass passages.*

Removal
Refer to illustrations 13.4, 13.6, 13.7a, 13.7b, 13.7c, 13.8, 13.9, 13.10 and 13.11
Warning: *Wait until the engine is completely cool before beginning this procedure.*

3   Disconnect the cable from the negative battery terminal (see Chapter 5).

4   Disconnect the air intake duct from the

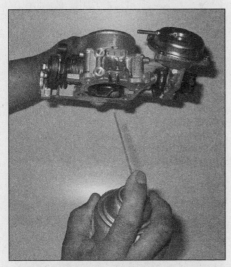

13.2a Clean out the area in the throttle body bore behind the throttle valve with carb cleaner or some other suitable aerosol solvent . . .

13.2b . . . but make sure that you don't allow any solvent to enter these air bypass passages; solvent and debris can damage the IAC motor, so if you're planning to do some heavy cleaning, it's a good idea to simply remove the IAC motor before cleaning the bore throttle body **(see illustration)**.

5   On 2003 and earlier models, disconnect the accelerator cable (see Section 10).

6   If equipped with cruise control, disconnect the cruise control cable vacuum hose **(see illustration)**. Disconnect any remaining vacuum lines.

7   Disconnect the main wiring harnesses from the throttle body **(see illustrations)**.

13.4 To disconnect the air intake duct from the throttle body, loosen this hose clamp screw and then pull off the air intake duct (1999 through 2003 model shown)

8   Disconnect the wiring from the IAC motor on 2003 and earlier models **(see illustration)**.

9   Partially drain the cooling system (see Chapter 1), then disconnect the coolant hoses from the throttle body **(see illustration)**.

10   Remove the throttle body mounting bolts from the throttle body, then remove the throttle body from the manifold **(see illustration)**.

11   Remove the throttle body gasket **(see illustration)**.

12   Remove all traces of old gasket material from the gasket mating surfaces of the throttle body and the air intake manifold.

13   If necessary, clean the throttle body as outlined in Step 2.

Installation

14   Using a new gasket, install the throttle body and tighten the throttle body mounting bolts to the torque listed in this Chapter's Specifications.

15   The remainder of installation is the reverse of removal. Add coolant as necessary to bring it to the appropriate level (see Chapter 1). On 2004 and later models, turn the ignition switch ON then turn it off and wait for at least 10 seconds. This is an electronic initialization procedure.

16   After installation, start the engine and

verify that the throttle body operates correctly and that there are no air leaks.

14   Fuel pressure regulator - removal and installation

Refer to illustrations 14.3a, 14.3b, 14.4, 14.5, 14.6a and 14.6b

Warning: *Gasoline is extremely flammable, so take extra precautions when you work on any part of the fuel system (see the* **Warning** *in Section 2).*

Note: *This procedure applies only to 2003 and earlier models. Later models have their fuel pressure regulator in the fuel tank as an integral part of the fuel pump module.*

1   Relieve the fuel system pressure (see Section 2).

2   Disconnect the cable from the negative battery terminal (see Chapter 5).

3   Disconnect the vacuum line from the fuel pressure regulator **(see illustrations)**.

4   Loosen the hose clamp **(see illustration)** and disconnect the fuel return line from the fuel pressure regulator.

5   Remove the fuel pressure regulator mounting bolts **(see illustration)** and remove the regulator from the fuel rail.

13.6 If the vehicle is equipped with cruise control, disconnect the vacuum line from the cruise control diaphragm (2003 and earlier models)

13.7a To disconnect the electrical connector from the Throttle Position (TP) sensor . . .

13.7b . . . pry this wire retainer open and pull off the connector (1999 through 2003 model shown)

13.7c The throttle body used on 2004 and later models is operated electrically - there are no cables used

13.8 Disconnect the electrical connector from the Idle Air Control (IAC) motor

13.9 Disconnect the coolant hoses from the throttle body

13.10 To separate the throttle body from the air intake manifold, remove these four bolts (1999 through 2003 2.4L SOHC model shown, other throttle bodies similar)

13.11 Be sure to remove and discard the old throttle body gasket, which might be stuck to the air intake manifold gasket mating surface or, as shown here, to the throttle body gasket mating surface; always use a new gasket when installing the throttle body to prevent air leaks

6   Remove and discard the old fuel pressure regulator O-ring **(see illustrations)**. Whether you're planning to reuse the old fuel pressure regulator or installing a new unit, be sure to install a new O-ring.

7   Installation is the reverse of removal. Be sure to install a new O-ring on the fuel pressure regulator and tighten the fuel pressure regulator mounting bolts to the torque listed in this Chapter's Specifications.

8   When you are finished working on the fuel system and all fuel lines are installed correctly, turn the ignition key to the ON position a few times to pressurize the system and check the serviced area for leaks.

14.3a Disconnect the vacuum line from the pressure regulator (1999 through 2003 2.4L SOHC model shown, earlier four-cylinder models similar)

14.3b To detach the fuel pressure regulator from the fuel rail on 2003 and earlier V6 models, disconnect this vacuum line, disconnect the fuel return hose (not visible in this photo) and remove the two pressure regulator mounting bolts

14.4 Loosen the hose clamp and disconnect the fuel return hose from the fuel pressure regulator (1999 through 2003 2.4L SOHC model shown, other models similar)

14.5 To detach the fuel pressure regulator from the fuel rail, remove these two bolts (1999 through 2003 2.4L SOHC model shown, other four-cylinder models similar)

14.6a Remove and discard the old fuel pressure regulator O-ring

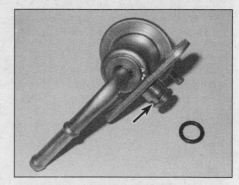

14.6b When installing a new O-ring, make sure that it's correctly installed in its groove on the fuel pressure regulator; also, coat the new O-ring with a little clean engine oil or gasoline so that it'll slide freely into its bore in the fuel rail

15.6a   To disconnect the fuel supply line from the fuel rail on 1999 through 2003 2.4L models, remove these two screws (other 2.4L models similar)

15.6b   To disconnect the fuel supply line from the fuel rail on V6 models, remove these two screws

15.7   To disconnect the electrical connector from each injector, press down on the "T" shaped end of this locking tab and pull off the connector

15   Fuel rail and injectors - removal and installation

Warning: *Gasoline is extremely flammable, so take extra precautions when you work on any part of the fuel system (see the **Warning** in Section 2).*

Removal

Refer to illustrations 15.6a, 15.6b, 15.7, 15.15a, 15.15b, 15.17, 15.18a, 15.18b, 15.19a, 15.19b, 15.19c and 15.19d

1   Relieve the fuel system pressure (see Section 2). Then disconnect the cable from the negative battery terminal (see Chapter 5).

2003 and earlier models

2   On 1994 and 1995 2.4L DOHC models, remove the spark plug wires.

3   On 1999 through 2003 models, drain the engine coolant (see Chapter 1).

4   On V6 models, remove the upper intake manifold (see Chapter 2B).

5   Disconnect the vacuum line and the fuel return hose from the fuel pressure regulator (see Section 14). (Unless you're planning to *replace* the fuel rail, it's not necessary to actually remove the fuel pressure regulator from the fuel rail in order to remove the fuel rail.)

6   Disconnect the fuel supply line from the fuel rail **(see illustrations)**.

7   Disconnect the electrical connectors from the fuel injectors **(see illustration)**.

8   On 1999 through 2003 four-cylinder models, remove the throttle body (see Section 13).

2004 and later models

Four-cylinder engines

9   Disconnect the wiring from the ignition coils and the injectors.

10   Disconnect the wiring from the EGR solenoid, the EVAP solenoid, the power steering pressure switch, the knock sensor, the throttle position sensor and the MAP sensor. Disconnect the PCV hose.

V6 engines

11   Refer to Chapter 2B and remove the upper intake manifold.

12   Disconnect the wiring from the injectors, then unbolt the wiring harness.

13   Remove the engine brace from the timing belt end of the engine.

All engines

14   Disconnect the fuel supply hose from the fuel rail.

All models

15   Remove the fuel rail mounting bolts **(see illustrations)**.

16   Using compressed air, blow off the area right around each injector or spray it with some carburetor cleaner to remove any dirt or debris that might fall into the injector holes in the manifold when the injectors are pulled out.

17   Remove the fuel rail and the fuel injectors as a single assembly **(see illustration)**.

18   There are spacers between the fuel rail

15.15a   To detach the fuel rail from a four-cylinder engine, remove these two bolts (1999 through 2003 2.4L model shown, other models similar)

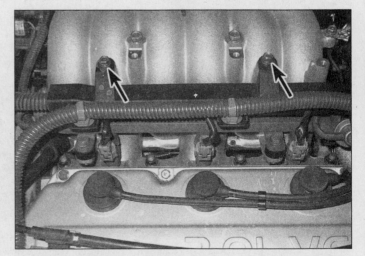

15.15b   To detach the fuel rail assembly from a V6 engine, remove these two bolts from the front fuel rail and remove the other two bolts (not shown) from the rear fuel rail

15.17 Remove the fuel rail and injectors as a single assembly

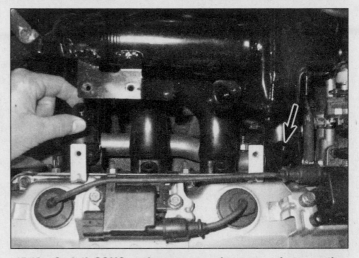

15.18a On 2.4L SOHC engines, remove the spacers between the fuel rail and the intake manifold and store them in a plastic bag until you're ready to install the fuel rail and injectors

and the intake manifold. It's a good idea to remove these spacers **(see illustrations)** and store them in a plastic bag so that you don't lose them while the fuel rail is removed.

19 On V6 models, remove the retaining clips and pull the injectors out of the fuel rail **(see illustrations)**. On 2.4L models, simply pull the injectors out of the fuel rail. On all models, remove the O-ring seals and discard them **(see illustrations)**. **Note:** *Whether you're replacing an injector or a leaking O-ring seal, it's standard practice to replace all the O-ring seals on all the injectors at the same time.*

15.18b On V6 engines, remove the spacers between the fuel rail and the intake manifold and store them in a plastic bag until you're ready to install the fuel rail and injectors

15.19a Using a small screwdriver, pry off the retainers . . .

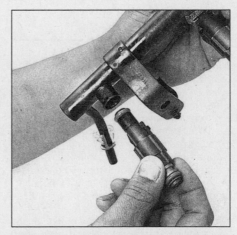

15.19b . . . and pull each injector out of the fuel rail (V6 models only; the injectors on 2.4L models don't use retainers)

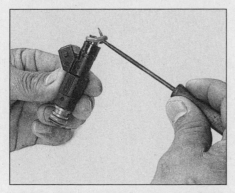

15.19c Remove the O-rings from each injector and discard them; always replace the O-rings with new ones to prevent fuel leaks

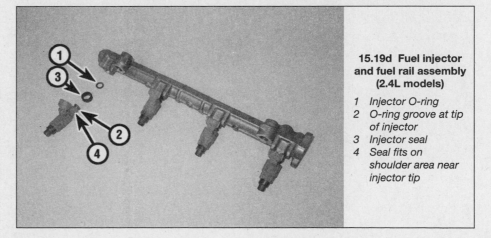

15.19d Fuel injector and fuel rail assembly (2.4L models)

1 Injector O-ring
2 O-ring groove at tip of injector
3 Injector seal
4 Seal fits on shoulder area near injector tip

Installation

20   Coat the new O-rings with clean engine oil and install them on the injectors, then insert each injector into its corresponding bore in the fuel rail. On V6 models, install the injector retaining clips.

21   Install the injector and fuel rail assembly on the intake manifold. Fully seat the injectors, then tighten the fuel rail mounting bolts to the torque listed in this Chapter's Specifications.

22   Connect the fuel supply line and the fuel return hose. Make sure that they are securely installed.

23   Connect the electrical connectors to each injector, referring to the numbered tags.

24   On V6 engines, clean and inspect the upper-to-lower manifold gasket surfaces. Install the upper intake manifold (see Chapter 2B).

25   The remainder of the installation is the reverse of removal.

26   After the injector/fuel rail assembly installation is complete, turn the ignition switch to ON (engine not running). Repeat this two or three times, then check the fuel lines and the injectors for leaks.

27   Refill the cooling system if it was drained (see Chapter 1).

16   Exhaust system servicing - general information

Refer to illustration 16.1

Warning: *Allow the exhaust system to cool completely before inspecting or repairing any exhaust components. Also, when working under the vehicle, make sure it is securely supported on jackstands.*

1   The exhaust system consists of the exhaust manifold, the catalytic converter, the resonator, exhaust pipe, muffler and all brackets, hangers and clamps. The exhaust system is attached to the body with mounting brackets and rubber hangers **(see illustration)**. If any of these parts are incorrectly installed, excessive noise and vibration might be transmitted to the body.

16.1 A typical rubber exhaust hanger used on the vehicles covered in this manual; to replace it, remove the bolt then slide it off the mounting bracket

Muffler and pipes

2   Conduct regular inspections of the exhaust system to keep it safe and quiet. Look for any damaged or bent parts, open seams, holes, loose connections, excessive corrosion or other defects which could allow exhaust fumes to enter the vehicle. Also check the catalytic converter when you inspect the exhaust system (see following). Deteriorated exhaust system components should not be repaired; they should be replaced with new parts.

3   Before trying to disassemble any exhaust components, spray the fasteners with a penetrating oil to help ease removal. If the exhaust system components are extremely corroded or rusted together, welding equipment will probably be required to remove them. The convenient way to accomplish this is to have a muffler repair shop remove the corroded sections with a cutting torch. If, however, you want to save money by doing it yourself (and you don't have a welding outfit with a cutting torch), simply cut off the old components with a hacksaw. If

you have compressed air, special pneumatic cutting chisels can also be used. If you decide to tackle the job at home, be sure to wear safety goggles to protect your eyes from metal chips and work gloves to protect your hands.

4   Here are some simple guidelines to follow when repairing the exhaust system:
   a) *Work from the back to the front when removing exhaust system components.*
   b) *Apply penetrating oil to the exhaust system component fasteners to make them easier to remove.*
   c) *Use new gaskets, hangers and clamps when installing exhaust systems components.*
   d) *Apply anti-seize compound to the threads of all exhaust system fasteners at reassembly.*
   e) *Be sure to allow sufficient clearance between newly installed parts and all points on the underbody to avoid overheating the floor pan and possibly damaging the interior carpet and insulation. Pay particularly close attention to the catalytic converter and heat shield.*

Catalytic converter

Warning: *The converter gets extremely hot during operation, and can remain very hot for hours after the engine has been turned off. Make sure it has cooled down before you touch it.*

Note: *See Chapter 6 for more information on the catalytic converter.*

5   Periodically inspect the heat shield for cracks, dents and loose or missing fasteners.

6   Remove the heat shield and inspect the converter for cracks or other damage.

7   If the converter must be replaced, detach the exhaust system from the exhaust manifold. Loosen the rear band clamp at the resonator and separate the converter from the exhaust system.

8   Installation is the reverse of removal. Be sure to use new gaskets and tighten the fasteners securely.

Chapter 5
Engine electrical systems

Contents

Specifications

Ignition system

Engine firing order
    Four-cylinder engines 1-3-4-2
    V6 engines 1-2-3-4-5-6
Ignition timing (models with distributors)
    1996 and earlier models
        Basic timing (with timing connector bridged) .... 5-degrees BTDC (± 3-degrees)
        Standard timing (computer controlled) .... 10-degrees BTDC (± 7-degrees)
    1997 and 1998 models
        Basic timing (requires scan tool) .... 5-degrees BTDC (± 3-degrees)
        Standard timing (computer controlled) .... 10-degrees BTDC (± 7-degrees)
    1999 through 2003 models
        Four-cylinder engine .... Not adjustable
        V6 engine
            Basic timing (requires scan tool) .... 5-degrees BTDC (± 3-degrees)
            Standard timing (computer controlled) .... 15-degrees BTDC (± 7-degrees)
    2004 and later models .... Not adjustable
Ignition coil resistance (approximate, at 70 to 80-degrees F)
    1994 through 1998 models
        2.4L DOHC engines (1994 and 1995)
            Primary resistance .... 0.67 to 0.81 ohms
            Secondary resistance .... 11.3 to 15.3 k-ohms
        2.4L SOHC engines
            Primary resistance .... 0.9 to 1.2 ohms
            Secondary resistance .... 20 to 29 k-ohms
    1999 through 2003 models
        2.4L SOHC engines
            1999 and 2000
                Primary resistance .... N/A (see Section 7)
                Secondary resistance .... 15.3 to 20.7 k-ohms
            2001 on
                Primary resistance .... N/A (see Section 7)
                Secondary resistance .... 8.5 to 11.5 k-ohms
        3.0L V6 engines
            Primary resistance .... 0.56 to 0.68 ohms
            Secondary resistance .... 9.4 to 12.8 k-ohms
    2004 and later models .... Cannot be checked with ohmmeter

Charging system

Charging voltage .... 13.9 to 14.9 volts (at 68-degrees [20-degrees C])
Output current .... 70 percent of normal output current

Torque specifications

	Ft-lbs	Nm
Starter motor mounting bolts (all engines)	22	30

1   General information, precautions and battery disconnection

The engine electrical systems include all ignition, charging and starting components. Because of their engine-related functions, these components are discussed separately from chassis electrical devices such as the lights, the instruments, etc. (which are included in Chapter 12).

Precautions

Always observe the following precautions when working on the electrical system:

a) *Be extremely careful when servicing engine electrical components. They are easily damaged if checked, connected or handled improperly.*

b) *Never leave the ignition switched on for long periods of time when the engine is not running.*

c) *Never disconnect the battery cables while the engine is running.*

d) *Maintain correct polarity when connecting battery cables from another vehicle during jump starting - see the "Booster battery (jump) starting" section at the front of this manual.*

e) *Always disconnect the negative battery cable from the battery before working on the electrical system, but read the following battery disconnection procedure first.*

It's also a good idea to review the safety-related information regarding the engine electrical systems located in the *"Safety first!"* section at the front of this manual, before beginning any operation included in this Chapter.

Battery disconnection

The battery is located in the engine compartment on all vehicles covered by this manual. To disconnect the battery for service procedures requiring power to be cut from the vehicle, disconnect the cable from the negative battery terminal. Make sure that you isolate the cable to prevent it from coming into contact with the battery negative terminal.

Several systems on the vehicle require battery power all the time, either to ensure their continued operation (radio, alarm system, power door locks, windows, etc.) or to maintain control unit memory (Powertrain Control Module, automatic transaxle control module, etc.) which would be lost if the battery were to be disconnected. Therefore, whenever the battery is to be disconnected, first note the following to ensure that there are no unforeseen consequences of this action:

a) *Before connecting or disconnecting the cable from the negative battery terminal, make sure that you turn the ignition key and the lighting switch to their OFF positions. Failure to do so could damage semiconductor components.*

b) *The engine management system's PCM will lose some of the information stored*

in its "map" (program) when the battery is disconnected. This includes idling and operating values, any diagnostic trouble codes that were stored in the PCM memory and system monitors required for emissions testing. Whenever the battery has been disconnected, allow the engine to idle for about ten minutes while the computer relearns its operating values (see Chapter 6 for more information about the PCM).

c) *On any vehicle with power door locks, it is a wise precaution to remove the key from the ignition and to keep it with you, so that it does not get locked inside if the power door locks should engage accidentally when the battery is reconnected!*

Devices known as "memory savers" (small, usually 9-volt, batteries) can be used to avoid some of the above problems. Typically, a memory saver is plugged into the cigarette lighter. Then you can disconnect the vehicle battery from the electrical system. The memory saver will deliver sufficient current to maintain security alarm codes and PCM memory, and it will also run unswitched (always on) circuits such as the clock and radio memory, while isolating the car battery in the event that a short circuit occurs while the vehicle is being serviced.

Warning: *If you're going to work around any airbag system components, disconnect the battery and do not use a memory saver. If you do, the airbag could accidentally deploy and cause personal injury.*

Caution: *Because memory savers deliver current to operate unswitched circuits when the battery is disconnected, make sure the circuit that you're going to service is actually open before working on it!*

2   Battery - emergency jump starting

Refer to the *Booster battery (jump) starting* procedure at the front of this manual.

3   Battery - check, removal and installation

Warning: *Hydrogen gas is produced by the battery, so keep open flames and lighted cigarettes away from it at all times. Always wear eye protection when working around a battery. Rinse off spilled electrolyte immediately with large amounts of water.*

Check

Refer to illustrations 3.1a, 3.1b and 3.1c

1   A battery cannot be accurately tested until it is at or near a fully charged state. Disconnect the negative battery cable from the battery and perform the following tests:

a) ***Battery state of charge test*** *- Visually inspect the indicator eye (if equipped) on the top of the battery. If the indicator eye is dark in color, charge the battery as*

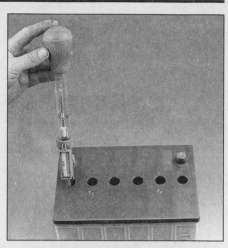

3.1a Use a battery hydrometer to draw electrolyte from the battery cell - this hydrometer is equipped with a thermometer to make temperature corrections

described in Chapter 1. If the battery is equipped with removable caps, check the battery electrolyte. The electrolyte level should be above the upper edge of the plates. If the level is low, add distilled water. DO NOT OVERFILL. The excess electrolyte may spill over during periods of heavy charging. Test the specific gravity of the electrolyte using a hydrometer **(see illustration)**. *Remove the caps and extract a sample of the electrolyte and observe the float inside the barrel of the hydrometer. Follow the instructions from the tool manufacturer and determine the specific gravity of the electrolyte for each cell. A fully charged battery will indicate approximately 1.270 (green zone) at 68-degrees F (20-degrees C). If the specific gravity of the electrolyte is low (red zone), charge the battery as described in Chapter 1.*

b) ***Open circuit voltage test*** *- Using a digital voltmeter, perform an open circuit voltage test* **(see illustration)**. *Connect the negative probe of the voltmeter to the negative battery post and the positive probe to the positive battery post. The battery voltage should be greater than 12.5 volts. If the battery is less than the specified voltage, charge the battery before proceeding to the next test. Do not proceed with the battery load test until the battery is fully charged.*

c) ***Battery load test*** *- An accurate check of the battery condition can only be performed with a load tester (available at most auto parts stores). This test evaluates the ability of the battery to operate the starter and other accessories during periods of heavy amperage draw (load). Install a special battery load-testing tool onto the battery terminals* **(see illustration)**. *Load test the battery according to the tool manufacturer's instructions. This*

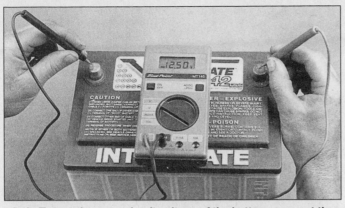

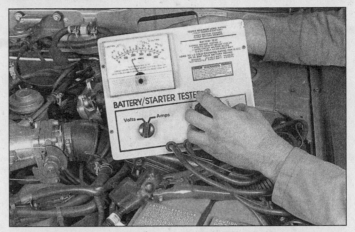

3.1b To test the open circuit voltage of the battery, connect the black probe of the voltmeter to the negative terminal and the red probe to the positive terminal of the battery - a fully charged battery should indicate approximately 12.5 volts depending on the outside air temperature

3.1c Some battery load testers are equipped with an ammeter which enables the battery load to be precisely dialed in, as shown - less expensive testers have a load switch and a voltmeter only

tool utilizes a carbon pile to increase the load demand (amperage draw) on the battery. Maintain the load on the battery for 15 seconds and observe that the battery voltage does not drop below 9.6 volts. If the battery condition is weak or defective, the tool will indicate this condition immediately. **Note:** *Cold temperatures will cause the minimum voltage requirements to drop slightly. Follow the chart given in the tool manufacturer's instructions to compensate for cold climates. Minimum load voltage for freezing temperatures (32 degrees F/0-degrees C) should be approximately 9.1 volts.*

d) *Battery drain test* - This test will indicate whether there's a constant drain on the vehicle's electrical system that can cause the battery to discharge. Make sure all accessories are turned Off. If the vehicle has an underhood light, verify it's working properly, then disconnect it. Connect one lead of a digital ammeter to the disconnected negative battery cable clamp and the other lead to the negative battery post. A drain of approximately 100 milliamps or less is considered normal (due to the engine control computers, clocks, digital radios and other components which normally cause a key-off battery drain). An excessive drain (approximately 500 milliamps or more) will cause the battery to discharge. The problem circuit or component can be located by removing the fuses, one at a time, until the excessive drain stops and normal drain is indicated on the meter.

Replacement

Refer to illustrations 3.2, 3.5 and 3.7
Caution: *Always disconnect the negative cable first and hook it up last, or the tool you're using to loosen the cable clamps might short the battery.*

2   Loosen the cable clamp nut **(see illustration)** and disconnect the ground cable from the negative battery post. Isolate the cable end to prevent it from accidentally

3.2 Before removing the battery, disconnect the ground cable (-), then the positive cable (+); to detach the battery from the battery tray, remove the two hold-down clamp nuts

coming into contact with the battery post.
3   Loosen the cable clamp nut and disconnect the positive battery cable from the positive battery post.
4   Remove the battery hold-down clamp nuts.
5   Remove the battery cover, if equipped **(see illustration)**.
6   Lift out the battery. Be careful - it's heavy.

3.5 Remove the battery cover, if equipped

Note: *Battery straps and handlers are available at most auto parts stores for a reasonable price. They make it easier to remove and carry the battery.*
7   While the battery is out, inspect the battery tray for corrosion. If corrosion exists, clean the deposits with a mixture of baking soda and water to prevent further corrosion. Flush the area with plenty of clean water and dry thoroughly. If the corrosion is too far advanced to save the battery tray, remove the tray **(see illustration)** and replace it.

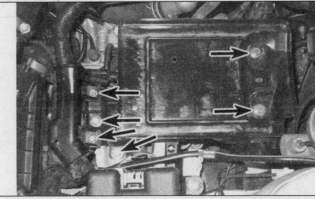

3.7 To detach the battery tray, remove these mounting bolts

Terminal end corrosion or damage.

Insulation cracks.

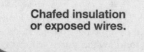

Chafed insulation
or exposed wires.

Burned or melted insulation.

4.2 Typical battery cable problems

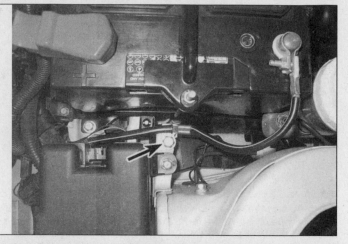

4.4a If the ground cable is attached to the engine compartment anywhere between the negative battery post and the ground bolt, detach it

4.4b When you trace the ground cable to its lower end, you'll find a ground bolt attaching the cable to the transaxle bellhousing

4.4c The positive battery cable is attached to the starter motor solenoid terminal by a nut, underneath this rubber cover

8   If you are replacing the battery, make sure you replace it with a battery with the identical dimensions, amperage rating, cold cranking rating, etc.

9   Installation is the reverse of removal. After connecting the cables to the battery, apply a light coating of petroleum jelly or grease to the connections to help prevent corrosion.

4   Battery cables - replacement

Refer to illustrations 4.2, 4.4a, 4.4b and 4.4c

1   Periodically inspect the entire length of each battery cable for damage, cracked or burned insulation and corrosion. Poor battery cable connections can cause starting problems and decreased engine performance.

2   Check the cable-to-terminal connections at the ends of the cables for cracks, loose wire strands and corrosion **(see illustration)**. The presence of white, fluffy deposits under the insulation at the cable terminal connection is a sign that the cable is corroded and should be replaced. Check the terminals for distortion, missing mounting bolts and corrosion.

3   When removing the cables always disconnect the negative cable from the negative battery post first and hook it up last or the tool

used to loosen the cable clamps may short the battery. Even if only the positive cable is being replaced, be sure to disconnect the negative cable from the negative battery post first (see Chapter 1 for further information regarding battery cable maintenance).

4   Disconnect the old cables from the battery (see Section 3), then disconnect each of them at the other end. It might also be necessary to detach the cables from cable brackets or clips before they can be removed. Trace each cable from the battery all the way down to its opposite end and detach the cables from any cable brackets or clips as necessary **(see illustrations)**. If either cable is bundled together with other wiring harnesses, remove the protective sheath and separate the cable from the other wires. Note the routing of both cables to ensure correct installation.

5   Positive cables are almost always red and larger in cross-section; ground cables are usually black and smaller in cross-section. But if you're replacing either or both of the cables, take them with you when buying new cables. It is vitally important that you replace the cables with the *identical* parts.

6   Clean the threads of the starter solenoid and/or ground connection with a wire brush

to remove rust and corrosion. Apply a light coat of battery terminal corrosion inhibitor or petroleum jelly to the threads to prevent future corrosion.

7   Attach the lower ends of the cables first, then connect the positive cable to the positive battery post (don't reconnect the ground cable to the negative battery post until you're completely finished). Before connecting a new cable to the battery, make sure that it reaches the battery post without having to be stretched.

8   If either cable is supposed to be secured to the engine compartment by any brackets or clips, make sure that you reattach them.

9   After both cables are completely installed, reconnect the ground cable to the negative battery post.

5   Ignition system - general information and precautions

General information

1   All vehicles covered in this manual are equipped with an electronic ignition system.

The ignition system on each of these vehicles includes the ignition switch, the battery, the ignition coils, the primary (low voltage) and secondary (high voltage) wiring circuits, the ignition wires, the spark plugs, the camshaft position sensor (except 1994 through 1998 2.4L SOHC models), the crankshaft position sensor, the power transistor and the Powertrain Control Module (PCM). The PCM controls the ignition timing and spark advance characteristics for the engine. The ignition timing is not adjustable.

2   There are two different electronic ignition systems on these vehicles. 1994 through 1998 2.4L SOHC models and all 3.0L V6 engines use a distributor. 3.8L V6, as well as 1994 and 1995 DOHC 2.4L models and 1999 and later 2.4L SOHC models are distributorless.

1994 through 1998 SOHC 2.4L models and 1999 through 2003 3.0L V6 models

3   These vehicles are equipped with a distributor to direct secondary voltage to each of the spark plugs at the appropriate time. The Powertrain Control Module (PCM) controls ignition timing based upon the information it receives from the following sensors and switches:

> Barometric pressure sensor (1997 and later models)
> Camshaft Position (CMP) sensor
> Crankshaft Position (CKP) sensor
> Closed throttle position switch (1997 through 2000 models)
> Engine Coolant Temperature (ECT) sensor
> Idle switch (1994 through 1996 models)
> Ignition switch (when starting the engine)
> Intake Air Temperature (IAT) sensor
> Knock sensor (2001 and later 3.0L V6 models)
> Park/Neutral Position (PNP) switch (automatics)
> Vacuum sensor (1994 through 1996 models)
> Vehicle Speed Sensor (VSS)
> Volume Air Flow sensor (1997 and later models)

4   The camshaft-driven distributor, which is located on the end of the cylinder head (end of the *rear* head on 3.0L V6 models), delivers ignition voltage to the cylinders in firing order. The distributor is not serviceable; if any component besides the cap, the rotor or the O-ring (which seals the distributor base) is defective, replace the distributor assembly. Besides the rotor, the distributor also houses the ignition coils, the Crankshaft Position (CKP) sensor (1994 and 1995 2.4L SOHC models) and the Camshaft Position (CMP) sensor (1994 through 1998 2.4L SOHC and all 3.0L V6 models).

5   The Camshaft Position (CMP) sensor and the Crankshaft Position (CKP) sensor are information sensors used by the PCM to monitor the positions of the camshaft and the crankshaft, in order to determine ignition timing (when to fire the spark plugs) and injector sequence (when to fire the injectors).

On 1994 and 1995 SOHC 2.4L models, the CKP sensor is an integral component of the distributor. On 1994 through 1998 2.4L models, the CMP sensor is an integral component of the distributor and the CKP sensor is mounted on the front of the block, above the crankshaft timing belt sprocket. On 3.0L V6 models, the CMP sensor is an integral component of the distributor and the CKP sensor is mounted near the front end of the crankshaft, above the crankshaft timing belt sprocket. Refer to Chapter 6 for replacement procedures for the CKP and CMP sensors.

1994 and 1995 DOHC 2.4L models and 1999 through 2003 2.4L SOHC models

6   These vehicles are "distributorless," i.e. they do not use a distributor. The Powertrain Control Module (PCM) calculates the firing order, ignition timing and injector sequence by using the information it receives from the following sensors:

> Atmospheric (or Barometric) Pressure sensor
> Camshaft Position (CMP) sensor
> Crankshaft Position (CKP) sensor
> Engine Coolant Temperature (ECT) sensor
> Idle Position switch (1994 and 1995 DOHC 2.4L models)
> Ignition switch (when starting the engine)
> Intake Air Temperature (IAT) sensor
> Knock sensor (1994 and 1995 DOHC 2.4L models)
> Park/Neutral Position (PNP) switch
> Vehicle Speed Sensor (VSS)
> Volume Air Flow sensor

7   The distributorless system uses a "waste spark" method of spark distribution. The firing order of these models is 1, 3, 4, 2. In a waste spark system, each cylinder is paired with its "companion" cylinder (1 and 4, 3 and 2). Each time the spark plug in the cylinder under compression is fired, the plug in its companion cylinder is also fired simultaneously. But the piston in the companion cylinder is on its exhaust stroke, so the plug in that cylinder uses very little voltage (because the resistance at the spark plug gap is low when there's no compression), leaving most of the voltage to fire the plug of the cylinder on its compression stroke.

8   The ignition coils are mounted on the valve covers. 1994 and 1995 2.5L DOHC models are equipped with a four-coil assembly. The high-tension terminal of each coil is connected to its corresponding spark plug by a plug wire. 1999 and later 2.4L SOHC models use two dual-coil units. One coil is positioned over and connected directly to the spark plug for cylinder No. 2 and the other is positioned over and connected directly to the spark plug for cylinder No. 4. Each of these coils is also connected to its companion cylinder spark plug by a plug wire. The second high-tension terminal for the coil over cylinder No. 2 is connected to cylinder No. 3 by a plug wire and the second high-tension terminal for the coil over cylinder No. 4 is connected to the spark plug

for cylinder No. 1 by a plug wire.

2004 and later models

9   These vehicles are also distributorless; however, they don't use a waste-spark system. Each cylinder has its own ignition coil connected to its spark plug and mounted on the valve cover. Refer to Step 6 in this Section for information about this PCM-controlled ignition system.

Precautions (all models)

10   When working on the ignition system take the following precautions:

a) *Do not keep the ignition switch on for more than 10 seconds if the engine will not start.*

b) *Always connect a tachometer in accordance with the manufacturer's instructions. Some tachometers may be incompatible with this ignition system. Consult an auto parts counterperson before buying a tachometer for use with this vehicle.*

c) *Never allow the ignition coil terminals to touch ground. Grounding the coil could result in damage to the power transistor and/or the ignition coil.*

d) *Do not disconnect the battery when the engine is running.*

---

6   Ignition system - check

Refer to illustrations 6.3a, 6.3b and 6.3c

Warning: *Because of the very high voltage generated by the ignition system (approximately 40,000 volts), use extreme care whenever performing an operation involving ignition components. This not only includes the coil and spark plug wires, but related items connected to the system as well, such as the electrical connectors, tachometer and any test equipment.*

Note: *The ignition system components on these models are expensive and difficult to diagnose. In the event of ignition system failure, if the checks do not clearly indicate the source of the ignition system problem, have the vehicle tested by a dealer service department or other qualified auto repair facility.*

1   If a malfunction occurs and the vehicle won't start, do not immediately assume that the ignition system is causing the problem. First, check the following items:

a) *Make sure the battery cable clamps, where they connect to the battery, are clean and tight.*

b) *Test the condition of the battery (see Section 3). If it does not pass all the tests, replace it with a new battery.*

c) *Check the external ignition coil (if equipped) wiring and connections.*

d) *Check the related fuses inside the fuse box (see Chapter 12). If they're burned, determine the cause and repair the circuit.*

2   If the engine turns over but won't start, make sure there is sufficient secondary ignition voltage to fire the spark plug.

3   Disconnect the spark plug wire from each

6.3a To test for spark, simply disconnect the spark plug boot from the plug, insert the calibrated ignition tester into the boot and clip the tester to a good ground (2.4L SOHC model shown)

6.3b Testing for spark on a 3.0L V6 engine

spark plug and attach it to a calibrated ignition tester (available at most auto parts stores) **(see illustrations)**. Connect the clip on the tester to a bolt or metal bracket on the engine. **Note 1:** *1999 and later 2.4L SOHC models have an ignition coil over cylinder No. 2 with a spark plug wire connecting it to its companion cylinder (No. 3) and another coil over cylinder No. 4 with a plug wire connecting it to its companion cylinder (No. 1). Because these coil assemblies actually fire two spark plugs simultaneously, you must check the spark at both high-tension terminals to test for sufficient secondary voltage. Testing at only one terminal will not conclusively tell you that one of these coils is operating correctly because there could be an open, or high resistance, in the circuit between the winding and the high tension terminal that you didn't test. So be sure to test both terminals of each coil on these models.* **Note 2:** *It is necessary to ground the coil assemblies on 1999 and later SOHC 2.4L models because they're grounded through the coil mounting bolts, so when you remove one of these coils to test for spark at the terminal that's plugged directly onto the top of the spark plug, run a jumper wire between the metal part of the coil (the boss for a mounting bolt) and a good ground such as the coil mounting bracket* **(see illustration)**.

4   Relieve the fuel pressure (see Chapter 4). Keep the fuel system disabled while performing the ignition system checks.

5   Crank the engine and watch the end of the tester to see if bright blue, well-defined sparks occur (weak spark or intermittent spark is the same as no spark).

6   If sparks occur, sufficient voltage is reaching the spark plug to fire it (repeat the check at the remaining spark plug wires to verify that all the ignition coils are functioning). However, the plugs themselves may be fouled, so remove and check them as described in Chapter 1 or install new ones.

7   If no sparks or intermittent sparks occur, check for battery voltage to the ignition coils (refer to the wiring diagrams at the end of Chapter 12). If battery voltage is present, check the ignition coil resistance (see Section 7).

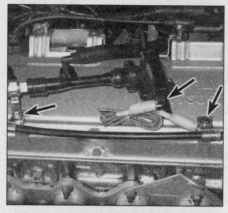

6.3c To test for spark at a high tension terminal that is connected directly (no spark plug wire) to a spark plug, remove the ignition coil, insert the calibrated ignition tester into the "boot" and clip the tester to a good ground and, on 1999 and later 2.4L SOHC models (shown), be sure to ground the coil's metal housing to a good ground with a jumper wire

8   Also, if no sparks or intermittent sparks occur, check the ignition wires to each spark plug (see Chapter 1).

9   If the checks are all correct, the Camshaft Position (CMP) sensor or Crankshaft Position (CKP) sensor might be defective (see Chapter 6 for CMP and CKP sensor replacement procedures).

7   Ignition coil - check and replacement

Check

Note: *The following checks should be made with the engine cold. If the engine is hot, the resistance will be greater.*

1994 and 1995 2.4L DOHC models

Refer to illustrations 7.4 and 7.5

1   Disconnect the electrical connector from the coil assembly.

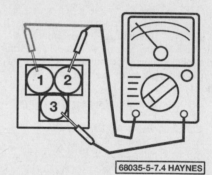

7.4 Ignition coil primary electrical connector terminal guide (1994 and 1995 2.4L DOHC models)

2   Clearly label the spark plug wires and then disconnect them from the coil pack.

3   Unbolt the coil assembly and remove it.

4   Measure the primary resistance of each coil winding **(see illustration)**. Connect an ohmmeter between terminal 3 (power) and each of the other two terminals (ground path for each primary coil winding, switched on and off by the power transistor) and note the resistance. Compare the indicated resistance with the primary resistance listed in this Chapter's Specifications. If the primary resistance for either coil winding is incorrect, replace the coil assembly.

5   Measure the secondary resistance between the high-tension terminals of each coil winding **(see illustration)**. Connect an ohmmeter between the high-tension terminals for spark plug Nos.1 and 4 and note the resistance. Repeat the check on terminals 2 and 3. Compare the indicated resistance with the secondary resistance listed in this Chapter's Specifications. If the secondary resistance for either coil winding is incorrect, replace the coil assembly.

6   Install the coil assembly and tighten the mounting bolts securely.

7   Reconnect the spark plug wires to the

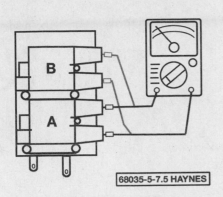

68035-5-7.5 HAYNES

7.5 Ignition coil secondary resistance check (1994 and 1995 2.4L DOHC models)

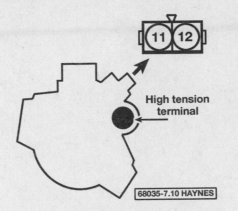

68035-7.10 HAYNES

7.10 Coil high tension terminal location and electrical connector terminal guide (1994 through 1996 2.4L SOHC models)

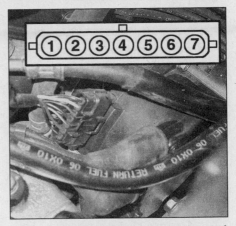

7.12 Ignition coil electrical connector and terminal guide (1999 and later 3.0L V6 models)

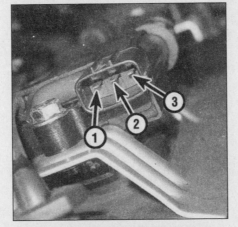

7.16a Ignition coil electrical connector terminal guide (1999 through 2003 2.4L SOHC models)

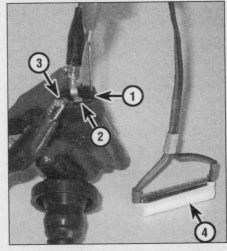

7.16b Here's the setup for testing the primary side of an ignition coil on 1999 through 2003 2.4L SOHC models:

1 Hook up the negative probe of an analog ohmmeter to terminal No. 1. Using spade connectors between the terminals and the alligator clips will "extend" the terminals so that you can clip onto them.

2 Hook up the positive ohmmeter probe to terminal No. 2 (with another spade connector). Then hook up the negative or ground wire for a 1.5-volt battery to this terminal (or to the spade connector, as shown).

3 Hook up the positive or power wire for the 1.5-volt battery to terminal No. 3.

4 You'll need a 1.5-volt battery and a couple of short leads to hook it up to terminals 2 and 3. We taped the ends of the leads to the battery so they'd stay put while we conducted the test.

coil assembly (see Chapter 1).

8   Reconnect the coil electrical connector.

1994 through 1998 2.4L SOHC models

Refer to illustration 7.10

9   Disconnect the electrical connector from the distributor.

10   Measure the coil primary resistance between connector terminals 11 and 12 on the distributor side of the connector **(see illustration)** and note the indicated resistance. Compare the indicated primary resistance with the primary resistance listed in this Chapter's Specifications. If the primary resistance for either coil winding is incorrect, replace the distributor (the coil is an integral component of the distributor).

11   Measure the secondary resistance between the coil high-tension terminal and connector terminal 11 or 12 **(see illustration 7.10)** and note the indicated resistance. Compare the indicated secondary resistance with the secondary resistance listed in this Chapter's Specifications. If the secondary resistance for either coil winding is incorrect, replace the distributor (the coil is an integral component of the distributor).

1999 and later 3.0L V6 models

Refer to illustration 7.12

12   Disconnect the electrical connector from the distributor **(see illustration)**.

13   Measure the coil primary resistance between connector terminals 1 and 2 on the distributor side of the connector **(see illustration 7.12)** and note the indicated resistance. Compare the indicated primary resistance with the primary resistance listed in this Chapter's Specifications. If the primary resistance for the coil winding is incorrect, replace the distributor (the coil is an integral component of the distributor).

14   Measure the secondary resistance between the coil high-tension terminal and connector terminal 1 **(see illustration 7.12)** and note the indicated resistance. Compare the indicated secondary resistance with the sec-

ondary resistance listed in this Chapter's Specifications. If the secondary resistance for the coil winding is incorrect, replace the distributor (the coil is an integral component of the distributor).

1999 through 2003 2.4L SOHC models

Refer to illustrations 7.16a, 7.16b and 7.17

15   Disconnect the electrical connector from the ignition coil assembly.

16   To check primary coil resistance (and to check the integral ignition power transistor), connect the negative probe of an *analog* ohmmeter to terminal 1 and the positive probe to terminal 2 while powering terminals 2 and 3 with a 1.5 volt battery **(see illustrations)**. **Caution:** *The following test must be performed quickly (10 seconds or less) to prevent damage to the coil and to the ignition power transistor.* When current is flowing from the battery to terminal 3 and from terminal 2 back to the battery, there should be continuity between terminals 1 and 2. When the battery circuit is opened, there should be no continuity between terminals 1 and 2. If the primary resistance is not as specified,

replace the coil.

17   To check coil secondary resistance, measure the resistance between the two high-tension terminals of the coil **(see illus-**

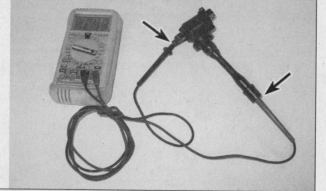

7.17 To measure the resistance on the secondary side of an ignition coil on 1999 through 2003 2.4L SOHC models, hook up the probes of an ohmmeter to the two high tension terminals

7.29 Disconnect the electrical connector from the ignition coil (1999 through 2003 2.4L SOHC models)

tration). Note the indicated resistance and compare your measurement to the secondary resistance listed in this Chapter's Specifications. If the secondary resistance is incorrect, replace the coil.

2004 and later models

18   These coils can't be checked using an ohmmeter because there is a diode in the circuit.
19   If an ignition coil is suspected of being faulty, you'll have to obtain a known good ignition coil or remove one from another cylinder.
20   Remove the suspected bad ignition coil,

7.30 To disconnect the spark plug wire for the companion cylinder from the ignition coil, simply pull it straight off the coil high tension tower (but don't pull on the spark plug wire, pull on the plug wire boot)

connect its wiring and connect a good spark plug to it. Ground the spark plug to the engine using a test lead.
21   Crank the engine and check for thick, blue sparks. If there is no spark, connect the known good coil and repeat the test to verify that the first coil is the problem.

Replacement

22   Disconnect the cable from the negative battery terminal.

1994 and 1995 2.4L DOHC models

23   Disconnect the electrical connector from the ignition coil assembly.
24   Clearly label and detach the spark plug wires (see Chapter 1).
25   Remove the ignition coil mounting bolts and detach the coil pack from the engine.
26   Installation is the reverse of the removal.

1994 through 1998 2.4L SOHC models

27   The coil on these models is not serviceable. Replace the distributor with a new or rebuilt unit (see Section 9).

1999 and later 3.0L V6 models

28   The coil on these models is not serviceable. Replace the distributor with a new or rebuilt unit (see Section 9).

1999 through 2003 2.4L SOHC models

Refer to illustrations 7.29, 7.30 and 7.31
29   Disconnect the electrical connector from the coil assembly **(see illustration)**.

30   Clearly label and detach the spark plug wire for the companion cylinder from the ignition coil assembly **(see illustration)**.
31   Remove the bolt(s) securing the coil/power transistor assemblies **(see illustration)**.
32   Installation is the reverse of removal.

2004 and later models

Refer to illustration 7.34
33   Disconnect the electrical connector from the ignition coil, then remove the mounting bolt.
34   Pull the coil straight up and out of the valve cover **(see illustration)**.
35   Installation is the reverse of removal.

8   Power transistor - check and replacement

1   All models use a power transistor (ignition control module) to control ignition timing. The power transistor is a separate module on 1994 and 1995 2.4L DOHC models. On 1994 through 1998 2.4L SOHC models and on 1999 and later 3.0L V6 models, the power transistor is an integral component of the dis-

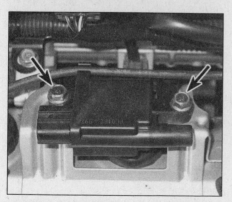

7.31 To detach the ignition coil from the valve cover, remove these two bolts (1999 through 2003 2.4L SOHC models)

7.34 On all 2004 and later models, there is an ignition coil mounted to each spark plug

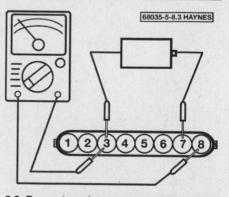

8.3 Power transistor test setup (No. 1 and 4 coil) and electrical connector terminal guide (1994 and 1995 2.4L DOHC models)

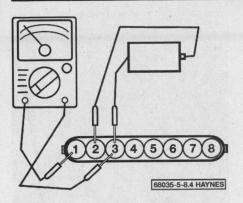

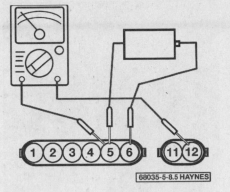

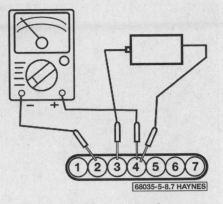

8.4 Power transistor test setup (No. 2 and 3 coil) and electrical connector terminal guide (1994 and 1995 2.4L DOHC models)

8.5 Power transistor test setup and electrical connector terminal guide (1994 through 1998 SOHC 2.4L SOHC models)

8.7 Power transistor test setup and electrical connector terminal guide (1999 and later 3.0L V6 models)

tributor. On 1999 and later 2.4L SOHC engines and all 3.8L V6 engines, it's an integral part of each ignition coil.

Check

2   Disconnect the power transistor electrical connector(s).

1994 and 1995 2.4L DOHC models

Refer to illustrations 8.3 and 8.4

3   To check the side of the power transistor that controls ignition timing for cylinders 1 and 4, connect the probes of an *analog* ohmmeter between terminals 3 and 8 **(see illustration)**. Then connect the negative side of a 1.5-volt battery to terminal No. 3 of the power transistor connector and the positive side of the battery to terminal No. 7. **Caution:** *Don't connect the 1.5-volt battery for more than 10 seconds or the power transistor might be damaged.* With the 1.5-volt battery connected, there should be continuity between terminals 3 and 8. But when the battery is disconnected, there should be no continuity between terminals 3 and 8. If the power transistor fails this check, replace it.

4   To check the side of the power transistor that controls ignition timing for cylinders 2 and 3, connect the probes of an *analog* ohmmeter between terminals 1 and 3 **(see illustration)**. Then connect the negative side of a 1.5-volt battery to terminal 3 of the power transistor connector and the positive side of the battery to terminal 2. **Caution:** *Don't connect the 1.5-volt battery for more than 10 seconds or the power transistor might be damaged.* With the 1.5-volt battery connected, there should be no continuity between terminals 1 and 3. But when the battery is disconnected, there should be no continuity between terminals 1 and 3. If the power transistor fails this check, replace it.

1994 through 1998 2.4L SOHC models

Refer to illustration 8.5

5   Connect the probes of an *analog* ohmmeter between terminal 5 (on the big connector) and terminal 12 (on the small connector)

(see illustration). Then connect the negative side of a 1.5 volt battery to terminal 5 and the positive side of the battery to terminal 6 (both on the big connector). **Caution:** *Don't connect the 1.5-volt battery for more than 10 seconds or the power transistor might be damaged.* With the 1.5-volt battery connected, there should be continuity between terminals 5 and 12. But when the battery is disconnected, there should be no continuity between terminals 5 and 12. If the power transistor fails this check, replace it.

1999 and later 2.4L SOHC models and all 3.8L V6 models

6   The power transistor is an integral component of each ignition coil on these models. To check the power transistor on one of these models, refer to Step 16 in Section 7. This test simultaneously checks the power transistor and the primary side of the ignition coil. If the power transistor doesn't operate as described, replace the ignition coil.

1999 and later 3.0L V6 models

Refer to illustration 8.7

7   The test on these models is similar to the tests described above, but the connections are made to the seven-pin terminal on the side of the distributor **(see illustration)**. Connect the negative probe of an analog ohmmeter to terminal 2 and the positive probe to terminal 4. Then connect the positive side of a 1.5-volt battery to terminal 3 and the negative side of the battery to terminal 4. **Caution:** *Don't connect the 1.5-volt battery for more than 10 seconds or the power transistor might be damaged.* With the 1.5-volt battery connected, there should be continuity between terminals 2 and 4. But when the battery is disconnected, there should be no continuity between terminals 2 and 4. If the power transistor fails this check, replace the ignition coil.

Replacement

1994 and 1995 2.4L DOHC models

8   Remove the center cover from the valve

cover (covers up the spark plug wires, which are routed along the center of the valve cover).

9   The power transistor is located on top of the valve cover, next to the ignition coil assembly. Disconnect the electrical connector from the power transistor, remove the mounting bolts and remove the power transistor.

10   Installation is the reverse of the removal steps.

1994 through 1998 2.4L SOHC models

11   The power transistor is an integral part of the distributor. Replace the distributor assembly (see Section 9).

1999 and later 2.4L SOHC models and all 3.8L V6 models

12   The power transistor is an integral part of each ignition coil. Replace the ignition coil (see Section 7).

1999 and later 3.0L V6 models

13   The power transistor is an integral part of the distributor. Replace the distributor assembly (see Section 9).

9   Distributor - removal and installation

1994 through 1998 2.4L SOHC models

Removal

Refer to illustrations 9.4, 9.5, 9.8a and 9.8b

1   Before removing the distributor, position the piston in the No. 1 cylinder at Top Dead Center (TDC) on the compression stroke and align the timing marks (see Chapter 2A).

2   Disconnect the cable from the negative battery terminal (see Section 3).

3   Remove the ignition wire cover, if equipped.

4   Disconnect the distributor electrical con-

9.4 Disconnect the distributor electrical connector (1994 through 1998 2.4L SOHC models)

9.5 Remove the bolt that secures the distributor wire harness and capacitor mounting bracket, then set the harness and the capacitor and bracket aside

9.8a Remove the two distributor hold-down nuts . . .

nector **(see illustration)**.

5   Remove the bolt that secures the distributor wire harness and the capacitor mounting bracket **(see illustration)** and then set the harness and capacitor aside.

6   Remove the distributor cap. It's not necessary to disconnect the spark plug wires.

7   Mark the position of the rotor in relationship to the distributor housing and mark the position of the distributor housing in relation to the engine.

8   Remove the distributor hold-down nuts and carefully remove the distributor from the cylinder head **(see illustrations)**. **Caution:** *DO NOT turn the crankshaft while the distributor is out of the engine, or the alignment marks will be useless.*

Installation

9   Install a new distributor housing O-ring and lubricate it with clean engine oil.

If the timing was not disturbed

10   Make sure that the rotor is aligned with the matchmark you made on the distributor housing and that the matchmark you made on the distributor housing is aligned with the matchmark you made on the engine.

11   Installation is otherwise the reverse of removal. Make sure that the distributor is fully seated and the distributor shaft is fully engaged. When you're done installing the distributor, adjust the ignition timing (see Section 10) and tighten the hold-down nuts to the torque listed in this Chapter's Specifications.

If the timing was disturbed

12   Position the engine so that the No. 1 piston is at Top Dead Center (TDC) on its compression stroke and the mark on the vibration damper is aligned with the "**0**" on the timing indicator.

13   Align the distributor housing and gear mating marks. Install the distributor in the engine so that the slot or groove in the distributor's mounting flange is aligned with the distributor mounting stud on the cylinder head. Make sure that the distributor is fully

9.8b . . . then carefully remove the distributor from the cylinder head

seated. Check the alignment of the distributor rotor. Make sure that the rotor is aligned with the position of the No. 1 ignition wire in the distributor cap. Adjust the ignition timing (see Section 10).

1999 and later 3.0L V6 models
Removal

Refer to illustration 9.19

14   Position the No. 1 cylinder at Top Dead Center (TDC) on the compression stroke (see Chapter 2B). Disconnect the negative battery cable from the battery (see Section 3).

15   Remove the air filter housing (see Chapter 4).

16   Disconnect the electrical connectors from the distributor.

17   Label each spark plug wire with its location in the distributor cap, then disconnect the wires.

18   Remove the spark plug wire routing bracket from the distributor.

19   Loosen the three screws and remove the distributor cap **(see illustration)**.

20   Mark the position of the rotor in relationship to the distributor housing and mark the position of the distributor housing in relation to the engine.

9.19 Distributor cap mounting screws (1999 and later 3.0L V6 models)

21   Remove the two nuts and washers securing the distributor and withdraw it from the cylinder head.

Installation

22   Install a new distributor housing O-ring and lubricate it with clean engine oil.

If the timing was not disturbed

23   Make sure that the rotor is aligned with the matchmark you made on the distributor housing and that the matchmark you made on the distributor housing is aligned with the matchmark you made on the engine.

24   Installation is otherwise the reverse of removal. Make sure that the distributor is fully seated and the distributor shaft is fully engaged. When you're done installing the distributor, adjust the ignition timing (see Section 10) and tighten the hold-down nuts to the torque listed in this Chapter's Specifications.

If the timing was disturbed

25   If engine was rotated while the distributor was removed, rotate the engine to Top Dead Center (TDC) for the number 1 piston (see Chapter 2), then align the rotor with the match-marks made in Step 20. Install the distributor as described in Step 23.

26   The remaining installation steps are the reverse of removal. Adjust the ignition timing (see Section 10).

10   Ignition timing - check and adjustment

Note: *If the information specified on your vehicle's VECI label differs from this procedure, use the information on the VECI label.*

1996 and earlier models

1   Start the engine and allow it to warm up to normal operating temperature, then turn off the engine.
2   Connect a timing light according to the manufacturer's specifications. Install the inductive pick-up onto the number one cylinder spark plug wire.
3   Disconnect the noise condenser connector from the distributor. Use a paper clip to bridge the terminals in the female side of the connector. Attach a tachometer (of the type that measures rpm through the primary side of the ignition) to the paper clip.
4   Locate the ignition timing adjustment connector; it's brown, and located at the firewall. Remove the cover from the connector and, using a jumper wire, bridge the terminal in the connector to a good ground.
5   Locate the timing marks on the timing belt cover and the crankshaft pulley.
6   Start the engine and check the ignition timing. Aim the timing light at the timing scale on the timing belt cover. Refer to the basic timing Specifications listed at the beginning of this chapter. If necessary, loosen the distributor hold-down bolt (see Section 9) and slowly rotate the distributor until the timing mark on the crankshaft pulley align with the specified mark on the cover. Tighten the hold-down bolt and recheck the timing.
7   Turn the engine off and remove the

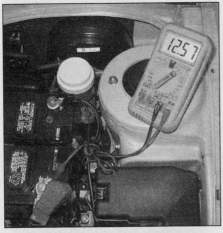

11.7 To measure "standing battery voltage" (engine turned off), attach the voltmeter leads to the battery terminals and note the indicated voltage; to measure charging voltage, start the engine and measure the voltage again

jumper wire from the timing adjustment connector. Recheck the ignition timing; although the timing is now being controlled by the PCM, it should be within the *standard* range listed in this Chapter's Specifications (if not, have the vehicle checked by a qualified technician).
8   Turn the engine off and remove the tachometer and the timing light.

1997 and later models

9   A proprietary scan tool is required to check the basic timing on 1997 and later models. Standard timing can be checked with a timing light, however, and can be used to get an approximate ignition timing setting. An automotive technician equipped with the proper scan tool will have to then set the basic timing to specification.

11   Charging system - general information, precautions and check

General information and precautions

1   The charging system includes the alternator, a charge indicator light, the battery, the voltage regulator and the wiring between all the components. The charging system supplies electrical power to maintain the battery at its full charge capacity. The alternator is driven by a drivebelt at the timing belt end of the engine.
2   The voltage regulator is an integral component of the alternator on the models covered in this manual. The purpose of the voltage regulator is to prevent the alternator's output voltage from exceeding a preset upper limit, thereby regulating the battery charging rate. This prevents power surges, circuit overloads, etc., during peak voltage output.
3   The charging system doesn't ordinarily require periodic maintenance. However, the drivebelt, battery, wires and connections should be inspected at the intervals outlined in Chapter 1.
4   The dashboard warning light should illuminate when the ignition key is turned to ON, but it should go off immediately after the engine is started. If it remains on, there is a malfunction in the charging system that must be diagnosed (see Step 6). The alternator is not serviceable. In the event of a malfunction, the alternator must be replaced. This includes the voltage regulator. If the regulator malfunctions, replace the alternator.
5   Be very careful when making connections in the charging circuit and note the following:

a) *When reconnecting wires to the alternator from the battery, be sure to observe correct polarity.*
b) *Before using arc-welding equipment to repair any part of the vehicle, disconnect the wiring from the alternator and the cables from the battery.*
c) *Never start the engine with a battery charger connected.*

d) *Always disconnect both battery cables before using a battery charger.*
e) *The alternator is turned by an engine drivebelt, which could cause serious injury if your hands, hair or clothes become entangled in it with the engine running.*
f) *Because the alternator is connected directly to the battery, it could arc or cause a fire if overloaded or shorted out.*

Check

Refer to illustration 11.7
6   If a malfunction occurs in the charging circuit, do not immediately assume that the alternator is causing the problem. First, check the following items:

a) *Make sure the battery cable clamps, where they connect to the battery, are clean and tight.*
b) *Test the condition of the battery (see Section 3). If it does not pass all the tests, replace it with a new battery.*
c) *Check the external alternator wiring and connections.*
d) *Check the drivebelt condition and tension (see Chapter 1).*
e) *Check the alternator mounting bolts for tightness.*
f) *Run the engine and check the alternator for abnormal noise.*
g) *Check the fusible links (if equipped) in the engine compartment fuse box (see Chapter 12). If they're burned, determine the cause and repair the circuit.*
h) *Check the charge light on the dash. It should illuminate when the ignition key is turned ON (engine not running). If it does not, check the circuit from the alternator to the charge light on the dash.*
i) *Check all the fuses that are in series with the charging system circuit. The location of these fuses and fusible links may vary from year and model but the designations are generally the same. Refer to the wiring schematics at the end of Chapter 12 for additional information.*

7   With the ignition key off check the battery voltage with no accessories operating **(see illustration)**. It should be approximately 12.5 volts. It may be slightly higher if the engine had been operating within the last hour.
8   Start the engine and check the battery voltage again. It should now be greater than the voltage recorded in Step 2, but not more than 14.5 volts. Turn on all the vehicle accessories (air conditioning, rear window defogger, blower motor, etc.) and increase the engine speed to 2,000 rpm - the voltage should not drop below the voltage recorded in Step 2.
9   If the indicated voltage is greater than the specified charging voltage, replace the voltage regulator.
10   If the indicated voltage reading is less than the specified charging voltage, the alternator is probably defective. Have the charging system checked at a dealer service department or other properly equipped repair facil-

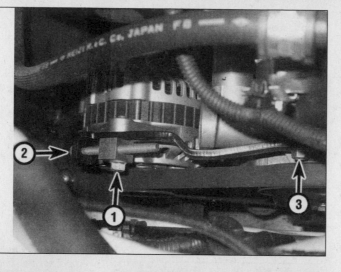

12.12 Upper alternator mounting bracket (1999 through 2003 four-cylinder models)

1   *Lock bolt*
2   *Upper alternator adjustment bolt*
3   *Upper mounting bracket bolt*

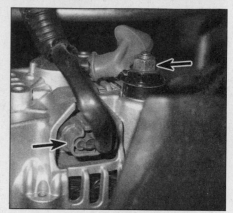

12.15 Alternator electrical connector and B+ (battery) connection (1999 through 2003 four-cylinder models)

12.16 Alternator lower mounting/pivot bolt and nut

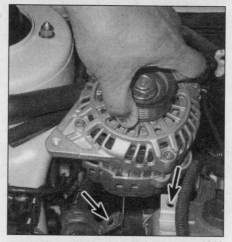

12.18 Unbolt the power steering pump pressure hose clamp from the valve cover, push the hose aside and then remove the alternator by pulling it out from the top (1999 through 2003 four-cylinder models)

12.27 Alternator wiring harness clamp (A) and connector (B) (2004 and later four-cylinder models)

ity. **Note:** *Many auto parts stores will bench test an alternator off the vehicle. Refer to your local auto parts store regarding their policy; many will perform this service free of charge.*

---

12   Alternator - removal and installation

Removal

1998 and earlier four-cylinder models

1   The alternator is located at the left front corner of the engine block.
2   Disconnect the cable from the negative battery terminal (see Section 3).
3   Loosen the left front wheel lug nuts. Raise the vehicle and support it on jackstands. Remove the left front wheel.
4   Remove the splash shield from the left wheel housing (see Chapter 11).
5   Loosen the alternator drivebelt adjustment bolt and remove the alternator drivebelt, then loosen the power steering pump drivebelt tension adjuster and remove the power steering drivebelt (see Chapter 1).
6   Remove the pulleys from the water

pump and from the power steering pump.
7   Disconnect the electrical connector and the "B+" (battery) cable from the alternator.
8   Remove the alternator mounting and pivot bolts.
9   Remove the alternator.

1999 through 2003 four-cylinder models

Refer to illustrations 12.12, 12.15, 12.16 and 12.18

10   Disconnect the cable from the negative battery terminal (see Section 3).
11   The alternator is located at the right rear corner of the engine block. The easiest way to remove the alternator is from above. The power steering pump pressure hose is the only thing in the way, so remove the clamp bolt that attaches the pressure hose to the valve cover and push the hose aside.
12   Loosen the lock bolt, the upper alternator adjustment bolt and the upper mounting bracket bolt **(see illustration)**.
13   Loosen the right front wheel lug nuts.

Raise the vehicle and support it on jackstands. Remove the right front wheel.
14   Remove the engine protection cover from below the engine compartment (see Chapter 2).
15   Disconnect the electrical connector and the B+ cable from the alternator **(see illustration)**.
16   Loosen the lower alternator pivot bolt and nut **(see illustration)** and remove the drivebelt.
17   Remove the upper and lower alternator mounting bolts and nuts and the upper mounting bracket.
18   Remove the alternator **(see illustration)**.

2003 and earlier V6 models

19   Disconnect the cable from the negative battery terminal (see Section 3).
20   The alternator is located at the right rear corner of the engine block. The easiest way to remove the alternator is from above. The power steering pump pressure hose is the only thing in the way, so remove the clamp bolt that attaches the pressure hose to the valve cover and push the hose aside.
21   Remove the alternator drivebelt (see Chapter 1).

22   Remove the dipstick tube bracket bolt and remove the engine oil dipstick and dipstick tube.
23   Disconnect the electrical connector and the "B+" cable from the alternator.
24   Remove the alternator mounting bolts.
25   Remove the alternator.

2004 and later 2.4L SOHC models
Refer to illustration 12.27
26   Raise the vehicle and support it securely on jackstands. Refer to Chapter 2A and remove the drivebelt from the alternator.
27   Disconnect the wiring harness clamp, then disconnect the wiring from the alternator **(see illustration)**.
28   Remove the alternator.
29   Installation is the reverse of removal.

2004 and later V6 models
30   Raise the vehicle and support it securely on jackstands. Remove the engine lower splash shield.
31   Refer to Chapter 1 and remove the drivebelt from the alternator.
32   Disconnect the wiring from the alternator.
33   Refer to Chapter 3 and unbolt the air conditioning compressor from its mount without disconnecting the refrigerant hoses. Secure the compressor out of the way with wire or twine.
34   Remove the alternator from its mount.
35   Installation is the reverse of removal. Securely tighten the front lower alternator mounting bolt first, followed by the other lower bolt, then the top bolt.

Installation (all models)
36   If you are *replacing* the alternator, take the old alternator with you when buying a replacement unit. Make sure that the new or rebuilt unit is identical to the old alternator. Look at the terminals: they should be the same in number, size and locations as the terminals on the old alternator. Then look at the identification markings: they should be stamped in the housing or printed on a tag or plaque affixed to the housing. Make sure that these numbers are the same on both alternators.
37   Many new and rebuilt alternators do not include a drive pulley, so you may have to swap the pulley from the old unit to the new or rebuilt one. When buying an alternator, find out the shop's policy regarding installation of pulleys. Some shops will perform this service free of charge.
38   Installation is the reverse of removal. Make sure that all alternator adjustment, mounting and pivot bolts and nuts are tightened securely.
39   Adjust the drivebelt tension (see Chapter 1).
40   Check the charging voltage to verify proper operation of the alternator (see Section 11).

---

13   Starting system - general information and precautions

The starting system consists of the battery, the ignition switch, the starter relay, the clutch start switch (manual transaxles), the Park/Neutral Position (PNP) switch (automatic transaxles), the starter motor solenoid, the starter motor and the wires that connect these components. The solenoid is located on the starter motor, which is located on the back side of the engine block on 1994 through 1998 models and on 1999 and later V6 models, and on the front side of the block on 1999 and later 2.4L SOHC models.

The starter motor on a vehicle with a manual transaxle can be operated only when the clutch pedal is depressed. The starter on a vehicle with an automatic transaxle can be operated only when the shift lever is in PARK or NEUTRAL. When the ignition key is turned to the START position, it closes the starter control circuit, which energizes the starter relay. (The starter relay is located on the right side of the engine compartment on 1994 through 1998 models or in the engine compartment fuse/relay center on 1999 and later models.) The starter relay closes the actual starter circuit between the battery and the starter solenoid, which energizes the solenoid, which moves a lever that engages the starter pinion gear with the flywheel ring gear to crank the engine.

Always observe the following precautions when working on the starting system:

a) *Excessive cranking of the starter motor can overheat it and cause serious damage. Never operate the starter motor for more than 15 seconds at a time without pausing for at least two minutes to allow it to cool.*
b) *The starter is connected directly to the battery and could arc or cause a fire if mishandled, overloaded or short-circuited.*
c) *Always detach the negative battery cable from the negative terminal on the battery before working on the starting system.*

---

14   Starter motor and circuit check

Refer to illustrations 14.3 and 14.4
1   If a malfunction occurs in the starting circuit, do not immediately assume that the starter is causing the problem. First, check the following items:

a) *Make sure the battery cable clamps, where they connect to the battery, are clean and tight.*
b) *Check the condition of the battery cables (see Section 4). Replace any defective battery cables with new parts.*
c) *Test the condition of the battery (see Section 3). If it does not pass all the tests, replace it with a new battery.*
d) *Check the starter solenoid wiring and connections. Refer to the wiring diagrams at the end of Chapter 12.*
e) *Check the starter mounting bolts for tightness.*
f) *Check the fusible links (if equipped) exiting the engine compartment fuse box (see Chapter 12). If they're burned, determine the cause and repair the circuit.*
g) *Check the operation of the Park/Neutral Position switch (automatic transaxle) or clutch start switch (manual transaxle). Make sure the shift lever is in PARK or NEUTRAL (automatic transaxle) or the clutch pedal is pressed (manual transaxle). Refer to Chapter 7 for the Park/Neutral Position switch check and adjustment procedure. Refer to Chapter 12 wiring diagrams, if necessary, when performing circuit checks. These systems must operate correctly to provide battery voltage to the ignition solenoid.*
h) *Check the operation of the starter relay. The starter relay is located either near the center console (2000 and earlier coupes) or in the fuse/relay box (all other models) inside the engine compartment. Refer to Chapter 12 for the testing procedure.*

Also, check the ignition switch circuit for correct operation (see Chapter 12).

2   If the starter does not actuate when the ignition switch is turned to the start position, check for battery voltage to the solenoid. This will determine if the solenoid is receiving the correct voltage signal from the ignition switch. Connect a test light or voltmeter to the starter solenoid positive terminal and while an assistant turns the ignition switch to the start position. If voltage is not available, refer to the wiring diagrams in Chapter 12 and check all the fuses and relays in series with the starting system. If voltage is available but the starter motor does not operate, remove the starter from the engine compartment (see Section 15) and bench test the starter (see Step 4).
3   If the starter turns over slowly, check the starter cranking voltage and the current draw from the battery. This test must be performed with the starter assembly on the engine. Crank the engine over (for 10 seconds or less) and observe the battery voltage. It should not drop below 8.0 volts on manual transaxle models or 8.5 volts on automatic transaxle models. Also, observe the current draw using an amp meter **(see illustration)**. It should not exceed 400 amps or drop below 250 amps.

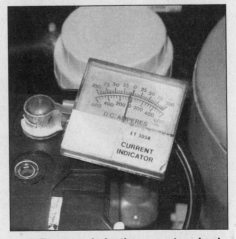

14.3 To use an inductive ammeter, simply hold the ammeter over the positive or negative cable (whichever cable has better clearance)

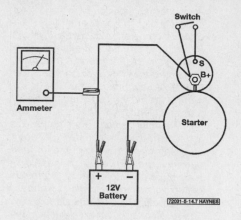

14.4 Starter motor bench testing details

Caution: *The battery cables might overheat because of the large amount of current being drawn from the battery. Discontinue the testing until the starting system has cooled down.* If the starter motor cranking amp values are not within the correct range, replace it with a new unit. There are several conditions that may affect the starter cranking potential. The battery must be in good condition and the battery cold-cranking rating must not be under-rated for the particular application. Be sure to check the battery specifications carefully. The battery terminals and cables must be clean and not corroded. Also, in cases of extreme cold temperatures, make sure the battery and/or engine block is warmed before performing the tests.

4   If the starter is receiving voltage but does not activate, remove and check the starter/solenoid assembly on the bench. Most likely the solenoid is defective. In some rare cases,

the engine may be seized so be sure to try and rotate the crankshaft pulley (see Chapter 2) before proceeding. With the starter/solenoid assembly mounted in a vise on the bench, install one jumper cable from the negative battery terminal to the body of the starter. Install the other jumper cable from the positive battery terminal to the B+ terminal on the starter. Install a starter switch and apply battery voltage to the solenoid S terminal (for 10 seconds or less) and see if the solenoid plunger, shift lever and overrunning clutch extends and rotates the pinion drive **(see illustration)**. If the pinion drive extends but does not rotate, the solenoid is operating but the starter motor is defective. If there is no movement but the solenoid clicks, the solenoid and/or the starter motor is defective. If the solenoid plunger extends and rotates the pinion drive, the starter/solenoid assembly is working properly.

---

15 Starter motor - removal and installation

Removal

Refer to illustrations 15.3, 15.5 and 15.6

1   Disconnect the cable from the negative battery terminal (see Section 3).

2   On some models, the resonators and/or air intake ducting for the air filter housing assembly might limit access to the starter assembly. If this applies to your vehicle, remove the air filter housing assembly and air intake duct (see Chapter 4).

3   On 1999 and later 2.4L SOHC models remove the heat shield from the starter **(see illustration)**.

4   Raise the vehicle and support it on jack-

stands. On 2004 and later V6 models, remove the engine lower splash shield. On 2004 and later four-cylinder models, remove the automatic transaxle cooler assembly.

5   Clearly label and disconnect the wires from the terminals on the starter motor solenoid **(see illustration)**.

6   Remove the starter motor upper mounting bolt **(see illustration)**. Then support the starter motor, remove the lower mounting bolt and remove the starter motor/solenoid assembly.

7   Installation is the reverse of removal. Be sure to tighten the starter mounting bolts to the torque listed in this Chapter's Specifications.

15.3 To detach the heat shield from the starter motor on a 1999 and later 2.4L SOHC model, remove these two bolts (exhaust manifold heat shield removed for clarity)

15.5 Disconnect the electrical connector and the battery cable from the terminals on the starter motor solenoid (1999 and later 2.4L SOHC shown, other models similar)

15.6 To detach the starter motor from the transaxle bellhousing, remove these two bolts (1999 and later 2.4L SOHC shown, other models similar)

Chapter 6
Emissions and engine control systems

Contents

Specifications

Torque specifications

	Ft-lbs	Nm
Engine Coolant Temperature (ECT) sensor (all models)	22	30
Knock sensor	16	22
Oxygen sensor (upstream and downstream)		
1994 through 1998	40	54
1999 on (all engines)	32	44

1.1 Typical emission control components (1999 and later 2.4L SOHC model shown)

1   Volume Air Flow sensor with integral Intake Air
    Temperature (IAT) sensor
2   Throttle Position (TP) sensor
3   Manifold Differential Pressure (MDP) sensor

4   Fresh air inlet hose for PCV system (between air intake
    duct and crankcase)
5   Positive Crankcase Ventilation (PCV) valve and PCV hose
    (between crankcase and intake manifold)

1   General information

Refer to illustrations 1.1, 1.5a and 1.5b

To prevent pollution of the atmosphere from incompletely burned and evaporating gases, and to maintain good driveability and fuel economy, a number of emission control systems are incorporated **(see illustrations)**. The Sections in this Chapter include general descriptions and replacement procedures for the following systems and their components:

Catalytic converter
Evaporative Emissions Control (EVAP)
    system
Exhaust Gas Recirculation (EGR) system
Multiport Fuel Injection (MFI) system
On-Board Diagnostic (OBD) II system
Positive Crankcase Ventilation (PCV)
    system

Before assuming that an emission control system or component is malfunctioning, check the fuel and ignition systems carefully. The diagnosis of emission control devices and systems requires specialized tools, equipment and training. If checking and servicing become too difficult, or if a procedure is beyond your ability, consult a dealer service department or other repair shop.

Remember, the most frequent cause of emissions problems is simply a loose or broken wire or vacuum hose, so always check the hose and wiring connections first.

This doesn't mean, however, that emissions control systems are particularly difficult to maintain and repair. You can quickly and easily perform many checks and do most of the regular maintenance at home with common tune-up and hand tools. **Note:** *Because of a Federally mandated warranty which covers the emission control system components, check with your dealer about warranty coverage before servicing any emission-related systems. Once the warranty has expired, you may wish to replace some components yourself to save money.*

Pay close attention to any special precautions outlined in this Chapter. Please note that, because of constant system and component changes made by the manufacturer during the production cycle (both annual changes and running changes made within a given model year), some of the photographs of various systems and components might not exactly match the system or component installed on your vehicle.

A Vehicle Emissions Control Information (VECI) label **(see illustration)** is attached to the underside of the hood. This label contains

important emissions specifications and adjustment information. Another label, the Vacuum Hose Routing Diagram **(see illustration)**, provides a vacuum hose schematic with emissions components identified. When servicing the engine or emissions systems, the VECI label and the vacuum hose routing diagram in your particular vehicle should always be checked for up-to-date information.

1.5a The Vehicle Emission Control Information (VECI) label contains such essential information as the types of emission control systems installed on the engine, and various specifications

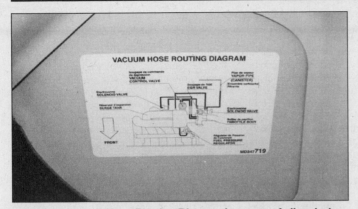

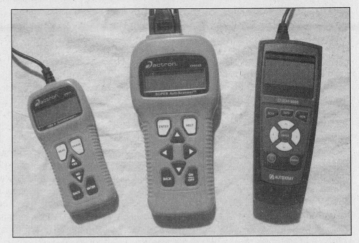

1.5b The Vacuum Hose Routing Diagram is a map of all emission-related vacuum hoses in the engine compartment; this is the most up-to-date information you can get for your car because it's specific to your exact model and because it includes any running changes made by the manufacturer during the production year

2.1 Hand-held scan tools like these can extract computer codes and also perform diagnostics

2.2 Simple code readers are an economical way to extract trouble codes when the CHECK ENGINE light comes on

2   On-Board Diagnostic (OBD) system and trouble codes

Scan tool information

Refer to illustrations 2.1 and 2.2

1   Hand-held scanners are the most powerful and versatile tools for analyzing engine management systems used on later model vehicles **(see illustration)**. Early model scanners handle codes and some diagnostics for many systems. Each brand scan tool must be examined carefully to match the year, make and model of the vehicle you are working on. Often, interchangeable cartridges are available to access the particular manufacturer (Ford, GM, Chrysler, Toyota etc.). Some manufacturers will specify by continent (Asia, Europe, USA, etc.). **Note:** *An aftermarket generic scanner should work with any model covered by this manual. However, some early OBD-II models, although technically classified as OBD-II compliant by the manufacturer and by the federal government, might not be fully compliant with all SAE standards for OBD-II. Some generic scanners are unable to extract*

all the codes from these early OBD-II models. Before purchasing a generic scan tool, contact the manufacturer of the scanner you're planning to buy and verify that it will work properly with the OBD-II system you want to scan. If necessary, of course, you can always have the codes extracted by a dealer service department or an independent repair shop with a professional scan tool.

2   With the arrival of the Federally mandated emission control system (OBD-II), a specially designed scanner has been developed. Several tool manufacturers have released OBD-II scan tools for the home mechanic **(see illustration)**. Ask the parts salesman at a local auto parts store for additional information concerning dates and costs.

OBD system general description

3   All models are equipped with an On-Board Diagnostic (OBD) system. This system consists of an on-board computer known as the Powertrain Control Module (PCM), and information sensors, which monitor various functions of the engine and send data to the PCM. This system incorporates a series of diagnostic monitors that detect and identify fuel injection and emissions control systems faults and store the information in the computer memory.

4   The PCM is the "brain" of the electronically controlled fuel and emissions system. It receives data from a number of sensors and other electronic components (switches, relays, etc.). Based on the information it receives, the PCM generates output signals to control various relays, solenoids (i.e. fuel injectors) and other actuators. The PCM is specifically calibrated to optimize the emissions, fuel economy and driveability of the vehicle.

5   It isn't a good idea to attempt diagnosis or replacement of the PCM or emission control components at home while the vehicle is under warranty. Because of a Federally mandated warranty which covers the emissions system components and because any owner-induced damage to the PCM, the sensors and/or the control devices may void this war-

ranty, take the vehicle to a dealer service department if the PCM or a system component malfunctions.

Information sensors

6   **Barometric pressure sensor** - The barometric pressure sensor measures atmospheric pressure. The PCM uses this data from the barometric pressure sensor to determine air density and altitude. The barometric pressure sensor, along with the Intake Air Temperature (IAT) sensor is an integral part of the Volume Air Flow sensor on all models. It cannot be replaced separately.

7   **Camshaft Position (CMP) sensor** - The CMP sensor produces a signal that the PCM uses to identify the number 1 cylinder and to time the firing sequence of the fuel injectors. On 1994 and 1995 DOHC models, the CMP sensor is located on the left (timing belt) end of the engine, adjacent to the intake camshaft timing belt sprocket. On 1994 through 1998 2.4L SOHC models and on 1999 and later 3.0L V6 models, the CMP sensor is located inside the distributor. On 3.8L V6, as well as 1999 and later 2.4L SOHC models, the CMP sensor is located on the left end (opposite end from the timing belt) of the cylinder head.

8   **Crankshaft Position (CKP) sensor** - The crankshaft sensor produces a signal that the PCM uses to determine the position of the crankshaft. On 1994 and 1995 DOHC models, the CKP sensor is located on the left (timing belt) end of the engine, adjacent to the crankshaft timing belt sprocket. On 1999 and later 2.4L SOHC and V6 models, the CKP sensor is located on the right (timing belt) end of the engine, adjacent to the crankshaft timing belt sprocket.

9   **Engine Coolant Temperature (ECT) sensor** - The ECT sensor is a thermistor (temperature-sensitive variable resistor) that sends a voltage signal to the PCM, which uses this data to determine the temperature of the engine coolant. The ECT sensor helps the PCM control the air/fuel mixture ratio and ignition timing, and it also helps the PCM

determine when to turn the Exhaust Gas Recirculation (EGR) system on and off. On 1994 and 1995 2.4L DOHC models, and on 1994 through 1998 2.4L SOHC models, the ECT sensor is located on the right end of the intake manifold. On 1999 and later 2.4L SOHC models, the ECT sensor is located on the left end (opposite the timing belt end) of the cylinder head. On 1999 and later V6 models, the ECT sensor is located at the left end of the engine, on the crossover portion of the thermostat housing.

10   **Fuel level sensor** - On 2002 and later models, the fuel level sending unit sends a signal not only to the fuel level gauge on the dash, but to the PCM as well, so it's referred to as the fuel level "sensor." The PCM uses this information to determine how much fuel remains in the tank, and when to turn on the low fuel level warning light. Since the fuel level "sensor" is actually the fuel level sending unit, which is located inside the fuel tank, and which is an integral component of the fuel pump assembly, it can be replaced separately once the fuel pump/fuel level sending unit has been removed from the fuel tank (see Chapter 4). On 2004 and later models, there is a secondary fuel level sensor beneath an access panel in the right side of the fuel tank.

11   **Fuel tank differential pressure sensor** - The fuel tank differential pressure sensor is a component of the Evaporative Emission Control (EVAP) system on 1996 and 1997 California models and on all 1998 and later models. It's used by the PCM to monitor any pressure build-up in the fuel tank. The PCM uses this data, along with information from other sensors, to turn the EVAP system purge solenoid valve on and off. The fuel tank differential pressure sensor is located on top of the fuel tank at the front right corner of the tank.

12   **Fuel temperature sensor** - The fuel temperature sensor is another component of the Evaporative Emission Control (EVAP) system on 2002 and later models. The PCM uses the data from the fuel temperature sensor, along with information from other sensors, to control the EVAP system purge solenoid. The fuel temperature sensor is located on top of the fuel tank.

13   **Intake Air Temperature (IAT) sensor** - The IAT sensor is a thermistor (a resistor which varies the value of its resistance in accordance with temperature changes). The IAT sensor provides the PCM with intake air temperature information. As the sensor temperature *increases*, the resistance *decreases*; as the sensor temperature *decreases*, the resistance *increases*. In other words, as the temperature goes up, the voltage output of the IAT sensor goes down; and vice versa. The PCM uses this information to control fuel flow, ignition timing and EGR system operation. The IAT sensor, along with the barometric pressure sensor, is an integral component of the Volume Air Flow sensor on all models. It cannot be replaced separately.

14   **Knock sensor** - The knock sensor is a piezoelectric crystal that oscillates in proportion to engine vibration. The oscillation of the piezoelectric crystal produces a voltage output that is monitored by the PCM, which retards the ignition timing when the oscillation exceeds a certain threshold. When the engine is operating normally, the knock sensor oscillates consistently and its voltage signal is steady. When detonation occurs, engine vibration increases, and the oscillation of the knock sensor exceeds a design threshold. (Detonation is an uncontrolled explosion, after the spark occurs at the spark plug, which spontaneously combusts the remaining air/ fuel mixture, resulting in a "pinging" or "slapping" sound.) If allowed to continue, detonation can cause serious engine damage. The knock sensor used on V6 engines is under the lower intake manifold. On 2004 and later four-cylinder engines as well as all DOHC four-cylinder engines, it's on the side of the block under the intake manifold.

15   **Manifold Differential Pressure (MDP) sensor/Manifold Absolute Pressure (MAP) sensor** - Mitsubishi uses different terms for this sensor, but they both do the same job. On 2003 and earlier models, it's called the MDP sensor; on 2004 and later models, it's called the MAP sensor. The sensor, which is located on the intake manifold, downstream from the throttle body, measures the actual amount (or volume) of air entering the engine. The PCM uses the data signal from the sensor for more precise fuel metering. The sensor is used on 1996 California 2.4L SOHC models, on 1997 and 1998 Federal 2.4L SOHC models and on all 1999 and later models.

16   **Oxygen sensors** - An oxygen sensor is a galvanic battery that generates a small variable voltage signal in proportion to the difference between the oxygen content in the exhaust stream and the oxygen content in the ambient air. The PCM uses the voltage signal from the upstream oxygen sensor to maintain a "stoichiometric" air/fuel ratio of 14.7:1 by constantly adjusting the "on-time" of the fuel injectors. There are *two* oxygen sensors on all 2.4L models (DOHC and SOHC) covered in this manual: one *upstream* sensor (ahead of the catalytic converter) and a *downstream* oxygen sensor (after the catalyst). There are two oxygen sensors (one upstream and one downstream) on 1999 and 2000 Federal 3.0L V6 models (these models use one catalyst). There are *four* oxygen sensors, one upstream and one downstream sensor for each cylinder head, on 1999 and 2000 California 3.0L V6 models and on all 2001 and later V6 models. On these models, there are three catalysts: a smaller "fast-light-off" cat right below each exhaust manifold and another larger downstream catalyst. The oxygen sensors are located upstream and downstream in relation to the two smaller catalysts.

17   **Park/Neutral Position (PNP) switch** - The PNP switch, which is located at the shift lever on top of the automatic transaxle, tells the PCM what gear the transaxle is in.

18   **Power Steering Pressure (PSP) switch** - The PSP sensor monitors the pressure inside the power steering system. When the front wheels are being turned at low speed there is more friction between the rubber tire treads and the road, so the pressure required to turn the wheels increases. The PCM uses the PSP sensor to determine when to increase engine idle speed during low-speed vehicle maneuvers. The PSP switch is located on the power steering pump.

19   **Throttle Position (TP) sensor** - The TP sensor, which is located on the throttle body, on the end of the throttle valve shaft, is a potentiometer that produces a variable voltage signal in accordance with the opening angle of the throttle valve. This voltage signal tells the PCM when the throttle is closed, in a cruise position, or wide open, or anywhere in between. The PCM uses this information, along with data from a number of other sensors, to calculate injector on-time.

20   **Vehicle Speed Sensor (VSS)** - The VSS, which is located on the transaxle, provides information to the PCM to indicate vehicle speed. Manual transaxles are equipped with one VSS. Automatics are equipped with an input and an output VSS (the PCM compares the difference, if any, between the two signals to predict transaxle failure).

21   **Volume Air Flow sensor** - The Volume Air Flow sensor measures the volume of the air being drawn into the engine. The Volume Air Flow sensor also contains the Intake Air Temperature (IAT) sensor and the barometric pressure sensor. If any of these three components fails, the Volume Air Flow sensor must be replaced. The Volume Air Flow sensor is located between the air filter housing and the air intake duct.

22   **Accelerator Pedal Position (APP) sensor** - This sensor reads the position of the accelerator pedal and provides that information to the PCM. It is an integral part of the accelerator pedal assembly. The PCM operates the throttle based on the APP sensor input as well as information from other sensors.

Output actuators

23   **EVAP purge control solenoid** - The EVAP purge control solenoid, which is controlled by the PCM, allows the fuel vapors in the EVAP canister to be drawn into the intake manifold for combustion when ordered to do so by the PCM. The purge control solenoid is located in the engine compartment. The EVAP purge control solenoid is attached to a bracket on the intake manifold.

24   **Exhaust Gas Recirculation (EGR) solenoid** - When the engine is put under a load (hard acceleration, passing, going up a steep hill, pulling a trailer, etc.), combustion chamber temperatures increase. When combustion chamber temperature exceeds 2500 degrees, excessive amounts of oxides of nitrogen (NOx) are produced. NOx is a "precursor" (constituent) of photochemical smog. When combined with hydrocarbons (HC), other "reactive organic compounds" (ROCs) and sunlight, it forms ozone, nitrogen dioxide and nitrogen nitrate and other nasty stuff. The EGR solenoid, which is controlled by the PCM, allows exhaust gases to be recirculated back to the intake manifold

where they dilute the incoming air/fuel mixture, which lowers the combustion chamber temperature and decreases the amount of NOx produced during high-load conditions. The EGR solenoid is located on the firewall on 1994 through 1998 models; on 1999 and later models, the solenoid is located adjacent to the EGR valve, which is located on the intake manifold.

25 **Idle air control (IAC) motor** - The IAC motor controls the amount of air allowed to bypass the throttle valve when the throttle valve is at its (nearly closed) idle position. It is only used on 2002 and earlier models equipped with cable-actuated throttle bodies. The IAC motor is controlled by the PCM. When the engine is placed under an additional load at idle (low-speed maneuvers or the air conditioning compressor, for example), the engine can run roughly, stumble and even stall. To prevent this from happening, the PCM opens the IAC motor pintle valve to increase the idle speed enough to overcome the extra load imposed on the engine. The IAC motor is mounted on the throttle body.

26 **Engine oil control valve** - This valve is used only on engines with the MIVEC system and is actuated by the PCM. When open, it allows engine oil pressure to activate the MIVEC system of the rocker arms for improved power at high engine speeds.

27 **Throttle actuator** - This actuator is an integral part of the throttle body on 2004 and later models and cannot be replaced separately. These later models do not have a throttle cable connected directly to the accelerator pedal. The actuator is operated by the PCM using inputs from the accelerator pedal position sensor, the cruise control switch and other sensors.

Obtaining and clearing Diagnostic Trouble Codes (DTCs)

28 All models covered by this manual are equipped with on-board diagnostics. When the PCM recognizes a malfunction in a monitored emission control system, component or circuit, it turns on the CHECK ENGINE or SERVICE ENGINE SOON light, also known as the Malfunction Indicator Light (MIL), on the dash. The PCM will continue to display the MIL until the problem is fixed and the Diagnostic Trouble Code (DTC) is cleared from the PCM's memory. On 1994 and 1995 models, Diagnostic Trouble Codes (DTCs) can be accessed by counting the number of flashes of the MIL. On 1996 and later models, you'll need a scan tool to access any DTCs stored in the PCM.

29 Before outputting any DTCs stored in the PCM, thoroughly inspect ALL electrical connectors and hoses. Make sure that all electrical connections are tight, clean and free of corrosion. And make sure that all hoses are correctly connected, fit tightly and are in good condition (no cracks or tears). Also, make sure that the engine is tuned up. A poorly running engine is probably one of the biggest causes of emission-related malfunctions. Often, simply giving the engine a good tune-up will correct the problem.

2.34 Location of the 16-pin Data Link Connector (DLC)

1994 and 1995 models
Accessing the DTCs

30 Locate the diagnostic connector, which is located under the dash, between the steering column cover and the center console. Using a jumper wire, ground the No. 1 terminal of the diagnostic connector (there are two rows of terminals on the diagnostic connector; No. 1 is at the upper left corner).

31 After three seconds, the Check Engine light/Malfunction Indicator Lamp (MIL) will begin flashing out any Diagnostic Trouble Code(s) stored in the PCM's memory. First, it will flash the tens place, and then it will flash the units place. For example, if a Code 24 is stored in the PCM memory:

1) *The Check Engine light will illuminate for 1.5 seconds.*
2) *Then it will go off for 0.5 second.*
3) *Then it will illuminate for another 1.5 seconds.*
4) *Then it will go off for about two seconds. This long pause indicates that the Check Engine light has completed its display of the tens place. To calculate the tens place number, simply count the number of long flashes (two) and you come up with 20 (three long flashes would indicate 30, four would indicate 40, etc.).*
5) *The Check Engine light will illuminate for 0.5 second.*
6) *Then it will go off for 0.5 second.*
7) *Then it will come on a second time for 0.5 second.*
8) *Then it will go off again for 0.5 second.*
9) *Then it will come on again for another 0.5 second.*
10) *Then it will go off again for 0.5 second.*
11) *Then it will come on again for 0.5 second.*
12) *This sequence will be followed by a three-second pause, which tells you that the Check Engine light has completed its display of the first DTC in the PCM's memory. Count the number of 0.5-second flashes and you get four. Add four to 20 and you get 24, or Code 24 (Vehicle Speed Sensor).*

13) *After the three-second pause, the Check Engine light will display the next DTC stored in the PCM's memory, if there is another one.*
14) *The Check Engine light will continue like this until it has flashed each stored DTC, after which it will pause three seconds and then repeat the entire sequence again. And it will continue to do so until the No. 1 terminal of the diagnostic connector is ungrounded.*
15) *Once you have outputted all of the stored DTCs, look them up on the accompanying DTC chart for 1994 and 1995 models.*

32 After troubleshooting the source of each DTC, make any necessary repairs or replace the defective component(s).

Clearing the DTCs

33 Clear the DTCs as follows:
1) *Disconnect the cable from the negative battery terminal for at least 10 seconds and then reconnect the cable.*
2) *Start the engine, warm it up and then run it at idle for 15 minutes.*

1996 and later models
Accessing the DTCs

Refer to illustration 2.34

34 On these models, all of which are equipped with On-Board Diagnostic II (OBD-II) systems, the Diagnostic Trouble Codes (DTCs) can only be accessed with a scan tool. Professional scan tools are expensive, but relatively inexpensive generic scan tools **(see illustrations 2.1 and 2.2)** are available at many auto parts stores. Simply plug the connector of the scan tool into the diagnostic connector **(see illustration)**, which is located under the left side of the dash and follow the instructions included with the scan tool to extract the DTCs.

35 Once you have outputted all of the stored DTCs, look them up on the accompanying DTC chart for 1994 and 1995 models.

36 After troubleshooting the source of each DTC, make any necessary repairs or replace the defective component(s).

Clearing the DTCs

37 Clear the DTCs with the scan tool in accordance with the instructions provided by the scan tool's manufacturer.

Diagnostic Trouble Codes

38 The accompanying tables are a list of the Diagnostic Trouble Codes (DTCs) that can be accessed by a do-it-yourselfer working at home (on 1996 and later models, there are many, many more DTCs available to dealerships with proprietary scan tools and software, but those codes cannot be accessed by a generic scan tool). If, after you have checked and repaired the connectors, wire harness and vacuum hoses (if applicable) for an emission-related system, component or circuit, the problem persists, have the vehicle checked by a dealer service department or a qualified repair shop.

OBD trouble codes (1994 and 1995 models)
Note: *Not all trouble codes apply to all models.*

Code	Probable cause
Code 11	Upstream heated oxygen sensor or circuit
Code 12	Volume air flow sensor or circuit
Code 13	Intake Air Temperature (IAT) sensor or circuit
Code 14	Throttle Position (TP) sensor or circuit
Code 21	Engine Coolant Temperature (ECT) sensor or circuit
Code 22	Crankshaft Position (CKP) sensor or circuit
Code 23	Camshaft Position (CMP) sensor or circuit
Code 24	Vehicle Speed Sensor (VSS) or circuit
Code 25	Barometric pressure sensor or circuit
Code 31	Knock sensor or circuit (DOHC engines)
Code 36	Ignition timing adjustment signal
Code 41	Injector or circuit
Code 43	EGR system malfunction
Code 44	Ignition coil, ignition power transistor unit or circuit (DOHC, cylinders 1 and 4)
Code 52	Ignition coil, ignition power transistor unit or circuit (DOHC, cylinders 2 and 3)
Code 55	Idle Air Control (IAC) valve position sensor or circuit (SOHC engines)
Code 59	Downstream heated oxygen sensor or circuit

OBD-II trouble codes (1996 and later models)
Note: *Not all trouble codes apply to all models.*

Code	Probable cause
P001A	Camshaft profile control (engine oil control valve) circuit
P0031	Oxygen sensor heater control circuit low (bank 1, sensor 1)
P0032	Oxygen sensor heater control circuit high (bank 1, sensor 1)
P0037	Oxygen sensor heater control circuit low (bank 1, sensor 2)
P0038	Oxygen sensor heater control circuit high (bank 1, sensor 2)
P003C	MIVEC system problem
P0051	Oxygen sensor heater control circuit low (bank 2, sensor 1)
P0052	Oxygen sensor heater control circuit high (bank 2, sensor 1)
P0057	Oxygen sensor heater control circuit low (bank 2, sensor 2)
P0058	Oxygen sensor heater control circuit high (bank 2, sensor 2)
P0069	Manifold pressure (MAP) sensor - barometric pressure correlation
P0100	Volume Air Flow circuit malfunction
P0101	Volume Air Flow sensor circuit out of range or performance problem

Code	Probable cause
P0102	Volume Air Flow sensor circuit, low input
P0103	Volume Air Flow sensor circuit, high input
P0105	Barometric pressure circuit malfunction
P0106	Barometric pressure circuit out of range or performance problem
P0107	Barometric pressure circuit, low input
P0108	Barometric pressure circuit, high input
P0110	Intake Air Temperature sensor circuit malfunction
P0111	Intake Air Temperature sensor out of range or performance problem
P0112	Intake Air Temperature sensor circuit, low input
P0113	Intake Air Temperature sensor circuit, high input
P0115	Engine Coolant Temperature sensor circuit malfunction or high input
P0116	Engine Coolant Temperature out of range or performance problem
P0117	Engine Coolant Temperature sensor circuit, low input
P0118	Engine Coolant Temperature sensor circuit, high input
P0120	Throttle Position sensor circuit malfunction
P0121	Throttle Position sensor circuit out of range or performance problem
P0122	Throttle Position sensor circuit, low input
P0123	Throttle Position sensor circuit, high input
P0125	Excessive time to enter closed loop fuel control (1996 through 2000)
P0125	Insufficient coolant temperature for closed loop fuel control (2002 on)
P0128	Coolant temperature below thermostat regulating temperature
P0130	Upstream heated oxygen sensor circuit problem[1]
P0131	Oxygen sensor circuit, low voltage (bank 1, sensor 1)
P0132	Upstream heated oxygen sensor circuit, high voltage[1]
P0133	Upstream heated oxygen sensor circuit, slow response[1]
P0134	Upstream heated oxygen sensor circuit, no activity detected[1]
P0135	Upstream oxygen sensor heater circuit problem[1]
P0136	Downstream heated oxygen sensor circuit problem[1]
P0137	Downstream heated oxygen sensor circuit, low voltage[1]
P0138	Downstream heated oxygen sensor circuit, high voltage[1]
P0139	Downstream heated oxygen sensor circuit, slow response[1]
P0140	Oxygen sensor circuit - no activity detected (bank 1, sensor 2)
P0141	Downstream oxygen sensor heater circuit problem[1]
P0150	Upstream heated oxygen sensor circuit malfunction[2]
P0151	Upstream heated oxygen sensor circuit, low voltage[2]

OBD-II trouble codes (1996 and later models) (continued)

Code	Probable cause
P0152	Upstream heated oxygen sensor circuit, high voltage[2]
P0153	Upstream heated oxygen sensor circuit, slow response[2]
P0154	Upstream heated oxygen sensor circuit, no activity detected[2]
P0155	Upstream oxygen sensor heater circuit problem[2]
P0156	Downstream heated oxygen sensor circuit problem[2]
P0157	Downstream heated oxygen sensor circuit, low voltage[2]
P0158	Downstream heated oxygen sensor circuit, high voltage[2]
P0159	Downstream heated oxygen sensor circuit, slow response[2]
P0160	Oxygen sensor circuit - no activity detected (bank 2, sensor 2)
P0161	Downstream oxygen sensor heater circuit malfunction[2]
P0170	Fuel trim malfunction[3]
P0171	System too lean[4]
P0172	System too rich[4]
P0173	Fuel trim malfunction[5]
P0174	System too lean[6]
P0175	System too rich[6]
P0181	Fuel temperature sensor circuit out of range or performance problem
P0182	Fuel temperature sensor circuit, low input
P0183	Fuel temperature sensor circuit, high input
P0201	Injector no. 1 circuit malfunction
P0202	Injector no. 2 circuit malfunction
P0203	Injector no. 3 circuit malfunction
P0204	Injector no. 4 circuit malfunction
P0205	Injector no. 5 circuit malfunction
P0206	Injector no. 6 circuit malfunction
P0222	Throttle position or pedal position sensor/switch B circuit, low input
P0223	Throttle position or pedal position sensor/switch B circuit, high input
P0300	Random misfire detected
P0301	Cylinder no. 1 misfire detected
P0302	Cylinder no. 2 misfire detected
P0303	Cylinder no. 3 misfire detected
P0304	Cylinder no. 4 misfire detected
P0305	Cylinder no. 5 misfire detected
P0306	Cylinder no. 6 misfire detected

Code	Probable cause
P0325	Knock sensor circuit malfunction
P0335	Crankshaft Position sensor circuit malfunction
P0340	Camshaft Position sensor circuit malfunction
P0400	Exhaust Gas Recirculation valve flow malfunction
P0401	Exhaust Gar Recirculation valve, insufficient flow detected
P0403	Exhaust Gas Recirculation valve control circuit or solenoid malfunction
P0420	Catalyst system efficiency below threshold
P0421	Warm-up catalyst efficiency below threshold[7]
P0431	Warm-up catalyst efficiency below threshold[8]
P0440	EVAP system malfunction
P0441	EVAP system, incorrect purge flow
P0442	EVAP system small leak detected
P0443	EVAP system purge control valve circuit malfunction
P0446	EVAP system vent control malfunction
P0450	EVAP system pressure sensor malfunction
P0451	EVAP system pressure sensor out of range or performance problem
P0452	EVAP system pressure sensor, low input
P0453	EVAP system pressure sensor, high input
P0455	EVAP system, big leak detected
P0456	EVAP system, very small leak detected
P0461	Fuel level sensor circuit out of ranger or performance problem
P0462	Fuel level sensor circuit, low input
P0463	Fuel level sensor circuit, high input
P050B	Ignition timing retard insufficient
P0500	Vehicle Speed Sensor malfunction
P0505	Idle control system malfunction
P0506	Idle control system rpm lower than expected
P0507	Idle control system rpm higher than expected
P0510	Closed throttle position switch malfunction
P0513	Immobilizer malfunction
P0551	Power steering pressure sensor circuit out of range or malfunctioning
P0554	Power steering pressure sensor circuit, intermittent input
P0603	Internal control module, keep alive memory (KAM) error
P0606	PCM processor fault
P0622	Alternator FR terminal, circuit malfunction

OBD-II trouble codes (1996 and later models) (continued)

Code	Probable cause
P0630	VIN not programmed or mismatch - ECM/PCM
P0638	Throttle actuator control range/performance (bank 1)
P0642	Engine control module (ECM), knock control - defective
P0657	Actuator supply voltage - circuit open
P0705	Automatic transaxle range sensor circuit malfunction (PRNDL input)
P0710	Automatic transaxle fluid temperature sensor circuit malfunction
P0712	Automatic transaxle fluid temperature sensor circuit, low input
P0713	Automatic transaxle fluid temperature sensor circuit, high input
P0715	Automatic transaxle input/turbine speed sensor circuit malfunction
P0720	Automatic transaxle output speed sensor circuit malfunction
P0725	Automatic transaxle engine speed input circuit system malfunction
P0731	Automatic transaxle, 1st gear, incorrect ratio
P0732	Automatic transaxle, 2nd gear, incorrect ratio
P0733	Automatic transaxle, 3rd gear, incorrect ratio
P0734	Automatic transaxle, 4th gear, incorrect ratio
P0735	Incorrect gear ratio, fifth gear
P0736	Automatic transaxle, Reverse gear, incorrect ratio
P0740	Automatic transaxle torque converter clutch system malfunction
P0741	Automatic transaxle torque converter clutch circuit problem, or stuck off
P0742	Automatic transaxle torque converter clutch circuit stuck on
P0743	Automatic transaxle torque converter circuit electrical problem
P0750	Automatic transaxle shift solenoid A electrical malfunction (2.4L four-cylinder)
P0753	Automatic transaxle shift solenoid A electrical malfunction (V6)
P0755	Automatic transaxle shift solenoid B electrical malfunction (2.4L four-cylinder)
P0758	Automatic transaxle shift solenoid B electrical malfunction (V6)
P0760	Automatic transaxle shift solenoid C electrical malfunction (2.4L four-cylinder)
P0763	Automatic transaxle shift solenoid C electrical malfunction (V6)
P0765	Automatic transaxle shift solenoid D electrical malfunction (2.4L four-cylinder)
P0768	Automatic transaxle shift solenoid D electrical malfunction (V6)
P0773	Shift solenoid E, electrical problem

OBD-II trouble codes (1996 and later models)

Notes:

1   *On V6 engines, this code refers to the oxygen sensor, or its circuit, for the rear cylinder head.*

2   *On V6 engines, this code refers to the oxygen sensor, or its circuit, for the front cylinder head.*

3   *On V6 engines, this code refers to the fuel trim function for the rear cylinder head. (The term "fuel trim" refers to the response of the Volume Air Flow sensor, the fuel injectors, the fuel pressure, the Engine Coolant Temperature sensor, the Intake Air Temperature sensor, the Barometric Pressure sensor and the oxygen sensor to intake air leaks or cracks in the exhaust manifold.)*

4   *On V6 engines, this code refers to the rear cylinder bank.*

5   *On V6 engines, this code refers to the fuel trim function for the rear cylinder head. (The term "fuel trim" refers to the response of the Volume Air Flow sensor, the fuel injectors, the fuel pressure, the Engine Coolant Temperature sensor, the Intake Air Temperature sensor, the Barometric Pressure sensor and the oxygen sensor to intake air leaks or cracks in the exhaust manifold.)*

6   *On V6 engines, this code refers to the front cylinder bank.*

7   *On V6 engines, this code refers to the warm-up catalyst for the rear cylinder head.*

8   *On V6 engines, this code refers to the warm-up catalyst for the front cylinder head.*

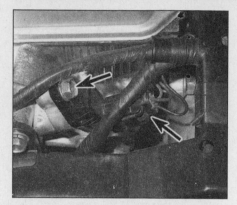

4.10a To detach the Camshaft Position (CMP) sensor from the cylinder head on a 1999 and later 2.4L SOHC model, disconnect the electrical connector and remove the sensor retaining bolt

4.10b Camshaft Position (CMP) sensor - 2004 and later four-cylinder engine

3 Barometric pressure sensor - replacement

1   The barometric pressure sensor is an integral component of the Volume Air Flow sensor. It cannot be replaced separately.
2   Remove the Volume Air Flow sensor (see Section 18).
3   Installation is the reverse of removal.

4 Camshaft Position (CMP) sensor - replacement

1   The CMP sensor determines the position of the cylinder for ignition start-up signals and for sequential fuel injection signals to each cylinder. The camshaft position sensor is mounted in several different places depending on the model.

a) On 1994 and 1995 2.4L DOHC models, the CMP sensor is mounted on the left (timing belt) end of the cylinder head, adjacent to the intake camshaft timing belt sprocket.
b) On 1998 and earlier 2.4L SOHC models and on 1999 and later 3.0L V6 engines,

the CMP sensor is located inside the distributor.
c) On 3.8L V6 and 1999 and later 2.4L SOHC models, the CMP sensor is mounted on the left end (opposite end from the timing belt) of the cylinder head.

2   Make sure that the ignition key is in the OFF position.

1994 and 1995 2.4L DOHC models

3   Remove the timing belt cover and the timing belt (see Chapter 2A).
4   Disconnect the electrical connector from the CMP sensor.
5   Remove the CMP sensor mounting bolts and detach the sensor from the cylinder head.
6   Installation is the reverse of removal.

1998 and earlier 2.4L SOHC models and 1999 and later 3.0L V6 models

7   Remove the distributor (see Chapter 5). The CMP sensor is not sold as an individual component. Replace the distributor assembly.
8   Installation is the reverse of removal.

1999 and later 2.4L SOHC models

Refer to illustrations 4.10a and 4.10b
9   Remove the air intake duct (see Chap-

ter 4).
10   Disconnect the electrical connector from the CMP sensor (**see illustrations**).
11   Remove the CMP sensor retaining bolt.
12   Remove the CMP sensor.
13   Installation is the reverse of removal.

2004 and later 3.8L V6 models

14   Disconnect the wiring from the sensor. It's located at the left end of the engine near the end of the front valve cover.
15   Remove the mounting bolt, then pull the sensor out. Remove the O-ring.
16   Installation is the reverse of removal.

5 Crankshaft Position (CKP) sensor - replacement

Refer to illustrations 5.5 and 5.6
1   The Crankshaft Position (CKP) sensor helps the PCM to determine the correct timing of the fuel injectors and the ignition spark for each cylinder. The CKP sensor is mounted in several different places depending on the year and model:

a) On 1994 and 1995 DOHC models and 1996 through 1998 SOHC four-cylinder models, the CKP sensor is located on the left (timing belt) end of the engine, adjacent to the crankshaft timing belt sprocket.
b) On 1994 and 1995 four-cylinder engines the CKP sensor is located inside the distributor.
c) On 1996 and later 2.4L SOHC models and on 1999 and later V6 models, the CKP sensor is located on the right (timing belt) end of the engine, adjacent to the crankshaft timing belt sprocket.

2   Make sure the ignition key is in the OFF position.
3   Refer to Chapter 2 and remove the lower timing belt cover. On 2003 and earlier models, remove the timing belt if necessary for clearance.
4   Raise the vehicle and support it securely on jackstands.
5   Disconnect the CKP sensor electrical connector (**see illustration**).

5.5 To find the electrical connector for the Crankshaft Position (CKP) sensor, trace the electrical leads from the sensor to the connector

5.6 To detach the CKP sensor from the engine block, remove these two bolts (1999 and later 2.4L SOHC model shown, other models similar)

6.1a On 1999 and later 2.4L SOHC models, the Engine Coolant Temperature (ECT) sensor is located on the left end of the cylinder head

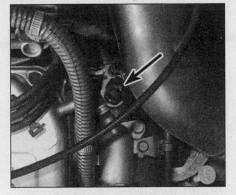

6.1b On 1999 and later 3.0L V6 models, the Engine Coolant Temperature (ECT) sensor is located on the crossover part of the thermostat housing

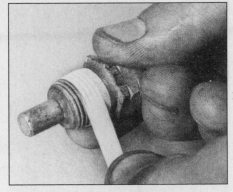

6.6 If the ECT sensor threads aren't already coated with some type of thread sealant, wrap the threads with Teflon tape

6   Remove the CKP sensor retaining bolts (see illustration) and detach the sensor.
7   Installation is the reverse of removal.

6   Engine Coolant Temperature (ECT) sensor - replacement

Refer to illustrations 6.1a, 6.1b and 6.6
Warning: *Wait until the engine has cooled completely before beginning this procedure.*
1   On 1994 and 1995 2.4L DOHC models, and on 1994 through 1998 2.4L SOHC models, the ECT sensor is located on the right end of the intake manifold. On 1999 and later 2.4L SOHC models, the ECT sensor (see illustration) is located on the left end (opposite the timing belt end) of the cylinder head. On 1999 and later V6 models, the ECT sensor (see illustration) is located at the left end of the engine, on the crossover portion of the thermostat housing.
2   Make sure that the ignition key is in the OFF position.
3   Drain about one gallon of coolant from the cooling system (see Chapter 1).
4   Disconnect the electrical connector from the ECT sensor.
5   Carefully unscrew the sensor.
6   Wrap the threads of the new sensor with Teflon sealing tape to prevent leakage and thread corrosion (see illustration).
7   Installation is the reverse of removal. Be sure to tighten the ECT sensor to the torque listed in this Chapter's Specifications.
8   When you're done, refill the cooling system (see Chapter 1).

7   Fuel level sensor - replacement

The fuel level sensor is simply a new name for the fuel level *sending unit* on 2002 and later models. On these models, the fuel level sensor is called a *sensor* because it's connected to the PCM. The fuel level sensor/sending unit is an integral component of the fuel pump. To remove it, refer to Section 5 in Chapter 4. To replace it, refer to Section 6 in Chapter 4. On 2004 and

later models, there is a secondary fuel level sensor in the right side of the fuel tank. It is serviced by removing the access cover under the right side of the rear seat. Refer to Chapter 4 for more information.

8   Fuel tank differential pressure sensor - replacement

Refer to illustration 8.3
1   The fuel tank differential pressure sensor is used on 1996 and 1997 California models and on all 1998 and later models. The fuel tank differential pressure sensor is located on top of the fuel tank. On 1996 and 1997 California models and on 1998 models, the sensor is bolted to the top of the fuel pump/fuel level sending unit mounting flange. On 1999 and later models, it's located at the front right corner of the fuel tank and is bolted directly to the top of the tank.
2   Remove the fuel tank (see Chapter 4).
3   Disconnect the electrical connector (see illustration) from the fuel tank differential pressure sensor.
4   Remove the fuel tank differential pressure sensor mounting nuts.
5   Remove the fuel tank differential pressure sensor.
6   Installation is the reverse of removal.

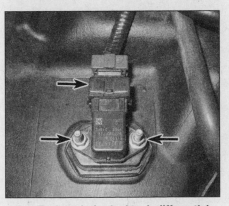

8.3 To detach the fuel tank differential pressure sensor, disconnect the electrical connector and remove these two nuts

9   Fuel temperature sensor - replacement

1   The fuel temperature sensor, which is used on later models, is an integral part of the fuel pump/fuel level sensor.
2   Remove the fuel pump/fuel level sensor (see Chapter 4).
3   Remove the fuel temperature sensor from the fuel pump/fuel level sensor.
4   Installation is the reverse of removal.

10   Intake Air Temperature (IAT) sensor - replacement

Refer to illustration 10.1
1   The IAT sensor (see illustration) is an integral part of the Volume Air Flow sensor. It cannot be replaced separately.
2   Remove the Volume Air Flow sensor (see Section 18).
3   Installation is the reverse of removal.

10.1 The Intake Air Temperature (IAT) sensor is an integral part of the Volume Air Flow sensor (air intake duct removed for clarity); to replace the IAT sensor, you'll have to replace the Volume Air Flow sensor

11.6 Typical knock sensor location - 2004 and later four-cylinder model

11 Knock sensor - replacement

Refer to illustration 11.6

Warning: *Wait for the engine to cool completely before performing this procedure.*

Note: *The following procedure applies only to V6 models, 2004 and later four-cylinder models and all DOHC four-cylinder models.*

1   The knock control system is designed to reduce spark knock during periods of heavy detonation. This allows the engine to use optimal spark advance to improve driveability. The knock sensor detects abnormal vibration in the engine and produces a voltage output, which increases with the severity of the knock. The voltage signal is monitored by the PCM, which retards ignition timing until the detonation ceases. The knock sensor is located underneath the intake manifold on V6 models.

2   Make sure that the ignition key is in the OFF position.

3   If you're working on a V6 model, drain the cooling system (see Chapter 1).

4   If you're working on a V6 model, re-move the intake manifold (see Chapter 2B). If you're working on a 2.4L DOHC model, remove the intake manifold stay.

5   Disconnect the knock sensor electrical connector.

6   Unscrew the knock sensor **(see illustration)**.

7   If you're going to reuse the old sensor, coat the threads with thread sealant. New sensors are pre-coated with thread sealant; do not apply any additional sealant or the operation of the sensor may be affected.

8   Install the knock sensor and tighten it to the torque listed in this Chapter's Specifications. Don't overtighten the knock sensor; overtightening it can damage it.

9   Plug in the knock sensor electrical connector.

10   If you're working on a V6 model, install the intake manifold (see Chapter 2B). If you're working on a 2.4L DOHC model, remove the intake manifold stay.

11   Refill the cooling system and check for leaks (V6 models).

12.1a The Manifold Differential Pressure (MDP) sensor is located on the front of the intake manifold on 1999 and later 2.4L SOHC models

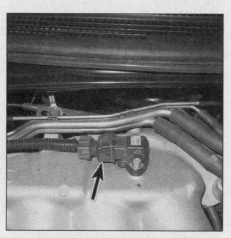

12.1b The Manifold Differential Pressure (MDP) sensor is located on top of the intake manifold on 1999 and later 3.0L V6 models

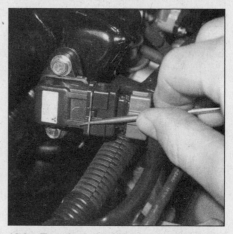

12.3a To unlock the MDP sensor electrical connector, pry open this wire retainer (1999 and later 2.4L SOHC model shown, other models similar)

12.3b Unplugging the electrical connector from the MDP sensor on a pre-1999 2.4L SOHC model

12.4a To detach the MDP sensor from the intake manifold, remove the two retaining bolts (1999 and later 2.4L SOHC model shown, other models similar)

12.4b Removing the two MDP sensor retaining bolts on a pre-1999 2.4L SOHC model

12 Manifold Differential Pressure (MDP)/Manifold Absolute Pressure (MAP) sensor - replacement

Refer to illustrations 12.1a, 12.1b, 12.3a, 12.3b, 12.4a, 12.4b and 12.5

1   The MDP/MAP sensor **(see illustrations)**, which is mounted on the intake manifold, is used on 1996 California 2.4L SOHC models, on 1997 and 1998 Federal 2.4L SOHC models and on all 1999 and later models.
2   Make sure the ignition key is in the OFF position.
3   Disconnect the electrical connector from the MDP/MAP sensor **(see illustrations)**.
4   Remove the MDP/MAP sensor retaining bolts **(see illustrations)**.
5   Remove the MDP/MAP sensor **(see illustration)**.
6   Inspect the tip of the MDP/MAP sensor. If it's clogged or damaged, replace the MDP/MAP sensor.
7   Installation is the reverse of removal.

13 Oxygen sensors - general information and replacement

General information

1   An oxygen sensor is a galvanic battery that produces a very small voltage output in response to the amount of oxygen in the exhaust gases. This voltage signal is the "input" side of the feedback loop between the oxygen sensor and the Powertrain Control Module (PCM). Without it, the PCM would be unable to correct the injector on-time (which determines the air/fuel ratio) to maintain the "perfect" (known as *stoichiometric*) air/fuel ratio of 14.7:1 that the catalyst needs for optimal operation.

12.5 Remove the MDP sensor from the intake manifold and inspect the tip of the sensor for damage; if the tip is clogged or damaged, replace the MDP sensor (pre-1999 2.4L SOHC model shown, other models similar)

On-Board Diagnostics II (OBD-II)

2   All 1996 and later vehicles covered by this manual have On-Board Diagnostics II (OBD-II) engine management systems, which means they have the ability to verify the accuracy of the basic feedback loop between the oxygen sensor and the PCM. They accomplish this by using an oxygen sensor *ahead of* the catalytic converter and another oxygen sensor *behind* the catalytic converter. By comparing the amount of oxygen in the post-catalyst exhaust gas to the oxygen content of the exhaust gas before it enters the catalyst, the PCM can determine the efficiency of the converter and can even predict when it will probably fail.

Four-cylinder models

3   All four-cylinder vehicles covered by this manual have *two* heated oxygen sensors. On all four-cylinder models (except 2001 and later), the upstream oxygen sensor is located in the front exhaust pipe, between the exhaust manifold and the catalytic converter; on 2001 and later models, the upstream sensor is located in the exhaust manifold. The downstream sensor is located *behind* the catalytic converter on all models. There are even two oxygen sensors on 1994 and 1995 (pre-OBD-II) models. Although these early models are not OBD-II compliant, there *is* a separate (two-digit) Diagnostic Trouble Code (DTC) for *each* oxygen sensor.

V6 models

4   1999 and 2000 *49-State* V6 models have *two* oxygen sensors: one upstream (ahead of the catalytic converter) and one downstream (after the converter). These models use only one catalytic converter, which is located downstream from the junction of the two exhaust pipes coming down from the exhaust manifolds. Locate the catalyst (under the vehicle) and you'll easily find both oxygen sensors.
5   1999 and 2000 *California* V6 models, and all 2001 and later V6 models, have *four* oxygen sensors: one upstream and one downstream *for each cylinder head*. These models have three catalysts: The two upstream catalysts are located in the down-pipes between the exhaust manifolds and the Y-junction where they connect to the main part of the exhaust system. The downstream catalyst is located in the same place (under the vehicle) as the single catalyst on 49-State models. The upstream oxygen sensor for the front cylinder head is located in the front exhaust manifold; the upstream sensor for the rear cylinder head is located at the top of the downpipe, at the flange between the exhaust manifold and the downpipe. The downstream oxygen sensors are located below the two smaller catalysts in the down-pipes.

All models

6   The upstream and downstream oxygen sensors on all models are heated to speed up the warm-up time during which

the sensors are unable to produce an accurate voltage signal. The circuit for each oxygen sensor heater is controlled by the PCM, which opens the ground side of the circuit to shut off the heater as soon as the sensor reaches its normal operating temperature.
7   Special care must be taken whenever a sensor is serviced.
a) Oxygen sensors have a permanently attached pigtail and an electrical connector that cannot be removed. Damaging or removing the pigtail or electrical connector will render the sensor useless.
b) Keep grease, dirt and other contaminants away from the electrical connector and the louvered end of the sensor.
c) Do not use cleaning solvents of any kind on an oxygen sensor.
d) Oxygen sensors are extremely delicate. Do not drop a sensor or throw it around or handle it roughly.
e) Make sure that the silicone boot on the sensor is installed in the correct position. Otherwise, the boot might melt and it might prevent the sensor from operating correctly.

Replacement

Refer to illustrations 13.10a, 13.10b, 13.11a, 13.11b, 13.11c and 13.11d
Note: *Because the oxygen sensors are installed in the exhaust system, which contracts as it cools down, the sensors can be difficult to loosen once the engine (and exhaust system) have cooled off. So, if you are planning to reuse an oxygen sensor (for example, you're only removing the sensor to replace a damaged section of exhaust pipe or a catalyst), instead of running the risk of damaging an oxygen sensor, run the engine for a minute or two, then shut it off. The oxygen sensor should now be easier to remove, but be careful not to burn yourself by touching any hot exhaust system parts.*
8   Make sure the ignition key is in the OFF position.
9   If you're planning to replace the *upstream* oxygen sensor on any 1994 model, on a 1995 through 2000 49-State 2.4L four-cylinder model, on any 2001 or later 2.4L model or on any 3.0L V6 model, raise the vehicle and place it securely on jackstands. It's not necessary to raise the vehicle to replace the upstream oxygen sensor on 1995 through 2000 California 2.4L four-cylinder models. If you're replacing the *downstream* sensor on any model, raise the vehicle and place it securely on jackstands.
10   Disconnect the oxygen sensor electrical connector **(see illustration)**. If you're replacing a *downstream* oxygen sensor, the electrical connector for the sensor is *inside the vehicle*, under the center console. Remove the center console (see Chapter 11) and have someone carefully wiggle the sensor harness from underneath the vehicle while you iden-

13.10a On 1999 and later 2.4L four-cylinder models, you'll find the electrical connector for the upstream oxygen sensor here; on other models, first locate the upstream oxygen sensor, then trace the electrical lead back to the electrical connector

13.10b If you're replacing a downstream oxygen sensor on any four-cylinder or V6 model, or the upstream sensor for the rear cylinder head on a 1999 or later V6 model, remove the center console, then locate the sensor connector by having someone wiggle the sensor harness from underneath so that you can identify the connector (1999 and later California model 2.4L model shown, other models similar)

13.11a Upstream oxygen sensor location on 1999 and later 2.4L SOHC models (1999 and later 3.0L V6 models similar, except that they have two upstream sensors: one above each upstream catalyst)

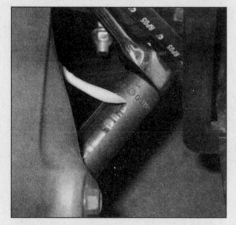

13.11b Use a special oxygen sensor socket to unscrew the upstream oxygen sensor; this special deep socket allows you to work in tight spaces where there's no room for a wrench, and the slot in the side of the socket protects the sensor harness from damage while you're loosening the sensor

13.11c It's not absolutely necessary to use an oxygen sensor socket on a downstream oxygen sensor, if you have enough room to put a wrench on it

13.11d Lower oxygen sensors (2004 and later four-cylinder models)

tify the connector **(see illustration)**.
11   Unscrew the sensor from the exhaust manifold or exhaust pipe **(see illustrations)**. **Note:** *The best tool for removing an oxygen sensor is a special slotted socket, especially if you're planning to reuse a sensor. If you don't have this tool, and you plan to reuse the sensor, be extremely careful when unscrewing the sensor.*
12   If you're planning to reuse an old oxygen sensor, recoat the threads with anti-seize compound to facilitate future removal. The threads of a new sensor should already be coated with this compound.
13   Install the oxygen sensor and tighten it to the torque listed in this Chapter's Specifications.
14   Reconnect the electrical connector of

the pigtail lead to the main wiring harness.
15   Lower the vehicle, if it was raised. Test drive the car and verify that no trouble codes have been set.

---

14   Park/Neutral Position (PNP) switch - replacement and adjustment

---

Replacement

Refer to illustrations 14.1, 14.3, 14.4 and 14.5
1   The Park/Neutral Position (PNP) switch **(see illustration)**, which is located on top of the transaxle, tells the Powertrain Control Module (PCM) what gear the automatic transaxle is in.

2   Make sure that the ignition key is in the OFF position.
3   Disconnect the electrical connector from the PNP switch **(see illustration)**.
4   Disconnect the shift cable from the PNP switch manual control lever **(see illustration)**.
5   Remove the nut from the manual lever shaft, then remove the lever and unscrew the PNP switch mounting bolts **(see illustration)**.
6   Remove the PNP switch.
7   Installation is the reverse of removal. Be sure to adjust the PNP switch when you're done.

Adjustment

Refer to illustrations 14.10a, 14.10b and 14.11
8   Put the shift lever inside the vehicle in the Neutral position.

14.1 The Park/Neutral Position (PNP) switch is located on top of the transaxle on all models equipped with an automatic (1999 and later model shown, other models similar)

14.3 Disconnect the electrical connector from the PNP switch

14.4 To disconnect the shift cable from the PNP switch, remove this nut

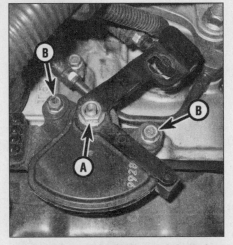

14.5 To detach the PNP switch from the transaxle, remove the manual lever nut (A) and the switch mounting bolts (B)

14.10a When the manual control lever is in the Neutral position, the hole in the end of the lever should be precisely aligned with the Neutral alignment hole in the PNP switch body flange, as shown

9   Loosen the shift cable-to-manual control lever adjusting nut **(see illustration 14.4)**.

10   Put the manual control lever in the Neutral position **(see illustration)**. When the manual control lever is in the Neutral position, the hole in the end of the lever should be precisely aligned with the Neutral alignment hole in the PNP switch body flange (as shown in the accompanying illustration). If the two holes aren't aligned, loosen the PNP switch mounting bolts **(see illustration 14.5)** and then rotate the PNP switch body so that the hole in the end of the manual control lever is aligned with the Neutral alignment hole in the PNP switch body flange. Once you get the two holes aligned, it's a good idea to insert a drill bit through both holes **(see illustration)** to maintain alignment until the PNP switch body mounting bolts and the transaxle control cable-to-manual lever nut are tightened.

11   Carefully pull the shift cable until it's taut **(see illustration)**, then tighten the shift cable-to-manual control lever adjusting nut securely.

14.10b If the two holes aren't aligned, loosen the PNP switch mounting bolts, then rotate the PNP switch body until the hole in the PNP switch body flange is aligned with the hole in the end of the manual control lever; once you get the two holes aligned, insert a drill bit through both holes to maintain alignment until the PNP switch body mounting bolts and the transaxle control cable-to-manual lever nut are tightened

14.11 Carefully pull the transaxle control cable (in the direction of the arrow) until it's taut, then tighten the cable adjustment nut securely

15.3 The Power Steering Pressure (PSP) switch is located on the front of the power steering pump on 1999 and later models (it's on top of the pump on earlier models); to replace the PSP switch, disconnect the electrical connector and unscrew the switch from the pump

15 Power Steering Pressure (PSP) switch - replacement

Refer to illustration 15.3

1   The Power Steering Pressure (PSP) switch is located on top of the power steering pump on 1994 through 1998 models. On 1999 and later models, the PSP switch is located on the front of the power steering pump.
2   Make sure that the ignition key is turned to the OFF position.
3   Disconnect the electrical connector from the PSP switch **(see illustration)**.
4   Unscrew the PSP switch. Have a pan ready to catch the power steering fluid that will leak out of the pump.
5   Be sure to install a new O-ring on the

16.1 The Throttle Position (TP) sensor is located on the throttle body, on one end of the throttle valve shaft (3.0L V6 model shown, other models similar)

PSP switch (even if you're planning to re-use the old PSP switch).
6   Coat the threads of the PSP switch with thread sealant or Teflon tape.
7   Install the PSP switch and tighten it securely.
8   Reconnect the electrical connector to the PSP switch.
9   When you're done, check the power steering fluid level (see Chapter 1) and top it up as necessary.

16 Throttle Position (TP) sensor - replacement

Refer to illustrations 16.1, 16.3a, 16.3b, 16.4a, 16.4b, 16.6, 16.9a and 16.9b
Note: *This procedure applies only to 2003*

and earlier models. The throttle position sensor on later models is an integral part of the throttle body and cannot be serviced separately. If there is a problem with the throttle position sensor, you'll have to replace the throttle body.

1   The Throttle Position (TP) sensor **(see illustration)** is located on the throttle body at the end of the throttle shaft. The TP sensor is a variable potentiometer that delivers an analog (infinitely variable) voltage signal to the PCM in accordance with the opening angle of the throttle valve inside the throttle body. By monitoring the output voltage from the TP sensor, the PCM can determine "driver demand" (the opening angle of the throttle valve), a vital piece of information for adjusting injector on-time (which in turn determines the amount of fuel squirted into the intake ports). A broken or loose TP sensor can cause intermittent bursts of fuel from the injectors and an unstable idle because the PCM thinks the throttle is moving.
2   Make sure that the ignition key is in the OFF position.
3   Disconnect the electrical connector from the TP sensor **(see illustrations)**.
4   Remove the TP sensor retaining screws **(see illustrations)**.
5   Before removing the TP sensor, note the orientation of the two screw holes and the angle of the electrical connector terminals; this is the installed position of the TP sensor. When you install the TP sensor, it must be reoriented to this exact same position (the TP sensor isn't adjustable).
6   To install the TP sensor, index the tabs on the back side of the sensor (the side that faces toward the throttle body) with the blade on the end of the throttle valve shaft **(see illustration)**. and then install the TP sensor. If you have indexed the tabs correctly with the blade, the TP sensor screw holes will not be lined up yet with the screw holes in the throt-

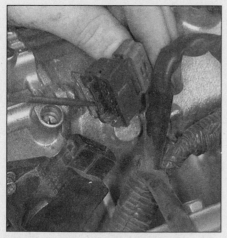

16.3a To disconnect the electrical connector from the TP sensor on a 1994 through 1998 model, pry open this wire retainer and carefully pull off the connector

16.3b To disconnect the electrical connector from the TP sensor on a 1999 and later model, pry open this wire retainer and carefully pull off the connector (2.4L SOHC model shown, 3.0L V6 models similar)

16.4a To detach the TP sensor from the throttle body on a 1994 through 1998 model, remove these two screws

16.4b To detach the TP sensor from the throttle body on a 1999 through 2003 model, remove these two screws (2.4L SOHC model shown, 3.0L V6 models similar)

16.6 When installing the TP sensor on the throttle body, make sure that the tabs on the back side of the sensor are correctly indexed with the blade on the end of the throttle valve shaft; one tab should be above the blade and one tab should be below it (3.0L V6 throttle body shown, other units similar; throttle body removed for clarity)

tle body. Now rotate the TP sensor 90 degrees clockwise and the screw holes in the TP sensor and the throttle body should be lined up.

7   With the screw holes in the TP sensor and the screw holes in the throttle body lined up, the throttle valve should be *closed*. If the throttle valve is open, the tabs on the TPS are indexed incorrectly. Repeat Step 6.

8   Install the TP sensor mounting screws and tighten them securely.

9   To verify that the TP sensor is correctly installed, hook up an ohmmeter between the indicated terminals of the electrical connector **(see illustrations)**, on the TP sensor side of the connector:

  a) *1994 through 1998 models - terminals 3 and 4*
  b) *1999 through 2003 models - terminals 1 and 3 or terminals 3 and 4.*

Then make sure that the continuity changes smoothly as you open and close the throttle valve.

10   Connect the TP sensor electrical connector.

17 Vehicle Speed Sensor (VSS) - replacement

Refer to illustrations 17.1a, 17.1b and 17.6

1   The Vehicle Speed Sensor (VSS) **(see illustrations)** is located on the transaxle. The VSS produces a pulsing voltage signal when the vehicle is moving. These voltage pulses are sent to the PCM, which uses this data to determine vehicle speed. On 1999 and later automatic transaxles, there are two sensors: an input shaft VSS and an output shaft VSS. The PCM compares the two signals so it can monitor the amount or torque converter clutch slippage.

2   Make sure the ignition key is in the OFF position.

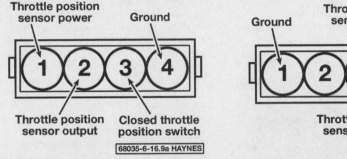

16.9a TP sensor electrical connector terminal guide (1994 through 1998 models)

16.9b TP sensor electrical connector terminal guide (1999 through 2003 models)

3   Disconnect the electrical connector from the VSS **(see illustration 17.1a or 17.1b)**.
4   Remove the VSS hold-down bolt.

5   Remove the VSS from the transaxle.
6   Replace the O-ring **(see illustration)**.
7   Installation is the reverse of removal.

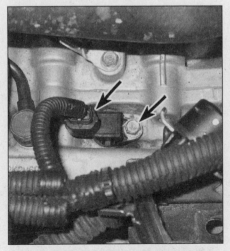

17.1a Input shaft Vehicle Speed Sensor (VSS) (1999 and later models with an automatic transaxle)

17.1b Output shaft Vehicle Speed Sensor (VSS) (1999 and later models with an automatic transaxle)

17.6 Be sure to replace the O-ring on the VSS

18.1 The Volume Air Flow sensor is located at the air filter housing (1999 and later model shown, earlier models similar)

18.5 To detach the Volume Air Flow sensor from the upper half of the air filter housing, remove these four nuts

18   Volume Air Flow sensor - replacement

Refer to illustrations 18.1 and 18.5

1   The Volume Air Flow sensor **(see illus-**

19.2 Accelerator Pedal Position (APP) sensor electrical connector (2004 and later models)

tration) is located in the air filter housing end of the air intake duct. The Volume Air Flow sensor circuit consists of a platinum hot wire, a "thermistor" (temperature-sensitive resistor) and the control circuit inside a plastic housing. The sensor uses a hot wire sensing element to measure the volume of air entering the engine. As the throttle valve opens, an increasing volume of air passes over the hot wire, which cools the wire. The sensor circuit is designed to maintain the hot wire at a constant preset temperature by controlling the current flow through the hot wire. So, as the wire cools, the PCM increases the flow of current through the hot wire in order to maintain the wire at a constant temperature. The output voltage signal of the sensor varies in accordance with this current flow. This voltage signal is measured by the PCM, which converts this signal into a digital wave form, calculates the fuel injector pulse width (duration) and turns the injectors on and off accordingly. On 1996 and later models, the Volume Air Flow sensor also incorporates the barometric pressure sensor and the Intake Air Temperature (IAT) sensor. If

you're replacing either of these sensors, replace the Volume Air Flow sensor.

2   Make sure that the ignition key is in the OFF position.

3   Disconnect the electrical connector from the Volume Air Flow sensor **(see illustration 18.1)**.

4   Remove the air intake duct and the air filter housing (see Chapter 4).

5   Remove the sensor retaining nuts **(see illustration)** and remove the MAF sensor.

6   Installation is the reverse of removal.

19   Accelerator Pedal Position (APP) sensor - replacement

Refer to illustration 19.2

Note: *This procedure applies only to 2004 and later models with electronically-controlled throttles. 2003 and earlier models have cable-operated throttles.*

Note: *The APP sensor is located at the upper end of the accelerator pedal assembly. The APP sensor and the accelerator pedal are*

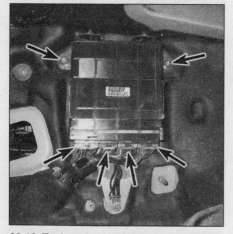

20.13 To detach the PCM from the firewall on 1999 and later models, disconnect the electrical connectors and remove the PCM mounting bracket bolts

20.17 The PCM on 2004 and later models is mounted near the battery in the engine compartment; it's protected by this cover (arrow)

20.20 Release the lock, then disconnect the wiring harnesses and remove the PCM from the engine compartment (2004 and later models)

serviced as a single assembly.

1   Disconnect the cable from the negative battery terminal (see Chapter 5).
2   Disconnect the APP sensor electrical connector **(see illustration)**.
3   Remove the mounting bolts and lift off the pedal/APP sensor assembly.
4   Installation is the reverse of removal. Tighten the mounting bolts securely.

20 Powertrain Control Module (PCM) - removal and installation

Warning: *The models covered by this manual are equipped with Supplemental Restraint systems (SRS), more commonly known as airbags. Always disable the airbag system before working in the vicinity of any airbag system components to avoid the possibility of accidental deployment of the airbag, which could cause personal injury (see Chapter 12).*
Caution: *To avoid electrostatic discharge damage to the PCM, handle the PCM only by its case. Do not touch the electrical terminals during removal and installation. If available, ground yourself to the vehicle with an anti-static ground strap, available at computer supply stores.*

1   The Powertrain Control Module (PCM) is located in the center of the dash on 1994 through 1998 models, and inside the dash, on the right end of the firewall on 1999 through 2003 models. On 2004 and later models, it's in the left side of the engine compartment.
2   Disconnect the cable from the negative battery terminal (see Chapter 5).

1994 through 1998 models
3   Remove the center trim bezel from the dash (see Chapter 11).
4   Remove the heater/air conditioner control assembly (see Chapter 3).
5   Remove the radio (see Chapter 12).
6   Disconnect the electrical connector from the PCM.
7   Remove the PCM mounting bracket bolts.
8   Carefully remove the PCM. **Caution:** *Avoid any static electricity damage to the computer by grounding yourself to the body before touching the PCM and using a special anti-static pad to store the PCM on once it is removed.*
9   Installation is the reverse of removal.
10   Reconnect the negative battery terminal (see Chapter 5).

1999 through 2003 models
Refer to illustration 20.13
11   Remove the glovebox (see Chapter 11). (It's not absolutely necessary to remove the glovebox to get to the PCM, but the glovebox is easy to remove, and removing it makes removing the PCM a lot easier.)
12   Remove the right side vent and the joint duct (which connects the heater core housing to the blower housing) and remove the blower housing (see *Heater core - removal and instal-*

lation in Chapter 3).
13   Disconnect the electrical connector from the PCM **(see illustration)**.
14   Remove the PCM mounting bracket bolts.
15   Carefully remove the PCM. **Caution:** *Avoid any static electricity damage to the computer by grounding yourself to the body before touching the PCM and using a special anti-static pad to store the PCM on once it is removed.*
16   Installation is the reverse of removal.

2004 and later models
Refer to illustrations 20.17 and 20.20
17   Remove the cover from the PCM **(see illustration)**.
18   Release the pivoting wiring connector clamps.
19   Remove the PCM mounting bracket.
20   Disconnect the wiring harnesses from the PCM, then lift it out of the engine compartment **(see illustration)**. **Caution:** *Avoid any static electricity damage to the PCM by grounding yourself to the body before touching the PCM and using a special anti-static pad to store the PCM on while it's removed.*
21   Installation is the reverse of removal. After connecting the PCM, perform the initialization by turning the ignition ON and then OFF. Keep it OFF for at least 10 seconds.
22   If the PCM has been replaced with a different one, it will be necessary to perform the idle-learn procedure. Start this procedure by first warming the engine completely.
23   Turn the ignition OFF, wait 10 seconds, then start the engine. Allow the engine to idle in Park for 10 minutes. The PCM should have learned the idle speed.

21 Idle Air Control (IAC) motor - replacement

Note: *This procedure applies only to 2003 and earlier models with cable-operated throttle bodies. Later models have electronically-controlled throttle bodies.*

21.11 Disconnect the electrical connector from the IAC motor (1999 through 2003 models; 2.4L SOHC model shown, 3.0L V6 models similar)

Note: *The minimum idle speed is pre-set at the factory and should not require adjustment under normal operating conditions. However if the throttle body has been replaced or you suspect the minimum idle speed has been tampered with (for example, if the idle speed screw was removed from the throttle body), have the vehicle checked by a dealer service department or other qualified automotive repair shop.*

1   The PCM controls engine idle speed with an output actuator known as the Idle Air Control (IAC) motor, which is mounted on the throttle body. When the engine is idling, the IAC motor meters the amount of air bypassing the closed throttle valve inside the throttle body bore in accordance with the "load" imposed on the engine. Typical loads at idle include running the air conditioning system, turning the wheels at low-speed or putting an automatic transaxle into gear. The PCM uses data from an array of information sensors to determine the correct amount of air needed to maintain idle speed during engine warm-up and when a load is placed on the engine, such as
2   Make sure that the ignition key is in the OFF position.
3   Remove the air intake duct (see Chapter 4).

1994 through 1998 models
4   Remove the throttle body (see Chapter 4).
5   Remove the IAC motor mounting screws.
6   Remove the IAC motor.
7   Remove the old IAC motor gasket.
8   Install a new IAC motor gasket.
9   Install the IAC motor and tighten the mounting screws securely.
10   Installation is the reverse of removal.

1999 through 2003 models
Refer to illustrations 21.11, 21.12 and 21.13
11   Disconnect the electrical connector from the IAC motor **(see illustration)**.
12   Remove the IAC motor mounting screws **(see illustration)** and detach the IAC motor from the throttle body.

21.12 To detach the IAC motor from the throttle body, remove these screws (1999 through 2003 models; 2.4L SOHC model shown, 3.0L V6 models similar)

21.13 Remove the old IAC motor O-ring and install a new O-ring (whether you plan to reuse the old IAC motor or install a new unit)

22.1 Engine oil control valve location for the MIVEC system (2004 and later four-cylinder engine)

13   Remove the old O-ring (see illustration) and install a new one. (Install a new O-ring regardless of whether you're going to reuse the old IAC motor or a new unit.)
14   Install the IAC motor and tighten the mounting screws securely.
15   Installation is otherwise the reverse of removal.

22   Engine oil control valve - replacement

Refer to illustration 22.1
1   The engine oil control valve controls engine oil pressure supply to the MIVEC system used on some later engines. This system provides substantial power increase at high engine speeds by using a secondary camshaft profile to alter intake valve timing and lift. There is one engine oil control valve mounted at the end of the cylinder head on four-cylinder models near the upper radiator hose and one at each end of 3.8L engines

(see illustration). The valves are electronically controlled by the PCM.
2   Disconnect the wiring from the valve. Remove the mounting screw, then carefully pull out the valve.
3   Discard the O-ring; it should be replaced with a new one. Tape the bottom part of the valve to prevent damage when installing the new O-ring.
4   Installation is the reverse of removal.
5   Remove the pipe plug at the top of the engine oil control valve housing, then remove the engine oil control valve filter. Check it, then clean or replace it. Replace the plug.

23   Catalytic converter

Note: *Because of a Federally-mandated extended warranty which covers emission-related components such as the catalytic converter, check with a dealer service department before replacing the converter at your own expense.*

General description

1   The catalytic converter is an emission control device in the exhaust system that reduces certain pollutants in the exhaust gas stream. There are two types of converters. The oxidation catalyst reduces hydrocarbons (HC) and carbon monoxide (CO). The reduction catalyst reduces oxides of nitrogen (NOx). Catalysts that can reduce all three pollutants are known as three-way catalysts. All the models covered by this manual are equipped with three-way catalysts.

Check

2   The test equipment for a catalytic converter (a "loaded-mode" dynamometer and a 5-gas analyzer) is expensive. If you suspect that the converter on your vehicle is malfunctioning, take it to a dealer or authorized emission inspection facility for diagnosis and repair.
3   Whenever you raise the vehicle to service underbody components, inspect the converter for leaks, corrosion, dents and

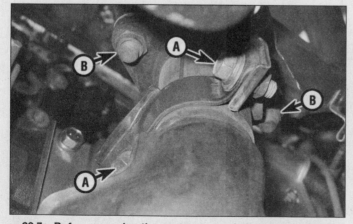

23.7a Before removing the upstream catalytic converter from most models, remove the two support bracket bolts (A) and the support bracket; to disconnect the upper end of the upstream catalyst from the exhaust manifold flange, remove the two nuts (B) (1999 and later 2.4L model shown, other models similar)

23.7b To disconnect the lower end of the upstream catalytic converter from the forward end of the downstream catalyst, remove these two nuts (1999 and later 2.4L model shown, other models similar)

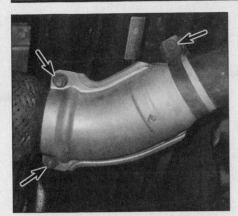

23.7c To remove the heat shield from the front end of the downstream catalyst, loosen this clamp bolt and remove these two nuts and bolts (1999 and later 2.4L model shown, other models similar)

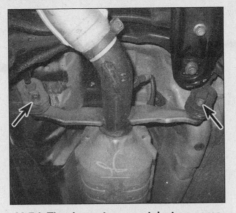

23.7d The downstream catalyst on some models might be secured to the vehicle underbody by a support bracket; to disconnect the bracket, remove these bolts

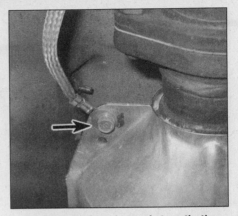

23.7e Look for a ground strap that's attached to the downstream catalyst; if the vehicle on which you're replacing the downstream catalyst is so equipped, disconnect the ground strap

other damage. Carefully inspect the welds and/or flange bolts and nuts that attach the front and rear ends of the converter to the exhaust system. If you note any damage, replace the converter.

4 Although catalytic converters don't break too often, they can become clogged or even plugged up. The easiest way to check for a restricted converter is to use a vacuum gauge to diagnose the effect of a blocked exhaust on intake vacuum.

a) *Connect a vacuum gauge to an intake manifold vacuum source (see Chapter 2).*

b) *Warm the engine to operating temperature, place the transaxle in Park (automatic models) or Neutral (manual models) and apply the parking brake.*

c) *Note the vacuum reading at idle and jot it down.*

d) *Quickly open the throttle to near its wide-open position, then quickly get off the throttle and allow it to close. Note the vacuum reading and jot it down.*

e) *Do this test three more times, recording your measurement after each test.*

f) *If your fourth reading is more than one in-Hg lower than the reading that you noted at idle, the exhaust system might be restricted (the catalytic converter could be plugged, OR an exhaust pipe or muffler could be restricted).*

Replacement

Refer to illustrations 23.7a, 23.7b, 23.7c, 23.7d, 23.7e and 23.7f

Note: *1999 and 2000 California 3.0L V6 models and all 2001 and later V6 models are equipped with a front exhaust pipe/catalytic converter unit bolted to each exhaust manifold (these catalysts are known as "fast-light-off" cats because they reach operating temperature quickly) and a larger catalyst mounted downstream near the center of the vehicle.*

5 Be sure to spray the exhaust flange bolt

or stud threads and the nuts with penetrant *well before* trying to break them loose. Exhaust and catalyst fasteners are invariably rusty, so loosening them can be difficult.

6 If you're going to remove the upstream catalyst from a 1994 through 2000 California 2.4L four-cylinder model or from a 1999 or later V6 model, remove the upstream oxygen sensor (see Section 13). Some other models might also have an upstream or downstream oxygen sensor installed in the front or rear end, respectively, of the catalyst housing; if the vehicle on which you're working is so equipped, remove the oxygen sensor(s) before removing the catalyst.

7 Remove the nuts and/or bolts and separate the catalytic converter from the exhaust system **(see illustrations)**.

8 It's a good idea to use new fasteners when installing the catalytic converter and to coat the threads of the new fasteners with anti-seize compound to facilitate removal the next time you have to loosen these fasteners.

9 Installation is otherwise the reverse of removal. Be sure to tighten everything securely.

10 When you're done, run the engine and check for exhaust leaks.

24 Evaporative emissions control (EVAP) system

General description

1 The Evaporative Emissions Control (EVAP) system prevents fuel system vapors from escaping into the atmosphere. On warm days, vapors trapped inside the fuel tank expand until the pressure reaches a certain threshold, at which point a fuel tank pressure control valve opens, allowing the fuel vapors to migrate from the fuel tank to a charcoal canister, where they're stored temporarily. When the conditions are right (engine warmed

23.7f To disconnect the rear end of the downstream catalyst from the exhaust system, remove these two nuts

up, vehicle up to speed, moderate or heavy load on the engine, etc.) the Powertrain Control Module (PCM) turns on the purge control solenoid, which allows fuel vapors to be drawn from the canister into the intake manifold, where they mix with the air/fuel mixture before being consumed in the combustion chambers.

2 The charcoal canister on 1994 through 1998 models is in the engine compartment, mounted on a bracket underneath the battery tray. 1994 through 1997 49-State models use a cylindrical canister; 1994 through 1997 California models and all 1998 models use a rectangular canister. These canisters are easy to replace once the battery and battery tray are removed. On 1999 and later models, the canister is mounted on the rear of the fuel tank. These canisters are a little more difficult to replace because the vehicle must be raised to access the canister. But the canisters on all vehicles are designed to be maintenance-free and should last the life of the vehicle.

3 1994 through 1997 49-State models are equipped with a single purge control solenoid, which is mounted on a bracket on the

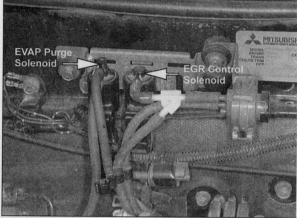

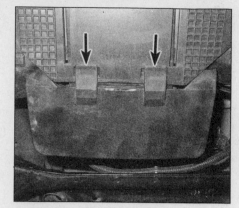

24.16 On 1994 through 1997 49-State models, the EVAP purge control solenoid is located on the firewall; on 1994 through 1996 California models, this is the No. 1 purge control solenoid (No. 2 is on the intake manifold)

24.31 To remove the EVAP system splash shield on 1999 and later models, pry open these two locking tabs and then pull the shield straight back (toward the rear of the vehicle)

firewall. 1994 through 1996 California models are equipped with *two* purge control solenoid valves, the one on the firewall ("No. 1") and another unit ("No. 2"), which is mounted on a bracket on the intake manifold. The purge control solenoids on all these models operate like switches (either they're ON or they're OFF). When the single purge solenoid on 49-State models is activated by the PCM, it meters vapor flow into the intake manifold. The dual purge solenoids on California models work exactly the same way as 49-State units, except that purging is more finely controlled: purge solenoid No. 1 meters smaller amounts of fuel vapor into the manifold when the engine is idling (and warmed up). Purge solenoid No. 2 meters larger amounts of fuel vapor at all other times.

4   1997 California models and all 1998 and later models are equipped with a single "duty-cycle" purge solenoid. This type of solenoid doesn't work like an ON/OFF switch. Instead, it's capable of regulating the flow of fuel vapors from the canister to the intake manifold at a variable and controllable rate that is determined by the PCM. The purge control solenoid on these models is on a mounting bracket located on the intake manifold.

5   1997 California models and all 1998 and later models are equipped with an OBD-II

leak monitoring system. If it detects a leak in the system, it will set a Diagnostic Trouble Code (DTC) in the PCM, which will illuminate the CHECK ENGINE or SERVICE ENGINE SOON/Malfunction Indicator Lamp (MIL) light on the instrument cluster. The most common cause of system pressure loss is a loose or poor sealing fuel filler cap. If the CHECK ENGINE or SERVICE ENGINE SOON light is illuminated, check the fuel filler cap first! Beyond inspecting the fuel filler cap, the EVAP lines and hoses and their connections, diagnosis of the leak monitoring system is beyond the scope of the home mechanic. If the leak monitoring system sets a DTC, have the vehicle EVAP system inspected and repaired by a dealer service department.

6   The most common symptom of a faulty EVAP system is a strong fuel odor (particularly during hot weather). If you smell fuel while driving or (more likely) right after you park the vehicle and turn off the engine, check the fuel filler cap first. Make sure that it's screwed onto the fuel filler neck all the way. If the odor persists on a 1994 through 1998 model, inspect all EVAP hose connections (both in the engine compartment and under the vehicle) and inspect the EVAP canister in the engine compartment. If the odor persists on a 1999 or later model, inspect all

EVAP hoses connections in the engine compartment, then raise the vehicle, place it securely on jackstands and inspect the rest of the EVAP system, most of which is located on the rear part of the fuel tank, or right behind the tank.

Replacement
1994 through 1998 models
Charcoal canister

7   Remove the fuel filler cap to relieve the pressure inside the fuel tank.

8   Remove the battery and the battery tray (see Chapter 5).

9   On California models, disconnect the electrical connector from the EVAP ventilation solenoid.

10   Clearly label and disconnect the vapor hoses from the canister.

11   On 49-State models, unsnap the canister retaining clamp and remove the canister.

12   On California models, disengage the canister mounting tabs from the canister mounting bracket.

13   Installation is the reverse of removal.

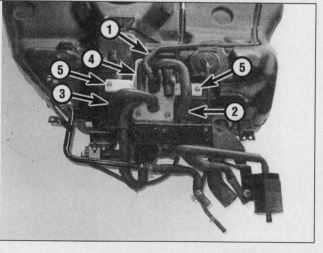

24.33 Removal and installation details for EVAP canister (1999 and later models)

1   Goes to purge solenoid (in engine compartment)
2   Goes to liquid separator
3   Goes to vent solenoid
4   Open hose for vent valve
5   EVAP canister mounting bolts

24.40 Ventilation solenoid (1) and vent (2) valve locations (1999 and later models)

24.41 Disconnect the electrical connector from the ventilation solenoid (1999 and later models)

24.42 Ventilation solenoid hoses (1999 and later models)

1   From charcoal canister
2   Goes to vent valve

24.43 To remove the ventilation solenoid, disconnect this lower vacuum hose and then remove the solenoid retaining nut

Purge control solenoid (1994 through 1997 49-State models) and No. 1 purge control solenoid (1994 through 1996 California models)

Refer to illustration 24.16

14   Remove the fuel filler cap to relieve the pressure inside the fuel tank.
15   Make sure that the ignition key is turned to OFF.
16   Locate the purge control solenoid (1994 through 1997 49-State models) or the No. 1 purge control solenoid (1994 through 1996 California models) on the firewall **(see illustration)**.
17   Disconnect the electrical connector from the purge control solenoid or from the No. 1 purge control solenoid.
18   Clearly label and disconnect the vapor hoses from the purge control solenoid or from the No. 1 purge control solenoid.
19   Detach the purge control solenoid or the No. 1 purge control solenoid from its mounting bracket on the firewall.
20   Installation is the reverse of removal.

Purge control solenoid (1997 California models and all 1998 models) and No. 2 purge control solenoid (1994 through 1996 California models)

21   Remove the fuel filler cap to relieve the pressure inside the fuel tank.
22   Make sure that the ignition key is turned to OFF.
23   Locate the purge control solenoid (1997 California models and all 1998 models) or the No. 2 purge control solenoid (1994 through 1996 California models) on its mounting bracket on the intake manifold.
24   Disconnect the electrical connector from the purge control solenoid or from the No. 2 purge control solenoid.
25   Clearly label and disconnect the vapor hoses from the purge control solenoid or from the No. 2 purge control solenoid.
26   Detach the purge control solenoid or the No. 2 purge control solenoid from its mount-

ing bracket on the intake manifold.
27   Installation is the reverse of removal.

1999 and later models

Charcoal canister

Refer to illustrations 24.31 and 24.33

28   Remove the fuel filler cap to relieve the pressure inside the fuel tank.
29   Make sure that the ignition key is turned to OFF.
30   Raise the vehicle and place it securely on jackstands.
31   Remove the EVAP system splash shield **(see illustration)**.
32   Remove the fuel tank (see Chapter 4).
33   Clearly label the vapor hoses on top of the canister **(see illustration)**, then disconnect them from the canister.
34   Remove the EVAP canister mounting bolts **(see illustration 24.33)**, then remove the canister.
35   Installation is the reverse of removal.

Ventilation solenoid

Refer to illustrations 24.40, 24.41, 24.42 and 24.43

36   Remove the fuel filler cap to relieve the pressure inside the fuel tank.
37   Make sure that the ignition key is turned to OFF.

38   Raise the vehicle and place it securely on jackstands.
39   Remove the EVAP system splash shield **(see illustration 24.31)**.
40   Locate the ventilation solenoid **(see illustration)**.
41   Disconnect the electrical connector from the ventilation solenoid **(see illustration)**.
42   Clearly label the vapor hoses connected to the ventilation solenoid **(see illustration)** then disconnect them.
43   Remove the ventilation solenoid from its mounting bracket **(see illustration)**.
44   Installation is the reverse of removal.

Vent valve

Refer to illustration 24.49

45   Remove the fuel filler cap to relieve the pressure inside the fuel tank.
46   Raise the vehicle and place it securely on jackstands.
47   Remove the EVAP system splash shield **(see illustration 24.31)**.
48   Locate the vent valve **(see illustration 24.40)**.
49   Clearly label the vapor hoses connected to the vent valve **(see illustration)**, disconnect them and then remove the vent valve.
50   Installation is the reverse of removal.

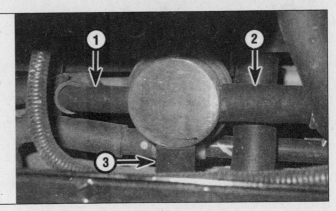

24.49 Vent valve hoses (1999 and later models)

1   Goes to air filter
2   Goes to ventilation solenoid
3   Outlet hose (vents to atmosphere)

24.55 To detach the EVAP ventilation solenoid/vent valve/air filter support bracket, remove these three bolts (1999 and later models)

24.56 Disconnect this hose from the air filter; to detach the air filter from the EVAP ventilation solenoid/vent valve/air filter support bracket, remove this nut (1999 and later models)

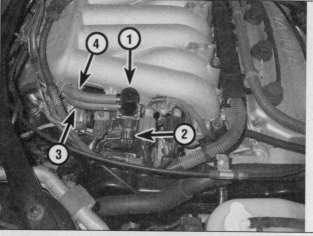

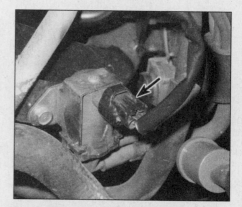

24.60 On V6 models, the purge solenoid is attached to a bracket on the right end of the intake manifold

1 Purge solenoid
2 Solenoid electrical connector
3 Vapor hose
4 Vapor hose

24.61 Disconnect the electrical connector from the purge solenoid (2.4L four-cylinder model shown, V6 models similar)

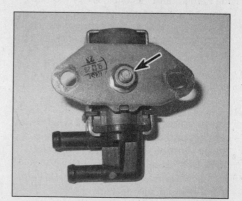

24.62 To detach the purge solenoid mounting bracket, remove these two bolts, then pull the purge solenoid assembly away from the manifold and disconnect the two vapor hoses from the solenoid (2.4L four-cylinder model shown, V6 similar)

24.64 To detach the purge solenoid from its mounting bracket, remove this nut (2.4L four-cylinder model shown, V6 similar)

Air filter

Refer to illustrations 24.55 and 24.56

51 Remove the fuel filler cap to relieve the pressure inside the fuel tank.

52 Raise the vehicle and place it securely on jackstands.

53 Remove the EVAP system splash shield **(see illustration 24.31)**.

54 Locate the air filter by tracing the hose that goes to the air filter **(see illustration 24.49)**.

55 Detach the EVAP ventilation sole-noid/

vent valve/air filter support bracket **(see illustration)** and lower it just enough to access the air filter retaining nut.

56 Disconnect the hose from the air filter **(see illustration)**.

57 Remove the air filter retaining nut (on top of the support bracket, but you should be able to access it once the bracket has been detached and lowered).

58 Installation is the reverse of removal.

Purge solenoid

Refer to illustrations 24.60, 24.61, 24.62 and 24.64

59 Make sure that the ignition key is turned to OFF.

60 On 2.4L models, the purge solenoid is attached to a bracket underneath the intake manifold. To get to it, remove the air intake duct (see Chapter 4). On V6 models, the purge solenoid is attached to the right end of

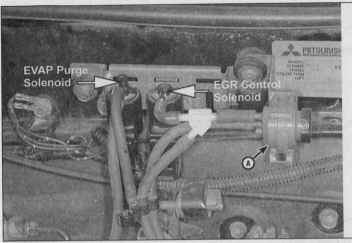

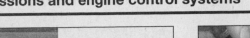

EVAP Purge Solenoid

EGR Control Solenoid

25.6 On 1994 through 1998 models, the EGR solenoid and the vacuum control valve (A) are located on the firewall

25.7 To detach the EGR solenoid from its mounting bracket, insert a screwdriver tip through this slot and release the solenoid retaining tab (1994 through 1998 models)

the intake manifold **(see illustration)**.

61   Disconnect the purge solenoid electrical connector **(see illustration)**.

62   Remove the purge solenoid mounting bracket bolts, then pull the solenoid and its bracket away from the intake manifold and disconnect the two vapor hoses from the solenoid **(see illustration)**.

63   Remove the purge solenoid and its mounting bracket as a single assembly.

64   Separate the purge solenoid from its mounting bracket **(see illustration)**.

65   Installation is the reverse of removal.

---

25   Exhaust Gas Recirculation (EGR) system

25.8a Clearly mark the hoses at the EGR solenoid . . .

25.8b . . . and disconnect the hoses from the solenoid (1994 through 1998 models)

General description

Note: *2004 and later models use only an EGR valve assembly that is electronically controlled by the PCM. No separate solenoid or vacuum control is used.*

1   When the combustion chambers reach about 2500 degrees F., they begin to produce excessive quantities of oxides of nitrogen (NOx). NOx, when combined with unburned hydrocarbons (HC), other volatile organic compounds and sunlight, forms ozone, nitrogen dioxide and nitrogen nitrate, otherwise known as photochemical smog. The Exhaust Gas Recirculation (EGR) system reduces (NOx) by recirculating exhaust gases from the exhaust ports through the EGR valve and back into the intake manifold, from which they're recycled back through the combustion chambers, which lowers the temperature during the combustion process.

2   The EGR system consists of the EGR valve, the EGR solenoid, the vacuum control valve, the Powertrain Control Module (PCM) and several information sensors, including the Crankshaft Position (CKP) sensor, the Engine Coolant Temperature (ECT) sensor, the Volume Air Flow sensor and, on 1994 and 1995 models, an EGR temperature sensor. The EGR valve is mounted on the intake manifold on all models. The EGR solenoid is mounted on the firewall (1994 through 1998

models) or on the intake manifold (1999 through 2003 models). The vacuum control valve is located in the vacuum line that connects the intake manifold to the vacuum line between the solenoid and the EGR valve. On 1994 and 1995 models, the EGR temperature sensor is an integral part of the EGR valve; it cannot be replaced separately.

3   Here's how the EGR system works: The EGR valve is vacuum-controlled, but the PCM-controlled solenoid determines whether the vacuum control valve and its circuit can maintain sufficient vacuum to open the EGR valve or not. When the engine is cold, not yet fully warmed up, idling or at wide-open throttle, the PCM prevents the EGR system from operating by keeping the solenoid turned off (when the solenoid is off, the vacuum control circuit *does not hold a vacuum*). Once the engine is warmed up, the PCM might turn on the solenoid at any time (*except* at idle or during wide-open throttle conditions), which allows the EGR valve to recirculate exhaust gases into the intake manifold (because when the solenoid is on, the vacuum control circuit *maintains* sufficient vacuum to open the EGR valve). The PCM determines when to energize the solenoid in accordance with engine speed (CKP sensor), coolant temperature (ECT sensor) and the volume of air being drawn into the intake manifold (Volume Air Flow sensor).

4   Typically, EGR systems are trouble-free. If

the EGR valve ever fails, it will do so while it's either closed or open. If the EGR valve is closed when it fails the EGR system will no longer work, but there will be no obvious symptom, other than the fact that the engine might run a little hotter under a load on a hot day (acceleration, passing, going up a hill or pulling a trailer). And when your vehicle is subjected to a biennial "loaded-mode" (dynamometer-type) smog test, the EGR system will fail. If the EGR valve is open when it fails, the symptom will be obvious. Exhaust gases metered into the combustion chambers during idle will cause the engine to run roughly and might even cause it to run so roughly that it stalls.

Component replacement
EGR solenoid

5   Make sure that the ignition key is turned to OFF.

1994 through 1998 models

Refer to illustrations 25.6, 25.7, 25.8a, 25.8b and 25.9

6   The EGR solenoid **(see illustration)** is located on the firewall.

7   To detach the EGR solenoid from its retaining bracket, release the retaining tab **(see illustration)**.

8   Clearly label the vacuum hoses, then disconnect them from the EGR solenoid **(see illustrations)**.

25.9 Disconnect the electrical connector and remove the solenoid (1994 through 1998 models)

25.11a On 1999 through 2003 2.4L models, the EGR solenoid (A) is located below and behind the intake manifold (this view is from underneath the engine, looking straight up); the vacuum control valve (B) is also located here

25.11b On 3.0L V6 models, the EGR solenoid (1) is located at the right end of the intake manifold; the vacuum control valve (2) is right next to the solenoid

9   Disconnect the electrical connector from the EGR solenoid (**see illustration**) and remove the solenoid.
10   Installation is the reverse of removal.

1999 through 2003 models

Refer to illustrations 25.11a, 25.11b, 25.12 and 25.15

11   On 2.4L models, the EGR solenoid is located below and behind the intake manifold (**see illustration**). On V6 models, the EGR solenoid is located at the right end of the intake manifold (**see illustration**).
12   Disconnect the electrical connector from the EGR solenoid (**see illustration**).
13   Clearly label and disconnect the upper vacuum hose from the EGR solenoid (**see illustration 25.12**).
14   Raise the front end of the vehicle and place it securely on jackstands.

15   Label and disconnect the lower vacuum hose from the EGR solenoid (**see illustration**).
16   Remove the EGR solenoid retaining nut (**see illustration 25.15**) and remove the solenoid.
17   Installation is the reverse of removal.

Vacuum control valve

Refer to illustration 25.19

18   The vacuum control valve is located on the firewall (**see illustration 25.6**) on 1994 through 1998 models. On 1999 and later 2.4L models, it's located behind and below the intake manifold, near the EGR solenoid (**see illustration 25.11a**). On 3.0L V6 models, the vacuum control valve is located at the right end of the intake manifold, next to the EGR solenoid (**see illustration 25.11b**).
19   To replace the vacuum control valve, clearly label the vacuum hoses (**see illustration**), dis-

connect them, then spread the re-taining tangs apart and pull out the vacuum control valve.
20   Installation is the reverse of removal.

EGR valve

Refer to illustration 25.21a, 25.21b, 25.23a and 25.23b

21   On 2003 and earlier models, disconnect the vacuum hose(s) from the EGR valve (**see illustrations**).
22   On 2004 and later four-cylinder models, disconnect all interfering wiring at the upper engine harness. On all 2004 and later engines, disconnect the wiring from the EGR valve.
23   Remove the EGR valve mounting bolts (**see illustrations**).
24   Remove the EGR valve and remove and discard the old EGR valve gasket.
25   Clean the gasket surfaces of the EGR valve and the intake manifold. If you're going

25.12 Disconnect the electrical connector and the upper vacuum hose from the EGR solenoid (1999 through 2003 2.4L model shown)

25.15 Disconnect the lower vacuum hose from the EGR solenoid, then remove the retaining nut and remove the solenoid (1999 through 2003 2.4L model shown)

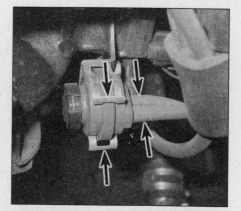

25.19 To replace a vacuum control valve, simply disconnect the vacuum hoses (be sure to label them first so they don't get accidentally switched during reassembly), then pry apart the retainer ends and pull out the vacuum control valve (1999 through 2003 2.4L model shown, other models similar)

25.21a On 1999 and later 2.4L models, disconnect these three hoses from the EGR valve

25.21b To detach the EGR valve from the intake manifold on a 3.0L V6 engine, disconnect the vacuum hose and remove the two mounting bolts (one bolt not visible in this photo)

to reuse the old EGR valve, clean the gasket mating surface of the valve mounting flange and, if necessary, remove any carbon build-up that might be present. If carbon build-up is excessive, replace the EGR valve.

26 Using a new gasket, install the EGR valve and tighten the bolts securely.

27 Reconnect the vacuum hose to the EGR valve.

26 Positive Crankcase Ventilation (PCV) system

Refer to illustrations 26.1a and 26.1b

1 The Positive Crankcase Ventilation (PCV) system **(see illustrations)** reduces hydrocarbon emissions by scavenging crankcase vapors. It does this by circulating fresh air from the air filter housing or air intake manifold to the crankcase, where it mixes with blow-by gases and from which it's routed through a PCV valve to the intake manifold.

2 The main components of the PCV system are a fresh air hose connecting ambient atmospheric air (usually the air filter housing or the intake manifold) to the crankcase (via a pipe on the valve cover), the PCV valve (usually located at the valve cover) and the hose connecting the PCV valve to an area of the intake manifold downstream from the throttle plate. Refer to Chapter 1 for more detailed information regarding the locations of the PCV valve on specific models.

3 To maintain idle quality, the PCV valve restricts the flow when the intake manifold vacuum is high. If abnormal operating conditions (such as piston ring problems) arise, the system is designed to allow excessive amounts of blow-by gases to flow back through the crankcase vent tube into the air cleaner to be consumed by normal combustion.

4 Checking and replacement of the PCV valve is covered in Chapter 1.

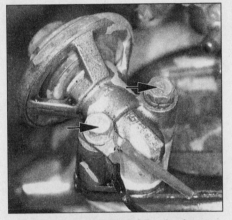

25.23a To detach the EGR valve from a 1994 through 1998 2.4L model, remove these two bolts

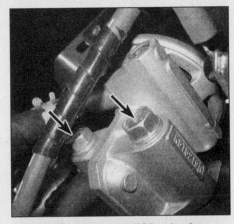

25.23b To detach the EGR valve from a 1999 or later 2.4L model, remove these two bolts

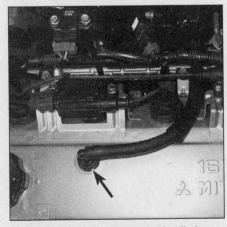

26.1a Positive Crankcase Ventilation (PCV) valve location (1999 and later 2.4L models)

26.1b Positive Crankcase Ventilation (PCV) valve location (V6 models)

Notes

Chapter 7 Part A
Manual transaxle

Contents

Specifications

Torque specifications	Ft-lbs	Nm
Centermember support bolts		
1994 through 1998 models		
Front mounting bolts	65	86
Rear mounting bolts	55	74
1999 and 2000 models		
Front mounting bolts	69	93
Rear mounting bolts	55	74
Transaxle-to-engine bolts		
Starter mounting bolts	22	30
All other bolts	35	48

1   General information

The vehicles covered in this manual are equipped with either a 5-speed manual, or a 4-speed or 5-speed automatic transaxle. Information on the manual transaxles are included in this Part of Chapter 7. Service procedures for the automatic transaxles are contained in Chapter 7, Part B.

The manual transaxle is a compact, two-piece, lightweight aluminum alloy housing containing both the transmission and differential assemblies.

Because of the complexity, unavailability of replacement parts and special tools necessary, internal repair procedures for the manual transaxle are beyond the scope of this manual. The bulk of information in this Chapter is devoted to removal and installation procedures.

2.9 Remove the cotter pins from the selector and shift cables, and slide the cable ends off of the lever pins

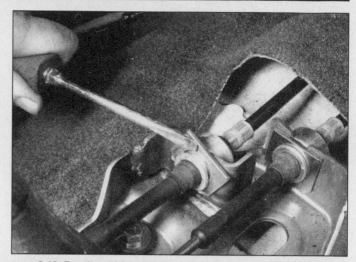

2.10 Pry the cable retaining clips out with a screwdriver

2.11 Remove the forward retainer bolts, detach the retainer from the firewall and pull the cable grommet through the firewall

2.12 Remove the cotter pins and the retainer clips

2 Shift cables - removal and installation

Removal

1   Disconnect the cable from the negative battery terminal (see Chapter 5).

2   Working inside the vehicle, unscrew the gearshift knob and remove the boot assembly. **Note:** *On 1999 and 2000 models, it will be necessary to remove the spring washer and nut from the lever to remove the boot assembly.*

3   Remove the center console and the center trim bezel (see Chapter 11).

1994 through 1998 models

4   Remove the PCM (see Chapter 6).

5   Remove the fuel pump relay module (California models only) (see Chapter 4).

1999 and 2000 models

6   Remove the heater/air conditioning control assembly from the passenger compartment (see Chapter 3).

All models

Refer to illustrations 2.9, 2.10, 2.11 and 2.12

7   Remove the air filter housing assembly (see Chapter 4).

8   If necessary, remove the battery and battery tray (see Chapter 5).

9   Remove the cotter pins from the shift and selector cables, and slide the cables off of the lever ends **(see illustration)**. **Note:** *1999 and 2000 models are equipped with a snap fit end on the select cable.*

10   Remove both cable retaining clips and remove the cables from the bracket **(see illustration)**.

11   At the firewall remove the forward retainer bolts **(see illustration)**.

12   At the transaxle, remove the cotter pins from the select and shift cables, and remove the cable retaining clips **(see illustration)**.

13   Pry the cable grommet out of the firewall and pull the cables through the firewall from the engine compartment side and remove the cable assembly from the vehicle.

Installation

14   Route the cables into place and install the forward retainer bolts.

15   Install new cable retaining clips and make sure they are properly seated in the cable grooves.

16   Place the transaxle levers in the neutral position (if they're not already there). Also place the shift lever in the passenger compartment in the neutral position.

17   Connect the select cable to the select lever in the passenger compartment so the flange side of the bushing is downward on the select lever.

18   When connecting the shift cable to the shift lever in the passenger compartment, make sure the slit in the bushing is straight up or straight down.

19   Shift the transaxle into all gear positions to make sure the cable is functioning properly. Readjust if necessary.

3 Shift lever - removal and installation

1   Disconnect the cable from the negative battery terminal (see Chapter 5).
2   Remove the center console assembly (see Chapter 11).
3   Disconnect the select and shift cables (see Section 2).
4   Unbolt the shift lever bracket bolts and remove the shift lever.
5   Installation is the reverse of removal.

4 Back-up light switch -replacement

Refer to illustration 4.1
1   The back-up light switch is located on top of the transaxle **(see illustration)**.
2   Disconnect the electrical connector from the back-up light switch.
3   Unscrew the switch from the case.
4   Wrap the threads of the new switch with Teflon tape, or equivalent.
5   Screw in the new switch and tighten it securely.
6   Connect the electrical connector.
7   Check the operation of the back-up lights.

5 Transaxle mounts - check and replacement

Refer to illustrations 5.3a and 5.3b
1   Insert a large screwdriver or prybar between the mount and the transaxle and pry up.
2   The transaxle should not move excessively away from the mount. If it does, replace the mount.
3   To replace a mount, support the transaxle with a jack, remove the nuts and bolts and remove the mount **(see illustrations)**. It may be necessary to raise the transaxle slightly to provide enough clear-

4.1 The back-up light switch is located on top of the transaxle

ance to remove the mount.
4   Installation is the reverse of removal.

6 Manual transaxle - removal and installation

Removal

1   Open the hood and place protective covers on the front fenders and cowl. Special fender covers are available, but an old bed-spread or blankets will also work.
2   Disconnect both cables from the battery terminals (see Chapter 5). **Caution:** *Always disconnect the negative cable first and hook it up last or the battery may be shorted by the tool being used to loosen the cable clamps.*
3   Remove the air filter housing (see Chapter 4).
4   Remove the battery and the battery tray (see Chapter 5).
5   Drain the transaxle oil (see Chapter 1).
6   Disconnect the shift cables from the transaxle and bracket (see Section 2).
7   Disconnect the vehicle speed sensor (see Chapter 6).
8   Disconnect the harness connector from the back-up light switch (see Section 4).
9   Remove the starter (see Chapter 5).
10   Remove the clutch release cylinder (see Chapter 8).

11   Working in the engine compartment, remove the transaxle mounting bracket.
12   Remove the transaxle-to-engine upper bolts.
13   Loosen the driveaxle/hub nuts (see Chapter 8) and front wheel lug nuts.
14   Raise the vehicle and place it securely on jackstands. Remove both front wheels and splash shields.
15   Support the engine from above with a hoist, or place a floor jack under the oil pan. Place a wood block on the jack head to spread the load on the oil pan.
16   Remove the transaxle mount through-bolt and bracket.
17   Remove the crossmember rear roll stopper through-bolt.
18   Remove the driveaxles (see Chapter 8).
19   If equipped, remove the two supports at the transaxle lower inspection cover.
20   Remove the lower inspection cover.
21   Remove any exhaust components that will interfere with transaxle removal (see Chapter 4).
22   Disconnect the stabilizer bar link from the transaxle side of the vehicle (see Chapter 10).
23   Disconnect the vehicle speed sensor (VSS) electrical connector on ABS models (see Chapter 6) and remove the front brake hose clamp behind the left wheel.
24   Disconnect the tie-rod end and the lower

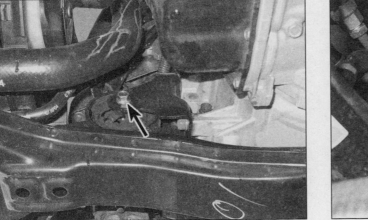

5.3a Front roll stopper through-bolt

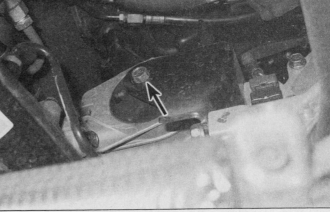

5.3b Rear roll stopper through-bolt

control arm balljoint from the transaxle side of the vehicle (see Chapter 10). **Note:** *On 1994 through 1998 models, disconnect the damper fork and the compression lower arm from the lower lateral arm (see Chapter 10).*

25   Support the transaxle with a transmission jack, if available, or use a floor jack. Secure the transaxle to the jack using straps or chains so it doesn't fall off during removal.

26   Remove the front roll stopper through-bolt.

27   Remove the bolts from the centermember assembly, the rear bracket (1994 through 1998 models) and remove the assembly from below the engine compartment.

28   Make a final check that all wires, hoses and brackets have been disconnected from the transaxle, then with the engine properly supported, remove upper transaxle mount, and lower the engine/transaxle assembly.

29   Remove the lower transaxle clutch housing-to-engine bolts. Make sure all clutch housing-to-engine bolts are removed.

30   Carefully lower the transaxle and remove it from under the vehicle. Make sure you keep the transaxle level. **Note:** *If necessary, have someone help with the removal procedure.*

Installation

31   Installation of the transaxle is the reverse of the removal procedure, but note the fol-

lowing points:

a) *Check the mounts and replace them if necessary.*

b) *Tighten all fasteners securely, or to the specified torque where given.*

c) *The front and rear roll stoppers should be temporarily tightened during installation, and then fully tightened after the vehicle is on the ground with the full weight of the engine on the body. Be sure the arrow on the roll stopper points toward the engine (1999 and 2000 models).*

d) *Refill the transaxle to the specified level (see Chapter 1).*

7   Manual transaxle overhaul - general information

1   Overhauling a manual transaxle unit is a difficult and involved job for the home mechanic. In addition to dismantling and reassembling many small parts, clearances must be precisely measured and, if necessary, changed by selecting shims and spacers. Internal transaxle components are also often difficult to obtain and in many instances, extremely expensive. Because of this, if the transaxle develops a fault or

becomes noisy, the best course of action is to have the unit overhauled by a transmission specialist or to obtain an exchange reconditioned unit.

2   Nevertheless, it is not impossible for the more experienced mechanic to overhaul the transaxle if the special tools are available and the job is carried out in a deliberate step-by-step manner, to ensure that nothing is overlooked.

3   The tools necessary for an overhaul include internal and external snap-ring pliers, bearing pullers, a slide hammer, a set of pin punches, a dial test indicator and possibly a hydraulic press. In addition, a large, sturdy workbench and a vise will be required.

4   During dismantling of the transaxle, make careful notes of how each component is fitted to make reassembly easier and accurate.

5   Before disassembling the transaxle, it will help if you have some idea of where the problem lies. Certain problems can be closely related to specific areas in the transaxle which can make component examination and replacement easier. Refer to the *Troubleshooting* Section in this manual for more information.

Chapter 7 Part B
Automatic transaxle

Contents

Specifications

Torque specifications

Torque specifications	Ft-lbs	Nm
Torque converter-to-driveplate bolts		
1994 through 1998 models	35	47
1999 and later models	37	49
Transaxle-to-engine bolts		
1994 through 1998 models		
Starter mounting bolts	22	30
All other bolts	35	48
1999 and later models		
Starter mounting bolts	22	30
All other bolts		
Four cylinder models	35	48
V6 models		
Front, top bolt	65	88
All other bolts	55	74

1   General information

All information on the automatic transaxle is included in this Part of Chapter 7. Information for the manual transaxle can be found in Part A of this Chapter.

The automatic transaxle and the differential are housed in a compact, lightweight, two-piece aluminum alloy housing.

Operation of the transaxle is controlled electronically by the Transmission Control Module (TCM) which is the "brain" of the transaxle. The TCM monitors engine and transaxle operating parameters through numerous sensors and generates output signals to various relays and solenoids to regulate hydraulic pressures, optimize driveability, provide efficient torque management and maintain maximum fuel economy. 1994 through 1998 models are equipped with a separate TCM mounted under the center console, while 1999 and later models are equipped with the transaxle control software built into the Powertrain Control Module (PCM). The TCM is part of the On-Board Diagnostic system. For more information see Chapter 6. **Note:** *If the power has been inter-*rupted (battery disconnected or has failed) the transaxle will shift roughly for the first few gear progressions while the TCM relearns the engine and transaxle parameters.

Because of the complexity of the automatic transaxles and the specialized equipment necessary to perform most service operations, this Chapter contains only those procedures related to general diagnosis, routine maintenance, adjustment and removal and installation.

If the transaxle requires major repair work, it should be left to a dealer service department or an automotive or transmission repair shop. Once properly diagnosed you can, however, remove and install the transaxle yourself and save the expense, even if the repair work is done by a transmission shop.

2   Diagnosis - general

1   Automatic transaxle malfunctions may be caused by five general conditions:

a) *Poor engine performance*
b) *Improper adjustments*
c) *Hydraulic malfunctions*
d) *Mechanical malfunctions*
e) *Malfunctions in the computer or its signal network*

2   Diagnosis of these problems should always begin with a check of the easily repaired items: fluid level and condition (see Chapter 1), shift cable adjustment and shift lever installation. Next, perform a road test to determine if the problem has been corrected or if more diagnosis is necessary. If the problem persists after the preliminary tests and corrections are completed, additional diagnosis should be performed by a dealer service department or other qualified transmission repair shop. Refer to the *Troubleshooting* section at the front of this manual for information on symptoms of transaxle problems.

Preliminary checks

3   Drive the vehicle to warm the transaxle to normal operating temperature.
4   Check the fluid level as described in Chapter 1:

a) *If the fluid level is unusually low, add enough fluid to bring the level within the designated area of the dipstick, then check for external leaks (see following).*

b) *If the fluid level is abnormally high, drain off the excess, then check the drained fluid for contamination by coolant. The presence of engine coolant in the automatic transmission fluid indicates that a failure has occurred in the internal radiator oil cooler walls that separate the coolant from the transmission fluid (see Chapter 3).*

c) *If the fluid is foaming, drain it and refill the transaxle, then check for coolant in the fluid, or a high fluid level.*

5   Check the engine idle speed. **Note:** *If the engine is malfunctioning, do not proceed with the preliminary checks until it has been repaired and runs normally.*

6   Check and adjust the shift cable, if necessary (see Section 4).

7   If hard shifting is experienced, inspect the shift cable under the center console and at the manual lever on the transaxle (see Section 4).

Fluid leak diagnosis

8   Most fluid leaks are easy to locate visually. Repair usually consists of replacing a seal or gasket. If a leak is difficult to find, the following procedure may help.

9   Identify the fluid. Make sure it's transmission fluid and not engine oil or brake fluid (automatic transmission fluid is a deep red color).

10   Try to pinpoint the source of the leak. Drive the vehicle several miles, then park it over a large sheet of cardboard. After a minute or two, you should be able to locate the leak by determining the source of the fluid dripping onto the cardboard.

11   Make a careful visual inspection of the suspected component and the area immediately around it. Pay particular attention to gasket mating surfaces. A mirror is often helpful for finding leaks in areas that are hard to see.

12   If the leak still cannot be found, clean the suspected area thoroughly with a degreaser or solvent, then dry it thoroughly.

13   Drive the vehicle for several miles at normal operating temperature and varying speeds. After driving the vehicle, visually inspect the suspected component again.

14   Once the leak has been located, the cause must be determined before it can be properly repaired. If a gasket is replaced but the sealing flange is bent, the new gasket will not stop the leak. The bent flange must be straightened.

15   Before attempting to repair a leak, check to make sure that the following conditions are corrected or they may cause another leak. **Note:** *Some of the following conditions cannot be fixed without highly specialized tools and expertise. Such problems must be referred to a qualified transmission shop or a dealer service department.*

Gasket leaks

16   Check the pan periodically. Make sure the bolts are tight, no bolts are missing, the gasket is in good condition and the pan is flat. Dents in the pan may indicate damage to the valve body inside.

17   If the pan gasket is leaking, the fluid

3.3 Using a large screwdriver or prybar, carefully pry the oil seal out of the transaxle (you may need to obtain a special seal removal tool - available at most auto parts stores - to do the job)

level or the fluid pressure may be too high, the vent may be plugged, the pan bolts may be too tight, the pan sealing flange may be warped, the sealing surface of the transaxle housing may be damaged, the gasket may be damaged or the transaxle casting may be cracked or porous. If sealant instead of gasket material has been used to form a seal between the pan and the transaxle housing, it may be the wrong type of sealant.

Seal leaks

18   If a transaxle seal is leaking, the fluid level or pressure may be too high, the vent may be plugged, the seal bore may be damaged, the seal itself may be damaged or improperly installed, the surface of the shaft protruding through the seal may be damaged or a loose bearing may be causing excessive shaft movement.

19   Make sure the dipstick tube seal is in good condition and the tube is properly seated. Periodically check the area around the sensors for leakage. If transmission fluid is evident, check the seals for damage.

Case leaks

20   If the case itself appears to be leaking, the casting is porous and will have to be repaired or replaced.

21   Make sure the oil cooler hose fittings are tight and in good condition.

Fluid comes out vent pipe or fill tube

22   If this condition occurs the possible causes are, the transaxle is overfilled, there is coolant in the fluid, the case is porous, the dipstick is incorrect, the vent is plugged or the drain-back holes are plugged.

---

3   Driveaxle oil seals - replacement

Refer to illustration 3.3 and 3.5

1   The driveaxle oil seals are located on the

3.5 Using a seal installer, drive the new seal squarely into the bore and make sure that it's completely seated

sides of the transaxle, where the inner ends of the driveaxles are splined into the differential side gears. If you suspect that a driveaxle oil seal is leaking, raise the vehicle and support it securely on jackstands. If the seal is leaking, you'll see lubricant on the side of the transaxle, below the seal.

2   Remove the driveaxle (see Chapter 8).

3   Using a screwdriver or prybar, carefully pry the oil seal out of the transaxle bore **(see illustration)**. **Note:** *Some driveaxle oil seals may require a slide hammer equipped with a hook-type tool for removal.*

4   If the oil seal cannot be removed with a screwdriver or prybar, a special oil seal removal tool, available at auto parts stores, will be required.

5   Using a seal installer, install the new oil seal. Drive it into the bore squarely until it bottoms.**(see illustration)**.

6   Install the driveaxle (see Chapter 8).

---

4   Shift cable - removal, installation and adjustment

Warning: *These models have airbags. Always disable the airbag system before working in the vicinity of any airbag system component to avoid the possibility of accidental deployment of the airbag, which could cause personal injury (see Chapter 12).*

1   Raise the hood and place a blanket over the fender to protect it.

2   Disconnect the cable from the negative battery terminal (see Chapter 5).

3   Remove the air filter housing (see Chapter 4).

4   Remove the trim panels from below the dash (see Chapter 11).

Removal

1994 through 1998 models

Refer to illustrations 4.9 and 4.10

5   Remove the center console (see Chapter 11).

6   Working inside the vehicle, remove the

4.9 Remove the cotter pin and pull the
cable off of the lever

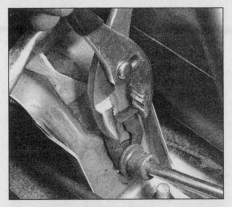

4.10 Use pliers to remove the shift cable
retaining clip

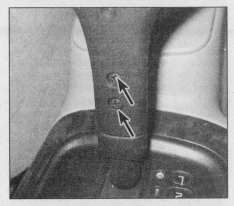

4.14 Remove the set screws and separate
the shift knob from the lever

4.18 Use a screwdriver to pry the shift cable from the select lever

4.19 Press the locking tabs and push the shift cable through the
console (metal bracket)

4.23 Remove the shift cable
adjustment nut

Powertrain Control Module (PCM) (see Chapter 6).

7   Remove the fuel pump relay (California models only) (see Chapter 4).

8   Remove the Transmission Control Module (TCM) (see Section 6) and the TCM bracket.

9   Remove the cotter pin that attaches the shift cable to the shift lever (see illustration).

10   Using a pair of pliers, remove the shift cable retaining clip (see illustration).

11   Working under the dash, remove the fasteners that attach the cable grommet at the firewall.

12   Working inside the engine compartment, remove the shift cable nut from the lever, the clip from the bracket and separate the shift cable from the transaxle.

13   Remove the shift cables from the vehicle.

1999 and later models

Refer to illustrations 4.14, 4.18, 4.19 and 4.23

Note 1: The shift cable replacement procedure on 1999 and later models requires the heater control unit be removed from the dash area. The airbags, the instrument panel and the heater control unit all must be removed to install the new shift cable through the dash area into the engine compartment. Refer to Chapter 3 for heater core/heater control unit information before attempting to change the shift cable.

Note 2: If the power has been interrupted (battery disconnected or has failed) the transaxle will shift roughly for the first few gear progressions while the PCM relearns the engine and transaxle parameters.

14   Working inside the vehicle, remove the shift knob set screw and remove the knob from the lever (see illustration).

15   Remove the center console (see Chapter 11).

16   Remove the shift trim bezel screws and the bezel.

17   Remove the gearshift indicator lamp from the shift trim bezel.

18   Remove the shift cable from the select lever (see illustration).

19   Remove the shift cable at the bracket (see illustration).

20   Remove the heater core/heater control unit (see Chapter 3).

21   Working under the dash, remove the fasteners that attach the cable grommet at the firewall.

22   Remove the battery and the battery tray (see Chapter 5).

23   Working in the engine compartment, disconnect the shift cable from the transaxle (see illustration).

24   Disconnect the shift cable from the bracket.

25   Remove the shift cables from the vehicle.

Installation and adjustment

26   Installation is the reverse of removal.

27   Place the shifter (passenger compartment) and the manual control lever (engine compartment) in the Neutral position. Attach the new shift cable to the shift lever.

28   Adjust the shift cable (see Chapter 6).

Note: The shift cable adjustment is included with the Park/Neutral Position switch adjustment in Chapter 6.

29   Verify that the shifter operates properly and the transaxle end of the cable functions in the range which corresponds to each position of the shift lever.

5   Shift interlock cable - removal, installation and adjustment

Warning: *These models have airbags. Always disable the airbag system before working in the vicinity of any airbag system component to avoid the possibility of accidental deployment of the airbag, which could cause personal injury (see Chapter 12).*

Removal

Refer to illustrations 5.8, 5.9, 5.10a, 5.10b and 5.11

Note 1: *The key interlock cable slides into the housing behind the lock cylinder and attaches to the shift lever base. The floor-shift interlock system is adjusted by a nut at the shift lever assembly. If the system must be adjusted (but not replaced), adjust it as described in Steps 21 through 23.*

Note 2: *These models use two cables in the shift interlock system. The shift interlock cable connects the brake pedal to the shift lever, and the key interlock cable connects the shift lever to the ignition key lock cylinder.*

1   Raise the hood and place a blanket over the fender to protect it.

2   Disconnect the cable from the negative battery terminal (see Chapter 5).

3   Remove the trim panels from below the dash (see Chapter 11).

4   Remove the shift knob (see Section 4).

5   Remove the center console (see Chapter 11).

6   Remove the steering column covers (see Chapter 12).

7   On 1994 through 1998 models, remove the hood release lever (see Chapter 12).

8   Remove the key and/or shift interlock cable from the shift lever **(see illustration)**.

9   Remove the cable housing from the shift lever base **(see illustration)**.

10   At the ignition key lock cylinder, squeeze the lock tabs on the interlock cable cover **(see illustration)** and remove the cable out of the slider **(see illustration)**.

11   At the shift lever base, remove the shift lock cable assembly **(see illustration)**.

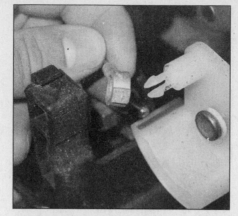

5.8 Separate the key shift interlock cable end from the shift lever

12   At the brake pedal, disconnect the cotter pin and remove the shift interlock cable.

Installation

Refer to illustrations 5.15 and 5.19

13   Route the key interlock cable from the ignition key lock cylinder, below the steering column and down to the shift lever base. Route the shift interlock cable from the shift lever to the brake pedal. Connect the cable eye to the brake pedal and install a new cotter pin.

14   Position the selector lever in Park.

15   At the shift lever base, tighten the shift lock cable in position with the end of the shift interlock cable above the red marking **(see illustration)**.

16   At the ignition key lock cylinder, turn the ignition key to the LOCK position and install the shift interlock cable.

17   At the shift lever base, install the key interlock cable onto the lock cam.

18   Install the spring and washer onto the shift interlock cable.

19   While pushing the cable coupling toward direction A, tighten the nut to fasten the shift interlock cable **(see illustration)**.

20   The remainder of installation is the reverse of removal.

5.9 Remove the nut and separate the cable housing from the shift lever base

Adjustment

21   Remove the center console (see Chapter 11).

22   With the shift lever in the Park position, the end of the shift lock cable should be positioned directly above the red marking **(see illustration 5.15)**. If not, loosen the shift lock cable locknut, reposition the cable as necessary and tighten the locknut.

23   Loosen the nut on the key interlock cable. Gently push the cable coupling toward direction A, then tighten the nut to fasten the shift interlock cable **(see illustration 5.19)**.

6   Transaxle oil cooler - removal and installation

Note: *1999 through 2003 models do not use an oil cooler.*

Removal

1994 through 1998 models

1   Disconnect both cables from the battery terminals (see Chapter 5). **Caution:** *Always disconnect the negative cable first and hook it up last or the battery may be*

5.10a Squeeze the lock tabs and lift the cover off the ignition switch housing

5.10b Remove the cable end from the slider

5.11 Remove the nut and separate the shift lock cable from the shift lever base

5.15 Position the shift interlock cable directly above the red marking

5.19 While pushing the key interlock cable coupling in the direction of the arrow, tighten the nut to fasten the shift interlock cable

shorted by the tool being used to loosen the cable clamps.

2   Remove the battery and the battery tray (see Chapter 5).

3   Drain the transaxle fluid (see Chapter 1).

4   Remove the front bumper (see Chapter 11).

5   Disconnect the transaxle fluid lines from the transaxle cooler. Be sure to place a pan below to catch any fluid that spills.

6   Remove the transaxle oil cooler mounting bolts.

7   Remove the transaxle cooler from the engine compartment.

2004 and later models

Four-cylinder models

8   Disconnect the cable from the negative battery terminal (see Chapter 5).

9   Drain the engine coolant (see Chapter 1).

10   Refer to Chapter 4 and remove the intake air duct.

11   Disconnect the transmission fluid and coolant hoses from the cooler unit. Plug the ends to avoid contamination.

12   Unbolt the cooler bracket and remove the assembly. Separate the cooler from its bracket if it needs to be replaced.

V6 models

Note: On 2004 and 2005 models, the cooler is an integral part of the radiator. The following procedure applies only to 2006 and later vehicles that use a separate heat exchanger/radiator to cool the transmission fluid.

13   Raise the vehicle and support it securely on jackstands. Remove the left lower engine splash shield

14   Refer to Chapter 4 and remove the intake air duct.

15   Remove the front bumper (see Chapter 11).

16   Disconnect both transmission fluid hoses from the cooler.

17   Remove the support bracket from the cooler.

18   Move the power steering cooler tubes

and the air deflector panel if necessary for clearance.

19   Remove the transmission fluid cooler.

Installation

20   Be sure to check all the hoses for cracks or damage. Replace the transaxle lines if necessary.

21   Installation is the reverse of removal.

22   Refill the transaxle with fluid (see Chapter 1).

23   Start the engine and check for leaks.

7   Transmission Control Module (TCM) (1994 through 1998 models) - removal and installation

Warning: These models have airbags. Always disable the airbag system before working in the vicinity of any airbag system component to avoid the possibility of accidental deployment of the airbag, which could cause personal injury (see Chapter 12).

Caution: The TCM is an Electro-Static Discharge (ESD) sensitive electronic device, meaning a static electricity discharge from your body could possibly damage electrical components. Make sure to properly ground yourself and the TCM before handling it. Avoid touching the electrical terminals of the TCM unless absolutely necessary.

Note: Do not interchange TCM's from different year vehicles. After replacing a TCM take the vehicle to your local dealer service department or other qualified transmission shop to have the TCM calibrated for your vehicle.

Removal

1   Disconnect the cable from the negative battery terminal (see Chapter 5).

2   Remove the trim panels from below the dash (see Chapter 11).

3   Remove the center console (see Chapter 11).

4   Remove the center trim bezel (see Chap-

ter 11).

5   Detach the electrical connector from the TCM. **Note:** The transaxle control module is located below the PCM (see Chapter 6) and the fuel pump relay (see Chapter 4).

6   Remove the mounting screws and withdraw the TCM from the vehicle.

Installation

7   Installation is the reverse of removal.

8   Automatic transaxle - removal and installation

Removal

Refer to illustrations 8.16, 8.18, 8.27a and 8.27b

1   Open the hood and place protective covers on the front fenders and cowl. Special fender covers are available, but an old bedspread or blankets will also work.

2   Disconnect both cables from the battery terminals (see Chapter 5). **Caution:** Always disconnect the negative cable first and hook it up last or the battery may be shorted by the tool being used to loosen the cable clamps.

3   Remove the air filter housing (see Chapter 4). On 2004 and later models, remove the strut tower reinforcement bar.

4   Remove the battery and the battery tray (see Chapter 5).

5   Drain the transaxle fluid (see Chapter 1). On 2004 and later models, remove the upper radiator hose (see Chapter 1).

6   Disconnect the shift cables from the transaxle and bracket (see Section 4).

7   Disconnect the Park/Neutral position switch (see Chapter 6).

8   Clearly label, then unplug, all electrical connectors. **Note:** 1999 and later models are equipped with electronic solenoids that control transaxle shift functions. Be sure to label each connector correctly.

9   Remove the transaxle dipstick tube. On 2004 and later V6 models, remove the upper intake manifold (see Chapter 2B). Also disconnect the oxygen sensor wiring and remove the engine oil dipstick if it interferes.

10   Loosen the hose clamps and disconnect the oil cooler hoses from the transaxle. Plug the hoses to prevent contamination and leaks.

11   Loosen the wheel lug nuts, raise the vehicle and support it securely on jackstands. Remove the wheels. Remove the engine lower splash shield.

12   Remove the starter motor (see Chapter 5).

13   Support the engine from above with a hoist or place a jack and a block of wood under the oil pan to spread the load.

14   Support the transaxle with a transmission jack, if available, or with a floor jack. Safety chains will help steady the transaxle on the jack. On 2004 and later models, remove the PCM.

15   Remove the transaxle mount throughbolt and bracket.

8.16 Remove the through-bolt from the rear roll stopper

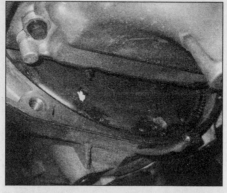

8.18 Before removing the driveplate-to-torque converter bolts, find a hole in the driveplate and match-mark the driveplate to the torque converter

8.27a Remove the bolts from the front . . .

8.27b . . . and from the rear of the centermember

16   Remove the crossmember rear roll stop-per through-bolt **(see illustration)**.
17   Remove the torque converter cover.
18   Mark the relationship of the torque converter to the driveplate so they can be installed in the same position **(see illustration)**.
19   Remove all three torque converter-to-driveplate bolts. Turn the crankshaft 120-degrees at a time for access to each bolt. After all three bolts are removed, push the torque converter into the bellhousing so it doesn't stay with the engine when the transaxle is removed.
20   Remove the upper transaxle-to-engine bolts.
21   Remove any exhaust components that will interfere with transaxle removal (see Chapter 4).
22   Remove both driveaxle assemblies (see Chapter 8).
23   Remove the remaining transaxle mounting bolts.
24   Disconnect the stabilizer link from the transaxle side of the vehicle (see Chapter 10).
25   Disconnect the wheel speed sensor electrical connector on ABS models (see Chapter 9) and remove the front brake hose clamp behind the wheel on the transaxle side.
26   Disconnect the tie-rod end and the lower control arm ball joint from the transaxle side of the vehicle (see Chapter 10). **Note:** *On 1994 through 1998 models, disconnect the damper fork and the compression lower arm from the lower lateral arm (see Chapter 10).*
27   Remove the bolts from the centermem-ber assembly **(see illustrations)**, the rear bracket (1994 through 1998 models) and remove the assembly from below the engine compartment.
28   Remove any remaining chassis or suspension components which will interfere with transaxle removal.
29   Remove the lower engine-to-transaxle bolts.
30   Make sure the torque converter is detached from the driveplate. Secure the torque converter to the transaxle so that it will not fall out during removal. Lower the transaxle from the vehicle.

Installation
Note: *The first few gear progressions while*

the TCM relearns the engine and transaxle parameters.
31   Install the fluid filler tube, if it was removed. Make sure the torque converter hub is securely engaged in the pump prior to installation. This can be confirmed by pushing on the torque converter and turning it. If it isn't seated completely, it will drop into place as this is done, evidenced by one or more "clunks".
32   With the transaxle secured to the jack, raise it into position. Be sure to keep it level so the torque converter does not slide forward.
33   Move the transaxle carefully into place until the dowel pins are engaged.
34   Turn the torque converter to line up the bolt holes with the holes in the driveplate. The match marks on the torque converter and driveplate, made during step 18, must line up.
35   Install the lower engine-to-transaxle bolt and the transaxle-to-engine bolts and tighten them to the torque listed in this Chapter's Specifications.
36   Install the torque converter-to-driveplate bolts and tighten them to the torque listed in this Chapter's Specifications. **Note:** *Install all of the bolts before tightening any of them.*
37   Install the upper transaxle-to-engine bolts and tighten them to the torque listed in this Chapter's Specifications.
38   Install the transaxle mounting bracket and tighten the bolts securely. **Note:** *The front and rear roll stoppers should be temporarily tightened during installation, and then fully tightened after the vehicle is on the ground with the full weight of the engine on the body. Be sure the arrow on the roll stopper points toward the engine (1999 and later models).*
39   Install the starter motor (see Chapter 5).
40   Install all suspension components that were removed. Tighten all suspension fasteners to the torque listed in the Chapter 10 Specifications.
41   Remove the jacks supporting the transaxle and the engine. Install any exhaust system components that were removed (see Chapter 4).
42   Install the wheels, remove the jack

stands and lower the vehicle.
43   Unplug the oil cooler hoses and reattach them to the transaxle.
44   Reconnect the shift cable to the manual lever (see Section 4).
45   Plug in all electrical connectors.
46   The rest of installation is the reverse of removal.
47   Fill the transaxle with fluid (see Chapter 1). Run the vehicle and check for fluid leaks.

9   Automatic transaxle overhaul - general information

In the event of a problem occurring, it will be necessary to establish whether the fault is electrical, mechanical or hydraulic in nature, before repair work can be contemplated. Diagnosis requires detailed knowledge of the transaxle's operation and construction, as well as access to specialized test equipment, and so is deemed to be beyond the scope of this manual. It is therefore essential that problems with the automatic transaxle are referred to a dealer service department or other qualified repair facility for assessment.

Note that a faulty transaxle should not be removed before the vehicle has been diagnosed by a knowledgeable technician equipped with the proper tools, as troubleshooting must be performed with the transaxle installed in the vehicle.

Chapter 8
Clutch and driveaxles

Contents

Specifications

Clutch pedal height
| 1994 through 1998 models | 7.00 to 7.10 inches (175 to 180 mm) |
| 1999 and 2000 models | 6.44 to 6.56 inches (163.5 to 166.5 mm) |

Clutch pedal freeplay
1/4 to 1/2 inch (6.0 to 13 mm)

CV inner boot adjustment length
1994 through 1998 models	3.15 inches (80 mm)
1999 through 2003 models	3.30 inches (85 mm)
2004 and later models	
2008 and 2009 V6 MIVEC models	3.74 inches (95 mm)
All others	3.35 inches (85 mm)

Axle damper adjustment length
1994 through 1998 models	
Right side	8.70 inches (221 mm)
Left side	14.37 inches (365 mm)
1999 through 2003 models	
Right side	10.0 inches (254 mm)
Left side	9.5 inches (242 mm)
2004 and later models	
Right side	16.0 inches (406 mm)
Left side	10.3 inches (260.5 mm)

Torque specifications
Note: *One foot-pound (ft-lb) of torque is equivalent to 12 inch-pounds (in-lbs) of torque. Torque values below approximately 15 foot-pounds are expressed in inch-pounds, because most foot-pound torque wrenches are not accurate at these smaller values.*

	Ft-lbs (unless otherwise noted)	Nm
Center bearing bracket bolts (V6 models)	30	40
Clutch-to-driveplate bolts	168 in-lbs	19
Driveaxle/hub nut	146 to 188	196 to 255
Wheel lug nuts	See Chapter 1	

1 General information

The information in this Chapter deals with the components that transmit power to the front wheels, except for the transaxle, which is dealt with in Chapter 7A and 7B. For the purposes of this Chapter, these components are grouped into two categories: clutch and driveaxles. Separate Sections within this Chapter offer general descriptions and checking procedures for both groups.

Since nearly all the procedures covered in this Chapter involve working under the vehicle, make sure it's securely supported on sturdy jackstands or a hoist where the vehicle can be easily raised and lowered.

2   Clutch - description and check

1   All vehicles with a manual transaxle use a single dry plate, diaphragm spring type clutch. The clutch disc has a splined hub which allows it to slide along the splines of the transaxle input shaft. The clutch and pressure plate are held in contact by spring pressure exerted by the diaphragm in the pressure plate.

2   The clutch release system is operated using hydraulic pressure. The hydraulic system consists of the clutch pedal, a master cylinder, the hydraulic line, a release-cylinder which actuates the clutch release lever and the clutch release (or throw-out) bearing.

3   When pressure is applied to the clutch pedal to release the clutch, hydraulic pressure is exerted against the outer end of the release lever, which pivots, moving the release bearing. The bearing pushes against the fingers of the diaphragm spring of the pressure plate assembly, which in turn releases the clutch plate.

4   Other than replacing components that have obvious damage, some preliminary checks should be performed to diagnose a clutch system failure:

a) *The first check should be of the clutch release system. Check the fluid level in the clutch master cylinder. If the fluid level is low, add fluid as necessary and inspect the hydraulic clutch system for leaks. If the master cylinder reservoir has run dry, bleed the system as described in Section 9 and re-test the clutch operation.*

b) *To check "clutch spin down time," run the engine at normal idle speed with the transaxle in Neutral (clutch pedal up - engaged). Disengage the clutch (pedal down), wait several seconds and shift the transaxle into Reverse. No grinding noise should be heard. A grinding noise would most likely indicate a problem in the pressure plate or the clutch disc.*

c) *To check for complete clutch release, run the engine (with the parking brake applied to prevent movement) and hold the clutch pedal approximately 1/2-inch from the floor. Shift the transaxle between 1st gear and Reverse several times. If the shift is not smooth, component failure is indicated.*

d) *Visually inspect the clutch pedal bushings at the top of the clutch pedal to make sure there is no sticking or excessive wear.*

3   Clutch master cylinder - removal and installation

Removal

1   Disconnect the cable from the negative battery terminal (see Chapter 5).

2   Working in the passenger compartment, remove the driver's side under cover from the dashboard (see Chapter 11), remove the clip that secures the clutch master cylinder pushrod to the clutch pedal and slide the pushrod off the clutch pedal pin. **Note:** *Inspect the plastic retainer for damage. Replace the retainer with a new part if necessary.*

3   From under the dash, remove the clutch master cylinder mounting nut(s) from the firewall. **Note:** *On 1998 and earlier models, only one mounting nut is accessible from under the dash (the other one is in the engine compartment).*

4   Working in the engine compartment, separate the hydraulic line from the clutch master cylinder. Use a flare-nut wrench, if available, to prevent rounding-off the corners of the fitting.

5   Remove the nut(s) securing the clutch master cylinder and fluid reservoir to the firewall.

6   Using care not to damage the hydraulic line, work the clutch master cylinder and reservoir from the engine compartment.

Installation

7   Place the clutch master cylinder pushrod through the firewall and install the fasteners finger tight.

8   Working inside the vehicle, connect the master cylinder pushrod to the clutch pedal pin and install a new clip.

9   Connect the master cylinder hydraulic line to the master cylinder.

10   The remainder of installation is the reverse of removal. Tighten the mounting fasteners securely.

11   Bleed the clutch hydraulic system (see Section 9).

12   Wash off any spilled brake fluid with water. **Caution:** *Don't allow brake fluid to come into contact with paint, as it will damage the finish.*

4   Clutch release cylinder - removal and installation

Removal

1   Disconnect the cable from the negative battery terminal (see Chapter 5).

2   Raise the vehicle and support it securely on jackstands.

3   Disconnect the hydraulic line from the release cylinder. Use a flare-nut wrench, if available, to prevent rounding-off the corners of the fitting. Have rags handy as some fluid will be lost when the line is removed. **Caution:** *Don't allow brake fluid to come into contact with paint as it will damage the finish.*

4   Remove the bolts securing the release cylinder to the transaxle.

Installation

5   Installation is the reverse of the removal, noting the following points:

a) *Install the release cylinder and tighten the mounting bolts securely.*

b) *Connect the hydraulic line and check the hydraulic fluid level in the reservoir, adding fluid if necessary, until the level is correct.*

c) *Bleed the clutch hydraulic system (see Section 9).*

5   Clutch components - removal and installation

Warning: *Dust produced by clutch wear and deposited on clutch components is hazardous to your health. DO NOT blow it out with compressed air and DO NOT inhale it. DO NOT use gasoline or petroleum-based solvents to remove the dust. Brake system cleaner should be used to flush the dust into a drain pan. After the clutch components are wiped clean with a rag, dispose of the contaminated rags and cleaner in a labeled, covered container.*

Removal

Refer to illustration 5.5

Note: *Access to the clutch components is normally accomplished by removing the transaxle, leaving the engine in the vehicle. If, of course, the engine is being removed for major overhaul, then the opportunity should always be taken to check the clutch for wear and replace worn components as necessary. However, the relatively low cost of the clutch components compared to the time and labor involved in gaining access to them warrants their replacement any time the engine or transaxle is removed, unless they are new or in near-perfect condition. The following procedures assume that the engine will stay in place.*

1   Remove the release cylinder (see Section 4). Hang it out of the way with a piece of wire - it's not necessary to disconnect the hydraulic line.

2   Remove the transaxle from the vehicle (see Chapter 7, Part A). Support the engine while the transaxle is out. Preferably, an engine hoist or support fixture should be used to support it from above. However, if a jack is used underneath the engine, make sure a piece of wood is used between the jack and oil pan to spread the load. **Caution:** *The pickup for the oil pump is very close to the bottom of the oil pan. If the pan is bent or distorted in any way, engine oil starvation could occur.*

3   The release fork and release bearing can remain attached to the transaxle for the time being.

4   To support the clutch disc during removal, install a clutch alignment tool through the clutch disc hub.

5   Carefully inspect the flywheel and pressure plate for indexing marks. The marks are usually an X, an O or a white letter. If they cannot be found, scribe marks yourself so

5.5 If you're going to re-use the same pressure plate, mark the relationship of the pressure plate to the flywheel

5.9 Inspect the clutch disc for signs of excessive wear such as smeared friction material, chewed-up rivets, worn hub splines and distorted damper cushions or springs

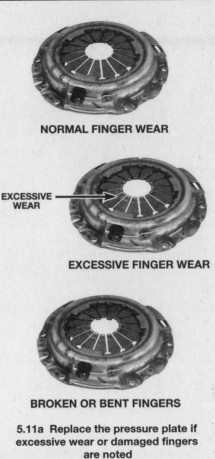

NORMAL FINGER WEAR

EXCESSIVE WEAR

EXCESSIVE FINGER WEAR

BROKEN OR BENT FINGERS

5.11a Replace the pressure plate if excessive wear or damaged fingers are noted

the pressure plate and the flywheel will be in the same alignment during installation **(see illustration)**.

6 Slowly loosen the pressure plate-to-flywheel bolts. Work in a diagonal pattern and loosen each bolt a little at a time until all spring pressure is relieved. Then hold the pressure plate securely and completely remove the bolts, followed by the pressure plate and clutch disc.

Inspection

Refer to illustrations 5.9, 5.11a and 5.11b

7 Ordinarily, when a problem occurs in the clutch, it can be attributed to wear of the clutch driven plate assembly (clutch disc). However, all components should be inspected at this time.

8 Inspect the flywheel for cracks, heat checking, score marks and other damage. If the imperfections are slight, a machine shop can resurface it to make it flat and smooth. Refer to Chapter 2 for the flywheel removal procedure.

9 Inspect the lining on the clutch disc. There should be at least 1/16-inch of lining above the rivet heads. Check for loose rivets, distortion, cracks, broken springs and other obvious damage **(see illustration)**. As mentioned above, ordinarily the clutch disc is replaced as a matter of course, so if in doubt about the condition, replace it with a new one.

10 The release bearing should be replaced along with the clutch disc (see Section 6).

11 Check the machined surface and the diaphragm spring fingers of the pressure plate **(see illustrations)**. If the surface is grooved or otherwise damaged, replace the pressure plate assembly. Also check for obvious damage, distortion, cracking, etc. Light glazing can be removed with emery cloth or sandpaper. If a new pressure plate is indicated, new or factory rebuilt units are available.

Installation

Refer to illustration 5.13

12 Before installation, carefully wipe the flywheel and pressure plate machined surfaces clean. It's important that no oil or grease is on these surfaces or the lining of the clutch disc. Handle these parts only with clean hands.

13 Position the clutch disc and pressure plate with the clutch held in place with an alignment tool **(see illustration)**. Make sure it's installed properly (most replacement clutch plates will be marked "flywheel side" or something similar - if not marked, install the clutch disc with the damper springs or cushion toward the transaxle).

14 Install the pressure plate-to-flywheel bolts only finger tight, working around the pressure plate.

15 Center the clutch disc by ensuring the alignment tool is through the splined hub and into the recess in the crankshaft. Wiggle the tool up, down or side-to-side as needed to

5.11b Examine the pressure plate friction surface for score marks, cracks and evidence of overheating

bottom the tool. Tighten the pressure plate-to-flywheel bolts a little at a time, working in a criss-cross pattern to prevent distortion of the cover. After all of the bolts are snug, tighten them to the torque listed in this Chapter's Specifications. Remove the alignment tool.

16 Using high-temperature grease, lubricate the inner groove of the release bearing (see Section 6). Also place grease on the

5.13 Center the clutch disc in the pressure plate with a clutch alignment tool or a wooden dowel of the appropriate diameter

6.4 Disengage the spring clip to release the bearing from the lever, then push the release lever in the direction of the arrow to free it from the ballstud

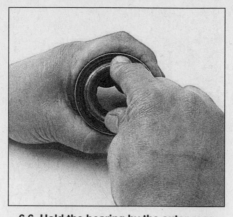

6.6 Hold the bearing by the outer race and rotate the inner race while applying pressure - if the bearing doesn't turn smoothly or if it's noisy, it must be replaced (it's a good idea to replace the bearing even if it checks out good)

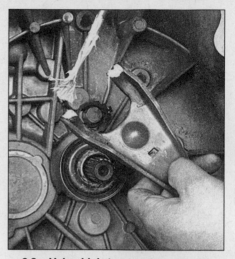

6.8a Using high-temperature grease, lubricate the release lever ends . . .

release lever contact areas and the transaxle input shaft bearing retainer.
17　Install the clutch release bearing (see Section 6.
18　Install the transaxle, release cylinder and all components removed previously, tightening all fasteners to the proper torque specifications.

6　Clutch release bearing and lever - removal, inspection and installation

Warning: *Dust produced by clutch wear and deposited on clutch components is hazardous to your health. DO NOT blow it out with compressed air and DO NOT inhale it. DO NOT use gasoline or petroleum-based solvents to remove the dust. Brake system cleaner should be used to flush it into a drain pan. After the clutch components are wiped clean with a rag, dispose of the contaminated rags and cleaner in a labeled, covered container.*

Removal
Refer to illustration 6.4
Note: *Because of the difficulty involved in removing the transaxle for release bearing replacement, we recommend routinely replacing the release bearing when the clutch components are replaced.*
1　Disconnect the cable from the negative terminal of the battery (see Chapter 5).
2　Remove the transaxle (see Chapter 7 Part A).
3　Move the lever and bearing so the lever is at a right angle to the input shaft.
4　Pull the ends of the spring clip out of the holes in the release lever to free the bearing from the lever, then push the lever away from the input shaft to disengage it from the ballstud **(see illustration)**. **Caution:** *Do not use a screwdriver or prybar to disengage the lever as the spring clip will be damaged.*

6.8b . . . the inner groove of the release bearing . . .

5　Slide the release bearing off the input shaft.

Inspection
Refer to illustration 6.6
6　Hold the bearing by the outer race and rotate the inner race while applying pressure **(see illustration)**. If the bearing doesn't turn smoothly or if it's noisy, replace the bearing assembly with a new one. Wipe the bearing with a clean rag and inspect it for damage, wear and cracks. Don't immerse the bearing in solvent - it's sealed for life and to do so would ruin it. Also check the release lever and fork for cracks and bends.
7　Check the release lever for wear or damage especially in the area where the lever contacts the release bearing. Also be sure to clean any dirt off the pivot ballstud and stud pocket in the release fork.

Installation
Refer to illustrations 6.8a, 6.8b and 6.8c
8　Lubricate the release lever ends, the inner diameter of the release bearing and the

6.8c . . . and the sleeve around the input shaft

input shaft **(see illustrations)**.
9　Install the release lever and bearing by reversing the procedure described in Step 4.
10　Install the transaxle (see Chapter 7 Part A).

7　Clutch pedal height and freeplay - check and adjustment

Refer to illustrations 7.1 and 7.3
1　Measure the clutch pedal height. The clutch pedal height is the distance from the top of the clutch pedal to the floor **(see illustration)**. The distance should be as listed in this Chapter's Specifications.
2　To adjust the clutch pedal height on 1994 through 1998 models, loosen the locknut and turn the bolt or clutch switch until the height is correct, then tighten the locknut. To adjust the clutch pedal height on 1999 and 2000 models, loosen the locknut and turn the pushrod until the height is correct, then tighten the locknut.

7.1 The clutch pedal height is the distance between the pedal pad and the floor

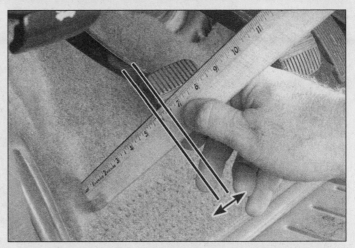

7.3 The clutch pedal freeplay is the distance the pedal travels before resistance is felt

3   Press down lightly on the clutch pedal and measure the distance that it moves freely before the clutch resistance is felt **(see illustration)**. The freeplay should be within the limits listed in this Chapter's Specifications. If it isn't, it must be adjusted.

4   The clutch pedal freeplay is not ad-just-able. If the freeplay measurement is incorrect, bleed the clutch hydraulic system and check for leaks (see Section 9). If the adjustment is still not correct, check and repair the clutch master cylinder and/or the clutch assembly.

8   Clutch start switch - check and replacement

Check

1   Verify that the engine will not start when the clutch pedal is released.

2   Verify that the engine will start when the clutch pedal is depressed all the way.

3   If the engine won't start with the pedal depressed, or starts with the pedal released, unplug the electrical connector to the switch. The clutch start switch is located near the top of the clutch pedal. Check continuity between the connector terminals with the clutch pedal depressed.

4   If there's continuity between the terminals with the pedal depressed, the switch is okay; if there's no continuity between the terminals with the pedal depressed, replace the switch. If there's continuity between the terminals when the clutch pedal is released, replace the switch.

Replacement

5   Remove the driver's side under cover from the instrument panel (see Chapter 11).

6   Unplug the switch electrical connector, if you haven't already done so.

7   Loosen the locknut and unscrew the switch from the clutch pedal bracket.

8   Installation is the reverse of removal. To adjust the switch, thread it into the bracket until there is a gap of 9/64-inch (3.5 mm) between the switch body and the tab on the clutch pedal, then tighten the locknut securely.

9   Verify that the starter will operate only when the clutch pedal is depressed.

9   Clutch hydraulic system bleeding

1   The hydraulic system should be bled of all air whenever any part of the system has been removed or if the fluid level has been allowed to fall so low that air has been drawn into the master cylinder. The procedure is very similar to bleeding a brake system.

2   Fill the clutch master cylinder with new brake fluid conforming to DOT 3 specifications. **Caution:** *Do not re-use any of the fluid coming from the system during the bleeding operation or use fluid which has been inside an open container for an extended period of time.*

3   Raise the vehicle and place it securely on jackstands to gain access to the release cylinder, which is located on the side of the transaxle.

4   Remove the dust cap which fits over the bleeder valve and push a length of plastic hose over the valve. Place the other end of the hose into a clear container with about two inches of brake fluid in it. The hose end must be submerged in the fluid.

5   Have an assistant depress the clutch pedal and hold it. Open the bleeder valve on the release cylinder, allowing fluid to flow through the hose. Close the bleeder valve when fluid stops flowing from the hose. Once closed, have your assistant release the pedal slowly.

6   Continue this process until all air is evacuated from the system, indicated by a full, solid stream of fluid being ejected from the bleeder valve each time and no air bubbles in the hose or container. Keep a close watch on the fluid level inside the clutch master cylinder reservoir; if the level drops too low, air will be sucked back into the system and the process will have to be started all over again.

7   Install the dust cap and lower the vehicle. Check carefully for proper operation before placing the vehicle in normal service.

10   Driveaxles - general information and inspection

1   Power is transmitted from the transaxle to the wheels through a pair of driveaxles. The inner end of each driveaxle is splined to the differential side gears. The driveaxles can be pulled out to replace the oil seals (see Chapter 7B). The outer ends of the driveaxles are splined to the front hubs and locked in place by a large nut.

2   Each driveaxle assembly consists of an inner and outer constant velocity (CV) joint connected together by a driveaxle shaft. The inner ends of the driveaxles are equipped with a tripod joint on all models. The design is capable of both angular and axial motion. In other words, the inner CV joints are free to slide in-and-out as the driveaxle moves up-and-down with the wheel. These joints can be disassembled and cleaned in the event of a boot failure, but if any parts are damaged, the entire driveaxle assembly must be replaced as a unit.

3   The outer CV joints use a ball-and-cage design, capable of angular but not axial movement. These joints can be cleaned and repacked if an outer boot is torn, but if any parts are damaged, the entire driveaxle assembly must be replaced as a unit.

4   The boots should be inspected periodically for damage and leaking lubricant. Torn CV joint boots must be replaced immediately or the joints can be damaged. Boot replacement involves removal of the driveaxle (see Sections 11 and 12). **Note:** *Some auto parts stores carry "split" type replacement boots, which can be installed without removing the driveaxle from the vehicle. This is a conve-*

11.2a   Remove the hub nut cotter pin . . .

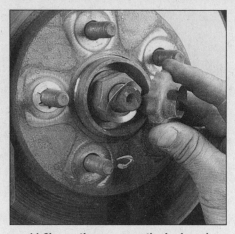

11.2b   . . . then remove the lock and spring washer

11.3   To prevent the hub from turning while you're loosening the driveaxle/hub nut, wedge a prybar between two of the wheel studs

nient alternative; however, the driveaxle should be removed and the CV joint disassembled and cleaned to ensure the joint is free from contaminants such as moisture and dirt which will accelerate CV joint wear. The most common symptom of worn or damaged CV joints, besides lubricant leaks, is a clicking noise in turns, a clunk when accelerating after coasting and vibration at highway speeds. To check for wear in the CV joints and driveaxle shafts, grasp each axle (one at a time) and rotate it in both directions while holding the CV joint housings, feeling for play indicating worn splines or sloppy CV joints. Also check the axleshafts for cracks, dents and distortion.

11   Driveaxle - removal and installation

Removal

Refer to illustrations 11.2a, 11.2b, 11.3, 11.6, 11.7 and 11.10

1   Loosen the front wheel lug nuts, raise the vehicle and support it securely on jack-stands. Remove the wheel.
2   Remove the hub nut cotter pin and discard it **(see illustration)**. Discard the old cotter pin - you'll need a new one for reassembly. Remove the driveaxle/hub nut lock and spring washer **(see illustration)**.
3   Loosen the driveaxle/hub nut with a large socket and breaker bar **(see illustration)**.
4   It's not absolutely necessary that you drain the transaxle lubricant prior to removing a driveaxle, but if the mileage on the odometer indicates that the transaxle is nearing the lubricant-change interval prescribed in Chapter 1, now is a good time to do it.
5   Remove the bolt and nut securing the balljoint to the steering knuckle then pry the lower control arm down to separate the components (see Chapter 10).
6   To loosen the driveaxle from the hub splines, tap the end of the driveaxle with a soft-faced hammer **(see illustration)**. If the driveaxle is stuck in the hub splines and won't move, it may be necessary to push it from the hub with a puller.

7   Pull out on the steering knuckle and detach the driveaxle from the hub **(see illustration)**. Suspend the outer end of the driveaxle on a bungee cord or piece of wire.
8   Before you remove the driveaxle, look for lubricant leakage in the area around the differential seal. If there's evidence of a leak, you'll want to replace the seal after removing the driveaxle (see Chapter 7B).
9   If you're removing a right-hand driveaxle on a V6 model, remove the center bearing bracket mounting bolts, then support the driveaxle assembly and slide the intermediate shaft out of the transaxle.
10   To remove either driveaxle on a four-cylinder model or a left driveaxle on a V6 model, position a prybar against the inner joint and carefully pry the joint off the transaxle side gear shaft **(see illustration)**. Do not use the driveaxle to pull on the inner joint. Doing so might damage the inner joint components. Pry straight out on the driveaxle to avoid damage to the transaxle oil seal. Remove the driveaxle assembly, being care-

11.6   To loosen the driveaxle from the hub splines, tap the end of the driveaxle with a soft-faced hammer

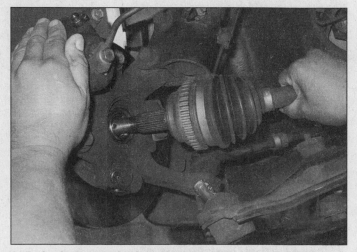

11.7   Angle the steering knuckle as required and pull the driveaxle from the wheel hub

ful not to over-extend the inner joint or damage the axleshaft boots.

11   Should it become necessary to move the vehicle while the driveaxle is out, place a large bolt with two large washers (one on each side of the hub) through the hub and tighten the nut securely.

12   If you noted evidence of a leaking driveaxle seal, refer to Chapter 7B for the seal replacement procedure.

Installation

13   Installation is the reverse of removal, but with the following additional points:

a) *Apply an even bead of multi-purpose grease around the splines of the inner joint.*

b) *When installing either driveaxle on a four-cylinder model or a left driveaxle on a V6 model, hold the driveaxle straight out, push it in sharply to seat the snap-ring that retains the inner CV joint. To make sure the snap-ring is properly seated, attempt to pull the inner CV joint out of the transaxle by hand. If the snap-ring is properly seated the inner joint will not move out.*

c) *On 3.0L V6 models, install the center bearing bracket and tighten the bolts to the torque listed in this Chapter's Specifications.*

d) *Clean all foreign matter from the driveaxle outer CV joint threads. Install the spring washer and the nut. Tighten the hub nut to the torque listed in this Chapter's specifications. Install the nut lock and a NEW cotter pin. Bend the ends over completely. **Note:** Tighten the nut to the lower torque figure given in this Chapter's Specifications, then, if necessary, tighten it a little more to allow cotter pin insertion (don't exceed the higher torque figure). Never loosen the nut to allow cotter pin insertion.*

e) *Install the wheel and lug nuts, then lower the vehicle. Tighten the lug nuts to the*

11.10 Using a large prybar, pry the inner CV joint out sharply to disengage it from the transaxle

torque listed in the Chapter 1 Specifications.

f) *Add transaxle lubricant as necessary (see Chapter 1).*

12   Driveaxle boot replacement and CV joint inspection

Note: *If the CV joints or boots must be replaced, explore all options before beginning the job. Complete, rebuilt driveaxles are available on an exchange basis, eliminating much time and work. Whichever route you choose to take, check on the cost and availability of parts before disassembling the vehicle.*

Inner CV joint

1   Remove the driveaxle (see Section 11).

2   Mount the driveaxle in a vise with wood-lined jaws, to prevent damage to the axleshaft. Check the CV joints for excessive play in the radial direction, which indicates worn parts. Check for smooth operation throughout the full range of motion for each CV joint. If a boot is torn, the recommended procedure is to disassemble the joint, clean the compo-

nents and inspect for damage due to loss of lubrication and possible contamination by foreign matter. If the CV joint is in good condition, lubricate it with CV joint grease and install a new boot.

Disassembly

Refer to illustrations 12.4, 12.5, 12.6 and 12.7

3   Cut the boot clamps with side-cutters, then remove and discard them.

4   Using a screwdriver, carefully pry up on the edge of the CV boot, pull it off the CV joint housing and slide it down the axleshaft, exposing the tripod spider assembly. To separate the axleshaft and spider assembly from the inner tripod joint housing, simply pull them straight out **(see illustration)**. **Note:** *When removing the spider assembly, hold the rollers in place on the spider trunnion to prevent the rollers and the needle bearings from falling free.*

5   Remove the spider assembly snap-ring with a pair of snap-ring pliers **(see illustration)**.

6   Mark the tripod to the axleshaft to ensure that they are reassembled properly **(see illustration)**.

12.4 Remove the boot from the inner CV joint and slide the tripod from the joint housing

12.5 Remove the snap-ring with a pair of snap-ring pliers

12.6 Mark the relationship of the tripod bearing assembly to the axleshaft

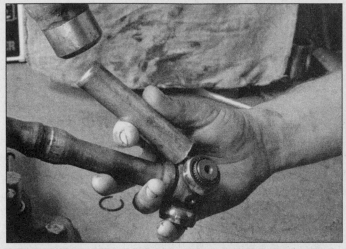

12.7 Drive the tripod joint off the axleshaft with a brass punch and hammer; be careful not to damage the bearing surfaces or the splines on the shaft

12.10a Wrap the axleshaft splines with electrical tape to prevent damaging the boot as it's slid onto the shaft

12.10b Install the tripod spider on the axleshaft (make sure your match mark is facing out)

12.10c Place grease at the bottom of the CV joint housing

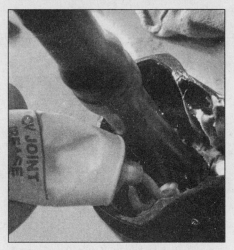

12.10d Install the boot and clamps onto the axleshaft, then insert the tripod into the housing, followed by the rest of the grease

12.11 Make sure that the thinnest groove on the axleshaft is the only one showing

7   Use a hammer and a brass drift to drive the spider assembly from the axleshaft **(see illustration)**.

8   Slide the boot off the shaft.

Inspection

9   Thoroughly clean all components with solvent until the old CV joint grease is completely removed. Inspect the bearing surfaces of the inner tripods and housings for cracks, pitting, scoring and other signs of wear. If any part of the inner CV joint is worn, you must replace the entire driveaxle assembly (inner tripod joint, axleshaft and outer CV joint). The only components that can be purchased separately are the boots themselves and the boot clamps. **Note:** *If you're working on a V6 model right-side driveaxle, check the center bearing for smooth operation. If it feels rough or is noisy when rotated, take the intermediate shaft to an automotive machine shop to have the old bearing pressed out and a new one pressed in. A press is also required to remove the inner CV joint housing from the shaft.*

Reassembly

Refer to illustrations 12.10a, 12.10b, 12.10c, 12.10.d, 12.11, 12.12 and 12.13

10   Wrap the splines on the inner end of the axleshaft with electrical or duct tape to protect the boots from the sharp edges of the splines and slide the clamps and boot onto the axleshaft **(see illustration)**. Remove the tape and place the tripod spider on the axleshaft with the chamfer toward the shaft **(see illustration)**. Tap the spider onto the shaft with a brass drift until it's seated and install the snap-ring. Apply grease to the tripod assembly and inside the housing **(see illustration)**. Insert the tripod into the housing and pack the remainder of the grease around the tripod **(see illustration)**.

11   Slide the boot into place, making sure the raised bead on the inside of the seal boot is positioned in the groove on the interconnecting shaft. If the driveaxle has multiple locating grooves on the shaft, position the

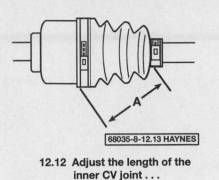

68035-8-12.13 HAYNES

**12.12 Adjust the length of the
inner CV joint . . .**

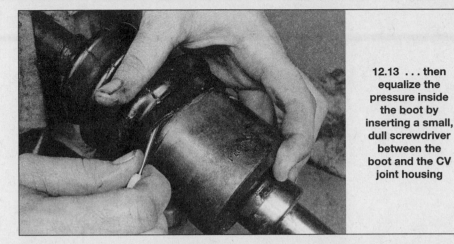

**12.13 . . . then
equalize the
pressure inside
the boot by
inserting a small,
dull screwdriver
between the
boot and the CV
joint housing**

boot so only one of the grooves (the thinnest)
is exposed **(see illustration)**. Position the
sealing boot into the groove on the tripod
housing retaining groove.

12   Adjust the length of the inner CV joint
boot **(see illustration)**. Refer to the Specifications listed in this Chapter for the correct
CV boot adjustment length.

13   Equalize the pressure inside the boot by
inserting a small, dull, flat screwdriver tip
between the boot and the CV joint housing
(see illustration).

14   Make sure each end of the boot is seated
properly, and the boot is not distorted.

15   Two types of clamps are used on the
inner CV joint. If a crimp-type clamp is used,
clamp the new boot clamps onto the boot
with a special crimping tool (available at most
automotive parts stores). Place the crimping
tool over the bridge of each new boot clamp,
then tighten the nut on the crimping tool until
the jaws are closed. If a low profile latching
type clamp is used, place the prongs of the
clamping tool (available at most automotive
parts stores) in the holes of the clamp and
squeeze the tool together until the top band
latches behind the tabs of the lower band.

16   The driveaxle is now ready for installation (see Section 11).

Outer CV joint

Disassembly

17   Remove the driveaxle (see Section 9).

18   Mount the driveaxle in a vise with wood-lined jaws to prevent damage to the axleshaft.

Check the CV joints for excessive play in the
radial direction, which indicates worn parts.
Check for smooth operation throughout the
full range of motion for each CV joint. If a boot
is torn, the recommended procedure is to
disassemble the joint, clean the components
and inspect for damage due to loss of lubrication and possible contamination by foreign
matter. If the CV joint is in good condition,
lubricate it with CV joint grease and install a
new boot.

19   Remove the inner CV joint and boot,
then cut off the clamps and slide the dynamic
damper off the axleshaft.

20   Cut the boot clamps with side-cutters,
then remove and discard them.

21   Slide the boot off the shaft.

Inspection

Refer to illustration 12.22

22   Rotate the outer CV joint housing at an
angle to the driveaxle to expose the bearings,
inner race and cage **(see illustration)**. Inspect
the bearing surfaces for signs of wear. If the
CV joint is worn, replace the driveaxle.

Reassembly

Refer to illustrations 12.24a and 12.24b

23   Slide the new outer boot onto the axle-shaft. It's a good idea to wrap tape around
the splines of the shaft to prevent damage to
the boot **(see illustration 12.10a)**. When the
boot is in position, add approximately four

ounces of CV joint grease to the outer joint
and the boot (pack the joint with as much
grease as it will hold and put the rest into the
boot). Slide the boot on the rest of the way
and install the new clamps. **Note:** *The length
of the outer joint isn't adjustable; just make
sure that each end of the boot is seated properly and that there are no dimples in the folds
in the boot.*

24   Slide the dynamic damper onto the shaft
to the specified distance **(see illustrations)**,
then secure it in place with new retaining
clamps.

25   Clean and reassemble the inner CV joint
by following Steps 9 through 16, then install
the driveaxle as outlined in Section 11.

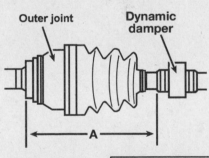

68035-8-12.12a HAYNES

**12.24a Dynamic damper positioning -
1994 through 1998 models**

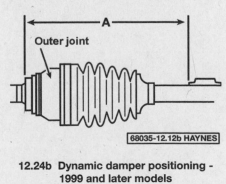

68035-12.12b HAYNES

**12.24b Dynamic damper positioning -
1999 and later models**

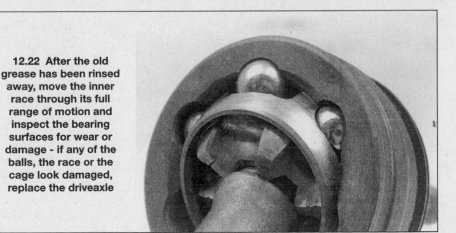

**12.22 After the old
grease has been rinsed
away, move the inner
race through its full
range of motion and
inspect the bearing
surfaces for wear or
damage - if any of the
balls, the race or the
cage look damaged,
replace the driveaxle**

Notes

Chapter 9 Brakes

Contents

Specifications

General
Brake fluid type .... See Chapter 1
Power brake booster pushrod-to-master cylinder piston clearance (see Section 9)
1998 and earlier models.. 0.024 inch (0.60 mm)
Power brake booster pushrod protrusion (see Section 9)
1999 and later model .... 0.404 to 0.415 inch (10.28 to 10.53 mm)

Brake pedal
Height.. 6.9 to 7.1 inches (175 to 180 mm)
Freeplay.. 0.12 to 0.31 inch (3 to 8 mm)
Reserve distance (minimum) .... 3.5 inches (90 mm)

Disc brakes
Minimum pad lining thickness....................................... See Chapter 1
Disc minimum thickness .... Cast into disc
Disc runout limit
1998 and earlier
Front .... 0.003 inch (0.07 mm)
Rear .... 0.003 inch (0.07 mm)
1999 and later
Front .... 0.002 inch (0.05 mm)
Rear .... 0.003 inch (0.07 mm)
Maximum disc thickness variation (parallelism) .... 0.0006 inch (0.01 mm)

Drum brakes
Shoe lining minimum thickness...................................... See Chapter 1
Maximum drum diameter .... Cast into drum

Torque specifications

Note: *One foot-pound (ft-lb) of torque is equivalent to 12 inch-pounds (in-lbs) of torque. Torque values below approximately 15 foot-pounds are expressed in inch-pounds, because most foot-pound torque wrenches are not accurate at these smaller values.*

	Ft-lbs (unless otherwise indicated)	Nm
Caliper guide pin/lock pin bolts		
Front		
1994 through 2000 models	54	74
2001 models		
Four-cylinder models	54	74
V6 models	28	38
2002 and later models	28	38
Rear		
1994 and 1995 models	36 to 43	49 to 59
1999 and later models	32	43
Caliper mounting bracket bolts		
Front		
1994 through 1998 models	65	88
1999 and later models	66 to 81	90 to 110
Rear		
1994 and 1995	54 to 65	74 to 88
1999 and later models	44	60
Brake hose inlet fitting bolt	22	29
Master cylinder-to-brake booster nuts		
1994 through 1998 models	89 in-lbs	10
1999 and 2000 models	124 in-lbs	14
2001 through 2003 models		
With traction control	113 in-lbs	13
Without traction control	89 in-lbs	10
2004 and 2005 models	16 to 20	23 to 27
2006 and later models	11 to 15	15 to 21
Power brake booster mounting nuts	124 in-lbs	14
Wheel cylinder mounting bolts	89 in-lbs	10

1   General information

The vehicles covered by this manual are equipped with a hydraulically operated brake system. The front brakes are disc type and the rear brakes are either drum or disc type. Both the front and rear disc brakes automatically compensate for disc and pad wear. As the pads wear down, the pistons gradually protrude farther from the calipers, but don't retract as far, automatically compensating for the thinner pads. Rear drum brakes have automatic adjusters, which compensate for wear of the brake shoes.

Hydraulic system

The hydraulic system consists of two separate circuits that are diagonally split (one circuit operates the left front and right rear brakes, while the other circuit operates the right front and left rear brakes). The master cylinder has separate reservoirs for the two circuits, and, in the event of a leak or failure in one hydraulic circuit, the other circuit will remain operative. A dual proportioning valve on the firewall provides brake balance between the front and rear brakes.

Power brake booster

The power brake booster is mounted on the firewall and utilizes engine manifold vacuum and atmospheric pressure to provide assistance to the hydraulically operated brakes.

Parking brake

The parking brake operates the rear brakes only, through cable actuation. A lever mounted in the center console activates it. The parking brake on rear disc brake models uses brake shoes and small brake drums integral with the rear brake discs.

Service

After completing any operation involving disassembly of any part of the brake system, always test drive the vehicle to check for proper braking performance before resuming normal driving. When testing the brakes, perform the tests on a clean, dry, flat surface. Conditions other than these can lead to inaccurate test results.

Test the brakes at various speeds with both light and heavy pedal pressure. The vehicle should stop evenly without pulling to one side or the other. Avoid locking the brakes, because this slides the tires and diminishes braking efficiency and control of the vehicle.

Tires, vehicle loads and wheel alignment is factors, which also affect braking performance.

2   Anti-lock Brake System (ABS) - general information and speed sensor removal and installation

General information

1   The anti-lock brake system is designed to maintain vehicle steerability, directional stability and optimum deceleration under severe braking conditions on most road surfaces. It does so by monitoring the rotational speed of each wheel and controlling the brake line pressure to each wheel during braking. This prevents the wheels from locking up.

2   The ABS system has three main components - the wheel speed sensors, the electronic control unit (ECU) and the hydraulic unit. Four wheel speed sensors - one at each wheel - send a variable voltage signal to the control unit, which monitors these signals, compares them to its program and determines whether a wheel is about to lock up. When a wheel is about to lock up, the control unit signals the hydraulic unit to reduce hydraulic pressure (or not increase it further) at that wheel's brake caliper. Electrically operated solenoid valves handle pressure modulation.

3   If a problem develops within the system, an "ABS" warning light will glow on the dashboard. Sometimes, a visual inspection of the ABS system can help you locate the problem. Carefully inspect the ABS wiring harness. Pay particularly close attention to the harness and connections near each wheel. Look for signs of chafing and other damage caused by incorrectly routed wires. If a wheel sensor harness is damaged, the sensor must be replaced. **Warning:** *Do NOT try to repair an ABS wiring harness. The ABS system is sensitive to even the smallest changes in resistance. Repairing the harness could alter resistance values and cause the system to malfunction. If the ABS wiring harness is damaged in any way, it must be replaced.* **Caution:** *Make sure the ignition is turned off before unplugging or reattaching any electrical connections.*

Diagnosis and repair

4   If a dashboard warning light comes on and stays on while the vehicle is in operation, the ABS system requires attention. Although special electronic ABS diagnostic testing tools are necessary to properly diagnose the system, you can perform a few preliminary checks before taking the vehicle to a dealer service department.

a) Check the brake fluid level in the reservoir.
b) Verify that the computer electrical connectors are securely connected.
c) Check the electrical connectors at the hydraulic control unit.
d) Check the fuses.
e) Follow the wiring harness to each wheel and verify that all connections are secure and that the wiring is undamaged.

5   If the above preliminary checks do not rectify the problem, the vehicle should be diagnosed by a dealer service department or other qualified repair shop. Due to the complex nature of this system, a qualified automotive technician must do all actual repair work.

Wheel speed sensor - removal and installation

Refer to illustration 2.9

6   Loosen the wheel lug nuts, raise the vehicle and support it securely on jackstands. Remove the wheel.

7   Make sure the ignition key is turned to the Off position.

8   Trace the wiring back from the sensor, detaching all brackets and clips while noting its correct routing, then disconnect the electrical connector.

9   Remove the mounting bolt and carefully pull the sensor out from the knuckle or brake backing plate **(see illustration)**.

10   Installation is the reverse of the removal procedure. Tighten the mounting bolt securely.

11   Install the wheel and lug nuts, tightening them securely to the torque listed in the Chapter 1 Specifications.

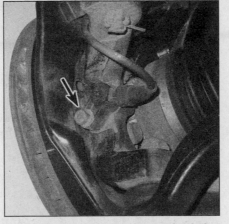

2.9 Wheel speed sensor mounting bolt

3.4 Always wash the brakes with brake system cleaner before working on them

---

3   Disc brake pads - replacement

Preliminary steps

Refer to illustrations 3.4 and 3.5

Warning: *Disc brake pads must be replaced on both front or rear wheels at the same time - never replace the pads on only one wheel. Also, the dust created by the brake system is harmful to your health. Never blow it out with compressed air and don't inhale any of it. An approved filtering mask should be worn when working on the brakes. Do not, under any circumstances, use petroleum-based solvents to clean brake parts. Use brake system cleaner only!*

Caution: *Don't depress the brake pedal with the caliper removed.*

1   Remove the cap from the brake fluid reservoir. Remove about two-thirds of the fluid from the reservoir, then reinstall the cap. **Warning:** *Brake fluid is poisonous - never siphon it by mouth. Use a suction gun or old poultry baster. If a baster is used, never again use it for the preparation of food.* **Caution:** *Brake fluid will damage paint. If any fluid is*

spilled, wash it off immediately with plenty of clean, cold water.

2   Loosen the wheel lug nuts, raise the end of the vehicle you're working on and support it securely on jackstands. Block the wheels that remain on the ground.

3   Remove the wheels. Work on one brake assembly at a time, using the assembled brake for reference if necessary.

4   Position a drain pan under the brake assembly and clean the caliper and surrounding area with brake system cleaner **(see illustration)**.

5   Push the piston back into its bore using a C-clamp **(see illustration)**. As the piston(s) is depressed to the bottom of the caliper bore, the fluid level in the master cylinder will rise as the brake fluid is displaced. Make sure it doesn't overflow. If necessary, siphon off some more of the fluid.

Brake pad replacement

Refer to illustrations 3.6a through 3.6l and 3.9

6   To replace the brake pads, follow the accompanying photos, beginning with **illus-**

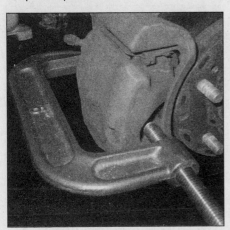

3.5 Push the piston back into the caliper bore with a large C-clamp

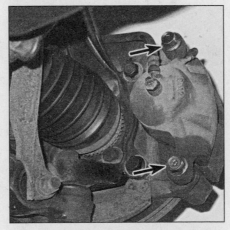

3.6a Remove the caliper guide pin (lower arrow) - it's only necessary to remove the lock pin (upper arrow) if you're removing the caliper

3.6b Swing the caliper up like this . . .

3.6c . . . and support it in this position with a piece of wire

3.6d Remove the inner pad and shim(s)

3.6e Remove the outer pad and shim(s)

tration 3.6a. Be sure to stay in order and read the caption under each illustration.

7   While the pads are removed, inspect the caliper for brake fluid leaks and ruptures of

the piston dust boot. Replace the caliper if necessary (see Section 4). Also inspect the brake disc carefully (see Section 5). If machining is necessary, follow the information in that

Section to remove the disc. Inspect the brake hoses for damage and replace if necessary (see Section 10).

8   Before installing the caliper guide pin,

3.6f Remove the anti-rattle clips, paying close attention to how they're installed in the mounting bracket

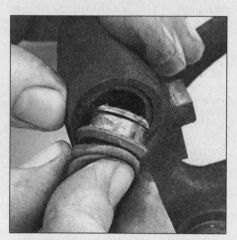

3.6g Remove the dust boots from the torque plate, inspect them for cracks and tears, and replace as necessary

3.6h Install the anti-rattle clips in the mounting bracket plate - make sure both arefully seated

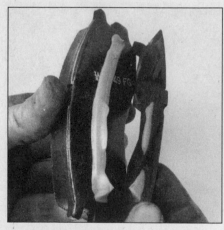

3.6i Apply anti-squeal compound (available at auto parts stores - follow the label instructions) to the back of the brake pads and install the anti-squeal shim(s)

3.6j Lubricate the guide pin with multi-purpose grease before installing it

3.6k Install the inner pad . . .

3.6l . . . and the outer pad into the mounting bracket - make sure both pads are fully seated, then swing the caliper down into place, install the guide pin and tighten it to the torque listed in this Chapter's Specifications

3.9 If you have removed the guide pin and lock pin, install them in the correct locations by referring to the letters stamped in the ends of the pins – they correspond with the letters cast into the caliper body (rear calipers they may not be marked)

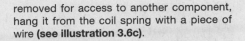

removed for access to another component, hang it from the coil spring with a piece of wire **(see illustration 3.6c)**.

Installation

5   Install the caliper by reversing the removal procedure. Remember to replace the sealing washers at the brake hose-to-caliper connection. Tighten the caliper guide/lock pins to the torque listed in this Chapter's Specifications.

6   Bleed the brake circuit according to the procedure in Section 11 (only if the brake hose was disconnected. Make sure there are no leaks from the hose connections. If you didn't disconnect the hose, be sure to pump the brake pedal several times to bring the pads into contact with the disc.

7   Test the brakes carefully before returning the vehicle to normal service.

---

5   Brake disc - inspection, removal and installation

---

clean the pin boots and check them for corrosion and damage. If they're significantly corroded or damaged, replace them.

9   If you removed both the guide pin and the lock pin, be sure to reinstall them in the correct locations **(see illustration)**. Tighten the guide pin and lock pin to the torque listed in this Chapter's Specifications.

10   Repeat the procedure on the opposite wheel, then install the wheels and lug nuts, lower the vehicle and tighten the lug nuts to the torque listed in the Chapter 1 Specifications.

11   Add the specified type of brake fluid to the reservoir until it's full (see Chapter 1).

12   Pump the brake pedal a few times to bring the pads into contact with the disc. Check the level of the brake fluid, adding some if necessary.

13   Check the operation of the brakes carefully before placing the vehicle into normal service. Try to avoid heavy brake application until the brakes have been applied lightly several times to seat the pads.

---

4   Disc brake caliper - removal and installation

Warning: *Dust created by the brake system is harmful to your health. Never blow it out with compressed air and don't inhale any of it. An approved filtering mask should be worn when working on the brakes. Do not, under any circumstances, use petroleum-based solvents to clean brake parts. Use brake system cleaner only.*

Note: *If replacement is indicated (usually because of fluid leakage), it is recommended that the calipers be replaced, not overhauled. New and factory rebuilt units are available on an exchange basis. Always replace the calipers in pairs - never replace just one of them.*

Removal

Refer to illustrations 4.2a and 4.2b

1   Loosen the wheel lug nuts, raise the vehicle and support it securely on jackstands. Remove the wheel.

2   If you're removing a front caliper, remove the fitting bolt and disconnect the brake hose from the caliper. Plug the brake hose to keep contaminants out of the brake system and to prevent losing any more brake fluid than is necessary **(see illustration)**. Discard the sealing washers - new ones should be used during installation **(see illustration)**. **Note:** *If the caliper is being removed for access to another component, don't disconnect the hose.*

3   If you're removing a rear caliper, remove the rear brake hose (see Section 10).

4   Refer to Section 3 for the caliper removal procedure (it's part of the brake pad replacement procedure). If the caliper is being

Inspection

Refer to illustrations 5.3, 5.4a, 5.4b, 5.5a and 5.5b

1   Loosen the wheel lug nuts, raise the vehicle and support it securely on jackstands. Remove the wheel and reinstall the lug nuts to hold the disc in place (washers may be required). If the rear brake disc is being worked on, release the parking brake.

2   Remove the brake caliper and pads (see Section 3) but don't disconnect the brake hose from the caliper, or you'll have to bleed the brakes when everything is reassembled. After removing the caliper bolts, suspend the caliper out of the way with a piece of wire **(see illustration 3.6c)**.

3   Visually inspect the disc surface for score marks and other damage. Light scratches and shallow grooves are normal after use and may not always be detrimental to brake operation, but deep scoring requires

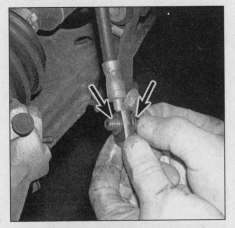

4.2a There is a sealing washer on either side of the brake hose inlet fitting; be sure to replace these with new ones when reconnecting the hose

4.2b The brake hose can be plugged using a snug-fitting piece of tubing

5.3 The brake pads on this vehicle were obviously neglected - they wore down completely and cut deep grooves into the disc (wear this severe means the disc must be replaced)

5.4a Use a dial indicator to measure disc runout - if the reading exceeds the maximum allowable runout limit, the disc will have to be machined or replaced

5.4b Using a swirling motion, remove the glaze from the disc surface with sandpaper or emery cloth

disc removal and refinishing by an automotive machine shop. Be sure to check both sides of the disc **(see illustration)**. If pulsating has been noticed during application of the brakes, suspect disc runout.

5.5a The minimum wear dimension is cast into the back side of the disc (typical)

4   To check disc runout, place a dial indicator at a point about 1/2-inch from the outer edge of the disc **(see illustration)**. Set the indicator to zero and turn the disc. The indicator reading should not exceed the specified allowable runout limit. If it does, the disc should be refinished by an automotive machine shop. **Note:** *The discs should be resurfaced regardless of the dial indicator reading, as this will impart a smooth finish and ensure a perfectly flat surface, eliminating any brake pedal pulsation or other undesirable symptoms related to questionable discs. At the very least, if you elect not to have the discs resurfaced, remove the glaze from the surface with emery cloth using a swirling motion* **(see illustration)**.
5   It's absolutely critical that the disc not be machined to a thickness under the specified minimum allowable thickness. The minimum thickness is cast into the inside of the disc **(see illustration)**. The disc thickness can be checked with a micrometer **(see illustration)**.

Removal

Refer to illustrations 5.6a and 5.6b
6   Remove the caliper mounting bracket **(see illustration)**. Remove the lug nuts, which were put on to hold the disc in place and remove the disc from the hub. Some models are equipped with threaded holes in the hub portion of the disc; if the disc sticks to the hub, screw in two bolts of the proper size and thread pitch and tighten them to force the disc off the hub **(see illustration)**.

Installation

7   Place the disc in position over the wheel studs. Install the mounting bracket, tightening the bolts to the torque listed in this Chapter's Specifications.
8   Install the brake pads and caliper (see Section 3). Tighten the caliper guide pin/lock pin to the torque listed in this Chapter's Specifications.
9   Install the wheel, lower the vehicle and tighten the lug nuts to the torque listed in the

5.5b Use a micrometer to measure disc thickness

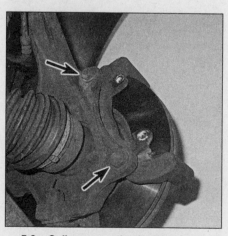

5.6a Caliper mounting bracket bolts (front shown, rear similar)

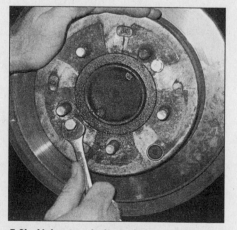

5.6b Using two bolts to force a stuck disc off the hub flange

6.4 Remove the spring from the automatic adjuster lever . . .

6.5 . . . then remove the adjuster lever

Chapter 1 Specifications.

10   Pump the brake pedal a few times to bring the brake pads into contact with the disc. Bleeding won't be necessary unless the brake hose was disconnected from the caliper. Check the operation of the brakes carefully before driving the vehicle.

6   Drum brake shoes - replacement

Refer to illustrations 6.4, 6.5, 6.6, 6.7, 6.8, 6.9, 6.13 and 6.14

Warning: *Drum brake shoes must be replaced on both wheels at the same time - never replace the shoes on only one wheel. Also, the dust created by the brake system is harmful to your health. Never blow it out with compressed air and don't inhale any of it. An approved filtering mask should be worn when working on the brakes. Do not, under any circumstances, use petroleum-based solvents to clean brake parts. Use brake system cleaner only!*

Note: *Work on one brake assembly at a time, using the assembled brake for reference if necessary.*

1   Loosen the rear wheel lug nuts, raise the rear of the vehicle and support it securely on jackstands. Block the front wheels to keep the vehicle from rolling. Release the parking brake and loosen and remove the rear wheels.

2   Remove the brake drum. If the drum won't come off, loosen the parking brake adjusting nut to remove the tension on the brake shoes (see Section 13).

3   Once the drum is removed, clean the brake assembly with brake system cleaner.

4   Using locking pliers, unhook the lever return spring from the adjuster lever and brake shoe **(see illustration)**.

5   Remove the adjuster lever **(see illustration)**.

6   Remove the retainer spring at the bottom of the shoes **(see illustration)**.

7   Using locking pliers, remove the upper return spring **(see illustration)**.

8   Remove the automatic adjuster assembly from between the brake shoes **(see illustration)**.

9   Remove the hold-down retainer and spring from each shoe **(see illustration)**.

10   Remove the leading shoe from the backing plate.

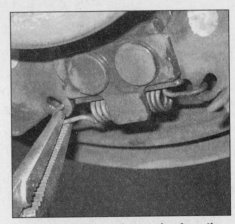

6.6 Detach the retainer spring from the bottom of the shoes

11   Remove the trailing shoe from the backing plate, then pry the retainer on the parking brake lever open just far enough to remove it. Detach the lever from the trailing shoe. Be careful not to lose the wave washer.

12   Check all parts for wear and damage, paying special attention to metal-to-metal contact points. Replace worn or damaged

6.7 Remove the upper return spring

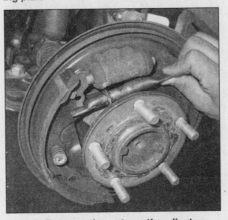

6.8 Remove the automatic adjuster assembly, noting which way it's installed

6.9 Using a hold-down spring tool, remove the hold-down spring retainer by pushing in and rotating it 1/4-turn

6.13 The maximum allowable diameter is stamped into the drum (typical)

6.14 Apply a small amount of high-temperature grease to the areas where the brake shoes contact the backing plate

parts. **Note:** *If the vehicle has high mileage, it's a good idea to replace all of the springs as well as any parts that have visible problems.*

13   Check the brake drum for score marks, cracks, deep scratches and hard spots, which will appear as small discolored areas. If the hard spots cannot be removed with sandpaper or emery cloth or if any of the other conditions are seen, the drum must be resurfaced by an automotive machine shop. **Note:** *Professionals recommend resurfacing the drum whenever a brake job is performed. Resurfacing will correct taper and out-of-roundness in the drums as well as removing visible problems. If the drums are so worn that they can't be resurfaced without exceeding the maximum allowable diameter stamped into the drum* **(see illustration)**, *then new ones will be required. At the very least, if you don't have the drums resurfaced, remove the glazing from the surface with emery cloth or sandpaper using a swirling motion.*

14   Apply a small amount of high-temperature brake grease to the shoe contact areas of the backing plate **(see illustration)**, the moving parts of the adjuster assembly and where the adjuster contacts the brake shoes.

15   Install the wave washer and attach the parking brake lever to the new trailing brake shoe. Place the retainer in the pin groove and secure it with pliers.

16   Reverse the removal steps to install the brake shoes. Expand the shoes, using the adjuster screw, until the drum will just fit over them.

17   Turn the drum and listen for the shoes dragging on the drum as it is turned. If they do rub, remove the drum and back-off the adjuster screw a little and try it again. Repeat this step until you don't hear any drag.

18   Install the drum, depress the brake pedal firmly several times, then rotate the drum to ensure that the brakes are not dragging. If they are, back off the star wheel a little more.

19   Repeat the brake shoe replacement procedure on the other rear wheel.

20   Install the wheels and lug nuts. Lower

the vehicle and tighten the lug nuts to the torque listed in the Chapter 1 Specifications.

21   Adjust the parking brake (see Section 13).

22   Start the engine, pump the brake pedal and operate the parking brake lever several times to actuate the automatic adjusters.

23   Carefully test brake operation before driving the vehicle in traffic.

7   Wheel cylinder - removal and installation

Refer to illustration 7.2

Note: *If replacement is warranted (usually because of fluid leakage or sticky operation) explore all options before beginning the job. New wheel cylinders are available, which makes this job quite easy. Never replace only one wheel cylinder. Always replace both of them at the same time.*

7.2 To detach the wheel cylinder from the brake backing plate, disconnect the brake line fitting, then remove the wheel cylinder bolts

Removal

1   Remove the rear brake shoes (see Section 6).

2   Using a flare-nut wrench (if available), disconnect the brake line fitting from the wheel cylinder **(see illustration)**. Don't pull the metal line out of the wheel cylinder - it could bend, making installation difficult.

3   Remove the two bolts securing the wheel cylinder to the backing plate and remove the wheel cylinder. Plug the end of the brake line to prevent the loss of brake fluid and the entry of dirt.

Installation

4   Installation is the reverse of removal. Tighten the wheel cylinder mounting bolts to the torque listed in this Chapter's Specifications. Tighten the line fitting securely.

5   Install the brake shoes and brake drum (see Section 6).

6   Bleed the brakes (see Section 11). Carefully test brake operation before resuming normal operation.

8   Master cylinder - removal and installation

Removal

Refer to illustration 8.6

1   The master cylinder is located in the engine compartment and mounted on the power brake booster. The fluid reservoir on earlier models is mounted on the firewall, next to the booster. On later models the reservoir is mounted directly on the master cylinder.

2   Remove the battery (see Chapter 5).

3   Using a large syringe or equivalent, siphon the brake fluid from the master cylinder reservoir and dispose of it properly. **Caution:** *Brake fluid will damage paint. Cover all painted surfaces and avoid spilling fluid during this procedure.*

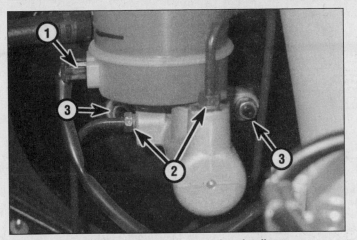

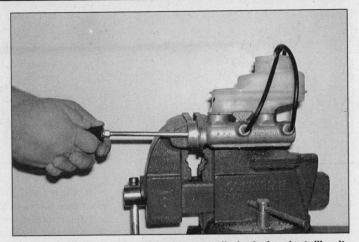

8.6 Master cylinder mounting details

1   *Electrical connector for*   2   *Brake line fittings*
     fluid level switch   3   *Mounting nuts*

**8.9 The best way to bleed the master cylinder before installing it
on the vehicle is with a pair of bleeder tubes that direct fluid into
the reservoir during bleeding**

4   Remove the windshield washer fluid reservoir. If equipped, unplug the electrical connector from the fluid level warning switch.
5   If the vehicle has a remote reservoir, place rags under the fittings and prepare caps or plastic bags to cover the ends of the lines once they're disconnected. **Caution:** *Brake fluid will damage paint. Cover all body parts and be careful not to spill fluid during this procedure.* Loosen the clamps that attach the brake hoses to the reservoir. Pull the fluid hoses away from the reservoir and plug the ends to prevent contamination.
6   Disconnect the fluid lines from the master cylinder with a flare nut wrench **(see illustration)**. On later models, disconnect the electrical connector from the fluid level sensor.
7   Remove the nuts attaching the master cylinder to the power booster and pull the master cylinder off the studs. Again, be careful not to spill the fluid as this is done.

Installation

Refer to illustration 8.9

8   Bench bleed the master cylinder before installing it. Mount the master cylinder in a vise, with the jaws of the vise clamping on the mounting flange. **Note:** *On models with a remote reservoir, this procedure will have to be performed after the master cylinder has been mounted to the power brake booster.*
9   Attach a pair of master cylinder bleeder tubes to the outlet ports of the master cylinder **(see illustration)**.
10   Fill the reservoir with brake fluid of the recommended type (see Chapter 1).
11   Slowly push the pistons into the master cylinder (a large Phillips screwdriver can be used for this, or on models with a remote reservoir, depress the brake pedal) - air will be expelled from the pressure chambers and into the reservoir. Because the tubes are submerged in fluid, air can't be drawn back into the master cylinder when you release the pistons.
12   Repeat the procedure until no more air

bubbles are present.
13   Remove the bleed tubes, one at a time, and install plugs in the open ports to prevent fluid leakage and air from entering. Install the reservoir cap.
14   Install the master cylinder over the studs on the power brake booster and tighten the nuts only finger-tight at this time. On models with a remote reservoir, connect the reservoir hoses to the inlet fittings and install the clamps.
15   Thread the brake line fittings into the master cylinder. Since the master cylinder is still a bit loose, it can be moved slightly so the fittings thread in easily. Don't strip the threads as the fittings are tightened.
16   Tighten the mounting nuts to the torque listed in this Chapter's Specifications. Tighten the brake line fittings securely.
17   Fill the master cylinder reservoir with fluid, then bleed the master cylinder and the rest of the brake system (see Section 11). To bleed the master cylinder on the vehicle, have an assistant depress the brake pedal and hold it down. Loosen the fitting to allow air and fluid to escape. Tighten the fitting, then allow your assistant to return the pedal to its rest position. Repeat this procedure on the other fit-

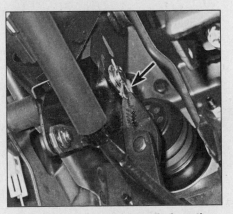

**9.9 Remove the retaining clip from the
pushrod clevis pin . . .**

tings until the fluid is free of air bubbles.
18   Reinstall the battery.
19   Re-check the brake fluid level, then check the operation of the brake system carefully before driving the vehicle in traffic.

9   Power brake booster - check, removal and installation

Operating check

1   Depress the brake pedal several times with the engine off and make sure that there is no change in the pedal reserve distance.
2   Depress the pedal and start the engine. If the pedal goes down slightly, operation is normal.

Airtightness check

3   Start the engine and turn it off after one or two minutes. Depress the brake pedal several times slowly. If the pedal goes down farther the first time but gradually rises after the second or third depression, the booster is airtight.
4   Depress the brake pedal while the engine is running, then stop the engine with the pedal depressed. If there is no change in the pedal reserve travel after holding the pedal for 30 seconds, the booster is airtight.
5   The power brake booster unit requires no special maintenance apart from periodic inspection of the vacuum hoses and the case.
6   The booster is not serviceable. If a problem develops, it must be replaced with a new one.

Removal

Refer to illustrations 9.9 and 9.10

7   Remove the battery (see Chapter 5).
8   Remove the brake master cylinder (see Section 8).
9   Locate the pushrod clevis connecting the booster to the brake pedal **(see illustration)**. It's accessible from inside the vehicle,

9.10 . . . then remove the four booster-to-firewall nuts

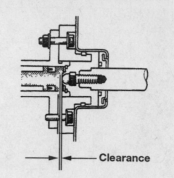

9.14a If there is there is too much clearance between the booster pushrod and the master cylinder piston, there will be excessive brake pedal travel, if there is interference between the two, the brakes may drag

9.14b Measure the distance that the pushrod protrudes from the brake booster at the master cylinder mounting surface (including the gasket, *if* one is used) - this is "dimension A"

under the dash on the driver's side. Remove the clevis pin retaining clip with pliers and pull out the pin.

10 Remove the four nuts holding the brake booster to the firewall **(see illustration)**.

11 Disconnect the hose leading from the engine to the booster. Be careful not to damage the hose when removing it from the booster fitting.

12 Slide the booster straight out from the firewall until the studs clear the holes.

Installation

13 Installation procedures are basically the reverse of removal. Be sure to install a new gasket between the booster and the firewall. Tighten the clevis locknut securely (if loosened) and the booster mounting nuts to the torque listed in this Chapter's Specifications. **Note:** *Apply a film of multi-purpose grease to the clevis pin before installing it.*

1998 and earlier models
Refer to illustrations 9.14a, 9.14b, 9.14c, 9.14d and 9.14e

14 If a new power brake booster unit is

being installed, check the pushrod clearance **(see illustration)** as follows:

a) *Measure the distance that the pushrod protrudes from the master cylinder mounting surface on the front of the power brake booster, including the gasket, if one is used. Write down this measurement* **(see illustration)**. *This is "dimension A."*

b) *Measure the distance from the mounting flange to the end of the master cylinder* **(see illustration)**. *Write down this measurement. This is "dimension B."*

c) *Measure the distance from the end of the master cylinder to the bottom of the pocket in the piston* **(see illustration)**. *Write down this measurement. This is "dimension C."*

d) *Subtract measurement B from measurement C, then subtract measurement A from the difference between B and C. This is the pushrod clearance.*

e) *Compare your calculated pushrod clearance to the pushrod clearance listed in this Chapter's Specifications. If neces-*

sary, adjust the pushrod length to achieve the correct clearance **(see illustration)**.

Proceed to Step 16.

1999 and later models
15 On these models, the only measurement that has to be taken is the amount the booster pushrod protrudes from the face of the booster **(see illustration 9.14b)**, with a vacuum of 19.6 in-Hg (-66.7 kPa) applied to the booster with a hand-held vacuum pump. Compare this dimension with the value listed in this Chapter's Specifications. If it doesn't fall within the specified range, adjust the length of the pushrod **(see illustration 9.14e)**.

All models
16 After the final installation of the master cylinder and brake hoses and lines, the system must be bled and the brake pedal height and freeplay must be adjusted. See the appropriate Sections of this Chapter for the procedures.

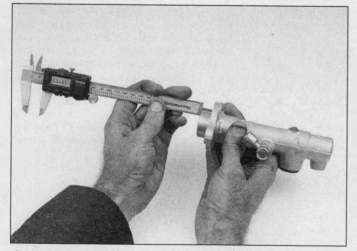

9.14c Measure the distance from the mounting flange to the end of the master cylinder - this is "dimension B"

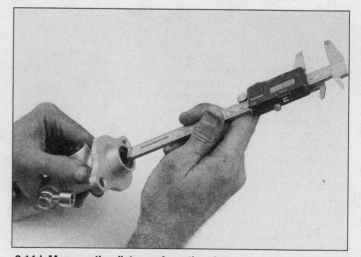

9.14d Measure the distance from the piston pocket to the end of the master cylinder - this is "dimension C"

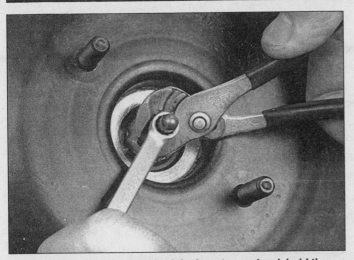

9.14e To adjust the length of the booster pushrod, hold the serrated portion of the rod with a pair of pliers and turn the adjusting screw in or out, as necessary, to achieve the desired setting

10.3 Loosening a brake line fitting from a front brake hose

10 Brake hoses and lines - inspection and replacement

Inspection

1   Whenever the vehicle is raised and supported securely on jackstands, the rubber hoses which connect the steel brake lines with the front and rear brake assemblies should be inspected for cracks, chafing of the outer cover, leaks, blisters and other damage. These are important and vulnerable parts of the brake system and inspection should be thorough. A light and mirror will be helpful for a complete check. If a hose exhibits any of the above conditions, replace it immediately.

Flexible hose replacement

Refer to illustration 10.3

2   Clean all dirt away from the hose fittings.

3   Using a flare-nut wrench, disconnect the metal brake line from the hose fitting **(see illustration)**. Be careful not to bend the frame bracket or line. If the threaded fitting is corroded, spray it with penetrating oil and allow it to soak in for about 10 minutes, then try again. If you try to break loose a fitting nut that's frozen, you will kink the metal line, which will then have to be replaced.

4   Remove the brake hose from the bracket (some are secured to a bracket with a retaining clip, others have an integral bracket/fitting). Detach the brake hose from the bracket or bracket from the vehicle as applicable. Immediately plug the metal line to prevent excessive leakage and contamination.

5   On hoses that are attached to the caliper with an inlet fitting bolt, unscrew the fitting bolt at the caliper and remove the hose, discarding the sealing washers on either side of the fitting.

6   If you're removing a rear hose on a model with disc brakes, remove the clip securing the hose to the bracket, then unscrew the hose from the caliper.

7   Attach the new brake hose to the caliper. **Note:** *When replacing the front brake hoses, always use new sealing washers.* Tighten the fitting bolt to the torque listed this Chapter's Specifications.

8   Insert the other end of the new hose through the bracket or loosely attach the fitting/bracket to the vehicle as applicable making sure the hose isn't kinked or twisted. Then fit the metal line to the hose (or hose fitting), tighten the hose bracket (if applicable) and tighten the brake tube fitting nut securely.

9   Carefully check to make sure the suspension or steering components don't make contact with the hose. Have an assistant push down on the vehicle while you watch to see whether the hose interferes with suspension operation. If you're replacing a front hose, have your assistant turn the steering wheel lock-to-lock while you make sure the hose doesn't interfere with the steering linkage or the steering knuckle.

10   After installation, check the master cylinder fluid level and add fluid as necessary. Bleed the brakes (see Section 11). Carefully test brake operation before resuming normal operation.

Metal brake lines

11   When replacing brake lines, be sure to use the correct parts. Do not use copper tubing for any brake system components. Purchase steel brake lines from a dealer parts department or auto parts store.

12   Prefabricated brake line, with the tube ends already flared and fittings installed, is available at auto parts stores and dealer parts departments. If it is necessary to bend a line, use a tubing bender to prevent kinking the line.

13   When installing the new line make sure it's well supported in the brackets and has plenty of clearance between moving or hot components. Make sure you tighten the fittings securely.

14   After installation, check the master cylinder fluid level and add fluid as necessary. Bleed the brakes (see Section 11). Carefully test brake operation before resuming normal operation.

11 Brake hydraulic system - bleeding

Refer to illustrations 11.7 and 11.9

Warning 1: *The following procedure is a manual bleeding procedure. This is the only bleeding procedure, which can be performed at home without special tools. However, if air has found its way into the hydraulic control unit, the entire system must be bled manually, then with a scan tool, then manually a second time. If the brake pedal feels "spongy" even after bleeding the brakes, or the ABS light on the instrument panel does not go off, or if you have any doubts whatsoever about the effectiveness of the brake system, have the vehicle towed to a dealer service department or other repair shop equipped with the necessary tools for bleeding the system.*

Warning 2: *Wear eye protection when bleeding the brake system. If the fluid comes in contact with your eyes, immediately rinse them with water and seek medical attention.*

Note: *Bleeding the hydraulic system is necessary to remove any air that manages to find its way into the system when it's been opened during removal and installation of a hydraulic component.*

1   It will be necessary to bleed the complete system if air has entered the system due to low fluid level, or if the brake lines have been disconnected at the master cylinder.

11.7 Have an assistant depress the brake pedal and hold it down, then loosen the fitting nut, allowing air and brake fluid to escape; repeat this procedure on the other fitting(s) until the fluid is clear of air bubbles

2   If a brake line was disconnected only at a wheel, then only that caliper or wheel cylinder must be bled.

3   If a brake line is disconnected at a fitting located between the master cylinder and any of the brakes, that part of the system served by the disconnected line must be bled. The following procedure describes bleeding the entire system, however.

4   Remove any residual vacuum from the brake power booster by applying the brake several times with the engine off.

5   Remove the cap from the master cylinder reservoir and fill the reservoir with brake fluid. Reinstall the cap(s). **Note:** *Check the fluid level often during the bleeding operation and add fluid as necessary to prevent the fluid level from falling low enough to allow air bubbles into the master cylinder.*

6   Have an assistant on hand, as well as a

11.9 When bleeding the brakes, a hose is connected to the bleed screw at the caliper or wheel cylinder and then submerged in clean brake fluid - air will be seen as bubbles exiting the tube (all air must be expelled before moving to the next wheel)

supply of new brake fluid, a clear container partially filled with clean brake fluid, a length of clear tubing to fit over the bleeder valve and a wrench to open and close the bleeder valve.

7   Begin the bleeding process by bleeding the master cylinder **(see illustration)**.

8   Moving to the first wheel in the bleeding sequence, loosen the bleeder valve slightly, then tighten it to a point where it is snug but can still be loosened quickly and easily. The bleeding sequence is as follows:

> Right rear
> Left front
> Left rear
> Right front

9   Place one end of the hose over the bleeder valve and submerge the other end in brake fluid in the container **(see illustration)**.

10   Have the assistant push the brake pedal slowly to the floor, then hold the pedal firmly depressed.

11   While the pedal is held depressed, open the bleeder valve just enough to allow a flow of fluid to leave the valve. Watch for air bubbles to exit the submerged end of the tube. When the fluid flow slows after a couple of seconds, close the valve and have your assistant release the pedal.

12   Repeat Steps 10 and 11 until no more air is seen leaving the tube, then tighten the bleeder valve and proceed to bleed the other calipers/wheel cylinders, in the proper sequence, using the same procedure. Be sure to check the fluid in the master cylinder reservoir frequently.

13   Never use old brake fluid. It contains moisture, which can boil, rendering the brakes inoperative.

14   Refill the master cylinder with fluid at the end of the operation.

15   Check the operation of the brakes. The pedal should feel solid when depressed, with no sponginess. If necessary, repeat the entire process. **Warning:** *If, after bleeding the system you do not have a firm brake pedal, or if the ABS light on the instrument panel does not go off, or if you have any doubts whatsoever about the effectiveness of the brake system, have it towed to a dealer service department or other repair shop to have the system bled.*

12 Parking brake shoes (models with rear disc brakes) - replacement

Refer to illustrations 12.4a and 12.4b
Warning: *Parking brake shoes must be replaced on both wheels at the same time - never replace the shoes on only one wheel. Also, the dust created by the brake system is harmful to your health. Never blow it out with*

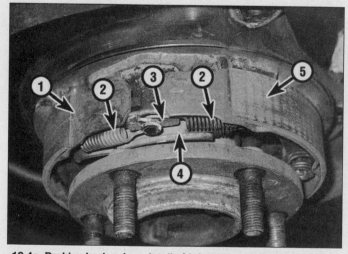

12.4a Parking brake shoe details (right side, viewed from above)

1	Trailing shoe	4	Strut
2	Upper return spring	5	Leading shoe
3	Anchor plate		

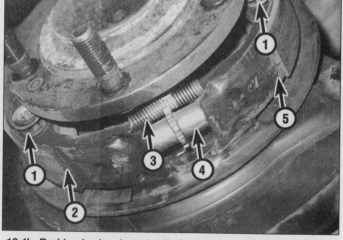

12.4b Parking brake shoe details (right side, viewed from below)

1	Hold-down spring and retainer	3	Lower return spring
2	Trailing shoe	4	Adjuster screw assembly
		5	Leading shoe

compressed air and don't inhale any of it. An approved filtering mask should be worn when working on the brakes. Do not, under any circumstances, use petroleum-based solvents to clean brake parts. Use brake system cleaner only!

1   Loosen the rear wheel lug nuts, raise the rear end of the vehicle and support it securely on jackstands. Block the front wheels to keep the vehicle from rolling. Release the parking brake and remove the rear wheels.

2   Remove the brake caliper, mounting bracket and brake disc (see Section 5).

3   Once the disc is removed, clean the parking brake assembly with brake system cleaner.

4   Using locking pliers, unhook and remove the springs **(see illustrations)**.

5   Remove the adjuster assembly (noting which end is facing forward) and strut from between the brake shoes.

6   Grasp one of the shoe hold-down cups with pliers and push it toward the brake backing plate to compress the hold-down spring. Twist the cup 1/4-turn to align the slot in the hold-down pin with the cup, then release the spring pressure (the pin will pass through the cup slot) and take off the cup and spring. Repeat this with the cup and spring on the other parking brake shoe.

7   Take the shoes off the backing plate. Disengage the parking brake lever from the cable.

8   Check all parts for wear and damage, paying special attention to metal-to-metal contact points. Replace worn or damaged parts. The parking brake lever is integral with the shoe it's attached to. **Note:** *If the vehicle has high mileage, it's a good idea to replace all of the springs as well as any parts that have visible problems.*

9   Check the parking brake drum surface inside the brake disc for score marks, cracks, deep scratches and hard spots, which will appear as small discolored areas. If the hard spots cannot be removed with emery cloth or if any of the other conditions are seen, the drum must be resurfaced by an automotive

machine shop. **Note:** *If you don't have the drums resurfaced, remove the glazing from the surface with emery cloth or sandpaper using a swirling motion.*

10   Apply a small amount of high-temperature brake grease to the friction points of the backing plate and adjuster screw assembly **(see illustration 6.14)**.

11   Reverse the removal steps to install the brake shoes. The shoe-to-anchor spring with the paint mark is installed with the paint mark toward the rear of the vehicle (for both left and right sides). Expand the shoes, using the automatic adjuster, until the drum will just fit over them.

12   Install the brake disc and caliper. Remove the rubber plug in the hub portion of the disc, then turn the adjuster screw until the disc will not turn. Now turn the adjuster in the opposite direction five notches.

13   Adjust the parking brake (see Section 13).

14   Install the wheel and lug nuts. Lower the vehicle and tighten the lug nuts to the torque listed in the Chapter 1 Specifications.

15   Check the operation of the parking brake.

13   Parking brake - adjustment

Refer to illustration 13.3

1   The parking brake lever, when properly adjusted, should travel five to seven clicks (rear drum brakes) or three to five clicks (rear disc brakes) when a moderate pulling force is applied. If it travels less than specified, there's a chance the parking brake might not be releasing completely and might be dragging on the drum. If the lever can be pulled up more than specified, the parking brake may not hold adequately on an incline, allowing the car to roll.

2   To gain access to the parking brake cable adjuster, remove the center console (see Chapter 11).

3   Turn the adjusting nut on the parking

brake cable all the way to the end of the cable **(see illustration)**.

4   If you're working on a vehicle with rear drum brakes, press the brake pedal firmly several times to operate the rear brake adjusters. The pedal stroke should change, then stop changing, as the pedal is pumped. If the automatic adjusters are working properly, this will adjust the parking brake, too.

5   If you're working on a vehicle with rear disc brakes, loosen the rear wheel lug nuts, raise the rear of the vehicle and support it securely on jackstands, then remove the rear wheels. Insert a screwdriver into the hole in the hub portion of the disc and turn the adjuster to lock the brake disc. Turn the adjuster back five notches. Install the rear wheels and leave the rear end jacked up.

6   Loosen or tighten the adjusting nut **(see illustration 13.3)** until the desired travel is attained. Tighten the nut. Make sure there's no play between the adjusting nut and the pin in the nut holder.

8   On drum brake models, jack up the rear end and support the vehicle on jackstands. Spin the rear wheels by hand and make sure the rear brakes don't drag. Lower the vehicle.

9   On rear disc brake models, install the wheel and lug nuts, then lower the vehicle and tighten the lug nuts to the torque listed in the Chapter 1 Specifications.

10   Install the console.

14   Brake light switch - check, replacement and adjustment

Check
Refer to illustrations 14.1a and 14.1b

1   The brake light switch is located on the brake pedal mounting bracket **(see illustrations)**. The switch activates the brake lights at the rear of the vehicle when the pedal is depressed. To gain access to the switch, remove the left-side under-dash panel and the heater/air conditioning duct.

13.3 Remove the center console for access to the parking brake cable adjuster nut

14.1 Brake light switch

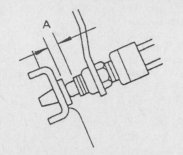

14.11 To adjust the brake light switch on 1998 and earlier models, adjust the position of the switch in its bracket until the gap between the switch body and the brake pedal is as specified

2   If the brake lights are inoperative, check the fuse first (see Chapter 12).

3   If the fuse is good, check for voltage to the switch on the feed wire (refer to the wiring diagrams at the end of this manual for the proper color wire to check). If no voltage is present, repair the wire between the switch and the fuse box.

4   If voltage is present, depress the brake pedal and check for voltage at the output wire terminal (again, refer to the wiring diagrams). If no voltage is present, replace the switch.

5   If voltage is present, check for power on the brake light wires at the tail light housings (with the brake pedal depressed). If voltage is not present, repair the circuit between the switch and the brake lights.

6   If voltage is present, check for a bad ground; using a jumper wire connected to a good ground, probe the ground wire terminal at the tail light connector. If the brake lights go on, repair the ground circuit (follow the ground wire from the tail light housing).

7   Keep in mind that the brake light bulbs *could* be burned out, but the likelihood of all the bulbs being burned out is very slim.

Replacement and adjustment

8   Disconnect the electrical connector from the brake light switch **(see illustration 14.1)**.

1998 and earlier models

Refer to illustration 14.11

9   Disconnect the electrical connector from the brake light switch.

10   Loosen the locknut and unscrew the switch from the bracket.

11   Installation is the reverse of removal. To adjust the switch, thread it into its bracket until it contacts the brake pedal, then unscrew it until there is a gap of 0.020 to 0.040-inch (0.5 to 1.01 mm) between the end of the switch body and the brake pedal **(see illustration)**.

12   Tighten the locknut securely.

1999 and later models

13   Rotate the switch counterclockwise slightly, so it unlocks from its holder, then pull it out of the holder.

14   To install the switch, insert it into its holder (canted slightly counterclockwise as during removal) and push it in until the switch body contacts the bracket on the brake pedal, then pull it back so there is approximately 3/64-inch (1 mm) clearance between the switch body and the bracket on the pedal. Rotate the switch clockwise to lock it into place.

15   Plug the electrical connector into the switch.

---

15   Brake pedal - adjustment

Brake pedal height

Refer to illustration 15.1

1   With the brake pedal fully released, measure the distance from the top of the pad to the floor **(see illustration)**.

2   If the height is not as listed in the Specifications Section at the beginning of this Chapter it must be adjusted.

3   Loosen the brake light switch (see Section 14).

4   Loosen the locknut just in front of the clevis on the power brake booster pushrod.

5   Turn the booster pushrod until the pedal height is correct.

6   Tighten the locknut.

7   After adjusting the pedal height, check the freeplay, then adjust the brake light switch (see Section 14).

Brake pedal freeplay

Refer to illustration 15.8

8   Press down lightly on the brake pedal and measure the distance that it moves freely before resistance is felt **(see illustration)**. The freeplay should be within the specified limits. If it isn't, check the clevis, clevis pin and the hole in the brake pedal arm for excessive wear. Also make sure the brake light switch is properly adjusted.

Brake pedal reserve distance

9   After checking and, if necessary, adjusting the pedal released height and freeplay, the pedal reserve distance must be checked.

10   With the engine running, press the brake pedal fully and measure the pedal pad-to-floor distance.

11   If the minimum depressed height is below that listed in the Specifications Section at the beginning of this Chapter, bleed the brakes to rule out the possibility of air in the system. If the reserve distance is still less than specified, check the rear brake automatic adjusters for proper operation (drum brake models only).

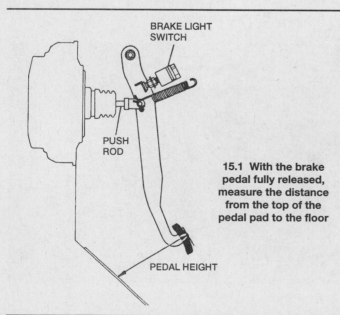

15.1 With the brake pedal fully released, measure the distance from the top of the pedal pad to the floor

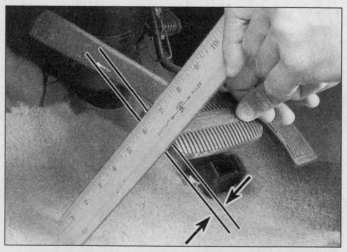

15.8 To measure brake pedal freeplay, press down lightly on the pedal and measure the distance that it moves freely before resistance is felt

Chapter 10
Suspension and steering systems

Contents

Specifications

Torque specifications

	Ft-lbs (unless otherwise indicated)	Nm
Front suspension (1998 and earlier models)		
Shock absorber		
Upper mounting nuts	32	44
Damper fork-to-shock absorber pinch bolt	75	103
Damper fork-to-lateral arm bolt/nut	64	88
Damper rod nut	18	25
Stabilizer bar		
Bracket bolts	28	39
Link nuts	28	39
Compression lower arm		
Balljoint nut	43 to 51	59 to 71
Pivot shaft bolts	60	83
Lateral lower arm		
Balljoint nut	43 to 51	59 to 71
To damper fork bolt	64	88
Pivot bolt/nut	71 to 85	98 to 118
Upper control arm		
Shaft-to-body nuts	62	86
Pivot bolt nuts	41	57
Balljoint nut	20	28
Hub and bearing assembly-to-steering knuckle bolts	65	88
Stiffener plate bolts	51 to 58	69 to 78
Driveaxle/hub nut	See Chapter 8	

Torque specifications

	Ft-lbs (unless otherwise indicated)	Nm

Note: *One foot-pound (ft-lb) of torque is equivalent to 12 inch-pounds (in-lbs) of torque. Torque values below approximately 15 foot-pounds are expressed in inch-pounds, because most foot-pound torque wrenches are not accurate at these smaller values.*

Front suspension (1999 through 2003 models)

	Ft-lbs	Nm
Strut		
Upper mounting nuts	33	44
Damper rod nut	44 to 51	59 to 69
Strut-to-steering knuckle bolts/nuts	203 to 239	275 to 324
Stabilizer bar		
Bracket bolts	32	44
Link nuts	32	44
Control arm		
Clamp-to-body bolts	60	81
Pivot bolt nut (front)	72 to 87	98 to 118
Rear bushing pivot nut	66 to 80	88 to 108
Balljoint-to-steering knuckle pinch bolt/nut	72 to 87	98 to 118
Hub and bearing assembly-to-steering knuckle bolts	65	88
Driveaxle/hub nut	See Chapter 8	

Front suspension (2004 and later models)

	Ft-lbs	Nm
Strut		
Upper mounting bolts	30 to 40	41 to 55
Strut-to-knuckle nuts	207 to 243	280 to 330
Damper rod nut	45 to 51	60 to 70
Stabilizer bar		
Bracket bolts	38 to 48	51 to 65
Link nuts	30 to 40	41 to 55
Control arm		
Front bolt	111 to 133	150 to 180
Rear nut	111 to 133	150 to 180
Control arm-to-knuckle nut	44 to 52	59 to 71
Hub and bearing assembly-to-knuckle bolts	67 to 81	90 to 110
Driveaxle/hub nut	See Chapter 8	

Rear suspension (1998 and earlier models)

	Ft-lbs	Nm
Rear stabilizer bar		
Clamp bolts	84 to 120 in-lbs	9 to 14
Link nuts	29	39
Shock absorber		
To body nuts	32	44
Lower mounting bolt/nut	71	98
Damper rod nut	14 to 20	20 to 25
Trailing arm-to-body bolt/nut	99 to 114	137 to 157
Trailing arm-to-knuckle bolt	85 to 99	118 to 137
Upper control arm-to-knuckle bolt/nut	71	98
Upper control arm-to-bracket pivot bolts/nuts	41	57
Upper control arm bracket-to-body bolts	28	39
Lower arm-to-crossmember bolt	71	98
Lower arm-to-knuckle bolt/nut	71	98
Toe control arm-to-crossmember bolt/nut	50 to 56	69 to 78
Toe control arm balljoint nut	20	28
Rear hub-to-knuckle bolts	60	81
Rear suspension crossmember-to-body nuts	64	86

Rear suspension (1999 through 2003 models)

	Ft-lbs	Nm
Rear stabilizer bar		
Clamp bolts	32	44
Link nuts	29	39
Shock absorber		
To body nuts	32	44
Lower mounting bolt/nut	72	98
Damper rod nut	15 to 18	20 to 25
Trailing arm-to-body bolt/nut	101 to 116	137 to 157
Trailing arm-to-knuckle bolt	87 to 101	118 to 137
Upper control arm-to-knuckle bolt/nut	72	98
Upper control arm-to-bracket pivot bolts/nuts	42	57
Upper control arm bracket-to-body bolts	29	39
Lower arm-to-crossmember bolt	72	98
Lower arm-to-knuckle bolt/nut	80	108
Toe control arm-to-crossmember bolt/nut	51 to 58	69 to 78

Toe control arm balljoint nut..	21	28
Rear hub-to-knuckle bolts..	55 to 65	74 to 88
Rear suspension crossmember-to-body nuts......................................	65	88

Rear suspension (2004 and later models)

Stabilizer bar		
Clamp bolts...	31 to 37	40 to 50
Link nuts...	27 to 33	35 to 45
Shock absorber		
Upper mounting nuts..	31 to 37	40 to 50
Lower mounting bolts...	67 to 81	90 to 110
Damper rod nut..	16 to 18	21 to 25
Trailing arm		
Trailing arm assembly-to-knuckle nut..	74 to 92	101 to 125
Trailing arm assembly-to-bracket nut..	74 to 92	101 to 125
Trailing arm bracket-to-body fasteners	67 to 81	90 to 110
Upper control arm		
Upper arm assembly-to-crossmember fasteners............................	74 to 92	101 to 125
Upper arm assembly-to-knuckle nut	74 to 92	101 to 125
Lower control arm		
Lower arm assembly-to-crossmember nut......................................	52 to 62	71 to 85
Lower arm assembly-to-knuckle nut	74 to 92	101 to 125
Lower arm assembly-to-stabilizer bar link nut................................	27 to 33	35 to 45
Toe control arm		
Toe control arm-to-crossmember nut	52 to 62	71 to 85
Toe control arm-to-knuckle nut	45 to 53	60 to 72
Rear suspension crossmember		
Crossmember-to-body bolts	70 to 92	95 to 125
Crossmember bracket mounting fasteners	52 to 70	71 to 95
Crossmember front brace bolts	31 to 37	40 to 50
Crossmember rear brace fasteners..	52 to 70	71 to 95

Steering system

Airbag bolts	84 in-lbs	9
Steering wheel nut..	30	41
Steering gear mounting bolts		
2003 and earlier models...	51	69
2004 and later models	52 to 70	71 to 95
Steering column mounting bolts	108 in-lbs	12
Steering column shaft pinch bolts..	156 in-lbs	18
Tie-rod end-to-steering knuckle nut...	18 to 25	25 to 33
Power steering pressure line-to-pump nut or bolt		
1998 and earlier models...	156 in-lbs	18
1999 and later models	42	57

1 General information

Refer to illustrations 1.1, 1.2, 1.3a, 1.3b and 1.3c

The front suspension on 1998 and earlier models uses a single upper and two lower control arms connected by a steering knuckle. Damping is provided by a coil spring/shock absorber unit, which is attached to the body at the top and through a damper fork to the compression lower control arm at the bottom **(see illustration)**.

On 1999 and later models the front suspension is a MacPherson strut design **(see illustration)**. The upper end of each strut is attached to the vehicle body. The lower end of the strut is connected to the upper end of the steering knuckle. The steering knuckle is attached to a balljoint in the outer end of the control arm. On all models, a front stabilizer bar is attached to the lower control arms to minimize body roll during cornering.

The rear suspension on all models also uses shock absorber/coil spring assemblies. The upper end of each shock is attached to the vehicle body. The lower end of the shock is attached to the rear knuckle. An upper control arm at the top, and two lateral links and a trailing arm at the bottom locate the knuckle. The basic design of the rear suspension is the same for all model years covered in this manual. Some components differ in appearance between models, but the overall design is the same **(see illustrations)**.

The rack-and-pinion steering gear is located below and behind the engine/transaxle assembly on the crossmember and actuates the tie-rods, which are attached to the steering knuckles. The steering column is designed to collapse in the event of an accident.

Frequently, when working on the suspension or steering system components, you may come across fasteners, which seem impossible to loosen. These fasteners on the underside of the vehicle are continually subjected to water, road grime, mud, etc., and can become rusted or "frozen," making them extremely difficult to remove. In order to unscrew these stubborn fasteners without damaging them (or other components), be sure to use lots of penetrating oil and allow it to soak in for a while. Using a wire brush to clean exposed threads will also ease removal of the nut or bolt and prevent damage to the threads. Sometimes a sharp blow with a hammer and punch will break the bond between a nut and bolt threads, but care must be taken to prevent the punch from slipping off the fastener and ruining the threads. Heating the stuck fastener and surrounding area with a torch sometimes helps too, but isn't recommended because of the obvious dangers associated with fire. Long breaker bars and extension, or "cheater," pipes will increase leverage, but never use an extension pipe on a ratchet - the ratcheting mechanism could be damaged. Sometimes tightening the nut or bolt first will help to break it loose. Fasteners that require drastic measures to remove should always be replaced with new ones.

1.1 Front suspension and steering components - 1998 and earlier models

1	Shock absorber/coil spring assembly	4	Lower Balljoints	7	Lower control arm mounts and bushings	10	Driveaxle
2	Steering knuckle	5	Compression lower control arm	8	Steering gear assembly	11	Upper balljoint
3	Hub and bearing assembly	6	Lateral arm	9	Stabilizer bar	12	Upper control arm

1.2 Front suspension and steering components - 1999 and later models

1	Strut/coil spring assembly	3	Balljoint	5	Steering gear
2	Steering knuckle	4	Lower control arm		

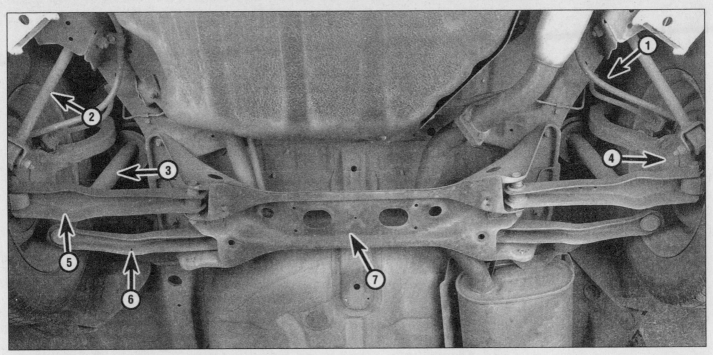

1.3a Rear suspension components - 1998 and earlier models

1   Upper control arm
2   Trailing arm
3   Shock absorber/coil spring assembly
4   Rear knuckle
5   Lower control arm
6   Toe control arm
7   Rear suspension crossmember

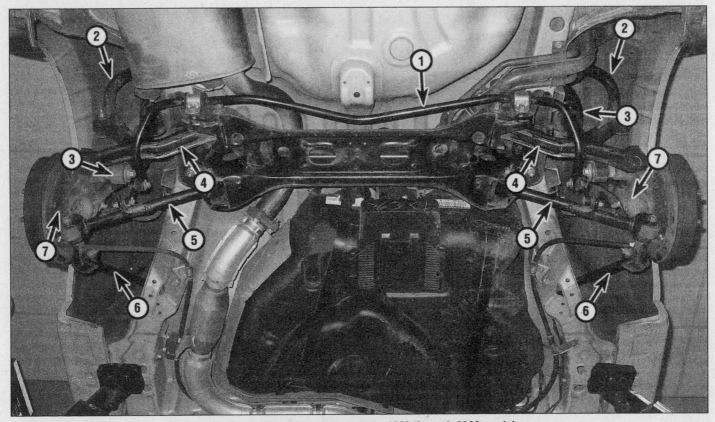

1.3b Rear suspension components - 1999 through 2003 models

1   Stabilizer bar
2   Upper control arm
3   Shock absorber/coil spring assembly
4   Toe control arm
5   Lower control arm
6   Trailing arm
7   Rear knuckle

1.3c Rear suspension components - 2004 and later models

A	Upper control arm	C	Toe control arm
B	Shock absorber/coil spring assembly	D	Lower control arm

E	Trailing arm
F	Rear knuckle

Since most of the procedures dealt with in this Chapter involve jacking up the vehicle and working underneath it, a good pair of jackstands will be needed. A hydraulic floor jack is the preferred type of jack to lift the vehicle, and it can also be used to support certain components during various operations. **Warning:** *Never, under any circumstances, rely on a jack to support the vehicle while working on it. Whenever any of the suspension or steering fasteners are loosened or removed they must be inspected and, if necessary, replaced with new ones of the same part number or of original equipment quality and design. Torque specifications must be followed for proper reassembly and component retention. Never attempt to heat or straighten any suspension or steering components. Instead, replace any bent or damaged part with a new one.*

---

2   Stabilizer bar and bushings (front) - removal, inspection and installation

---

Removal

2003 and earlier models

Refer to illustrations 2.2a, 2.2b and 2.3

1   Loosen the front wheel lug nuts, raise

the front of the vehicle and support it securely on jackstands. Apply the parking brake and block the rear wheels to keep the vehicle from rolling off the stands. Remove the front wheels.

2   Remove the nuts and the stabilizer bar attaching link assemblies from the damper forks (1998 and earlier models) or the strut (1999 and later models) **(see Illustrations)**. **Note:** *Use an Allen wrench to prevent the ballstud from turning when removing the attaching link nut.*

3   Remove the stabilizer bar bushing retainer bolts **(see illustration)**.

4   Remove the stabilizer bar from the vehicle. On some models it'll be necessary to unbolt the center member (see Chapter 2 and Section 22) and stiffener plates from between the crossmember and the floorpan to allow removal of the bar **(see illustrations 22.7a, 22.7b and 22.9)**. Also, on 1999 through 2003 four-cylinder models, the front portion of the exhaust system must be removed.

2004 and later models

5   Raise the vehicle and support it securely on jackstands. Aim the front wheels straight ahead to avoid damaging the airbag clockspring when installing it.

6   Remove the engine lower splash shield.

7   Disconnect the engine roll-stopper mounts, then remove the longitudinal center crossmember.

8   Refer to Section 8 and remove the front lower control arms.

9   Refer to Section 18 and remove the steering wheel assembly.

10   Remove the console, the front door threshold trims, the kick panel trims, the trunk lid opener cover and the accelerator pedal stopper (see Chapter 11). Pull back the carpet as necessary.

11   Disconnect the ends of the stabilizer bar from the links.

12   Disconnect the steering tie-rods from the steering knuckle (see Section 20).

13   Remove the steering column base cover, then disconnect the steering shaft from the steering gear. **Note:** *Paint matchmarks on the parts so they can be assembled in the same way.*

14   Disconnect the power steering lines from the pump. Place a drain pan underneath to contain spillage.

15   Unbolt the engine rear roll-stopper bracket from the roll-stopper bushing.

16   Place a floor jack under the center of the engine crossmember to support it. Unbolt the steering column (see Section 22), then pinch the column shaft clip using pliers and pull the column rearward to disengage it from the steering gear.

17   Remove the end bolts from the front crossmember, then remove the crossmember braces.

18   Slowly lower the engine crossmember.

2.2a On 1998 and earlier models the stabilizer bar link is connected to the damper fork

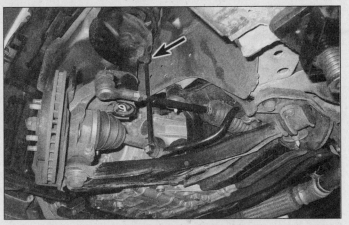

2.2b The stabilizer bar link on 1999 and later models connects to the strut

19   Remove the steering linkage guard from V6 models.

20   Unbolt the stabilizer bar brackets and remove the stabilizer bar.

Inspection

21   Inspect for cracked, torn, or distorted stabilizer bar bushings, bushing retainers, and worn or damaged stabilizer bar links.

22   To replace damaged stabilizer bar bushings, remove the retainer, open the bushing slit and peel the bushing from the stabilizer bar. On some models it will be necessary to bend back the tabs holding the retainer together. **Caution:** *Install the new bushings with the slits facing the same way that the original bushing slits faced.*

Installation

23   Guide the stabilizer bar into position. Install the retainer bolts, tightening them to the torque listed in this Chapter's Specifications.

24   Connect the stabilizer bar links to the damper forks or struts, as applicable, and install the retaining nuts. Tighten the nuts to the torque in this Chapter's Specifications.

25   The remainder of installation is the reverse of removal.

26   Install the wheels and lug nuts. Lower the vehicle and tighten the lug nuts to the torque listed in the Chapter 1 Specifications.

27   On 2004 and later models, make sure to refill and bleed the power steering system as necessary (see Section 24). Also take care to correctly align the steering gear input shaft with the steering column shaft (see Section 22).

---

3   **Shock absorber/coil spring assembly (front) (1998 and earlier models) - removal, inspection and installation**

Removal

Refer to illustrations 3.4 and 3.5

1   Loosen the wheel lug nuts, raise the front of the vehicle, support it securely on

jackstands and remove the front wheels.

2   Mark the shock absorbers LEFT and RIGHT if you're going to remove both of them at the same time. Unclip the brake hose from its bracket and detach the ABS wheel speed sensor bracket from the steering knuckle, as applicable.

3   Remove the nut and detach the stabilizer bar link from the damper fork **(see illustration 2.2a)**.

4   Remove the pinch bolt that secures the lower end of the shock absorber to the damper fork. Also remove the nut and through-bolt that secures the lower end of the damper fork to the suspension arm **(see illustration)**. **Note:** *After removing the nut, drive the bolt out with a hammer and punch (don't turn it, because it has a serrated shoulder).*

5   Remove the upper mounting nuts that secure the shock absorber to the body **(see illustration)**. **Warning:** *Do not remove the shock absorber damper rod nut (the nut in the center of the upper mount).* Separate the damper fork from the shock absorber, using a brass hammer if necessary, and remove them both from the vehicle. It may be necessary to push down on the steering knuckle/lower control arm(s), but be careful not to

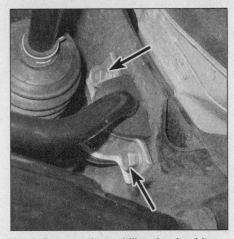

2.3 Remove the stabilizer bar bushing retainer bolts

strain the brake hose. **Note:** *If you're working on a convertible or sedan model, the upper control arm will come out with the shock absorber assembly.*

Inspection

6   Check the shock absorber/coil spring assembly for leaking fluid, dents, cracks and

3.4 Unscrew the nut from the damper fork-to-control arm bolt, then drive the bolt out with a hammer and punch

3.5 Shock absorber upper mounting nuts

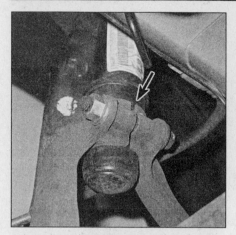

3.8 When installing the damper fork to the shock absorber, make sure the tab on the shock engages with the slot in the fork, and that it seats completely

other obvious damage, which would warrant replacement.

7   Check the coil spring for chips and corrosion. Replace it if any undesirable symptoms are found. See Section 5 for the shock absorber or coil spring replacement procedure.

Installation

Refer to illustration 3.8

8   Installation is the reverse of the removal steps. When installing the damper fork to the shock absorber, make sure it is properly aligned and fully seated against the locating tab on the shock absorber body **(see illustration)**. Tighten the fasteners to the torque values listed in this Chapter's Specifications. Tighten the lug nuts to the torque listed in the Chapter 1 Specifications. **Note:** *Before tightening the damper fork-to-lower control arm bolt, raise the lower control arm with a floor jack to simulate normal ride height (this will prevent bushing wind-up).*

---

4   Strut assembly (front) (1999 and later models) - removal, inspection and installation

---

Removal

Refer to illustration 4.2

1   Loosen the wheel lug nuts, raise the vehicle and support it securely on jackstands. Remove the wheel.

2   Detach the brake hose from the strut. If the vehicle is equipped with ABS, also detach the speed sensor wiring harness from the strut **(see illustration)**. On 2004 and later models, disconnect the stabilizer bar link from the strut.

3   Remove the strut-to-knuckle nuts and knock the bolts out with a hammer and punch. **Note:** *Mark the locations of the bolts, as special camber adjusting bolts may have*

been installed at some point. Also mark the relationship of the strut to the steering knuckle.

4   Separate the strut from the steering knuckle. Be careful not to overextend the inner CV joint. Also make sure you don't push down too far on the control arm or you could overextend - and damage - the ABS speed sensor wiring harness and the brake hose. **Caution:** *Don't allow the steering knuckle and hub assembly to swing outward as this could strain the brake hose also.*

5   Support the strut and spring assembly with one hand and remove the three strut upper mounting nuts (similar to those shown in **illustration 3.5**). Remove the assembly from the fenderwell.

Inspection

6   Check the strut body for leaking fluid, dents, cracks and other obvious damage, which would warrant repair or replacement.

7   Check the coil spring for chips or cracks in the spring coating (this will cause premature spring failure due to corrosion). Inspect the spring seat for cuts, hardness and general deterioration.

8   If any undesirable conditions exist, proceed to the strut disassembly procedure (see Section 5).

Installation

9   Guide the strut assembly up into the fenderwell and insert the three mounting studs through the holes in the strut tower. Once the three studs protrude from the shock tower, install the nuts so the strut won't fall back through. This is most easily accomplished with the help of an assistant, as the strut is quite heavy and awkward.

10   Slide the steering knuckle into the strut flange and insert the two bolts. Install the nuts, line-up the marks you made on the strut and the knuckle, then tighten the nuts to the torque listed in this Chapter's Specifications.

11   Attach the brake hose to the strut. If the vehicle is equipped with ABS, attach the speed sensor wiring harness bracket.

12   Install the wheel and lug nuts, then lower the vehicle and tighten the lug nuts to the torque listed in the Chapter 1 Specifications.

13   Tighten the upper mounting nuts to the torque listed in this Chapter's Specifications.

14   It's a good idea to have the front end alignment checked and, if necessary, adjusted.

---

5   Shock absorber/strut or coil spring - replacement

---

1   If the shock absorbers/struts or coil springs exhibit the telltale signs of wear (leaking fluid, loss of damping capability, chipped, sagging or cracked coil springs) explore all options before beginning any work. The strut/shock absorber portions of the assemblies are not serviceable and must be replaced if a problem develops. The coil springs and strut/shock absorber assemblies can be replaced separately, using the procedures in this Section. In the case of struts, you'll need a special tool or equivalent to hold the spring seat while you unscrew the nut. Strut/shock absorber assemblies complete with springs may be available on an exchange basis, which eliminates much time and work. Whichever route you choose to take, check on the cost and availability of parts before disassembling your vehicle. **Warning:** *Disassembling a strut/shock absorber assembly is potentially dangerous and utmost attention must be directed to the job, or serious injury may result. Use only a high quality spring compressor and carefully follow the manufacturer's instructions furnished with the tool. After removing the coil spring, set it aside in a safe, isolated area.*

Disassembly

Refer to illustrations 5.3, 5.5, 5.6, 5.7 and 5.8

2   Remove the front shock absorber/coil spring assembly (see Section 3), the strut and spring assembly (see Section 4) or the rear shock absorber/coil spring assembly (see Section 13). Mount the assembly in a vise. Line the vise jaws with wood or rags to prevent damage to the unit and don't tighten the vise excessively.

3   Following the tool manufacturer's instructions, install the spring compressor (which can be obtained at most auto parts stores or equipment yards on a daily rental basis) on the spring and compress it sufficiently to relieve all pressure from the spring seats insulator **(see illustration)**. This can be

4.2 Remove the clip and detach the brake hose from the strut (not visible here); unbolt the ABS speed sensor from the strut, if equipped; remove the two large nuts and drive out the strut-to-knuckle bolts (1999 and later models)

5.3 Install the spring compressor following the tool manufacturer's instructions; compress the spring until all pressure is relieved from the spring seat

5.5 Remove the damper rod nut (you'll probably have to prevent the rod from turning by holding the spring seat with a pin spanner type tool that engages with the holes in the seat)

5.6 Lift the upper mount off the rod

verified by wiggling the spring.

4   If you're working on a shock absorber/ coil spring assembly, hold the flat on the damper rod with a wrench and unscrew the nut with another wrench.

5.7 Remove the upper spring seat and the upper pad from the damper rod

5   If you're working on a strut, you'll probably have to use a special tool with pins that engage with the holes in the spring seat to prevent the damper rod from turning while unscrewing the nut. Loosen the damper rod nut with a socket wrench **(see illustration)**.

6   Remove the nut and the upper mount **(see illustration)**. Inspect the bearing in the mount for smooth operation. If it doesn't turn smoothly, replace the mount. Inspect the rubber portion of the mount for cracking and general deterioration. If there is any separation of the rubber, replace it.

7   Lift the upper spring seat and upper pad from the damper rod **(see illustration)**. Check the spring seat for cracking and hardness, replacing it if necessary.

8   Carefully lift the compressed spring from the assembly and set it in a safe place **(see illustration)**. **Warning:** *Never place your head near the end of the spring!* Slide the rubber bumper and dust cover off the damper rod.

Reassembly

Refer to illustrations 5.11, 5.13a and 5.13b

9   If the lower insulator is being replaced, set it into position with the dropped portion seated in the lowest part of the seat.

10   Extend the damper rod to its full length and install the rubber bumper and dust cover.

11   Carefully place the coil spring onto the lower insulator, with the end of the spring resting in the lowest part of the insulator **(see illustration)**.

12   Install the upper pad and spring seat.

13   Install the upper mount onto the damper shaft. If you're working on a front shock absorber of a 1998 or earlier model, make sure the studs of the upper mount are aligned correctly with the pinch bolt that secures the damper fork to the shock absorber body **(see illustration)**. If you're working on a rear shock absorber assembly, make sure the upper mount bracket is

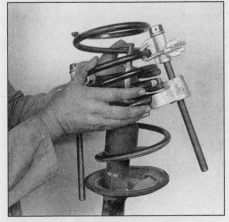

5.8 Remove the compressed spring from the strut/shock absorber assembly - keep the ends of the spring pointed away from your body

5.11 When installing the spring, make sure the end fits into the recessed portion of the lower seat

DAMPER FORK
INSTALLATION
BOLT

INSIDE OF THE BODY

25040-10-5.14A HAYNES

5.13a On 1998 and earlier model front shock absorbers, the damper fork bolt must align with the three upper mounting studs

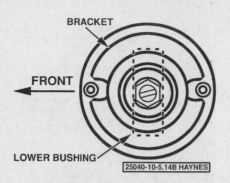

5.13b On 1998 and earlier model rear shock absorbers, align the lower bushing with the upper bracket like this before tightening the damper rod nut

6.3 Use a two-jaw puller to break the ball joint loose from the steering knuckle. Loosen the nut a few turns, but leave it in place to prevent a violent separation

6.4 Upper control arm-to-body nuts (1998 and earlier models)

properly aligned with the lower mounting bushing of the shock absorber **(see illustration)**.

14   Install the damper rod nut and tighten it to the torque listed in this Chapter's Specifications. Slowly release the spring compressor.

15   Install the strut/shock absorber and coil spring assembly following the procedure in Section 3, 4 or 13.

6   Upper control arm (front) (1998 and earlier models) - removal, inspection and installation

Removal

Refer to illustration 6.3 and 6.4

1   Loosen the wheel lug nuts on the side to be disassembled, raise the front of the vehicle, support it securely on jackstands and remove the wheel.

2   Support the suspension from below with a jack.

3   Loosen the nut from the upper control arm balljoint stud. Using a two-jaw puller or balljoint separator, break the balljoint loose from the steering knuckle, then remove the nut and detach the arm **(see illustration)**.

4   Working in the engine compartment, remove the nuts from the control arm shafts **(see illustration)** and remove the control arm.

Inspection

5   Check the control arm for wear. If the arm is bent or the pivot shafts or bolts are worn, replace them. Don't try to straighten a bent control arm. Also check the balljoint (see Section 9). If a balljoint is worn out, you'll have to replace the control arm; the balljoint is not available separately. **Note:** *If you remove the pivot bolts, be sure to install them facing in the correct direction (with the bolt heads facing towards each other.*

Installation

Refer to illustration 6.6

Warning: *The manufacturer recommends replacing self-locking nuts with new ones whenever they are removed.*

6   If you have removed the pivot bolts, the pivot shafts must be installed in a certain position before tightening the nuts **(see illustration)**.

7   Installation is the reverse of removal. Tighten all of the fasteners to the torque val-

ues listed in this Chapter's Specifications.

8   Install the wheel and lug nuts, lower the vehicle and tighten the lug nuts to the torque listed in the Chapter 1 Specifications.

9   It's a good idea to have the front wheel alignment checked, and if necessary, adjusted after this job has been performed.

7   Lower control arms (front) (1998 and earlier models) - removal, inspection and installation

Refer to illustrations 7.3, 7.4 and 7.5

1   These models have two lower control arms; a lateral lower arm and a compression lower arm.

Removal

2   Loosen the wheel lug nuts on the side to be disassembled, raise the front of the vehicle, support it securely on jackstands and remove the wheel.

3   Remove the nut from the balljoint stud on the arm you're removing **(see illustration)**. Using a large ball peen hammer (and

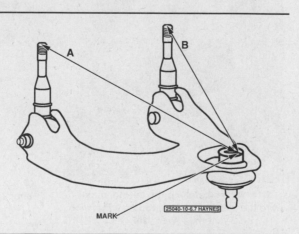

6.6 When installing the pivot shafts on a 1998 and earlier model, position them as shown before tightening the bolts/nuts

A   11.8 inches (299.9 mm)
B   9.2 inches (234.0 mm)

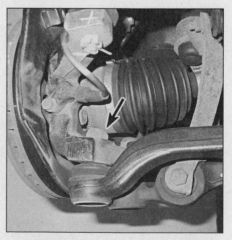

7.3 Compression lower arm-to-steering knuckle nut (1998 and earlier models)

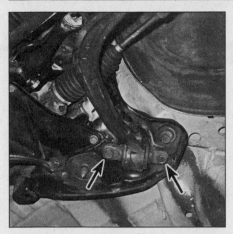

7.4 Compression lower arm-to-body bolts (1998 and earlier models)

7.5 Lateral lower arm-to-crossmember bolt/nut (1998 and earlier models)

8.2 Unscrew the nut and remove the pinch bolt completely (1999 through 2003 models)

wearing goggles to protect your eyes), give the steering knuckle a few good whacks in the vicinity of the balljoint stud to break the stud loose from the knuckle. Use a prybar to disconnect the control arm from the steering knuckle. If that doesn't work, use a tie-rod or balljoint separator. These tools can usually be rented from rental outlets and some auto parts stores.

4   To remove the compression lower arm, remove its bushing bolts and separate it from the vehicle **(see illustration)**.

5   To remove the lateral lower arm, remove the nut and bolt that secure it to the damper fork **(see illustration 3.4)**, then remove the pivot bolt and nut **(see illustration)**. Work the arm free of its pivot point in the body and take it out of the vehicle.

Inspection

6   Check the control arms for distortion and the bushings for wear. If the arm is bent or any of the bushings are cracked, torn or worn out, replace the control arm. These parts are not replaceable and you can't straighten a bent control arm. Also check the balljoint (see Section 10). If a balljoint is worn out, you'll have to replace the control arm; the balljoint is not available separately.

Installation

7   Installation is the reverse of removal. Do NOT reuse self-locking nuts. Replace them with new ones. Tighten all of the fasteners to the torque values listed in this Chapter's Specifications. **Note:** *Before tightening the lateral lower arm pivot bolt, raise the outer end of the arm with a floor jack to simulate normal ride height, then tighten the pivot bolt/ nut to the specified torque.*

8   Install the wheel and lug nuts, lower the vehicle and tighten the lug nuts to the torque listed in the Chapter 1 Specifications.

---

8   Control arm (front) (1999 and later models) - removal, inspection and installation

Removal

Refer to illustrations 8.2 and 8.3

1   Loosen the wheel lug nuts on the side to be disassembled, raise the front of the vehicle, support it securely on jackstands and remove the wheel.

1999 through 2003 models

2   Completely remove the nut and pinch

bolt from the balljoint stud that's connected to the steering knuckle **(see illustration)**. Use a prybar to disconnect the control arm from the steering knuckle.

3   Remove the nut and washer from the control arm forward pivot bolt **(see illustration)**. Pull out the pivot bolt.

4   Remove the heat shield (if equipped), and the two nuts and bolts from the clamp for the rear control arm bushing.

5   Remove the control arm and rear clamp from the vehicle.

2004 and later models

6   Loosen the balljoint nut several turns but don't remove it. Install a special balljoint removal tool to break it loose, then separate the control arm from the steering knuckle.

7   Remove the two control arm mounting bolts and lift it free.

Inspection

8   On 2003 and earlier models, remove the nut that secures the rear clamp and bushing to the control arm. Slide the bushing off the control arm stud.

9   Check the control arm for distortion and the bushings for wear. If the arm is bent or the forward bushing is cracked, torn or worn out, replace the control arm. These parts are not replaceable and you can't straighten a bent control arm.

10   If the bushing in the clamp is worn or damaged, have it pressed out and a new one pressed in by a dealer service department or machine shop.

11   Also check the balljoint (see Section 9). If a balljoint is worn out, you'll have to replace the control arm; the balljoint is not available separately.

Installation

12   Installation is the reverse of removal. Do NOT reuse self-locking nuts. Replace them with new ones. Tighten all of the fasteners to the torque values listed in this Chapter's Specifications. **Note:** *Before tightening the control arm pivot bolt, raise the outer end of*

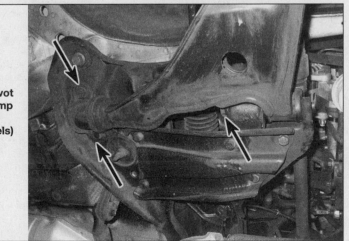

8.3 Control arm pivot bolt (right) and clamp bolts (left) (1999 through 2003 models)

the control arm with a floor jack to simulate normal ride height.

13   Install the wheel and lug nuts, lower the vehicle and tighten the lug nuts to the torque listed in the Chapter 1 Specifications.

14   Have the front wheel alignment checked, and if necessary, adjusted after this job has been performed.

9   Balljoints - check and replacement

Check

Lower balljoint(s)

1   Raise the front of the vehicle and support it securely on jackstands. Apply the parking brake and block the rear wheels to keep the vehicle from rolling off the jackstands.

2   On 1998 and earlier models, remove the damper fork-to-control arm nut and bolt.

3   Place a large prybar under the balljoint and resting on the wheel, then try to pry the balljoint up while feeling for movement between the balljoint and steering knuckle. Now, pry between the control arm and the steering knuckle and try to lever the control arm down while feeling for movement between the balljoint and steering knuckle. If any movement is evident in either check, the balljoint is worn.

4   Have an assistant grasp the tire at the top and bottom and move the top of the tire in-and-out. Touch the balljoint stud nut. If any looseness is felt, suspect a worn balljoint stud or a widened hole in the steering knuckle boss. If the latter problem exists, the steering knuckle should be replaced as well as the balljoint/control arm.

Upper balljoint (1998 and earlier models)

5   Loosen the wheel lug nuts, raise the front of the vehicle and support it securely on jackstands. Remove the wheel.

6   Place a floor jack under the lower balljoint(s) and raise it slightly.

7   Using a prybar, attempt to pry the upper control arm up and down while feeling for play in the balljoint. If any play is felt, replace the control arm.

All balljoints

8   Separate the control arm from the steering knuckle (Section 6, 7 or 8. Using your fingers (don't use pliers), try to twist the stud in the socket. If the stud turns, replace the balljoint.

Replacement

9   The balljoints are not replaceable separately (the entire control arm must be replaced).

10   The balljoint dust boot can be replaced separately. This should not be done if the dust boot has cracked or been damaged while the vehicle is in use, since dirt has prob-

10.5 With the driveaxle out of the way, unscrew the hub-to-steering knuckle bolts

ably gotten into the balljoint. However, if the dust boot was damaged during removal of the control arm, the dust boot can be replaced. To do this, pry off the old dust boot. Grease the balljoint stud and the upper lip of the dust boot. Push the dust boot onto the balljoint with a special tool or a socket the same diameter as the dust boot. On 1999 and later models, push the dust boot upper lip down with a smaller socket until it locks into the groove in the bottom of the balljoint stud.

11   Install the wheel and lug nuts (if removed) and lower the vehicle. Tighten the lug nuts to the torque listed in the Chapter 1 Specifications.

10   Hub and bearing assembly (front) - removal and installation

Refer to illustration 10.5
Warning: *Dust created by the brake system is harmful to your health. Never blow it out with compressed air and don't inhale any of it. Do not, under any circumstances, use petroleum-based solvents to clean brake parts. Use brake system cleaner only.*

1   Loosen the wheel lug nuts, raise the vehicle and support it securely on jackstands. Remove the wheel.

2   Remove the driveaxle/hub nut (see Chapter 8). If the vehicle is equipped with ABS, remove the wheel speed sensor (see Chapter 9).

3   Remove the brake caliper and support it with a piece of wire as described in Chapter 9. Remove the caliper mounting bracket and separate the brake disc from the hub.

4   Separate the lower balljoint(s) from the steering knuckle (see Section 7). Pivot the knuckle outward and push the driveaxle from the hub to provide removal access for the hub mounting bolts. Support the end of the driveaxle with a piece of wire.

5   Unbolt the hub from the knuckle **(see illustration)**. Remove the hub from the vehicle.

6   If necessary, remove the brake disc shield from the knuckle.

7   Check the hub bearing for wear or damage. Spin it with your fingers and check for rough, loose or noisy rotation. The bearing can't be replaced separately, so if the bearing is bad or any other problems are found, replace the hub as an assembly.

8   Installation is the reverse of removal. Tighten the hub bolts and balljoint fasteners to the torque listed in this Chapter's Specifications. Tighten the driveaxle/hub nut to the torque listed in the Chapter 8 Specifications (and on models so equipped, be sure to use a new cotter pin), the brake fasteners to the torque listed in Chapter 9 and the wheel lug nuts to the torque listed in Chapter 1.

11   Steering knuckle - removal and installation

Warning: *Dust created by the brake system is harmful to your health. Never blow it out with compressed air and don't inhale any of it. Do not, under any circumstances, use petroleum-based solvents to clean brake parts. Use brake system cleaner only.*

Removal

1   Loosen the wheel lug nuts, raise the vehicle and support it securely on jackstands. Remove the wheel.

2   Remove the brake caliper and support it with a piece of wire as described in Chapter 9. If the vehicle is equipped with ABS, unbolt and remove the wheel speed sensor from the knuckle. Remove the caliper mounting bracket, separate the brake disc from the hub, and then remove the driveaxle/hub nut (see Chapter 8).

3   Separate the tie-rod end from the steering knuckle arm (see Section 20).

4   Separate the control arm(s) from the knuckle (see Sections 6 and 7 [1998 and earlier models], Section 8 [1999 and later models]).

5   Push the driveaxle from the hub as described in Chapter 8. Support the end of the driveaxle with a piece of wire.

6   If you're working on a 1999 or later model, remove the bolts and carefully sepa-

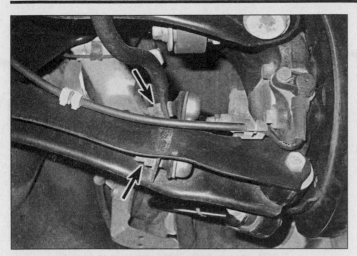

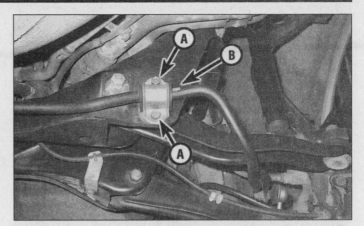

12.3 Stabilizer bar clamp bolts (A); approximately 13/32-inch (10 mm) of the alignment mark (B) must be showing past the outside of each bushing when installing the bar

12.2 Stabilizer bar link nuts

rate the steering knuckle from the strut (see Section 4).

7   If necessary, unbolt the hub from the knuckle.

Installation

8   Installation is the reverse of the removal steps. Tighten all suspension and steering fasteners to the torque values listed in this Chapter's Specifications. Tighten the drive-axle/hub nut to the torque listed in the Chapter 8 Specifications (and be sure to use a new cotter pin), the brake fasteners to the torque listed in Chapter 9 and the wheel lug nuts to the torque listed in Chapter 1.

12   Stabilizer bar and bushings (rear) - removal, inspection and installation

Removal

Refer to illustrations 12.2 and 12.3

1   Loosen the wheel lug nuts, raise the vehicle and support it securely on jackstands. Remove the wheels.

2   Remove the nuts attaching the stabilizer links to the stabilizer and lower control arm **(see illustration)**.

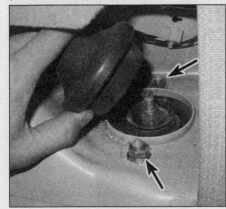

13.3 Rear shock absorber upper mounting nuts (typical)

3   Unbolt the stabilizer bar clamps from the crossmember **(see illustration)**. Remove the stabilizer bar from the vehicle.

Inspection

4   Inspect the stabilizer bushings for cracks and tears. If the bushings are damaged, distorted or excessively worn, replace them. Also, inspect the link balljoints for damage or excessive looseness.

Installation

5   Installation is the reverse of the removal steps. Position the stabilizer bar in the brackets so its alignment mark is within the specified distance of the bushing **(see illustration 12.3)**. Tighten all fasteners to the torque listed in this Chapter's Specifications.

13   Shock absorber/coil spring assembly (rear) - removal, inspection and installation

Removal

Refer to illustrations 13.3 and 13.4

1   Loosen the wheel lug nuts, raise the vehicle and support it securely on jack-

13.4 Shock absorber lower mounting bolt (2003 and earlier models)

stands. Remove the wheel.

2   Open the trunk, peel back the carpet or, remove the seat back for access to the upper mount (see Chapter 11).

3   Support the trailing arm with a floor jack. Raise the jack just enough to take the load off the shock absorber, then remove the shock absorber upper mounting nuts **(see illustration)**. **Warning:** *Don't remove the nut from the damper rod (the center nut).*

4   Remove the shock absorber lower mounting bolt and remove the shock **(see illustration)**.

Inspection

5   Follow the inspection procedures described in Section 3. If the shock absorber assembly must be disassembled for replacement of the shock or the coil spring, refer to Section 5.

Installation

6   Maneuver the shock absorber assembly up into the fenderwell and insert the mounting studs through the holes in the body. Install the nuts, but don't tighten them yet.

7   On 1999 and later models, position the lower end of the shock so the flanged portion of the bushing is toward the outside of the vehicle. On all other models, push the lower end of the shock into its bracket on the knuckle, install the bolt and tighten it to the torque listed in this Chapter's Specifications.

8   Install the wheel and lug nuts, lower the vehicle and tighten the lug nuts to the torque listed in the Chapter 1 Specifications.

9   Tighten the two upper mounting nuts to the torque listed in this Chapter's Specifications. Reinstall the trim panels.

14   Rear suspension arms - removal and installation

1   Loosen the wheel lug nuts, raise the vehicle and support it securely on jackstands. Remove the wheels.

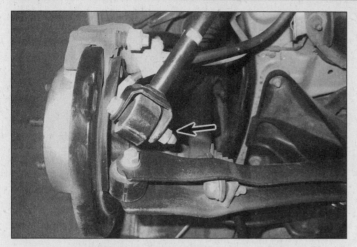

14.2a   Trailing arm-to-rear knuckle nut/bolt

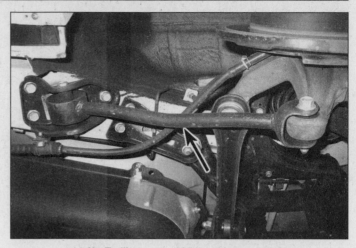

14.2b   Trailing arm - 2004 and later models

Trailing arm

Refer to illustrations 14.2a, 14.2b and 14.3

2   Remove the nut, washer and bolt that attach the rear end of the trailing arm to the rear knuckle **(see illustrations)**.

3   Remove the plug at the front end of the trailing arm on 2003 and earlier models **(see illustration)**. Remove the nut, washer and bolt that attach the front end of the trailing arm to the body, then remove the trailing arm.

4   Inspect the bushings in the front end of the trailing arm and in the knuckle for cracks and deterioration. Replace parts as necessary.

5   Installation is the reverse of removal. Make sure you install the bolts with the heads facing outward. Raise the rear knuckle with a floor jack to simulate normal ride height and tighten the bolts/nuts to the torque listed in this Chapter's Specifications.

6   Tighten the lug nuts to the torque listed in the Chapter 1 Specifications.

Lower and toe control arms

Removal

Refer to illustrations 14.9a, 14.9b, 14.9c, 14.10 and 14.11

Lower control arm

7   Remove the nut that connects the stabi-lizer bar link to the lower control arm **(see illustration 12.2)**.

8   If you're working on a vehicle equipped with ABS, unbolt the clamp that secures the wheel speed sensor wiring harness.

9   Remove the nut, lockwasher and bolt that secure the outer end of the lower control arm to the knuckle. Do the same thing at the inner end, then remove the control arm from the vehicle **(see illustrations)**.

Toe control arm

10   Mark the position of the eccentric at the inner end of the toe control arm before removing it **(see illustration)**.

11   Loosen the nut on the toe control arm balljoint **(see illustration)**. Strike the knuckle in the vicinity of the balljoint several times with a hammer to free the balljoint stud, then pry it loose with a pry bar. If that doesn't work, use a tie-rod or balljoint separator.

12   Remove the toe control arm pivot bolt, lockwasher and nut and take the arm out.

Inspection

13   Check the bushing in the inner end of each arm, and the lower control arm bushing in the knuckle, for wear or damage. Replace parts as necessary.

14   Refer to Section 9 to inspect the balljoint in the outer end of the toe control arm.

Installation

15   Installation is the reverse of the removal steps. Align the marks made on the eccentric and rear suspension crossmember. Raise the rear knuckle with a floor jack to simulate normal ride height and tighten the bolts/nuts to the torque listed in this Chapter's Specifications.

16   Tighten the lug nuts to the torque listed in the Chapter 1 Specifications.

17   Have the rear wheel alignment checked and, if necessary, adjusted.

Upper control arm

Removal

Refer to illustrations 14.19, 14.20a and 14.20b

18   Loosen the wheel lug nuts, raise the vehicle and support it securely on jackstands. Remove the wheels.

19   Remove the bolt, nut and washer that

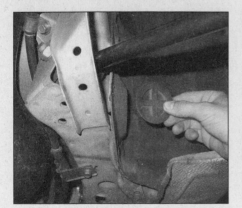

14.3   Remove this plug for access to the trailing arm pivot bolt nut (2003 and earlier models)

14.9a   Lower control arm-to-rear knuckle nut/bolt

14.9b   Lower control arm inner pivot bolt/nut

14.9c Lower control arm (2004 and later models)

14.10 Mark the position of the toe adjuster cam to the rear crossmember (when installing the toe control arm, line-up these marks)

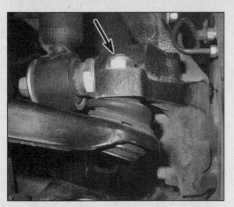

14.11 Toe control arm balljoint-to-knuckle nut

14.19 Upper control arm-to-rear knuckle nut/bolt

14.20a Upper control arm-to-body bolts (2003 and earlier models)

attach the upper control arm to the knuckle **(see illustration)**.

20   Unscrew the bolts that attach the upper control arm pivots to the body **(see illustrations)**. Remove the upper control arm from the vehicle. Don't allow the knuckle to fall outward - the brake hose could be damaged.

21   If necessary, remove the pivot bolts and nuts and separate the brackets from the control arm.

Inspection

Refer to illustration 14.23

22   Check the control arm for cracks or bending and check the bushings for wear or damage. Replace the control arm and bushings as an assembly if any problems are found.

23   On 2003 and earlier models, if the brackets have been separated from the arm, place them at the correct angle **(see illustration)**. The vertical distance between the outer control arm pivot point and the inner pivot point should be 1.46 +/-0.080 inch. With this distance set correctly, tighten the pivot bolts

and nuts to the torque listed in this Chapter's Specifications.

Installation

24   Installation is the reverse of the removal steps. Install the arm and tighten the mounting bracket bolts to the torque listed in this Chapter's Specifications. Raise the rear knuckle with a floor jack to simulate normal ride height and tighten the arm-to-knuckle bolt/nut to the torque listed in this Chapter's Specifications.

25   Tighten the lug nuts to the torque listed in the Chapter 1 Specifications.

14.20b Upper control arm mounting bolts (2004 and later models)

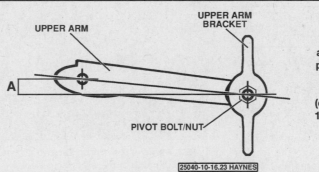

UPPER ARM

UPPER ARM BRACKET

A

PIVOT BOLT/NUT

25040-10-16.23 HAYNES

14.23 With the upper arm mounting brackets positioned properly, the vertical distance between the pivots (dimension A) should be 1.46 +/- 0.080 inch (2003 and earlier models)

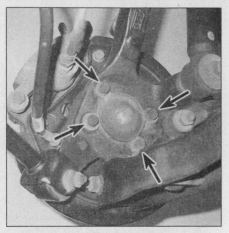

15.3 Hub and bearing assembly-to-rear knuckle bolts

15 Hub and bearing assembly (rear) - removal and installation

Refer to illustration 15.3

Warning: *Dust created by the brake system is harmful to your health. Never blow it out with compressed air and don't inhale any of it. Do not, under any circumstances, use petroleum-based solvents to clean brake parts. Use brake system cleaner only.*

1   Loosen the wheel lug nuts, raise the vehicle and support it securely on jackstands. Remove the wheel.

2   Remove the rear brake caliper and disc or rear brake drum and shoes and, on vehicles equipped with an ABS braking system, remove the rear wheel speed sensor (see Chapter 9).

3   Remove the hub bolts **(see illustration)** and detach the hub from the knuckle.

4   Check the hub bearing for wear or damage. Spin it with your fingers and check for rough, loose or noisy rotation. The bearing can't be replaced separately, so if the bearing is bad or any other problems are found, replace the hub as an assembly.

5   Installation is the reverse of removal. Tighten the hub bolts to the torque listed in this Chapter's Specifications.

6   Install the wheel and lug nuts. Lower the vehicle and tighten the lug nuts to the torque listed in the Chapter 1 Specifications.

16 Knuckle (rear) - removal, inspection and installation

Warning: *Dust created by the brake system is harmful to your health. Never blow it out with compressed air and don't inhale any of it. Do not, under any circumstances, use petroleum-based solvents to clean brake parts. Use brake system cleaner only.*

Removal

1   If the vehicle is equipped with ABS, remove the rear wheel speed sensor (see Chapter 9).

2   Remove the rear brake caliper, bracket and disc (disc brakes) or brake drum and shoes (drum brakes) (see Chapter 9).

3   Remove the rear hub and bearing assembly (see Section 15).

4   Disconnect the shock absorber, trailing arm, lower control arm, toe control arm and the upper control arm from the knuckle as described elsewhere in this Chapter. Remove the knuckle from the vehicle.

Inspection

5   Check the bushings in the knuckle for wear and damage. Replace the knuckle if problems are found.

6   Check the knuckle for cracks or bending. Don't try to repair any damage; replace the knuckle if there are visible problems.

7   Refer to Section 9 to inspect the balljoint at the outer end of the toe control arm.

Installation

8   Installation is the reverse of the removal steps. Tighten all suspension fasteners to the torque listed in this Chapter's Specifications. Tighten the brake fasteners to the torque listed in the Chapter 9 Specifications. **Note:** *Before tightening the pivot bolts that attach the suspension arms to the knuckle, raise the suspension with a floor jack to simulate normal ride height, then tighten the fasteners to the specified torque.*

9   Tighten the lug nuts to the torque listed in the Chapter 1 Specifications.

17 Steering system - general information

All models are equipped with power rack-and-pinion steering. The steering gear is bolted to the crossmember and operates the steering arms via tie-rods. Rubber boots which should be inspected periodically for secure attachment, tears and leaking lubricant, protects the inner ends of the tie-rods.

The power assist system consists of a

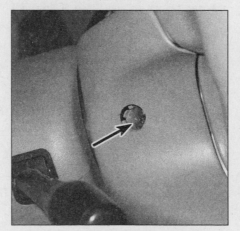

18.3 Remove the airbag Torx bolt from each side of the steering wheel

belt-driven pump and associated lines and hoses. The fluid level in the power steering pump reservoir should be checked periodically (see Chapter 1).

The steering wheel operates the steering shaft, which actuates the steering gear through universal joints. Looseness in the steering can be caused by wear in the steering shaft universal joints, the steering gear, the tie-rod ends and loose retaining bolts.

18 Steering wheel - removal and installation

Removal

Refer to illustrations 18.3, 18.5, 18.7, 18.8 and 18.9

Warning 1: *These models have airbags. Always disable the airbag system before working in the vicinity of the impact sensors, steering column or instrument panel to avoid the possibility of accidental deployment of the airbag, which could cause personal injury (see Chapter 12).*

Warning 2: *Do not use a memory saving device to preserve the ECM's memory when working on or near airbag system components.*

1   Park the vehicle with the front wheels pointing straight ahead.

2   Disconnect the cable from the negative terminal of the battery. Wait at least two minutes before proceeding (the airbag system has a back-up capacitor that must fully discharge).

3   Remove the airbag by unscrewing the Torx retaining bolt from each side of the steering wheel, but don't attempt to remove the bolts from their casings **(see illustration)**.

4   Remove the airbag module from the steering wheel.

5   Remove the lock from the airbag clockspring electrical connector and disconnect the electrical connector from the back of the airbag module **(see illustration)**. **Warning:** *When*

18.5 Disengage the connector lock and unplug the electrical connector from the airbag module

18.7 Mark the steering shaft to steering wheel relationship

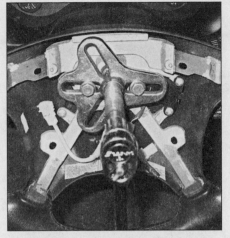

18.8 Use a steering wheel puller to remove the steering wheel from the shaft

18.9 Airbag clockspring mounting screws (some models have four screws)

handling the airbag module, make sure that at no time any source of electricity is allowed near the inflator on the back of the airbag module; when carrying the airbag module, the trim cover must be pointed away from your body or any other person; if the airbag module is placed on a workbench or any other surface, the trim cover must face upwards. When removing the airbag module, tag or mark all fasteners, screws, bolts, and other parts for the airbag module with their location as removed, for correct installation later.

6　Disconnect the airbag clockspring and horn wires from the airbag mounting bracket. Unbolt the cruise control switch and disconnect its electrical connector.

7　Remove the steering wheel retaining nut. Mark the steering column shaft and the steering wheel for correct positioning when reinstalling later **(see illustration)**.

8　Remove the steering wheel with a steering wheel puller - do not bump or hammer on the steering wheel or steering column in an attempt to remove the wheel **(see illustration)**.

9　If necessary for access to other components, remove the airbag clockspring **(see illustration)**. **Note:** *The steering column covers will have to be removed first (see Chapter 11).* **Warning:** *Don't allow the steering shaft to rotate with the steering wheel removed.*

Installation

10　Before installing the steering wheel, make sure the front wheels are pointing straight ahead and the airbag clockspring is centered, as follows:

　　1994 and 1995 models - Turn the hub in either direction until it stops (don't apply too much force). Now, rotate the hub in the other direction, counting the number of turns it takes to reach the opposite stop. Divide that number by two, then turn the hub back that many turns. Now, with the front wheels in the straight-ahead position, align the clockspring Neutral position indicator with its mating mark, then install the clockspring.

　　1996 through 1998 models - Turn the

clockspring rotor clockwise by hand until it stops (don't apply too much force), then turn the rotor counterclockwise approximately 3-1/3 turns until the arrows on the clockspring body and rotor are in alignment.

　　1999 through 2002 models - Turn the clockspring rotor clockwise by hand until it stops (don't apply too much force), then turn the rotor counterclockwise approximately 3 turns until the arrows on the clockspring body and rotor are in alignment.

　　2003 and later models - Turn the clockspring rotor clockwise by hand until it stops (don't apply too much force), then turn the rotor counterclockwise approximately 3-1/2 to 3-3/4 turns until the arrows on the clockspring body and rotor are in alignment. **Caution:** *2010 models and other late models also have a steering wheel position sensor mounted under the combination switch. This sensor is accessed by removing the combination switch assembly. If you disassemble the steering column, be sure that this sensor is centered using the same procedure as for the clockspring with the front wheels pointing straight ahead. Failure to do this can damage the mechanism or prevent the steering wheel from turning completely.*

11　Lower the steering wheel into position, feeding the clockspring wiring harness through the opening in the wheel.

12　Place the steering wheel on the shaft, aligning the marks. Install the nut or bolt and tighten it to the torque listed in this Chapter's Specifications.

13　Correctly route and reconnect electrical connectors such as the cruise control switch electrical leads from the clockspring to switch openings in the steering wheel.

14　Plug in the horn and airbag module electrical connectors. Press the cruise control wires into the retaining channels on the steering wheel, if applicable.

15　Install the airbag module electrical lead from the clockspring into the connector on the airbag module. Insert the locking tab in the back of the airbag module connector. **Warning:** *Make sure the electrical connector*

from the clockspring is securely latched into the airbag module connector. The fasteners, screws, bolts, and other parts for the airbag module are specifically designed and must never be replaced with anything other than genuine factory part number replacements.

16　Install the airbag module into the center of the steering wheel and install the mounting bolts, tightening them to the torque listed in this Chapter's Specifications.

17　Connect the cable to the negative terminal of the battery.

19　Steering column - removal and installation

Refer to illustrations 19.12 and 19.13

Warning 1: *These models are equipped with airbags. Always disable the airbag system before working in the vicinity of any airbag system component to avoid the possibility of accidental deployment of the airbag(s), which could cause personal injury (see Chapter 12).*

Warning 2: *Do not use a memory saving device to preserve the ECM's memory when working on or near airbag system components.*

Removal

1　Park the vehicle with the wheels in the straight-ahead position. Disconnect the cable from the negative terminal of the battery. Wait at least two minutes before proceeding (the airbag system has a back-up capacitor that must fully discharge).

2　Remove the steering wheel (see Section 18).

2003 and earlier models

3　Remove the lower instrument panel trim (under the steering column), the knee bolster and the heater/air conditioning duct (see Chapter 11).

4　Remove the steering column covers (see Chapter 11).

5　Remove the airbag system clockspring (see Section 18).

19.12 Steering column shaft-to-steering gear input shaft pinch bolt

19.13 Steering column upper mounting bolts

6   Remove the multi-function switch (see Chapter 12).

7   On models equipped with an automatic transmission, detach the shift interlock cable from the ignition lock cylinder (see Chapter 7B).

2004 and later models

8   Remove the lower instrument panel (see Chapter 11). Also remove the console, the trunk lid opener cover, the accelerator pedal stopper, the door sill covers and the kick panel trim covers. Pull back the carpet as necessary.

9   Refer to Chapter 11 and remove the steering column covers.

10   Remove the combination switch (see Chapter 12).

11   Remove the steering column pad from the base of the column.

All models

12   Mark the relationship of the steering column shaft to the steering gear input shaft, then remove the pinch bolt **(see illustration)**.

13   Remove the steering column mounting bolts **(see illustration)**, then guide the column out from the instrument panel.

Installation

14   Guide the column into position, con-
necting the U-joint with the steering gear input shaft. Be sure to align the mark made in Step 8.

15   Install the mounting bolts/nuts, tightening them to the torque listed in this Chapter's Specifications.

16   Install the pinch bolt and tighten it to the torque listed in this Chapter's Specifications.

17   The remainder of installation is the reverse of the removal procedure. When installing the steering wheel, be sure the airbag clockspring is centered (see Section 18), and tighten the steering wheel nut or bolt to the torque listed in this Chapter's Specifications. Also tighten the airbag mounting bolts to the torque listed in this Chapter's Specifications.

20   Tie-rod ends - removal and installation

Refer to illustrations 20.2 and 20.4

Removal

1   Loosen the wheel lug nuts, raise the front of the vehicle and support it securely on jackstands. Apply the parking brake and block the rear wheels to keep the vehicle
from rolling off the jackstands. Remove the wheel.

2   Loosen the tie-rod end jam nut **(see illustration)**.

3   Mark the relationship of the tie-rod end to the threaded portion of the tie-rod. This will ensure the toe-in setting is restored when reassembled.

4   Remove the cotter pin (if so equipped) and loosen the nut from the tie-rod end ball-stud a few turns. Disconnect the tie-rod end from the steering knuckle arm with a puller **(see illustration)**.

5   Remove the nut from the ballstud, separate the tie-rod end from the steering knuckle, and then unscrew the tie-rod end from the tie-rod.

Installation

6   Thread the tie-rod end onto the tie-rod to the marked position and connect the tie-rod end to the steering arm. Install the nut on the ballstud and tighten it to the torque listed in this Chapter's Specifications. Install a new cotter pin or a new locknut if no cotter pin was used. **Note:** *If necessary, tighten the nut a little more to allow insertion of the cotter pin. Never loosen the nut to align the cotter pin holes.*

7   Tighten the jam nut securely and install the wheel. Lower the vehicle and tighten the lug nuts to the torque listed in the Chapter 1 Specifications.

8   Have the front end alignment checked and, if necessary, adjusted.

21   Steering gear boots - replacement

1   Loosen the lug nuts, raise the vehicle and support it securely on jackstands. Remove the wheel.

2   Remove the tie-rod end and jam nut (see Section 20).

3   Remove the steering gear boot clamps and slide the boot off. **Note:** *Check for the presence of power steering fluid in the boot. If there is a substantial amount, it means the rack*

20.2 Loosen the tie-rod end jam nut far enough to mark its position on the tie-rod

20.4 Using a puller, separate the ballstud from the steering knuckle

seals are leaking and the power steering gear should be replaced with a new or rebuilt unit.

4   Before installing the new boot, wrap the threads and serrations on the end of the steering rod with a layer of tape so the small end of the new boot isn't damaged.

5   Slide the new boot into position on the steering gear until it seats in the grooves, then install new clamps.

6   Remove the tape and install the tie-rod end (see Section 20).

7   Install the wheel and lug nuts. Lower the vehicle and tighten the lug nuts to the torque listed in the Chapter 1 Specifications.

8   Have the front end alignment checked and, if necessary, adjusted.

22   Steering gear - removal and installation

Warning: *These models are equipped with airbags. Always disable the airbag system before working in the vicinity of airbag system components (see Chapter 12). Make sure the steering column shaft is not turned while the steering gear is removed or you could damage the airbag system clockspring. To prevent the shaft from turning, turn the ignition key to* the lock position before beginning work, and run the seat belt through the steering wheel and clip it into its latch.

Removal

Refer to illustration 22.6, 22.7a, 22.7b, 22.7c, 22.7d and 22.9

1   Disconnect the cable from the negative terminal of the battery.

2   Drain the power steering fluid from the reservoir. This can be accomplished with a suction gun or poultry baster. **Warning:** *If a poultry baster is used, never again use it for the preparation of food.*

3   Loosen the front wheel lug nuts, raise the front of the vehicle and support it securely on jackstands. Apply the parking brake and remove the wheels.

2003 and earlier models

4   On 1999 and later models, remove the front exhaust pipe (see Chapter 4). **Note:** *Although not absolutely necessary, removing the front exhaust pipe on 1998 and earlier models will make steering gear removal easier.*

5   Mark the relationship of the universal joint to the steering gear input shaft. Remove the steering column shaft pinch bolt **(see illustration 19.12).**

6   Place a drain pan under the steering gear. Detach the power steering pressure and return lines and cap the ends to prevent excessive fluid loss and contamination **(see illustration).**

7   Remove the stiffener plates from under the steering gear **(see illustrations).** Also remove the transaxle rear roll stopper (mount) and center member **(see illustrations)** (see Chapter 2) and the stabilizer bar (see Section 2).

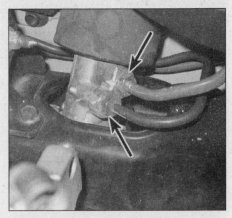

22.6 Disconnect the fluid lines from the steering gear housing

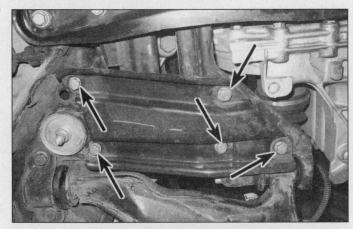

22.7a Remove the bolts from the left side . . .

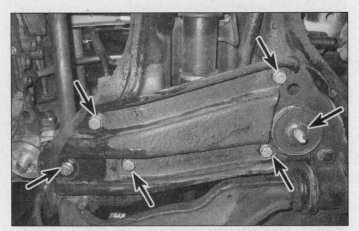

22.7b . . . and right side stiffener plates

22.7c Remove the bolts from the front . . .

22.7d . . . and rear of the center member

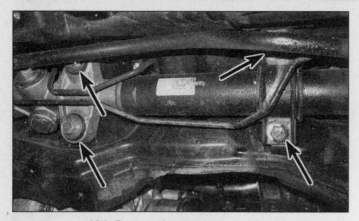

22.9 Remove the steering gear bolts

**23.2 Power steering pressure switch
(2004 and later four-cylinder models)**

8   Separate the tie-rod ends from the steering knuckle arms (see Section 20).
9   Support the steering gear and remove the steering gear-to-crossmember mounting bolts and clamps **(see illustration)**. Separate the intermediate shaft from the steering gear input shaft and guide it out from under the vehicle.

2004 and later models

10   Refer to Section 2 and perform all the steps necessary to remove the stabilizer bar. **Note:** *The stabilizer bar does not need to be detached from the crossmember.*
11   Unbolt the steering gear from the cross-member.

All models

12   Check the steering gear mounting grommets for excessive wear or deterioration, replacing them if necessary.

Installation

13   Center the steering gear before instal-

ling it. To do this, turn the steering gear input shaft counterclockwise until it stops, then count the number of turns as you turn the shaft clockwise until it stops. Divide that number by two, then turn the shaft counterclockwise that amount.
14   Raise the steering gear into position and connect the U-joint, aligning the marks.
15   Install the mounting brackets and bolts and tighten them to the torque listed in this Chapter's Specifications.
16   Connect the tie-rod ends to the steering knuckle arms (see Section 20).
17   Install the U-joint pinch bolt and tighten it to the torque listed in this Chapter's Specifications.
18   Connect the power steering pressure and return hoses to the steering gear.
19   The remainder of installation is the reverse of the removal steps.
20   Lower the vehicle, fill the power steering pump reservoir with the recommended fluid (see Chapter 1) and bleed the steering sys-

tem (see Section 24).
21   Tighten the lug nuts to the torque listed in the Chapter 1 Specifications.

23   Power steering pump - removal and installation

Refer to illustrations 23.2, 23.4a and 23.4b

1   Disconnect the cable from the negative terminal of the battery.
2   Using a large syringe or suction gun, suck as much fluid out of the power steering fluid reservoir as possible. On 2004 and later models, raise the vehicle and support it securely on jackstands, then disconnect the wiring from the pressure switch on the pump **(see illustration)**. Remove the right side lower splash shield. On 3.8L V6 models, remove the strut tower support bar.
3   Place a drain pan under the vehicle to catch any fluid that spills out when the hoses are disconnected.

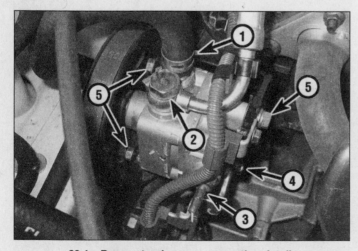

**23.4a Power steering pump mounting details
(1999 four-cylinder model shown)**

1   Return hose
2   Pressure line union bolt
3   Pressure switch
4   Harness bracket bolt
5   Mounting bolts (front bolts are accessed through holes in pulley)

**23.4b Power steering pump mounting details
(2004 and later four-cylinder models)**

A   Through-bolts
B   Bracket bolts

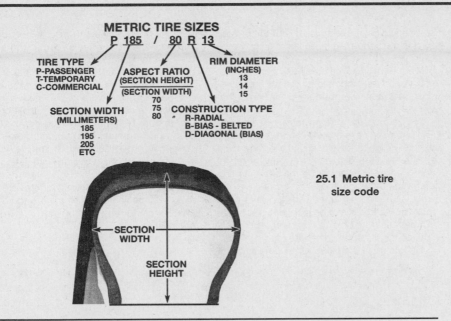

METRIC TIRE SIZES

P 185 / 80 R 13

TIRE TYPE
P-PASSENGER
T-TEMPORARY
C-COMMERCIAL

ASPECT RATIO
(SECTION HEIGHT)
―――――――――
(SECTION WIDTH)
70
75
80

RIM DIAMETER
(INCHES)
13
14
15

SECTION WIDTH
(MILLIMETERS)
185
195
205
ETC

CONSTRUCTION TYPE
R-RADIAL
B-BIAS - BELTED
D-DIAGONAL (BIAS)

SECTION
WIDTH

SECTION
HEIGHT

**25.1 Metric tire
size code**

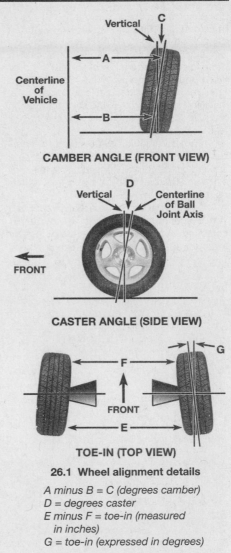

CAMBER ANGLE (FRONT VIEW)

CASTER ANGLE (SIDE VIEW)

TOE-IN (TOP VIEW)

26.1 Wheel alignment details

A minus B = C (degrees camber)
D = degrees caster
*E minus F = toe-in (measured
  in inches)*
G = toe-in (expressed in degrees)

4   Disconnect the power steering pump hoses **(see illustrations)**. Cap the hoses and the power steering pump ports.

5   On models with a pump-mounted pressure switch, unplug the electrical connector from the switch. On 3.8L V6 models, disconnect the stabilizer bar from its links and remove the steering gear and linkage shield.

6   Loosen the pump mounting bolts and remove the drivebelt. **Note:** *Some models have mounting bolts at the rear of the pump as well as the front..*

7   Unscrew the mounting bolts and remove the power steering pump.

8   If you're installing a new pump, you may need a special puller to remove the pulley from the old pump and another special tool to install it on the new pump. These tools are available at most auto parts stores. **Caution:** *Install the pulley onto the new pump to the exact same position as on the old one.*

9   Installation is the reverse of removal, noting the following points:

a) *Install and adjust the drivebelt, then tighten the pump mounting bolts securely.*
b) *Tighten the pressure line union fitting bolt to the torque listed in this Chapter's Specifications.*
c) *Fill the power steering fluid reservoir with the recommended fluid (see Chapter 1), then bleed the system (see Section 24).*

---

24   Power steering system - bleeding

1   Following any operation in which the power steering fluid lines have been disconnected, the power steering system must be bled to remove all air and obtain proper steering performance.

2   With the front wheels in the straight ahead position, check the power steering fluid level and, if low, add fluid until it reaches the Cold mark on the dipstick or reservoir (see Chapter 1, if necessary).

3   Start the engine and allow it to run at fast idle. Recheck the fluid level and add more if necessary to reach the Cold mark.

4   Bleed the system by turning the wheels from side to side, without hitting the stops. This will work the air out of the system. Keep the reservoir full of fluid as this is done.

5   When the air is worked out of the system, return the wheels to the straight ahead position and leave the vehicle running for several more minutes before shutting it off.

6   Road test the vehicle to be sure the steering system is functioning normally and noise free.

7   Recheck the fluid level to be sure it is up to the Hot mark on the dipstick or reservoir while the engine is at normal operating temperature. Add fluid if necessary (see Chapter 1).

---

25   Wheels and tires - general information

Refer to illustration 25.1

1   Vehicles covered by this manual are equipped with metric-sized radial tires **(see illustration)**. Use of other size or type of tires may affect the ride and handling of the vehicle. Don't mix different types of tires, such as radials and bias belted, on the same vehicle as handling may be seriously affected. It's recommended that tires be replaced in pairs on the same axle, but if only one tire is being replaced, be sure it's the same size, structure and tread design as the other.

2   Because tire pressure has a substantial effect on handling and wear, the pressure on all tires should be checked at least once a month or before any extended trips (see Chapter 1).

3   Wheels must be replaced if they are bent, dented, leak air, have elongated bolt holes, are heavily corroded, out of vertical symmetry or if the lug nuts won't stay tight. Wheel repairs that use welding or peening are not recommended.

4   Tire and wheel balance is important in the overall handling, braking and performance of the vehicle. Unbalanced wheels can adversely affect handling and ride characteristics as well as tire life. Whenever a tire is installed on a wheel, a shop with the proper equipment should balance the tire and wheel.

---

26   Wheel alignment - general information

Refer to illustration 26.1

A wheel alignment refers to the adjustments made to the wheels so they are in proper angular relationship to the suspension and the ground. Wheels that are out of proper alignment not only affect vehicle control, but also increase tire wear.

The front end should be measured for camber, caster and toe-in **(see illustration)**. Toe-in can be adjusted by turning the tie-rods in or out. On 1998 and earlier models, front camber and caster is not adjustable; if camber and caster aren't within the specified dimensions, suspension parts are bent or worn and must be replaced. On 1999 and later models, camber can be adjusted by installing special bolts in the strut-to-steering knuckle lower mounting holes, but caster isn't adjustable.

The rear should be measured for camber and toe-in. Toe-in is adjusted by an eccentric cam at the inner end of the toe control arm. Camber and caster is not adjustable.

Getting the proper wheel alignment is a very exacting process, one in which complicated and expensive machines are necessary to perform the job properly. Because of this,

you should have a technician with the proper equipment perform these tasks. We will, however, use this space to give you a basic idea of what is involved with a wheel alignment so you can better understand the process and deal intelligently with the shop that does the work.

Toe-in is the turning in of the wheels. The purpose of a toe specification is to ensure parallel rolling of the wheels. In a vehicle with zero toe-in, the distance between the front edges of the wheels will be the same as the distance between the rear edges of the wheels. The actual amount of toe-in is normally only a fraction of an inch. Incorrect toe-in will cause the tires to wear improperly by making them scrub against the road surface.

Camber is the tilting of the wheels from

vertical when viewed from one end of the vehicle. When the wheels tilt out at the top, the camber is said to be positive (+). When the wheels tilt in at the top the camber is negative (-). The amount of tilt is measured in degrees from vertical and this measurement is called the camber angle. This angle affects the amount of tire tread which contacts the road and compensates for changes in the suspension geometry when the vehicle is cornering or traveling over an undulating surface.

Caster is the tilting of the front steering axis from the vertical. A tilt toward the rear is positive caster and a tilt toward the front is negative caster.

Chapter 11 Body

Contents

1 General information

The models covered by this manual feature a "unibody" layout, using a floor pan with front and rear frame side rails which support the body components, front and rear suspension systems and other mechanical components. Certain components are particularly vulnerable to accident damage and can be unbolted and repaired or replaced. Among these parts are the body moldings, bumpers, front fenders, the hood and trunk lids and all glass. Only general body maintenance practices and body panel repair procedures within the scope of the do-it-yourselfer are included in this Chapter.

2 Body - maintenance

1 The condition of the vehicle's body is very important, because the resale value depends a great deal on it. It's much more difficult to repair a neglected or damaged body than it is to repair mechanical components. The hidden areas of the body, such as the wheel wells, the frame and the engine compartment, are equally important, although they don't require as frequent attention as the rest of the body.
2 Once a year, or every 12,000 miles, it's a good idea to have the underside of the body steam cleaned. All traces of dirt and oil will be removed and the area can then be inspected carefully for rust, damaged brake lines, frayed electrical wires, damaged cables and other problems.
3 At the same time, clean the engine and the engine compartment with a steam cleaner or water-soluble degreaser.
4 The wheel wells should be given close attention, since undercoating can peel away and stones and dirt thrown up by the tires can cause the paint to chip and flake, allowing rust to set in. If rust is found, clean down to the bare metal and apply an anti-rust paint.
5 The body should be washed about once a week. Wet the vehicle thoroughly to soften the dirt, then wash it down with a soft sponge and plenty of clean soapy water. If the surplus dirt is not washed off very carefully, it can wear down the paint.
6 Spots of tar or asphalt thrown up from the road should be removed with a cloth soaked in solvent.
7 Once every six months, wax the body and chrome trim. If a chrome cleaner is used to remove rust from any of the vehicle's plated parts, remember that the cleaner also removes part of the chrome, so use it sparingly.

3 Vinyl trim - maintenance

Don't clean vinyl trim with detergents, caustic soap or petroleum-based cleaners. Plain soap and water works just fine, with a soft brush to clean dirt that may be ingrained. Wash the vinyl as frequently as the rest of the vehicle. After cleaning, application of a high-quality rubber and vinyl protectant will help prevent oxidation and cracks. The protectant can also be applied to weatherstripping, vacuum lines and rubber hoses, which often fail as a result of chemical degradation, and to the tires.

4 Upholstery and carpets - maintenance

1 Every three months remove the floor mats and clean the interior of the vehicle (more frequently if necessary). Use a stiff whiskbroom to brush the carpeting and loosen dirt and dust, then vacuum the upholstery and carpets thoroughly, especially along seams and crevices.
2 Dirt and stains can be removed from carpeting with basic household or automotive carpet shampoos available in spray cans. Follow the directions and vacuum again, then use a stiff brush to bring back the "nap" of the carpet.
3 Most interiors have cloth or vinyl upholstery, either of which can be cleaned and maintained with a number of material-specific cleaners or shampoos available in auto supply stores. Follow the directions on the product for usage, and always spot-test any upholstery cleaner on an inconspicuous area (like the bottom edge of a back seat cushion) to ensure that it doesn't cause a color shift in the material.
4 After cleaning, vinyl upholstery should be treated with a protectant. **Note:** *Make sure the*

protectant container indicates the product can be used on seats - some products may make a seat too slippery. **Caution:** Do not use a protectant on vinyl-covered steering wheels.

5   Leather upholstery requires special care. It should be cleaned regularly with saddle soap or leather cleaner. Never use alcohol, gasoline, nail polish remover or thinner to clean leather upholstery.

6   After cleaning, regularly treat leather upholstery with a leather conditioner, rubbed in with a soft cotton cloth. Never use car wax on leather upholstery.

7   In areas where the interior of the vehicle is subject to bright sunlight, cover leather-seating areas of the seats with a sheet if the vehicle is to be left out for any length of time.

---

5   Body repair

Minor damage
Repair of scratches

1   If the scratch is superficial and does not penetrate to the metal of the body, repair is very simple. Lightly rub the scratched area with a fine rubbing compound to remove loose paint and built up wax. Rinse the area with clean water.

2   Apply touch-up paint to the scratch, using a small brush. Continue to apply thin layers of paint until the surface of the paint in the scratch is level with the surrounding paint. Allow the new paint at least two weeks to harden, then blend it into the surrounding paint by rubbing with a very fine rubbing compound. Finally, apply a coat of wax to the scratch area.

3   If the scratch has penetrated the paint and exposed the metal of the body, causing the metal to rust, a different repair technique is required. Remove all loose rust from the bottom of the scratch with a pocket knife, then apply rust inhibiting paint to prevent the formation of rust in the future. Using a rubber or nylon applicator, coat the scratched area with glaze-type filler. If required, the filler can be mixed with thinner to provide a very thin paste, which is ideal for filling narrow scratches. Before the glaze filler in the scratch hardens, wrap a piece of smooth cotton cloth around the tip of a finger. Dip the cloth in thinner and then quickly wipe it along the surface of the scratch. This will ensure that the surface of the filler is slightly hollow. The scratch can now be painted over as described earlier in this Section.

Repair of dents
See photo sequence

4   When repairing dents, the first job is to pull the dent out until the affected area is as close as possible to its original shape. There is no point in trying to restore the original shape completely as the metal in the damaged area will have stretched on impact and cannot be restored to its original contours. It is better to bring the level of the dent up to a point, which is about 1/8-inch below the level of the surrounding metal. In cases where the dent is very shallow, it is not worth trying to pull it out at all.

5   If the back side of the dent is accessible, it can be hammered out gently from behind using a soft-face hammer. While doing this, hold a block of wood firmly against the opposite side of the metal to absorb the hammer blows and prevent the metal from being stretched.

6   If the dent is in a section of the body which has double layers, or some other factor makes it inaccessible from behind, a different technique is required. Drill several small holes through the metal inside the damaged area, particularly in the deeper sections. Screw long, self tapping screws into the holes just enough for them to get a good grip in the metal. Now pulling on the protruding heads of the screws with locking pliers can pull out the dent.

7   The next stage of repair is the removal of paint from the damaged area and from an inch or so of the surrounding metal. This is easily done with a wire brush or sanding disk in a drill motor, although it can be done just as effectively by hand with sandpaper. To complete the preparation for filling, score the surface of the bare metal with a screwdriver or the tang of a file or drill small holes in the affected area. This will provide a good grip for the filler material. To complete the repair, see the subsection on *filling and painting*.

Repair of rust holes or gashes

8   Remove all paint from the affected area and from an inch or so of the surrounding metal using a sanding disk or wire brush mounted in a drill motor. If these are not available, a few sheets of sandpaper will do the job just as effectively.

9   With the paint removed, you will be able to determine the severity of the corrosion and decide whether to replace the whole panel, if possible, or repair the affected area. New body panels are not as expensive as most people think and it is often quicker to install a new panel than to repair large areas of rust.

10   Remove all trim pieces from the affected area except those which will act as a guide to the original shape of the damaged body, such as headlight shells, etc. Using metal snips or a hacksaw blade, remove all loose metal and any other metal that is badly affected by rust. Hammer the edges of the hole on the inside to create a slight depression for the filler material.

11   Wire brush the affected area to remove the powdery rust from the surface of the metal. If the back of the rusted area is accessible, treat it with rust inhibiting paint.

12   Before filling is done, block the hole in some way. This can be done with sheet metal riveted or screwed into place, or by stuffing the hole with wire mesh.

13   Once the hole is blocked off, the affected area can be filled and painted. See the following subsection on *filling and painting*.

Filling and painting

14   Many types of body fillers are available, but generally speaking, body repair kits which contain filler paste and a tube of resin hardener are best for this type of repair work. A wide, flexible plastic or nylon applicator will be necessary for imparting a smooth and contoured finish to the surface of the filler material. Mix up a small amount of filler on a clean piece of wood or cardboard (use the hardener sparingly). Follow the manufacturer's instructions on the package, otherwise the filler will set incorrectly.

15   Using the applicator, apply the filler paste to the prepared area. Draw the applicator across the surface of the filler to achieve the desired contour and to level the filler surface. As soon as a contour that approximates the original one is achieved, stop working the paste. If you continue, the paste will begin to stick to the applicator. Continue to add thin layers of paste at 20-minute intervals until the level of the filler is just above the surrounding metal.

16   Once the filler has hardened, the excess can be removed with a body file. From then on, progressively finer grades of sandpaper should be used, starting with a 180-grit paper and finishing with 600-grit wet-or-dry paper. Always wrap the sandpaper around a flat rubber or wooden block, otherwise the surface of the filler will not be completely flat. During the sanding of the filler surface, the wet-or-dry paper should be periodically rinsed in water. This will ensure that a very smooth finish is produced in the final stage.

17   At this point, the repair area should be surrounded by a ring of bare metal, which in turn should be encircled by the finely feathered edge of good paint. Rinse the repair area with clean water until all of the dust produced by the sanding operation is gone.

18   Spray the entire area with a light coat of primer. This will reveal any imperfections in the surface of the filler. Repair the imperfections with fresh filler paste or glaze filler and once more smooth the surface with sandpaper. Repeat this spray-and-repair procedure until you are satisfied that the surface of the filler and the feathered edge of the paint are perfect. Rinse the area with clean water and allow it to dry completely.

19   The repair area is now ready for painting. Spray painting must be carried out in a warm, dry, windless and dust free atmosphere. These conditions can be created if you have access to a large indoor work area, but if you are forced to work in the open, you will have to pick the day very carefully. If you are working indoors, dousing the floor in the work area with water will help settle the dust, which would otherwise be in the air. If the repair area is confined to one body panel, mask off the surrounding panels. This will help minimize the effects of a slight mismatch in paint color. Trim pieces such as chrome strips, door handles, etc., will also need to be masked off or removed. Use masking tape and several thickness of newspaper for the masking operations.

20   Before spraying, shake the paint can thoroughly, then spray a test area until the spray painting technique is mastered. Cover the repair area with a thick coat of primer.

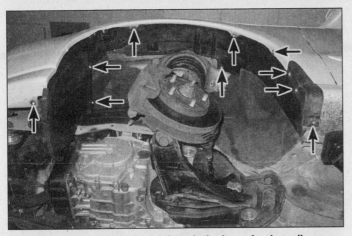

8.2 Remove the screws and detach the inner fenderwell cover

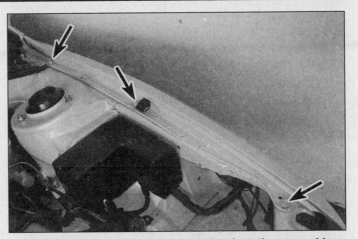

8.3a Remove the fender retaining bolts along the upper side

The thickness should be built up using several thin layers of primer rather than one thick one. Using 600-grit wet-or-dry sandpaper, rub down the surface of the primer until it is very smooth. While doing this, the work area should be thoroughly rinsed with water and the wet-or-dry sandpaper periodically rinsed as well. Allow the primer to dry before spraying additional coats.

21   Spray on the top coat, again building up the thickness by using several thin layers of paint. Begin spraying in the center of the repair area and then, using a circular motion, work out until the whole repair area and about two inches of the surrounding original paint is covered. Remove all masking material 10 to 15 minutes after spraying on the final coat of paint. Allow the new paint at least two weeks to harden, then use a very fine rubbing compound to blend the edges of the new paint into the existing paint. Finally, apply a coat of wax.

Major damage

22   Major damage must be repaired by an auto body shop specifically equipped to perform unibody repairs. These shops have the specialized equipment required to do the job properly.
23   If the damage is extensive, the body must be checked for proper alignment or the vehicle's handling characteristics may be adversely affected and other components may wear at an accelerated rate.
24   Due to the fact that all of the major body components (hood, fenders, etc.) are separate and replaceable units, any seriously damaged components should be replaced rather than repaired. Sometimes the components can be found in a auto salvage or wrecking yard that specializes in used vehicle components, often at considerable savings over the cost of new parts.

6   Hinges and locks - maintenance

Once every 3000 miles, or every three months, the hinges and latch assemblies on the doors, hood and trunk should be given a few drops of light oil or lock lubricant. The

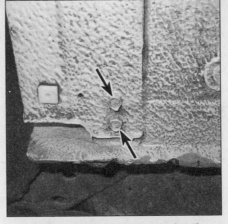

8.3b Remove the bolts located at the lower rear of the fender

door latch strikers should also be lubricated with a thin coat of grease to reduce wear and ensure free movement. Lubricate the door and trunk locks with spray-on graphite lubricant.

7   Windshield and fixed glass - replacement

Replacement of the windshield and fixed glass requires the use of special fast-setting adhesive/caulk materials and some specialized tools and techniques. These operations should be left to a dealer service department or a shop specializing in glass work.

8   Front fender - removal and installation

Refer to illustrations 8.2, 8.3a, 8.3b, 8.3c and 8.3d

1   Remove the headlight, turn signal light assembly and the front bumper (see Chapter 12 and Section 12).
2   Remove the inner fenderwell cover **(see illustration)**. On some 2004 and later models, it may be necessary to remove the door

8.3c Remove the bolts retaining the front fender to the bumper cover

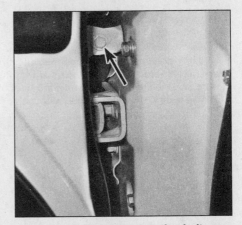

8.3d The fender rear mounting bolt can be reached with the door open (2004 and later models)

mirror inner cover and the small molding at the upper rear of the fender.
3   Remove the retaining bolts and detach the fender **(see illustrations)**.
4   The manufacturer recommends applying 3M™ silicone sealant tape number 8625 or equivalent between the fender and the inner fenderwell cover. The remainder of installation is the reverse of removal.

These photos illustrate a method of repairing simple dents. They are intended to supplement *Body repair - minor damage* in this Chapter and should not be used as the sole instructions for body repair on these vehicles.

1 If you can't access the backside of the body panel to hammer out the dent, pull it out with a slide-hammer-type dent puller. In the deepest portion of the dent or along the crease line, drill or punch hole(s) at least one inch apart . . .

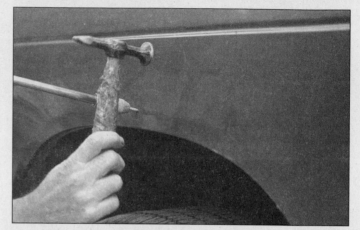

2 . . . then screw the slide-hammer into the hole and operate it. Tap with a hammer near the edge of the dent to help 'pop' the metal back to its original shape. When you're finished, the dent area should be close to its original contour and about 1/8-inch below the surface of the surrounding metal

3 Using coarse-grit sandpaper, remove the paint down to the bare metal. Hand sanding works fine, but the disc sander shown here makes the job faster. Use finer (about 320-grit) sandpaper to feather-edge the paint at least one inch around the dent area

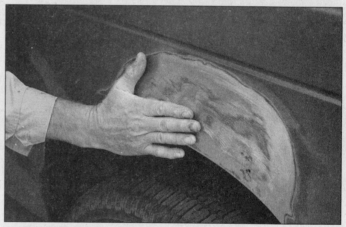

4 When the paint is removed, touch will probably be more helpful than sight for telling if the metal is straight. Hammer down the high spots or raise the low spots as necessary. Clean the repair area with wax/silicone remover

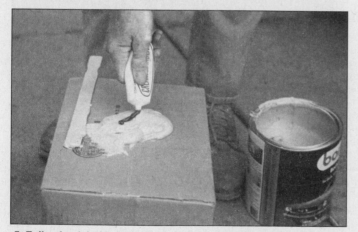

5 Following label instructions, mix up a batch of plastic filler and hardener. The ratio of filler to hardener is critical, and, if you mix it incorrectly, it will either not cure properly or cure too quickly (you won't have time to file and sand it into shape)

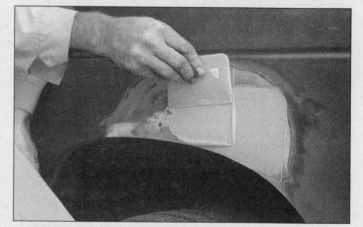

6 Working quickly so the filler doesn't harden, use a plastic applicator to press the body filler firmly into the metal, assuring it bonds completely. Work the filler until it matches the original contour and is slightly above the surrounding metal

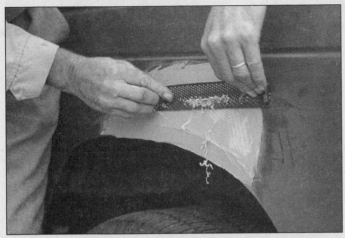

7 Let the filler harden until you can just dent it with your fingernail. Use a body file or Surform tool (shown here) to rough-shape the filler

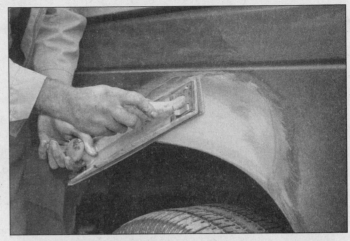

8 Use coarse-grit sandpaper and a sanding board or block to work the filler down until it's smooth and even. Work down to finer grits of sandpaper - always using a board or block - ending up with 360 or 400 grit

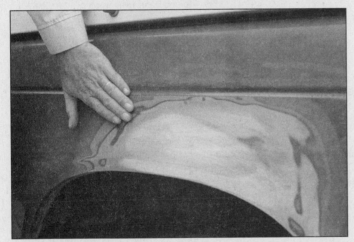

9 You shouldn't be able to feel any ridge at the transition from the filler to the bare metal or from the bare metal to the old paint. As soon as the repair is flat and uniform, remove the dust and mask off the adjacent panels or trim pieces

10 Apply several layers of primer to the area. Don't spray the primer on too heavy, so it sags or runs, and make sure each coat is dry before you spray on the next one. A professional-type spray gun is being used here, but aerosol spray primer is available inexpensively from auto parts stores

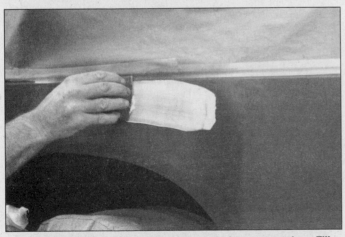

11 The primer will help reveal imperfections or scratches. Fill these with glazing compound. Follow the label instructions and sand it with 360 or 400-grit sandpaper until it's smooth. Repeat the glazing, sanding and respraying until the primer reveals a perfectly smooth surface

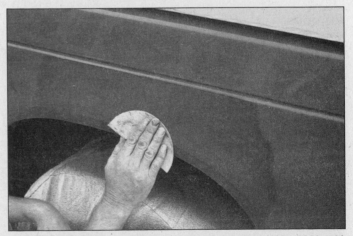

12 Finish sand the primer with very fine sandpaper (400 or 600-grit) to remove the primer overspray. Clean the area with water and allow it to dry. Use a tack rag to remove any dust, then apply the finish coat. Don't attempt to rub out or wax the repair area until the paint has dried completely (at least two weeks)

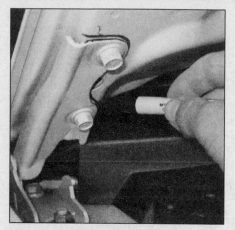

9.3 Paint or mark around the hood hinge before removing the bolts

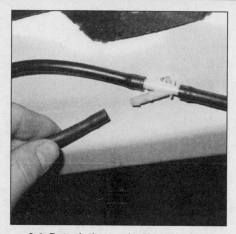

9.4 Detach the washer hose before removing the hood

9.5 Support the hood with your shoulder while removing the hood bolts

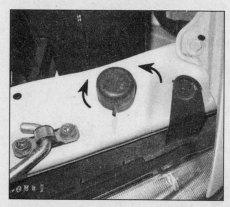

9.11 Screw the rubber hood bumpers in-or-out to adjust the hood until it is flush with the fenders

9   Hood - removal, installation and adjustment

Note: *The hood is heavy and somewhat awkward to remove and install - at least two people should perform this procedure.*

Removal

Refer to illustration 9.3, 9.4 and 9.5

1   Use blankets or pads to cover the cowl area of the body and both fenders. This will protect the body and paint as the hood is lifted off.
2   Open the hood and support it on the prop rod.
3   Scribe alignment marks around the bolt heads and hinges to aid alignment during installation **(see illustration)**.
4   Disconnect the under hood lamp connector (if equipped) and windshield washer hose **(see illustration)**.
5   Have an assistant support one side of the hood while you support the other. Simultaneously remove the hinge-to-hood bolts **(see illustration)**.
6   Lift off the hood. **Note:** *A good place to store the hood is on the roof of the vehicle. Place blankets or pads on the roof first and lay the hood painted-side down on the blankets.*

Installation

7   Installation is the reverse of removal. Align the marks around the hinges and bolts (one side at a time) and then check for proper clearance. Readjust as necessary (see below).

Adjustment

Refer to illustration 9.11

8   Fore-and-aft and side-to-side adjustment of the hood is done by moving the hood in relation to the hinge plate after loosening the bolts. The hood must be aligned so there is an equal gap to each front fender and flush with the top surface.
9   Scribe or trace a line around the entire hinge plate so you can judge the amount of movement **(see illustration 9.3)**.
10   Loosen the bolts and move the hood into correct alignment. Move it only a little at a time. Tighten the hinge bolts and carefully lower the hood to check the alignment.
11   Adjust the hood bumpers on the radiator support so the hood is flush with the fenders when closed **(see illustration)**.
12   The hood latch assembly can also be adjusted up-and-down and side-to-side after loosening the nuts. Make sure you place alignment marks around the hood latch assembly

10.2a Mark the hood latch position with paint or a permanent type marking pen

before loosening the mounting nuts.
13   The hood latch assembly, as well as the hinges, should be periodically lubricated with white lithium-base grease to prevent sticking and wear.

10   Hood latch and cable - removal and installation

Warning: *These models have airbags. Always disable the airbag system before working in the vicinity of any airbag system components to avoid the possibility of accidental deployment of the airbag, which could cause personal injury (see Chapter 12).*

Latch

Removal

Refer to illustrations 10.2a, 10.2b and 10.3

1   Open the hood and support it on the prop rod.
2   Scribe alignment marks around the hood latch assembly to aid alignment during installation (a permanent-type felt-tip marker or paint will also work for this) **(see illustrations)**.
3   Remove the bolts/nuts and detach the

10.2b Remove the front bumper and grille assembly for access to the hood latch on 2004 and later models

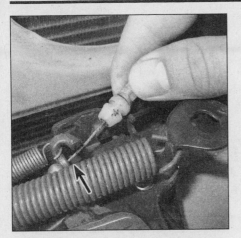

10.3 Slide the cable housing from the keyhole slot and detach the cable

latch assembly from the radiator support, then disconnect the release cable from the hood latch assembly **(see illustration)**.

Installation

4   Installation is the reverse of removal. Align the hood latch assembly with the marks on the radiator support and then tighten the nuts. Check hood latch operation. Readjust as necessary.

Cable

Removal

Refer to illustration 10.7

5   Disconnect the release cable from the hood latch (see Steps 1 through 3).
6   Detach the cable from the clips securing it to the radiator support.
7   Remove the screws retaining the release lever **(see illustration)**.
8   Under the dash, locate and disengage the push-in retainer and cable grommet from the firewall.
9   Connect a piece of heavy string or flexible wire to the engine compartment end of the cable, then from inside the vehicle, pull the cable with string or wire attached through the firewall into the vehicle. Disconnect the

10.7 Lift up the release lever for access to the retaining screws

string or wire from the old cable.

Installation

10   Connect the string or wire to the new cable and carefully pull it through the firewall into the engine compartment.
11   The remaining installation steps are the reverse of removal.

---

11   Radiator grille - removal and installation

Warning: *These models have airbags. Always disable the airbag system before working in the vicinity of any airbag system components to avoid the possibility of accidental deployment of the airbag, which could cause personal injury (see Chapter 12).*

2003 and earlier models

Refer to illustrations 11.2 and 11.3

1   Open the hood and support it on the prop rod.
2   Use a screwdriver to detach the retaining clips **(see illustration)**.
3   Remove the grille by pulling it straight out **(see illustration)**.

4   Reinstall the clips on the grille then place it in position and push it into place until the clips lock.

2004 through 2006 models

5   Open the hood, then pull out the heads of the pushpin retainers that are around the perimeter of each grille.
6   Remove each section by pulling it forward.
7   To install, push each pushpin into place, then push their center pins in to lock them.

2007 and later models

8   Refer to Section 12 and remove the front bumper.
9   The grille is retained by claw-type clips and screws. Remove all screws, then use a screwdriver to release all the clips.
10   Remove the grille. It can be further disassembled to replace individual pieces.
11   Installation is the reverse of removal.

---

12   Bumpers - removal and installation

Warning: *These models have airbags. Always disable the airbag system before working in the vicinity of any airbag system components to avoid the possibility of accidental deployment of the airbag, which could cause personal injury (see Chapter 12).*

Front bumper

Removal

2003 and earlier models
Refer to illustrations 12.6a and 12.6b

1   Open the hood and support it on the prop rod.
2   Remove the radiator grille (see Section 11).
3   Remove the fasteners securing the front fender inner splash shields to the lower section of the bumper cover.
4   Pull the splash shields away from the fenderwell as necessary to remove the bolts

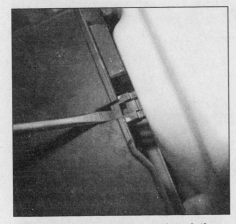

11.2 Use a screwdriver to detach the grille clips (2003 and earlier models)

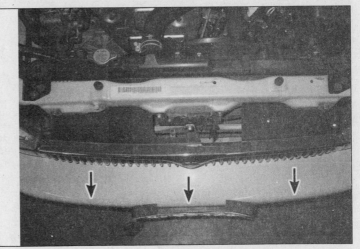

11.3 After the clips have been disengaged, detach the grille by pulling it straight out (2003 and earlier models)

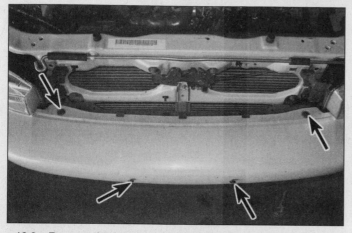

12.6a Remove the fasteners along the top of the bumper cover (2003 and earlier models)

12.6b Remove the fasteners along the bottom of the bumper cover (2003 and earlier models)

securing the bumper cover to the front fender.

5   If equipped, disconnect the foglight wiring harness connectors and remove the foglight assemblies.

6   Remove the fasteners securing the bumper cover **(see illustrations)**.

12.12 To remove the front bumper cover, remove the lower splash shields (A), the inner fender splash shields (B) and the top and bottom retainers (C) - there are also screws at the upper ends of the bumper

2004 through 2006 models

7   Remove the grille (see Section 11).

8   Raise the vehicle and support it securely on jackstands. Remove the two bumper lower splash shields.

9   Remove the license plate support if necessary.

10   Disconnect the fog light wiring connectors.

11   Remove the bumper cover screws and pushpin retainers.

2007 and later models

Refer to illustrations 12.12, 12.15a and 12.15b

12   Raise the vehicle and support it securely on jackstands. Remove the two bumper lower splash guards **(see illustration)**.

13   Remove the license plate support if necessary.

14   Remove the fog lights, if so equipped.

15   Remove the two bumper cover screws at each upper end of the bumper **(see illustration)**. Remove the top and bottom pushpin retainers **(see illustration)**.

All models

16   Remove the bumper cover from the vehicle. **Note:** *If you are performing this job*

alone, place some blankets or other suitable padding on the ground below the bumper cover to protect the paint should it fall during removal.

17   If required, the bumper reinforcement can be removed at this time.

Installation

18   Installation is the reverse of removal.

Rear bumper
Removal

2003 and earlier models

Refer to illustrations 12.20a, 12.20b and 12.21

19   Open the trunk lid.

20   Detach the trunk trim fasteners and remove the panels for access to the inner body-to-bumper cover fasteners **(see illustrations)**.

21   Remove the fasteners securing the lower part of the bumper cover **(see illustration)**.

2004 and later models

Refer to illustration 12.27

22   Refer to Chapter 12 and remove the taillight assemblies.

23   Detach the trunk inner trim panels for

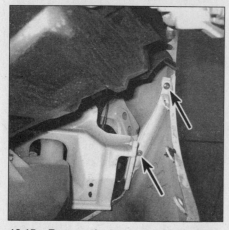

12.15a Remove the inner wheel well splash shields to access these bumper screws

12.15b Bumper upper push-pin retainers (2007 and later models)

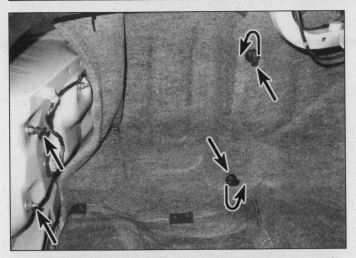

12.20a Remove the trunk trim fasteners and remove the panels for access to the bumper cover retainers

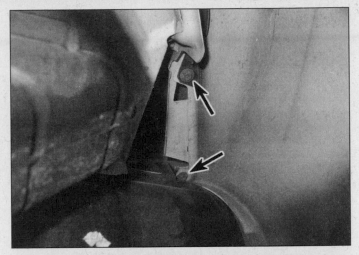

12.20b Inside the trunk, remove the nuts retaining the bumper cover to the body (2003 and earlier models)

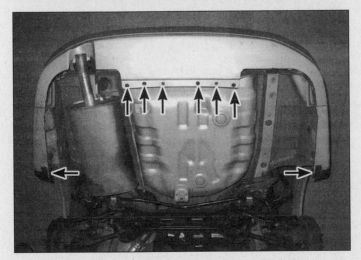

12.21 Remove the bumper cover retaining bolts and screws (typical)

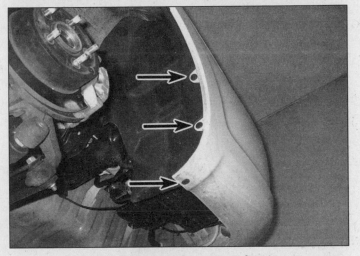

12.27 Typical rear bumper retainers

access to the bumper cover fasteners.

24   Raise the vehicle and support it securely on jackstands. Remove the rear wheels if necessary for clearance, then remove the inner rear wheel well splash shields. **Note:** *The shields can be pulled back for access to the screws so they don't have to be removed completely.*

25   Pry the upper parts of the end sections of the bumper cover upward to release them.

26   Push down at the front of the upper center section of the bumper cover to release the claw-type latches.

27   Remove the bumper cover screws and pushpin retainers **(see illustration).**

All models

28   Slide the bumper cover rearward to remove it from the vehicle. **Note:** *If you are performing this job alone, place some blankets or other suitable padding on the ground below the bumper cover to protect the paint should it fall during removal.*

29   If required, the bumper reinforcement can be removed at this time.

Installation

30   Installation is the reverse of removal.

13   Door trim panel - removal and installation

Removal

Refer to illustration 13.2

Note: *This procedure applies to both the front and rear doors.*

1   Open the door and completely lower the window glass.

2   On manual window models, remove the window crank using a special tool (available at most auto parts stores) or by working a cloth back-and-forth behind the handle to dislodge the retaining clip **(see illustration).**

2003 and earlier models

Refer to illustrations 13.3a, 13.3b, 13.4 and 13.5

3   Pry open the screw covers and remove

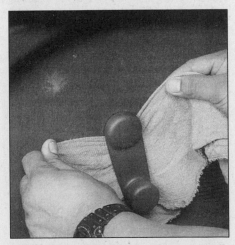

13.2 If you don't have a window crank removal tool (which is available at most auto parts stores and relatively inexpensive), place a shop cloth behind the window crank handle and work it back-and-forth to dislodge the retaining clip

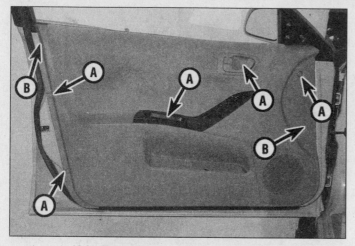

13.3a Front door trim panel screw locations

A   *2003 and earlier models*
B   *Additional screw locations on 1998 and earlier models*

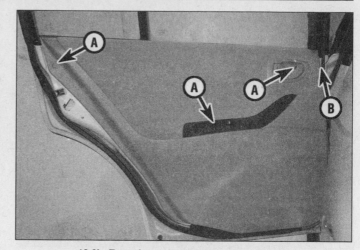

13.3b Rear door trim panel screw locations

A   *2003 and earlier models*
B   *Additional screw location on 1998 and earlier models*

the screws at the front and rear edges of the door trim panel **(see illustrations)**.

4   In the pull handle pocket, remove the screw **(see illustration)**. On 1998 and earlier

models with "flat" door trim panels, also remove the two screws securing the armrest to the door.

5   Pull the inner door handle away and remove the screw **(see illustration)**.

2004 and later models

Refer to illustrations 13.6a, 13.6b, 13.9a, 13.9b and 13.9c

6   Remove the screw under the door latch handle bezel **(see illustration)**. Use a plastic trim tool or a screwdriver wrapped with tape to pry the front part of the bezel **(see illustration)**. Press inward on the claw-type latches at the rear of the handle to release it.

7   Use the same tool to pry the front of the power window switch assembly up. Press inward on the claw-type latches around the switch assembly to release it. Lift the switch assembly out, then disconnect the wiring.

8   On 2006 and earlier models, carefully pry the screw cap from the large pull handle and remove the screw below it.

9   On 2007 and later models, remove the bottom cover from the hand grip pocket **(see**

illustration). Remove the screw under the cover. Also pry off the reflector lens from the rear of the door and remove the screw behind it **(see illustration)**. Remove the screw at the bottom rear of the panel (there is a cover over the screw on 2007 and later models) **(see illustration)**. Check to make sure all screws have been removed.

All models

Refer to illustrations 13.10, 13.12, 13.13a, 13.13b, 13.13c and 13.13d

10   Carefully pry around the door trim panel to disengage it from the retaining clips **(see illustration)**.

11   Grasp the trim panel, pull up and detach it from the door.

12   Disconnect the electrical connector and remove the trim panel **(see illustration)**. **Caution:** *Do not allow the trim panel to hang from the electrical wires.*

13   If necessary for access to the inner door, remove the panel bracket and inner door handle and carefully remove the plastic watershield **(see illustrations)**.

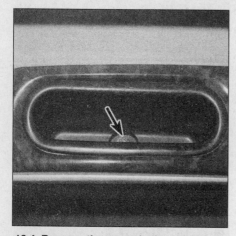

13.4 Remove the screw in the pull handle pocket area (2003 and earlier models)

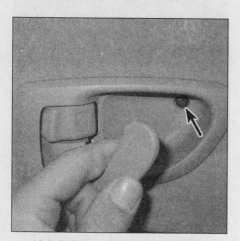

13.5 Pull the door handle away for access, then remove the screw (2003 and earlier models)

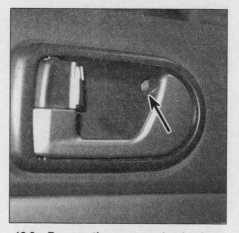

13.6a Remove the screw under the door latch handle

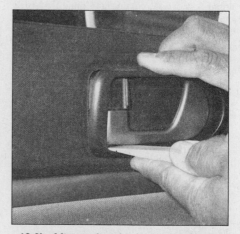

13.6b After prying the front of the bezel out, use a plastic tool to release the hooks at the rear (2004 and later models)

13.9a On 2004 and later models, there is a screw in the bottom of the door pull handle

13.9b Remove the door reflector, then remove the panel screw under it (2004 and later models)

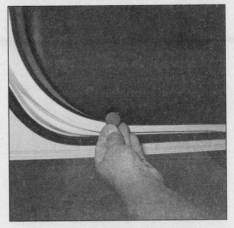

13.9c Door panel lower rear screw location

Installation

14   Reconnect any electrical connectors and install the latch linkage into the door handle. Secure it with the retaining clip.

15   When reinstalling the watershield, make sure there is enough adhesive remaining to seal properly. Replace the adhesive if necessary.
16   Engage the top of the trim panel into the

door and press it into place, seating all clip fasteners.
17   The remaining installation steps are the reverse of removal.

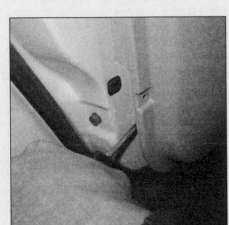

13.10 Carefully pry around the door trim panel to disengage it from the retaining clips

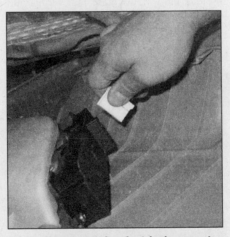

13.12 Disconnect the electrical connector from the door trim panel

13.13a Remove the screws and detach the trim panel bracket

13.13b Remove the screws and detach the inner door handle (2003 and earlier models)

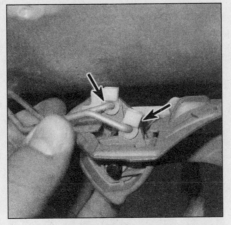

13.13c Disconnect the door handle connecting links

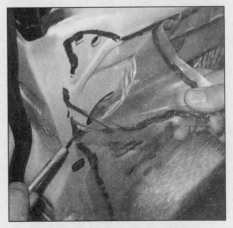

13.13d Carefully peel the plastic watershield from the door

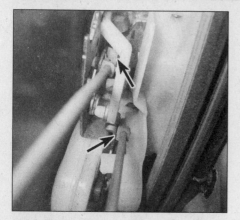

14.4 Door latch linkage rod connections (2003 and earlier models)

14.6 The door latch is retained by three screws

14.7 Unclip the inside door latch handle (2004 and later models)

14 Door latch, outside handle and lock cylinder - removal and installation

Note: *This procedure applies to both the front and rear doors.*

Latch

1   Remove the door trim panel (see Sec-

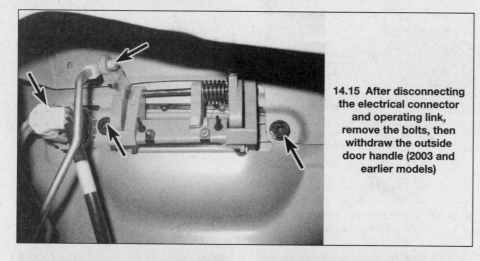

14.15 After disconnecting the electrical connector and operating link, remove the bolts, then withdraw the outside door handle (2003 and earlier models)

tion 13). On vehicles equipped with power windows, close the window before disconnecting the door trim panel electrical connectors.
2   On vehicles with manual windows, install the window crank (without the retaining clip) and roll up the window.
3   If you are removing a rear door latch, remove the window glass rear vertical run channel.

2003 and earlier models
Refer to illustrations 14.4 and 14.6
4   Disconnect the lock cylinder, lock button and latch release operating rods from the door latch **(see illustration)**.
5   On vehicles equipped with power door locks, disconnect the electrical connector.
6   Remove the three mounting screws from the end of the door and remove the door latch **(see illustration)**. Installation is the reverse of removal.

2004 and later models
Refer to illustration 14.7
7   Disconnect the cables, then remove the inside door handle **(see illustravtion)**.
8   Remove the plastic watershield.
9   Remove the lower rear vertical window channel.
10   Disconnect the two rods from the outer door handle, then remove the latch assembly **(see illustration 14.6)**.
11   Installation is the reverse of removal.

Outside handle
12   Remove the door trim panel (see Section 13). On vehicles equipped with power windows, close the window before disconnecting the door trim panel electrical connectors.
13   On vehicles with manual windows, install the window crank (without the retaining clip) and roll up the window.

2003 and earlier models
Refer to illustration 14.15
14   On vehicles so equipped, disconnect the central locking electrical connector.
15   Remove the two bolts **(see illustration)**.
16   Withdraw the handle from the door and disconnect the electrical connector. Installation is the reverse of removal.

2004 and later models
Refer to illustration 14.19
17   Remove the plastic watershield.
18   Disconnect the rods from the outer door handle.
19   Remove the door handle mounting bolt **(see illustration)**.
20   Pull the door handle out a little to access

14.19 Outside door handle mounting bolt (2004 and later models)

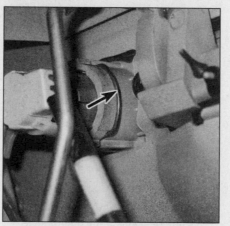

14.26 Pry out the lock cylinder retaining clip

15.7 Remove the screws securing the regulator arm to the glass

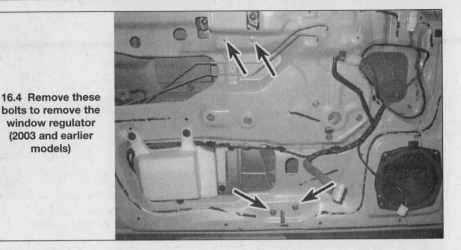

16.4 Remove these bolts to remove the window regulator (2003 and earlier models)

the key cylinder, then spread the pin apart and remove the key lock cylinder.
21 Remove the door handle.
22 Installation is the reverse of removal.

Lock cylinder

Refer to illustration 14.26
Note: *This procedure applies only to 2003 and earlier models. See Step 20 to remove the key lock cylinder from later models.*
23 Remove the outside door handle (see earlier in this Section).
24 Detach the operating rod retaining clip and operating rod from the lock cylinder.
25 Disconnect the electrical connector (if equipped).
26 Using a screwdriver, pry off the lock cylinder retainer and withdraw it from the door or handle **(see illustration).**
27 Installation is the reverse of removal.

15 Door window glass - removal and installation

Removal

Refer to illustration 15.7
1 Remove the door trim panel (see Section 13).
2 Carefully remove the plastic watershield from the door (see Section 13).
3 If you are removing the rear door glass, remove the window glass rear run channel.
4 On vehicles equipped with power windows, remove the switch from the door trim panel and connect it to the wiring harness. This will allow you to move the window as necessary.
5 On vehicles with manual windows, install the window crank (without the retaining clip). This will allow you to move the window as necessary.
6 Lower the window for access to the glass retaining screws.
7 Remove the screws securing the regulator to the glass then maneuver the glass out of the opening in the top of the door **(see illustration).**

Installation

8 Installation is the reverse of removal. Make sure there is enough adhesive remaining on the watershield to seal properly. Replace the adhesive if necessary.

16 Door window regulator - removal and installation

Refer to illustration 16.4
Note: *This procedure applies to both the front and rear doors and both manual and power operated windows.*
1 Remove the door trim panel (see Section 13).
2 Detach the glass from the window regulator (see Section 15), then move the glass all the way up in its channel and secure it there by placing a couple strips of masking tape from one side of the glass, over the top of the door, to the other side of the glass.
3 On power window models, disconnect the window motor electrical connector.
4 Remove the retaining bolts and remove the regulator assembly through the access hole in the door **(see illustration). Warning:** *On power window models, do not remove the motor from the regulator assembly without first clamping the sector gear to the mounting*

17.2 Remove the bolts and detach the check strap from the door pillar

plate or serious personal injury may result.
5 Installation is the reverse of removal.

17 Door - removal and installation

Note 1: *This procedure applies to both the front and rear doors.*
Note 2: *The door is heavy and somewhat awkward to remove and install - at least two people should perform this procedure.*

Removal

Refer to illustrations 17.2 and 17.4
1 Use a plastic trim tool or a screwdriver wrapped with tape to remove the interior sill trim and the kick panel trim panels, then disconnect the door wiring harness from under the instrument panel.
2 Remove the bolt and detach the check strap from the door pillar **(see illustration).**
3 Place a jack under the door or have an assistant on hand to support it when the hinge bolts are removed. **Note:** *If a jack is used, place a rag and a piece of wood between it and the door to protect the door's painted surfaces.*
4 Mark around the hinges, then remove the bolts and remove the door **(see illustration). Note:** *Place scribe marks around the hinges before loosening the bolts to maintain a reference point.*

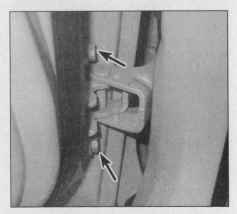

17.4 Remove the door hinge bolts

18.3 For a reference point at installation, outline the hinges on the trunk lid with a felt tip marker

Installation

5   Installation is the reverse of removal.
6   Install the bolts/nuts and tighten them securely. Check door fit and adjust by loosening the hinge bolts and moving the door, as necessary.

---

18   Trunk lid - removal, installation and adjustment

Note: *The trunk lid is heavy and somewhat awkward to remove and install - at least two people should perform this procedure.*

Removal

Refer to illustration 18.3

1   Open the trunk lid and cover the edges of the trunk compartment with pads or cloths to protect the painted surfaces when the lid is removed.
2   Disconnect any electrical connectors attached to the trunk latch and center brake light. To aid with installation, attach a length of flexible wire to the connector end of the harness and then carefully pull it out of the trunk lid. Disconnect the guide wire from the

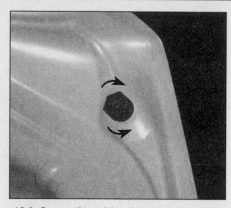

18.8 Screw the rubber bumpers in or out to adjust the trunk height

harness and secure it at both openings of the trunk lid.
3   Use a permanent type marking pen to make alignment marks around the hinges **(see illustration)**.
4   On 2004 and later models, disconnect the gas-filled support struts from the trunk lid by using a small screwdriver to pull out the flat spring at the ball socket. Have an assistant support one side of the trunk lid while you support the other. Simultaneously remove the hinge-to-trunk lid bolts.
5   Lift off the trunk lid.

Installation

Refer to illustration 18.8

6   Installation is the reverse of removal.
Note: *When reinstalling the trunk lid, align the marks made during removal.* After installation, close the lid and see if it's in proper alignment with the surrounding panels and adjust if necessary.

Adjustment

7   Fore-and-aft and side-to-side adjustments of the lid are controlled by the position of the hinge bolts in the holes. To adjust it, loosen the hinge bolts, reposition the lid and

retighten the bolts. Make sure to mark the position of the hinges before loosening the bolts.
8   The height of the lid in relation to the surrounding body panels can be adjusted by screwing the trunk lid bumpers in or out **(see illustration)**.
9   Installation is the reverse of removal.

---

19   Dashboard trim panels and glove box - removal and installation

Warning: *These models have airbags. Always disable the airbag system before working in the vicinity of any airbag system components to avoid the possibility of accidental deployment of the airbag, which could cause personal injury (see Chapter 12).*
Caution: *The following trim covers can be easily scratched; take care in removing them to avoid damage.*

Dashboard end caps

Refer to illustrations 19.1 and 19.2

1   On early models, you don't need a tool to remove the left cap **(see illustration)**. On later models, use a plastic trim tool or a screwdriver wrapped with tape to pry the cap off.
2   Pry off the right end cap using the tool **(see illustration)**.
3   Installation is the reverse of removal.

Driver's side under cover

Refer to illustrations 19.4, 19.5a and 19.5b

4   Remove the left end cap (see Step 1) and the hood latch handle **(see illustration)**.
5   Remove the screws and detach the under cover panel, then disconnect the electrical connectors and remove the panel **(see illustrations)**. **Note:** *On 2004 and later models, the upper part of the panel is secured with clips. Use a plastic trim tool or a screwdriver wrapped with tape to pry the upper section loose. Installation is the reverse of removal.*

19.1 Pull out on left side end cap and rotate it away from the dashboard

19.2 The right side dashboard end cap doesn't have a finger hold, so you'll have to pry it out a little with a screwdriver before you can get your fingers on it.

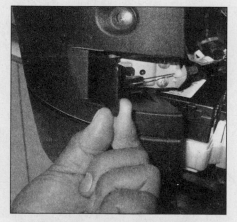

19.4 Remove the hood latch release handle to detach the driver's lower trim panel

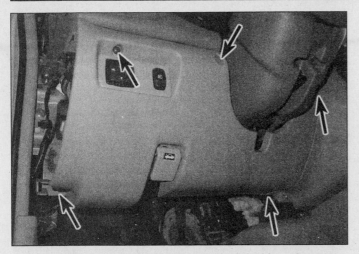

19.5a Remove the screws and detach the left side under cover (2003 and earlier models)

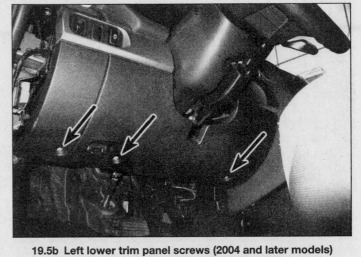

19.5b Left lower trim panel screws (2004 and later models)

Center bezel hood (2004 and later models)

Refer to illustration 19.6

6   Use a plastic trim tool or a screwdriver wrapped with tape to pry up the edge of the hood nearest the rear of the car **(see illustration)**. Push forward to release the clips at the front edge and lift it off.

7   Installation is the reverse of removal.

Center bezel

2003 and earlier models

Refer to illustration 19.8

8   Detach the clips at each corner by gripping inside of the bezel securely and pulling out sharply **(see illustration)**.

9   Install the bezel by placing it in position, then pushing in sharply until the clips lock in place.

2004 and later models

Refer to illustration 19.14

10   Refer to Step 6 and remove the bezel hood.

11   Use a plastic trim tool or a screwdriver wrapped with tape to release the clips at each corner of the heater control assembly

and radio trim panel. There are also claw-type clips at the center of each side.

12   Pull the unit out and disconnect the wiring.

13   Remove the sound system components (see Chapter 12).

14   Remove the mounting screws from the bezel **(see illustration)**. Pull the center bezel rearward to detach it. Installation is the reverse of removal.

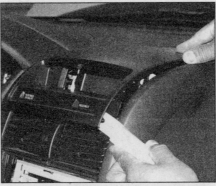

19.6 Always use a non-scratching tool to pry any plastic interior panel - the center bezel hood on 2004 and later models must be released at the rear end first

Glove box

Refer to illustrations 19.15a and 19.15b

15   Open the glove box, squeeze in on the sidewalls while rotating the glove box door all the way down, then lift the hinge hooks at the base out of the slots in the instrument panel **(see illustrations)**.

16   Insert the hinge hooks into the slots and rotate the glove box up sharply until the

19.8 Grasp the center bezel securely inside the opening and pull back sharply to detach the retaining clips

19.14 Center trim panel mounting screws (2004 and later models)

19.15a Squeeze the glove box sides inward and rotate it down

19.15b Rotate the glove box hinge hooks out of the slots in the dash

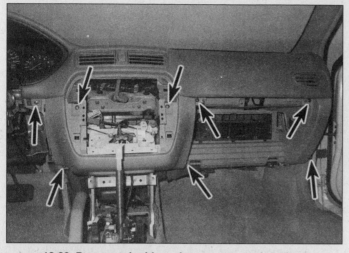

19.20 Passenger's side under cover screw locations (2003 and earlier models)

19.23 Remove the glove box door, then remove the screws . . .

retainers snap into place.

17   To remove the glove box itself, remove the door, then remove the mounting screws.

18   Use a plastic trim tool or a screwdriver wrapped with tape to pry the glove box rearward to release the clips at the center of each end. Installation is the reverse of removal.

Passenger's side under cover (1999 through 2003 models)

Refer to illustration 19.20

19   Remove the driver's side under cover (see Steps 4 and 5). Also remove the glove box and right side dashboard end cap.

20   Remove the upper and lower retaining screws and remove the under cover **(see illustration)**.

21   Installation is the reverse of removal.

Passenger's side lower trim panel (2004 and later models)

Refer to illustrations 19.23 and 19.24

22   Remove the center bezel, the right end cap and the glove box assembly.

23   Remove the mounting screws from the lower and left edges of the trim panel **(see illustration)**.

24   Use a plastic trim tool or a screwdriver wrapped with tape to pry the panel rearward and release the 5 clips around its perimeter **(see illustration)**.

25   Installation is the reverse of removal.

---

20   Instrument cluster bezel - removal and installation

Refer to illustration 20.2

Warning: *These models have airbags. Always disable the airbag system before working in the vicinity of any airbag system components to avoid the possibility of accidental deployment of the airbag, which could cause personal injury (see Chapter 12).*

Note: *This procedure applies only to 2003 and earlier models. The bezels of later models are integral with the cluster assembly.*

1   Disconnect the battery cable from the negative battery terminal.

2   Remove the screws securing the bezel to the top of the cluster, detach the clips at the lower edge and remove the bezel **(see illustration)**. Disconnect the electrical connector from the rheostat, if equipped.

3   Place the bezel in position, press in until the clips engage, then install the retaining screws.

---

21   Instrument panel - removal and installation

Warning: *These models have airbags. Always disable the airbag system before working in the vicinity of any airbag system components to avoid the possibility of accidental deployment of the airbag, which could cause personal injury (see Chapter 12).*

Note: *It is not necessary, but it is suggested to remove both front seats to allow additional working space and lessen the chance of damage to the seats during this procedure.*

1   Disconnect the battery cable from the negative battery terminal.

2   Remove the left and right dashboard end caps (see Section 19).

19.24 . . . and pull the passenger's lower trim panel rearward

20.2 Remove the retaining screws at the top of the instrument cluster bezel, then detach and remove the bezel (typical)

21.8a Detach the front trim pillar rubber molding . . .

21.8b . . . then carefully pry off the trim pieces

21.13a Remove the bolts from the left side . . .

2003 and earlier models

Refer to illustration 21.8a, 21.8b, 21.13a and 21.3b

3   Remove the hood latch release lever (see Section 10).

4   Remove the dashboard trim panels and glove box (see Section 19). Remove the steering column cover (see Section 22).

5   On 1998 and earlier models, remove the center console.

6   Remove the driver's airbag and the steering wheel (see Chapter 10).

7   Remove the radio (see Chapter 12).

8   Detach the front pillar trim pieces **(see illustrations)**.

9   Remove the passenger side airbag (see Chapter 12). **Warning:** *Carry the airbag with the trim cover side FACING AWAY from your body to minimize injury if the airbag module accidentally deploys. Store the airbag module aside in a safe, isolated location with the trim cover side facing UP.*

10   Remove the instrument cluster bezel (see Section 20), then the instrument cluster (see Chapter 12).

11   Remove the center air outlet and heating and air conditioning control assembly (see

Chapter 3).

12   On 1998 and earlier models remove the bolts attaching the instrument panel center console base to the floor.

13   Remove the instrument panel retaining bolts **(see illustrations)**.

14   Lift up on the instrument panel and pull it rearward and withdraw it from the vehicle.

15   Installation is the reverse of removal.

2004 and later models

Refer to illustrations 21.19 and 21.23

16   Refer to Section 9 and remove all of the instrument panel trim panels and the glove box.

17   Remove the instrument cluster bezel, then the instrument cluster (see Chapter 12).

18   Use a plastic trim tool or a screwdriver wrapped with tape to pry off the windshield pillar trim panel.

19   Pry off the speaker trim panels from each end of the instrument panel **(see illustration)**. Remove the tweeter speakers and disconnect their wiring.

20   Remove the screws from the side air outlets and remove them.

21   Remove the steering wheel, clockspring

and the column covers (see Section 22 and Chapter 10).

22   Remove the interior temperature sensor from the driver's side of the instrument panel.

23   Carefully pry up the long trim panel at the windshield edge of the instrument panel **(see illustration)**. Work slowly to release each clip. Disconnect the light sensor as you remove the panel.

24   Remove the screws from the lower instrument panel braces and remove them.

25   Refer to Section 23 and remove the console.

26   Remove the door sill trim panels and the kick panels.

27   Disconnect the wiring from the passenger's airbag module.

28   Remove the instrument panel screws and bolts.

29   Check that all wiring and other components have been disconnected.

30   Get an assistant to help you pull the instrument panel rearward, then slide it carefully out the passenger's side of the vehicle.

31   Installation is the reverse of removal.

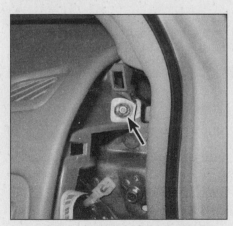

21.13b . . . and the right side of the instrument panel (2003 and earlier models)

21.19 Remove the speaker trim panel to access the instrument panel mounting screws under them

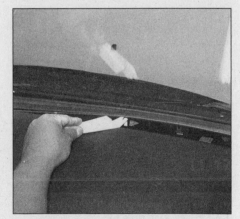

21.23 Carefully pry off the windshield trim panel using a plastic tool

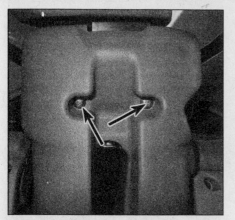

**22.3 Steering column cover
screw locations (typical)**

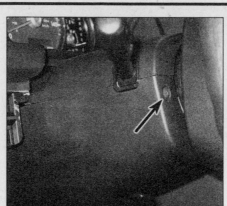

**22.6 These two column cover screws
(one on each side) can be removed
when the steering wheel is turned**

**23.5a Use a screwdriver to detach
the clips at each corner
(2003 and earlier models)**

**23.5b Once the shift panel trim clips have
been detached, lift it off**

22 Steering column covers - removal and installation

Warning: *These models have airbags. Always disable the airbag system before working in the vicinity of any airbag system components to avoid the possibility of accidental deploy-*

ment of the airbag, which could cause personal injury *(see Chapter 12).*
Caution: *These covers can be easily scratched, take care when removing them to avoid damage.*
1   Disconnect the cable from the negative battery terminal (see Chapter 5).

2003 and earlier models
Refer to illustration 22.3
2   Refer to Section 20 and remove the instrument cluster bezel. Also remove the driver's knee bolster trim panel (see Section 19).
3   Remove the two screws from the lower column cover, then separate them **(see illustration).**
4   Installation is the reverse of removal.

2004 and later models
Refer to illustration 22.6
5   Remove the screws from the lower column cover.
6   Rotate the steering wheel for access to the two screws behind the steering wheel, then remove them **(see illustration).**
7   Separate the column covers and remove them.
8   Installation is the reverse of removal.

23 Center console - removal and installation

Warning: *These models have airbags. Always disable the airbag system before working in the vicinity of any airbag system components to avoid the possibility of accidental deployment of the airbag, which could cause personal injury (see Chapter 12).*
Caution: *The center console can be easily scratched. Take care in removing the assembly to avoid damage.*
1   Disconnect the negative cable from the battery.
2   Completely raise the parking brake lever.

2003 and earlier models
Refer to illustrations 23.5a, 23.5b 23.6a, 23.6b, 23.7a, 23.7b, 23.7c and 23.8
3   Remove the instrument panel center bezel (see Section 19).
4   On vehicles equipped with a manual transaxle, pull the boot down and unscrew the gear shift knob.
5   Detach the console shift panel trim **(see illustrations).**
6   Remove the retaining screws and remove

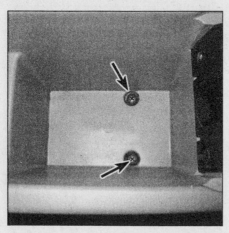

**23.6a Remove the screws and detach the
inner console cover**

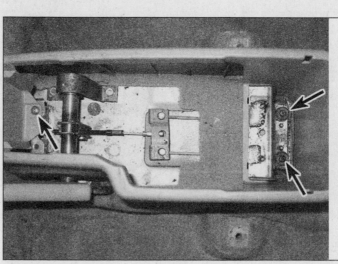

**23.6b Remove the
console screws
(1999 through 2003
models shown. On
1998 and earlier
models, the screws
are on the outside
of the console box**

23.7a Use a screwdriver to detach the center lower panel (typical)

23.7b Disconnect the electrical connectors and remove the panel

23.7c Remove the console-to-dashboard retaining screws (2003 and earlier models)

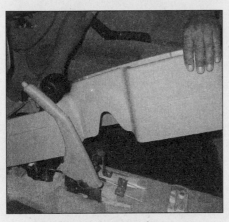

23.8 Rotate the console up over the shift lever

23.10 Use a plastic tool to pry up the rear of the console top panel to avoid scratching it

23.11 The console front storage box can be pulled out by hand

the center console **(see illustrations)**.

7   Detach the center lower panel and ashtray, remove the screws and detach the front of the console to the dashboard **(see illustrations)**.

8   Lift the center console up over the shift lever and remove it from vehicle **(see illustration)**.

9   Installation is the reverse of removal.

2004 and later models
Refer to illustrations 23.10, 23.11, 23.12 and 23.13

10   Use a plastic trim tool or a screwdriver wrapped with tape to carefully pry up the shift lever upper panel **(see illustration)**. Disconnect the wiring harnesses as you lift it.

11   Pry out the storage box at the front of the console **(see illustration)**.

12   Lift the trim plate from the bottom of the console rear storage box **(see illustration)**.

13   Remove all the console mounting screws **(see illustration)**, then carefully lift the console main body.

14   Installation is the reverse of removal.

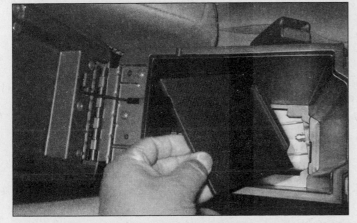

23.12 Lift the bottom cover from the console storage box; there are screws beneath it

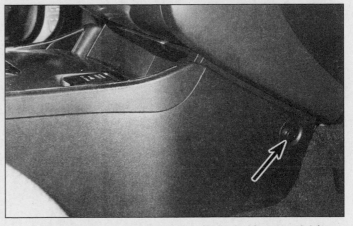

23.13 Console mounting location (2004 and later models)

24.1 Insert a screwdriver into the mirror base to detach it

24.4 Insert a small screwdriver under the edge of the mirror cover and pry it off

24.5 Remove the exterior mirror mounting nuts (typical)

24 Mirrors - removal and installation

Interior

Refer to illustration 24.1

1   Insert a small flat blade screwdriver into the notch in the mirror bracket, push up toward the top of the windshield to release the internal spring and remove the mirror **(see illustration)**.

2   Slide the mirror base onto its mount until the internal spring locks it in place. **Note:** *If the support base for the mirror has come off the windshield, it can be reattached with a special mirror adhesive kit available at auto parts stores. Clean the glass and support base thoroughly and follow the directions on the adhesive package, allowing the base to bond overnight before attaching the mirror.*

Exterior

Refer to illustrations 24.4 and 24.5

3   On models so equipped, it will be nec-

essary to remove the tweeter cover, base and speaker.

4   Pry off the mirror cover with a small screwdriver **(see illustration)**. On vehicles equipped with power mirrors, disconnect the mirror electrical connector.

5   Remove the retaining nuts and detach the mirror from the door **(see illustration)**.

6   Installation is the reverse of removal.

25 Cowl cover - removal and installation

Refer to illustration 25.2

1   Remove the trim caps from the windshield wiper arms and mark the positions of the arms to their shafts (see Chapter 12, Section 11), then detach the wiper arm retaining nuts and remove the wiper arms.

2   Remove the retainers on each side of the cowl cover and carefully lift it from the vehicle **(see illustration)**. **Note:** *On 2004 and later models, the rear of the cowl clips onto*

the lower edge of the windshield glass.

3   Installation is the reverse of removal.

26 Seats - removal and installation

Front

Refer to illustrations 26.1, 26.2, 26.3a and 26.3b

Warning: *Some models are equipped with side-impact airbags located in the exterior sides of the front seats. On these models, be sure to disable the airbag system before removing a front seat. Also, do not disassemble these seats.*

Warning: *The manufacturer recommends that the vehicle have an accuracy check done on the passenger seat occupant classification sensor (located within the seat) whenever it's removed.*

1   Move the seat fully rearward and remove the seat track front bolts **(see illustration)**.

2   Move the seat fully forward, remove the covers and unscrew the seat track rear bolts **(see illustration)**.

25.2 Cowl cover retainer locations (hood removed for clarity) (typical)

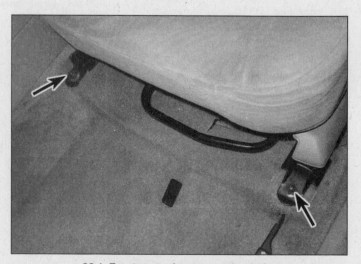

26.1 Front seat - front mounting bolts

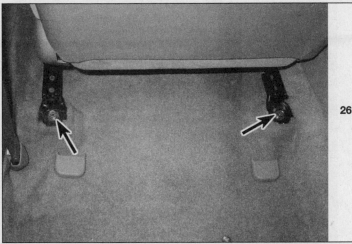

26.2 Front seat - rear mounting bolts

26.3a Be sure to disconnect any electrical connectors before removing the seat

26.3b Later models have several wiring harnesses that must be disconnected before removing a front seat

26.5 Remove the rear seat cushion by pulling out on the release rings while lifting up on the cushion (2003 and earlier models)

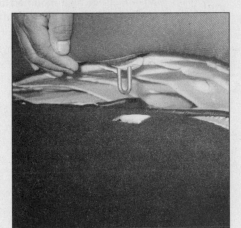

26.6 On 2004 and later models, pull the forward edge of the rear seat cushion up to release it

3   Disconnect the wiring for the seat belt switch and the seat slide sensor **(see illustration)**. If the vehicle is equipped with heated seats, power seats and/or side impact airbags, disconnect the electrical connector and lift the seat out of the vehicle **(see illustration)**.

4   Installation is the reverse of removal.

Rear

Seat cushion

Refer to illustrations 26.5 and 26.6

5   On 2003 and earlier models, pull out on the two release rings at the bottom edge while lifting the cushion to detach it **(see illustration)**.

6   On 2004 and later models, pull upward on the front edge of the cushion, then slide it forward to disengage the rear clips **(see illustration)**.

7   Installation is the reverse of removal. Press down firmly over the seat retainers to ensure they are fully engaged in the floorpan.

Seat back

Refer to illustrations 26.8a and 26.8b

8   Remove the seat cushion, then remove the bolts and lift the seat back up off the

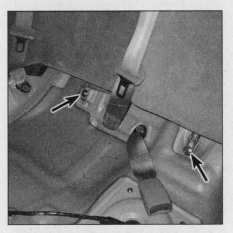

26.8a Remove the bolts at the base of the seat back

retainer hooks **(see illustrations)**.

9   Installation is the reverse of removal. Press firmly over the seat retainers to ensure they are fully engaged.

26.8b Lift the seat back up and off these retaining hooks

27.2 Remove the electrical connector and the two retaining nuts and detach the high-mounted brake light (2003 and earlier models)

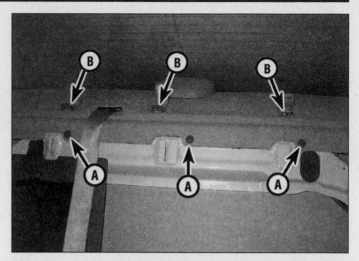

27.3 Remove the retainers along the front edge of the rear shelf trim panel (A) and the child seat anchors (B), if equipped

27   Rear shelf trim panel - removal and installation

Refer to illustrations 27.2 and 27.3

1   Remove the rear seat cushion and seat back (see Section 26).

2003 and earlier models

2   Open the trunk and remove the high-mounted brake light **(see illustration)**.
3   Detach the roof pillar trim pieces on both sides, then remove the retainers, child seat anchors (if equipped) and detach the shelf **(see illustration)**.

2004 and later models

4   Use a plastic trim tool or a screwdriver wrapped with tape to detach the rear pillar side trim panels.

5   Pry off the covers for the child restraint fitting and the rear shelf speakers. Remove the seat belt end cover.
6   Remove the screws from the rear shelf and carefully remove it.

All models

7   Installation is the reverse of removal.

Chapter 12
Chassis electrical system

Contents

1 General information

The electrical system is a 12-volt, negative ground type. Power for the lights and all electrical accessories is supplied by a lead/acid-type battery, which is charged by the alternator.

This Chapter covers repair and service procedures for the various electrical components not associated with the engine. Information on the battery, alternator, distributor and starter motor can be found in Chapter 5.

It should be noted that when portions of the electrical system are serviced, the cable should be disconnected from the negative battery terminal (see Chapter 5) to prevent electrical shorts and/or fires.

2 Electrical troubleshooting - general information

Refer to illustrations 2.5a, 2.5b, 2.6 and 2.9

A typical electrical circuit consists of an electrical component, any switches, relays, motors, fuses, fusible links or circuit breakers related to that component and the wiring and connectors that link the component to both the battery and the chassis. To help you pinpoint an electrical circuit problem, wiring diagrams are included at the end of this Chapter.

Before tackling any troublesome electrical circuit, first study the appropriate wiring diagrams to get a complete understanding of what makes up that individual circuit. Noting if other components related to the circuit are operating properly, for instance, can often narrow trouble spots, down. If several components or circuits fail at one time, chances are the problem is in a fuse or ground connection, because several circuits are often routed through the same fuse and ground connections.

Electrical problems usually stem from simple causes, such as loose or corroded connections, a blown fuse, a melted fusible link or a failed relay. Visually inspect the condition of all fuses, wires and connections in a problem circuit before troubleshooting the circuit.

If test equipment and instruments are going to be utilized, use the diagrams to plan ahead of time where you will make the necessary connections in order to accurately pinpoint the trouble spot.

The basic tools needed for electrical troubleshooting include a circuit tester or voltmeter (a 12-volt bulb with a set of test leads can also be used), a continuity tester, which includes a bulb, battery and set of test leads, and a jumper wire, preferably with a circuit breaker incorporated, which can be used to bypass electrical components **(see illustrations)**. Before attempting to locate a problem with test instruments, use the wiring diagram(s) to decide where to make the connections.

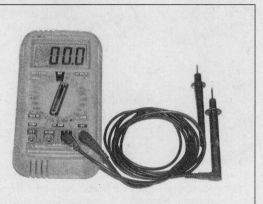

2.5a The most useful tool for electrical troubleshooting is a digital multimeter that can check volts, amps, and test continuity

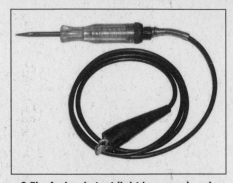

2.5b A simple test light is a very handy tool for testing voltage

Voltage checks

Voltage checks should be performed if a circuit is not functioning properly. Connect one lead of a circuit tester to either the negative battery terminal or a known good ground. Connect the other lead to a connector in the circuit being tested, preferably nearest to the battery or fuse **(see illustration)**. If the bulb of the tester lights, voltage is present, which means that the part of the circuit between the connector and the battery is problem free. Continue checking the rest of the circuit in the same fashion. When you reach a point at which no voltage is present, the problem lies between that point and the last test point with voltage. Most of the time the problem can be traced to a loose connection. **Note:** *Keep in mind that some circuits receive voltage only when the ignition key is in the Accessory or Run position.*

Finding a short

One method of finding shorts in a live circuit is to remove the fuse and connect a test light in place of the fuse terminals (fabricate two jumper wires with small spade terminals, plug the jumper wires into the fuse box and connect the test light). There should

be voltage present in the circuit. Move the suspected wiring harness from side-to-side while watching the test light. If the bulb goes off, there is a short to ground somewhere in that area, probably where the insulation has rubbed through.

Ground check

Perform a ground test to check whether a component is properly grounded. Disconnect the battery and connect one lead of a continuity tester or multimeter (set to the ohms scale), to a known good ground. Connect the other lead to the wire or ground connection being tested. If the resistance is low (less than 5 ohms), the ground is good. If the bulb on a self-powered test light does not go on, the ground is not good.

Continuity check

A continuity check is done to determine if there are any breaks in a circuit - if it is passing electricity properly. With the circuit off (no power in the circuit), a self-powered continuity tester or multimeter can be used to check the circuit. Connect the test leads to both ends of the circuit (or to the "power" end and a good ground), and if the test light comes on the circuit is passing current properly **(see illustration)**. If the resistance is low (less than 5 ohms), there is continuity; if the reading is 10,000 ohms or higher, there is a break somewhere in the circuit. The same procedure can be used to test a switch, by connecting the continuity tester to the switch terminals. With the switch turned On, the test light should come on (or low resistance should be indicated on a meter).

Finding an open circuit

When diagnosing for possible open circuits, it is often difficult to locate them by sight because the connectors hide oxidation or terminal misalignment. Merely wiggling a connector on a sensor or in the wiring har-

ness may correct the open circuit condition. Remember this when an open circuit is indicated when troubleshooting a circuit. Intermittent problems may also be caused by oxidized or loose connections.

Electrical troubleshooting is simple if you keep in mind that all electrical circuits are basically electricity running from the battery, through the wires, switches, relays, fuses and fusible links to each electrical component (light bulb, motor, etc.) and to ground, from which it is passed back to the battery. Any electrical problem is an interruption in the flow of electricity to and from the battery.

Connectors

Most electrical connections on these vehicles are made with multiwire plastic connectors. The mating halves of many connectors are secured with locking clips molded into the plastic connector shells. The mating halves of large connectors, such as some of those under the instrument panel, are held together by a bolt through the center of the connector.

To separate a connector with locking clips, use a small screwdriver to pry the clips apart carefully, then separate the connector halves. Pull only on the shell, never pull on the wiring harness as you may damage the individual wires and terminals inside the connectors. Look at the connector closely before trying to separate the halves. Often the locking clips are engaged in a way that is not immediately clear. Additionally, many connectors have more than one set of clips.

Each pair of connector terminals has a male half and a female half. When you look at the end view of a connector in a diagram, be sure to understand whether the view shows the harness side or the component side of the connector. Connector halves are mirror images of each other, and a terminal shown on the right side end-view of one half will be on the left side end view of the other half.

2.6 In use, a basic test light's lead is clipped to a known good ground, then the pointed probe can test connectors, wires or electrical sockets - if the bulb lights, the circuit being tested has battery voltage

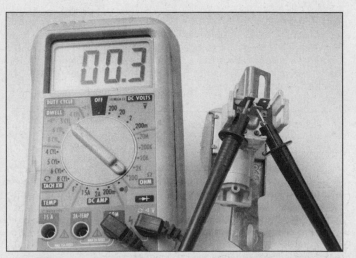

2.9 With a multimeter set to the ohms scale, resistance can be checked across two terminals - when checking for continuity, a low reading indicates continuity, a high reading or infinity indicates lack of continuity

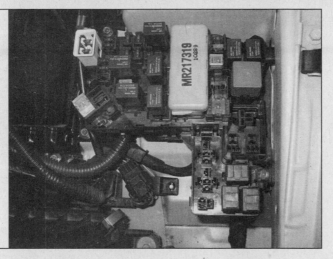

3.1a The main engine compartment fuse/relay box is located on left side of the engine compartment on 1999 and later models (on earlier models it's on the right side)

3.1b On 1999 and later models the interior fuse box is located in the left end of the instrument panel

3 Fuses and fusible links - general information

Fuses

Refer to illustrations 3.1a, 3.1b and 3.3

The electrical circuits of the vehicle are protected by a combination of fuses, circuit breakers and fusible links. Fuse blocks are located in the engine compartment and on the end of, or under, the left side of the instrument panel **(see illustrations)**.

Each of the fuses is designed to protect a specific circuit, and the various circuits are identified on the fuse panel cover.

Miniaturized fuses are employed in the fuse blocks. These compact fuses, with blade terminal design, allow fingertip removal and replacement. If an electrical component fails, always check the fuse first. The best way to check a fuse is with a test light. Check for power at the exposed terminal tips of each fuse. If power is present on one side of the fuse but not the other, the fuse is blown. A blown fuse can also be confirmed by visually inspecting it **(see illustration)**.

Be sure to replace blown fuses with the correct type. Fuses of different ratings are physically interchangeable, but only fuses of the proper rating should be used. Replacing a fuse with one of a higher or lower value than specified is not recommended. Each electrical circuit needs a specific amount of protection. The amperage value of each fuse is molded into the fuse body.

If the replacement fuse immediately fails, don't replace it again until the cause of the problem is isolated and corrected. In most cases, this will be a short circuit in the wiring caused by a broken or deteriorated wire.

Fusible links

Some circuits are protected by fusible links. The links are used in circuits which are not ordinarily fused, or which carry high current.

Cartridge type fusible links are located in the engine compartment fuse/relay box and are similar to a large fuse. After discon-

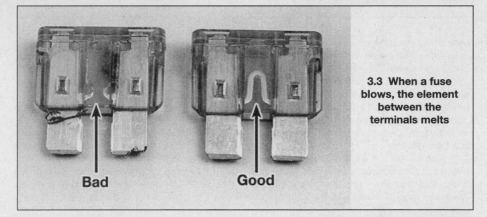

3.3 When a fuse blows, the element between the terminals melts

Bad   Good

necting the negative battery cable, simply unplug and replace a fusible link with one of the same amperage.

4 Circuit breakers - general information

Circuit breakers protect certain circuits, such as the power windows or heated seats. Depending on the vehicle's accessories, there may be one or two circuit breakers, located in the fuse/relay box in the engine compartment **(see illustration 3.1a)**.

Because the circuit breakers reset automatically, an electrical overload in a circuit-breaker-protected system will cause the circuit to fail momentarily, then come back on. If the circuit does not come back on, check it immediately.

For a basic check, pull the circuit breaker up out of its socket on the fuse panel, but just far enough to probe with a voltmeter. The breaker should still contact the sockets.

With the voltmeter negative lead on a good chassis ground, touch each end prong of the circuit breaker with the positive meter probe. There should be battery voltage at each end. If there is battery voltage only at one end, the circuit breaker must be replaced.

Some circuit breakers must be reset manually.

5 Relays - general information and testing

General information

1 Several electrical accessories in the vehicle, such as the fuel injection system, horns, starter, and fog lamps use relays to transmit the electrical signal to the component. Relays use a low-current circuit (the control circuit) to open and close a high-current circuit (the power circuit). If the relay is defective, that component will not operate properly. Most relays are mounted in the engine compartment fuse/relay box, with some specialized relays located above the interior fuse box in the dash **(see illustrations 3.1a and 3.1b)**. If a faulty relay is suspected, it can be removed and tested using the procedure below or by a dealer service department or a repair shop. Defective relays must be replaced as a unit.

Testing

Refer to illustrations 5.2a and 5.2b

2 Most of the relays used in these vehicles are of a type often called "ISO" relays, which refers to the International Standards Organization. The terminals of ISO relays are numbered to indicate their usual circuit connections and functions. There are two basic lay-

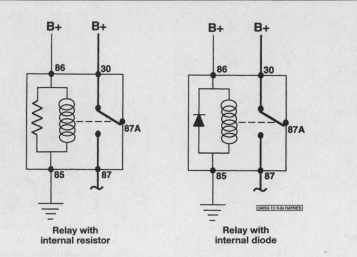

Relay with internal resistor

Relay with internal diode

5.2a Typical ISO relay designs, terminal numbering and circuit connections

5.2b Most relays are marked on the outside to easily identify the control circuits and the power circuits - four terminal type shown

outs of terminals on the relays used in the covered vehicles **(see illustrations)**.

3   Refer to the wiring diagram for the circuit to determine the proper connections for the relay you're testing. If you can't determine the correct connection from the wiring diagrams, however, you may be able to determine the test connections from the information that follows.

4   Two of the terminals are the relay control circuit and connect to the relay coil. The other relay terminals are the power circuit. When the relay is energized, the coil creates a magnetic field that closes the larger contacts of the power circuit to provide power to the circuit loads.

5   Terminals 85 and 86 are normally the control circuit. If the relay contains a diode, terminal 86 must be connected to battery positive (B+) voltage and terminal 85 to ground. If the relay contains a resistor, terminals 85 and 86 can be connected in either direction with respect to B+ and ground.

6   Terminal 30 is normally connected to the battery voltage (B+) source for the circuit loads. Terminal 87 is connected to the circuit leading to component being powered. If the relay has several alternate terminals for load or ground connections, they usually are numbered 87A, 87B, 87C, and so on.

7   Use an ohmmeter to check continuity through the relay control coil.

  a) *Connect the meter according to the polarity shown in the illustration for one check; then reverse the ohmmeter leads and check continuity in the other direction.*

  b) *If the relay contains a resistor, resistance will be indicated on the meter, and should be the same value with the ohmmeter in either direction.*

  c) *If the relay contains a diode, resistance should be higher with the ohmmeter in the forward polarity direction than with the meter leads reversed.*

  d) *If the ohmmeter shows infinite resistance in both directions, replace the relay.*

8   Remove the relay from the vehicle and use the ohmmeter to check for continuity between the relay power circuit terminals. There should be no continuity between terminal 30 and 87 with the relay de-energized.

9   Connect a fused jumper wire to terminal 86 and the positive battery terminal. Connect another jumper wire between terminal 85 and ground. When the connections are made, the relay should click.

10   With the jumper wires connected, check for continuity between the power circuit terminals. Now, there should be continuity between terminals 30 and 87.

11   If the relay fails any of the above tests, replace it.

---

6   Turn signal and hazard flasher - check and replacement

Warning: *These models have airbags. Always disable the airbag system before working in the vicinity of any airbag system component to avoid the possibility of accidental deployment of the airbag, which could cause personal injury* (see Section 24).

1   On 1998 and earlier models the turn signal and hazard flasher is a single combination unit, mounted under the left end of the instrument panel on the fuse panel/junction block. On 1999 and later models the turn signals and hazard flashers are controlled by the ETACS-ECU and a small electronic module incorporated into the switch.

2   When the flasher unit is functioning properly, an audible click can be heard during its operation. If the turn signals fail on one side or the other and the flasher unit does not make its characteristic clicking sound, or if a bulb on one side of the vehicle flashes much faster than normal but the bulb at the other end of athe vehicle (on the same side) doesn't light at all, a faulty turn signal bulb may be indicated.

3   If both turn signals fail to blink, the problem may be due to a blown fuse, a faulty flasher unit, a defective switch or a loose or

open connection. If a quick check of the fuse box indicates that the turn signal fuse has blown, check the wiring for a short before installing a new fuse.

4   On 1998 and earlier models the flasher is located on the interior fuse block. To replace the flasher, simply unplug it from the fuse block and install the new one. Make sure that the replacement unit is identical to the original. Compare the old one to the new one before installing it.

5   On 1999 and later models, diagnosis and replacement should be performed by a dealer service department or other qualified technician equipped with the necessary tools.

---

7   Steering column switches - replacement

Warning: *These models have airbags. Always disable the airbag system before working in the vicinity of any airbag system component to avoid the possibility of accidental deployment of the airbag, which could cause personal injury* (see Section 24).

1   These models have steering column mounted switches that can be removed separately with the steering wheel in place. In the event of problems with the main switch body (i.e. defective canceling cam), it will be necessary to remove the steering wheel for replacement.

2   There are two switches with levers; the left side controls the signaling and the lighting, and the right side controls the wipers and washer system. An additional control lever on cruise control-equipped models is located on the steering wheel hub, to the rear of the wiper/washer lever.

Turn signal and wiper/washer switches

Refer to illustration 7.5

3   Disconnect the cable from the negative battery terminal.

4   Remove the steering column covers (see Chapter 11). On 2003 and earlier models, also remove the driver's lower dash covers (see Chapter 11).

5   Depress the retaining clips and pull the

7.5 Press the retaining clips and detach the turn signal switch by pulling it straight out

7.9 Remove the screws (A) securing the steering wheel trim, remove the trim from the wheel, then remove the switch retaining screws (B) (typical)

switch straight out to detach it **(see illustration)**.
6   Place the new switch into position, push it in until it is securely locked in place.
7   The remainder of installation is the reverse of removal.

Cruise control switch
Refer to illustration 7.9
8   Disconnect the electrical connector from the switch. Remove the airbag and steering wheel (see Chapter 10).
9   Remove the screws and detach the trim piece from the back of the steering wheel, then remove the switch securing screws and detach the switch **(see illustration)**.
10   Installation is the reverse of removal.

8   Ignition switch and key lock cylinder - replacement

Warning: *These models have airbags. Always disable the airbag system before working in the vicinity of any airbag system component to avoid the possibility of accidental deployment of the airbag, which could cause personal injury (see Section 24).*

Ignition switch
Removal

2003 and earlier models
Refer to illustration 8.7
1   Disconnect the cable from the negative battery terminal.
2   Remove the driver's side under cover (see Chapter 11).
3   Remove the steering column covers (see Chapter 11).
4   Disconnect the electrical connector from the ignition switch.
5   Remove the key lock cylinder (see Steps 9 through 12).
6   On models with a key reminder switch, disconnect the switch and remove the assembly from the ignition switch and the lock cylinder. **Note:** *On models equipped with the anti-theft system, disconnect the key ring antenna and remove the immobilizer ECU harness from the below the dash.*
7   Remove the retaining screws and detach the switch from the steering column **(see illustration)**.

2004 and later models
8   Refer to Chapter 10 and remove the steering wheel, the airbag module and

the clockspring.
9   Remove the steering column covers (see Chapter 11).
10   Remove the steering column switch assembly (see Section 7).
11   Disconnect the wiring harness from the switch. Remove the mounting screws and remove the ignition switch.

Installation
12   Installation is the reverse of removal. Make sure the switch and lock cylinder are in the ACC position before installation. Tighten the switch mounting screws securely.

Lock cylinder
Removal
Refer to illustration 8.16
13   Disconnect the cable from the negative battery terminal.
14   Remove the driver's side under cover and the steering column covers (see Chapter 11).
15   Insert the ignition key and turn the switch to the ACC position.
16   Depress the retaining tab with a thin tool and withdraw the lock cylinder from the housing **(see illustration)**.

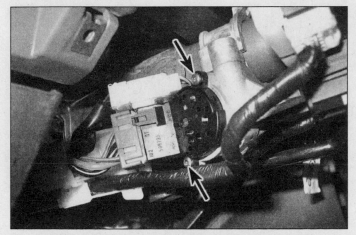

8.7 Location of the ignition switch mounting screws

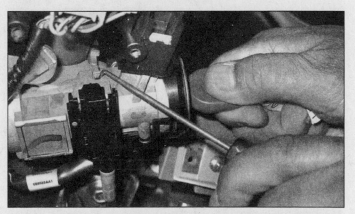

8.16 With the lock cylinder in the ACC position, depress the retaining pin with a thin tool, then pull straight out to remove the lock cylinder (typical)

8.17 Make sure the slot in the switch is positioned at the same exact angle as the ignition key lock cylinder (both must be in the ACC position)

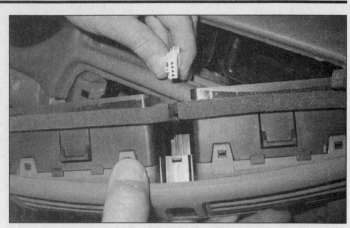

9.7 Disconnect the electrical connector then push the switch out from the rear

Installation

Refer to illustration 8.17

17   Make sure the slot in the ignition switch is in the ACC position and insert the lock cylinder into the housing until the retaining tab locates the housing **(see illustration)**. Check key operation.

18   The remaining installation steps are the reverse of removal. **Note:** *On models equipped with the anti-theft system, if the immobilizer ECU is replaced, attach a new immobilizer serial number identification sticker onto the glove box panel.*

---

9   Instrument panel switches - replacement

Hazard warning switch

1998 and earlier models

1   Remove the dash center air outlet assembly.

2   Disconnect the cool air bypass and air bypass damper lever from the center outlet assembly.

3   Disconnect the electrical connector from the hazard warning switch.

4   Separate the hazard warning switch from the center outlet assembly.

5   Installation is the reverse of removal

1999 through 2003 models

Refer to illustration 9.7

6   Remove the radio (see Section 12).

7   Remove the center air outlet by pushing up on the retaining tabs on the underside of the ducts, then disconnect the electrical connector **(see illustration)**.

8   Remove the switch from the outlet by pushing the bottom of the switch out from the backside with a screwdriver, then push the top of the switch out. Install the new switch by pushing it straight in until it snaps into place.

2004 and later models

9   Refer to Chapter 11 and remove the glove box, the hood release lever, the instrument panel center bezel hood and the center bezel.

10   Push the hazard light out from the rear. Installation is the reverse of removal.

Power mirror/fog light switch

Refer to illustrations 9.11a and 9.11b

11   Use a small screwdriver to pry the switch panel from the trim panel **(see illustrations)**.

12   Insert a small screwdriver between the

switch body and the panel to disengage the retaining tabs, then push the switch out the front of the panel.

13   Installation is the reverse of the removal procedure.

Instrument cluster dimmer rheostat

Refer to illustrations 9.15a and 9.15b

Note: *This procedure applies only to 2003 and earlier models. On 2004 and later models, the instrument cluster dimmer is mounted in the switch panel with the mirror and fog light switches. Follow the same procedures as for the other switches.*

14   Remove the cluster bezel (see Chapter 11).

15   Disconnect the electrical connector, remove the screws and remove the rheostat **(see illustrations)**.

16   Installation is the reverse of the removal procedure.

---

10   Instrument cluster - removal and installation

Warning: *These models have airbags. Always*

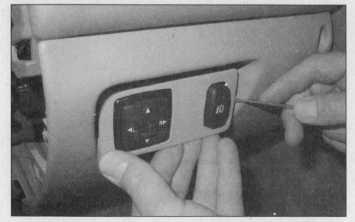

9.11a Carefully pry the power mirror/fog light control switch panel from the panel (2003 and earlier models)

9.11b On 2004 and later models, the switch arrangement is changed but the removal procedure is the same - you can either remove the instrument panel end trim panel and push the switch out from the rear or use a non-scratching plastic trim tool to pry it out from the front

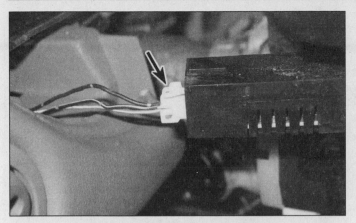

9.15a Disconnect the rheostat connector

9.15b Remove the rheostat retaining screws

10.4 Remove the instrument cluster mounting screws

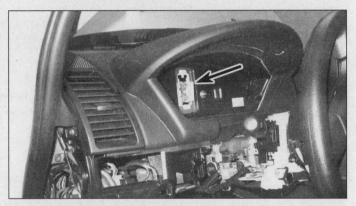

10.8 On 2004 and later models, the instrument cluster is secured by two screws at the top of the bezel - the rear of the cluster plugs into this connector (arrow)

disable the airbag system before working in the vicinity of any airbag system component to avoid the possibility of accidental deployment of the airbag, which could cause personal injury (see Section 24).

1   Disconnect the cable from the negative battery terminal.

2003 and earlier models

Refer to illustration 10.4

2   Remove the instrument cluster bezel (see Chapter 11).

3   Cover the steering column with a cloth to protect the trim covers.

4   Remove the cluster mounting screws and pull the instrument cluster towards the steering wheel **(see illustration)**.

5   Disconnect the electrical connectors, then remove the instrument cluster from the vehicle.

6   Installation is the reverse of removal.

2004 and later models

Refer to illustration 10.8

7   Lower the steering column to its lowest position. Remove the two mounting screws from the top of the cluster.

8   Carefully pull the cluster rearward to disengage it from the electrical connector

behind it **(see illustration)**.

9   Installation is the reverse of removal.

---

11 Wiper motor - check and replacement

Refer to illustrations 11.2a, 11.2b and 11.4

1   Disconnect the cable from the negative battery terminal.

11.2a Pry off the covers for access to the wiper arm retaining nuts

2   Carefully pry off the covers and mark the positions of the wiper arms, then remove the wiper arms **(see illustrations)**.

3   Remove the cowl cover (see Chapter 11), then unscrew the nut and detach the wiper linkage from the wiper motor arm.

4   Disconnect the electrical connector and

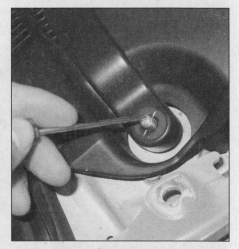

11.2b Paint an alignment mark over the stud and the wiper arm for correct reassembly

11.4 Remove the wiper motor mounting bolts

12.3 Remove the mounting screws and remove the heater control assembly

unscrew the wiper motor mounting bolts **(see illustration)**.
5   Lift the windshield wiper motor assembly from the cowl area.
6   Installation is the reverse of removal.

12   Radio and speakers - removal and installation

Warning: *These models have airbags. Always disable the airbag system before working in*

the vicinity of any airbag system component to avoid the possibility of accidental deployment of the airbag, which could cause personal injury (see Section 24).

Radio

2003 and earlier models
Refer to illustrations 12.3, 12.4a, 12.4b, 12.5 and 12.6
1   Disconnect the cable from the negative battery terminal.

2   Remove the dashboard center bezel (see Chapter 11).
3   Remove the heater control panel **(see illustration)**.
4   Remove the radio bracket retaining screws and pull the radio rearward to access the rear **(see illustrations)**.
5   Disconnect the electrical connectors and the antenna lead and remove the radio unit **(see illustration)**.
6   If it is necessary to replace the radio, remove the screws and detach the mounting

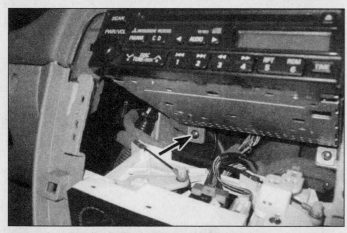

12.4a Remove radio retaining screw . . .

12.4b . . . pull the radio out of the dash . . .

12.5 . . . then disconnect the antenna lead and the electrical connector (2003 and earlier models)

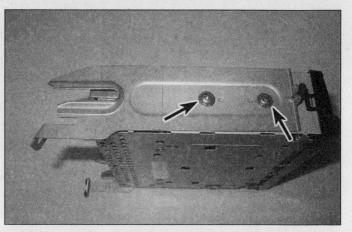

12.6 If necessary remove the screws and detach the mounting bracket from the radio

12.9 On 2004 and later models, the heater control/radio assembly can be removed by carefully releasing the hooks and clips at each side; the radio can be separated by removing the screws at the rear of the assembly

12.14 Disconnect the electrical connector and remove the speaker screws

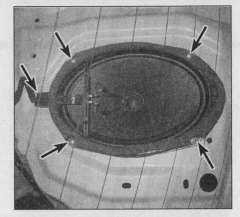

12.17 Disconnect the rear shelf speaker electrical connector and remove the screws

brackets **(see illustration)**.

7   Installation is the reverse of removal.

2004 and later models

Refer to illustration 12.9

8   Refer to Chapter 11 and remove the center panel hood trim panel.

9   Use a plastic trim tool or a screwdriver wrapped with tape to release the clips at each corner of the radio/heater control trim panel **(see illustration)**. There are also claw-type clips at the center of each side.

10   Pull the unit out and disconnect the wiring.

11   Remove the sound system components by removing the screws at the rear of the unit.

12   Installation is the reverse of removal.

Speakers

Door speakers

Refer to illustration 12.14

13   Remove the door trim panel (see Chapter 11).

14   Remove the speaker screws, disconnect the electrical connector and remove the speaker from the vehicle. **(see illustration)**.

15   Installation is the reverse of removal.

Rear shelf speakers

Refer to illustration 12.17

16   On 2003 and earlier models, refer to Chapter 11 and remove the rear shelf trim panel. On 2004 and later models, pry off the speaker covers.

17   Remove the speaker screws, disconnect the electrical connector and remove the speaker from the vehicle **(see illustration)**.

18   Installation is the reverse of removal.

Instrument panel speakers

19   Pull loose the front door weatherstrip in the area of the windshield pillar.

20   Use a plastic trim tool or a screwdriver wrapped with tape to carefully pry off the windshield trim panels.

21   Remove the speaker cover, then remove the speaker, disconnecting the wiring as you lift it out.

22   Installation is the reverse of removal.

---

13   Antenna - replacement

Warning: *These models have airbags. Always disable the airbag system before working in the vicinity of any airbag system component to avoid the possibility of accidental deployment of the airbag, which could cause personal injury (see Section 24).*

Note: *Some models are equipped with an antenna built into the rear window glass. If a problem arises with radio reception due to a break in the antenna grid, take the vehicle to a dealer service department or automotive glass specialist for repair.*

1   Open the trunk and remove the side trim panel.

2   If you're removing a fixed-mast antenna, unscrew the mast from the antenna base.

3   Unscrew the mounting nut from the top of the antenna and remove the adapter. **Note:** *It's a good idea to cover the area around the nut with masking tape to prevent scratching the paint.*

4   If you're removing a power antenna, disconnect the electrical connector from the antenna motor.

5   Unplug the antenna lead from the antenna base.

6   Remove the mounting bolt or nut from the antenna and remove the antenna from the trunk.

7   Installation is the reverse of removal.

---

14   Rear window defogger - check and repair

---

1   The rear window defogger consists of a number of horizontal elements baked onto the glass surface.

2   Small breaks in the element can be repaired without removing the rear window.

Check

Refer to illustrations 14.4, 14.5 and 14.7

3   Turn the ignition switch and defogger system switches to the ON position. Using a voltmeter, place the positive probe against the defogger grid positive terminal and the negative probe against the ground terminal. If battery voltage is not indicated, check the fuse, defogger switch and related wiring. If voltage is indicated, but all or part of the defogger doesn't heat, proceed with the following tests.

4   When measuring voltage during the next two tests, wrap a piece of aluminum foil around the tip of the voltmeter positive probe and press the foil against the heating element with your finger **(see illustration)**. Place the negative probe on the defogger grid ground terminal.

5   Check the voltage at the center of each

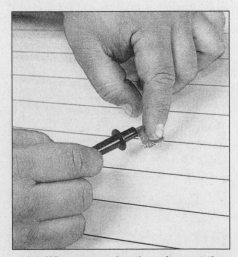

14.4 When measuring the voltage at the rear window defogger grid, wrap a piece of aluminum foil around the positive probe of the voltmeter and press the foil against the wire with your finger

14.5 To determine if a heating element has broken, check the voltage at the center of each element - if the voltage is 5 or 6-volts, the element is unbroken. If the voltage is 10 or 12-volts, the element is broken between the center and the ground side. If there is no voltage, the element is broken between the center and the positive side

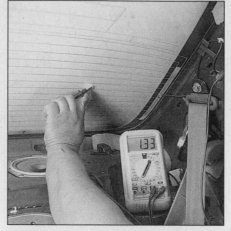

14.7 To find the break, place the voltmeter negative lead against the defogger ground terminal, place the voltmeter positive lead with the foil strip against the heating element at the positive terminal end and slide it toward the negative terminal end - the point at which the voltmeter reading changes abruptly is the point at which the element is broken

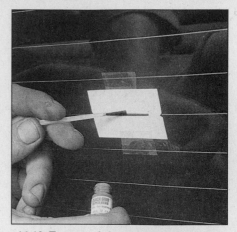

14.13 To use a defogger repair kit, apply masking tape to the inside of the window at the damaged area, then brush on the special conductive coating

14   Allow the repair to cure for 24 hours before removing the tape and using the system.

heating element **(see illustration)**. If the voltage is 5 or 6-volts, the element is okay (there is no break). If the voltage is 0-volts, the element is broken between the center of the element and the positive end. If the voltage is 10 to 12-volts the element is broken between the center of the element and ground. Check each heating element.

6   Connect the negative lead to a good body ground. The reading should stay the same. If it doesn't, the ground connection is bad.

7   To find the break, place the voltmeter negative probe against the defogger ground terminal. Place the voltmeter positive probe with the foil strip against the heating element at the positive terminal end and slide it toward the negative terminal end. The point at which the voltmeter deflects from several volts to zero is the point at which the heating element is broken **(see illustration)**.

Repair
Refer to illustration 14.13

8   Repair the break in the element using a repair kit specifically recommended for this purpose, available at most auto parts stores. Included in this kit is plastic conductive epoxy.

9   Prior to repairing a break, turn off the system and allow it to cool off for a few minutes.

10   Lightly buff the element area with fine steel wool, then clean it thoroughly with rubbing alcohol.

11   Use masking tape to mask off the area being repaired.

12   Thoroughly mix the epoxy, following the instructions provided with the repair kit.

13   Apply the epoxy material to the slit in the masking tape, overlapping the undamaged area about 3/4-inch on either end **(see illustration)**.

15   Headlight bulb - replacement

Warning: *Halogen gas filled bulbs are under pressure and may shatter if the surface is scratched or the bulb is dropped. Wear eye protection and handle the bulbs carefully, grasping only the base whenever possible. Do not touch the surface of the bulb with your fingers because the oil from your skin could cause it to overheat and fail prematurely. If you do touch the bulb surface, clean it with rubbing alcohol.*
Note: *On some models it may be necessary to remove the coolant reservoir for access to the right side headlight bulb.*

2003 and earlier models
Refer to illustrations 15.1, 15.2 and 15.3

1   Reach behind the headlight assembly and disconnect the electrical connector **(see illustration)**.

2   Remove the bulb cover **(see illustra-**

15.1 Disconnect the headlight electrical connector

15.2 Grasp the bulb cover securely and pull it off (later model)

15.3 Detach the spring and remove the bulb from the housing

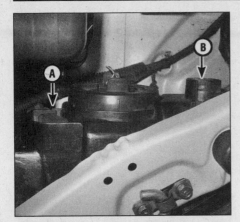

16.1 Headlight vertical (A) and horizontal (B) adjusting screw location (2001 and earlier models)

tion). On 1998 and earlier models the cover is removed by turning it counterclockwise. On 1999 and later models it's removed by pulling it straight off.

3   Remove the bulb holder by rotating the holder counterclockwise (earlier models) or detaching the locking spring **(see illustration)**.

4   Insert the new bulb assembly into the headlight housing. **Note:** *Don't touch the surface of the bulb with your fingers because the oil from your skin could cause it to overheat and fail prematurely. If you happen to touch the bulb surface, clean it with rubbing alcohol.*

5   Plug in the electrical connector.

2004 and later models

6   If you're working on the driver's side, it may be necessary to remove the electrical relay box for clearance.

7   Disconnect the headlight wiring connector.

8   Twist the bulb holder counterclockwise and pull it out of the housing.

9   Remove the bulb from the bulb holder and replace it without touching the new one with your fingers (see **Warning** above).

10   Installation is the reverse of removal.

16   Headlights - adjustment

Refer to illustrations 16.1 and 16.3
Note: *The headlights must be aimed correctly. If adjusted incorrectly they could blind the driver of an oncoming vehicle and cause a serious accident or seriously reduce your ability to see the road. The headlights should be checked for proper aim every 12 months and any time a new headlight is installed or front end body work is performed. It should be emphasized that the following procedure is only an interim step, which will provide temporary adjustment until a properly equipped shop can adjust the headlights.*

1   Some models have a horizontal adjustment screw located on the outer end of the headlight housing and a vertical screw located on the inner end of the headlight housing **(see illustration)**. Insert a Phillips

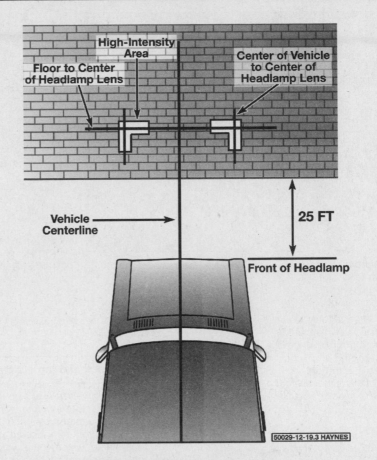

16.3 Headlight adjustment details

screwdriver into the gear-drive mechanism to turn the screw. On 2002 and later models only vertical adjustment is possible.

2   There are several methods of adjusting the headlights. The simplest method requires masking tape, a blank wall and a level floor.

3   Position masking tape vertically on the wall in reference to the vehicle centerline and the centerlines of both headlight bulbs **(see illustration)**.

4   Position a horizontal tape line in reference to the centerline of all the headlights. **Note:** *It may be easier to position the tape on the wall with the vehicle parked only a few inches away.*

5   Adjustment should be made with the vehicle parked 25 feet from the wall, sitting level, the gas tank half-full and no unusually heavy load in the vehicle.

6   Starting with the low beam adjustment, position the high intensity zone so it is two inches below the horizontal line and two inches to the side of the headlight vertical line, away from oncoming traffic. Turning the vertical adjusting screw to raise or lower the beam makes adjustment. The horizontal adjusting screw should be used in the same manner to move the beam left or right.

7   With the high beams on, the high intensity zone should be vertically centered with the exact center just below the horizontal line.

Note: *It may not be possible to position the headlight aim exactly for both high and low beams. If a compromise must be made, keep in mind that the low beams are the most used and have the greatest effect on driver safety.*

8   Have the headlights adjusted by a dealer service department or service station at the earliest opportunity.

17   Headlight housing - replacement

Warning: *These vehicles are equipped with halogen gas-filled headlight bulbs, which are under pressure and may shatter if the surface is damaged or the bulb is dropped. Wear eye protection and handle the bulbs carefully, grasping only the base whenever possible. Do not touch the surface of the bulb with your fingers because the oil from your skin could cause it to overheat and fail prematurely. If you do touch the bulb surface, clean it with rubbing alcohol.*

2003 and earlier models
Refer to illustration 17.5
1   Remove the headlight bulb (see Section 15).

2   Disconnect the electrical connector (see Section 15).

3   On 1998 and earlier models, remove the front bumper (see Chapter 11).

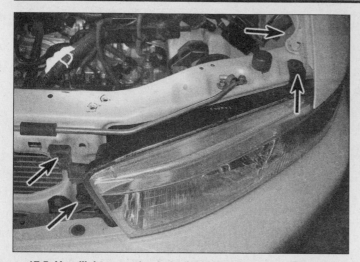

17.5 Headlight mounting bolts (1999 and later model shown)

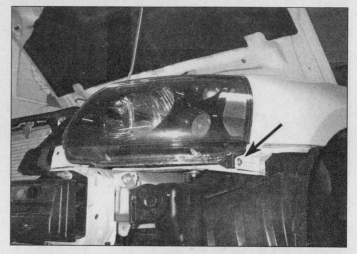

17.8 The front bumper must be removed from 2004 and later models in order to remove the lower headlight mounting screw (arrow)

4   On 1999 and later models, remove the radiator grille (see Chapter 11).

5   Remove the retaining bolts, detach the headlight housing and withdraw it from the vehicle **(see illustration)**.

6   Installation is the reverse of removal. Be sure to check headlight adjustment (see Section 16).

2004 and later models

Refer to illustration 17.8

7   Raise the vehicle and support it securely on jackstands. Remove the plastic splash shield from below the headlight you're removing. Disconnect the headlight wiring.

8   On 2004 through 2006 models, remove the grille (see Chapter 11). On all models, remove the mounting screws and clips of the inner fender splash shield and the bumper cover **(see illustration). Note:** *These parts don't need to be removed as long as they can be moved aside enough for access to the headlight mounting screws.*

9   Disconnect the fog light wiring.

10   Remove the headlight assembly mounting screws, then lift it out.

---

18   Horn - check and replacement

Warning: *These models have airbags. Always disable the airbag system before working in the vicinity of any airbag system component to avoid the possibility of accidental deployment of the airbag, which could cause personal injury (see Section 24).*

Check

Note: *Check the fuses before beginning electrical diagnosis.*

1   Disconnect the electrical connector from the horn.

2   To test the horn, connect battery voltage to the horn terminal with a jumper wire. If the horn doesn't sound, replace it.

3   If the horn does sound, check for voltage at the terminal when the horn button is depressed. If there's voltage at the terminal, check for a bad ground at the horn.

4   If there's no voltage at the horn, check the relay (see Section 5).

5   If the relay is OK, check for voltage to the relay power and control circuits. If either of the circuits is not receiving voltage, inspect the wiring between the relay and the fuse panel.

6   If both relay circuits are receiving voltage, depress the horn button and check the circuit from the relay to the horn button for continuity to ground. If there's no continuity, check the circuit for an open. If there's no open circuit, replace the horn button.

7   If there's continuity to ground through the horn button, check for an open or short in the circuit from the relay to the horn.

Replacement

Refer to illustrations 18.9 and 18.10

8   On 1998 and earlier models, the horns are accessible in the engine compartment. On 1999 through 2003 models, the air filter housing must be removed for access to them (see Chapter 4).

9   On 2004 and later models, the right horn is in the right side of the engine compartment

18.9 On 2004 and later models, the left horn is behind the front bumper

18.10 Disconnect the electrical connector and remove the horn retaining bolt

19.2 Disconnect the electrical connector and rotate the turn signal bulb holder 1/4 turn counterclockwise to remove it

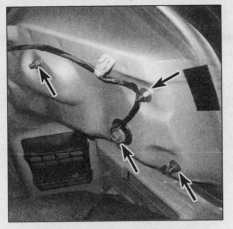

19.6 Remove the retaining nuts, disconnect the electrical connector and detach the tail light housing for access to the bulbs

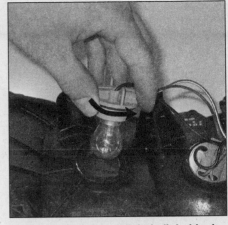

19.8a Remove the tail light bulb holder by rotating it counterclockwise

and the left horn is behind the bumper **(see illustration)**. On these models, remove the left inner fender and lower splash shields and, if necessary, the front bumper (see Chapter 11).
10   To replace the horns, disconnect the wiring and remove the bracket bolt **(see illustration)**.
11   Installation is the reverse of removal.

19 Bulb replacement

Front park/turn signal lights
Refer to illustration 19.2
1   Disconnect the turn signal/parking bulb holder electrical connector.
2   Remove the bulb holder by turning the socket counterclockwise **(see illustration)**. Remove the bulb from the holder.
3   Installation is the reverse of removal.

Rear tail light/brake light/turn signal
Refer to illustrations 19.6, 19.8a and 19.8b
4   Open the trunk.
5   Separate the trunk lining from the rear panel.

6   Disconnect the electrical connector, then unscrew and remove the nuts securing the tail light assembly to the rear panel **(see illustration)**.
7   Withdraw the tail light assembly from the rear panel.
8   To replace a bulb, rotate the bulb holder counterclockwise and withdraw it from the assembly, then pull the bulb from the holder **(see illustrations)**.
9   Installation is the reverse of removal.

High-mounted brake light
2003 and earlier models
Refer to illustrations 19.10 and 19.11
10   On rear shelf mounted brake lights, open the trunk, rotate the bulb holder counterclockwise and lower it from the housing (see Chapter 11) **(see illustration)**. **Note:** *On spoiler mounted lights, remove the screws and detach the lens to access the high mounted brake light assembly.*
11   Pull the bulb straight out of the holder **(see illustration)**.
12   Installation is the reverse of removal.

19.8b Push the bulb in and rotate it counterclockwise to remove it

2004 and later models
Refer to illustration 19.13
13   On spoiler-mounted lights, remove the entire spoiler assembly, then remove the brake light. **Note:** *Later models do not have replaceable bulbs. Replace the entire unit* **(see illustration)**.

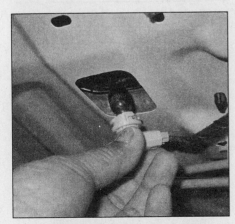

19.10 Rotate the bulb holder counterclockwise and lower it from the high-mounted brake light assembly

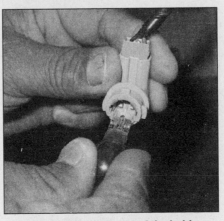

19.11 Pull the bulb out of the holder

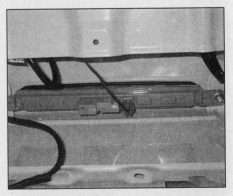

19.13 Most 2004 and later models don't have replaceable bulbs in the center brake light; check for power to the unit with a test light and replace the light as a complete assembly if it's faulty

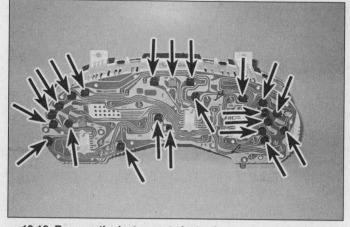

19.16 Remove the instrument cluster for access to the bulbs (2003 and earlier models)

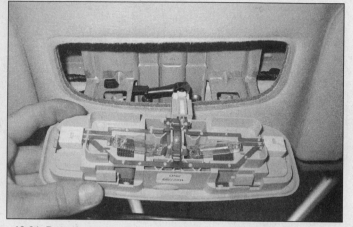

19.21 Detach the reading light bulbs by spreading the end clips

14   On models with trunk lid-mounted brake lights, open the trunk and pull the bulb holder from its socket. **Note:** *Later models do not have replaceable bulbs. Replace the entire unit.*

Instrument cluster lights

Refer to illustration 19.16

Note: *This procedure applies only to 2003 and earlier models. Later models do not have replaceable bulbs.*

15   The instrument cluster will have to be removed (see Section 10) to gain access to the instrument cluster illumination bulbs. The bulbs can then be removed and replaced from the rear of the cluster.

16   Rotate the bulb holder counterclockwise to remove it **(see illustration)**.

17   Installation is the reverse of removal.

Reading light

1998 and earlier models

18   Remove the lens from the light by depressing the tabs and pulling the lens down.

19   Remove the bulb from the holder by pulling it straight out.

20   Installation is the reverse of removal.

19.28 Rotate the bulb holder counterclockwise and withdraw it from the fog light housing

1999 and later models

Refer to illustration 19.21

21   Carefully pry the reading light housing from the headliner, then rotate it down and remove the bulb(s) by spreading the clips at each end **(see illustration)**.

22   Installation is the reverse of removal.

License plate light

23   Open the trunk, reach up behind the license plate light assembly and remove the license plate bulb holder by rotating it counterclockwise. Remove bulb by pulling it straight out of the holder socket.

24   Installation is the reverse of removal.

Fog light

Refer to illustrations 19.28

25   Raise the vehicle and support it securely on jackstands. On 2003 and later models, remove the plastic splash shield from below the end of the bumper.

26   From behind the bumper, disconnect the fog light electrical connector.

27   On 1998 and earlier models, remove the two screws at the top and withdraw the fog light from the bumper. Detach the retaining spring and remove the bulb holder.

28   On 1999 and later models disconnect the electrical connector, then rotate the bulb holder and withdraw it from the housing **(see illustration)**.

29   Installation is the reverse of the removal.

---

20   Electric side view mirrors - description

---

1   Most electric rear view mirrors use two motors to move the glass; one for up and down adjustments and one for left-right adjustments.

2   The control switch has a selector portion which sends voltage to the left or right side mirror. With the ignition ON but the engine OFF, roll down the windows and operate the

mirror control switch through all functions (left-right and up-down) for both the left and right side mirrors.

3   Listen carefully for the sound of the electric motors running in the mirrors.

4   If the motors can be heard but the mirror glass doesn't move, there's a problem with the drive mechanism inside the mirror.

5   If the mirrors do not operate and no sound comes from the mirrors, check the fuse (see Chapter 1).

6   If the fuse is OK, remove the mirror control switch. Have the switch continuity checked by a dealership service department or other qualified automobile repair facility.

7   Test the ground connections. Refer to the wiring diagrams at the end of Chapter 12.

8   If the mirror still doesn't work, remove the mirror and check the wires at the mirror for voltage.

9   If there's not voltage in each switch position, check the circuit between the mirror and control switch for opens and shorts.

10   If there's voltage, remove the mirror and test it off the vehicle with jumper wires. Replace the mirror if it fails this test.

---

21   Cruise control system - description

---

1   The cruise control system maintains vehicle speed with an electrically controlled, vacuum operated servo in the engine compartment. On 1998 and earlier models the vacuum servo is connected to the throttle lever by a cable. On 1999 through 2003 models the vacuum servo is mounted on the throttle body and is connected by a hose to the vacuum pump. On 2004 and later models, the throttle is controlled electronically by the cruise control logic in the PCM. Some features of this system require special testers and diagnostic procedures, which are beyond the scope of this manual. Listed below are some general procedures that maybe used to locate common problems.

2   Check the fuses (see Section 3).

3   Have an assistant operate the brake lights while you check their operation (voltage from the brake light switch deactivates the cruise control).

4   If the brake lights don't come on or stay on all the time, correct the problem and retest the cruise control.

5   On 1998 and earlier models, inspect the control cable between cruise control servo and the throttle linkage for free movement. Replace it if necessary.

6   Check the vacuum hose and vacuum servo for leaks.

7   The cruise control system uses inputs from the Vehicle Speed Sensor (VSS). Refer to Chapter 6 for more information on the VSS.

8   Test drive the vehicle to determine if the cruise control is now working. If it isn't, take it to a dealer service department or an automotive electrical specialist for further diagnosis.

22   Power window system - description

1   The power window system operates electric motors, mounted in the doors, which lower and raise the windows. The system consists of the control switches, relays, the motors, regulators and associated wiring.

2   The power windows can be lowered and raised from the master control switch by the driver or by remote switches located at the individual windows. Each window has a separate motor that is reversible. The position of the control switch determines the polarity and therefore the direction of operation.

3   The circuit is protected by a fuse and a circuit breaker. Each motor is also equipped with an internal circuit breaker; this prevents one stuck window from disabling the whole system.

4   The power window system will only operate when the ignition switch is ON. In addition, many models have a window lockout switch at the master control switch that, when activated, disables the switches at the rear windows and, sometimes, the switch at the passenger's window also. Always check these items before troubleshooting a window problem.

5   These procedures are general in nature, so if you can't find the problem using them, take the vehicle to a dealer service department or other properly equipped repair facility.

6   If the power windows won't operate, always check the fuse and circuit breaker first.

7   If only the rear windows are inoperative, or if the windows only operate from the master control switch, check the rear window lockout switch for continuity in the unlocked position. Replace it if it doesn't have continuity.

8   Check the wiring between the switches and fuse panel for continuity. Repair the wiring, if necessary.

9   If only one window is inoperative from the master control switch, try the other control switch at the window. **Note:** *This doesn't*

apply to the driver's door window.

10   If the same window works from one switch, but not the other, check the switch for continuity.

11   If the switch tests OK, check for a short or open in the circuit between the affected switch and the window motor.

12   If one window is inoperative from both switches, remove the trim panel from the affected door and check for voltage at the switch and at the motor while the switch is operated.

13   If voltage is reaching the motor, disconnect the glass from the regulator (see Chapter 11). Move the window up and down by hand while checking for binding and damage. Also check for binding and damage to the regulator. If the regulator is not damaged and the window moves up and down smoothly, replace the motor. If there's binding or damage, lubricate, repair or replace parts, as necessary.

14   If voltage isn't reaching the motor, check the wiring in the circuit for continuity between the switches and motors. You'll need to consult the wiring diagram for the vehicle. If the circuit is equipped with a relay, check that the relay is grounded properly and receiving voltage.

23   Power door lock system - description

1   A power door lock system operates the door lock actuators mounted in each door. The system consists of the switches, actuators, a control unit and associated wiring. Diagnosis can usually be limited to simple checks of the wiring connections and actuators for minor faults that can be easily repaired.

2   Power door lock systems are operated by bi-directional solenoids located in the doors. The lock switches have two operating positions: Lock and Unlock. When activated, the switch sends a ground signal to the door lock control unit to lock or unlock the doors. Depending on which way the switch is activated, the control unit reverses polarity to the solenoids, allowing the two sides of the circuit to be used alternately as the feed (positive) and ground side.

3   Some vehicles may have an anti-theft system incorporated into the power locks. If you are unable to locate the trouble using the following general Steps, consult a dealer service department or other qualified repair shop.

4   Always check the circuit protection first. Some vehicles use a combination of circuit breakers and fuses.

5   Operate the door lock switches in both directions (Lock and Unlock) with the engine off. Listen for the click of the solenoids operating.

6   Test the switches for continuity. Remove the switches and have them checked by a dealer service department or other quali-

fied automobile repair facility.

7   Check the wiring between the switches, control unit and solenoids for continuity. Repair the wiring if there's no continuity.

8   Check for a bad ground at the switches or the control unit.

9   If all but one lock solenoids operate, remove the trim panel from the affected door (see Chapter 11) and check for voltage at the solenoid while the lock switch is operated. One of the wires should have voltage in the Lock position; the other should have voltage in the Unlock position.

10   If the inoperative solenoid is receiving voltage, replace the solenoid.

11   If the inoperative solenoid isn't receiving voltage, check the relay for an open or short in the wire between the lock solenoid and the control unit. **Note:** *It's common for wires to break in the portion of the harness between the body and door (opening and closing the door fatigues and eventually breaks the wires).*

Keyless entry system

12   The keyless entry system consists of a remote control transmitter that sends a coded infrared signal to a receiver, which then operates the door lock system. On models so equipped, the transmitter may also engage the alarm system and provide a "panic" button, which flashes the lights and blows the horn for emergencies.

13   Replace the transmitter batteries when the red LED light on the case doesn't light when the button is pushed. As the batteries deteriorate with age, the distance at which the remote transmitter operates will diminish.

14   Remove the screw and use a coin or small screwdriver to carefully separate the case halves for battery replacement.

15   Replace the lithium battery with the same type as originally installed, observing the polarity diagram on the case.

16   Snap the case halves together.

24   Airbag system - general information

General information

Refer to illustrations 24.1a, 24.1b and 24.1c

1   All models are equipped with a Supplemental Restraint System (SRS), more commonly known as an airbag. This system is designed to protect the driver, and the front seat passenger, from serious injury in the event of a head-on or frontal collision and on some later models side impact as well. On earlier models it consists of airbag sensors mounted on the front unibody frame members and a sensing/diagnostic electronic control module mounted in the center of the vehicle, under the floor console. Later models use a single SRS ECU to detect G force impact. Models equipped with side impact airbags have impact sensors in the center pillars. The airbag assemblies are mounted on the steer-

24.1a The driver's side airbag is located in the center of the steering wheel

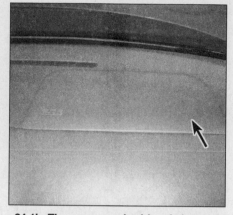

24.1b The passenger's airbag is located on the dashboard above the glove box

24.1c On 1999 and later models the SRS ECU is mounted under the center of the instrument panel

ing wheel **(see illustration)**, the right side, top surface of the passenger's side dash **(see illustration)** and, on the side impact airbags used on some later models, in the sides of the front seats. The Supplemental Restraint System Electronic Control unit (SRS ECU) is mounted below the instrument panel under the front of the center console **(see illustration)**.

Airbag module

Driver's side

2   The airbag inflator module contains a housing incorporating the cushion (airbag) and inflator unit, mounted in the center of the steering wheel The inflator assembly is mounted on the back of the housing over a hole through which gas is expelled, inflating the bag almost instantaneously when an electrical signal is sent from the system. A clockspring assembly on the steering column under the steering wheel carries this signal to the module.

3   This clockspring assembly can transmit an electrical signal regardless of steering wheel position. The igniter in the airbag con-

verts the electrical signal to heat and ignites the powder, which inflates the bag.

Passenger's side

4   The airbag is mounted above the glove compartment and designated by the letters SRS (Supplemental Restraint System). It consists of an inflator containing an igniter, a bag assembly, a reaction housing and a trim cover.

5   This airbag is considerably larger than the steering wheel-mounted unit and is supported by the steel reaction housing. The trim cover has a molded seam, which splits when the bag inflates.

Side impact

6   These airbags are mounted in the sides of the front seat backs. In the event of severe side impact they inflate, ripping open the front seat back side trim covers. It consists of an inflator containing an igniter, a bag assembly, a reaction housing and a trim cover.

SRS ECU

7   The airbag control module supplies the current to the airbag system in the event of the collision, even if battery power is cut off.

It checks this system every time the vehicle is started, causing the "SRS" light to go on then off, if the system is operating properly. If there is a fault in the system, the light will go on and stay on, flash, or the dash will make a beeping sound. If this happens, the vehicle should be taken to your dealer immediately for service.

Disarming the system and other precautions

Warning: *Failure to follow these precautions could result in accidental deployment of the airbag and personal injury.*

8   Whenever working in the vicinity of the steering wheel, steering column or any of the other SRS system components, the system must be disarmed. To disarm the system:

a) *Point the wheels straight ahead and turn the key to the Lock position.*

b) *Disconnect the cable from the negative battery terminal. Position the cable so it can't accidentally come in contact with the battery terminal.*

c) *Wait at least two minutes for the back-up power supply to be depleted.*

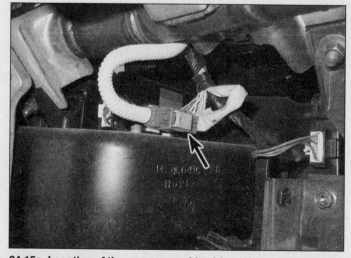

24.15a Location of the passenger side airbag electrical connector

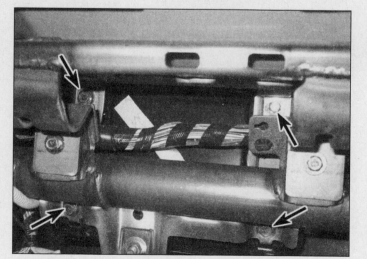

24.15b Passenger side airbag retaining bolt locations

9   Whenever handling an airbag module, always keep the airbag opening (the trim side) pointed away from your body. Never place the airbag module on a bench or other surface with the airbag opening facing the surface. Always place the airbag module in a safe location with the airbag opening facing up.

10   Never measure the resistance of any SRS component. An ohmmeter has a built-in battery supply that could accidentally deploy the airbag.

11   Never use electrical welding equipment on a vehicle equipped with an airbag without first disconnecting the airbag electrical connector, located under the steering column near the combination switch connector (driver's airbag) and behind the glove box (passenger's airbag), and under each front seat (on models with side-impact airbags).

12   Never dispose of a live airbag module. Return it to a dealer service department or other qualified repair shop for safe deployment and disposal.

Component removal and installation

Driver's side airbag module and clockspring

13   Refer to Chapter 10, *Steering wheel - removal and installation*, for the driver's side airbag module and clockspring removal and installation procedures.

Passenger's side airbag module

Refer to illustrations 24.15a and 24.15b

14   Disarm the airbag system as described previously in this Section.

15   Remove the glove box and passenger side under cover (see Chapter 11). The airbag fasteners are now accessible. Remove the fasteners, unplug the electrical connector and detach the airbag module from the instrument panel. Be sure to heed the precautions outlined previously in this Section.

16   Installation is the reverse of the removal procedure. Tighten the airbag module mounting fasteners securely.

Side impact airbag

17   This procedure will require removal and disassembly of the seat(s). Under normal circumstances there would never be a reason to remove a seat airbag. However, if it has been determined that there is a problem with the seat airbag module, the work should be left to a dealer service department or other qualified repair shop.

Side curtain airbag

18   This procedure requires removal of the headliner. If it has been determined that there is a problem with a side curtain airbag module, the work should be left to a dealer service department or another qualified repair shop.

25 Wiring diagrams - general information

Since it isn't possible to include all wiring diagrams for every year covered by this manual, the following diagrams are those that are typical and most commonly needed.

Prior to troubleshooting any circuits, check the fuse and circuit breakers (if equipped) to make sure they're in good condition. Make sure the battery is properly charged and check the cable connections (see Chapter 1).

When checking a circuit, make sure that all connectors are clean, with no broken or loose terminals. When unplugging a connector, do not pull on the wires. Pull only on the connector housings themselves. **Note:** *You may find that some of the wire colors in the wiring diagrams do not exactly match those on your vehicle. This is due to running changes made by the manufacturer from year-to-year and model-to-model. However, the circuitry, components and their terminals still function as shown on the diagrams; if you encounter a wire on your vehicle whose color doesn't match the corresponding circuit on the wiring diagram, pencil in the correct color on the diagram to help you avoid confusion.*

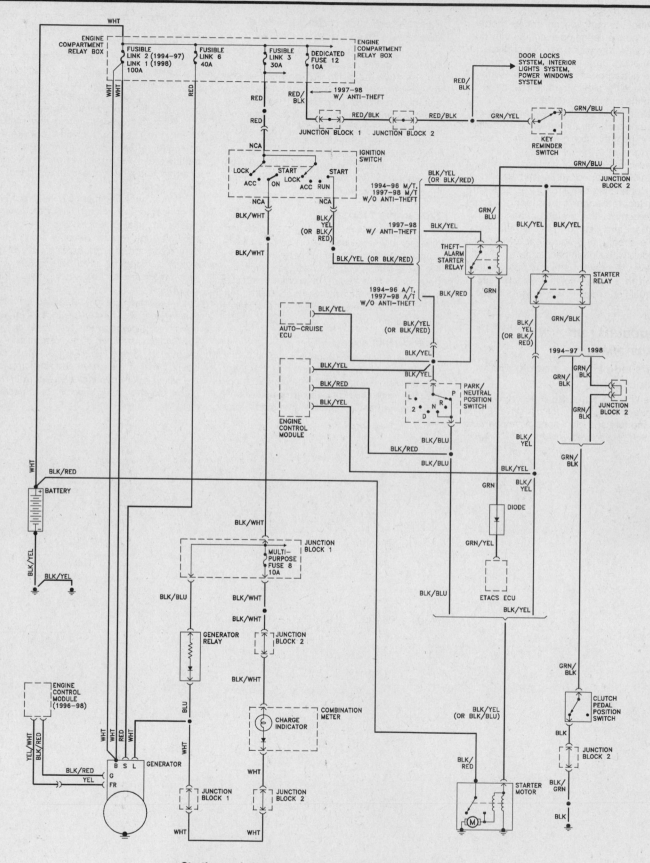

Starting and charging systems (1998 and earlier models)

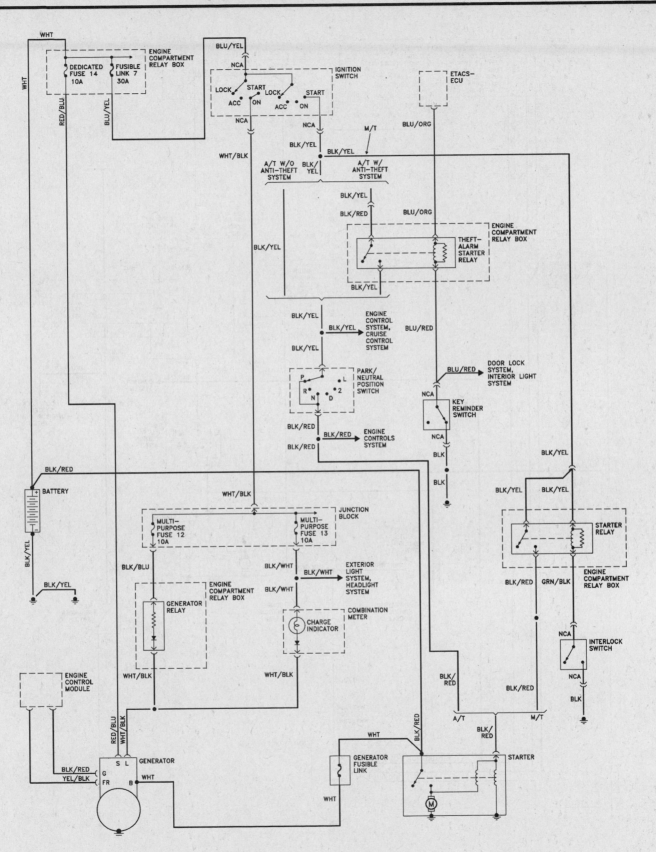

Starting and charging systems (1999 models)

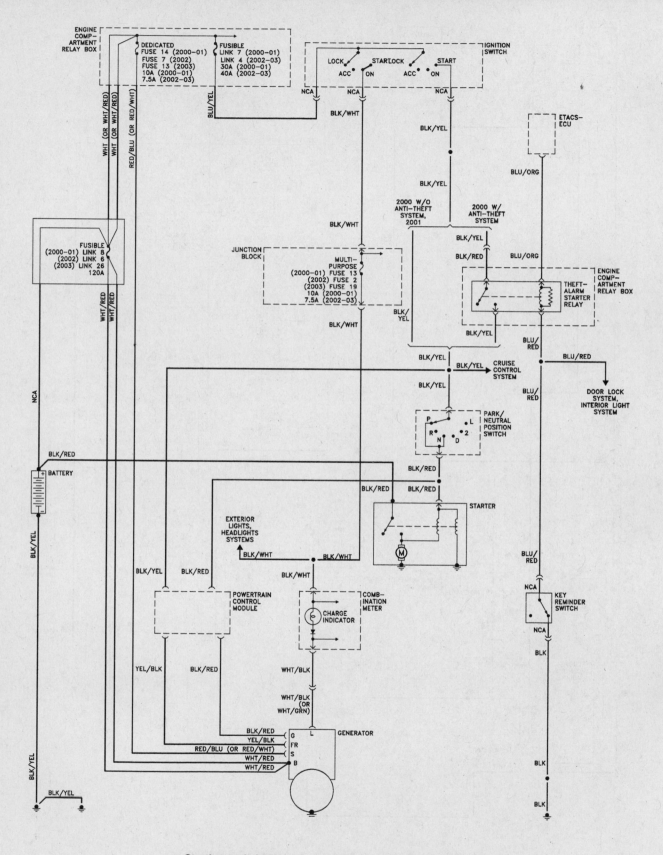

Starting and charging systems (2000 and later models)

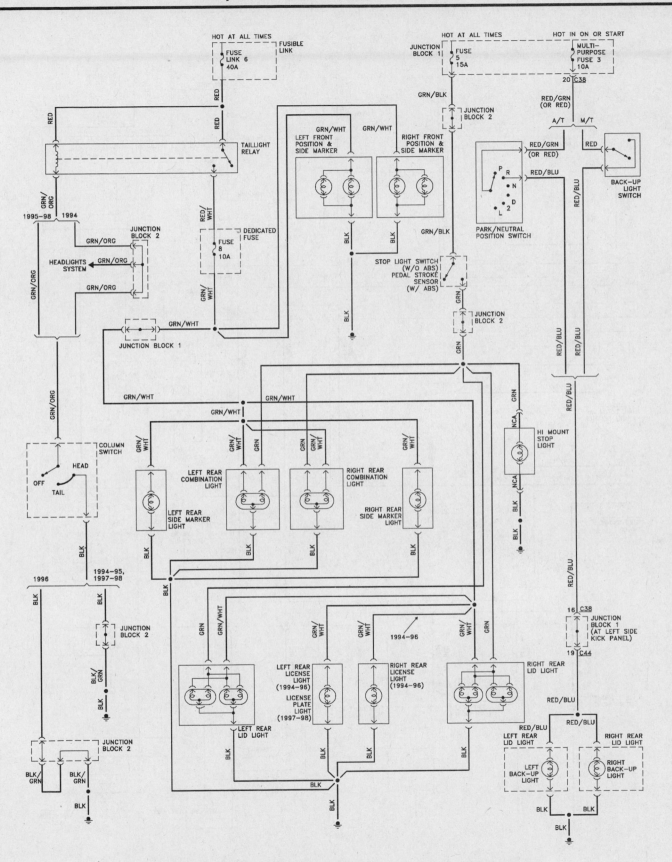

Exterior lighting system (except headlights) - 1998 and earlier models (1 of 2)

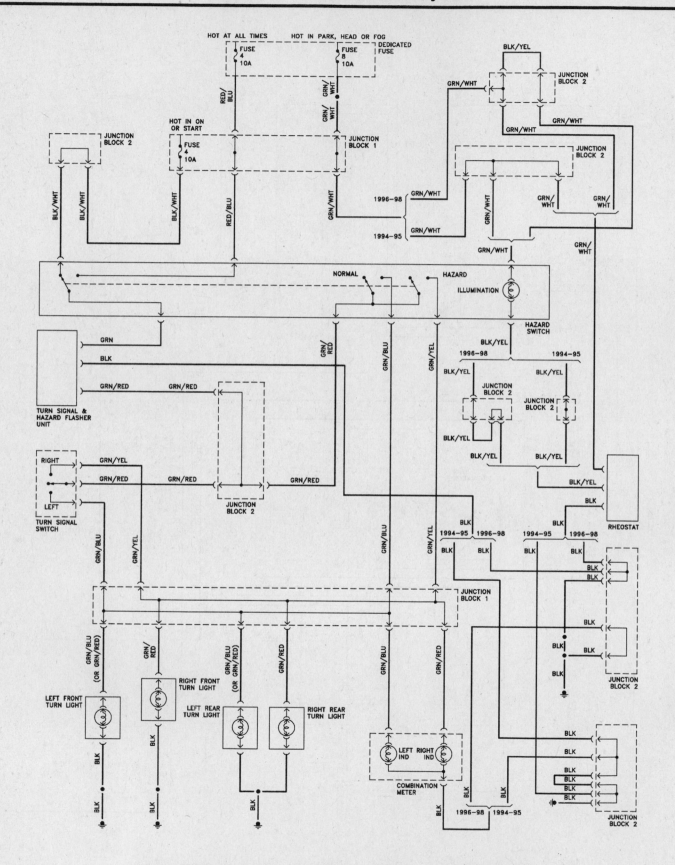

Exterior lighting system (except headlights) - 1998 and earlier models (2 of 2)

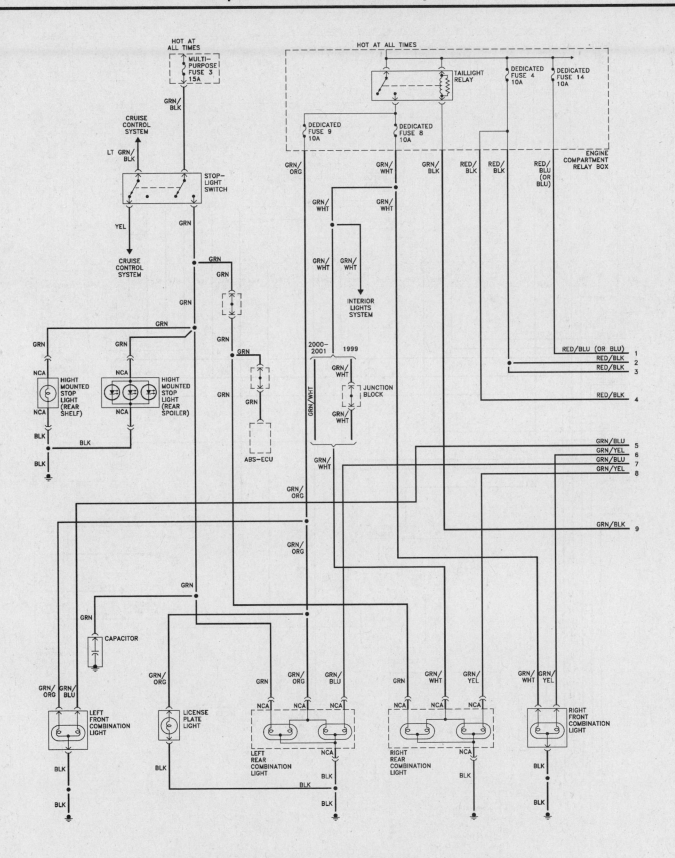

Exterior lighting system (except headlights) - 1999 through 2001 models (1 of 2)

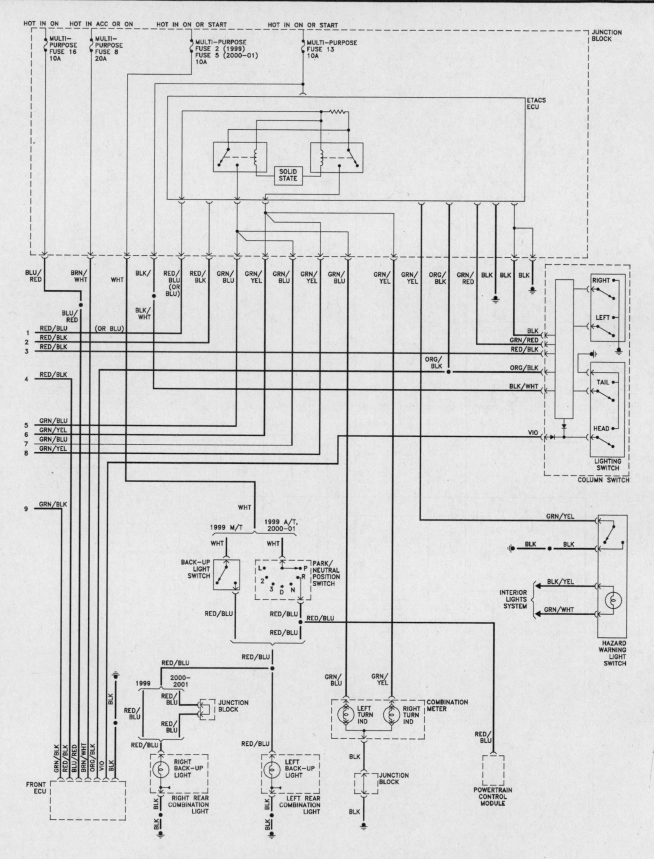

Exterior lighting system (except headlights) - 1999 through 2001 models (2 of 2)

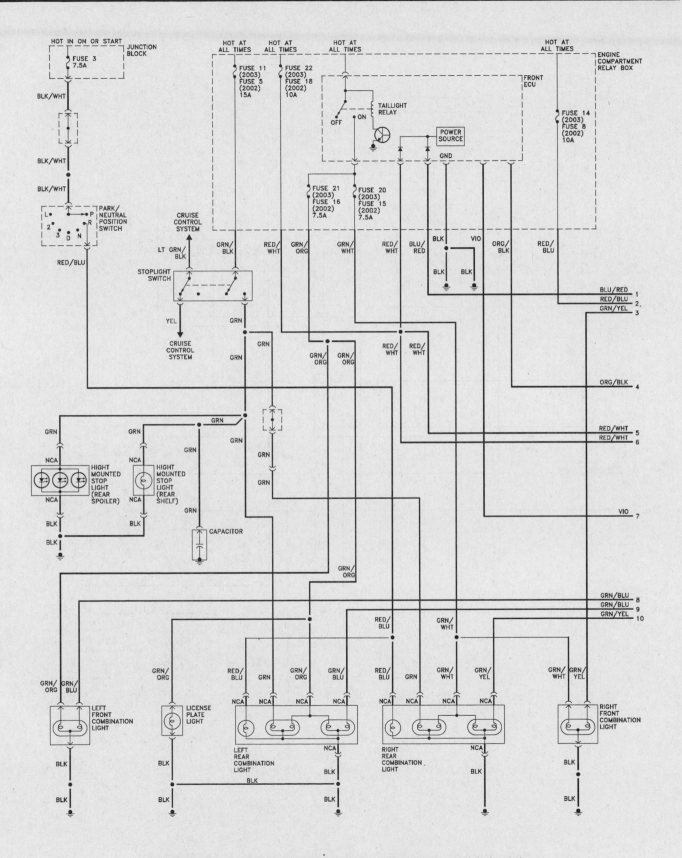

Exterior lighting system (except headlights) - 2002 and later models (1 of 2)

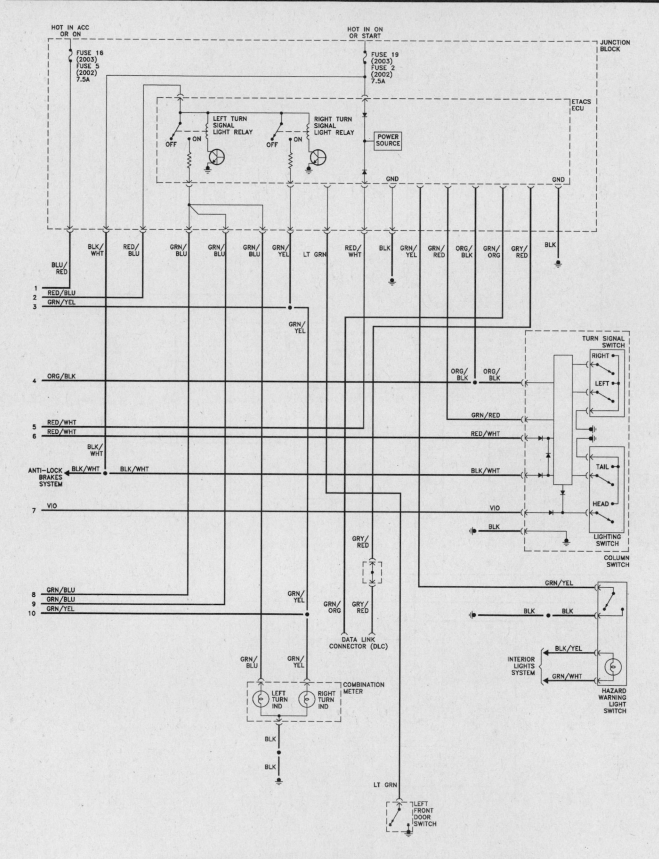

Exterior lighting system (except headlights) - 2002 and later models (2 of 2)

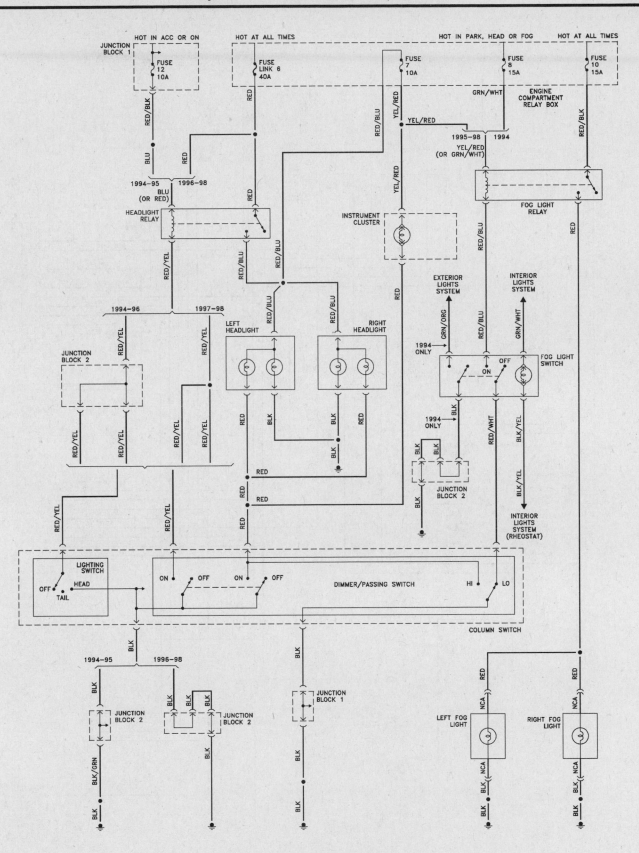

Headlight system (1998 and earlier models)

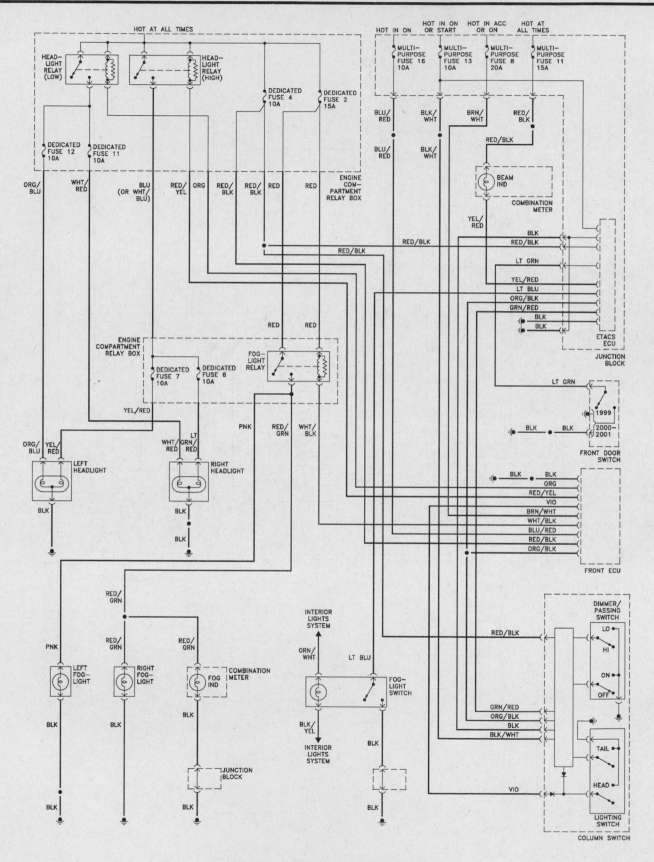

Headlight system (1999 through 2001 models)

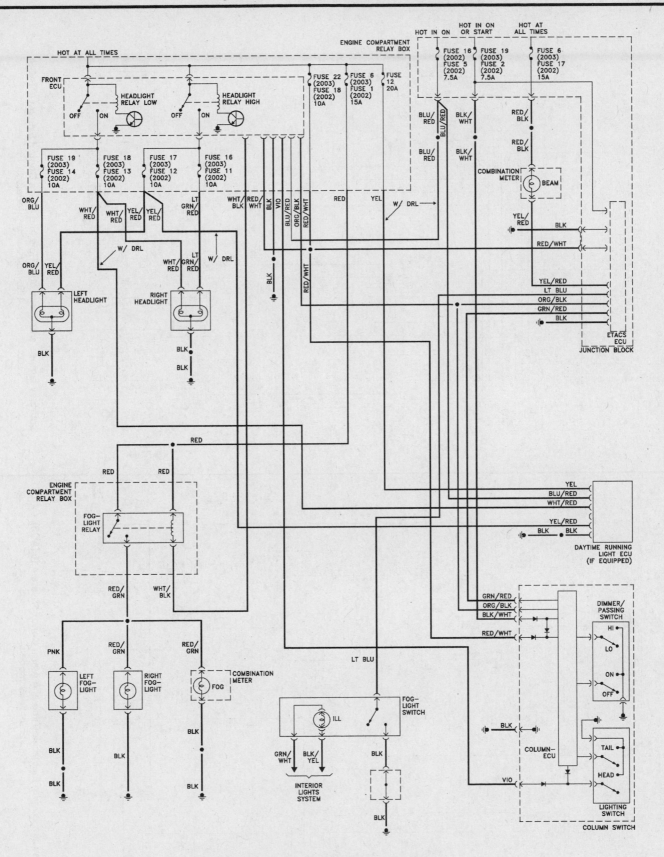

Headlight system (2002 and later models)

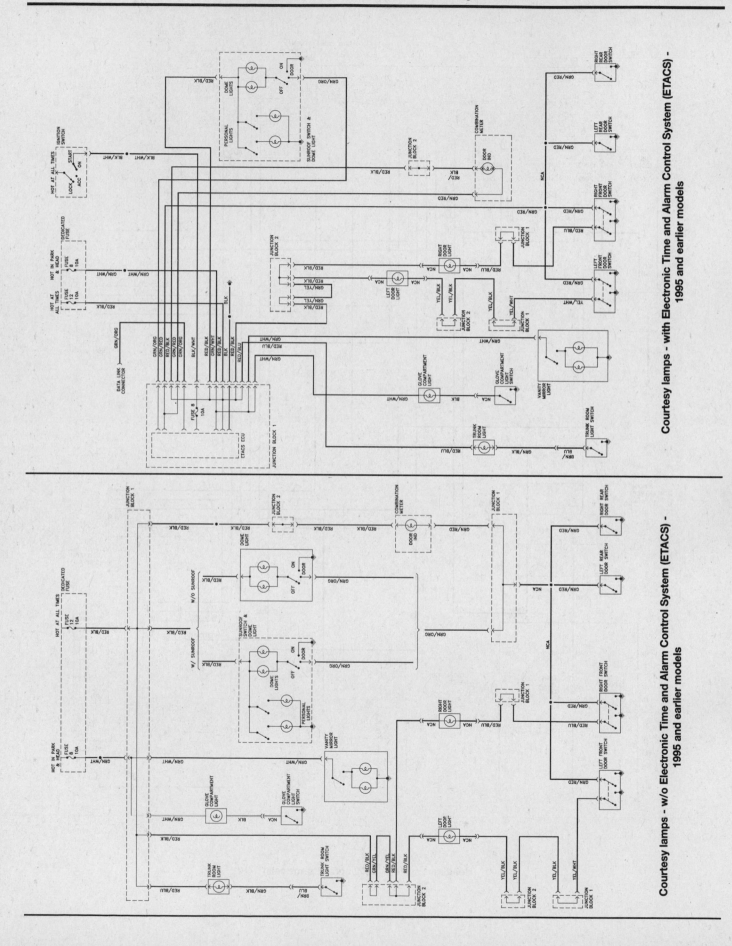

Courtesy lamps - with Electronic Time and Alarm Control System (ETACS) - 1995 and earlier models

Courtesy lamps - w/o Electronic Time and Alarm Control System (ETACS) - 1995 and earlier models

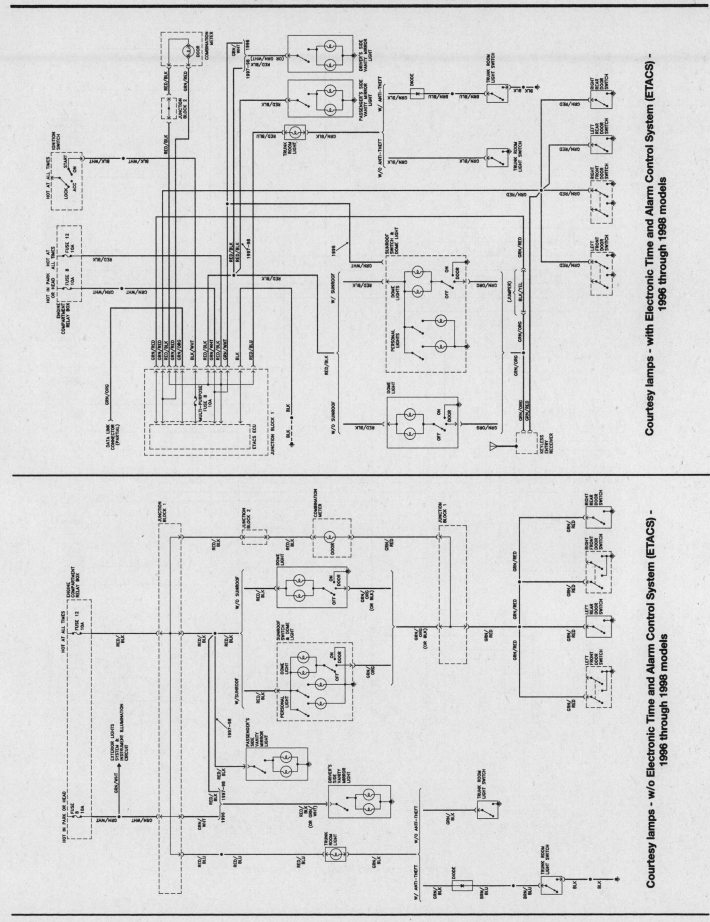

Courtesy lamps - with Electronic Time and Alarm Control System (ETACS) - 1996 through 1998 models

Courtesy lamps - w/o Electronic Time and Alarm Control System (ETACS) - 1996 through 1998 models

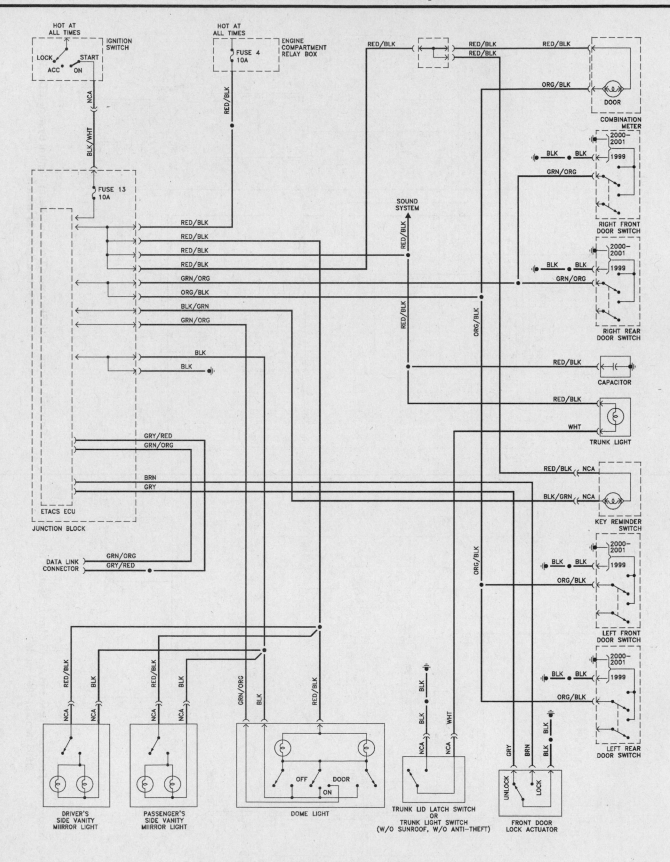

Courtesy lamps (1999 through 2001 models)

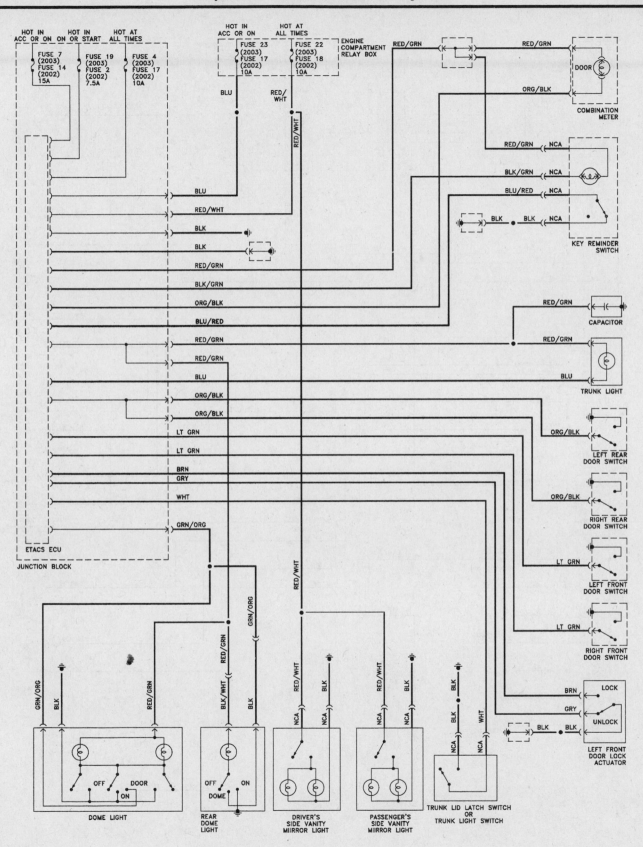

Courtesy lamps (2002 and later models)

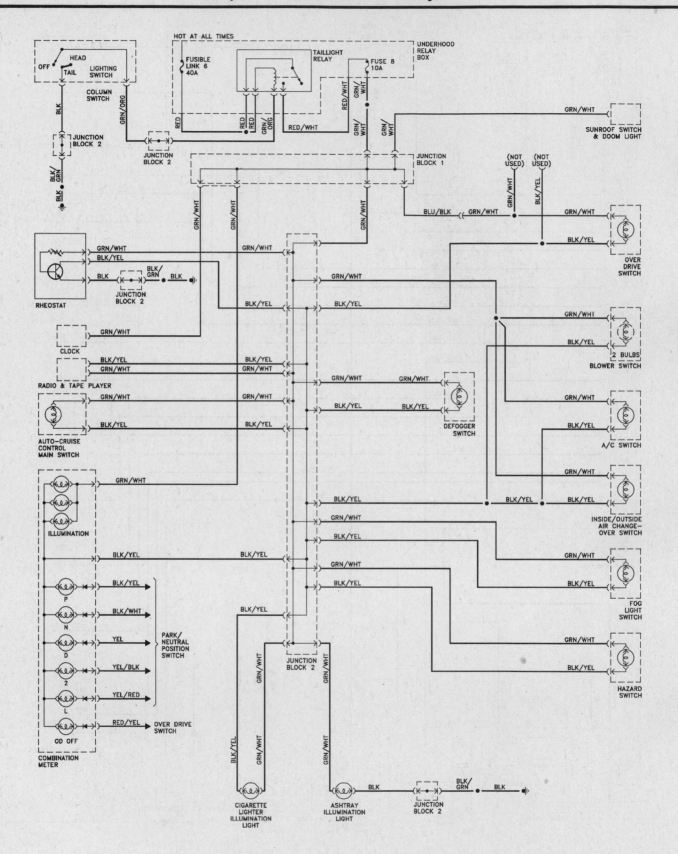

Instrument panel illumination (1995 and earlier models)

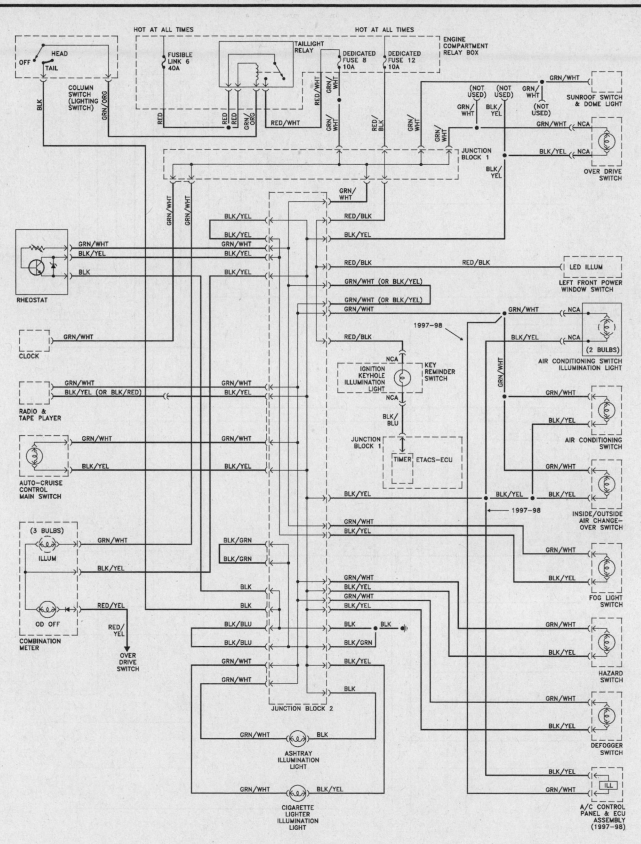

Instrument panel illumination (1996 through 1998 models)

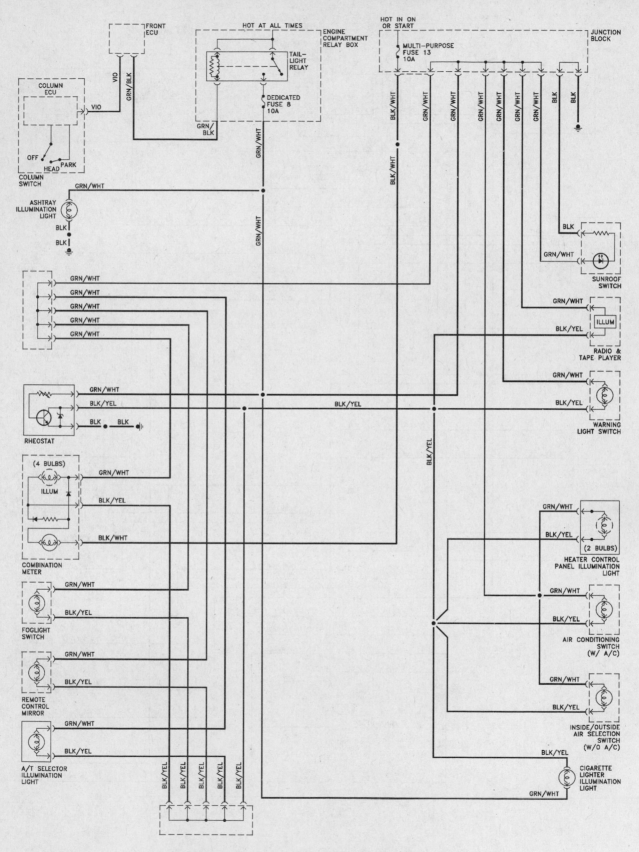

Instrument panel illumination (1999 through 2001 models)

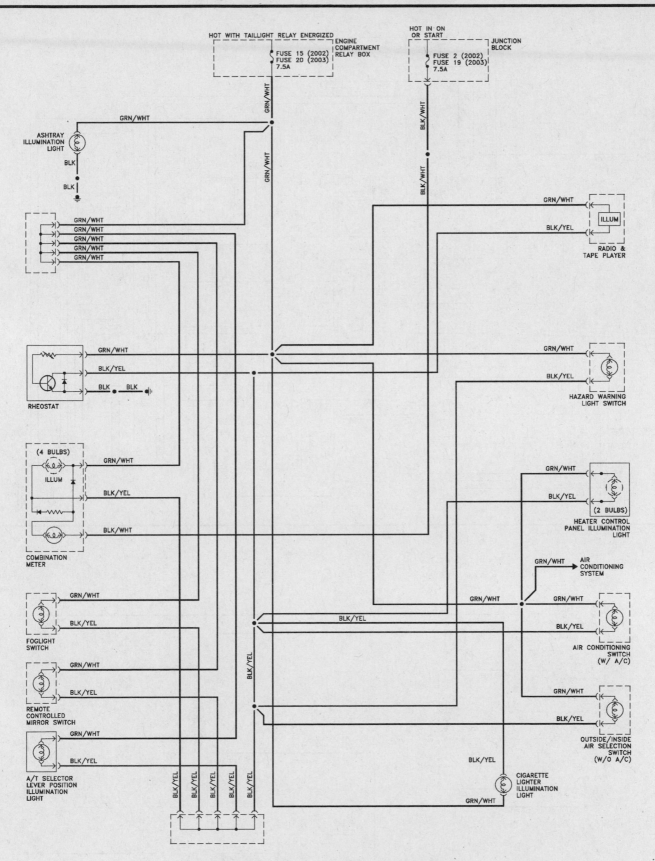

Instrument panel illumination (2002 and later models)

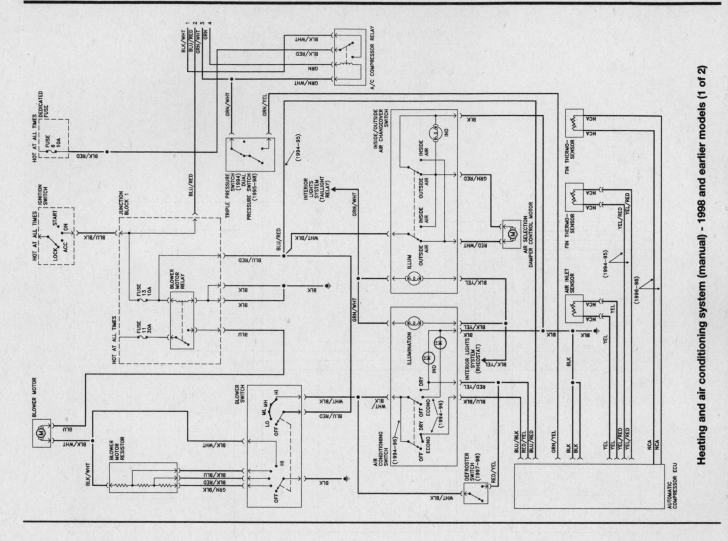

Heating and air conditioning system (manual) - 1998 and earlier models (1 of 2)

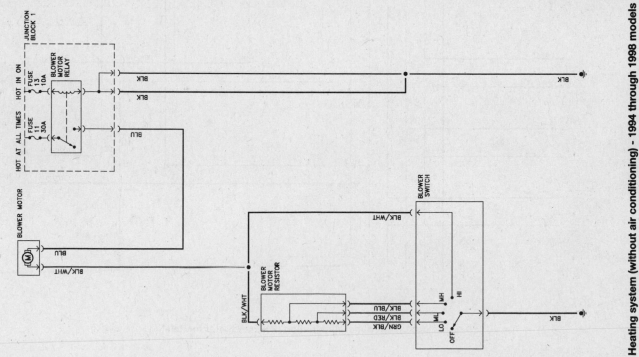

Heating system (without air conditioning) - 1994 through 1998 models

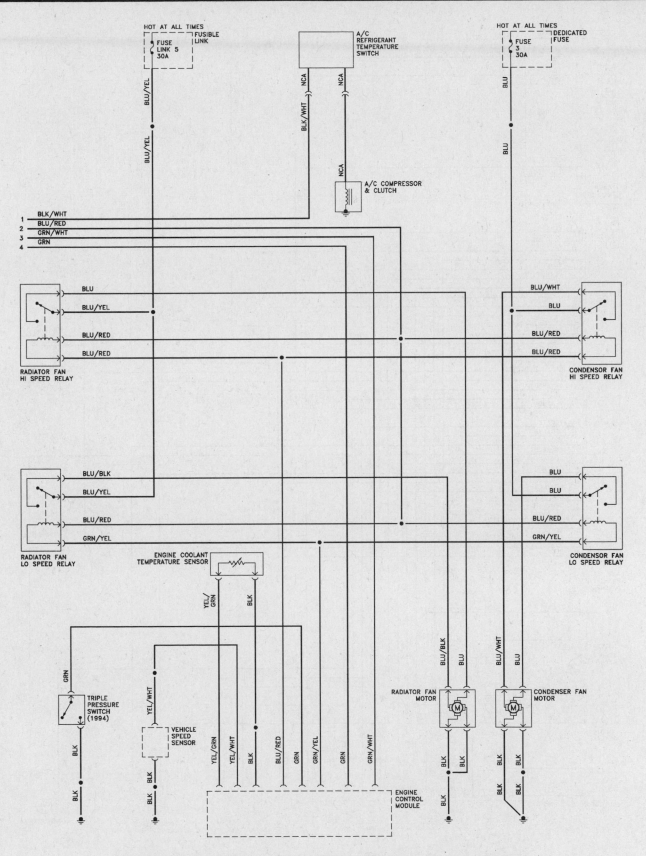

Heating and air conditioning system (manual) - 1998 and earlier models (2 of 2)

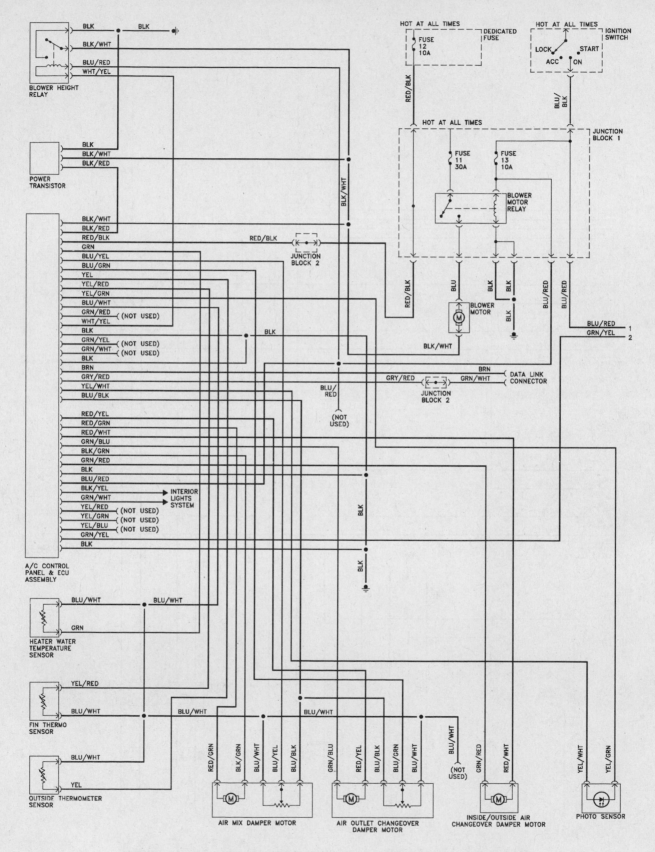

Heating and air conditioning system (automatic) - 1998 and earlier models (1 of 2)

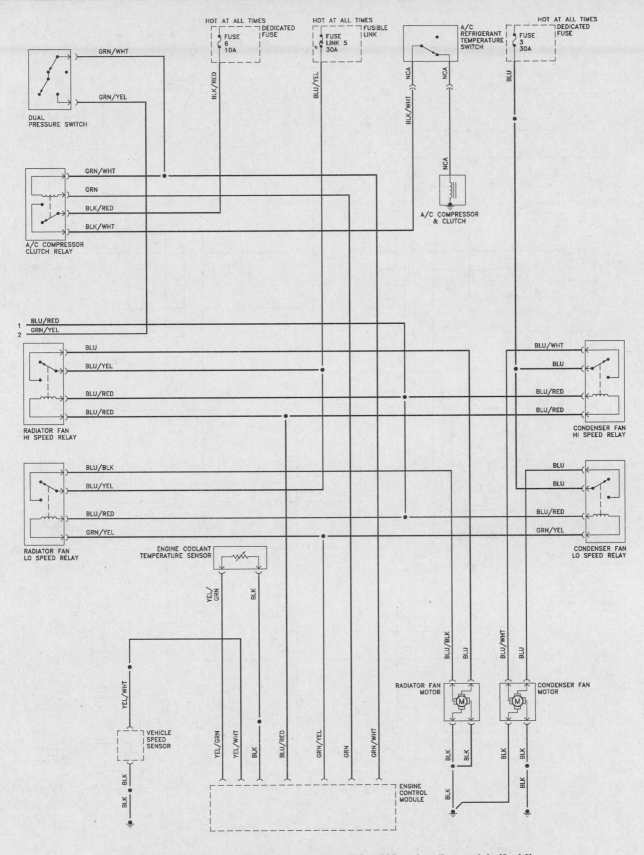

Heating and air conditioning system (automatic) - 1998 and earlier models (2 of 2)

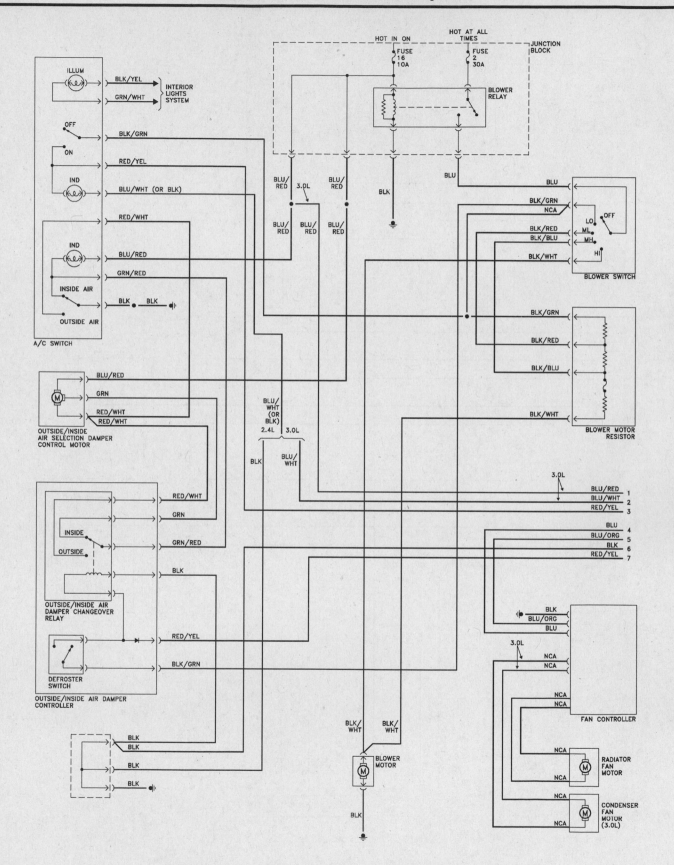

Heating and air conditioning system (manual) - 1999 models (1 of 2)

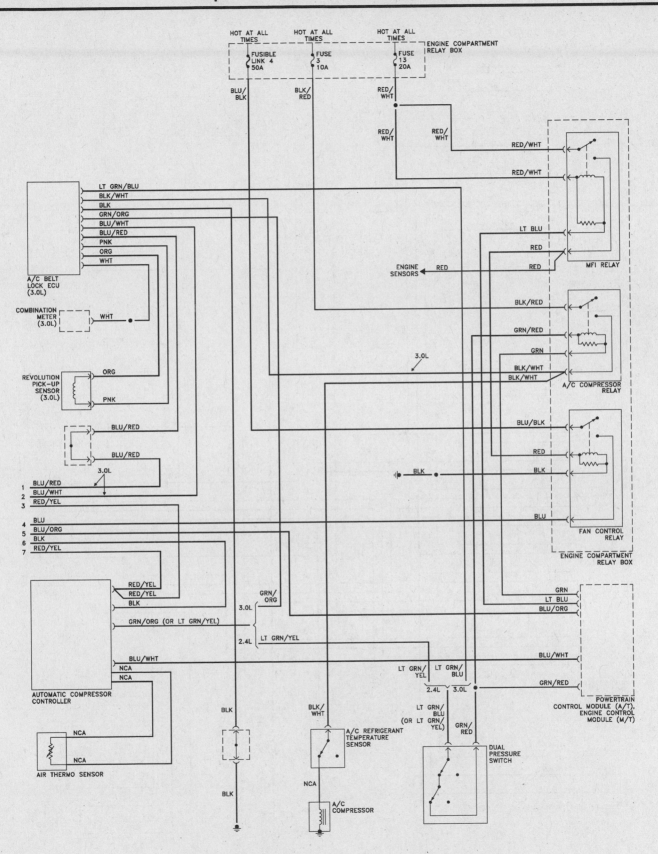

Heating and air conditioning system (manual) - 1999 models (2 of 2)

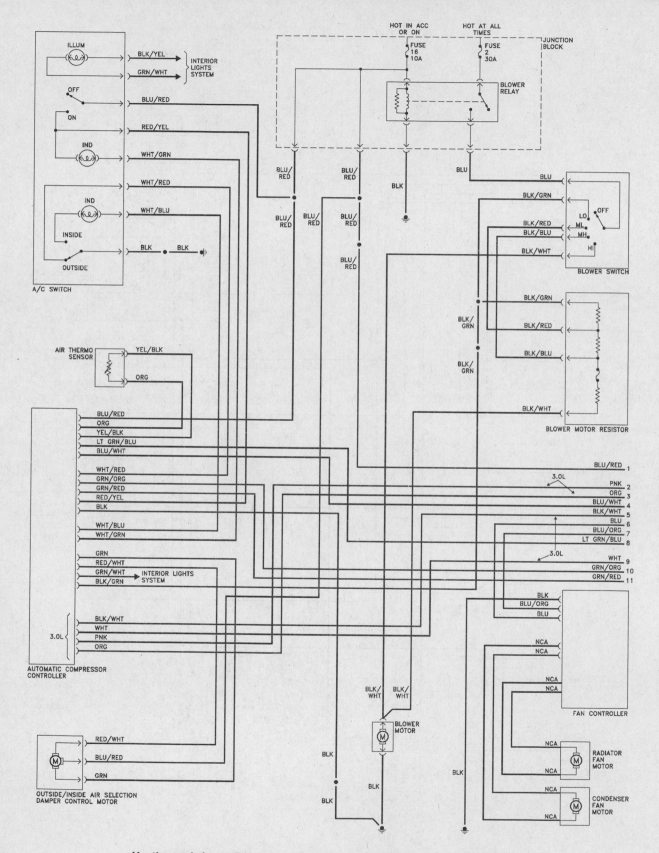

Heating and air conditioning system (manual) - 2000 and 2001 models (1 of 2)

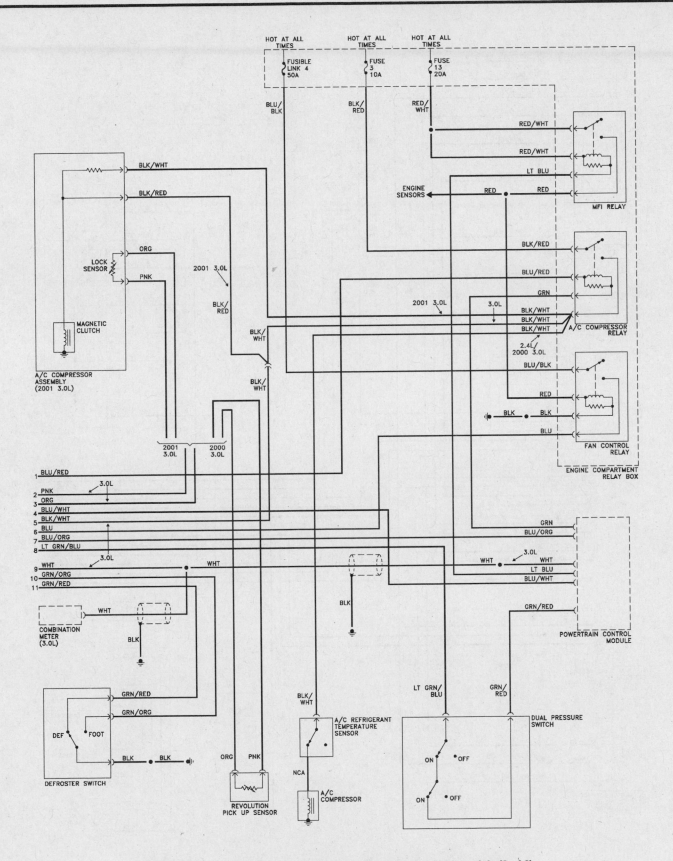

Heating and air conditioning system (manual) - 2000 and 2001 models (2 of 2)

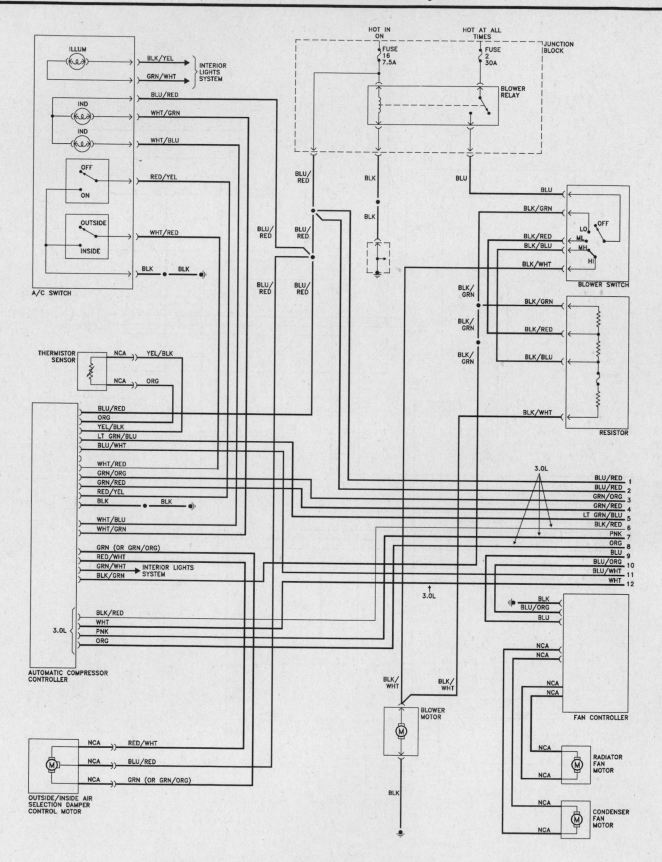

Heating and air conditioning system (manual) - 2002 and later models (1 of 2)

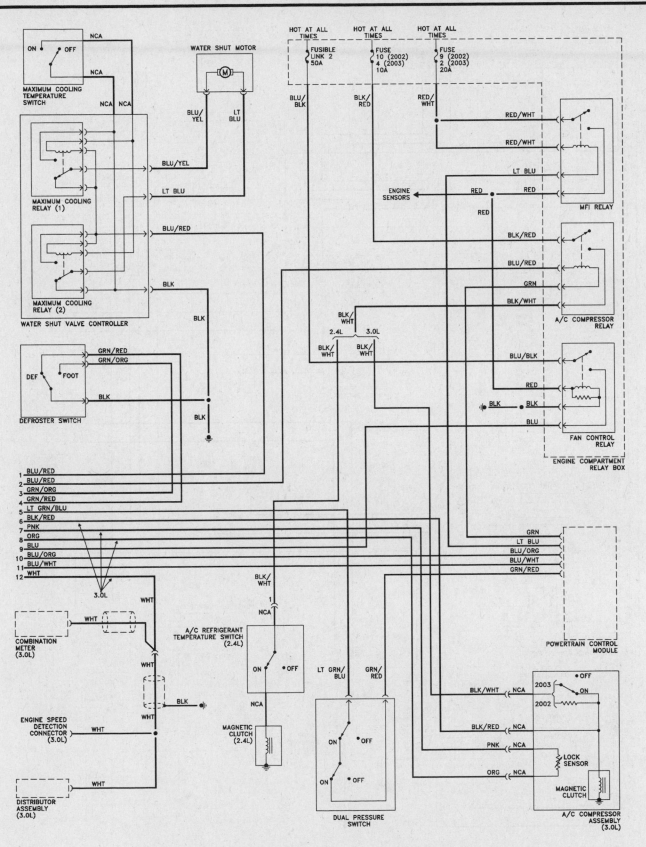

Heating and air conditioning system (manual) - 2002 and later models (2 of 2)

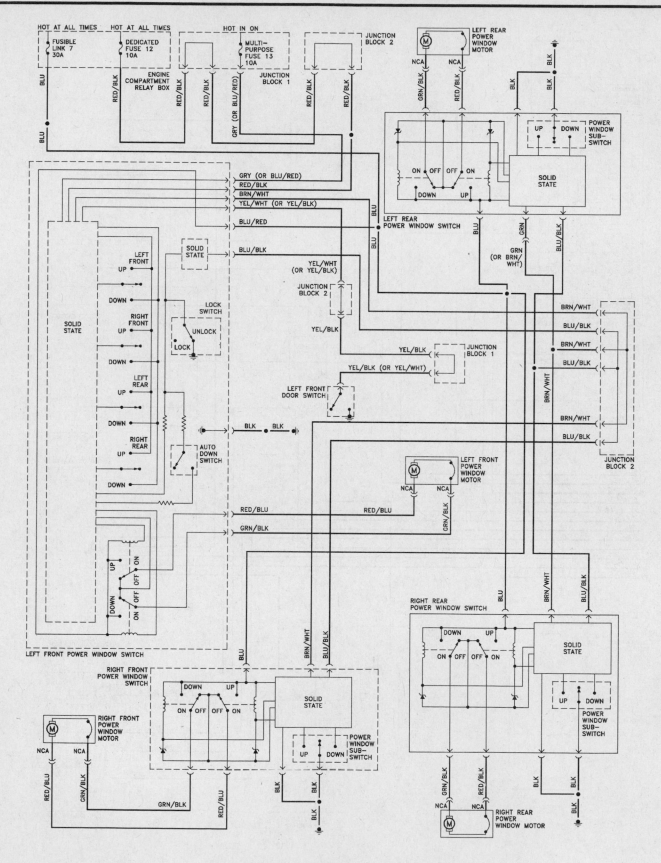

Power window system (1998 and earlier models)

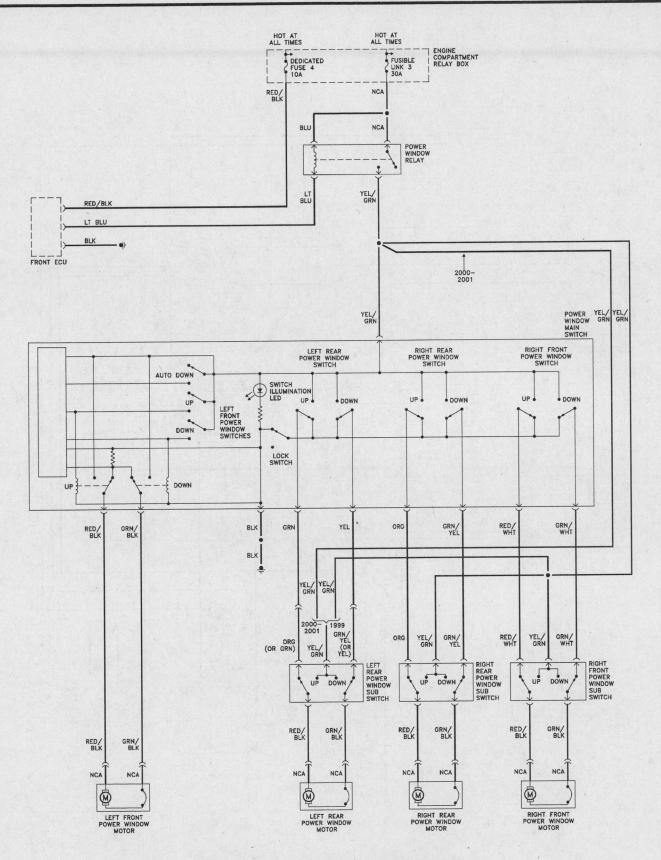

Power window system (1999 through 2001 models)

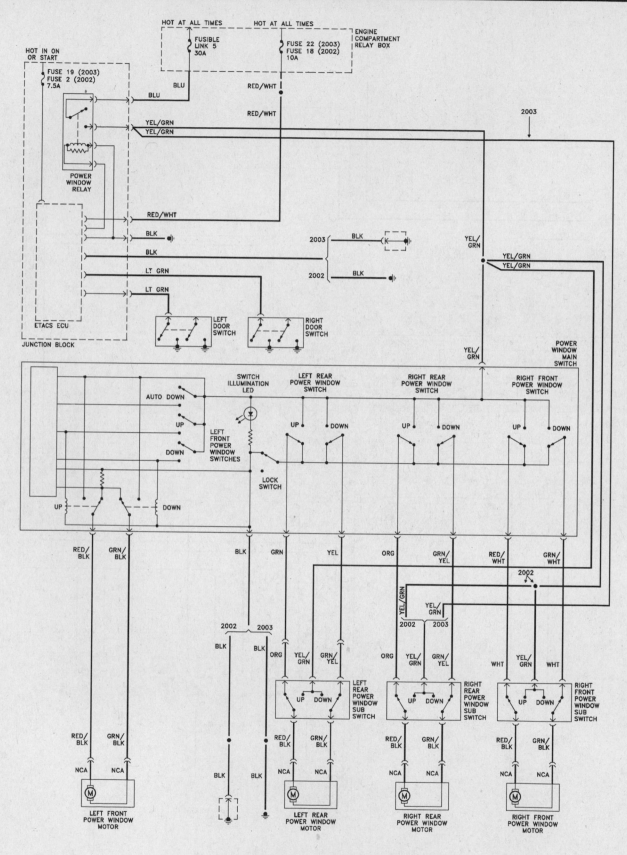

Power window system (2002 and later models)

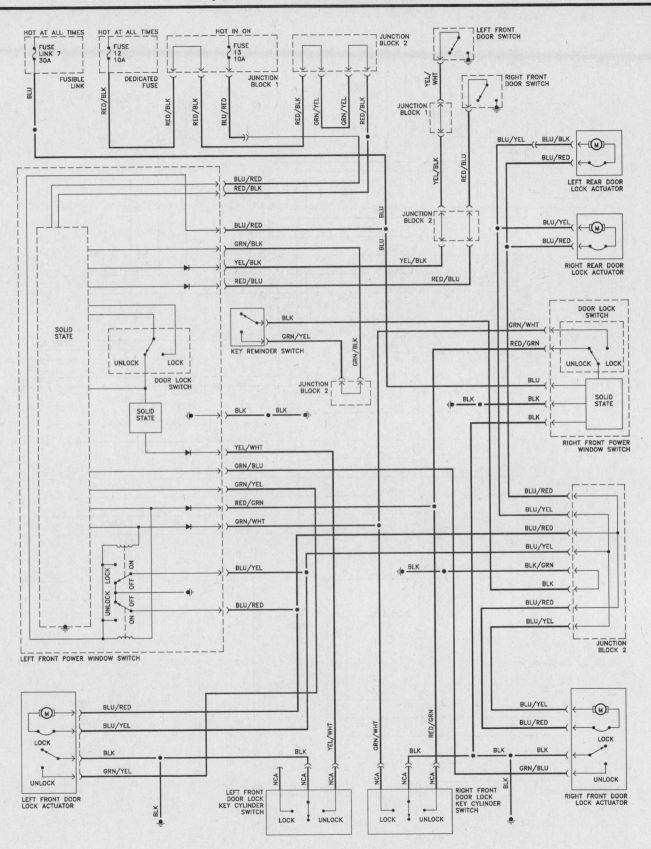

Power door lock system (1995 models)

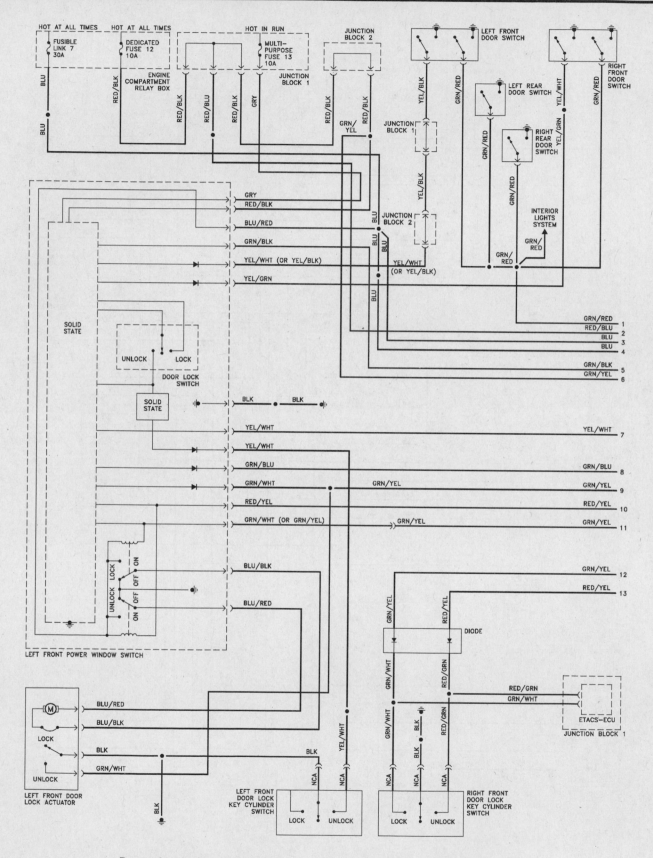

Power door lock system (with keyless entry) - 1996 through 1998 models (1 of 2)

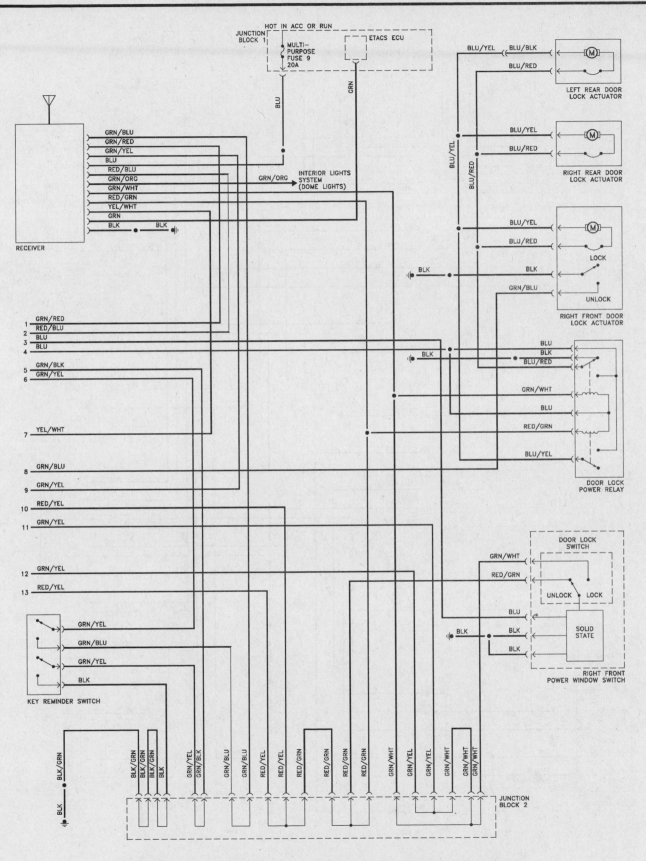

Power door lock system (with keyless entry) - 1996 through 1998 models (2 of 2)

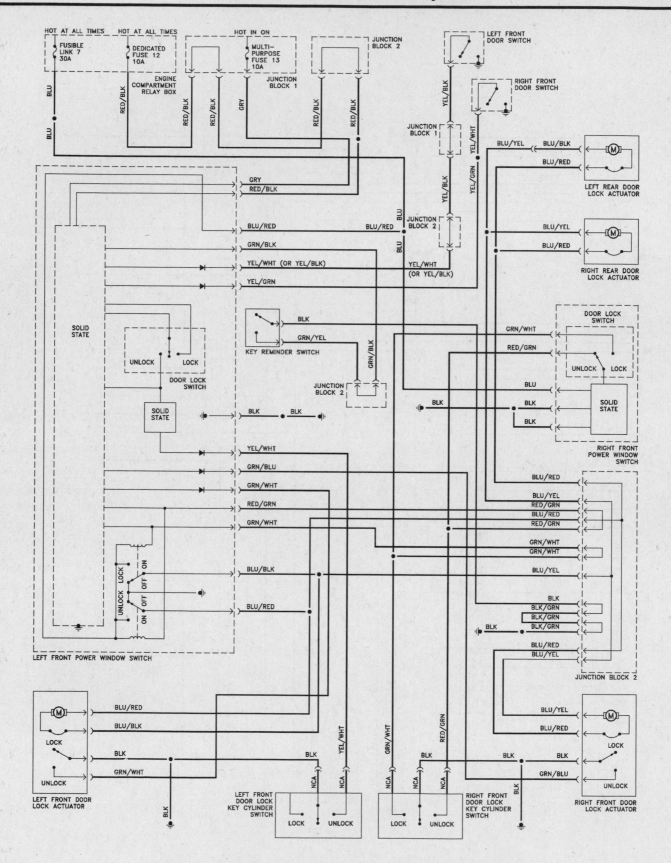

Power door lock system (w/o keyless entry) - 1996 through 1998 models

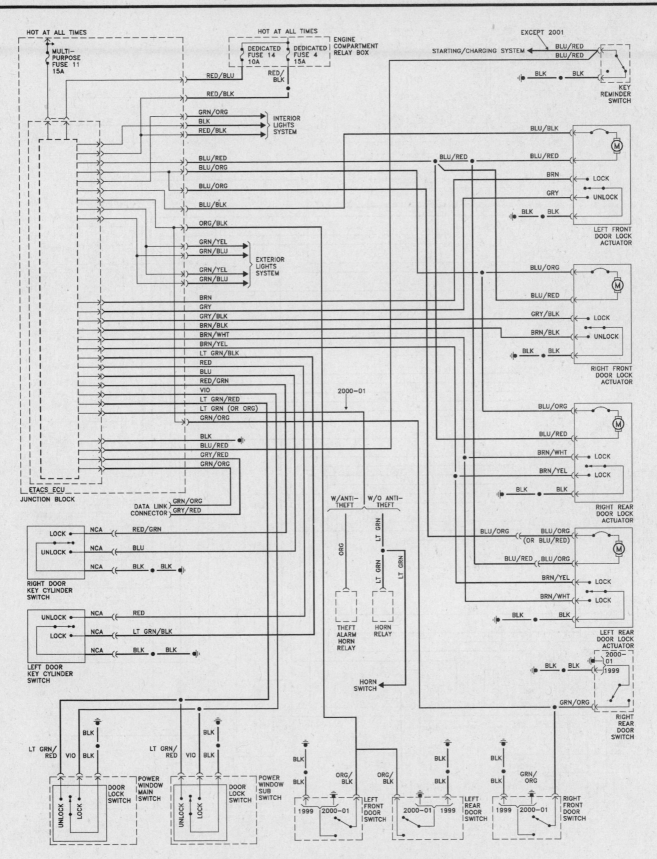

Power door lock system (1999 through 2001 models)

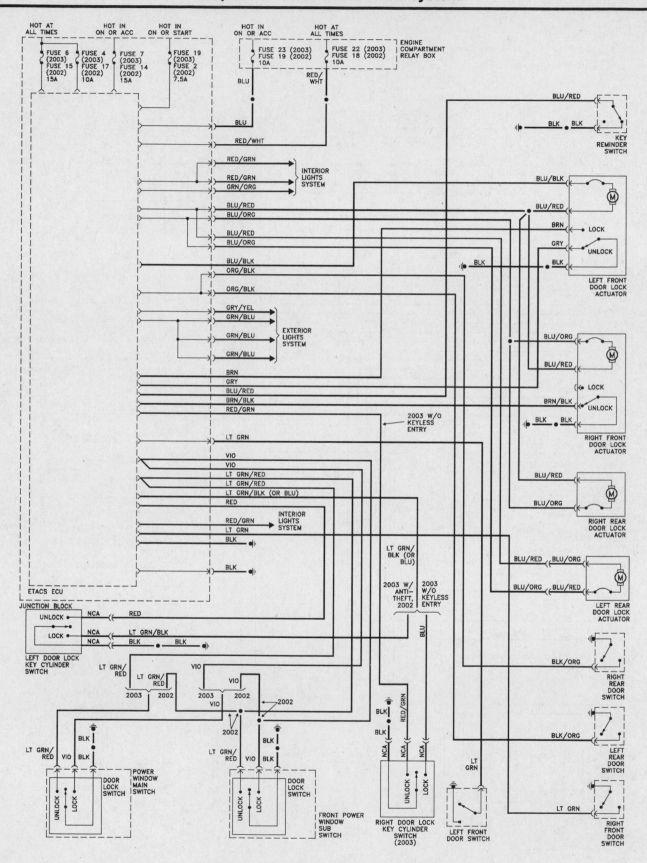

Power door lock system (2002 and later models)

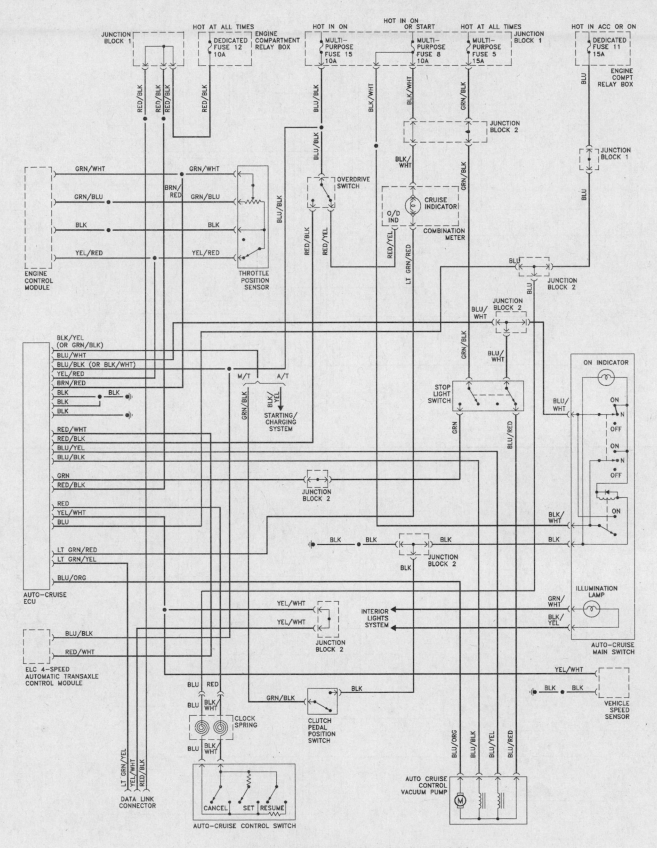

Cruise control system (1998 and earlier models)

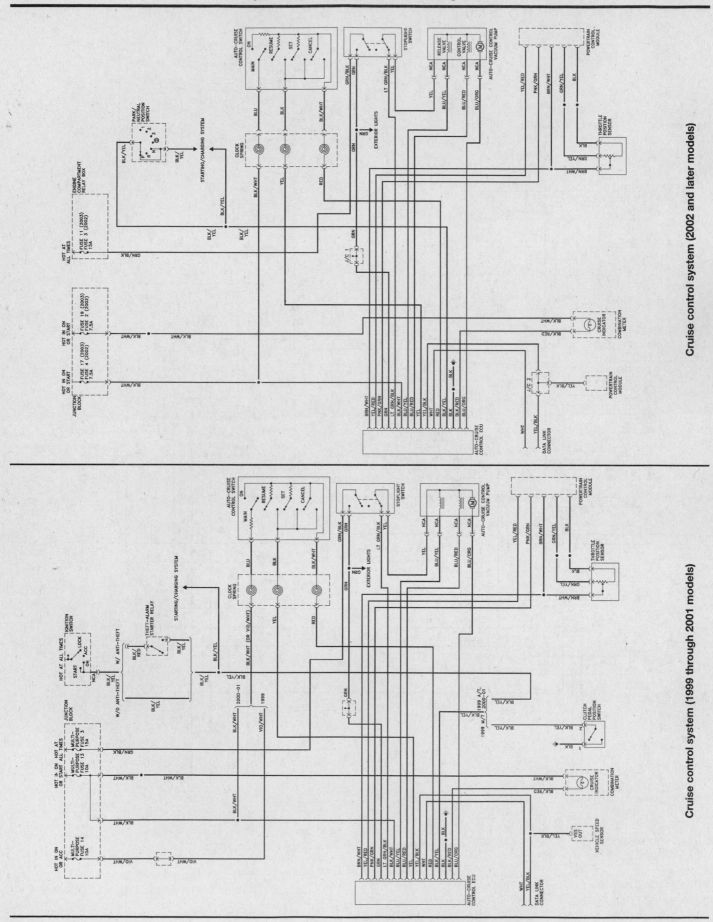

Cruise control system (2002 and later models)

Cruise control system (1999 through 2001 models)

Index

Haynes Automotive Manuals

NOTE: If you do not see a listing for your vehicle, consult your local Haynes dealer for the latest product information.

ACURA
12020 **Integra** '86 thru '89 **& Legend** '86 thru '90
12021 **Integra** '90 thru '93 **& Legend** '91 thru '95
    Integra '94 thru '00 - see *HONDA Civic (42025)*
    MDX '01 thru '07 - see *HONDA Pilot (42037)*
12050 **Acura TL** all models '99 thru '08

AMC
    Jeep CJ - see *JEEP (50020)*
14020 **Mid-size models** '70 thru '83
14025 **(Renault) Alliance & Encore** '83 thru '87

AUDI
15020 **4000** all models '80 thru '87
15025 **5000** all models '77 thru '83
15026 **5000** all models '84 thru '88
    Audi A4 '96 thru '01 - see *VW Passat (96023)*
15030 **Audi A4** '02 thru '08

AUSTIN-HEALEY
    Sprite - see *MG Midget (66015)*

BMW
18020 **3/5 Series** '82 thru '92
18021 **3-Series** incl. Z3 models '92 thru '98
18022 **3-Series** incl. Z4 models '99 thru '05
18023 **3-Series** '06 thru '10
18025 **320i** all 4 cyl models '75 thru '83
18050 **1500 thru 2002** except Turbo '59 thru '77

BUICK
19010 **Buick Century** '97 thru '05
    Century (front-wheel drive) - see *GM (38005)*
19020 **Buick, Oldsmobile & Pontiac Full-size**
    (Front-wheel drive) '85 thru '05
    Buick Electra, LeSabre and Park Avenue;
    Oldsmobile Delta 88 Royale,
    Ninety Eight and Regency; **Pontiac** Bonneville
19025 **Buick, Oldsmobile & Pontiac Full-size**
    (Rear wheel drive) '70 thru '90
    Buick Estate, Electra, LeSabre, Limited,
    Oldsmobile Custom Cruiser, Delta 88,
    Ninety-eight, **Pontiac** Bonneville,
    Catalina, Grandville, Parisienne
19030 **Mid-size Regal & Century** all rear-drive
    models with V6, V8 and Turbo '74 thru '87
    Regal - see *GENERAL MOTORS (38010)*
    Riviera - see *GENERAL MOTORS (38030)*
    Roadmaster - see *CHEVROLET (24046)*
    Skyhawk - see *GENERAL MOTORS (38015)*
    Skylark - see *GM (38020, 38025)*
    Somerset - see *GENERAL MOTORS (38025)*

CADILLAC
21015 **CTS & CTS-V** '03 thru '12
21030 **Cadillac Rear Wheel Drive** '70 thru '93
    Cimarron - see *GENERAL MOTORS (38015)*
    DeVille - see *GM (38031 & 38032)*
    Eldorado - see *GM (38030 & 38031)*
    Fleetwood - see *GM (38031)*
    Seville - see *GM (38030, 38031 & 38032)*

CHEVROLET
10305 **Chevrolet Engine Overhaul Manual**
24010 **Astro & GMC Safari Mini-vans** '85 thru '05
24015 **Camaro V8** all models '70 thru '81
24016 **Camaro** all models '82 thru '92
24017 **Camaro & Firebird** '93 thru '02
    Cavalier - see *GENERAL MOTORS (38016)*
    Celebrity - see *GENERAL MOTORS (38005)*
24020 **Chevelle, Malibu & El Camino** '69 thru '87
24024 **Chevette & Pontiac T1000** '76 thru '87
    Citation - see *GENERAL MOTORS (38020)*
24027 **Colorado & GMC Canyon** '04 thru '10
24032 **Corsica/Beretta** all models '87 thru '96
24040 **Corvette** all V8 models '68 thru '82
24041 **Corvette** all models '84 thru '96
24045 **Full-size Sedans** Caprice, Impala, Biscayne,
    Bel Air & Wagons '69 thru '90
24046 **Impala SS & Caprice and Buick Roadmaster**
    '91 thru '96
    Impala '00 thru '05 - see *LUMINA (24048)*
24047 **Impala & Monte Carlo** all models '06 thru '11
    Lumina '90 thru '94 - see *GM (38010)*
24048 **Lumina & Monte Carlo** '95 thru '05
    Lumina APV - see *GM (38035)*
24050 **Luv Pick-up** all 2WD & 4WD '72 thru '82
    Malibu '97 thru '00 - see *GM (38026)*
24055 **Monte Carlo** all models '70 thru '88
    Monte Carlo '95 thru '01 - see *LUMINA (24048)*
24059 **Nova** all V8 models '69 thru '79
24060 **Nova and Geo Prizm** '85 thru '92
24064 **Pick-ups** '67 thru '87 - Chevrolet & GMC
24065 **Pick-ups** '88 thru '98 - Chevrolet & GMC

24066 **Pick-ups** '99 thru '06 - Chevrolet & GMC
24067 **Chevrolet Silverado & GMC Sierra** '07 thru '12
24070 **S-10 & S-15 Pick-ups** '82 thru '93,
    Blazer & Jimmy '83 thru '94,
24071 **S-10 & Sonoma Pick-ups** '94 thru '04, includ-
    ing Blazer, Jimmy & Hombre
24072 **Chevrolet TrailBlazer, GMC Envoy &**
    Oldsmobile Bravada '02 thru '09
24075 **Sprint** '85 thru '88 **& Geo Metro** '89 thru '01
24080 **Vans - Chevrolet & GMC** '68 thru '96
24081 **Chevrolet Express & GMC Savana**
    Full-size Vans '96 thru '10

CHRYSLER
10310 **Chrysler Engine Overhaul Manual**
25015 **Chrysler Cirrus, Dodge Stratus,**
    Plymouth Breeze '95 thru '00
25020 **Full-size Front-Wheel Drive** '88 thru '93
    K-Cars - see *DODGE Aries (30008)*
    Laser - see *DODGE Daytona (30030)*
25025 **Chrysler LHS, Concorde, New Yorker,**
    Dodge Intrepid, **Eagle** Vision, '93 thru '97
25026 **Chrysler LHS, Concorde, 300M,**
    Dodge Intrepid, '98 thru '04
25027 **Chrysler 300, Dodge Charger &**
    Magnum '05 thru '09
25030 **Chrysler & Plymouth Mid-size**
    front wheel drive '82 thru '95
    Rear-wheel Drive - see *Dodge (30050)*
25035 **PT Cruiser** all models '01 thru '10
25040 **Chrysler Sebring** '95 thru '06, **Dodge** Stratus
    '01 thru '06, **Dodge** Avenger '95 thru '00

DATSUN
28005 **200SX** all models '80 thru '83
28007 **B-210** all models '73 thru '78
28009 **210** all models '79 thru '82
28012 **240Z, 260Z & 280Z** Coupe '70 thru '78
28014 **280ZX** Coupe & 2+2 '79 thru '83
    300ZX - see *NISSAN (72010)*
28018 **510 & PL521 Pick-up** '68 thru '73
28020 **510** all models '78 thru '81
28022 **620 Series Pick-up** all models '73 thru '79
    720 Series Pick-up - see *NISSAN (72030)*
28025 **810/Maxima** all gasoline models '77 thru '84

DODGE
    400 & 600 - see *CHRYSLER (25030)*
30008 **Aries & Plymouth Reliant** '81 thru '89
30010 **Caravan & Plymouth Voyager** '84 thru '95
30011 **Caravan & Plymouth Voyager** '96 thru '02
30012 **Challenger/Plymouth Saporro** '78 thru '83
30013 **Caravan, Chrysler Voyager, Town &**
    Country '03 thru '07
30016 **Colt & Plymouth Champ** '78 thru '87
30020 **Dakota Pick-ups** all models '87 thru '96
30021 **Durango** '98 & '99, **Dakota** '97 thru '99
30022 **Durango** '00 thru '03 **Dakota** '00 thru '04
30023 **Durango** '04 thru '09, **Dakota** '05 thru '11
30025 **Dart, Demon, Plymouth Barracuda,**
    Duster & Valiant 6 cyl models '67 thru '76
30030 **Daytona & Chrysler Laser** '84 thru '89
    Intrepid - see *CHRYSLER (25025, 25026)*
30034 **Neon** all models '95 thru '99
30035 **Omni & Plymouth Horizon** '78 thru '90
30036 **Dodge and Plymouth Neon** '00 thru '05
30040 **Pick-ups** all full-size models '74 thru '93
30041 **Pick-ups** all full-size models '94 thru '01
30042 **Pick-ups** full-size models '02 thru '08
30045 **Ram 50/D50 Pick-ups & Raider and**
    Plymouth Arrow Pick-ups '79 thru '93
30050 **Dodge/Plymouth/Chrysler RWD** '71 thru '89
30055 **Shadow & Plymouth Sundance** '87 thru '94
30060 **Spirit & Plymouth Acclaim** '89 thru '95
30065 **Vans - Dodge & Plymouth** '71 thru '03

EAGLE
    Talon - see *MITSUBISHI (68030, 68031)*
    Vision - see *CHRYSLER (25025)*

FIAT
34010 **124 Sport Coupe & Spider** '68 thru '78
34025 **X1/9** all models '74 thru '80

FORD
10320 **Ford Engine Overhaul Manual**
10355 **Ford Automatic Transmission Overhaul**
11500 **Mustang** '64-1/2 thru '70 Restoration Guide
36004 **Aerostar Mini-vans** all models '86 thru '97
36006 **Contour & Mercury Mystique** '95 thru '00
36008 **Courier Pick-up** all models '72 thru '82
36012 **Crown Victoria & Mercury Grand**
    Marquis '88 thru '10
36016 **Escort/Mercury Lynx** all models '81 thru '90
36020 **Escort/Mercury Tracer** '91 thru '02

36022 **Escape & Mazda Tribute** '01 thru '11
36024 **Explorer & Mazda Navajo** '91 thru '01
36025 **Explorer/Mercury Mountaineer** '02 thru '10
36028 **Fairmont & Mercury Zephyr** '78 thru '83
36030 **Festiva & Aspire** '88 thru '97
36032 **Fiesta** all models '77 thru '80
36034 **Focus** all models '00 thru '11
36036 **Ford & Mercury Full-size** '75 thru '87
36044 **Ford & Mercury Mid-size** '75 thru '86
36045 **Fusion & Mercury Milan** '06 thru '10
36048 **Mustang V8** all models '64-1/2 '73
36049 **Mustang II** 4 cyl, V6 & V8 models '74 thru '78
36050 **Mustang & Mercury Capri** '79 thru '93
36051 **Mustang** all models '94 thru '04
36052 **Mustang** '05 thru '10
36054 **Pick-ups & Bronco** '73 thru '79
36058 **Pick-ups & Bronco** '80 thru '96
36059 **F-150 & Expedition** '97 thru '09, **F-250** '97
    thru '99 & **Lincoln Navigator** '98 thru '09
36060 **Super Duty Pick-ups, Excursion** '99 thru '10
36061 **F-150** full-size '04 thru '10
36062 **Pinto & Mercury Bobcat** '75 thru '80
36066 **Probe** all models '89 thru '92
    Probe '93 thru '97 - see *MAZDA 626 (61042)*
36070 **Ranger/Bronco II** gasoline models '83 thru '92
36071 **Ranger** '93 thru '10 & **Mazda Pick-ups** '94 thru '09
36074 **Taurus & Mercury Sable** '86 thru '95
36075 **Taurus & Mercury Sable** '96 thru '05
36078 **Tempo & Mercury Topaz** '84 thru '94
36082 **Thunderbird/Mercury Cougar** '83 thru '88
36086 **Thunderbird/Mercury Cougar** '89 thru '97
36090 **Vans** all V8 Econoline models '69 thru '91
36094 **Vans** full size '92 thru '10
36097 **Windstar Mini-van** '95 thru '07

GENERAL MOTORS
10360 **GM Automatic Transmission Overhaul**
38005 **Buick Century, Chevrolet Celebrity,**
    Oldsmobile Cutlass Ciera & Pontiac 6000
    all models '82 thru '96
38010 **Buick Regal, Chevrolet Lumina,**
    Oldsmobile Cutlass Supreme &
    Pontiac Grand Prix (FWD) '88 thru '07
38015 **Buick Skyhawk, Cadillac Cimarron,**
    Chevrolet Cavalier, Oldsmobile Firenza &
    Pontiac J-2000 & Sunbird '82 thru '94
38016 **Chevrolet Cavalier &**
    Pontiac Sunfire '95 thru '05
38017 **Chevrolet Cobalt & Pontiac G5** '05 thru '11
38020 **Buick Skylark, Chevrolet Citation,**
    Olds Omega, Pontiac Phoenix '80 thru '85
38025 **Buick Skylark & Somerset,**
    Oldsmobile Achieva & Calais and
    Pontiac Grand Am all models '85 thru '98
38026 **Chevrolet Malibu, Olds Alero & Cutlass,**
    Pontiac Grand Am '97 thru '03
38027 **Chevrolet Malibu** '04 thru '10
38030 **Cadillac Eldorado, Seville, Oldsmobile**
    Toronado, Buick Riviera '71 thru '85
38031 **Cadillac Eldorado & Seville, DeVille, Fleetwood**
    & Olds Toronado, Buick Riviera '86 thru '93
38032 **Cadillac DeVille** '94 thru '05 & **Seville** '92 thru '04
    Cadillac DTS '06 thru '10
38035 **Chevrolet Lumina APV, Olds Silhouette**
    & Pontiac Trans Sport all models '90 thru '96
38036 **Chevrolet Venture, Olds Silhouette,**
    Pontiac Trans Sport & Montana '97 thru '05
    General Motors Full-size
    Rear-wheel Drive - see *BUICK (19025)*
38040 **Chevrolet Equinox** '05 thru '09 **Pontiac**
    Torrent '06 thru '09
38070 **Chevrolet HHR** '06 thru '11

GEO
    Metro - see *CHEVROLET Sprint (24075)*
    Prizm - '85 thru '92 see *CHEVY (24060)*,
    '93 thru '02 see *TOYOTA Corolla (92036)*
40030 **Storm** all models '90 thru '93
    Tracker - see *SUZUKI Samurai (90010)*

GMC
    Vans & Pick-ups - see *CHEVROLET*

HONDA
42010 **Accord CVCC** all models '76 thru '83
42011 **Accord** all models '84 thru '89
42012 **Accord** all models '90 thru '93
42013 **Accord** all models '94 thru '97
42014 **Accord** all models '98 thru '02
42015 **Accord** '03 thru '07
42020 **Civic 1200** all models '73 thru '79
42021 **Civic 1300 & 1500 CVCC** '80 thru '83
42022 **Civic 1500 CVCC** all models '75 thru '79

(Continued on other side)

Haynes North America, Inc., 861 Lawrence Drive, Newbury Park, CA 91320-1514 • (805) 498-6703 • http://www.haynes.com

Haynes Automotive Manuals (continued)

NOTE: If you do not see a listing for your vehicle, consult your local Haynes dealer for the latest product information.

42023 **Civic** all models '84 thru '91
42024 **Civic & del Sol** '92 thru '95
42025 **Civic** '96 thru '00, **CR-V** '97 thru '01,
Acura Integra '94 thru '00
42026 **Civic** '01 thru '10, **CR-V** '02 thru '09
42035 **Odyssey** all models '99 thru '10
Passport - see ISUZU Rodeo (47017)
42037 **Honda Pilot** '03 thru '07, **Acura MDX** '01 thru '07
42040 **Prelude CVCC** all models '79 thru '89

HYUNDAI
43010 **Elantra** all models '96 thru '10
43015 **Excel & Accent** all models '86 thru '09
43050 **Santa Fe** all models '01 thru '06
43055 **Sonata** all models '99 thru '08

INFINITI
G35 '03 thru '08 - see NISSAN 350Z (72011)

ISUZU
Hombre - see CHEVROLET S-10 (24071)
47017 **Rodeo, Amigo & Honda Passport** '89 thru '02
47020 **Trooper & Pick-up** '81 thru '93

JAGUAR
49010 **XJ6** all 6 cyl models '68 thru '86
49011 **XJ6** all models '88 thru '94
49015 **XJ12 & XJS** all 12 cyl models '72 thru '85

JEEP
50010 **Cherokee, Comanche & Wagoneer Limited**
all models '84 thru '01
50020 **CJ** all models '49 thru '86
50025 **Grand Cherokee** all models '93 thru '04
50026 **Grand Cherokee** '05 thru '09
50029 **Grand Wagoneer & Pick-up** '72 thru '91
Grand Wagoneer '84 thru '91, **Cherokee &
Wagoneer** '72 thru '83, **Pick-up** '72 thru '88
50030 **Wrangler** all models '87 thru '11
50035 **Liberty** '02 thru '07

KIA
54050 **Optima** '01 thru '10
54070 **Sephia** '94 thru '01, **Spectra** '00 thru '09,
Sportage '05 thru '10

LEXUS
ES 300/330 - see TOYOTA Camry (92007) (92008)
RX 330 - see TOYOTA Highlander (92095)

LINCOLN
Navigator - see FORD Pick-up (36059)
59010 **Rear-Wheel Drive** all models '70 thru '10

MAZDA
61010 **GLC Hatchback** (rear-wheel drive) '77 thru '83
61011 **GLC** (front-wheel drive) '81 thru '85
61012 **Mazda3** '04 thru '11
61015 **323 & Protegé** '90 thru '03
61016 **MX-5 Miata** '90 thru '09
61020 **MPV** all models '89 thru '98
Navajo - see Ford Explorer (36024)
61030 **Pick-ups** '72 thru '93
Pick-ups '94 thru '00 - see Ford Ranger (36071)
61035 **RX-7** all models '79 thru '85
61036 **RX-7** all models '86 thru '91
61040 **626** (rear-wheel drive) all models '79 thru '82
61041 **626/MX-6** (front-wheel drive) '83 thru '92
61042 **626, MX-6/Ford Probe** '93 thru '02
61043 **Mazda6** '03 thru '11

MERCEDES-BENZ
63012 **123 Series Diesel** '76 thru '85
63015 **190 Series** four-cyl gas models, '84 thru '88
63020 **230/250/280** 6 cyl sohc models '68 thru '72
63025 **280** 123 Series gasoline models '77 thru '81
63030 **350 & 450** all models '71 thru '80
63040 **C-Class:** C230/C240/C280/C320/C350 '01 thru '07

MERCURY
64200 **Villager & Nissan Quest** '93 thru '01
All other titles, see FORD Listing.

MG
66010 **MGB** Roadster & GT Coupe '62 thru '80
66015 **MG Midget, Austin Healey Sprite** '58 thru '80

MINI
67020 **Mini** '02 thru '11

MITSUBISHI
68020 **Cordia, Tredia, Galant, Precis &
Mirage** '83 thru '93
68030 **Eclipse, Eagle Talon & Ply. Laser** '90 thru '94
68031 **Eclipse** '95 thru '05, **Eagle Talon** '95 thru '98
68035 **Galant** '94 thru '10
68040 **Pick-up** '83 thru '96 & **Montero** '83 thru '93

NISSAN
72010 **300ZX** all models including Turbo '84 thru '89
72011 **350Z & Infiniti G35** all models '03 thru '08
72015 **Altima** all models '93 thru '06
72016 **Altima** '07 thru '10
72020 **Maxima** all models '85 thru '92
72021 **Maxima** all models '93 thru '04
72025 **Murano** '03 thru '10
72030 **Pick-ups** '80 thru '97 **Pathfinder** '87 thru '95
72031 **Frontier Pick-up, Xterra, Pathfinder** '96 thru '04
72032 **Frontier & Xterra** '05 thru '11
72040 **Pulsar** all models '83 thru '86
Quest - see MERCURY Villager (64200)
72050 **Sentra** all models '82 thru '94
72051 **Sentra & 200SX** all models '95 thru '06
72060 **Stanza** all models '82 thru '90
72070 **Titan pick-ups** '04 thru '10 **Armada** '05 thru '10

OLDSMOBILE
73015 **Cutlass** V6 & V8 gas models '74 thru '88
*For other OLDSMOBILE titles, see BUICK,
CHEVROLET or GENERAL MOTORS listing.*

PLYMOUTH
For PLYMOUTH titles, see DODGE listing.

PONTIAC
79008 **Fiero** all models '84 thru '88
79018 **Firebird** V8 models except Turbo '70 thru '81
79019 **Firebird** all models '82 thru '92
79025 **G6** all models '05 thru '09
79040 **Mid-size** Rear-wheel Drive '70 thru '87
Vibe '03 thru '11 - see TOYOTA Matrix (92060)
*For other PONTIAC titles, see BUICK,
CHEVROLET or GENERAL MOTORS listing.*

PORSCHE
80020 **911** except Turbo & Carrera 4 '65 thru '89
80025 **914** all 4 cyl models '69 thru '76
80030 **924** all models including Turbo '76 thru '82
80035 **944** all models including Turbo '83 thru '89

RENAULT
Alliance & Encore - see AMC (14020)

SAAB
84010 **900** all models including Turbo '79 thru '88

SATURN
87010 **Saturn** all S-series models '91 thru '02
87011 **Saturn Ion** '03 thru '07
87020 **Saturn** all L-series models '00 thru '04
87040 **Saturn VUE** '02 thru '07

SUBARU
89002 **1100, 1300, 1400 & 1600** '71 thru '79
89003 **1600 & 1800** 2WD & 4WD '80 thru '94
89100 **Legacy** all models '90 thru '99
89101 **Legacy & Forester** '00 thru '06

SUZUKI
90010 **Samurai/Sidekick & Geo Tracker** '86 thru '01

TOYOTA
92005 **Camry** all models '83 thru '91
92006 **Camry** all models '92 thru '96
92007 **Camry, Avalon, Solara, Lexus ES 300** '97 thru '01
92008 **Toyota Camry, Avalon and Solara and
Lexus ES 300/330** all models '02 thru '06
92009 **Camry** '07 thru '11
92015 **Celica** Rear Wheel Drive '71 thru '85
92020 **Celica** Front Wheel Drive '86 thru '99
92025 **Celica Supra** all models '79 thru '92
92030 **Corolla** all models '75 thru '79
92032 **Corolla** all rear wheel drive models '80 thru '87
92035 **Corolla** all front wheel drive models '84 thru '92
92036 **Corolla & Geo Prizm** '93 thru '02
92037 **Corolla** all models '03 thru '11
92040 **Corolla Tercel** all models '80 thru '82
92045 **Corona** all models '74 thru '82
92050 **Cressida** all models '78 thru '82
92055 **Land Cruiser FJ40, 43, 45, 55** '68 thru '82
92056 **Land Cruiser FJ60, 62, 80, FZJ80** '80 thru '96
92060 **Matrix & Pontiac Vibe** '03 thru '11
92065 **MR2** all models '85 thru '87
92070 **Pick-up** all models '69 thru '78
92075 **Pick-up** all models '79 thru '95
92076 **Tacoma, 4Runner, & T100** '93 thru '04
92077 **Tacoma** all models '05 thru '09
92078 **Tundra** '00 thru '06 & **Sequoia** '01 thru '07
92079 **4Runner** all models '03 thru '09
92080 **Previa** all models '91 thru '95
92081 **Prius** all models '01 thru '08
92082 **RAV4** all models '96 thru '10
92085 **Tercel** all models '87 thru '94
92090 **Sienna** all models '98 thru '10
92095 **Highlander & Lexus RX-330** '99 thru '07

TRIUMPH
94007 **Spitfire** all models '62 thru '81
94010 **TR7** all models '75 thru '81

VW
96008 **Beetle & Karmann Ghia** '54 thru '79
96009 **New Beetle** '98 thru '11
96016 **Rabbit, Jetta, Scirocco & Pick-up** gas
models '75 thru '92 & Convertible '80 thru '92
96017 **Golf, GTI & Jetta** '93 thru '98, **Cabrio** '95 thru '02
96018 **Golf, GTI, Jetta** '99 thru '05
96019 **Jetta, Rabbit, GTI & Golf** '05 thru '11
96020 **Rabbit, Jetta & Pick-up** diesel '77 thru '84
96023 **Passat** '98 thru '05, **Audi A4** '96 thru '01
96030 **Transporter 1600** all models '68 thru '79
96035 **Transporter 1700, 1800 & 2000** '72 thru '79
96040 **Type 3 1500 & 1600** all models '63 thru '73
96045 **Vanagon** all air-cooled models '80 thru '83

VOLVO
97010 **120, 130 Series & 1800 Sports** '61 thru '73
97015 **140 Series** all models '66 thru '74
97020 **240 Series** all models '76 thru '93
97040 **740 & 760 Series** all models '82 thru '88
97050 **850 Series** all models '93 thru '97

TECHBOOK MANUALS
10205 **Automotive Computer Codes**
10206 **OBD-II & Electronic Engine Management**
10210 **Automotive Emissions Control Manual**
10215 **Fuel Injection Manual** '78 thru '85
10220 **Fuel Injection Manual** '86 thru '99
10225 **Holley Carburetor Manual**
10230 **Rochester Carburetor Manual**
10240 **Weber/Zenith/Stromberg/SU Carburetors**
10305 **Chevrolet Engine Overhaul Manual**
10310 **Chrysler Engine Overhaul Manual**
10320 **Ford Engine Overhaul Manual**
10330 **GM and Ford Diesel Engine Repair Manual**
10333 **Engine Performance Manual**
10340 **Small Engine Repair Manual, 5 HP & Less**
10341 **Small Engine Repair Manual, 5.5 - 20 HP**
10345 **Suspension, Steering & Driveline Manual**
10355 **Ford Automatic Transmission Overhaul**
10360 **GM Automatic Transmission Overhaul**
10405 **Automotive Body Repair & Painting**
10410 **Automotive Brake Manual**
10411 **Automotive Anti-lock Brake (ABS) Systems**
10415 **Automotive Detailing Manual**
10420 **Automotive Electrical Manual**
10425 **Automotive Heating & Air Conditioning**
10430 **Automotive Reference Manual & Dictionary**
10435 **Automotive Tools Manual**
10440 **Used Car Buying Guide**
10445 **Welding Manual**
10450 **ATV Basics**
10452 **Scooters 50cc to 250cc**

SPANISH MANUALS
98903 **Reparación de Carrocería & Pintura**
98904 **Manual de Carburador Modelos
Holley & Rochester**
98905 **Códigos Automotrices de la Computadora**
98906 **OBD-II & Sistemas de Control Electrónico
del Motor**
98910 **Frenos Automotriz**
98913 **Electricidad Automotriz**
98915 **Inyección de Combustible** '86 al '99
99040 **Chevrolet & GMC Camionetas** '67 al '87
99041 **Chevrolet & GMC Camionetas** '88 al '98
99042 **Chevrolet & GMC Camionetas
Cerradas** '68 al '95
99043 **Chevrolet/GMC Camionetas** '94 al '04
99048 **Chevrolet/GMC Camionetas** '99 al '06
99055 **Dodge Caravan & Plymouth Voyager** '84 al '95
99075 **Ford Camionetas y Bronco** '80 al '94
99076 **Ford F-150** '97 al '09
99077 **Ford Camionetas Cerradas** '69 al '91
99088 **Ford Modelos de Tamaño Mediano** '75 al '86
99089 **Ford Camionetas Ranger** '93 al '10
99091 **Ford Taurus & Mercury Sable** '86 al '95
99095 **GM Modelos de Tamaño Grande** '70 al '90
99100 **GM Modelos de Tamaño Mediano** '70 al '88
99106 **Jeep Cherokee, Wagoneer & Comanche**
'84 al '00
99110 **Nissan Camioneta** '80 al '96, **Pathfinder** '87 al '95
99118 **Nissan Sentra** '82 al '94
99125 **Toyota Camionetas y 4Runner** '79 al '95

Over 100 Haynes
motorcycle manuals
also available

7-12